MUSEUMS AND THEIR DEVELOPMENT

The European Tradition 1700–1900

Volume 8

Edited and Introduced by
Susan M. Pearce
University of Leicester

Museums and their Development
The European Tradition 1700–1900

Edited and Introduced by Susan M. Pearce
University of Leicester

Volume 1
*Musaeum Tradescantianum, or, a Collection of Rarities,
Preserved at South-Lambert neer London* (1656)
John Tradescant

Volume 2
*Museographia, oder Anleitung zum rechten Begriff und
nützlicher Anlegung der Museorum, oder Raritäten-Kammern* (1727)
Caspar Friedrich Neickel [*pseud.,* i.e. C. F. Einckel]

Volume 3
Reflections on the Painting and Sculpture of the Greeks (1765)
Johann Winckelmann

Volume 4
Travels in Southern Europe and the Levant, 1810–1817 (1903)
Charles Robert Cockerell

Volumes 5–7
*Treasures of Art in Great Britain, being an Account of the Chief
Collections of Paintings, Drawings, Sculptures, Illuminated MSS., &c.,*
(1854)
Gustav Waagen

Volume 8
*Galleries and Cabinets of Art in Great Britain…, forming a
Supplemental Volume to the Treasures of Art in Great Britain* (1857)
Gustav Waagen

Printed in England by Antony Rowe Ltd, Chippenham

GALLERIES AND CABINETS
OF ART IN GREAT BRITAIN

forming a Supplemental Volume
to the Treasures of Art in
Great Britain

Gustav Waagen

ROUTLEDGE/THOEMMES PRESS

This edition published by Routledge/Thoemmes Press, 1999

Routledge/Thoemmes Press
11 New Fetter Lane
London EC4P 4EE

Museums and their Development
8 Volumes : ISBN 0 415 19307 9

© Routledge, 1999

Reprinted from the 1857 edition

Routledge/Thoemmes Press is a joint imprint
of Routledge Ltd and Thoemmes Ltd

British Library Cataloguing-in-Publication Data
A CIP record of this title is available from the British Library

Publisher's Note

The Publisher has gone to great lengths to ensure the
quality of this reprint but points out that some
imperfections in the original book may be apparent.

This book is printed on acid-free paper, sewn, and
cased in a durable buckram cloth.

GALLERIES AND CABINETS OF ART

IN

GREAT BRITAIN:

BEING AN ACCOUNT OF MORE THAN FORTY COLLECTIONS OF

PAINTINGS, DRAWINGS, SCULPTURES, MSS.,

&c. &c.

VISITED IN 1854 AND 1856, AND NOW FOR THE FIRST TIME DESCRIBED.

BY DR. WAAGEN,

DIRECTOR OF THE ROYAL GALLERY OF PICTURES, BERLIN.

FORMING A SUPPLEMENTAL VOLUME TO THE 'TREASURES OF ART IN GREAT BRITAIN,'
THREE VOLUMES.

LONDON:

JOHN MURRAY, ALBEMARLE STREET.

1857.

LONDON: PRINTED BY WILLIAM CLOWES AND SONS, STAMFORD STREET,
AND CHARING CROSS.

PREFACE.

ALTHOUGH the works of art of every kind contained in the public and private galleries of Great Britain, and described in my 'Treasures of Art,' published in 1854, are of almost incredible amount, yet, no sooner had those three somewhat bulky volumes appeared than I was invited to visit collections and inspect pictures of the existence of which I had been previously unaware. Knowing, further, that numerous already-described collections had, since the publication of my work, received considerable additions, I formed the resolution, with the kind encouragement of Mr. Murray, whose desire it is to promote in every way the knowledge of the art-treasures in this country, of adding a fourth volume to those already before the public. My visit to England in 1854, followed up by one in 1856, and another in 1857, enabled me to collect fresh materials, the abundance of which will astonish all who have hitherto taken interest in my researches. This fourth volume consists therefore partly of additions to collections already described, partly of collections not known to me before. In both respects, no less in London than in the country, I have adhered to the same plan of arrangement pursued in the first three volumes. The reflection that time would impart an especial value to this work has induced me, as far as leisure possibly permitted, to give such a description of every work of art as might suffice in future to identify it. This is the more important from the number of pictures which necessarily change their owners; such, for instance, since the publication of my former volumes, has been the fate of the pictures belonging to

Lord Colborne—the collections of Mr. Rogers, of his sister Miss
Rogers, of the Earl of Orford, the Earl of Shrewsbury, and
others. But though I may justly claim to have done all in my
power to make myself acquainted with the treasures of art in
this country, yet I am well aware how far I am, even now, from
having had cognizance of much that is worthy of notice; so that
a follower in the same path, who may bring more knowledge and
equal love to the task, will still reap a considerable harvest.

I cannot conclude this short Preface without here expressing
my gratitude to all those who have served not only me, but the
cause of art in this land, by the kindness with which they have
promoted and facilitated my labours.

CONTENTS OF VOL. IV.

THE

TREASURES OF ART IN GREAT BRITAIN.

LETTER I.

ADDITIONS TO THE BRITISH MUSEUM.

British Museum — Antiquities — Objects of art belonging to the Middle Ages
— Additions to the collection of miniatures — Byzantine — Bedford Missal
— Henry VI.'s Psalter — Divina Commedia — Drawings of the Italian,
Early Netherlandish, Early German, and later Netherlandish schools —
Engravings : Italian, Early German — Block-books.

SINCE the publication of my work 'The Treasures of Art in Great
Britain,' the arrangement of the sculpture in the British Museum
has been greatly improved. The Egyptian and Assyrian monuments have, in the first place, been disposed in that chronological
succession which alone best unites the highest instruction with the
greatest enjoyment. With the Assyrian monuments are also seen
other antiquities of the same nation and of the same period—the
ivory reliefs and the bronze vessels being deposited in glass cases
along the centre of the same gallery. The arrangement of the
Greek and Roman marbles, though the space did not permit of so
strictly chronological an order as with the foregoing, is also much
more satisfactory. The chief alteration consists in the fact that the
sculptures from the pediments of the Parthenon have been removed
from the hall containing the reliefs from the Parthenon, into a
neighbouring room, which, though smaller, is also lighted from
above. Besides this, room has thus been gained so to place the
sculptures from the two pediments—here seen opposite each other
—as to leave about the same spaces as the missing portions would
have occupied ; by which means the relation between what has
been preserved and what has perished is shown, as well as the
original extent of the pediments. At the same time the reliefs
in the great hall have perhaps benefited more than any other
objects by this change. Now for the first time are they seen so

free from all impediment, that the spectator can view them at a proper distance from any part; while the apartment itself, which, with the statues, and the models of the Parthenon and other buildings, looked more like a warehouse than a gallery, now presents a *coup-d'œil* worthy of these universally celebrated works of art. The Greco-Roman and the Roman sculptures are now also more strictly divided, and favourably seen in spaces lighted from above and proportioned to their size. The entrance gallery devoted to the Roman marbles, and which is now being appropriately decorated, is, it is true, not so favourable in point of lighting as might be desired, though sufficiently so for their subordinate value in point of art. All these changes have been executed with great discrimination by Mr. Oldfield. As regards the antiquities also, the Greek, Etruscan, and Roman bronzes and terracottas have greatly gained by the new arrangements. And here I first insert some earlier notices of Greek and Roman antiquities, which, owing to an omission on my part, were not printed in my first volume of the 'Treasures of Art.'

Vol. I. p. 93, line 18 from the top.

By far the greater number of the antiquities are contained in a large apartment lighted from above.

A shallow basin of Parian marble of considerable size is remarkable for elegance of form; a priestess of Bacchus, of great beauty, is treated in flat relief in the centre, and a graceful wreath of vine-leaves surrounds the border.

Next to this may be observed a bronze statuette of the infant Bacchus, seated, placed upon the stove. He is leaning with his right hand on a sceptre, one shoulder covered with the nebris. The softness and animation of the forms correspond with the beauty of the motive.

Among the numerous specimens of small sculptures in metal, especially in bronze, are many of the highest artistic merit. I enumerate a few which struck me as particularly remarkable. Foremost among the Etruscan bronzes are four reliefs from the well-known chariot—a votive offering—found in 1812 between Perugia and Cortona (Case 87). These agree in the whole style of art—namely in the profiles with the sloping lines of forehead and nose—with the vases of the archaic period. The mode of workmanship is very remarkable. The reliefs consist of thin plates of silver, on some parts of which gold plates are fastened with rivets. On the reverse they appear as if beaten out over moulds of some solid material, most probably wood. This kind of work was called by the ancients Empæstic.

Next in order, as an excellent example of the developed art of the Etrurians, may be mentioned a statuette of Mars, found in the Lake of Monte Falterona in Tuscany (Case 71).

Among the bronzes of the highest Grecian art the following are particularly distinguished.

------

* Vol. I. p. 94.

An Apollo, drawing his bow, of the greatest elegance and highest finish (Case 78). Two statuettes of Jupiter (Case 77). An hermaphrodite, and the spirited bust of a sea-god. These, with the following and others, were found at Paramythia, in Epirus, in the neighbourhood of the ancient Dodona.

A Venus of animated action, very graceful, of singular softness in the forms, and of the finest surface. The right arm and the lower part of the legs are unfortunately wanting.

Mercury, with a small gold chain round his neck—invention and execution both admirable. (Both these last in Case 84.)

A Minerva, in a striding position, without arms.

A youthful Hercules Bibax, with the cantharus in his hand.

A Hercules in full manhood—the left arm wanting.

The Hercules Farnese. Many a celebrated but now perished work has served as a model for statuettes like this last.

A circular relief.

Hercules reposing, surrounded by Cupids. This is a very attractive composition. The epidermis is unfortunately much injured.

Of the metallic mirrors, of which the British Museum possesses a large and admirable selection (Cases 74 and 75), I may particularly notice one, Bacchus embracing Ariadne, the outlines of which are not, as usually, incised, but in relief, in the ancient Greek style. It is remarkable for the excellent workmanship, and for the already free and noble form of the heads.

In the well-furnished collection of ancient weapons, I must mention a helmet with a gold laurel-wreath (Cases 44 and 45).

Among the numerous bronze vessels is a circular one of considerable size, on which, above, are the statuettes of two comic actors, with Silenus masks, of great animation.

Also one much smaller, with three bacchanalian figures, and another, on which a corpulent Pan is defending himself from a serpent, deserve favourable notice.

The collection of beautiful candelabra contains one with two bacchanalian figures on the top, of very spirited motive.

Finally, the department of tripods and lamps in bronze is richly represented, and displays some particularly fine examples.

The collection of glass vessels is not large, but offers various choice specimens, including some balsam vases of oriental alabaster.

The number of antique mosaics is small; among them is a Silenus mask of great beauty.

Masks, Tesseræ, and Lamps in terracotta are here in considerable numbers. On the other hand, the collection of figures, reliefs, ornaments, &c., of terracotta, is but moderate in extent when compared with other collections of the kind; some very remarkable statuettes from Athens are, however, to be seen on Shelf 2.

A group of female figures, one of whom is playing the tambourine, the other dancing, is most charming and animated in motive. Athenian Hydriophoræ, or female water-bearers, and the muse Polyhymnia, who corresponds entirely in motive with a marble statue in the Berlin Museum, are admirable. A comic actor also in the character of Hercules is of delightful humour.

Various departments have also, during this lapse of time, received considerable additions, to which I now proceed to call attention.

OBJECTS OF ART BELONGING TO THE MIDDLE AGES, AND TO MODERN TIMES.

This title applies in the widest sense to those objects which the indefatigable exertions of Mr. Franks—a gentleman who unites in no common degree the qualities of zeal and discrimination—have gathered together, and which have grown from small beginnings into a very important collection. The most important is perhaps a circular disk of rock-crystal, with the history of Susannah engraved on it. According to an inscription this work was executed for

King Lothaire. Of the three Carlovingian princes of this name, the latest, who was King of France from 954 to 986, judging from style of art and excellence of motive, is probably the one referred to. The finished and delicate execution in so hard a material displays the technical skill of that period in a surprisingly favourable light. From the Bernal Collection.

Another engraving on the same material is far ruder. It represents the Crucifixion, with the Virgin and St. John on each side, and the sun and the moon in the sky. Judging from the style of art, it belongs also to the 10th century.

The purchase of Mr. Maskell's collection of carvings in ivory, together with the few but excellent specimens already possessed by the Museum, have combined worthily to represent this important branch of art. I must be satisfied with noticing a few of the most important.

Reliefs.—Four pieces which had belonged to a box.

1. Pilate washing his hands, Christ bearing the Cross, and Peter denying Christ, with the Maid and the Cock. 2. Judas hanging, and the Crucifixion, with the Virgin, St. John, and the Centurion. 3. The two Maries, and the two Guards at the Sepulchre, which is represented as a separate building, with a kind of chapel. 4. Christ teaching in the centre of four Apostles. The whole style of art, motives, expression, and drapery, agree so entirely with the early Christian sarcophagi, that these reliefs, which approach the round in depth, cannot be ascribed to a later period than the 5th or 6th century. From the very short proportions, I believe them to be of the 6th century, and of Italian origin. The colour of the ivory has become a dark brown.

The combat of Perseus with the Chimæra, whom he is piercing with a spear in the back. The motive and drawing are both good. The ground is perforated ; the style of flat relief very good. Nevertheless, the two conventional mushroom-shaped trees, and the horseshoe arches of a gallery above, forbid my assigning to it an earlier date than the 9th century.

An ivory tablet—originally, probably, the cover of a book— divided into two compartments,—the upper one containing the Marriage at Cana, with the Virgin telling Christ that the wine is come to an end ; and the lower one the giver of the feast, two youths filling six vessels with water, and Christ in the act of per-

forming the miracle. The motives are speaking, the draperies
tasteful, the high relief in good style, and the workmanship careful.
The style of art inclines me to believe this a Carlovingian work of
the 9th century.

Of the same period and style is the half of a Diptych, with the
Annunciation above, the Visitation in the centre, and the Nativity
below. The motive and style of the flat relief are good, the proportions short.

The Raising of Lazarus: a very careful but dry Byzantine
work, which may belong to the 12th century. This relief was
formerly in the possession of Chevalier Bunsen.

The cover of a book, about 4 in. wide, and 6 in. high, with
thirty Scriptural events represented in five rows, in perforated
work, beginning below from the left, and ending above on the
right. This small relief, which belongs to the 14th century, is
quite unique. Style and composition are good, and the execution
of the little figures, not more than two-thirds of an inch high, of
marvellous delicacy and precision.

Some covers of mirrors, of good workmanship, may also be mentioned.

Next in order to these I must notice a complete jewel-casket,
the cover of which contains on the top a tournament, with numerous animated female figures in the balcony; a hunting party,
three girls bathing, and similar subjects on the sides. This is a
good work of the 15th century.

Finally, I beg to call attention to a chef-d'œuvre of ivory
carving in the picturesque style that prevailed at a later time.
The subject is the Temptation, of indescribable finish and
richness of details, especially in the landscape. The head of
Christ is also singularly noble for the period.

Ivory objects in the round. The statuette of the Virgin with
the Child on her arm, about 5 in. high. The composition is
remarkably beautiful, and the execution equally fine. This agrees
so entirely with the statue of the Virgin by Neri Pisano, in the
little church of the Maria della Spina, at Pisa, that, if not by that
sculptor himself, it must have been executed in his time and under
his influence, i. e. in the 13th century.

Statuette of one of the Wise Virgins—the lamp in her right
hand—about 8 in. high. Slender and noble in form, of earnest and

dignified head, and the drapery of admirable style.   In my opinion
a German work of the 13th century.

A painted statuette of the Virgin enthroned, about 4 in. high,
with the Child standing at the breast.   The style good, and the
head of the Virgin very lovely.   Most probably French, of the
13th century.

Statuette of the Virgin enthroned, almost a foot high, with the
Child undraped, and again standing at the breast.   The Child is
remarkable for the well-understood and full forms.   The drapery
is especially excellent, and the execution very careful.   This is
probably German, of the 14th century.

Among the ivory vessels a circular one with a lid is distinguished for its beautiful and broad decorations in the Romanesque
style.

A series of those beautiful medallions, executed by Vittore
Pisano and others in the 15th century, with some fine medals and
coins of the 16th century, merit a close inspection.

Many fine specimens of the enamels of the middle ages, with
which shrines especially were decorated, are to be seen here.

But one of the most imposing portions of this new department
of art consists of those tasteful vessels and plates which art has
enriched.   Of the celebrated Limoges manufactory—metal vessels
and plates with enamels—some beautiful specimens are here preserved.   The manufacture of majolica is also represented by a
series of plates and dishes of the 15th to the 17th century, which,
for size, beauty of form, style of decoration, and in many, also, of
figures, are very remarkable.   Nor are specimens wanting of the
fine Palissy ware.

ADDITIONS TO THE COLLECTION OF MINIATURES.

Vol. I. p. 97.

A Byzantine MS., in quarto, purchased at the sale of Mr. Borell's
collection, in 1853, containing the psalter and hymns, with the
date 1066, displays some of the most interesting miniatures that
I have seen of the kind.   The subjects of many of these extend the
in every way important field of Byzantine art.   At the same time
they serve to prove that even after the middle of the 11th century

the Byzantine painter adhered frequently, more or less, to the art
of the first Christian centuries, so intimately allied as it was with
the purely antique school of painting; while, at the same time, in
general character, we observe that ascetic severity of conception,
that dryness and elongation in the forms, those mechanical arrangements of the drapery, and that gloominess of colouring, which all
bear witness to the local Byzantine school. The laying on of the
colours alone is throughout broad, solid, and careful. The text
consists of 208 leaves in one column, and is written in a full
minuscule letter. Only the three first pages and the superscriptions
of all the chapters are in golden capitals; first executed,—as it appears from some portions where the gold has fallen off,—in crimson
colour, and afterwards covered with gold. The pretty tendrils
which, in eight compartments upon a gold ground, surround the
superscription ΥΜΝΟС ΤΟΥ ΔΑΥΙΔΟΥ ΠΡΟΦΗΤΟΥ, give no
evidence, as in most Byzantine ornamentation after the year 1000,
of Arabian influence, but still point to antique tradition. The
same may be said of two gryphons next an altar over the inscription. Unfortunately the numerous miniatures which decorated the
borders have greatly suffered; and occasionally we find that, owing
to a mutilation of the upper borders, some of them are entirely
lost. The importance attached to the pictures is seen by red
signs in the text corresponding with others next the pictures
referred to. The miniatures of the first page are also much
injured : those on the border probably represented the Three
Persons of the Trinity, in human figures. This, at least, is
deducible from the inscription ὁ παλαιος ἡμερων near a figure
enthroned in a blue mandorla, showing that it is intended for
the First Person. The dress is of dark purple, with the forms
of the folds in gold, and the mantle vermilion; the head is
obliterated. The inscription ĪĊ and X̄P̄ shows that the figure
below represents the Second Person. All that can be seen of
the third figure is that it was also human. Some much ruined
representations—for instance, the Nativity and the Annunciation
to the Shepherds, Leaf 2a—still serve to show that the conception
in every way corresponds with the Byzantine treatment of these
subjects. An interesting example of Pagan forms adopted by
Christian art is seen in a picture L. 3a, with the inscription
ὕπνος, where an angel, who is fanning the sleeping David with a

circular gold fan, is meant to represent sleep.   It is also worthy of
remark that the local Byzantine style is especially applied in its
complete development to Byzantine saints, the representation of
whom, by means of art, necessarily belongs to a somewhat later
period.   Thus, for example, St. Basil is given standing before a
singing-desk, with a burning taper in his right hand, in precisely
those dry forms and in that brown colour indicative of pure
Byzantine art.   In L. 8a, representing Christ enthroned and
blessing, with purple robe and blue mantle, the angels on each
side are new to me.   These have four large wings, folded over
each other, above and below, partly in beautiful colour and partly
in gold, out of which the heads with golden glories, and the
graceful hands and feet, are alone seen.   Upon their shoulders are
heads of animals vomiting fire from the open jaws.   Probably
these represent that order of angels called by the Byzantine
church the τετραμορφοι, as uniting the four attributes of the
Evangelists.   This accounts for the head of the lion and bull on
their shoulders : the eagle's head, which they should bear between
their upper wings, may have been obliterated.   The head of one
of the angels which is preserved is delicate in form and dignified
in expression.   L. 11a contains the often repeated subject of
David prostrate in prayer before the First Person.   This is conspicuous for its good preservation and for the very successful
expression of adoration in the head of David, a figure in regal
attire, with vermilion coat bordered with gold, a purple mantle,
and a flat golden crown.   Especially remarkable are the pictures
of the Apostles and Evangelists, SS. Peter, Paul, John, Matthew,
Mark, Luke, Simon, Andrew, James, Philip, Thomas, and Bartholomew, their names inscribed next them, LL. 19b and 20a.
Each of these are enthroned, with a number of figures with their
right hands raised, before them, to whom they are preaching the
Gospel.   In the case of St. Thomas these figures are black men,
in reference to his conversion of the Moors.   St. Peter appears
here in the well-known type, only, as in the earlier form, without a
bald head, though his hair is already white.   St. Paul's is also
white.   Unfortunately the lower part of the face is obliterated.
St. John is also represented as an old man.   St. James has a long
brown beard.   The dress of St. Peter consists here, as later, of a
blue tunic and yellow toga, inclining to orange—that of St. Paul

of a light blue tunic and a toga of dark purple. The subject of
Hezekiah appointed by the grace of God king over the Jews,
L. 21a, is very peculiarly expressed. Hezekiah is seen held aloft
by three men of war upon a steel shield with a golden border,
dressed in a purple tunic with broad gold stripes, while an angel
flying down from a blue segment of a circle, well known as the
symbol of Heaven, places a gold crown with red stones on his
head. The king holds a long sceptre in his hand, which terminates in a square with four small circles at the corners. The
Ascension, L. 25b, is another remarkable picture. Above, in a
large blue circle with red stars, are seen two angels holding
sumptuous hangings in gold with bright purple patterns. The
inscription, ἀι πυλαι τοῦ ὁυρανου, informs us that these represent the
gates of Heaven. The Saviour, attired in a dark purple tunic, is
seen in a blue mandorla, borne upwards by two angels of good
action and dressed in the light-coloured drapery of antique art.
L. 27b is again one of the most remarkable pictures. Above
are two saints, with the inscription Νικηφορος ὁ πρῖαρχος (abbreviation for πατριαρχος) and Σωπηρος, holding between them a circle,
with the bust-picture of Christ. This latter is severe but dignified in character. Further below are the same saints next an
enthroned Byzantine emperor, obviously interceding for the worship
of pictures. Near them are three aged priests, somewhat successfully dressed in light-coloured garments, one of whom is striking
a similar picture of Christ with his staff. The inscription ὁι
ἐικονομαχοι informs us that these figures represent the Iconoclasts.
This is the only instance I know of such an allusion in Byzantine
miniatures. L. 28a exhibits David as a slender youth standing
in a short light blue coat and light purple chlamys, with naked
thighs and swathed legs and feet, the crook in his right hand,
and a lyre of very simple form in his left. Five goats and rams,
which compose his flock, are too large in proportion to himself.
These, with a wolf which is carrying off a ram, and a dog which
is pursuing—both of admirable action—are obviously by another
hand, as seen in the heavy and dark tone of colour. L. 31b,
the Raising of Lazarus, shows quite the earliest mode of conception as found in the catacombs, only that the proportions
are very tall, and the features quite youthful. L. 32a contains
Christ and David standing conversing together, twice over.

L. 32b, the Resurrection of Christ, is also remarkable. The sepulchre, a tower-like building, is obviously the original of a similar form of conception in occidental miniatures. The circumstance, however, of the angel dressed in blue stooping from the segment of a circle, typical of Heaven, and holding his hands to raise up the Saviour, who is still standing on the earth, is new to me. Two guards are reposing; one of whom, who is supporting himself on a circular golden shield, and looking upwards, is very animated and natural. L. 35b represents SS. Basil and Chrysostom, and a third saint, who, with their gloomy severity of expression, and heavy brown tone of flesh and drapery, are again perfect types of the later Byzantine style. L. 38a, the Stoning of St. Stephen, is the earliest example I know of a Byzantine representation of this subject. While three Jews are stoning the kneeling martyr, Saul, already in the type of St. Paul, is seated upon a rock in the strict Byzantine conventional form, and is stretching out his hand in encouragement to them. L. 47b, the Repentant Peter; very speaking in action, and dressed, contrary to custom, in a light blue tunic, and a toga of pink shot material, which he is holding before his mouth. Near him is a large cock, and over him, in token that his repentance is accepted, the hand of the Almighty is extended in benediction from the segment of the circle. L. 50a, the Last Supper, unfortunately much damaged, but perhaps the earliest representation of this subject in Byzantine form which has descended to us. It is remarkable that the antique custom of a recumbent position at a meal is here preserved; the Saviour is also quite on the right-hand side of the table, which is of semicircular form. L. 51a, the beginning of the psalm, "As thirsteth the hart," &c., is a proof that the ancient Greek mode of expression had not died away by the 11th century. We here observe a stag of very good action, with a blue stripe indicating water, and a purple rock and bush, the rest of the landscape. Above this is David, addressing these words to the bust-picture of the Almighty, who appears in a golden circle, denoting heaven, in the mosaic type of Christ, accompanied even, as frequently, with the letters I. C. and X. C. L. 51b, the Ascension of Elijah. The car, which is drawn by four horses, is here painted vermilion, to indicate the fiery light. Elijah himself, attired in bright colours, is in admirable action. L. 55b shows a peculiar Byzantine representation of the Trinity. The hand of the Almighty is seen above proceeding from a dark blue segment of a circle, and giving the benediction, after ʹthe Greek fashion. In a broad light-blue ray, issuing from the hand, is seen the Holy Ghost, as a Dove, while below, in a gold circle, is the Saviour as a child upon the lap of the Virgin, who is conceived in a dark purple robe with golden folds, in the strictest Byzantine form. L. 56a, the youthful type of the enthroned Saviour, in very good action, shows that this form of conception, though of Western origin, was occasionally admitted into Byzantine art. On the other hand, the equally youthful David below him, a very good figure, appears already in the over-laden and tasteless costume of a Byzantine monarch. L. 56b, the Annunciation. This is one of the most successful pictures: the Virgin, in a light blue tunic and dark purple mantle, is seated on a golden chair. The movement of her hands speakingly expresses the words—" What a salutation is this ! "—which she addresses to the angel, who is very nobly conceived. The figure of David, as the head of her line, standing behind her in act of benediction, shows that the whole conception is symbolical. L. 58b, the Ascension. Christ is represented very small, borne upwards in a blue mandorla by four angels. Below, under trees, is the Virgin ; at her side are the figures of the apostles, very much injured. The peculiar broad antique treatment is obvious in the tolerably pre-served heads. L. 61b, the representation of the God of the Sun, very circumstantially given, with the words ὁ ἥλιος, strikingly recalling that in the Abbess Herrad von Landsberg's ' Hortus Delitiarum,' only that here the antique form is much more closely adhered to. A youthful figure, taken quite in front, and sur-rounded with rays, stands out from behind a semicircular car. In his right hand he holds a whip ; in the left the sun's disk—a circle with rays proceeding from it. The four horses are galloping two and two at the sides. Below are the shining wheels, with their axletree. To express also the warmth of the light, the whole sub-ject is carried out in a light red colour. Below, in the centre, in a golden circle, is Christ, with Habakkuk and David on each side. L. 62b, Abraham visited by the Three Angels, two of them standing at the table. Unfortunately the greater portion of Abra-ham is ruined. L. 63b. Here the words, ὁ Δαυιδ ἐλεγχομενος, inform us that the figure standing before the enthroned David is

the prophet Nathan, upbraiding him in the name of the Most High
for the murder of Uriah. Behind David is an angel of great
beauty of form, motive, and colour. Christ washing the feet of his
Disciples. Here, in the earliest Byzantine representation of this'
subject I know, we already find that significant gesture of Peter—
pointing with his right hand to his head—which, as I have elsewhere pointed out, may be traced in all representations of this
subject down to the 17th century. L. 67b, St. Macarius, in supplication, with a white beard; also L. 75b, another saint—are
again of that severe ascetic character peculiar to Byzantine art.
L. 82b and 83a, the Delivery of the Souls of the Patriarchs from
Purgatory. Here Christ is seen in a blue mandorla, which Satan
—a figure of dark colour, but entirely human—touches in his fall.
A very aged man and woman next Christ are probably Adam and
Eve. L. 85a, Philip baptizing the Eunuch; this latter is
standing up to his neck in a pyramid of water, the usual form in
the earliest representations of Christ's baptism. Philip is clothed
in purple. Close by, the two are seen in a chariot with four horses
driving away at full gallop. A youthful saint on horseback, with
the inscription Θ πρoκõς (abbreviation for Procopos), to whom a
golden cross appears from out the segment of a circle in the sky, is
conspicuous for elevation of conception. L. 87b, the Crucifixion.
Here we have the great length and meagreness of the Byzantine
mode of treatment in the body of our Saviour; but, singular to
say, not yet the sunken head and swayed-out figure. On the contrary, the Saviour is quite upright, and still alive. From this it
appears that this treatment, which Rumohr first pronounced characteristic of the Byzantine school, was, after the middle of the
11th century, by no means universally accepted in it. On the
other hand, we find here the four nails and the unusually wide
footboard. Christ is also, with the exception of hands and feet,
wrapped in a purple robe with the folds indicated in gold. The
only figures about the cross are Longinus the centurion piercing
the side with his spear, and the Jew giving him the sponge.
L. 85a, two more figures, striking at a bust-picture of Christ, which
they hold between them; with the inscription, Ἐικονομαχοι. L. 91a,
the youthful figure of Solomon, of very earnest and stately conception, is very remarkable, showing on the one hand the costume
of a Byzantine monarch, and on the other the antique tradition of

the hands lifted in prayer. The Annunciation below is peculiar, as representing the Virgin on the outside of the house, with a spindle. L. 92b, the Adoration of the Kings. The word μαιγοι shows that they are still treated as wise men. Instead of the later crown, they have still caps on their heads, corresponding obviously with the antique Roman conception of all foreign persons as Phrygians—namely, the cap, the crimson trowsers, the short coat, and the blue boots. The somewhat large but meagre Child is here draped. Below this are the three wise men galloping away, the ass behind them, carrying their baggage, not being forgotten. L. 96b, another Crucifixion. Here the Saviour is alive as before, but with the body slightly bent, and a large white cloth round the loins. The centurion is on the right, St. John and the Virgin on the left. The representation of Paradise below, as a garden, and enclosed by a ruin, which, in the absence of all perspective, appears to run up both sides, is quite new to me. At the ends of the river are two river gods, of the colour of water, with gold crowns on their heads of singular form. The intention doubtless is to express that Paradise, which was lost by sin, is only to be recovered by the death of Christ. L. 99b, the Giving the Law on Mount Sinai. This occupies a whole page, and is without doubt the repetition of some much earlier original. The Almighty is represented in the mosaic type of Christ, in tunic and toga of blue colour, with naked feet, and the right hand raised in benediction. The figure is highly dignified and noble in expression and motive. Moses also, with light blue and pink drapery, gives the impression of an antique painting. The tables of the law do not appear. L. 100a, at the heading of the Psalm of Asaph appears the figure of that personage enthroned, and pointing to a book. At the sides are the audience, three and three. Above, sidewards, in a circle, is the bust-picture of the Almighty in the unbearded type of Christ. L. 101b, Moses on a hill, of youthful conception. From a staff which he holds up flows a stream, from which three men below are drinking. L. 102a, the Giving of the Manna. This is a very peculiar representation. An angel of good action is giving the manna to a man, in the form of the sacred wafer ; thus showing an allusion to the holy communion. At the same time the subject is repeated at the side in its historical form—namely, by a blue semicircle, with the two golden doors of heaven, from which proceed a rain of green spots, caught by four men below, one of whom, with a large black beard, admirably represents the Jewish type. L. 104a, the first Six Plagues of Egypt, represented in a very simplified manner : for instance, the conversion of the waters into blood, by two reddish river gods, with horns after the fashion of demons, who are pouring a red stream from an urn. Next one of these river gods are three men with gestures of sorrow ; four frogs, eight flies, and, below the river, six locusts upon a corn-field, indicate the other plagues. Below is a dark greenish segment of a circle, from which fall hail and rain upon one ox, one horse, two rams, and a pig. L. 104b represents the Seventh Plague, the death of all the first-born. Here again we find antique feeling, though in a Christian form—namely, two avenging angels, flying, and piercing two men with spears. L. 106a. Here is doubtless some symbolic intention, which is not quite clear to me. Above are the Virgin and Child, half-length figures, before a building, in the strict Byzantine treatment ; below is a rock, and, lower still, David anointed by Samuel. By way of indication of his shepherd condition, a herd of six animals are introduced, and a dog barking. L. 107b, the Almighty enthroned between two angels, with the patriarch Jacob, as an old man in a purple robe, and Joseph holding Benjamin by the hand, as indicated by the names written at each side. This subject is also new to me. L. 109b, Abraham as a dignified old man in a purple dress, with the folds drawn in gold, bending in adoration before the figure of the Almighty, who is giving him the benediction. This is also very remarkable. The same may be said of L. 110a, Christ in act of benediction upon a rock, whence flows the water of life, of which two persons are drinking. Behind Christ stands a youthful saint. L. 110b, the youthful Christ in act of benediction, enthroned between two large angels with red sceptres. This is one of the most interesting pictures : the Christ is strikingly like that on the well-known Dalmatic—a work of Byzantine origin—in St. Peter's at Rome. Three armed figures in blue, standing on pillars, with the inscription, δι Θεοι τῶν εθνων, are also remarkable as showing how much the traditionary forms of representation of the ancient gods had already degenerated. L. 113a. This is the earliest representation I know of Zacchæus, who is depicted as an old man with purple tunic and vermilion toga, sitting in a tree, the leaves of which are copied from ivy. Below is Christ, looking up to him.

The feast at Zacchæus's house is lower down, and, as required by
the space, is much simplified, only Christ and St. Peter being seen
reclining at the table, with two other persons behind the table,
and Zacchæus entering by the door, with a dish. L. 114a, the
Visitation. The Virgin in a blue tunic and purple mantle; Elizabeth in a light brown petticoat and a dark brown mantle. This is
conspicuous for the heartiness with which the women embrace. At
the same time we recognise in the late antique forms of the
buildings the model of the architecture prevailing in occidental
miniatures from the 8th up to the 12th century—consequently at
a time when the Romanesque architecture was fully developed.
This is another proof of the tenacity of Byzantine influence.
Above the building, in symbolic allusion, is the figure of Christ
in the act of benediction, with St. John kneeling in adoration;
both as boys. The inscription of the latter is ὁ προδρομος.
L. 115a, the bust-picture of Christ, with the cross thus, ✠; doubtless conveying some meaning. Next the cross is David standing
in adoration. L. 116a, the Entombment. This is peculiarly
conceived. Joseph of Arimathea and Nicodemus, as the written
names inform us, are carrying the very diminutive body of the
Saviour, which is wrapped up like a mummy, to the gate-like
opening in a brown rock, to which an angel, descending from the
segment of a circle, is pointing. Below, in very speaking gestures
of sorrow, are the Virgin and two women (ἀι γυναικες). L. 118a
contains one of the earliest representations of the Transfiguration,
with the inscription ἡ μεταμορφοσης, which, doubtless being of
very early Byzantine invention, became a model for all times,
and even for Raphael. In the centre, in a circle of dark steel-
blue colour, is Christ. On his right hand Elijah depicted as
an old man—on his left Moses youthfully conceived; both with
their heads bowed in adoration. Far below, kneeling upon a rock,
are the three disciples: St. Peter, according to the well-known
type, but already as an old man; another, probably St. John,
youthful; the third, and therefore St. James, with a brown beard.
L. 121a, the Flight into Egypt: the Virgin and Child, very
statelily conceived, are seated on the ass, before which, which is
new to me, walks a figure in short red coat and purple trowsers,
with the inscription denoting St. James. Joseph, who follows the
Virgin, is given as an old man, but in antique costume, in blue

tunic, purple toga, and with bare feet. L. 125a contains again two river gods, blue figures with crowns, and the inscription ὁι ποταμοι. L. 134b, Christ weeping over Jerusalem. Before the figure of Christ, who is in the act of benediction, and projecting from the architectural indication of the city, with the inscription CIWN, is a female head, with an expression of grief, and with a flat purple crown—obviously the personification of Jerusalem. Her future destruction is however fully expressed in the antique manner; for below is a black compartment, with the inscription ὁ ἁδης, denoting therefore the lower world, within which is a prostrate figure, doubtless typifying Je-rusalem, of which unfortunately only the outline is left. L. 135b, an attempt to represent the universe, by a figure of which I have here tried to give an idea. This is one of the remarkable objects in this rich codex. In the outer blue ring of this circle the stars are indicated: within the same is the inscription ὁ ὁυρανος, with the sun of a red, and the moon of a blue colour. In the centre of the circle is the earth.

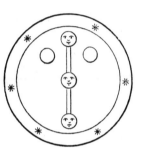

The two heads which are connected with the earth are, we are informed by the inscription, ἀντιποδες, the antipodes. L. 137a, a Dying Man; a naked child coming from his mouth, with the inscription ψυχη του ἀμᵾ—the abbreviation for ἀμῶμου, the spot-less, or, as we call it, the righteous;—an angel flying down is in the act of receiving it, while another angel stands at the head of the couch. This proves that this mode of representing the soul, which obtained so much among the western nations, was ori-ginally conceived in the Byzantine school. At all events, I know of no earlier representation of this subject. L. 138a. Here we find again a very similar picture of the antipodes, accompanied with three full-length undraped little figures. L. 140a, SS. Peter and John the Evangelist; the former, both in head and dress, quite according to the earliest tradition. St. John, however, is almost in the type of St. Paul, only with grey hair and beard. L. 143. However worthy of remark the subject of this and the following pictures from the history of Moses—the Passage of the Red Sea, the Worship of the Golden Calf, &c.—I must content myself with saying that Moses is throughout represented as youthful, and Aaron always as aged. On the other hand, I must call attention to the Ascension, L. 149a, which is remarkable for the conception, for the very pure antique feeling for colour, and for the broad execution. Christ is here alone, dressed in a vermilion tunic and purple toga, with the folds given in gold (doubtless to express the heavenly glory), his right hand raised in benediction, within a blue mandorla with three stars, borne up by two angels of very beautiful motives, at the lower point of the mandorla. L. 150a, the Death of Judas. This is a remarkable picture, his moral depravity not being given, as elsewhere, in any outward expression. His head is youthful, his figure refined, his costume of delicate shot material, and quite Roman. He is held up by a black demon, with a black band round his throat, in order to hang him upon a tree. A dignified figure with a glory on the opposite border, appears from the inscription, μχτ, to be St. Matthew, the narrator of the death of Judas. L. 151a. This is the earliest representation I know of the Temptation of St. Anthony. Unfortunately the figure is much injured, and only in the head is seen a good expression of entreaty. Behind him is a black winged demon of colossal size, and before him, retreating, are two smaller ones of the same character. But one of the most important pictures of this MS. is the Last Supper. L. 152a. Beneath a pent-house, supported on columns, as seen in old Basilicas, above the altar—only here more in the form of a cupola—is Christ, standing in the centre, with a flesh-coloured wafer in his right hand. This he is giving to one of the disciples, who is bending in the act of receiving it with both hands. In the left hand of Christ is a similar wafer. Before him is an altar with a beautiful red cloth. . Behind the disciple mentioned are five others with upraised hands. On the left of the Saviour are six others, the foremost drinking from the chalice. Behind them, as appears from the inscription, is Melchizedec, a youthful figure with a crown, holding a golden cup, with a golden ewer. Corresponding with Melchizedec, on the opposite side, and with the name given, is David, also youthfully conceived. The motives are throughout good, the costumes of the disciples quite antique, as is the style of colouring. The whole has a far earlier look than that in many respects similar representation on the sleeves of the above-mentioned Imperial Dalmatic, and thus affords another proof of the later period to which that belongs. L. 152 contains the original of the representation of St. Onofrius, as an old man, naked, and only girded with leaves, who is kneeling in prayer to a segment of a circle, from which the hand of the Almighty proceeds. Palm Sunday is represented in a very simple form. Christ is seen on the ass, accompanied only by Peter; a small Jewish figure is spreading out his purple dress; while in the gateway, of antique form, is an old man holding a large palm-branch, with some companions. L. 158a shows us five saints, in good and lively action, adoring the bust-picture of Christ, which appears in the sky in a circle, and in the act of benediction. The inscription, πεντε, teaches us that the saints represented are the martyrs Eustratius, Auxentius, Mardarius, Eugenius, and Orestes. L. 162, the Creation of Adam and Eve, is very remarkable: the Almighty in the mosaic type of Christ, and very dignified in expression, dressed in a purple tunic, with a toga of subdued blue, and sandals, is seen bending over the figure of Adam on the ground, and is touching his head with his left hand, while he blesses him with the right. The garden of Eden is expressed by flowering trees, which surround the figures, and the gate by a red compartment, in which is a cherub. L. 163b, and l. 165b, containing the figures of St. Euphemia and St. Thecla, are very characteristic as representations of female saints—somewhat rare in comparison with male—in strict Byzantine style. They are seen praying with upraised hands, and therefore in antique form, both in brown dresses. L. 176, the Jewish Captivity in Babylon. This is probably the earliest representation of this subject. Two river gods, personifying doubtless the Euphrates and the Tigris, are here introduced as before, only with the unembellishing addition of the stream proceeding from the mouth. By these are palm-trees, with golden harps leant against them. Some Jews reclining are unfortunately much injured. Four standing figures are better preserved. Two men in golden helmets represent doubtless Babylonian soldiers, who are guarding the Jews. The history of David, in a series of pictures, contains also much that is interesting. L. 183 displays David in the act of slinging, with Goliah in a red shirt of mail, with golden scales, striking at him in a lame manner with his lance. L. 189b shows us the Almighty enthroned between two angels, and sending the one on his right to David. Below is the same angel, and David with his flock, blowing the flute exactly as it is blown to this day. Lower still he is seen following the angel. L. 190a, David again with his flock, conversing with the angel. Below, the same, opposite to the aged Samuel, who holds a large horn with the anointing oil; and lower still, David being anointed in presence of his father, Jesse, and others, in whom the expression of astonishment is well given. L. 190b, the same subject in similar form, only that the spectators are designated as Jesse and the brethren of David. Also on a much larger scale, Saul, enthroned and possessed with an evil spirit, surrounded by five soldiers, with the inscription, θαυμαζον καὶ οἱ ἀρχοντες. L. 191a. On the same scale of size, David, in a tunic of light purple, and a fluttering blue chlamys, kneeling upon Goliah, and holding him by the hair as he cuts off his head. Next this, the Philistines fleeing. Below, three virgins with harp, violin, and timbrel, celebrating the triumph of David. L. 192a contains a strange representation, arranged in the fashion of a mosaic, but rendered indistinct by the state of figures and inscriptions. L. 199. This is a remarkable example of subjects conceived in the earliest period of Byzantine art, undergoing a change and becoming weaker in execution with the lapse of time. The representation, namely, of the Prophet Isaiah, between the personifications of Night and Dawn, is well known to all lovers of art by the engraving in D'Agincourt's work, from a Byzantine MS. of the 10th century in the library of the Vatican. Another still finer example, though agreeing in all essentials with the above, is in the celebrated Byzantine MS. of the Psalter in Paris, of which I gave a circumstantial account in 1839.* Both point to one common earlier and justly prized original. Here we find, it is true, the subject again, with the same motives; the boy has even the same inscription—ὀρθρος; the figure of Night, however, is quite suppressed, while the bust-picture of the Almighty, in the mosaic type of Christ, in a golden circle, is introduced instead of the hand blessing, and proceeding from the segment of a circle. Finally, the execution, as compared with the others, especially with the Paris Psalter, is of very barbarous effect. L. 202a, and the following, display in great detail the history of the Three Children in

* See Kunstwerke und Künstler in Paris, p. 223.

the Fiery Furnace: they are represented, as in the catacombs, under youthful forms, and are also thus inscribed—παιδες. They are protected in the furnace by an angel. Their arms are raised in prayer to Heaven, which is represented as a large blue half-circle, with two rude profiles in white and red, and the words σελην and ηλιος. Their heads are of good expression. L. 206b contains, finally, a very stately and truly Byzantine representation of the Virgin standing with the Child.

Vol. I. p. 127.

A renewed examination of the Bedford Missal in 1854, and a somewhat more extended knowledge of early miniatures, enable me in some respect to correct as well as to add to my notice of that most important MS. made as early as the year 1835. I there-fore feel myself especially called upon to do so. There is no doubt that English, French, and Netherlandish artists united their skill in this work. Although, therefore, so thoroughly competent a judge as Mr. Bond pronounces the text to be English, the fact, on the other hand, that all the chief French saints—St. Genoveva, St. Martin, St. Germain, and St. Denis—are distinguished by golden letters in the Calendar, while St. Thomas of Canterbury is the only English one so favoured, is apparently an evidence of the volume having been executed in France. The borders have also far more a French than an English character. Further, I may observe that the pictures in the Calendar, the small circular pictures in the borders, St. John the Evangelist (l. 19a), St. Luke (l. 20b), and the majority of the large pictures, are by a French, though by no means a distinguished painter. Numerous small pictures in the borders also show a French hand, and one of a far more mechanical order. The Days of the Creation (l. 14), the Crucifixion (l. 144a), and the Last Judgment (l. 157a), appear to me, judging from the character of the heads, the glutinous nature of the colours, and the admirable impasto, to be the work of a Netherlander. The two best artists, however, who have taken part in this work, I am per-suaded were both English. The first is seen in the building of the ark. The whole tendency is here more realistic, the heads more individual and decided, and the colouring strikingly resembling that in authentic English miniatures. The following pictures are

also by the same hand:—The Building of the Tower of Babel
(l. 17b), the Departure from the Ark, and the Drunkenness of
Noah (l. 18b), the suppliant David (l. 96a), and finally various
small pictures in the borders—for instance, l. 186a. To the other
English, and incomparably superior hand I attribute the three
pictures which I was formerly disposed to give to Jan van Eyck,
viz. the two with the portraits of the Duke and Duchess (l. 256b),
and (257b) King Clovis, to whom the Almighty is sending the
coat-of-arms with the three lilies from Heaven. My especial
reasons for thus deciding are the slender proportions, delicate melting of the flesh-tones, the copious use of vermilion, the general
gaiety of colouring, and the character of the delicate ornamentation
on St. George's armour. All these peculiarities I have since learnt
in my studies of undoubted English miniatures in the British
Museum, and also in the Bodleian, in 1851, to be characteristic of
English work at this period.

———

Vol. I. p. 130.

My notice already given of Henry VI.'s Psalter is, when compared with the artistic importance of the MS., far too short. An
error in it also calls for correction. This octavo work contains
286 leaves, written in one column, in a large and powerful minuscule letter. The border decorations have an English character,
and St. George, the patron saint of England, is distinguished in
the calendar by golden letters; that the same distinction is here
bestowed on those French saints named in the Bedford Missal, is a
circumstance which may be explained by the fact that Henry VI.
was also King of France. The pictures bear witness partly to a
Netherlandish, partly to a French hand, and are interesting as
specimens of the length of time during which the idealistic tendency,
dating from 1350, maintained its power side by side with the
realistic, dating from about 1380. For as Henry VI. appears
here crowned—his coronation took place in Paris, 1431—and yet
still as a child, it is evident that the execution of this work belongs
to the years immediately following 1431, when the chef-d'œuvre of
the realistic art of the 15th century, namely, the altarpiece representing the Adoration of the Lamb, by the brothers Van Eyck, had
been already completed. By far the greater number of the pictures
partake of the idealistic tendency, and in my opinion were executed

by a French artist.   To these belong the Virgin enthroned (l. 49a), where the royal figure in a blue mantle with lilies, standing behind Henry VI., is not, as I have stated, the Duke of Bedford, but Louis IX., called St. Louis ; also the Virgin with the Child, who is giving a scroll to the youthful kneeling king; another, termed in my book the Coronation of the Virgin ; and finally (l. 205a), a very remarkable representation of the king, who, kneeling, entreats the intercession of the Madonna, who, kneeling in her turn, is praying to Christ, while she points with her left hand to her undraped breast, and with the other to herself.   Her prayer is heard, for Christ is seen above, enthroned next the Almighty, pointing to the wound in his side as symbol of the atonement. Two angels on the throne with the instruments of the Passion have the same meaning.   The different pictures of monks and nuns, of which I mentioned a few, are, on the other hand, entirely realistic in character, and show the hand of a Netherlander.   The picture with King David (l. 204b) is drier, and obviously by an inferior artist.   The combat between David and Goliah is remarkable as taking place within barriers, as at a tournament, with King Saul looking on from a tribune.   The delicate chess-board ground is also a relic of an older period, though occasionally the elements of a new era in art are seen side by side with it in a simple land-scape, and oftener in that species of architecture representing the interior of a church.

Vol. I. p. 206.

The following manuscripts are new acquisitions :—

The Vulgate (Addit. 18,720) folio, in two columns, on very fine parchment, beautifully written in a strong and full minuscule letter. This MS. is remarkable inasmuch as, though decidedly belonging to the 14th century, the eight pictures from the Old Testament, and the nine from the New, show no signs of the style of art prac-tised by Giotto, but partake entirely of that Byzantine character which prevailed in Italy in the 13th century.   The tone of the flesh is generally brown, the remaining portions of a dark and gloomy colour.   All evidence proves this work to have been exe-cuted in Northern Italy, most probably in Bologna.   Considered in an artistic sense the pictures are of little value.

Dante's Divina Commedia (Addit. 19,587), a folio volume of

174 sheets, in one column, with a broad border, written in a strong minuscule letter; the lower border, as far as l. 99a, containing pen drawings delicately shaded in colour and Indian ink. The picture l. 99b is incomplete in colour, and after that only outlines occur. The inventions are, however, clever; the motives generally very dramatic and graceful; the drawing of the nude—the period (about the middle of the 14th century) considered—good; the faces in many cases already emancipated from the Giottesque type, and striving successfully at individuality. In the *Inferno*, the representations even of the demons are not, as in the pictures by Bernardo Orcagna, caricatures; only the Satan at the end shows in form, as well as in motive, namely, in the devouring of the condemned, a similarity to that painter, though quite independent of him. I select a few of the single pictures: l. 2a represents the youthfully conceived Dante pointing to the figure of Virgil, who appears as an old man in a blue mandorla, with a golden Gothic frame; l. 3a, a female form, praying, probably Beatrice, with a nimbus of scolloped Gothic shape surrounded with rays, is very noble in motive, expression, and cast of drapery. At the commencement of the *Purgatorio* (l. 62a) the rich decoration of the border in beautifully coloured tendril-work points to Tuscany; below in a horizontal oblong is the Archangel Michael weighing two souls; other souls are kneeling. The picture of three knights (l. 77a) is particularly successful. This MS. represents probably one of the earliest attempts to embody the poems of Dante that has descended to us, and is on that account also very remarkable.

The following miniatures, extracted from MSS., which in 1834 I saw and described, in the possession of the late Mr. Young Ottley, and which, after his death, became the property of Mr. Rogers the poet, were fortunately acquired for the Museum at the sale of that gentleman's collection. They are thus secured from further wanderings, and have become accessible to every lover of art.

Border decorations, executed, as we are informed by an inscription, in 1489, for Antonio Pallavicini, Cardinal of St. Praxede. The beauty of the arabesques, enriched with classical motives, and the splendour of the colours and of the gilding, render these admirable specimens of the taste for MS. ornamentation of this period.

The same remark applies, as regards the middle of the 16th

century, to some borders with the following inscription:—" Apollonius de Bonfratellis de Capranica Capellæ et Sacristiæ Apostolicæ Miniator fecit, Anno Domini MDLXIV. mense Julio, sedente Pio IV. Pont. Opt. Max. de Medicis Mediolanense V." Here we see that Renaissance style in miniature painting first developed by Don Giulio Clovio, in which the most graceful arabesques are executed in gold, brown, and other colours, intermingled with small pictures and bronze cameos.

The original document, in the most elegant writing, on the finest parchment, containing the jointure settled by Lodovico Sforza, Lord of Milan, on his wife Beatrice d'Este: it is dated 1494, and signed by Sforza himself. In the centre of the wide upper border are the arms of Il Moro, supported by two beautiful angels of graceful action; at each side of which, in circles, are the portraits of himself and Beatrice in profile; both, and especially hers, display a refinement of taste, a delicacy of feeling for nature, and a technical completion seldom met with in this mode of art. Both the side borders are decorated with arabesques; the right one more in the earlier taste of the 15th century; the left one of that freer and more spirited character which points already to the 16th century, with very graceful figures introduced on purple or dark-green grounds. In the whole we perceive the influence of Leonardo da Vinci, then working in Milan. They were probably executed by that Maestro Girolamo whom Vasari praises as the greatest miniature-painter of that time in Milan.

Allied in character to the foregoing are the contents of a volume (Addit. 20,916) purchased at the sale of Lord Stuart de Rothesay's library; they consist chiefly of what are called in Italian *Ducali*, or instructions by the Signory of Venice, some of the 15th, but chiefly of the 16th and 17th centuries, all headed by a miniature. Some of these are very remarkable, especially the portraits. Upon the whole, these *Ducali* afford, like the deed of settlement above described, very interesting examples of that feeling in the middle ages which not only sought to adorn works of ecclesiastical and secular intention, but even bestowed the cheerful accompaniments of art upon documents of mere business import. They also show how long this custom continued. Among the miniatures, two are particularly remarkable: the one represents a sage in a carriage drawn by two owls, and accompanied by children. The invention is good, the colouring very powerful, and the execution admirable. The painter Francho, whose name we gather from the following inscription—" Dii faveant opus Franchi Miniatoris "—appears from the style of art to have belonged to the Milanese school of the latter part of the 15th century. The other miniature, a large combat, also bears witness to a very skilful Lombard artist of about 1480. This one has unfortunately much suffered.

DRAWINGS OF THE ITALIAN SCHOOL.

Vol. I. p. 224.

The additions made to the collection of drawings and engravings in the two years since the publication of my work, are, both in number and quality, very considerable.

Owing to the ceaseless and successful exertions of Mr. Carpenter, several miniatures extracted from MSS. have been acquired for his department.

The earliest is the initial O, $9\frac{3}{4}$ inches in diameter, and obviously belonging originally to a large Cantionale. In style of art and stage of development it may be adjudged to the Tuscan school of the time of Andrea Orcagna, and consequently to the latter half of the 14th century. In the middle is St. Bernard of Clairvaux, enthroned on his right St. Bernardin, on his left two other canonised monks of his order. The composition is dignified; the execution in body colours careful, and the grounds gilt. The body of the O is vermilion with green foliage, and flowers in the corners.

Next in importance is a miniature by Don Giulio Clovio, representing the martyrdom of St. Bartholomew. The influence of Michael Angelo is seen in the motive. On the other hand, the manner in which the blood is running down from the one already flayed leg is vulgarly realistic and very disgusting. The guards appear in the antique Roman costume. A stone idol is falling. The heads are pleasing, but of no character; the finish is great. A prayer on the other side appears to be by the same hand as the writing on the pictures by Clovio bequeathed by Sir Charles Greville to the library of the British Museum. About $5\frac{6}{8}$ in. high, by $7\frac{7}{8}$ in. wide.

Two miniatures of the time of Clovio, and allied to him in style, are also remarkable. The subjects are dancing children, and angels playing on musical instruments. The drawing of the one, where the angels are draped, is better than in the other, where the forms of the children are too full. Both are very soft and tender in treatment.

This is also the fitting place to notice a very beautiful drawing of the Crucifixion in red chalk, which Mr. Carpenter, in my opinion rightly, ascribes to Don Giulio Clovio. The rich composition of ten figures contains some few fine motives. It has, however, that eclectic character peculiar to this artist. In some parts Raphael may be recognised as the model for imitation, in others Parmigianino. The soft modelling agrees also with the manner of Clovio.

———

Pesellino (?).—A youthful female head looking down towards the right side; drawn with the point of the brush in a green-blueish tone, and on one side set off by a dark-blue ground. This is of very great delicacy, and may perhaps be, as Mr. Carpenter believes, by the hand of this rare scholar of Fra Filippo Lippi.

Jacobo Bellini.—The most important recent acquisition is decidedly the book of drawings by this master, with which lovers of art had been made acquainted by means of Dr. Gaye's long article in No. 23 of the 'Kunst Blatt' of 1840, published by Cotta in Stuttgart. This book had been since 1813 in Venice, in the possession of M. Domenico Mantovani. It consists of one folio volume of 100 leaves, of a thick and coarsely-grained paper, 99 of which, and most of them on both sides, are drawn upon in black chalk and pencil. In many cases one drawing runs through two opposite pages. On the first page is an inscription by the hand of the master, "De mano de mi iacobo bellino veneto 1430, in Venetia." I agree entirely with Dr. Gaye in his opinion that this date refers only to the commencement of these drawings, at which he doubtless continued to work for a series of years from this period. Considering the general dearth of pictures of the Venetian school belonging to the first half of the 15th century, a book of this kind, containing such a store of artistic ideas by the chief master of the school, becomes of the greatest importance, and the more so as scarcely a picture by his hand can be with certainty pointed out. The contents are divided into subjects for ecclesiastical art, subjects from mythology, and others from common life, animals, landscapes, and architecture; thus giving us a comprehensive view of the position occupied by the Venetian school at that time in all these different departments of painting. In the conception of his ecclesiastical subjects he frequently shows the influence of his master, Gentile da Fabriano. The Adoration of the Kings, p. 19, is an example of this; and still more so another representation of the same subject further on, with the rich suite of the kings on horseback. Other drawings, on the other hand, exhibit the development of a peculiar and highly dignified mode of treatment in sacred subjects. For instance, Christ in the Mandorla, p. 61; the Entombment, p. 23; the Almighty between Adam and Eve, p. 43; Judith, p. 35; and the Death of the Virgin, p. 67. The drawing of the Baptism of Christ is remarkable for the four angels playing on musical instruments; in the representation of which Giovanni Bellini and his school afterwards took so much delight. Upon the whole, however, we here perceive that realistic conception both of figures, and also in the ample rendering of space, which is so characteristic of the Venetian school. This peculiarity is already apparent in the frescoes of Jacopo d'Avanzo, but it is much further developed in these drawings. In many of the sacred subjects the landscape or architecture is by far the principal object, the very small figures playing only a subordinate part. Specimens of this treatment may be seen in the Annunciation, p. 13; in the same subject, p. 76; in the Flagellation, pp. 71 and 74; in the Judgment of Solomon, p. 47; and, finally, in the Twelve Disciples, p. 88. The monotony of the landscapes is striking, consisting, with some exceptions, of formless and clumsy hills.

In the conception of mythological subjects, with the exception of a fight between Lapithæ and Centaurs, where the master has obviously made use of an antique model, he shows an ignorance of all antique examples, amounting to an almost ridiculous naïveté. The Triumph of Bacchus is an instance of this. In this respect the contrast between these drawings and the Paduan school is very decided. To Squarcione, surrounded as he was with antique sculpture, such a mode of conception must have appeared quite puerile; and the hatred which, according to Vasari, that painter entertained for Jacobo Bellini was doubtless not the result of personal dislike only, but of the great difference which existed between their respective artistic tendencies. While Squarcione followed the newly awakened antique impulse, Jacobo Bellini adhered with enthusiasm to the marvellous and fantastic, and to the chivalry of the departing middle ages. This is shown by his drawings of all kinds of fabulous dragons, by his predilection for the subject of St. George and the Dragon (four drawings of which occur in this book), and by his spirited and veracious representation of the military commanders and soldiers of his period. While Squarcione, as all the works of his school prove, sought to apply the plastic laws of ancient sculpture to painting, Jacobo Bellini's efforts were all directed to the picturesque only. For this his feeling was so strong that he even sacrificed to it the moral importance of his subject; as, for instance, in the Crucifixion, p. 77, where the foreground is occupied with horsemen seen from behind, in the strongest foreshortenings, while the chief event takes place in the middle distance, so that the picture is principally devoted to solving the most intricate lessons in perspective. Thus again, in the Nativity, we find him taking delight in elaborate and overladen constructions in wood, in which the connoisseur of the early Venetian school may recognise the original model of similar erections by Giovanni Bellini and his followers, to wit, in the Adoration of the Shepherds by Girolamo da Santa Croce in the Berlin Museum, No. 24. In no respect, however, is his feeling for the picturesque seen to such advantage as in his draperies, which are frequently of a purity and freedom surpassing the later and best works of the great Andrea Mantegna, who never quite emancipated himself from his youthful practice acquired in the school of Squarcione, in which a disposition of drapery fitted only for sculpture was applied to painting. At the same time we recognise from this and other drawings the source of that powerful and beneficial influence which Jacobo Bellini exerted over Mantegna after he became his father-in-law. This influence may be traced in the greater picturesqueness of invention and truth of colour seen in the frescoes of the martyrdom and death of St. Christopher in the Chapel of the Eremitani at Padua, executed immediately after Mantegna's marriage with Bellini's daughter. To this fact I have drawn attention in my treatise on Andrea Mantegna, though I erroneously ascribed the change to Squarcione's criticism on the misapplied imitation of sculpture apparent in Mantegna's earlier pictures executed in Padua. The great development of the picturesque and realistic feeling in most of Mantegna's later works may now without question be ascribed to his connection with Jacobo Bellini. Various figures indeed occur—for instance, the archers in the Martyrdom of St. Sebastian, p. 11, and in another representation of the same subject—in which we plainly recognise Mantegna's models; while the conception of several single heads displays the strongest resemblance to the series of pen drawings by Mantegna, formerly in the possession of Mr. Samuel Woodburn, and now in that of Mr. Barker.

Scenes from the most various departments of common life are conceived with great truth and animation. I may mention especially a youth on horseback, and ladies also on horseback, one of whom has a falcon on her hand, p. 20; a fight between a knight and a lion, p. 22; a tournament, p. 36; milk-women, p. 34; and two men carrying a tub. The representation of animals, horses and lions, were evidently his favourite subjects; many studies of each are here, and both animals are frequently very successful.

Upon the whole, I may observe that in subjects requiring lively action he shows less aptitude; thus, in representing a combat, the thrusts are lame, and do not reach their mark. But in quiet figures, on the other hand, he deserves especial admiration. This is the case with St. Paul, p. 28—a sketch for an altarpiece, of three figures—who is positively grand in design. Also, though figures occur which are too meagre, we find equal examples of full forms, though his proportions incline frequently to the over slender. All things considered, he shows himself here as a very good draughtsman. Unfortunately a large portion of these drawings are very much rubbed, and others much obliterated.

ANDREA MANTEGNA.—The Virgin fainting, and two other women. A study executed with a broad pen for the group in the well-known engraving of the Entombment. The head of the Virgin is especially spirited; $9\frac{1}{2}$ in. high, $6\frac{5}{8}$ in. wide. Two youths, one holding a club in the left hand, and looking at the other, who has the left hand on his companion's shoulder, and a sword in his right hand. Obviously a fragment, the figures being cut off at the knees, and only the hilt of the sword seen. Of masterly execution in the sloping lines peculiar to Mantegna, with the brush and bistre, and showing the form of art he practised in his later time. 9 in. high, 10 in. wide.

PIETRO PERUGINO.—1. To this master I agree with Mr. Carpenter in ascribing a slight but spirited sketch for an Adoration of the Kings, of rich composition, and with much architecture. Formerly in the collection of Mr. Richardson, who erroneously held it to be by Giovanni Bellini. 7⅞ in. high, 7⅛ in. wide.

2. A Prophet seated, his left hand supported on a book—doubtless his Prophecies—his right hand pointing to it. This fine drawing has been wrongly ascribed both to Taddeo Gaddi and Benedetto da Majano. I am inclined, however, to consider it by Perugino.

LEONARDO DA VINCI.—1. The Virgin seated, holding the Child on her arm, who is hugging a cat. Close by, only in outline, another sketch of her head more in profile. Most spiritedly executed with pen and brush in sepia. On the back, only far slighter, a similar motive, but taken from the other side, so that the Virgin looks at the Child. About 4½ in. high, 3 in. wide. Purchased in 1856.

2. A page with slight but very spirited sketches in pen and sepia. Two horsemen in full gallop, a lion seizing a horse, and the strongly foreshortened figure of a horseman dying.

LORENZO DI CREDI.—Head of an old and bald man, almost three-fourths the size of life; admirably drawn on green paper with a silver point, and heightened with white.

MICHAEL ANGELO.—1. Study of a powerful man, much bent, and bound. Slightly drawn in red chalk, with a broad and masterly hand.

2. A powerful youth, seated, looking at a picture which he holds with the left hand. Most spiritedly and broadly thrown on the paper with the brush and sepia.

3. A head, life size, looking sidewards, and with open mouth. Of broad and masterly drawing in black chalk, heightened with white, most of which is now effaced.

RAPHAEL.—1. A seated figure, the hands above the head, as if bound. Judging from the inscription, a study for the well-known fresco of the Battle of Ostia. The right leg is separately repeated. Finely drawn in black chalk, though, from a defect in the forms of the left shoulder, rather questionable in my eyes.

2. The beautiful pen drawing of the group in the Entombment who are carrying the body. Bequeathed by Mr. Chambers Hall,

who has died since my work was published. Formerly in the Lawrence Collection, afterwards in that of the King of Holland.

Baccio Bandinelli.—A rich composition of much action, spiritedly drawn with pen and bistre.

Beccafumi.—Drawing for the well-known composition of Moses striking the Rock, on the floor of the cathedral at Siena. Of broad and spirited execution with the pen and brush in bistre, and hatched in the masses. This drawing quite agrees with the engraving by Laelius Cosatti. In the form of a frieze. $9\frac{5}{8}$ in. high, 5 ft. 3 in. wide.

Pellegrino da Modena.—A Pietà, of unusual composition, the Christ being in the centre, with the Magdalen kissing his feet, and with the Virgin, St. John, and seven other men and women in actions of lamentation on each side. The motives are noble, though the heads are somewhat insipid. The execution very careful, with the brush, in bistre, and heightened with white. Formerly in the Richardson collection.

Federigo Baroccio.—1. Study for his well-known Entombment. Of picturesque and masterly drawing, in red-brown colour on reddish paper, and heightened with white.

2. Study for his St. Francis receiving the *Stigmata*. Very broad, in Indian ink, on green paper. From the Sagredo Collection.

Correggio.—1. The Virgin, with the very graceful Child, and Joseph. In red chalk, of soft and picturesque treatment.

2. A figure in lively action, the left hand pointing to himself, the right upwards. Very pleasing. In red chalk.

3. The Virgin with the Child, who, turning upwards, is kissing and caressing her. A new and charming motive. In sepia, with a broad pen and brush.

These are on sheets of parchment, from the collection of Sir Peter Lely.

Parmigianino.—1. Jupiter upon a pedestal, holding the thunderbolt, and worshipped by numerous figures. Opposite to him the statue of Minerva enthroned. With pen and brush and bistre. Very spirited.

2. The infant Christ being bathed, a composition of six figures. Arbitrary in composition, but of very graceful motives. Of masterly drawing in sepia and red chalk.

Giorgione.—Above is a saint thrown down; according to Mr.

Carpenter's opinion, St. James the Less.   Below are numerous figures in fear and astonishment.   Very animated and speaking in motives, of good style in the draperies, and of masterly drawing in sepia with a broad pen.   Also ascribed to Titian.

PAUL VERONESE.—1. A Riposo.   The Virgin, looking down on the sleeping Child, is holding her breast with her right hand. Joseph is on the right, the ass on the left.   Of unusual elevation of feeling in the head of the Virgin.   The drawing broad and masterly, on greenish paper, with the pen and Indian ink, and heightened with white.   Of considerable size.

2. St. George before the throne of some potentate, which is surrounded with warriors and courtiers.   On the other side a group, with horsemen.   Like the foregoing drawing, only in sepia.   About 1 ft. high, 1 ft. 8 in. wide.

ANDREA SCHIAVONE, called MELDOLLA.—The Marriage of St. Catherine, with Joseph and three angels.   The proportions slender and the motives graceful in the style of Parmigianino. With pen and sepia on light brown paper, heightened with white, and very spirited and soft.   About 9 in. high, 7 wide.

CAMILLO PROCACCINI. — David celebrating his victory over Goliah.   A rich and attractive composition, in pen and Indian ink, slightly shaded.   Engraved by Ryland.

OTTAVIO LEONI.—Three portraits.   Very softly drawn, in his usual manner, with black and red chalk.

DRAWINGS OF THE EARLY NETHERLANDISH AND EARLY GERMAN SCHOOLS.

The sale of Mr. Woodburn's collection afforded Mr. Carpenter the opportunity of purchasing some miniatures of the Passion, which had been extracted from a MS.   These consist of Pilate washing his hands; the Flagellation; the Bearing of the Cross; the Descent from the Cross; and the Entombment.   They are executed with great skill in chiaroscuro, with modest indications of green trees and blue sky.   Judging from the drapery, which is still soft in its folds, from the already individualised heads, and from the character of the initials and text, they may have been executed in Belgium, on the French frontier, between 1430 and

1440. The heads are generally delicate in form and expression, but the proportions too short.

HANS MEMLING.—Sketch for the lower part of a rich composition of the Crucifixion, in which, however, the Cross is not even indicated, though the Magdalen is looking up to it in entreaty. The group of the fainting Virgin supported by St. John and a young female, bears, as well as the Magdalen, great resemblance to the beautiful small picture by Memling in the collection of the Rev. J. Fuller Russell. The same remark applies to the riders, five on horses and one on a camel. The horseman, also, seen in front, occurs in Memling's well-known Crucifixion in the Church of Our Lady at Lübeck. Two of the same, one of whom is holding a handkerchief to his face, are piercing the side. All the heads are very animated, and those of the believers and of the centurion very noble. The horses, which are very skilfully drawn, correspond most with those in the picture of the Seven Joys of the Virgin, by Memling, in the Munich Gallery. The execution is careful and delicately felt. Drawn with the pen and point of the brush in Indian ink, on white paper, with frequent hatchings. About 10 in. high, 11¾ in. wide. This drawing is the most important I know of the whole school of the Van Eycks.

EARLY DUTCH SCHOOL. — Most probably by Gerhart von Harlem. The youthful Christ teaching in the Temple, which is treated in the Romanesque style. A very admirable drawing in Indian ink with the point of the brush, but not complete. The figure of Christ is scarcely indicated. In the middle distance are the Virgin and Joseph, who have just entered. In the decidedly realistic character of the Scribes a certain humour is apparent. The drapery is sharp, but otherwise of good style. None of the feet are given, and only one indicated. 11¼ in. high, 8⅞ in. wide.

MARTIN SCHONGAUER.—Christ, as the teacher of the world, giving the benediction with his right hand,—in the left the Book of Life. A finished and masterly pen-drawing, 8⅛ in. high; almost 5 in. wide. Upon the drawing, in an early hand, which Mr. Hartzen rightly recognises as that of Albert Durer, is the following inscription : "Das hat hübsch Martin gemacht im 1469 jor." The head alone appears to me not quite worthy of this great master. The ink is of unusual blackness.

IN THE MANNER OF MARTIN SCHONGAUER.—The Virgin, with Joseph, seated on a block, and holding the Infant on her lap. Joseph is kissing his right hand. The head of the Virgin partakes much of Martin Schongauer in feeling and beauty; but, as also the Child, is fuller in the forms. The folds of the drapery are, it is true, sharp, though each single one is softly modelled. The execution, in Indian ink upon a reddish paper, is throughout masterly. The white with which it is heightened is now partially turned black. 8½ in. high, 8 in. wide.

By the master E. S. (?)—The Announcing Angel. Of very peculiar conception ; being represented holding a document with two seals in the left hand, and pointing to it as the warrant for his mission with the other. Of light and spirited touch with a broad pen. The above designation, which proceeds from so approved a connoisseur as Mr. Hartzen, is probably right. The character of the head only appears to me to be somewhat foreign to this master. 10 in. high, 5⅝ in. wide.

SCHOOL OF ALBERT DURER.—Adoration of the Shepherds. In the foreground of a landscape are seen the Virgin and Joseph adoring the Child, who lies on a cloth on the ground. Close by, under a tree, is a stately shepherd with a club : at his feet a sheep, and two smaller shepherds, one of them looking up to an angel with a scroll hovering over the house. In the middle distance, beneath a penthouse, are the ox and the ass. Upon a small tablet, hanging on the branch of a tree, is a monogram, and the date 1.5.1.4. Unfortunately spotted. In Christ's 'Lexicon of Monograms' he assigns this to Michael Wohlgemuth, and says that it occurs on his copper plates with the same date. On the other hand, Brulliot states that no plate so inscribed ever met his eye. Setting aside the fact that Wohlgemuth was never known as an engraver, and also the improbability of his engraving a plate at the age of 80, it may be remarked that this drawing, with which the engravings in question would doubtless agree, displays the fully developed style of Albert Durer. The unknown artist may therefore be classed as one of his very skilful followers.

HANS HOLBEIN.—The harvest of drawings by this great master is by far the most important of the recent acquisitions ; at the same time they equally exemplify the high development and rich variety of his powers.

1. Design for the Triumph of Riches, which, with its companion, the Triumph of Poverty, Holbein executed in body colours on the walls of the hall of the Easterling Merchants, in the Steelyard, London. Drawn with the pen, and slightly washed with Indian ink. The composition is known by the engraving in Van Mechel's work, which gives, however, no idea of the freedom, breadth, decision, and spirit of the drawing. In point of style and artistic merit it stands midway between Mantegna and Raphael, and is more than any other of his works calculated to prove Holbein to be *the* master in whom German art attained the free forms of the cinquecento; also that, had the circumstances of his life been as favourable to him as to Raphael, or, in other words, had he not been required to earn his daily bread by painting portraits, his name, as an historical painter, might have stood next that of the great Italian. About 9 in. high, 2 ft. wide. The best representation of the picture itself is, however, conveyed by Vostermann's copy in the possession of Sir Charles Eastlake, and, next to that, by the careful drawing in sepia, by De Bischop, in the print-room of the British Museum.

2. A female seated, and seen in front, with a kind of barett cap; an infant on her lap; on her right is a girl speaking to her; on her left, a boy with cap and feathers. The motives and indications of the forms are worthy of Raphael. The head of the woman, of a melancholy expression, is the slightest in execution; the rest is very broadly drawn with the pen, and slightly washed in Indian ink. In the handwriting of the master is this inscription:—" Exultate cedrus H. Holbein." A drawing of the first class, about 4 in. high, 6 in. wide.

3. Five musicians in a gallery, playing on wind instruments. Motives and expression of the greatest animation; of similar style to the last, only still broader and more powerful in treatment.

4. Henry VIII. alone at table beneath a canopy. Two persons approaching him; others are dispersed in the space. On the right is the buffet with various vessels : $3\frac{3}{4}$ in. high, $4\frac{3}{8}$ in. wide ; inscribed in capital letters, " Holbein invent :" a true picture of the time. The little heads are very spirited, and expressed with great mastery; while the light striking through the window, rendered with Indian ink, gives the whole a picturesque effect.

5. Portrait of a woman, drawn only in slight outline with the

silver point upon coloured paper, but with the most delicate feeling for nature.

6. A woman in bed; behind her an infant swathed in a cradle. Five other children are also present; the youngest naked and standing by the bed, two seated on the floor, and two bringing a vessel and a saucer for drinking. Next the house is an interwoven fence. Attached to a hut and a tree is a stake on which rags are hanging. $5\frac{3}{8}$ in. high, $7\frac{1}{2}$ in. wide. Signed " H. Holbein," in delicate writing. Very cleverly composed ; the children true and full in forms; and the execution with the pen broad and masterly.

7. Design for a clock; on the foot below, two Tritons ; above, two boys pointing to tablets with numbers, and bearing on their heads the dial-plate with a crown; in the centre a kind of satyr with a painful expression. About 1 ft. 6 in. high, 10 in. wide. The following inscription, not entirely legible, in pale ink :—" . . . hora . . . facta pro Anthony deny Camerario regis quod in initio novi anni 1544 regi dedet." This design, which is drawn in a very delicate Renaissance taste, in pen and Indian ink, was bought at the Strawberry Hill sale (Horace Walpole's), and is mentioned by him as having formerly belonged to the Mariette collection. The English name of the individual alluded to in the inscription is Sir Anthony Denny. A no less beautiful design for a clock, though somewhat different, may be seen (No. 86) in a MS. belonging to the British Museum : Sloane, No. 5308.

8. Design for the sheath of a dagger, with hilt; on the top are two Genii—half-length figures; on the sheath the history of Mutius Scævola, but of simpler treatment than in the drawing already described in my book. Lower down is a female figure, and also several half-length figures. The decorations, which display the later Renaissance taste, indicate the last period of the master, who, besides pen and Indian ink, has here employed a little sepia. $11\frac{3}{4}$ in. high, $2\frac{1}{4}$ in. wide.

9. A highly finished architectural design for a mantel-piece, in two stories, divided by an entablature of antique form, each story with two columns at the sides; the upper Ionic. In the centre space of the lower story is a half-circle, containing a circle with Esther and King Ahasuerus, and a fight of horsemen on each side ; in the angles are the busts of a warrior and a woman ; in the upper story, in the centre, above, are the royal arms in a circle, with a

lion and a dragon opposite supporting the shield ; at the sides, a
scroll and arabesques ; below, in the centre, and very spirited,
a combat of horsemen ; at the sides, a Charity with three children
(very beautiful), and Justice, with her feet upon criminals. The
division of the space shows how admirable an architect was Holbein.
In the motives of the figures the greatest freedom and the most
natural grace prevail ; the ornaments are of the choicest taste of
the Renaissance style. The execution with pen, Indian ink, and
sepia, is a model of precision and power. $21\frac{1}{2}$ in. high, $16\frac{3}{4}$ in. wide.
This drawing was formerly in the possession of Sir Joshua Reynolds,
and was also purchased from the Strawberry Hill collection ; it is
now framed and glazed and hung up.

St. Ursula with her suite in a ship, attacked by archers on the
shore ; in front, in a corner, upon a stone, is a T and another
letter which may be read as a b or a h. This drawing is nearly
allied to the earlier time of Holbein ; it is animatedly conceived
and of masterly execution with the point of the brush in Indian
ink, heightened with white.

ALBERT DURER.—1. Sketch for a Last Judgment, in two semi-
circles, one within the other. Above, in the centre, in the mandorla, is Christ enthroned, giving the benediction with the right
hand, and threatening with the other ; at his side, in corresponding
significance, are the lily and the sword ; next him, on each side,
the Apostles enthroned and Saints ; somewhat lower down, the
Virgin on the right, and John the Baptist on the left ; between
them, under the feet of Christ, are four other persons ; lower down
are two trumpeting angels, very grand and spirited ; below, on
the left, are the jaws of hell, with demons ; on the right, the
blessed conducted to heaven by angels. Signed with the monogram, and with the date 1513. This slight but very animated
drawing, with the point of the brush upon white paper, abounds
with original and beautiful motives. The Christ greatly resembles
that in Albert Durer's well-known engraving, where he is represented seated with scales and sword upon a lion : one of the
demons, however, is like that in the plate of the Knight, Death,
and the Devil. $10\frac{5}{8}$ in. high, 1 ft. $4\frac{6}{8}$ in. wide.

2. Scene from a legend with which I am unacquainted—a
canonised nun pointing with the right hand from a window to a
monk below in the water, who is holding a jug in his left hand,

and is being drawn out of the water by another monk.   A masterly drawing in Indian ink, with the point of the brush; the house slightly coloured of a blueish, the trees of a greenish tint.   9 in. high, $6\frac{1}{2}$ in. wide.   Erroneously inscribed with the name of Israel von Mecheln.

3. A kind of pillar, as a candelabra.   At the foot is a man seated; above, a goat leaping.   Inscribed 1510.   Broadly and softly drawn in Indian ink with the point of the brush, and slightly coloured. $11\frac{7}{8}$ in. high, $2\frac{5}{8}$ in. wide.

HANS BROSAMER.—Adam just created, and blessed by the Holy Trinity.   The First Person in papal robes, and with a sceptre, is giving the benediction on one knee ; the other Persons similarly attired and occupied, are hovering in the air.   In the corner on the left is a piece of architecture in the taste of the Renaissance.   The background is a landscape, with animals.   A very finished drawing, in a stiff and somewhat minute pen. $9\frac{2}{8}$ in. high, $6\frac{1}{2}$ in. wide.   I entirely agree with the designation above given by Mr. Carpenter.

GEORGE PENS.—1. The Sacrifice of Isaac.   A very spirited drawing in sepia with the pen and brush, and quite corresponding with the engravings by this master. $2\frac{1}{8}$ in. high, $3\frac{3}{8}$ in. wide.

2. Two Emperors; both in their robes, and with the imperial globe ; the one holding a sceptre, the other a sword.   2 in. high, $1\frac{1}{2}$ in. wide.

LUCAS VAN LEYDEN.—1. Lucretia kneeling, and stabbing herself, in the costume of the painter's time.   In the background is represented the cause for this deed.   In a circle about 4 inches in diameter, of masterly and careful drawing, on yellow paper, in pen and Indian ink, with slight heightening of white.   The whole style of art greatly recalls his master Engelbrechtsen, and bears witness to his earlier period.   On the back is the same subject, by an inferior but closely allied hand.

2. Judith putting the head of Holofernes into a bag.   The very mannered motive, and the broad use of the otherwise masterly pen, all point to the later time of the master.

PIETER KOECK.—Pen-drawing for an altarpiece with wings.   In the centre the Baptism of Christ ; a very rich composition.   Skilful and masterly.   This artist shows the influence of Bernhard van Orley.   Dated 1553.   Besides this there are 6 large drawings in pen and Indian ink of the History of David, with much architecture in the taste of the Renaissance.

" MARTINUS VAN HEEMSKIRK, inventor, 1561." This is the inscription on a very careful, though feebly executed pen-drawing, representing David reproved by Nathan, which quite corresponds with the known style of this master.

HENRICK GOLZIUS.—Colossal portrait of a man, of broad and masterly execution in pen and sepia, in the style of his engravings, with monogram, and the date 1608.

JERONYMUS BOSCH.—A fat man being shaved. Of vulgar humour, and drawn with a broad pen.

PIETER AERTZEN.—An old woman entreating a smith to patch an old pair of bellows. Pen and bistre. Dated 1570. The style of vulgar waggishness in which this drawing is conceived makes me attribute it to this master.

PIETER BREUGHEL THE ELDER.—Representation of some Dutch proverb, unknown to me. A man is searching with a lantern under bales of goods; another is looking into a tub; a third into a sack, &c. In the distance is an army. Full of character, and carefully drawn with pen and brush in bistre.

JAN BREUGHEL.—1 & 2. Landscapes, with travellers attacked by robbers. Two very good drawings.

DRAWINGS BY THE LATER MASTERS OF THE NETHERLANDISH SCHOOL.

RUBENS.—1. Portrait of a woman in black and red chalk. Slight and spirited.

2. Very slight but masterly sketch in the same style of a flat Flemish landscape.

VANDYKE.—1. Study for the portrait of the Earl of Arundel, seated, full length. Very easy in motive, and thrown on to the paper with the most masterly hand in black chalk.

2. Another sketch, of similar treatment, of a man seated, a child at his side.

JACOB JORDAENS.—Adoration of the Shepherds. A rich and dramatic composition, of bold and masterly execution with chalk and brush. Of unusual size.

Teniers.—1. A Knifegrinder at his work. Slight and broad, in black chalk.

2. Landscape, with a village church. Of similar treatment.

Peter de Hooghe.—A woman, taken in profile, instructing four little girls in the art of knitting. The heads are very animated. The light, falling in, is admirably expressed, though only in red chalk. Drawings by this master, especially of such a size, are very rare.

Philip Wouvermans.—Camp scene, with six horsemen, and other figures on foot. A trumpeter is blowing his instrument. This drawing, which is executed with great breadth only with the brush and Indian ink—the masses of light and shade admirably indicated—is a striking contrast to his delicately-finished pictures. It is well known how seldom drawings by this master occur.

Hobbema.—A water-mill, with reflections. Of admirable chiaroscuro, and broad and spirited execution with chalk and the stump. Exceedingly rare.

C. Poelemburg.—The Finding of Moses. His love of depicting the female form undraped is here indulged by representing Pharaoh's daughter and her companions as bathing. In sepia, and of the same tenderness and delicacy as his oil pictures.

Franz van Mieris the Elder.—1. An old woman seated in prayer. Opposite to her a child in strong lighting. In black chalk and the stump, and of such masterly treatment of chiaroscuro as to approach in effect the etchings of his master Rembrandt. Upon parchment, and signed "Mieris."

2. His own portrait, marvellously soft and delicate ; in the same style and on the same material as the foregoing, and obviously the original of the engraving by A. Blotelinck, which is preserved with it.

Jan Lievens.—1. A male portrait, almost to the knees. Of great truth of nature, and carefully and softly treated with black chalk and the stump.

2. A landscape. In front a drawbridge ; houses and trees behind. An effect of chiaroscuro is here produced with sepia, bistre, and a little colour, worthy of Rembrandt.

School of Rembrandt.—View of Bacharach on the Rhine. The foreground in clear light, the background in chiaroscuro. Of masterly execution in bistre and Indian ink.

" PIETER SANREDAM, 1661, 31 MAY."—This is the signature in the interior of a church, executed in Indian ink, and a little colour, and quite worthy of the author.

ALBERT CUYP.—Piece of water, with a sailing vessel and a boat. The luminous effect, and the fine reflections in the water, which are so admired in this artist's pictures, are also expressed here with great spirit and sketchy breadth. Drawings by Cuyp are very rare. Signed " A. C."

WILLIAM VAN DER VELDE.—1. Large drawing for a sea-fight, in chalk and the stump.

2. A smaller drawing of a similar subject, treated in the same way, but more slightly.

3. A calm sea, with several vessels. Signed " W. v. V. F." Of the same treatment, and of great charm.

SIR BALTHASAR GERBIER.—Portrait of Frederick, Elector of the Palatinate and King of Bohemia; in an oval form, and with tasteless decorations. Extremely delicate, but somewhat stiffly drawn with the pen upon parchment. Signed " Gerbier fet."

GONZALES COQUES.—Portrait of a woman seated, in Indian ink, on parchment. In an oval form. Very animated.

J. HULSWITT.—Exterior of an old picturesque house. Finely executed with the pen and brush and bistre. Of Rembrandt-like power.

" KORNELI VAN BORSUM, 1624."—This is the inscription in a drawing-book in 4to., containing a number of drawings with the pen, with the brush, in Indian ink, or in bistre ;—of landscapes with animals, and especially fowls ; sea-pieces ;—and lastly of scenes, in a circular form, representing the months of January and February. This book affords us a fresh example of the astonishing number of skilful artists who flourished in Holland in the 17th century, nothing else being known by this master.

ENGRAVINGS.

Besides the six engravings from the Otto Collection in Leipsic (of which I gave an account, vol. i. p. 254), ten more have been obtained from the same source ; so that the British Museum now possesses 16 out of the whole series of 24. They are as follows :

A female figure recumbent, and almost undraped. Upon a

scroll is this inscription: "Amor vuol fe, e dove fe nonn e, amor non puo." (Bartsch, xiii. p. 43, 1.)

A circle, in the centre of which is a stout young man crowned with vine-leaves; half-length. Festoons of fruit form a border around. (Bartsch, xiii. p. 143, 3.) $4\frac{1}{2}$ in. in diameter. A coarse, mechanical work, intended perhaps for Bacchus.

A circle, with Cupid, represented as a youth, with bandaged eyes, and bound to a tree by four women, two on each side, who are playing him tricks. (Bartsch, xiii. p. 144, 5.) $6\frac{2}{12}$ in. in diameter. The Cupid is very elevated both in motive and forms, and, as well as the rest of the drawing, points to Sandro Botticelli.

A circle. In the centre, opposite each other, are two heads, of a man and woman, both caricatures, and looking at one another. In a border of leaves and tendrils are eight ovals, each containing one amorino playing on a musical instrument. The words " Da mi conforto," written by hand on a scroll, are to be considered as proceeding from the mouth of each of these caricatures, and well express the original humorous intention of the design. (Bartsch, xiii. p. 144, 6.) $6\frac{9}{12}$ in. in diameter.

A circle, in the centre of which is a fight of five large dogs with a bear. The border is a wreath of fruit. The balls, from the arms of the Medici, are drawn with the pen in two compartments. (Bartsch, xiii. p. 145, 8.) $7\frac{6}{12}$ in. in diameter. The conception is very animated. It is very interesting to compare this plate with another of an upright form, and containing the same composition; with this advantageous difference, that, instead of one of the dogs, a huntsman is introduced, who is spearing the bear.

A circle, with a hideous face. (Bartsch, xiii. p. 146, 10.) $6\frac{8}{12}$ in. in diameter.

A circle, with two medallions. In the one, the head of a man in profile; in the other, that of a woman in front. Above and below are three hunting subjects. (Bartsch, xiii. p. 146, 11.) $5\frac{8}{12}$ in. in diameter.

A circle, with a youth and a maiden in a landscape, and a young man blowing the shawm and beating the drum. (Bartsch, xiii. p. 148, 15.) $5\frac{3}{12}$ in. in diameter. Very attractive for naïveté and simplicity.

A circle, with a youth bound to a tree, and a maiden holding up a heart before him. (Bartsch, xiii. p. 149, 19.)　$3\frac{8}{12}$ in. in diameter. Very animated and naïve.

A horizontal oval. Two amorini, holding a festoon of fruit and leaves. In the centre is Cupid standing with bandaged eyes and outspread wings; in one hand a bow, in the other an arrow. (Bartsch, xiii. p. 150, 21.)　$3\frac{9}{12}$ in. high, $7\frac{9}{12}$ in. wide. In this beautiful little plate the composition is prettier, and the forms softer and fuller, than in the others.

These plates, with the before described other six, are especially important as rare examples of non-ecclesiastical subjects at so early a period of Italian engraving.

The Crucifixion. The Saviour, with the head already sunk. On the right the Virgin, with folded hands; and, what is new to me, on the left St. John the Baptist, with a long sceptre, terminating in a cross, looking at the spectator, and pointing upward to the Cross. About 8 in. high, 6 in. wide. Conception and expression remind me most of Andrea del Castagno. The draperies are of pure taste, though the still niello-like treatment is very hard. From the De Bammeville Collection.

BALDINI.—The Virgin, upon a moderately high throne, is holding with her right hand the Child, who is seated on her knee. Two flying angels hold a crown over her head. On the right, directly close to the throne, and about the height of the Child, is a female saint, holding a flower and the model of a church; on the left St. Lucy. More in the foreground, on the right, are St. Anthony of Padua and St. Catherine; on the left, Peter Martyr, and the Magdalen with her hands folded, and the box of ointment at her feet. In the centre, quite in front, is St. Dominic kneeling, with the rosary. Above the wall which runs behind the throne are seen four cypresses. The whole engraving, with obtuse angles, is enframed by a wreath of laurel and ribbon. About 6 in. high, 5 in. wide. The rich composition corresponds very nearly with Sandro Botticelli, and the treatment, as Mr. Carpenter rightly observes, entirely with the manner of Baldini. The printing ink is dull and grey; the drapery of the Magdalen coloured with dark crimson. Some other portions are also feebly coloured.

POLLAIUOLO.—An impression of the plate of Hercules with the Giants (Bartsch, No. 3), in the same unfinished state, with the white ground left on the left hand, like that in the Imperial Collection at Vienna. From the De Bammeville Collection.

Andrea Mantegna.—1. Impression of the Virgin in the Grotto. (Bartsch, No. 9.) Of the rarest power and beauty.

2. Impression of the first state of the plate of the Virgin and Child. (Bartsch, No. 8.) I have nowhere seen a proof of such warmth, freshness, and power. The fine shadings in the heads, which are here perfectly rendered, show the degree of artistic excellence at which Mantegna had arrived. From the Mund Collection.

Girolamo Mocetto.—1. John the Baptist in the Desert. (Bartsch, No. 5.) This is the model for the more frequent plate by Giulio Campagnola, who only altered the landscape background; incomparably nobler in the head, and of freer and better understood drawing. The treatment also for this period is very broad and masterly. Judging from conception, expression, and rendering of forms, this is decidedly from a drawing by Andrea Mantegna. From the Mund Collection.

2. The third portion of a plate representing a large combat of horsemen, with the signature " Mocettus." Another third is in the Imperial Collection in Paris; the remaining portion in the Imperial Collection at Vienna. From the Mund Collection.

St. Bernard of Siena, standing below an arch of the most elegant Renaissance taste—the angles, however, perforated—pointing with his right hand to an open book in his left, in which are the words, " Pater manifestabi nomen tuum hominibus." On the wall is his attribute, the I. H. S., with the cross above the H. In front are two boys with large cornucopias; behind, upon a parapet, three mitres and a flower-pot. The portrait-like head, as well as all the rest, is admirably drawn. The whole style of art shows an affinity with Andrea Mantegna; but the taste of the drapery is purer, and the technical treatment more developed. In all probability the work of one of his followers. The impression is singularly powerful and fine.

A Pietà. Christ seen more than half-length above a sarcophagus, of antique decoration, showing, with an expression of rigid sorrow, and with somewhat lively action, the wounds in his hands. Next above is the Holy Spirit in form of a dove; then the Almighty in the mosaic type of Christ, with a crown, formed of three lilies, and

surrounded by a glory, on his head; the arms outstretched. In
the air, on each side, in very pleasing motives, is a kneeling angel.
Below, before the sarcophagus, is John the Baptist, looking up, the
cross above his right shoulder, his hands folded. The folds of his
mantle are of very good taste. The goatskin is only seen upon the
chest; the right advanced leg is nude. On the left is a youthful
saint, quite in the costume of the time, with a naked sword, the
point of which touches the ground, under his left arm; his hands
are folded. In the centre of the sarcophagus is a wreath of laurel
with four ribbons; in the centre the word IESV. Round the whole
plate is a border of laurel-leaves. $8\frac{5}{12}$ in. high, $6\frac{7}{12}$ in. wide.
From the Mund Collection; and in that catalogue erroneously
given to Baldini. I agree rather with Mr. Carpenter in recognising in the characters of the heads, and in the drawing and
treatment, a striking likeness to the so-called *Gioco* by Mantegna.
At the same time the whole style of art strikes me as somewhat
less refined, the drawing not so good, and the treatment somewhat
harder and more antiquated, namely, the crossing of the lines at
right angles, in the style of a niello. In all probability a unique
specimen.

NICOLLETTO DA MODENA.—The God Mars, youthfully conceived, with the armour and weapons of the period, standing in a
quiet posture, looking down; the right hand inclined towards the
hip; a standard in the left hand, with S. P. Q. R. and a trophy. On
the right is a dry tree, on which is a small tablet with the name
NICOLETO DA MODENA. At the foot of the tree are two shields
and a drum. On the left side is a ruin. On a projection in the
form of a pedestal is a helmet, and leaning against it a battleaxe.
On one of the surfaces of the pedestal is the inscription DIVO MARTI.
In the middle distance is a large piece of water, and behind that a
landscape with two hills.   About $4\frac{1}{2}$ in. high, 3 in. wide.   This
plate, which is not mentioned by Bartsch, is of great delicacy of
feeling, and more elegant in drawing than most of the works of this
engraver.

IN THE MANNER OF ANTONIO OF BRESCIA.—The youthful
Bacchus, his left hand, according to the well-known antique motive,
above his head; the right hand upon the shoulder of a very hideous
follower of Pan. On the left is a male satyr blowing the horn and
the double flute. At the feet of Bacchus is a dog biting a serpent.

Next the follower of Pan is a *cista mystica* with two snakes coming out of it, and a tree on which hangs a Pan's-pipe. About 5 in. high, 4½ in. wide. The treatment of this very powerful engraving shows much affinity, as Mr. Carpenter rightly remarks, with the above-mentioned master. The indication of the forms is hard.

The Holy Family. In the centre is the Virgin, of pathetic expression, sitting with her hands folded ; before her is the very beautiful Child, sweeping away the dust and dirt with a broom. More behind is St. Joseph sawing a beam. In the background are two women, whose gestures express surprise. In the distance is the high line of the sea, with a vessel. The sun is seen in the sky. On the right, quite in front, is a short stump of a tree, on which is a small anvil with a hammer upon it. Against the tree is a stake. In the centre on the floor is a shell. About 6 in. high, 5 in. wide. The full and decided forms bear witness to an excellent artist of Raphael's time. The technical treatment also of the engraving is on a par with Marc Antonio. At the same time, this domestic conception of the subject is very unusual in Italian art ; the feeling, however, is very elevated. An admirable impression.

Marc Antonio.—1. Leda with the Swan. Quite the same composition which Bartsch (xiv. p. 187, No. 232) describes as in the manner of Agostino Veneziano. It is however so far more spirited, of such delicate drawing and superior chiaroscuro, and in all these respects so entirely resembling Marc Antonio, that Mr. Carpenter appears to me to be perfectly right in recognising in this plate a specimen of the master, and in that mentioned by Bartsch a copy from it. Bartsch is of opinion that the design was by Giulio Romano. If that be the case, he borrowed the chief motive from the well-known composition by Michael Angelo.

2. A very fine impression of the Triumph of Titus (Bartsch, No. 213), with this difference, that the fillet upon the trophy held by the warrior seen from behind, and who is pointing to the child, is left partially white, while in the common state of the plate this portion is quite in shadow.

3. A woodcut of excellent workmanship, from the engraving of the Martyrdom of St. Lawrence by Marc Antonio (Bartsch, No. 104), the size of the original. An admirable impression. From the Mund Collection.

ENGRAVINGS OF THE EARLY GERMAN SCHOOL.

The well-known subject of St. Hubert kneeling before the stag with a crucifix between its horns, here represented with a few peculiarities new to me. On the right of the kneeling saint, and next to the stag opposite him, only the foremost half of which is seen, is a boy kneeling, of a monkey-like face. In front of the saint is a dog kneeling with his fore-legs, while the hind-legs still express the act of running. Further behind, and only partially seen, are two other dogs, the foremost of the two also kneeling. Quite on the right, and in the middle distance, is the horse turning his head round. An angel is seen descending with a stole painted of a crimson colour. The other portions also, with the exception of the flesh, are almost all illuminated. Along the upper border, in a Gothic minuscule letter, difficult to read, is the following inscription :—" Sanctus Hupertus zu atre (?) in lotringen." Hanging by threads to this inscription are two slightly-indicated coats-of-arms, $7\frac{1}{12}$ in. high, $4\frac{11}{12}$ in. wide. Drawing and motives are good, and the treatment very simple ; for besides the tolerably delicate outlines, there is only a very modest indication of shadows. The printing-ink is powerful. Judging from all circumstances, the work can hardly be much later than 1440.

The Virgin with her hands crossed, lamenting over the body of the Saviour—a very meagre figure stretched upon her lap, the head lying towards the right side of the engraving. In the background is the cross, on which hang a scourge and a rod, and against which lean the pole, with the sponge and the spear. On each side are rocks indicated in the early Byzantine form. $7\frac{2}{12}$ in. high, $4\frac{10}{12}$ in. wide. The ink is rather pale, and the very moderate execution like the German editions of block-books. The folds in the drapery of the Virgin are much overladen, and with sharp breaks. The execution may be assigned to about 1460-70. This impression is illuminated. Both these engravings just described are on wood.

An acquisition of great interest for the art of copper-engraving in Germany consists of 27 small plates on parchment, cut out of a surrounding text, as the writing on the back of some of them testifies. They represent—1. The youthful Christ teaching in the Temple. 2. Christ washing the feet of the Apostles. 3. The Last Supper. The figures are seated at a round table. On the left, in the foreground, is Judas Iscariot, with Satan entering his open mouth in the shape of a fly. On the stone bench on which he is seated is the inscription LVII 10r, indicating, as Mr. Carpenter agrees with me, the date 1457. All other evidence also is in favour of this supposition. In style of art, and in the still soft folds of pure taste, these little prints recall the small Passion by Meister Wilhelm in the Berlin Museum. At the same time the treatment is very simple, and does not extend beyond a pale outline. Most of the compositions have something awkward: on the other hand, single motives are speaking. The powerful colouring applied, and the large glories laid on with leaf-gold, with borders and decorations painted in black, bring these little prints in close affinity to miniatures. Here evidently we see a kind of transition from the art of miniature-painting to that of engraving on copper. 4. Christ on the Mount of Olives. He is here represented lying on the ground with outstretched arms. Before him, on a green eminence, is the chalice. From a cloud, resembling the earlier segment of a circle in form, proceeds the hand of the Almighty, holding the cross of St. Anthony **T**. The three sleeping disciples are clumsily arranged. 5. Judas kissing Christ. 6. The guards, three in number, lying as if dead before Christ on the ground. 7. Christ before Caiaphas, who is rending his garment. 8. The maid-servant of the High Priest accusing Peter. Her gesture is particularly speaking. 9. Christ before Pilate. 10. Christ before Herod. 11. Christ mocked. 12. The Scourging. 13. The Crowning with Thorns. 14. The Ecce Homo. 15. Pilate washing his hands. 16. The disrobing of Christ. 17. Christ disrobed, and sitting next the Cross, which lies on the ground. A very rare form of representation. 18. Christ being attached to the Cross. 19. Christ on the Cross. 20. The Descent from the Cross. 21. The Dead Christ lamented. 22. The Entombment. 23. The Descent into the Limbus. 24. The Ascension. 25. The Three Women at the Sepulchre. The angel is drawing the winding-sheet from the empty tomb, in order to show that the Lord is no longer there. 26. The Noli me tangere. 27. The Incredulity of Thomas. The difference between the youthful Christ teaching in the Temple and the Christ washing the feet of the Apostles is so great that other plates may be supposed to have filled up the text between them. Each plate, including a border $\frac{2}{12}$ of an inch wide, is

$3\frac{5}{12}$ in. high, $2\frac{6}{12}$ in. wide. · These engravings appear to have been executed in the Rhine country, probably in Cologne.   They afford a fresh proof of the early exercise of the art of engraving on copper in Germany.

The Master of 1466.—I am glad here to make good an error committed in vol. i. p. 293, where I reported that the British Museum did not possess the chief work of this master, the Virgin of Einsiedlen (Bartsch, No. 35).   On the contrary, a remarkably fine impression of the same is here.

2. The Adoration of the Kings, a different composition to that described by Bartsch, No. 14.   The Child, seated on the lap of the Virgin, is here showing her a gold piece which he has taken from the open casket of the King kneeling before him in profile.   Between the Virgin and this King, and more behind, is the second King, standing, and taken in front ; and next to him, also standing, and seen in profile, the third King, looking up at the star, and holding in his right hand a vessel in the form of a horn, his left hand up-raised.   On the right, in the ruin in the background, is Joseph, with his right hand on a crutch, a candle in the left.   On his right are the ox and ass.   Finally, in the landscape are two shepherds, also looking up at the star.   About $4\frac{1}{2}$ in. high, 3 in. wide.   A good though somewhat spotted impression.   The composition shows in a high degree the influence of the Van Eyck school.   The treat-ment displays the middle time of the master.   This plate, an im-pression of which is in the collection of engravings in the Berlin Museum, is a free and diminished copy from a plate in *abraded work*, of which an excellent impression exists in the collection of M. Sotz-mann at Berlin.   The essential difference between the two lies in the landscape background.   That in the abraded plate contains a town and two mountain castles, and, besides the shepherds, the figures of three horsemen, and three pedestrians, one of whom, carrying a sack, is attacked by a lion.   In this engraving, on the other hand, there is only one mountain castle, and, on the stream at its feet, a ship, with the indication of some figures.   The abraded plate is $6\frac{4}{12}$ in. high, $4\frac{4}{12}$ in. wide ; and is also surrounded with a border of foliage work of an inch wide.

3. A couple of lovers, in the open air ; mentioned by Bartsch (vol. x. p. 53, No. 29), under the name of " l'Amant," as anonymous. This plate is with justice assigned by Mr. Carpenter to the Master

of 1466. Judging from drawing and treatment, it belongs decidedly to his earlier time.

Lucas van Leyden.—Among the plates of this master, presented to the British Museum, as mentioned in vol. i. p. 299, by H. T. Brooke, Esq., there are two, of the utmost rarity, to which I omitted to call attention, viz. the large plate of Hagar and the "Uylenspiegel."

I must also here mention, and chiefly for its great rarity, a plate of the early French school, by Jean Duvet. It is a circle of about 6 in. in diameter, containing three horses rearing ; the one seen half in profile, the other two from behind. On the right is a horseman, nude ; another figure, also nude, is holding the throat of the horse on the left. Below, on the left, is a dog's head in profile ; on the right, the upper portion of another dog seen from behind. A good impression, though with a small piece cut off on the left side. M. Dumenil himself never saw this plate, but only mentions it as existing, at the close of the preface to his well-known Catalogue.

In other departments, also, the last three years have brought many additions. The collection of Hollar's etchings has now, by means of a considerable number of new specimens, among which are some of his chief and rarest, become one of the richest and finest in the world.

Of Rembrandt's etchings also it may be unhesitatingly said that the finest collection is here. The same applies to the other Netherlandish etchings, which have received their last completion by new and very valuable additions to Mr. Sheepshanks' splendid collection, purchased some years ago by the Museum of Mr. Smith.

Of several German engravers — such as Dietrich, Bode, Carl Baron von Vitinghof, and Weirotter—who had before been quite absent, or only very sparingly represented, whole collections have been purchased.

As regards the Block-books, I have been publicly accused of having described them as belonging also to the Print Room. I may observe therefore here that this was by no means my intention. The misunderstanding is merely owing to the circumstance that in the superscription, vol. i. p. 300, " Block-books and single woodcuts in the British Museum," the words " the library of printed books in " were omitted after the word " in."

Although not belonging to the department of Block-books, I may here notice a very great rarity with Italian woodcuts, in the same library. This is a quarto vol. of 66 leaves, with the title, " Philippi de Barbariis opuscula, MCCCCLXXXI. ;" and the further particular title, " Tractatus solennis et utilis editus per religiosum virum." The 28 therein contained woodcuts are very simply treated, but nobly composed and well drawn. They show the strong influence of Andrea Mantegna.

LETTER II.

National Gallery — Florentine, Umbrian, Paduan, Venetian schools, &c. — Lord Elcho's collection — Lord Yarborough's collection — Mr. Barker's collection — Tuscan and Umbrian schools — Book of Drawings by Mantegna — Collection of Marquis of Hertford — Italian, Spanish, French, Netherlandish, and English schools — Grosvenor Gallery — Mr. Baring's collection — Florentine, Roman, Bolognese, Venetian, French, Early German and Netherlandish, Flemish, Dutch, and English schools — Mr. Holford's collection — Lord Ward's collection — Collection of H. Danby Seymour, Esq. — Collection of Right Hon. Henry Labouchere — Mr. Morrison's collection — Sir Charles Eastlake's pictures — Mr. Sackville Bale's collection — Sir John Soane's collection.

ADDITIONS TO THE NATIONAL GALLERY.
Vol. I. p. 315.

In the two years that have elapsed since the publication of my work, the National Gallery has been enriched by legacies from Lord Colborne and Mr. Rogers, and by very important purchases. The latter give evidence of a systematic plan which every lover of art will gladly recognise, namely, that of supplying to the Gallery those schools and periods which have hitherto been wanting, and which alone can contribute to give it the completeness worthy of so great and wealthy a nation. With this view admirable works of the great Italian masters of the 15th century—of Perugino—Mantegna—Giovanni Bellini—upon whose shoulders Raphael, Titian, and Correggio may be said to have been upraised—have been obtained. How difficult also it is to procure pictures of this class at the present day no one can better appreciate than myself, to whom, as regards a public gallery, a similar task has been assigned.

I proceed to consider the new pictures in the same order of schools as in my book.

THE FLORENTINE SCHOOL.

BENOZZO GOZZOLI.—Altarpiece. The Virgin enthroned, holding the Child standing on her lap. Behind her are four angels. At the sides are John the Baptist, with SS. Zenobio,

Jerome, Peter, Dominic, and Francis. This work, according to a recently published contract,* dated October 14, 1461, was executed in tempera for the *Oratorio* of the Brotherhood of the Purification of the Virgin, consequently at a time when the painter, born 1424, was 37 years of age. The picture is unequal in its parts. The Child is the least interesting in motive and forms, while the head of the kneeling St. Jerome, which, in intensity of feeling, recalls Fiesole, the master of Benozzo Gozzoli, is very attractive. The same may be said of the angels, and especially of the small figures on the worked robe of one of the figures. The preservation is, in every essential part, excellent. As all authentic easel pictures by Benozzo Gozzoli are exceedingly rare, the acquisition of this is the more important for a public gallery.

FRA FILIPPO LIPPI.—St. Bernard of Clairvaux adoring the Virgin, who appears to him with the infant Christ. Of the highest elevation and refinement of feeling. Judging from this quality, from the characters of the heads, and the drawing, I am inclined to consider this picture, which is dull in colour, an early work of the master. From the collection of M. de Bammeville.

SANDRO BOTTICELLI.—The Virgin standing, and holding with both hands the Child before her. On the right is John the Baptist, as a child, with a crimson mantle over his goatskin, his hands folded, and his eyes cast down. On the left is an angel. The background is sky. According to the inscription on the back of the picture—"M. Giuliano da S. Ghallo"—it was probably once in the possession of that artist, mentioned by Vasari as having, with his brother, formed a collection. The expression of purity in the youthful and portrait-like head of the Virgin, is admirable; the same may be said of that of humble adoration in the Baptist and angel. The Child is modelled with particular care. Most of the hands are unusually graceful in form and motives. The picture is in excellent preservation.

JACOPO PACCHIAROTTO.—The Virgin offering the breast to the Child, who is looking round. The background a landscape. Easel pictures by this Sienese master rarely occur. The maternal expression in the portrait-like head of the Virgin is very success-

---

* Zanobbi Bicchierai. Alcuni documenti artistici. Firenze, 1855.

ful, and the Child is carefully executed in a warm tone.   From
the collection of M. de Bammeville.

THE UMBRIAN SCHOOL.

LORENZO DI S. SEVERINO.—The Virgin enthroned with the
Child, and surrounded with four saints. Signed. Lanzi rightly
remarks that this painter, who flourished about 1470, remained
inferior in the rendering of artistic form to the average standards
of Italian art. In earnest and dignified character of heads,
however, in good drawing and careful execution, he shows himself to be an able master. In excellent preservation. From the
de Bammeville Collection.

NICCOLO ALUNNO.—The head of Christ, as the Ecce Homo,
in body colours on plaster. The refined and genuine religious
feeling for which the pictures of this rare master are celebrated
is well exemplified in the noble features of this head.

PIETRO PERUGINO.—The three lower and principal compartments
of the altarpiece painted, according to Vasari, for a chapel in the
Certosa of Pavia. The centre compartment represents the Virgin
kneeling in adoration before the Child, who is lying on a cushion,
supported by a youthful angel. Three angels are in the sky
above. The compartment on the right contains the Archangel
Michael, in full armour; that on the left the Archangel Raphael
with the youthful Tobit. The background consists of a landscape
running through each picture. Of the three upper compartments
the centre contained the First Person of the Trinity, with the
Holy Ghost as the dove doubtless below him; those at the sides
the announcing angel Gabriel and the Virgin. The altarpiece
consequently comprehended originally the Trinity, the Virgin,
and the three archangels. At the dissolution of the monastery
of the Certosa, these three lower and principal compartments were
purchased by the ducal family of Melzi, and transferred to Milan,
where they remained until 1856, when the present Duke Melzi
sold them to the National Gallery. These pictures possess in the
highest degree the feeling for beauty, purity, and earnestness in
which the essence of Perugino's art may be said to consist, combined at the same time with a depth and warmth of colouring, a
delicacy of modelling, and a carrying out of detail, such as is
most rarely met with in the works of this master. In both the

side compartments especially, the forms of the school peculiar to this master are developed with an animation which led both Rumohr and Passavant to believe that the hand of the youthful Raphael had been engaged upon them. I agree with them as to the co-operation of the great master, though inclined to assign to it a more definite limit; for the great elevation and refinement, the soft melancholy which pervades the expression, the tender modelling, and the marvellous feeling for beauty—all charac-teristics of Raphael—appear to me to shine forth especially in the left compartment [right of the spectator] and more particu-larly in the head of the archangel Raphael. In my notice of the beautiful drawing for this picture at Oxford (vol. iii. p. 56) I have supposed it to be executed about the year 1501. At all events, no later date than 1502 can be assigned, for Passavant proves that the Coronation of the Virgin, executed by Raphael for the Oddi family of Perugia, and now in the Vatican, cannot have been produced later than 1503. In truth, the Coronation of the Virgin exhibits, in point of feeling, style of modelling, and power of tone, much affinity with this left compartment, which at all events was one of the last works executed by the young Raphael in the atelier of his master, as he painted the picture for the Oddi family on his own account. Thus the period of the execution of the whole altarpiece, of which we have hitherto had no evidence, may be also determined. This may be assigned to no earlier a time than that of Perugino's location in Perugia, when, according to the custom of the day, his scholars assisted in the works he had undertaken. That they did so in this instance is further proved by the three angels in the sky, in the centre picture, which exhibit a coldness and crudeness of colour differing from all the rest of the work, and also from all the authentic examples of Perugino before the year 1500, and are probably by the hand of Spagna. The landscape is especially worthy of admiration in point of forms, fulness, and depth of tone. The name of the master is on the compartment which contains the archangel Michael.

Lo SPAGNA.—An altarpiece. The Virgin and Child upon a lofty throne, surrounded with angels. At the foot of the throne are two little angels seated, and playing on musical instruments. The picture is semicircular above. From the collection of Lord

Orford. The composition is of simple and antiquated form, but the separate motives are free and graceful; the head of the Madonna mild and lovely; the expression of the angel looking up from below inspired; the modelling careful; the colouring powerful and very clear, and the preservation in all essentials excellent. The pictures of this master, who, next to Raphael, was the most gifted scholar of Perugino, are rarely found even in Italy.

SCHOOL OF PADUA.

ANDREA MANTEGNA.—This highly original school, founded by Francesco Squarcione, about 1430, was formerly not represented in the National Gallery at all. The difficulty of discovering authentic works by this its chief master, makes it the more fortunate that the gap should have been filled by such an example as this altarpiece. The Virgin is seen enthroned under a vermilion canopy, holding the Child standing on her lap. On the right is John the Baptist with a delicate cross in the right hand, round the lower part of which is entwined a scroll, with the "Ecce Agnus," on the inner side of which, in elegant characters, is the inscription —" Andreas Mantinia, C. P. F." (i. e. civis patavinus fecit). He is clad in the goatskin, and in the left hand holds a light-coloured drapery around him. On the left is the Magdalen, with blonde, grandly-flowing hair, looking upwards with an air of inspiration, holding in her right hand the vase of ointment, and grasping her mantle with her left. On the ground are separate stones and plants, and on each side of the throne pomegranate and orange trees in flower. The background is sky. The figures are three-fourths the size of life. The general effect of this picture, which is painted in tempera, is unusually light. Nevertheless the saints, both in the light draperies and in the flesh parts, are most delicately modelled, and carried out in every detail with as much knowledge as care. The style of the very tender folds strikingly recalls the picture of the Madonna della Vittoria in the Louvre, and, as well as other qualities, bears witness to the latest and ripest time of the master. The Madonna's head however, as we occasionally find in pictures by the master—a circumstance for which it is difficult to account—is inferior to the rest. The preservation is excellent. According to the evidence of Borroni, this picture passed from the possession of Cardinal Cesare

Monti, by legacy, into the Andreani family. Later it became the property of the Mellerio family; and last of all that of the family of Sommaglia, who sold it to a picture-dealer in 1855.

BARTOLOMMEO VIVARINI.—The Virgin, with the Child on her lap. St. Paul on the right—St. Jerome on the left. Half-length figures. An unusually good picture by this master, who adhered to the practice of tempera, and to the antiquated forms of art, at a time when Giovanni Bellini, availing himself of the use of oil, introduced a more powerful modelling, a far greater force and depth of colouring, and a melting execution. This picture is more refined in the physiognomies, and executed with greater attention to roundness and reflected lights, than his usual works. Formerly in the Contarini Collection. Of unusual excellence of preservation. Inscribed below "OPUS BARTOLOMEI VIVARINI DE MURANO."

GIOVANNI BELLINI.—The Virgin holding the Child on her right arm, with a pomegranate in her left hand, on which the Child has also placed his right hand. On each side of the curtain behind the Virgin is landscape; in front a parapet of brown marble, on which is a *cartellino*, with the inscription—" Joannes Bellinus P." A prophetic sense of the Saviour's sufferings, which the painter has signified by the symbol of the pomegranate, is touchingly depicted in the unusually beautiful features of the Virgin, who has her eyes cast down, and in the highly expressive countenance of the Child. At the same time the painter has exerted all his powers in the modelling of every part, and especially of the nude. The colouring, with the full brownish flesh-tones with dark shadows, the deep blues and crimsons of the drapery, and the green of the curtain, harmonises with obvious intention with the intense pathos of the moral conception. The tone of the landscape also is serious, and even gloomy. The preservation is so perfect as still to show unchanged that enamel-like surface, and those ridges in the draperies, which resulted from the nature of certain colours used by the old masters. Purchased at Venice in 1855, from Baron Galvagna.

MARCO BASAITI.—St. Jerome, in a rich rocky landscape, kneeling before a crucifix. Among the scholars of Giovanni

Bellini who adhered to his types, Basaiti occupies a prominent place. In delicacy and solidity of execution, this picture strikingly recalls the smaller works of Antonello da Messina, nay even shows an affinity to Van Eyck. The tone is, at the same time, of a deep and full harmony, and the preservation leaves nothing to be desired.

FRANCESCO TACHONI.—The Virgin with the Child on her lap. Signed, " Op. Francisci Tachoni, 1489 Octu." This rare Cremonese painter is here seen as a conscientious follower of Giovanni Bellini, with an affinity to Cima da Conegliano. He is refined in feeling, and able in composition, though dull in colouring. The preservation is good.

GIROLAMO DAI LIBRI.—The Virgin and Child. Particularly pleasing in the heads, and unusually animated in colour. This Veronese master is known to have received his cognomen from his also decorating books with miniatures.

GIORGIONE, AND VINCENZO CATENA.—The Virgin Enthroned, with the Child on her lap. Before her on the ground in the attitude of adoration is a warrior. Further back his page with a horse. The peculiar animation and poetry of the invention breathe quite the spirit of Giorgione. Judging also from the glow of colour and energy of treatment, I am inclined to attribute the figure of the warrior and his page to his hand. The expression, however, and light tone of the Virgin and Child, and the style of folds, display so much of Vincenzo Catena, his fellow-scholar, that I believe those portions to be by him. It is quite possible that Giorgione may have had occasion to avail himself of Catena's assistance.

GIORGIONE.—Small full-length figure of St. George. Elevated and powerful in head and form, of unusual vigour in the glow of tone, and of broad and masterly treatment. I have not been so fortunate as to visit Castelfranco, but I have learnt that this little picture is a study for the St. George in the altarpiece painted by Giorgione for his native town—only that the saint is there represented with a helmet on. Bequeathed by Mr. Rogers.

TITIAN.—1. Christ appearing to Mary Magdalen. See vol. ii. p. 76. Bequeathed by Mr. Rogers.

2. The Tribute-money. Signed. From the Soult Collection. This picture is particularly important as an example of the manner in which Titian treated biblical subjects in his later years. As

respects moral refinement, it can bear no comparison with the well-known " *Cristo della Moneta* " of his earlier time in the Dresden Gallery. The head of our Saviour, though fine, is worldly; the tone of the flesh less transparent and at the same time redder, but of singular power and depth; and the treatment, finally, broader and more marrowy. The preservation is remarkably good.

GIACOMO BASSANO.—The Good Samaritan. Very rarely did this unequal master combine such admirable modelling, such carefully carried out and yet broad execution, with so much general brightness and transparency of colouring. The preservation is perfect. Bequeathed by Mr. Rogers.

BARTOLOMMEO VENETO.—Portrait of a young man in the costume of a member of the Compagnia della Calza. Inscribed, " Ludov: Marti. (Martinengo) Ann: xxi. Bartol: Venetus faciebat MDXXX. XVI. Jun." This otherwise unknown master shows himself thoroughly worthy of the great period of art in which he lived. The conception is serious and elevated, and, as well as the powerful and warm colouring and strict carrying out, shows an affinity to Giorgione and to the earlier portraits of Titian. In good preservation. Purchased at Venice in 1855 of the heir of the Count Girolamo Martinengo.

PAUL VERONESE.—The Adoration of the Kings; a rich composition, inscribed with the date MDLXXIII., and originally executed for the church of S. Silvestro * in Venice. There it remained until 1837, at which time it was removed on account of repairs to the church, which, having entailed alterations rendering the space too small for it, the picture passed into the hands of Signor Angelo Toffoli, from whom it was purchased for the National Gallery in 1855. The painter has here followed the old symbolical conception, according to which the Nativity as well as the Adoration of the Kings was represented as taking place in the ruins of an antique temple, signifying that Christianity was founded upon the ruins of Paganism. Here, as in the Marriage of Cana, in the Louvre, and many other works by the master, the architecture occupies a principal part; so that the composition is confined to the lower portion of the picture. At the same time the composition is incomparably more artistic in arrangement, and more varied in the lines, than in either of the other two pictures of the same subject by the painter,

* Venetia citta nobilissima, MDLXXXI, p. 65.

known to me, in the Dresden Gallery, and in Devonshire House. These two, which greatly resemble each other, are not, like the work before us, quadrangular in form, but more in the shape of a frieze, while the composition corresponds by assuming more the style of a bas-relief. On the other hand, the golden tones render them far more effective than this grey and coolly-treated picture. Nevertheless, however monotonous in general tone, the colours are here most delicately balanced. Thus the decided mass of a silvery tone, produced by the foremost king and the page on the one side, is agreeably balanced by the broken red of the Virgin's dress, and the orange colour of her mantle; while, on the other hand, the powerful crimson robe of the second king not only forms a happy contrast to the cool colouring of the first, but an excellent transition to the deep but transparent mass of shadow on the right side of the picture. The motives are very animated; the heads, as in general with this painter, decidedly realistic in character; and the treatment very broad. Seldom do we find a sky by Paul Veronese in which the blue has been so well preserved—a circumstance which contributes much to the delicate keeping of the whole. The merits of this picture have been recognised by the most esteemed Venetian writers on art of all times. Boschini calls it " il famosissimo quadro di mano di Paolo Veronese;" * and Zanetti, in his enumeration of the works of the master, with the localities to which they belonged, thus mentions it: " Un celebre quadro di Paolo con la visita de' Re Maggi. Bella e ricca composizione." † But there is no greater proof of the reputation this picture enjoyed in Venice than the fact of its having been engraved on copper by Carlo Sacchi in 1649. As the removal from the church in 1837 necessitated its being folded, the marks thus occasioned have had to be repaired. Small retouches can also be discerned; but there is no sign of any larger over-paintings.

BOLOGNESE SCHOOL.

GUIDO RENI.—The Ecce Homo bequeathed by the late Mr. Rogers. Pure and elevated in feeling, and broadly and spiritedly executed in his finest silvery tone.

NEAPOLITAN SCHOOL.

RIBERA.—See vol. ii. p. 241. Bequeathed by Lord Colborne.

* Guida di Venezia, 1664, p. 253.   † Della Pittura Veneziana, MDCCLXXI, p. 189.

EARLY GERMAN SCHOOL.

ALBERT DURER.—A male portrait with white beard. With the monogram and 1514. Although this picture belongs to the less finished and drily-coloured works of the master, it is still, considering the extreme scarcity of his pictures, a valuable acquisition. From the collection of M. de Bammeville.

NETHERLANDISH SCHOOL.

RUBENS.—1. Triumph of Julius Cæsar, after Andrea Mantegna. See vol. ii. p. 79. Bequeathed by Mr. Rogers.

2. An Allegory of War, study for the Pitti picture. See vol. ii. p. 79. Bequeathed by same.

REMBRANDT.—See vol. ii. p. 240. Bequeathed by Lord Colborne.

TENIERS.—See vol. ii. p. 239. Backgammon-players. Bequeathed by same.

BERGHEM.—See same page. Bequeathed by same.

ARTUS VAN DER NEER.—See same page. Bequeathed by same.

ENGLISH SCHOOL.

SIR DAVID WILKIE.—See vol. ii. p. 240. Bequeathed by Lord Colborne.

———

LORD ELCHO'S COLLECTION.

Vol. II. p. 82.

Since the appearance of my book Lord Elcho has succeeded in adding the following valuable pictures to those previously in his possession. They are distributed with much taste in the different apartments of the house.

SEBASTIAN DEL PIOMBO.—Portrait of Pope Clement VII. in a chair; almost to the knees. Painted on stone. Grandly conceived. The hands of admirable action and drawing. The colours much broken.

JACOBO PONTORMO (?).—1. Portrait of a young man, holding a paper in his hand, on which is the name Jacopo.

2. Portrait of a beautiful young woman, companion to the above. The conception of each is very elevated; the drawing refined. Judging from the style of the *sfumato*, and from the generally cool

colouring, which is pale in the flesh-tones, I am inclined to attribute these very attractive pictures rather to the hand of FRANCIABIGIO, rival of Andrea del Sarto. From the circumstance of the inscription, Lord Elcho is disposed to believe them the work of Pontormo, and they partake, it is true, in some measure, of the manner of this master, who was scholar to Andrea del Sarto. In colouring, however, they appear nearer to Franciabigio, while the inscription, according to the custom of the period, refers more probably to the Christian name of the person portrayed than to that of the artist.

TITIAN.—1. St. Sebastian. This is almost a repetition of the large picture already described in Lord Elcho's possession, but on a smaller scale. The comparison of the two pictures is very interesting. The lesser one is in no way inferior in depth of tone, and but little so in making out. It is also in good preservation.

2. Venus and Adonis, the same composition as that in the National Gallery. This picture has unfortunately suffered in most parts, though such as are preserved—for instance, the arm of Adonis—show a delicacy of modelling, and a transparency of warm tone, surpassing that in the National Gallery, proving this picture to have been unquestionably a fine work by the master.

PARIS BORDONE.—Venus reposing. Now a half-length, but originally, as the form shows, a full-length figure. The head was furnished by a model of uncommon beauty, which is somewhat marred by an undue space between the right eye and the nose. The colouring, however, displays in full measure that truly luminous power and warmth which rendered the master so popular among the Venetian fair sex.

ANDREA SCHIAVONE.—The newborn Jupiter, attended by nymphs, who are playing on musical instruments. The size and spirit of the composition, the, for him, unusually light local tones of the flesh, and, finally, the grand and beautiful landscape in the manner of his master, Titian, render this one of the most important pictures I know by Schiavone. Like other Venetian painters, he was no adept in the difficult task of depicting the human foot, so that in this picture no feet are visible.

MURILLO.—A Monk of the mendicant order, kneeling, and receiving a loaf of bread in a scrip from the infant Christ, who is appearing unto him. In the sky are angels with more loaves. The background is a landscape, which is rendered somewhat more in detail than usual. The figures full-length and life-size. The feeling in the head of the monk is of great intensity. The tone of colouring corresponds with the solemnity of the subject; the execution is careful, and the whole in so far remarkable as displaying the master's power in the delineation of saints, children, and landscape. From the collection of Louis Philippe.

Zurbaran.—The Virgin and Child in Glory: two saints at their side. The Virgin is almost too tenderly conceived; the saints are very animated, and the effect very powerful.

Giorgio Vasari.—Christ on the Mount of Olives. Of moderate size. Far happier in composition than usual; of astonishing power of colouring for him, and careful in execution.

Finally, I must mention the head of a youthful Bacchus, executed in marble, and with the species of bandeau called the *credemnon* about his head. The ideal conception of this god is here rendered with uncommon beauty, and, with the admirable workmanship, displays the hand of a Greek artist of no ordinary skill. The greater portion of the nose, and almost the whole lower lip, are modern.

LORD YARBOROUGH'S COLLECTION.

Vol. II. p. 86.

By the kind intervention of Sir Charles Anderson, I succeeded in obtaining a satisfactory inspection of Lord Yarborough's pictures in his house in Arlington Street. I therefore give the following completed description of the collection, introducing, for the convenience of those readers who may take this work as a guide, such pictures as I before described in their appropriate places.

DRAWING-ROOM.

Ribera.—St. Catherine. Although somewhat secular in general character, yet the forms are more elevated than usual for the master, and the drawing particularly refined.

Sir Anthony More.—1. Portrait of the Earl of Essex. To the knees. A sitting figure. One of the best specimens of this celebrated portrait-painter. Very true and animated in conception, and of particularly solid execution—namely, in the hands.

Bartolommeo Schidone.—The Virgin and Child. St. Joseph

quite on one side of the picture, with a quantity of grey hair. For astonishing power of chiaroscuro and freedom of handling, this is one of the best examples of a composition which the master frequently repeated in various scales of size.

Ventura Salimbeni.—St. Catherine, seated, a palm-branch in her hand. Pictures signed with the name of this pleasing but not profound master of the later Sienese school are seldom seen out of Italy. The head is of a pretty, but very worldly character. The clear, warm, and delicate colouring shows the study of Correggio.

Tintoretto.—1. Consecration of a Bishop. A rich and fortunate composition; whole-length figures, the size of life. Full of animated heads, and of very careful execution.

Sofonisba Angusciola.—A nun, in the white robes of her order. A signed picture. This is a nobly conceived and delicately coloured specimen of this rare female artist, who is justly praised by Vasari.

Titian.—1. The repentant Magdalen. Among the various repetitions of this composition which I have met with in European galleries, this may be considered as an original. With few exceptions it surpasses all others, not only in transparency and warmth of colouring and spirited treatment, but also in elevation of expression. The landscape background is also of great beauty.

Annibale Carracci.—1. John the Baptist, whole-length figure, seated. Very dramatic in action, but forcibly recalling an Academy figure, and rather dark in the shadows.

Sir Anthony More.—2. Portrait of Catholic Queen Mary. Companion to the foregoing, and in the delicacy and rendering of all portions certainly one of his best female portraits.

Tintoretto.—2. The dead body of the Saviour mourned by the disciples. Of his later time. Spirited, but sketchy, and treated in a uniform brown tone.

Salvator Rosa.—1. St. Jerome, in a rocky landscape. The conception of the saint is far more elevated than usual with this master; to which is added a peculiarly powerful, warm, and transparent colouring, and a proportionably careful treatment.

Domenichino.—The Martyrdom of St. Stephen, treated as a landscape. This little picture is genuine, but belongs to those by the master in which a cold red, and a generally heavy tone of colour predominates.

Andrea del Sarto (?).—The Virgin holding the Child before her, who is adored by the Baptist. The rather hard heads of the Virgin and Child incline me to believe that this often-repeated composition is a good work of the school.

Annibale Carracci.—2. The well-known composition of Christ mourned by six figures, with an angel pointing to the wound in one hand. The master, it is certain, seldom attained such elevation of feeling as in this composition, which he executed the size of life. This example, which is a cabinet size, and painted on wood, is also very attractive for clearness of colouring and careful carrying out.

Titian.—2. Christ with the Disciples at Emmaus. This is essentially the same composition as that known by the name of "la Nappe," in the Louvre, though with a few alterations. The heads, to my view, have something too uncertain and woolly in quality for Titian, while the very clear and warm colouring, as well as the treatment of all the other parts, indicate the picture to have proceeded from the master's atelier.

Garofalo.—The Circumcision. The rich composition of this cabinet picture is very happy ; the heads elevated in feeling, the colouring warm, and the execution very careful.

Rembrandt.—The portrait of an old woman seated in an armchair, with white collar. To the knees. The conception very animated and delicate, and carefully executed in a light and very transparent golden tone.

Titian.—3. The original sketch for the picture of Actæon and Diana in the Bridgewater Gallery. Highly spirited, warm, and clear, and having the advantage of the finished picture in being admirably preserved.

THE STAIRCASE.

Guercino.—The Annunciation. Whole-length figures, the size of life. A picture of the first quality, and particularly characteristic of the master in the great power of colouring and the free and spirited treatment.

Juan de Pareja, also called "the Slave of Velasquez."— Portraits of Philip and Isabella of Bourbon. Whole-length figures, the size of life, animated and well preserved.

Sir Joshua Reynolds.—1. Portrait of Sir Richard Worsley,

the well-known collector, whose treasures of art were inherited by Lord Yarborough. Full-length figure, life-size. A good and careful specimen of the master.

PIETRO DELLA VECCHIA.—1. The Nativity, in a long and narrow form, composed in the taste of Giacomo Bassano, and of extraordinary power of colouring.

SALVATOR ROSA.—2. A large landscape; grand hills rising in the middle distance, and crowned with a castle; robbers in the foreground. Highly poetic in lines and in warmth of lighting, and a chef-d'œuvre of the master. The pendant to it is in the National Gallery.

HANS HOLBEIN.—1. Portrait of Edward VI. as an infant. A bust-picture with the hands; presented by Henry VIII. to an ancestor of Lord Yarborough. Of very naïve and natural conception, and especially careful in execution. The little hands are incomparable.

GASPAR POUSSIN.—1. Landscape with a town; a waterfall in the foreground. The poetical feeling of the master is here combined in a rare degree with delicacy of tone, clearness of colouring, and careful execution.

HANS HOLBEIN.—2. King Henry VIII. A perfectly front view; to the knees; like the picture in Warwick Castle: not so transparent and careful in detail as that picture, but more powerful in modelling. Also presented by that monarch to the family.

FRANCESCO ALBANI.—The Repose in Egypt. Joseph is holding an open book, to which the Virgin points; numerous angels are around. Of very pleasing composition, warm and clear in colouring, and careful in execution.

GUIDO RENI.—David holding the head of Goliah. Of the earlier and better time of the master; nobly conceived, and carefully carried out in a powerful and clear tone.

CLAUDE LORRAINE.—1. Trees and a single figure in the foreground; a chain of hills in the distance. The picture is animated by numerous and well-drawn figures. This is one of the works which display the master in his whole greatness. The distance is of marvellous airiness; the colouring clear and powerful; the execution careful. It was painted for Pope Urban VIII., who died in 1644, and therefore belongs to Claude's middle and best time. It was afterwards in the possession of Louis XVI., when it was engraved under the title of "la Récompense du Village." The preservation is unusually good.

NICOLAS POUSSIN.—1. A very poetic landscape, but with the figures obviously by another and inferior hand.

ALBERT CUYP.—A winter landscape : a broad frozen stream, with the ruin of a massive tower on the shore, and a gay multitude with skates and sledges. The happy composition, the striking effect of sunlight, and the broad and masterly treatment, render this one of the finest works of the best time of the master.

SIR JOSHUA REYNOLDS.—2. Portrait of Mrs. Pelham, feeding chickens; full-length figure, life-size. Most delicately conceived, and of a subdued warmth of colouring.

CLAUDE LORRAINE.—2. A large landscape. The cold tone is little attractive. It is placed too high for any positive opinion.

JOSEPH VERNET.—A sea-piece, with a stranding boat. Of unusual power for him.

ANDREA SCHIAVONE.—Adam and Eve expelled from Paradise. An excellent example of the painter, for, in addition to his warm and powerful colouring, we have here the (for him) rare quality of careful execution.

GIUSEPPE PORTA, named, after his master, DEL SALVIATI.— The Annunciation. The works of this painter are not often met with out of Venice. In this little picture he has been singularly successful in combining the graceful feeling of the Florentine school in his motives with the full warm colouring of the Venetian school. The execution is also very careful.

DIETRICH.—1 and 2. Two genuine and good pictures by this many-sided master.

PIETRO DELLA VECCHIA.—2. The Adoration of the Kings. Companion to the before-mentioned picture, and of similar character and merit.

RAPHAEL (?).—A male portrait with hands, with a landscape background, signed " R. A. S. MDXVI. R." Nominally the portrait of the well-known Caradosso Foppa, of Milan, who in the time of Julius II. executed a large and very beautiful medal in Rome. At all events this is a very good work of that golden age of art. For any more precise opinion the place where it hangs is too dark.

GUIDO RENI.—2. The daughter of Herodias receiving the head of the Baptist on a dish. A specimen of the often-repeated picture.

The expression of the head is dignified and tender, and the colouring more powerful and warm than in other examples.

NICOLAS BERGHEM.—His own portrait as a huntsman. Next to him his dog. Very animatedly conceived, and of warm colouring and careful execution.

CLAUDE LORRAINE.—3. A ruin, with pillars. On the left of the foreground are Hagar and Ishmael, with the angel appearing to them : on the right trees, with a flock feeding : in the distance a view of the sea. Of pleasing composition and warm and delicate tone.

NICOLAS POUSSIN.—2. The Virgin and Child, the little St. John, and Joseph ; whole-length figures, the size of life. Although Poussin seldom attempted such a large scale, which is far less adapted to him than his usual size, this picture is nevertheless remarkable for beauty of composition and very careful execution. The heads, however, have something empty.

ADRIAN VAN DER WERFF.—Venus and Cupid in a landscape ; pleasing and highly finished.

TENIERS.—1. A landscape, recalling the style of Momper. Mass is being performed in a cave, with numerous figures. Poetically conceived, and of spirited treatment.

GREUZE.—A young girl seated, holding a letter before her. To the knees. Execution of uncommon solidity is here combined with his pleasing conception.

TITIAN.—4. The Virgin and Child in a landscape, surrounded with the Baptist, SS. Elizabeth, Catherine, and Joseph. Figures about two-thirds the size of life. It is much to be regretted that this promising-looking picture is so darkly placed as to render any more decided opinion impossible.

TENIERS. – 2. Cooking and feasting are going on beneath a ruin. A very original and beautiful picture.

GIAMBATTISTA MORONI.—Portrait of a man about to write. The background of a landscape character. A Latin inscription upon a label declares all the happiness of the individual portrayed to be in himself. The true and delicate conception of this great portrait-painter is here united to a particularly delicate and warm colouring.

LEONARDO DA VINCI (?).—A repetition of the well-known picture in the Louvre, of the Virgin on the lap of St. Anna. An old and fine work, but somewhat heavy in the colouring. I am inclined to consider this the work of Salaino.

PAUL VERONESE.—Christ driving the Money-changers from the Temple. The conception is very dramatic, though not free from undignified motives. The colouring is clear and warm.

DRAWING-ROOM.

JACOB JORDAENS.—Three Flemish musicians. This so often vulgar master is here quite in his element. The humour is as genuine as it is delightful; the colour of the greatest power and transparency; and the execution in a solid impasto, and altogether masterly.

GASPAR POUSSIN.—2. Landscape, with rising ground in the middle distance, crowned with a castle; in the foreground two figures resting. In poetry of conception and feeling for lines a picture of the first quality.

3. The companion to the above, and but little inferior to it.

VANDYCK.—The sketch for a Crucifixion. The painter has here not advanced beyond the most general idea, so that the heads are only very undecidedly given. Composition and treatment are spirited.

VAN DER HELST.—Portraits of a Dutch family. In truth of nature, kindliness of feeling, warmth of colouring, and delicacy of carrying out, this is a real gem of art, and recalls the beautiful picture in the Louvre, No. 197.

TURNER.—1. A very large landscape, with the commencement of the vintage of Mâcon. In the foreground are figures dancing and occupied with the vintage. Inscribed 1803. In the highest style of landscape, recalling both Claude and Poussin, and at the same time solidly and carefully carried out.

2. Wreck of the Minotaur, a transport-ship, upon the Haak Sands. Dated 1810. Although at the period of my visit in 1854 this picture was not in its place, being at that time in the hands of the engraver, yet I had it fully before my memory as another master-work of the same rank as the foregoing, showing affinity to the great Dutch sea-painters, and namely to William van de Velde.

THE HALL.

The arrangement of sculpture in this space gives it a very stately appearance. Portrait busts by NOLLEKENS here display the great English statesmen of the latter half of the last century and the beginning of the present, such as Pitt and Fox. Here are also a group of Venus and Cupid by NOLLEKENS, and the statue of a young girl, and the well-known huntsman, by GIBSON. Also the Prodigal Son embraced by his Father, by THEED, in which the speaking earnestness of the motive is especially worthy of remark.

Finally I may mention a very spirited work by BERNINI—the statue of Neptune, from the Colonna Palace at Rome, executed with the greatest decision, only with the chisel.

COLLECTION OF ALEXANDER BARKER, ESQ.
Vol. II. p. 125.

Since the appearance of my book Mr. Barker has continued to increase his collection with pictures of the same class, namely, with the Italian and Netherlandish masters of the 15th and beginning of the 16th centuries. Some few of these I am not able to describe with any detail, having unfortunately mislaid the notices taken of them in 1854. This gentleman has also added a series of interesting sculptures in ivory, and a number of beautiful majolica plates. I take the pictures in the order I have already observed.

TUSCAN SCHOOL.

DELLO FIORENTINO (?).—The Adoration of the Kings, who appear in the richest costume of the times, and whose truly portrait-like heads are said to represent members of the Accajuoli family. On the hut, within which are seen the ox and ass, is a peacock; in the sky are two falcons aiming at a heron; in the rocky landscape are several horsemen. Of circular form. So very little that is authentic exists of this master, who belongs to the earliest part of the 15th century, that I do not venture to decide as to the painter of this picture. At all events it is an interesting memorial of his time and style of art. The Virgin is very maidenly in physiognomy and expression. In the other and very animated heads an aim at individuality is evident, and the modelling, in a powerful and somewhat heavy tone, is very good for the period.

FRA FILIPPO LIPPI.—Six saints enthroned, one beside the other. A picture in which the master appears in the full excellence of his art; the heads are noble, animated, and individual, the drawing excellent, the motives speaking and graceful, the draperies in choice taste, and the execution highly solid.

SANDRO BOTTICELLI.—1. The Virgin standing and looking at the Child, who is seated and looking up at her. Also the little St. John. Large life-size, to the knees. A work of the first class by this so unequal master. The forms have something grand. The expression of the heads is that of a deep and mysterious melancholy; the carrying out is of great decision and mastery, and the keeping excellent. From the Bammeville collection.

2. Venus, in light white drapery, stretched on a couch, her right arm leaning on a red cushion, on which a pomegranate and some roses are held by an *amorino*, on whom her left arm is laid. The *amorino* has his left hand on a bunch of grapes, which lie on the person of the goddess, and which she is holding with the fingers of her right hand. Lower down is another *amorino*, kneeling on his right knee, looking round very animatedly at Venus, and with his right hand in a basket of red and white roses. Behind him is a third, with a similar action of head, holding a bunch of roses. Quite in the foreground are flowers. The background is a rocky landscape of insipid tone. This is one of the most remarkable of Sandro Botticelli's mythological pictures. The forms are grand in conception, though the head, hands, and feet of the goddess show that they were taken from a living model. The drapery may have been painted in by a later hand. Æsthetically speaking, the two *amorini* at her feet are the most successful. The motives are graceful, the forms of beautiful fulness, and the modelling very careful, in a prevailing brown tone. Only the roses are somewhat unsatisfactory.

ANDREA VEROCCHIO.—A circular picture of about 5 ft. in diameter, divided vertically into three parts. In the centre, and relieved by the clear sky of the background, is the Virgin, a slender and noble figure, of fine action of head, folding the tips of her fingers; her dress, which consists of a veil, a dark violet dress, and a dark blue mantle with yellow lining, affords a peculiarly earnest and pleasing harmony of colour. Before her, on the ground, on a piece of dark-green drapery, is the Infant, which she is adoring. The forms of the Child are too full, which is especially seen in the fingers, those of the right hand pointing to his mouth, with the well-known meaning—" I am the Word:"

those of the left hand holding a goldfinch. In the left compartment is a youthful angel kneeling, his hands crossed on his breast; in the right compartment is another angel, taken in front, his hands raised in wonder as he looks at the Child. On the right, kneeling next him, is St. John the Baptist, as a child, the cross in his left hand, and pointing with his right to the Virgin. In the middle distance is Joseph. The landscape background contains a town, a large piece of water, and mountains. Figures almost life-size. The modelling, in a clear brownish flesh-tone, is very careful. This is the most important picture I know by this rare master.

Lorenzo di Credi.—Here are various pictures by this scholar of Verocchio, who, though noble and pure in feeling, graceful in motives, of pleasing heads, very clear colouring, and careful execution, was nevertheless rather monotonous in character. None of these specimens, however, show him in his full force.

1. An altarpiece of considerable size. The Virgin enthroned with the Child, with two saints at her side. Figures life-size. Of great clearness of general tone. The forms of the Child too full. The heads very pleasing.

2. The Virgin kneeling and adoring the Child, who is lying on the ground, with a wheat-sheaf, at which a goldfinch is pecking, under the upper part of his body. Next him, and in reference doubtless to the transitoriness of all things, a dandelion with its light seed-vessel, which a breath can carry away. On the left is Joseph seated. Figures about three-fourths life-size. Very clear in colouring, but of less delicate rendering.

3. The Virgin holding the Child upon her lap, who is blessing the little St. John, led up to him by an angel on the right. On the left is another angel holding flowers in his robe. The background is a landscape with buildings. A circular picture. This unfavourably hung work is noble and refined in the heads, and particularly careful in execution.

4. The Virgin and Joseph are kneeling in adoration before the Child, who is lying on the ground. Circular picture. The head of the Virgin beautiful. Of more powerful modelling than usual, and broader in the folds of the drapery.

Luca Signorelli.—1. Two fresco pictures, with figures about half-life size, which have been successfully transferred from wall to canvas; both signed " Luca Coritius," in allusion, as often with him, to his native town of Cortona. The one represents the Triumph of Chastity, represented by a female figure in the foreground, drawn by two white unicorns in a car, on which Cupid is bound. Behind come a tumultuous troop of maidens, one of them holding aloft the youthful figure of Love. In the foreground is Love again as an undraped youth, kneeling and being bound by virgins, some of whom are plucking the feathers from his wings, while another breaks his bow, and a third is aiming at him with two of his own arrows. The motives here are very animated, and the troop of girls behind of very momentary action. On the left, as quiet spectators, are three knightly figures.

2. Coriolanus being overcome by the entreaties of his mother and wife. The expression of joy in his face, of entreaty in that of the women, and of rage in the leaders of the Volscians, and especially in one old man, is very admirable. The throughout less complete rendering of the forms, which in some parts are even deficient, show these works to be of the earlier time of the master.

UMBRIAN SCHOOL.

PIETRO DELLA FRANCESCA.—The profile portrait of Isotta, wife of the art-loving but cruel tyrant of Rimini—Sigismondo Malatesta—well known to all connoisseurs by Vittore Pisani's admirable medal. In the features, and in the rich dress, it entirely agrees with that medal; in conception and treatment with the fresco portrait of her husband in the Chapel of the Relics, Church of S. Francesco, Rimini. Unfortunately the flesh parts have been stippled over by an Italian restorer.

PINTURICCHIO.—A fresco successfully taken from a wall, the subject of which Mr. Barker believes to be the Return of Ulysses to Penelope. I am inclined, however, to consider it the visit of Collatinus to Lucretia. The subject is treated in the costume and manners of the painter's time. On the right is Lucretia busied at a large loom, and next her a young female attendant winding yarn from a skein, with which a cat is playing. Opposite to her are seven youths, just entered at the door, and evidently surprised at her occupation; the foremost, decidedly Collatinus, bearing, in Mr. Barker's opinion, the features of Raphael. The fact of his being represented with light hair is sufficient, to my view, however, to overturn this supposition, as the authentic portrait of Raphael, by himself, in the Gallery of the Uffizi at Florence, shows that his hair was at an early age of a dark brown. The youth behind the foremost figure, with a falcon on his wrist, represents doubtless Sextus Pompeius. The view of a seaport with vessels, and surrounded with hills, seen through a window, on which Mr. Barker chiefly grounds his opinion of the subject, is, I believe, merely an accidental accessory. The figures are about three-fourths life-size. The whole is a no less remarkable than charming specimen of the treatment by the Umbrian school of a scene in profane history. The modesty and domestic character of the women are admirably expressed. The heads of the youths, the foremost of whom is very elegant in form, show entirely the well-known and attractive type of this school.

Besides this, Mr. Barker possesses several more pictures of a frieze-like form, which he also attributes to Pinturicchio. As my mislaid notices refer to these, my memory only serves to state that two of them represent scenes from a tale with which I am unacquainted, that they are full of animated and often very graceful motives, unequal in execution, sometimes careful and sometimes sketchy. Generally speaking the proportions are of a length, compared with the small heads, such as I have never seen in the authentic pictures by Pinturicchio.

Portrait of a young man in black dress, entitled a MASACCIO, but in my opinion of later date, and also too feeble for him. The forms are too empty and the hands too small.

An example of the often repeated Leda with the Swan, attributed to LEONARDO DA VINCI, and believed by Mr. Barker to be the work of that master. This I believe to be the careful work of an excellent master of the Cologne school, who first painted in the style of Quentin Matsys, as may be seen in his best picture of that time, the well-known Death of the Virgin in the Pinacothek at Munich. He afterwards devoted himself to the imitation of the great Italian masters, relinquishing his warm and clear colouring for the better study of modelling, and spending, as it appears, some time in Lombardy. Evidence of this is seen in the imitation of Leonardo's Cena in the Predella of a Pietà in the Louvre, No. 601 of the Catalogue of 1854, and in the picture before us, the style and treatment of the landscape background of which strikingly correspond with that one. For Leonardo himself, or even for one of his school, the drawing is too weak. The position of the eyes is incorrect, the feet badly foreshortened, and the swan too heavy and coarse.

Finally, I am inclined to believe that an undraped Juno, holding in her left hand the neck of a peacock standing next to her, attributed to Razzi, is too feeble for that master, although said to have passed under his name in the Orleans Gallery. How is it to be believed that a painter who often rivalled Raphael in feeling for beauty and grace should have represented the Queen of the Gods under the aspect of a short and stout model? In the character of the head, in the colouring, and the style of the very careful modelling, this picture reminds us most of Marco Oggione, one of the second-rate scholars of Leonardo da Vinci.

EARLY NETHERLANDISH AND GERMAN SCHOOL.

QUENTIN MATSYS.—The Virgin enthroned, holding the Child on her lap, who, with his right hand on a page, is placing an open book in the hands of the kneeling St. Catherine beside him, and with his left hand showing his mother the blossom of an iris. On the left is St. Margaret seated reading a book, with the dragon, her attribute, stretched upon her blue mantle. Both the saints are in the rich costume of the painter's time. Above the head of the Virgin are two angels holding a rich gold crown; within the throne, which terminates in a semicircular form, and more towards the outer edge, are roses, and in the centre admirably painted grapes; on each side is the view of a landscape—on the right, towers and blue hills, and on the left a town, and the sea, on which is a large ship; at the side is a frieze of violet colour, with boys, three and three, holding festoons. That this beautiful picture of the latest and best time of Quentin Matsys should, owing to a small monogram of A and D upon it, have been, even when in the possession of Mr. Samuel Woodburn, attributed to Albert Durer, to whose monogram also it bears no likeness, is a proof how small is the knowledge of this master even among tried connoisseurs. Those who are acquainted with Albert Durer's authentic pictures will agree with me that no trace of his style is to be found here. On the other hand, it agrees in the most remarkable manner with the known works of Quentin Matsys : the same aim at tenderness and beauty in the heads, the same narrowness of the female hands, and delicacy of the luminous flesh-tones, the same peculiar arrangement of the colours of the draperies, and the same tender pinks, and style of the golden patterns on the red robes of St. Catherine. Finally, the preservation of this miniature-like picture of moderate size leaves nothing to be desired.

HANS HOLBEIN.—Portrait of a man of a type of features resembling the House of Habsburg, with long hair hanging down on each side, and a broad-brimmed hat, on which a medal is fastened ; a white shirt with delicate border reaches to the throat; one-half of the coat is red with slashings of cloth of gold, the other half of cloth of gold with red slashings. The blue mantle, now become almost black, has a turned-down collar with a golden pattern. In his right hand is a paper with the profile in slight outline of a male head; the ground is a blueish green ; the face is of great decision of forms, and admirably modelled in a full brownish tone. The hands, however, are dry and empty, the treatment of all accessories of great precision.

Mr. Barker has recently become the possessor of a number of pictures from the well-known Manfrini collection in Venice, including some of the chefs-d'œuvre of the gallery. They were not arrived before I left England.

The sale of Mr. Samuel Woodburn's collection afforded Mr. Barker also the opportunity of acquiring a book containing 50 leaves, with pen-drawings on each, by ANDREA MANTEGNA, belonging to various periods of his career, and showing his genius in various aspects. Thus a Madonna, holding the Child standing before her on a cushion, with two angels playing on musical instruments, is obviously of a very early time. Again, a sheet with four compositions upon it, all of the same subject, in the two upper of which the Child is represented sleeping, shows by its fuller forms and freer motives a somewhat later time. He appears in his maturity in four compositions of the same kind on a third sheet; of these, the two lower ones, in which the Child is represented at the breast, and fretting, but for the puffy character of the drapery, belong entirely to the freer forms of the cinquecento, and in point of beauty are worthy of Raphael. Another series of leaves, with scenes from common life, and bust-pictures in profile, belong to Mantegna's realistic side, and show in the most striking manner, when compared with many of the drawings in the book by Jacobo Bellini, already described in the print-room of the British Museum, the great influence which the Venetian exercised upon the Paduan master. Next in order, and of the highest charm, are a number of drawings with children and *amorini*, sometimes playing, sometimes fighting. But the palm of superiority must be given to two allegorical subjects, one of which displays two slightly draped female figures and an *amorino* striking a man who is already on his knees; the other a prostrate female, who is attacked with blows by two *amorini* with arrows and a burning torch. The purity of the drawing, the freedom and grace of the motive, the beauty of the forms, and the more picturesque style of the draperies, agree entirely with the beautiful picture with the dancing figures in the Louvre, and display the master in his latest time and highest perfection.

I now proceed to the sculptures in Mr. Barker's possession:— The bust of a young Florentine woman by a very skilful hand, and showing in conception and workmanship the latter time of the 15th century, is the only specimen in marble. The delicate features express great modesty; the round and elevated forehead is the least individualised part.

Various specimens of ivory are also here, of which I can only notice those which appeared to me particularly interesting. The following are of Italian origin:—

Statuette of a female Saint crowned, holding a lily in her right hand in the form of French *fleur-de-lys*. About 9 in. high. Of very noble head, excellent drapery, and careful execution. About the middle of the 13th century, and, judging from the slender and meagre form, Florentine.

Statuette of the Virgin and Child; about 1 ft. high. Of admirable style of drapery. 13th century.

Barnaba Galazzo Visconti, enthroned as judge, four figures at his side, and his coat-of-arms. A very careful work, with a border of a tasteful pattern. All in relief.

A small tablet of peculiar form, with the profiles of Sigismondo Malatesta, and Isotta his wife, opposite each other, in very flat relief; below, their united ciphers. The ground of dark mother-of-pearl, and around a very tasteful frame-work of enamel. The original leather case is here also, and remarkable for its pretty decorations. The same may be said of two ivory dagger-sheaths, with the initials of Sigismondo, Pandolfo, and Malatesta. Also an ivory mortar, with a pestle, shows by its pretty form how the feeling for elegance pervaded everything at that time.

Statuette of the Virgin and Child, of the unusual height, for ivory, of about 1 ft. 6 in. This I consider to be a French work of the beginning of the 14th century. The motive is of a conventional Gothic, the heads tolerably advanced in the not pleasing type of that period, and the drapery of good invention and of masterly execution.

Finally, sixteen majolica plates are well worthy of observation. Several by MAESTRO GIORGIO DA GUBBIO are of great beauty. The best is one representing the Birth of Adonis. For this, however, Mr. Barker paid the sum of 60l.

***

COLLECTION OF THE MARQUIS OF HERTFORD.

Vol. II. p. 154.

By a particular kindness on the part of the Marquis of Hertford, I find myself enabled to describe a number of valuable pictures belonging to his Lordship's collection, which I saw partly in 1854 and partly in 1856, in Manchester House and in a house in Berkeley Square. To these I may add three pictures which the Marquis purchased in Paris in 1855, at the sale of Baron Mecklenburg's collection. These had been long known to me.

ITALIAN SCHOOL.

BERNARDINO LUINI.—The Virgin looking at the Child, whom she holds with both hands on her lap. The Child is taken quite in front and is gazing out of the picture. A landscape background. A picture of very attractive heads and motives, and of very careful execution. The colours of the drapery have, however, rather a crude effect for him. From the Fesch Gallery.

PAUL VERONESE.—Perseus and Andromeda. She is fastened to the rock on the left, while he, mounted on Pegasus, is attacking the monster. Figures life-size. The conception is very animated; the dragon of admirable invention; the colouring of a power seldom seen in his pictures, and approaching Titian. The landscape also, which occupies a large portion of the picture, is admirable.

DOMENICHINO.—The Sibyl. From the Stowe collection. Half-length figure. The fine features are taken from a model from whom this master frequently drew. The expression of inspiration, the unusual power and warmth of colouring, the refined drawing, and the solid execution, combine to render this well-preserved picture very attractive.

ALBANO.—Venus reposing on a light cloud and kissing Cupid. *Amorini* surround the group. A piece of violet drapery forms a kind of sail over her. This little picture, a flat oval in shape, belongs in point of elegance of forms and motives, and light and harmonious colouring, to the most charming examples of the master. From the collection of Count Montcalm.

CANALETTO.—1. A view of the Piazetta, with a festivity going on.

2. The Bridge of the Rialto.

3 and 4. Two Venetian views. These are the four pictures already mentioned as inherited by Lord Hertford. They are remarkable for great power and freshness. The first only is somewhat crude.

5 and 6. Two other pictures by Canaletto, about $4\frac{1}{2}$ ft. high by 6 ft. wide, belong for choice of subject and admirable keeping to his chefs-d'œuvre.

7 and 8. Two other views of Venice, by the same master, may finally be mentioned, in which buildings and figures are on an unusually small scale. These are of a delicacy of keeping and precision of rendering seldom observed in his pictures.

SASSOFERRATO.—Marriage of St. Catherine, with an angel. Full-length figures, life-size. In composition, beauty of heads, warmth of colour, and equality of careful rendering, this is one of the most admirable pictures of the master. From Lord Orford's collection.

SPANISH SCHOOL.

VELASQUEZ.—1. Portrait of an Infant of Spain, about three years old, in grey dress, with violet scarf with a sword attached, the hilt of which is held by the left hand. In the right is a sort of general's bâton, which serves the child for a stick. Upon a cushion is a cap and feather. Full-length figure, life-size. The background consists of a darkly-treated curtain. From the Standish collection. This picture has a marvellous charm. The conception is highly animated, the delicate flesh-tones positively luminous, and the careful execution of every part unusually sustained.

2. Portrait of an Infanta of Spain. Standing figure, in black dress with white sleeves, the right hand upon a table covered with a red cloth. Full-length life-size figure. Hangings in the background, with a bit of landscape. 5 ft. high, 3 ft. 6 in. wide. The head is painted in a luminously warm tone, the hair very broadly treated. The general keeping admirable. From the Higginson collection.

3. Don Balthasar, son of Philip IV. of Spain. In a black and white dress with a crimson scarf, on a black charger. A cavalier attended by a page, and other figures around. The royal mews are seen in the background. Purchased at the sale of the collection of the late Samuel Rogers, Esq., for 1210 guineas. Of very animated conception, powerful colouring, and masterly keeping. A portrait of this prince, very similar to this but still finer, is in the Grosvenor Gallery.

4. Portrait of a lady, in black neckerchief and brown dress ; gloves on both hands, in the right hand a fan. The background consists of a dark sky. Almost to the knees, and the size of life. From the Aguado collection. This picture displays the warmest golden tones of the master, and also a far more careful execution and solid impasto than is usually found in his portraits. It is of astonishing animation.

MURILLO.—1. The Annunciation. The Virgin is kneeling at her faldstool, the angel kneeling upon a light cloud a little above the floor. About three-quarters the size of life. Of unusual power and clearness of colouring, though the greenish-blue and violet drapery of the angel makes a somewhat gaudy effect. Very well preserved. From the Aguado collection.

2. The Marriage of the Virgin. A composition of twelve small figures. The Virgin is dressed in white, with a blue mantle which scarcely conceals her dress. Behind her are four maidens. Between her and Joseph—who is attired in a blue

coat and orange-coloured mantle, and accompanied by five male figures, one of whom is breaking a withered staff—is the High Priest. Behind is a crimson curtain with a ray of light falling from above, and the Holy Spirit in form of a dove before it. The draperies are in particularly fine taste, the execution equal and very careful. This is by far the most important example of the few cabinet pictures by Murillo known to me.

3. The Virgin in Glory. In white dress and azure mantle. Several angels at her feet. Her head is of unusual elevation of character, and the effect of the whole earnest and powerful. Small figures. From the Stowe collection.

4. The Virgin holding the Child. Life-size, to the knees; of oval form. I know few pictures by the master where the draperies are treated so finely, and where the colours are of such luminous transparency. At the same time the treatment is very careful. From the collection of Casimir Perrier.

5. The Virgin and Child. Half-length figures. A good picture, though not so important as the foregoing.

6. The Adoration of the Shepherds. Represented as a night scene, with the light proceeding from the Child. Around are the figures of St. Joseph, two shepherds, a shepherdess carrying a basket with two pigeons, a boy, and two angels. Below, in the foreground, are a lamb and a dog. About three-quarters size. The Virgin is of unusual elevation both of form and expression, and the other heads very animated. The red-brownish tones of the flesh are transparent, and the general effect admirable.

7. The Holy Family. The Virgin is kneeling and contemplating the Child lying on the floor before her, who, looking up to the adoring little St. John, points to the scroll with the " Ecce Agnus Dei." St. John grasps the scroll in token that he accepts the mission. On the right is Joseph standing with an open book, and looking at the children. Behind him are trees; on the other side a lightly treated hill and sky. This is a very remarkable work of the master. The Virgin, who is painted in a warm, silvery tone, is refined and noble both in feature and expression. The Child is very lovely, and, like the St. John, warmly and transparently coloured. Joseph alone is of a cool reddish flesh-tone. At the same time the execution, especially in the Virgin and

Child, is very careful, though a lamb may be pointed out as feebly treated. Formerly in the Casimir Perrier collection.

8. Joseph sold by his Brethren. A rich composition of figures of small life-size. The motives are animated and of great truth of detail. Nevertheless this is one of those pictures by the master in which expression and forms are of that common character appertaining more to a *genre* than to a biblical subject.

FRENCH SCHOOL.

FRANÇOIS CLOUET, called JANET.—Portrait of a Lord Hertford in black dress and black cap with white feather. The background is green. Below is this inscription—" Le Comte de Hertford." This small picture belongs to the few genuine works of a painter to whom so many mediocre pictures of his time are erroneously ascribed. The conception is very delicate and animated, the colouring clear, and the execution very tender.

GASPAR POUSSIN.—A rich, hilly landscape, with a waterfall in the foreground. Unquestionably one of the finest works of the master, in whom we seldom find the high poetry of his art combined with so much detail, with such warmth and transparency of tone, and so equal and happy an execution. Formerly in Lord Ashburnham's collection.

WATTEAU.—1. A landscape, with figures of ladies and cavaliers in the foreground, listening to the sound of a theorbo played by a male figure standing before them. In power and transparency, and broad and spirited treatment, this picture is one of the most admirable by the master.

2. A wood, with four ladies and a gentleman resting in the foreground; another gentleman standing. At different distances from the eye are similar groups. The very tasteful composition, truly luminous and harmonious colouring, tender aërial perspective, and very refined carrying-out, render this also one of the chefs-d'œuvre of the master. From the collection of Count de Morny.

3. A wood with tall stems, with cheerful figures of ladies and cavaliers in various groups. On the right is the statue of a stout female figure on a pedestal. For tasteful distribution of the figures, power of chiaroscuro, delicate aërial perspective, and clever and yet careful treatment, we have here again one of the most

superb specimens of the master. From the de Morny collection, where I had already seen and admired it.

Lancret.—Eight figures of ladies and cavaliers, one of them with a mask, in the open air, before a pedestal. On the right a fountain with sculpture. Beautiful and powerful trees are in the landscape. The figures, which are of an unusually large scale for this painter, are warmly coloured, and finished with unusual industry. The whole picture is characterised by much air and light. I had previously seen this fine work in the Standish collection. The present possessor purchased it for 750l., the highest price, I imagine, yet given for the master.

Pater.—A landscape, with a party of ladies and gentlemen resting in the foreground under trees. One of the figures, dressed in white silk, quite in front, is very remarkable, and strongly relieved by another figure in black. On the right is the recumbent figure of a Venus on a pedestal, at the base of which are three children. On the same side, in the background, is a distant view. In every respect—composition, power, clearness of colouring, and finish—this is the finest picture I know by the master.

Greuze.—1. A young girl kneeling in adoration before a statue of Cupid with a garland. Various accessories at the foot of the pedestal. A landscape background. Whole-length figure, three-quarters size. This picture in every way merits the high reputation it enjoyed in the collection of Cardinal Fesch. The slender form, beautiful features, lovely expression, and warm and clear tints of the girl, render this work attractive in no common degree. The execution is also careful, and the preservation perfect.

2, 3, 4, and 5. These are specimens of Greuze's most frequent subjects; half-length figures of young girls, all of great power, transparency, beauty, and finish. In one of them especially, who is looking sorrowfully upward, the expression is admirably given.

I was agreeably surprised, also, to find in this collection fine specimens of the most approved masters of the modern French school.

Horace Vernet.—1. One of those mounted shepherds, here on a grey horse, who drive the oxen to Rome, is following a stray member of the herd, which is seen with other drivers in the background. He is aiming a blow with a pike at the animal, which with its head turned aside is trying to avoid the thrust. Signed and dated " Romæ, 1829." About 3 ft. high and 4 ft. wide. This picture, which was painted in the master's freshest period, unites with that animation and truth of action in which no other living master approaches him a transparent and sunny effect, and a treatment as careful as it is spirited.

2. A scene in Algiers, with ten Arabians and a boy, in their white bernousses, encamped in a circle. Next them stands a woman with a vessel of water on her head. About 3½ ft. high by 4 ft. wide. Signed and dated " Romæ, 1833." This is incomparably one of the finest pictures I know by Horace Vernet. No modern painter has seized the peculiar character of the Arabians in so masterly a manner, and in this picture he surpasses himself. The animation and variety of the heads, preserving at the same time the national type of character, are truly admirable. The keeping and lighting are masterly, and the execution of a solid impasto. The hilly landscape, also, forming the background, deserves praise.

3. French soldiers storming a gateway. Some Arabians lie vanquished on the ground. Probably an episode in the storming of Constantine. This is a very small picture, painted on slate, of very lively motives and careful execution.

DECAMPS.—A crowd of Arabian horsemen and pedestrians under the white walls of a town. Signed and dated 1837. This picture belongs to the best time of this justly celebrated master, and combines the full glow of his colouring and the force of his effect with a more precise and solid execution of details than is observable in many of his later works.

PAUL DELAROCHE.—A woman with a child asleep on her lap. The background a landscape. Full-length figures, three-quarters size. Signed and dated " Rome, 1844." Whether the painter intended to depict Hagar and Ishmael, or some other biblical event, I know not. At all events it is one of the best of his pictures, as far as I am acquainted with them. The expression of the mother, who is looking up, is dignified, the sleep of the child very natural, the drawing excellent in every part, the modelling throughout very careful, and finally, what can seldom be said of his pictures, the colouring of great transparency and delicacy.

LEON COIGNET.—The original of the masterly and well-known engraving of the Abduction. Signed and dated 1828. The engraving promises more than the picture fulfils; for, with all the animation of motive, admirable expression, and careful execution, the crudeness of the colour is unpleasingly conspicuous. The figures are small.

ST. JEAN.—1. A large flower-piece, chiefly composed of poppies and roses. Signed and dated 1846.

2. The companion picture, a fruit-piece in a dish. These both belong to the most successful works of this painter, who stands first in rank in the modern French school in this walk of art.

NETHERLANDISH SCHOOL.

RUBENS.—1. The celebrated "Rainbow" landscape. From the collection of Lord Orford. See vol. iii. p. 434.

2. Portrait of an old man, almost *en face*, with white beard and black dress, with his left hand holding a glove about the centre of his breast. Half-length. The ground is a greyish-brown. One of the finest portraits I know of the master. The conception is so animated that the eyes are really luminous, and the flesh-tones so transparent that one can see the blood under the skin. At the same time the transparency of the shadows, which are very deep but treated in the local flesh-tone, is almost the most remarkable feature.

3. Battle between Constantine and Maxentius. One of the twelve sketches from the history of Constantine, once in the Orleans Gallery. A raging combat of horsemen upon the broken bridge, now called Ponte Molle. This sketch is more powerful in colour than usual, and in action and spiritedness of execution recalls the famous Battle of the Amazons of Munich. Formerly in the Orleans Gallery. Later in the collection of Lord Ranelagh. Purchased at the sale of Mr. Rogers's pictures for 260 guineas.

VANDYCK.—1. Portrait of a young man in black dress; the background a red curtain; full-length figure, standing, life-size; of animated conception, and carefully executed in his fused Genoese manner.

2. Portrait of a lady with pretty features, in a black silk dress

with yellow stomacher, seated in a chair, her right hand on the arm of the chair. The ground dark. To the knees. Of the master's best middle period, and as lively in conception as careful in execution. From the Wells collection.

3 and 4. Portraits of Charles I. and Henrietta Maria, inherited by the Marquis of Hertford. These are decidedly not entirely by Vandyck's hand. Portions of the execution are weak; for instance, the dress of the king.

PHILIPPE DE CHAMPAGNE.—The Adoration of the Shepherds; an altarpiece. Besides the Virgin and Joseph the figures include five shepherds and three angels. A lamb is on the ground. The light proceeds from the Child. This picture is of the painter's later time; it is happily composed, delicately drawn for him, and very carefully finished. The effect, on the other hand, is crude, and the colouring unusually cool. From the collection of Count Montcalm at Montpellier. Purchased for 367*l*.

REMBRANDT.—1. The Unjust Steward. The master, dressed in red, with a red and orange-coloured turban, is seated behind a table with papers. Three persons stand before him, the centre one of whom is the culprit; next him is a soldier about to lead him to prison. The ground is dark; figures life-size. This picture, formerly well known in the Stowe collection, is of the most striking effect. The power, warmth, and transparency of the colouring are astonishing, and the treatment broad and masterly in the most solid impasto.

2. Portrait of a young man with hat and feather; bust-picture; carefully executed in a clear, yellowish tone.

3. Portrait of a negro as huntsman, half-length figure, very animated, solid and careful. From the Stowe collection.

GABRIEL METZU.—1. A fishmonger, and a girl bargaining with him; above them a kind of bower; the background architecture. Very carefully finished in a clear tone.

2. Single figure of a girl; a small but pretty picture.

GASPAR NETSCHER.—A room, with a girl in crimson bodice, and dark-green petticoat, making lace. About 1 ft. high, 10 in. wide. This picture is as characteristic of the master as it is admirable, and of his best time. He is rarely seen with such power of colour and force of effect.

PETER DE HOOGHE.—A woman peeling apples, seated beneath

a window; a little girl standing before her is trying to take the peel of the apple she is engaged upon. Behind is a saucepan. upon the fire. About 2 ft. 3 in. high, 1 ft. 10 in. wide. Very naïve and domestic in feeling, and as sunny and clear as it is powerful in effect.

SCHALCKEN.—A girl by candlelight. Very agreeable.

TENIERS.—1 and 2. These two pictures, though genuine, are not of that class which one rightly expects in a collection of such masterpieces of the greatest painters. One of them represents peasants in an interior.

ADRIAN BROUWER.—A peasant seated asleep; almost entirely seen in front; behind him a wooden partition; in the background are two more peasants. By far the finest example of this rare master I know. The figure, which is of an unusually large size for him, is of the most surprising truth, admirably drawn, very careful, though broad and soft in treatment, and of a delicacy of harmonious arrangement which places him in this respect higher than any other *genre* painter, and quite explains the admiration that Rubens had for him.

ADRIAN VAN OSTADE.—1. Five peasants round a table before a tavern; in the background three more, and a woman who is pouring out liquor. On wood. About 1 ft. 6 in. high, by 1 ft. 3 in. wide. Signed and dated, though the date is illegible. The figures are well distributed in the space, and the clear chiaroscuro, treated in a delicate golden tone, is admirable.

2. A peasant before the door of his house cleaning a fish; his wife and three children, the youngest of whom she holds in her arms, are attentively watching this interesting occupation. On wood. About 1 ft. 2 in. high, 1 ft. 1 in. wide. The figures are truthful and animated, and the colouring of singular power and clearness.

ISAAC VAN OSTADE.—View of a town, with figures of men and animals. Among the latter a grey horse is especially remarkable; on the left is a church, before which is a cart with a brown horse. On wood. About 2 ft. high, 3 ft. wide. The colouring of this picture is of unusual power, even for this master, and the treatment very careful.

PHILIP WOUVERMANS.—1. A smithy in a cavern, with a horse being shod before it; behind is a cart. An unusual effort of the master, and approaching Isaac Ostade in warmth and energy of tone. Also very carefully carried out.

2. A large landscape, with a sandy hill on the left, in the manner of his master Wynants. Water in the foreground, with a small foot-bridge, with a man passing over; on the shore a man on a grey horse which is drinking. About 2 ft. 3 in. high, 2 ft. wide. This picture is in his third manner, and is carried out in his softest and most delicate silver tone.

3. The well-known horse-market, from the collection of Baron de Mecklenburg at Paris. In point of size, richness of composition, agreeable motives, delicacy of keeping, and equality of careful execution, one of the chief works of the master's third period. This is the only way to explain the enormous sum of 80,000 francs, or 3200l., given for it by Lord Hertford at the sale of that collection.

Albert Cuyp.—View of the river Maas by Dortrecht. On the right is the church with its blunt tower; on the left, in the foreground, in the river, a ship manned with soldiers. About 3 ft. 6 in. high, 5 ft. 8 in. wide. This masterpiece possesses in full measure all the great qualities of this painter. The effect of morning is of the sunniest transparency, the reflections in the water marvellous, the colouring powerful, and the execution marrowy.

Nicolas Berghem.—A rocky landscape, with a shepherdess on horseback, and her herd. This picture, of an upright form, belongs, in point of tasteful composition and airy delicacy of gradations, to the best examples of the master.

Karel Dujardin.—1. The interior of a court, in which stand two horses laden—a grey and a brown horse. Above the wall is the view of a landscape. On canvas. About 1 ft. 6 in. high, 1 ft. 8 in. wide. Very warm and clear in tone, and of peculiarly soft touch.

2. A group of children, one singing, another jumping; behind them a wall and a piece of sky. Of upright oval form, very prettily conceived, and sketchily but very cleverly treated in a warm tone, approaching Adrian van de Velde. From the Duval collection.

3. Portrait of a young man. Very animated and delicate.

Hobbema.—A piece of clear water on the right, and behind, a village in sunshine; quite on the left a house with three figures before it, with a wood at the side; in the centre another house among trees, and a flat distance. This picture is of considerable size and very happy composition. The bright lighting of the whole right side with the clouds, forms a fine contrast to the powerful and clearly treated shadow of the left. The execution is also most careful. From the Fesch collection.

JAN WYNANTS.—On the right a dead tree, with a piece of water at its foot; behind are two sportsmen by ADRIAN VAN DE VELDE, who painted also the other figures in this picture; on the left is his favourite sand-hill; in the centre of the middle distance are two light trees. About 2 ft. high, 2 ft. 8 in. wide. The charm of true nature in this picture, the great softness, harmony, and transparency of the tone, and the very delicate execution, render it quite a little chef-d'œuvre.

JACOB RUYSDAEL.—A landscape with a waterfall almost in the foreground; in the middle distance on the left a hill; on the right a distant view, with slight elevation of ground and bright horizon; some clouds in the sky. Of charming effect, and clear and true in the highest degree; the treatment broad and spirited. From the Denon collection.

ARTUS VAN DER NEER.—A warm sunset over a Dutch canal, with houses and trees along it. Inscribed with the monogram of the master. The marvellous warmth and transparency, and the precise though soft execution, render this one of the finest works of the painter.

WILLEM VAN DE VELDE.—1. A calm sea; a large vessel on the left is firing a gun; close by is another vessel; in the centre a manned boat; on the right a smaller sailing-vessel. Every part of this picture, including the sky, is of a truly luminous and silvery tone.

2. A fresh breeze at sea. In the foreground small fishing-boats. On the right a large vessel lying on its side. In the tone of this fine picture the influence of Simon de Vlieger is recognisable.

JAN WEENIX.—Two dead hares and dead birds in the centre. On the right a dog seated, and above, a white dove in the air. On the left a sarcophagus, with two children in high relief. The background a landscape. About 5 ft. high, 6 ft. wide. This is the finest specimen of the master I know. His usual high finish is here combined with admirable keeping. The dog is of peculiar animation.

Melchior Hondekoeter.—A cock, a peacock, and other birds. A good but not first-rate picture by the artist.

I here take the opportunity of correcting a few erroneous notices in vol. ii. p. 160, regarding pictures of the Netherlandish school.

The landscape by Hobbema, from the collection of the King of Holland, was purchased, not for 1000*l*. but for 2400*l*. The two pictures by Vander Heyden, for 1000*l*. not for 300*l*. Finally, for the Duval collection " in Ghent," the reader must substitute " in Geneva."

ENGLISH SCHOOL.

Sir Joshua Reynolds.—Portrait of Nelly O'Brien. Taken quite in front, with a straw hat and black mantle, a reddish-coloured quilted dress, and an apron over it of a transparent material. The background is a dark landscape. To the knees. This picture may be considered a *tour de force* of the utmost skill, after the manner of Rubens' *Chapeau de Paille*, in Sir Robert Peel's collection, for here also the head is in shadow, with strong reflected sunny light, which is treated with exquisite refinement and transparency. The rest of the picture, also, is of bright and harmonious colour, the landscape very powerful and juicy, and the whole a model of taste and complete mastery of the art. This was one of the pictures inherited by Lord Hertford.

2. The Strawberry Girl. See vol. ii. p. 75. Formerly in the collection of Samuel Rogers, Esq., and sold at the sale of that gentleman's pictures in 1856 for 2100 guineas, a proof that no nation so appreciate the works of their distinguished painters as the English.

3. A little girl holding a dog. Background a landscape of enchanting truth and naïveté of conception, and of truly sunny effect. Though, in my opinion, equal in beauty to the Strawberry Girl, to which it forms an admirable companion, yet, being less famous, it cost the Marquis only 1000*l*.

Gainsborough.—Portrait of a lady in a white dress seated in a chair. Next her a little dog. Background a landscape. Whole-length figure, life-size. Of great charm of conception, only the disposition of the feet tasteless. Carefully executed in a cool but harmonious tone.

Hilton.—Diana and her nymphs bathing, while Venus descends to them through the air. Cupid is upon a tree. Very attractive in composition, and of much feeling for beauty in forms and motives. The colouring clear, though a little pale in some of the figures. The fine landscape is composed in the manner of Titian. From the collection of Lord Charles Townshend, and purchased for 640*l.*

Sir David Wilkie.—The Highland Toilette. An interior, with a girl in a Scotch dress seated at a window dressing her hair: next her is another girl. In the background, next a fireplace, is a man smoking his pipe. Charmingly composed, admirable in lighting, and clear in colour. The treatment shows the later period of the master. Purchased for 567*l.*

Bonnington.—A sea-coast, with a grey and a brown horse in the foreground, and chalk rocks in the background. Carried out in a silvery tone, with a delicate feeling for harmony. The price, 231*l.*, shows how much the works of this painter are esteemed.

THE GROSVENOR GALLERY.

Vol. II. p. 161.

Rubens.—Two children. Spiritedly conceived and slightly treated. This hangs too high to admit of a more decided opinion.

Rembrandt.—As regards the fine landscape which I formerly (vol. ii. p. 166) only considered as a work of his school, I am glad to perform the pleasing duty of stating that subsequent close examination has convinced me of its being an unquestionable work by the master.

Philip de Koninck.—A landscape, which, in extent, lighting, refinement of sky and linear perspective, and power and transparency of colouring, is one of his most important works.

Claude Lorraine.—The specimens of this master, of which this is the eighth, are very significant of his course of development. We here see how much Claude, in his earlier period, formed himself on the model of Paul Brill. In the far more finished execution, showing a realistic tendency and aim at truth in detail, which gradually declined in his later works, a striking resemblance to that master is seen. This is especially applicable to the great transparency of the sky.

Velasquez.—This portrait (vol. ii. p. 172) does not represent Philip IV. of Spain, as I have erroneously stated, but the son of that monarch, the Infant Don Balthasar.

DINING-ROOM.

In this apartment are various good pictures of the Italian school of the 15th century, among which I especially noticed the following :—

Carlo Crivelli.—The Virgin and Child enthroned; a saint on each side. Altarpiece. Signed "Carolus Crivelli, 1491." The head of the Virgin is unusually noble for him, and the execution as usual very finished.

Andrea Verocchio.—The Virgin and Child, with saints. A circular picture. The style of physiognomies, the drawing, careful modelling, and powerful colouring, are all evidences of this rare master, of whom this is an unusually good specimen.

MR. BARING'S COLLECTION.

Vol. II. p. 174.

No collection in England known to me has, since my visit in 1851, received such numerous and important additions of various epochs and schools as that of Mr. Baring. I continue my account of these acquisitions in the same order I observed in the description of the collection.

FLORENTINE SCHOOL.

Fra Bartolommeo.—The Virgin holding on her lap the Child, who is in lively movement, and in the act of benediction. On the right is the Baptist stretching out his hand. Upon his right shoulder is the hand of Joseph, who is standing behind a parapet. The two children alone, who are pleasing in the forms and elevated in the expression of the heads, are carried out with careful modelling in colour. Otherwise the ground is only covered with a thin surface of brown lake, with the outlines drawn in with the brush in dark-brown colour. In the Virgin are seen indications of grey shadows. The background is black. In a technical point of view this picture is very interesting.

ROMAN SCHOOL.

JULIO ROMANO (?).—The Virgin holding the Child, who is clinging to her. This picture is original and attractive in motive, admirable in drawing, and of powerful, warm brown tone of flesh; but the shot stuffs, in the style of fresco-painting, are rather crude. Judging from conception, colouring, and treatment, I consider this to be a very good work by the hand of PERINO DEL VAGA.

LOMBARD SCHOOL.

FRANCESCO MARIA RONDANI.—Marriage of St. Catherine, in the style of Parmigianino, with very dark shadows. Judging from authentic works in Parma, I attribute this picture to the above-named painter—a little-known but excellent scholar of Correggio. I know not on what authority it is here given to Pietro Paolini, a Lucca painter who flourished in the 17th century, and who painted, as far as his works are known to me, in a very different manner.

BOLOGNESE SCHOOL.

FRANCESCO FRANCIA.—1. Lucretia, with her eyes, which are red with weeping, cast up towards the left, is stabbing herself with the right hand in the right breast, while she touches the other breast with the other hand. Her hair is reddish, her dress violet. A golden armlet with precious stones is round her left arm. The background is a landscape, with a horseman and two male figures on foot. Half-length figure, the size of life. On wood. This picture, which possesses great charm of form and expression, is painted in a bright golden tone in the latest time of the master.

2 (?).—The Virgin enthroned, showing the Child an apple, to which it is pointing. On the right is Joseph, his hands leaning on a crutch; on the left St. Francis of Assisi, with a crucifix in his right hand. On the throne is the following inscription in golden letters:—" F. Francia Aurifex faciebat anno MDXII." About 11 in. high by 10 in. wide. A very pretty and careful picture, though too cold and crude in colouring, and not intense enough in feeling, for this master. From the colour of the gold I consider the inscription not to be genuine, and the picture rather by the hand of his son, GIACOMO FRANCIA.

This is the fitting place to introduce two pictures of the school of Romagna.

LODOVICO MAZZOLINO.—The youthful Christ teaching in the Temple. A rich composition. of the often-repeated subject by Mazzolino. A baboon and an owl are here introduced. The Berlin Museum possesses the same composition of almost the same size by the master. Mr. Baring's picture is, however, far deeper and more glowing in colour.

MARCO PALMEZZANO DA FORLI.—I am inclined to consider an undraped figure of John the Baptist drinking out of a bowl the work of this master. The motive is peculiar and pleasing, and the execution careful. About 2 ft. high, 1 ft. 3 in. wide.

VENETIAN SCHOOL.

CARLO CRIVELLI.—1. The Virgin holding the Child, who tands before her on a parapet, and is pressing towards himself a goldfinch with both hands. Behind the Virgin is a curtain, and on each side views of a landscape. Signed " Opus Karoli Crivelli, Veneti." The Virgin, who is of his usual type of feature, is here very refined in expression, and delicately finished. On the other hand, the head of the Child is without expression, and also badly foreshortened. The fruit also, upon a festoon before the curtain, is too large for the figures, which are about a fourth the size of life. The same may be said of a fly, otherwise of the utmost truth, upon the parapet.

2. The Ascension, with three sleeping guards. Seldom has this master attained the elevation and grandeur remarkable in the head of the Saviour. At the same time every portion of the work shows a greater attention to truth, while the execution is very careful. The strange form of this picture, which is shaped below like a heart, has doubtless some symbolical meaning.

TITIAN.—Charles V. in complete armour on a black horse, with a lance in his right hand. The horse is in gallop, with a crimson saddle-cloth. The figure of Charles is about 2 ft. high. A warm evening light is in the landscape. Spiritedly conceived, and executed with a marrowy touch in a solemn and deep tone. From the collection of Mr. Rogers.

GIOVANNI BATTISTA MORONI.—Portrait of a general in armour. The left hand on the hilt of his sword, the right on his helmet, which lies on a broken pillar, on which is the inscription, "Marius Benve^t sub Carolo V. imperat. dux." The background consists of architecture and sky. To the knees. The action easy, and the animated head coloured and conceived much in the feeling of his master Moretto. The hands of great truth, and the armour of masterly treatment.

GIACOMO BASSANO.—A picture in which, as usual with him, cattle play the chief part, and with a particularly fine landscape background.

SPANISH SCHOOL.

VELASQUEZ.—Philip IV. of Spain galloping on a brown horse. A picture of moderate size, but of clever conception and solid execution. From the collection of Mr. Rogers.

ALONSO SANCHEO COELLO.—Portrait of a small sickly-looking child, probably an Infant of Spain, in a splendid white patterned dress. In the left hand a wooden horse. Full-length figure, life-size. I am acquainted with too few specimens of this master, who is seldom seen out of Spain, to pronounce as to the correctness with which this is named. The truth, however, of every portion, and the care of the execution, are worthy of the high reputation as a portrait-painter which Coello bore at the court of Philip II.

ZURBARAN.—A monk, with his face entirely shaded by his cowl, is contemplating a skull which he holds in his clasped hands. About 2 ft. high, 1 ft. 4 in. wide. This is quite a congenial subject for the chief painter of Spanish asceticism. It is admirably conceived and of broad and masterly rendering in a solid impasto, with strong contrasts of light and shadow.

ALONSO CANO.—The Virgin and Child. Of very realistic treatment, but pleasing and animated. The excellent drawing of the hands reminds us that this master was sculptor as well as painter. At the same time the colouring is as powerful as it is clear, and the execution careful.

FRENCH SCHOOL.

WATTEAU.—1. Pierrot, in his white dress, surrounded with ladies and cavaliers. The background a garden. This picture, which is about 2 ft. high by 3 ft. wide, is of such vivacity in the heads, clearness and warmth of colouring, and carefulness of execution, that I do not hesitate to pronounce it one of the most remark-

able works of the master I know. It recalls the picture in my
friend M. de Lacaze's fine collection in Paris, only that there the
figures are as large as life.

2. A landscape, animated with numerous figures. In the
foreground is a carriage drawn by three grey horses. Their
trappings, however, are not indicated. This picture, which is of
considerable size, is treated in a clever though sketchy manner.

3 and 4. Two smaller pictures, which for composition, transparency and power of colour, and spirited and careful finish, belong
to his best works.

OLD GERMAN AND OLD NETHERLANDISH SCHOOL.

JAN VAN EYCK.—See vol. ii. p. 78. From the collection of
Mr. Rogers.

HANS HOLBEIN.—1. Portrait of the painter Johann Herbster,
with a powerful beard, a cap of a fine red colour, and a black
dress. At the sides are two pillars, with a winged boy on each,
holding two festoons fastened together in the centre of an arch.
Upon a parapet, sustained by the pillars, is the inscription " Johann
Herbster, pictor Operini pater." Also, above the heads, on two
other festoons, are two little tablets, one containing the date 1516,
the other doubtless the now obliterated monogram. This picture
is most carefully executed, especially the beard, in those yellowish
flesh-tones formerly peculiar to Holbein, and is of great animation.
The architecture is of a golden tone. It has much affinity to the
altarpiece of S. Sebastian, dated 1512, in the gallery at Augsburg, although of more delicate rendering. Historically speaking,
also, it is of interest, as we gather from it that the migration of
Holbein from Augsburg to Basle took place at latest in 1516, for
the painter Herbster was a native of Basle, and his son Operinus
the famous printer of that city.

LUCAS CRANACH.—1. " Suffer little children to come unto me."
This is one of the many examples of the treatment of this subject
by Lucas Cranach, and in point of richness of composition, happy
infantine motives, power and clearness of colouring, and careful
finish, it is one of the best. From the collection of M. de Bammeville.

2 and 3 (?).—The small portraits of the Electors of Saxony,
Frederick the Wise and John the Constant. These are two spe-

cimens of the numerous portraits of these two princes executed in the school of Lucas Cranach in 1532. The German verses, setting forth the merits of these individuals as leaders of the Reformation, are here, for once, perfectly preserved. These superficial and mechanically painted pictures were decidedly never touched by the hand of Cranach.

JOHANN MABUSE.—1. The Virgin with the Child, enthroned beneath a canopy of the latest and most mannered Gothic taste, with pleasing sculpture. Six angels are around, one holding flowers, while the others are engaged in music. The heads are more attractive than is usually the case in the later pictures by Mabuse; the colouring of a fine warm brown tone; and the execution of uncommon precision.

2. The Virgin and Child on a throne of the richest forms of the Renaissance. The heads are here of very indifferent feeling, but the colouring of the flesh and of the architecture very warm, and the numerous details of the latter of masterly execution.

FLEMISH AND DUTCH SCHOOL OF THE 17TH AND 18TH CENTURIES.

RUBENS.—A landscape, with a cart and two horses in the foreground. The evening light is expressed with marvellous warmth and transparency. From the collection of Mr. Rogers.

VANDYCK.—A male figure in black dress, with a plain white collar and cuffs, seated in a chair in an easy position, with his feet crossed, and playing the lute. A room is faintly indicated in the dark background. Whole-length, life-size. In conception and colouring this picture is as original as it is attractive. The feeling in it is refined and elevated, the colours very harmonious, but unusually broken for Vandyck, and the treatment quite masterly.

REMBRANDT.—1. Portrait of an aged Rabbi. Half-length. Painted in a delicate and clear, but for him cool tone. The shadows only are very dark.

2. A small landscape with buildings, overshadowed with rainclouds, leaving one portion only of foreground and background in light. Highly poetical and melancholy in feeling, and of great power and depth of chiaroscuro.

GERARD DOW.—A room by candlelight, with a man looking close into the face of a laughing girl. Of admirable truth in the expression of the light, and especially in the subdued gleam of a lantern.

PETER DE HOOGHE.—On the left a man sitting at a meal, and about to drink. A maidservant, who is taking care of a child with a go-cart, is reaching a glass to another gentleman, who is coaxing the head of a parrot in a cage. This picture is treated in a very cool tone, which in the figure eating is almost dark, but has, nevertheless, a great charm. The maidservant, who is seen in profile, is unusually pretty for the master. The execution is very careful.

ADRIAN VAN OSTADE.—An uproar at a card-table. Six persons are round the table, two of whom have seized knives. One of them, who is already on his legs, is held back by his wife,—the other is kept down in his chair by a man. All the other individuals are in great excitement as well. In the foreground is a child. Signed. Seldom has such a scene been treated by the master with such animation. The chiaroscuro is also unrivalled in warmth and depth, and the execution shows a breadth, a softness, and a care seldom seen united.

JACOB RUYSDAEL.—1. A windmill in the foreground, close to a piece of water. In the background a church with a tower, and two other towers. Although somewhat dark in general effect, this picture has a bright sky, recalling Hobbema, which gives it a wonderful charm of nature. The slight reflections of the objects in the smooth water are quite incomparable.

2. View of the plain before Haarlem, with buildings on the right, and a bleaching-ground, on which a gleam of sun is falling. The clouds in the sky are somewhat grey, but light, and illuminated by the sun. This picture takes a high place among this class of Ruysdael's works. It possesses great truth of effect, and the execution, though careful, is free and spirited.

3. A landscape, with a waterfall in the foreground, and fir-trees in the background. A cloud in the partially clear sky is lighted by the sun. The whole composition shows the influence of his somewhat older contemporary Everdingen. The effect is somewhat cold, the execution careful.

VAN KESSEL.—A landscape, with a tree on the right hand, a dark piece of water in the foreground, and a bright gleam of sunshine in the middle distance. This is an excellent work, in the taste of Ruysdael.

ENGLISH SCHOOL.

SIR JOSHUA REYNOLDS.—A landscape. To the left, in front under trees, are cattle and sheep reposing. In the middle distance a piece of water, houses, a wood, and a hill. In the distance a slight indication of mountains. Sir Joshua, it is well known, very seldom painted a landscape. Here, in the glowing tone and warm reflection of an evening sky, we are reminded of Rembrandt. The treatment of the detail is conventional and slight. From Mr. Rogers's collection.

SIR DAVID WILKIE.—Dead stag, with a huntsman, a boy, and a girl, on the left. A piper in highland dress, blowing his bagpipe, on the right, and a woman with a child on her arm. Behind are slightly indicated hills. Signed and dated 1821. A very spirited sketch.

MULREADY.—1. Two girls, with their elbows on their knees, are watching a little boy who steps timidly forward to give a penny to two gipsies, one of whom is stretching out a hand. The background a landscape. The motive is very animated and true, the colouring very lively, and the execution extremely careful.

2. Girls bathing. The chief figure is a girl seated in the foreground, arranging her hair. The next in interest is one rising from the water, and one sitting on the bank looking on. Two others are seen already dressed, and also a woman with a child. In the distance on the rock is a man, whose presence disturbs some of the girls. The heads and forms of the figures are very pretty, and are conceived in a purely artistic and modest taste. They are most carefully modelled, in full daylight. A red dress near the chief figure recalls Paul Veronese, both in colour and form. The painter has not availed himself, however, of the resources of oil-painting in this picture, which has the effect of a very lightly treated water-colour drawing. The execution also is stippled in the shadows.

3. The companion to the foregoing, only that the chief figure is here seen from behind. This is also most carefully studied, and of masterly modelling in the details. It has the same characteristics as its companion.

COLLECTION OF R. S. HOLFORD, ESQ.

Vol. II. p. 193.

Although Mr. Holford has not continued to add to his treasures of art of late years in the same ratio as formerly, yet some pictures of so fine a quality have been acquired, that I cannot pass them over in silence.

ITALIAN SCHOOL.

Fra Bartolommeo.—The Virgin and Child. The heads, forms, and motives of great elevation, and in a high degree characterised by the warm colouring peculiar to him.

Titian.—A female portrait, purporting to be Catherine Cornaro. Of animated conception, and carefully carried out in a somewhat subdued flesh-tone.

Paul Veronese.—A portrait ascribed by me to this master (p. 197) is also said to represent Catherine Cornaro.

Lodovico Carracci.—Our Saviour healing the blind man. The well-known picture from the Giustiniani Gallery, and more recently from the Gallery of the Duke of Lucca. The composition is very skilful, and the forms, namely, the Saviour's head, of uncommon beauty.

Agostino Carracci.—Christ raising the Widow's Son. Companion to the foregoing, and also from the same collection. This picture shows the profound knowledge and masterly execution of the painter, and is the more valuable from the rarity of his works. The only reason why I did not previously mention these two pictures is because I was under the erroneous impression in 1851 that the purchase of them had not been concluded with Mr. Buchanan.

FRENCH SCHOOL.

Nicolas Poussin.—A landscape. The elevated poetry of composition which renders Nicolas Poussin the greatest master of landscape-painting is here combined with very powerful colouring and an unusual carefulness of execution.

Antoine Watteau.— A very attractive party of ladies and cavaliers in the open air.

NETHERLANDISH SCHOOL.

RUBENS.—1. Portrait of a young woman, with hands; purporting to be that of a poetess. The thoughtfulness of the expression well corresponds with this title. This picture is also characterised by a very delicate and pure feeling for nature; the modelling is very careful, and the colouring combines great transparency with a truthful and subdued tone.

The sketch by RUBENS mentioned p. 199 is not of the Descent from the Cross, but of the Elevation of the Cross at Antwerp.

KAREL DUJARDIN.—A landscape, with a cow and some sheep in the foreground, and a wood in the middle distance. The animals exhibit a truth and solidity of impasto approaching Paul Potter. The keeping has, however, been somewhat disturbed by the after-darkening of the mass of trees, and bubbles have appeared on many parts of the surface.

BACKHUYSEN.—A very agitated sea, with numerous vessels. A remarkable work in every respect—composition, effect, and execution.

ADDITIONS TO LORD WARD'S COLLECTION.
Vol. II. p. 229.

RAPHAEL.—The Three Graces. Not having seen this little picture when compiling my work on the Treasures of Art in England, I only made a slight allusion to it (p. 233). Since then, in 1856, I have had the opportunity of inspecting it in the possession of Mr. Munro, to whom Lord Ward intrusted it for a time.

Most completely can I confirm Passavant's statement of its being taken from the well-known antique group of the Graces in the Libreria of the Cathedral at Siena. The delicate feeling of the painter has however led him to treat his subject according to the laws of pictorial style. Though preserving the slender proportions of the figures, he has yet given them somewhat more fulness, while the effect of the fine flesh tones is heightened by a golden ball in the hand of each, and by the coral which he has placed in the hair of two of the figures, and round the throat of the third. In the heads also, which are of marvellous beauty, all the peculiar type of Raphael is apparent. The group is admirably relieved by the landscape background. From the character of the modelling, which is in a fine impasto, I agree with Passavant in assigning the date of the work to 1506. This precious little picture belonged to the Borghese Gallery, and was purchased from it in Rome by a M. Reboul. It passed later into the possession of the Messrs. Woodburn, who sold it to Sir Thomas Lawrence. After his death it was acquired by the late Lord Dudley and Ward, from whom the present Lord Ward inherited it.

RAZZI.—The Virgin, with the Child lying on a parapet before her, and grasping with his right hand her right breast. On the right is the little St. John. This very attractive picture is most arbitrarily assigned to Schidone.

BAGNACAVALLO. — St. Augustin. Whole-length figure, life-size. This picture displays the energy of conception and power of colouring characteristic of this scholar of Raphael. The flesh tones however, as usual with him, are somewhat too red.

Finally, I have a mistake to rectify. After renewed and careful study of the fine picture of Christ on the Mount of Olives, which I attributed to Mostaert, I have come to the conclusion that it is a work of the best time of JOACHIM PATENIER.

COLLECTION OF HENRY DANBY SEYMOUR, ESQ., M.P.

Vol. II. p. 241.

GAROFALO.—St. Christopher. A very clever fresco painting.

LUCA DELLA ROBBIA.—A statue of Charity, with a child upon her arm and another at her feet. Purchased from the collection of M. de Bammeville. As the clay of which this is formed has from some reason not been glazed in the flesh parts, the forms have remained more delicate and sharp, while, in point of naïveté of feeling, slenderness and delicacy of proportions, and infantine grace, the whole work may be classed as one of the most attractive specimens of the master.

I take this opportunity of correcting a mistake which I have committed in my former notice of Mr. Seymour's collection—namely, in attributing to Sir Joshua Reynolds a beautiful female portrait by HOGARTH. The fact of such a mistake having been possible proves that in point of colouring this picture is a particularly choice work of the master.

ADDITIONS TO THE WORKS OF ART BELONGING TO THE RIGHT HON. HENRY LABOUCHERE.

Vol. II. p. 287.

Since the publication of my work I have had the opportunity of inspecting some new acquisitions made by this gentleman.

DRAWING-ROOM.

GAROFALO.—The Circumcision. A very choice cabinet picture by the master. The composition is as original as it is fortunate, the heads are noble, the draperies of very pure taste, the colouring harmonious and of uncommon power, and the execution delicately felt and careful.

JAN MABUSE (?).—The Mass of Pope Gregory. A small picture, very animated and expressive in the heads, of great force of colour, and masterly execution in a solid impasto. The rich architecture is in the taste of Bernhard van Orley. Decidedly unlike Mabuse, but by some excellent painter of the Netherlandish school, soon after the beginning of the 16th century, unknown to me.

MARTIN SCHAFNER.—1 and 2. Two very delicate pictures of religious subjects by this clever master, who flourished at Ulm at the end of the 15th and beginning of the 16th century.

ROMNEY.—Portrait of Lady Hamilton as Cassandra. The marvellous beauty of her features is especially seen in this spirited sketch.

GREUZE.—Head of a young girl. A drawing of the most tender charm.

A small picture of a girl resting on her arm, from the school of Madame Lebrun, shows a very pure and delicate feeling for nature.

I also found here, in 1856, the fine Baptism by FRANCIA, and the portrait by MORONI, which I formerly described at Stoke (see vol. ii. p. 419).

DINING-ROOM.

ALONSO CANO.—Portrait of Calderon. From the Louis Philippe Collection. The noble and intellectual features are admirably rendered.

The large picture by SEBASTIAN DEL PIOMBO, which I have only slightly mentioned, represents Amerigo Vespucci submitting maps of his discoveries to various gentlemen. One of these individuals is seated in an arm-chair ; three others are standing.   The head of Vespucci, seen in profile, shows features of noble character, expressive of resolution and enterprise.   The table and the table-cloth are rudely executed, and betray the hand of a scholar.

I profit by this opportunity to correct some mistakes in my description of Mr. Labouchere's collection at Stoke (see vol. ii. p. 417), which I greatly regret.

1. The Virgin and Child, with the little St. John and four singing angels, which I consider a youthful work by Michael Angelo, is not *circular* but *quadrangular* in form.

2. The statue of Venus, which on very slight examination I mistook for an original repetition by Canova, is a very faithful and careful copy by Rossi.

On the other hand, the bust of Napoleon, by Canova, is here ; and the head of the Vestal Tuccia, as we are informed by an inscription.

3. The boy on the dolphin, which I attributed to Canova, is by Thorwaldsen, and represents one of the four Elements, the remaining three being also at Stoke.

CATALOGUE OF THE COLLECTION OF OBJECTS OF ART BELONGING TO JAMES MORRISON, ESQ.,

In his house, 57, Upper Harley Street.

A short notice of this collection appeared in vol. ii. p. 260. Subsequent opportunities, however, have enabled me to give the following and fuller account.

DINING-ROOM.

Jan van Huysum.—A bouquet of flowers, comprising roses, tulips, poppies, hyacinths, and convolvuluses, in a bronze vase, decorated with a relief of pretty *amorini*.   Other flowers, especially auriculas, are lying on the table on which the vase stands.   A niche forms the background.   On wood, 2 ft. 10 in. high, 2 ft. 1¼ in. wide.   The flowers are executed with the usual skill of this eminent master, and the whole picture exhibits a greater certainty in the distribution of the masses of light and shade than is usua. with this painter.

SIR JOSHUA REYNOLDS.—The portrait of Dr. Johnson, at an advanced period of life, and evidently suffering from illness. He is seated in an arm-chair, dressed in black; a pen in his right hand, and his left resting on a sheet of paper on a table. On canvas, 4 ft. 1 in. high, 3 ft. 3 in. wide. The suffering state of the lexicographer is strongly expressed both in the features and in the colouring. The treatment is broad and masterly.

PETER PAUL RUBENS.—St. Francesco de Paula is rising through the air in the presence of a large number of people, most of whom are gazing at him with signs of adoration. Many figures are on a bridge; others stand somewhat lower. Quite below are three persons—two men and a woman—possessed by evil spirits, who are writhing in convulsive movements. Several persons are endeavouring to restrain them. On wood, 3 ft. 6½ in. high, 2 ft. 6 in. wide. This sketch is rich and dramatic in composition, and also exhibits careful drawing, and a more than usual power of colouring.

LIBRARY.

On a dumb waiter, and protected by a glass, is a painted Greek vase, with a complete representation of the combat for the body of Achilles. This belongs to the so-called archaic style, the heads as well as the figures being, according to a uniform antique type, black upon a yellow ground. The chief group represents the body of Achilles lying on the ground, his name, as well as those of all the other personages, being inscribed in large capital letters close by. This vase, which is about 1½ ft. high, and in excellent preservation, is one of the most interesting of this style known to me. The motives are very speaking and animated, and the execution very careful.

On the bookcases are eight vases from the province of Basilicata, in the kingdom of Naples, some of them large, and with ruder paintings.

FRONT DRAWING-ROOM.

FRANCESCO ALBANI.—A pleasing landscape, with a woman seated beneath a tree, from which she is plucking fruit. A boy with fruit in his hand is clinging to her, while another child lies sleeping at her feet. On the right is a palm-tree with a child seated upon it, and two more standing below. On the left is a superb fountain surmounted by the figure of a child. On canvas, 2 ft. 4 in. high, 3 ft. 2 in. wide. Of pleasing motives and attractive heads ; warm and soft in colouring, and careful in execution.

Teniers.—A crowd of country people are amusing themselves in various ways before a village tavern. On the left, next the door, are some couples seated, and some more standing. In the centre are three couples dancing; behind them lookers-on. On the right, on a tub, is a piper; around him are other groups, with two women, who are supporting their drunken husbands. In the background is the village, with the church. A portion of a rainbow is in the sky. Signed. On wood, 2 ft. high, 3 ft. 2 in. wide. Formerly in the collection of Lord Ashburton. Very happily arranged, full of speaking and animated motives, and carefully and spiritedly treated in a light, warm flesh tone.

Gaspar Poussin.—A landscape, with a large tree to the left in the foreground ; in the centre a shepherd with some sheep and goats. In the middle distance is a still piece of water with buildings reflected on its smooth surface. A lofty chain of rocks terminates the horizon. On canvas, 3 ft. $2\frac{1}{4}$ in. high, 4 ft. 4 in. wide. The noble character of the composition is here combined with great clearness, softness, and delicacy of tone.

Adrian van Ostade.—A lawyer in black dress and velvet cap reading a letter thoughtfully in a room. Writing materials, documents, and a book, on the table. A map of Europe on the wall. Signed and dated 1671. On wood, 8 in. high, $8\frac{3}{4}$ in. wide. Very true and animated in expression, admirable in the clear daylight effect, and the flesh harmoniously executed in a subdued golden tone.

Isaac van Ostade.—A man on a grey horse is halting before a village tavern. Another on a black horse is paying the ostler. A group of five persons are at the door. On the road, quite in the foreground, are two dogs. In the landscape is a peasant on a cart, and two on foot. Inscribed. On wood, 1 ft. 4 in. high, 1 ft. $3\frac{1}{2}$ in. wide. Of fine and powerful effect, especially the man on the grey horse, and carefully executed in an excellent impasto.

Il Parmigianino.—The Virgin seated, and holding with her left hand the Child, who is standing before her, supported by a female saint, and worshipped by the little St. John. The background is formed by a landscape of thick foliage, with a view of a hilly distance. On wood, 3 ft. 5¾ in. high, 2 ft. wide. An admirable picture by this very unequal master. The heads pleasing, especially that of the female saint; the motives happy, carefully modelled in a warm tone, and in excellent preservation.

GERARD DOW.—A sage writing in his study. On the table is a large open book resting against a globe; also a skull. Signed. On wood, 9½ in. high, 7½ in. wide. Of the highest finish, and admirable keeping in a subdued light.

JAN WYNANTS.—Two men and a woman driving four cows along a road skirting a sandhill. Trees in the middle distance, rising ground behind. On wood, 1 ft. 3¼ in. high, 1 ft. wide. The harmonious effect, the style of lighting, the careful execution, and the admirable figures by ADRIAN VAN DE VELDE, render this picture highly attractive.

LEANDRO BASSANO.—The Adoration of the Shepherds. The cattle, as usual, play a conspicuous part. On canvas, 2 ft. 6 in. high, 4 ft. 6 in. wide. A picture remarkable for clearness of colour and careful execution.

PHILIP WOUVERMANS.—A tent on the sea-shore; before it a horse being laden; also a baggage-waggon. Several persons conversing before the tent. On the shore are two washwomen, and a rude pole on which is a lantern. Signed. On wood, 1 ft. 9¼ in. high, 2 ft. 8½ in. wide. A very picturesque composition in his second manner, executed in a tone which is rather dark in the foreground.

JAN STEEN.—Saying grace. On a table, on which falls a bright light from an open window, is seated a woman with her back to the window in a grey jacket and white cap, with a child on her arm. Opposite to her sits her husband saying grace, with his hat held before him. Bread and cheese are on the table, and a ham close by upon a barrel. On the window-sill a jug; and written on the wall a verse from Proverbs, ch. xxx. ver. 8. Signed and dated 1660. On wood, 1 ft. 9 in. high, 1 ft. 6¼ in. wide. A remarkable specimen of the fact that this uproarious master could also occasionally represent the touching scenes of humble but happy domestic life. In other respects also, excellence of drawing, decision of forms, equal carefulness of execution in a solid impasto, and great transparency, this picture belongs to the finest works of the master. It was brought to England by Mr. Chaplin, 1831.

WILLIAM VAN DE VELDE.—A sea-coast scene, in a perfect calm. On the left a small Dutch vessel-of-war; on the right, in the distance, a large ship. Also a number of larger and smaller boats. On canvas, 1 ft. 9¼ in. high, 2 ft. 1 in. wide. The reflections of the vessels in this charming picture are of the utmost transparency. The execution is very careful.

VANDYCK.—The infant Christ caressing the little St. John, who worships him. Both standing figures. On wood, 2 ft. 1 in. high, 1 ft. 5½ in. wide. Of beautiful motive and intense expression; warm and powerful in colour. The glass which protects the picture allows, however, no opinion on treatment and preservation.

NICHOLAS BERGHEM.—A woman on a mule in the centre of the foreground; a man near her; another man engaged in loading another mule. Behind are a cow, a goat, and sheep. On the right is a man with a donkey; close to a gate, through which a landscape is seen, another man and a woman. On the right are grand ruins of a classical character. On wood, 1 ft. 9¾ in. high, 2 ft. 2½ in. wide. Formerly in the collection of Lord C. Townshend. A rich and picturesquely arranged composition of careful execution, of the later time of the master.

CLAUDE LORRAINE.—A sea-coast. On the right, through trees, buildings are seen, with a hill behind. In the distance above the line of the sea are other hills. On the left are trees. In the foreground is Europa on a white bull, approaching the sea, and followed by an attendant, who is joined by another female. Two others are seated near the stems of two trees. Three cows are feeding, and two are resting. On canvas, 1 ft. 10¾ in. high, 2 ft. 7½ in. wide. The freshness of morning seen in this beautiful picture is admirably expressed in silvery tones of the utmost delicacy and transparency. Although this picture agrees in many respects with a larger work by the master of the same subject in the Royal collection, yet it has also many points of dissimilarity. It was originally executed for M. Courtois, and is dated 1658.

RUBENS.—The four Evangelists setting forth on the divine behest to preach the Gospel. Foremost are St. Matthew and St. Luke; St. Mark follows with the open book; and St. John is last. On wood, 2 ft. 1½ in. high, 2 ft. 3 in. wide. This very spirited sketch for the large pictures in the Grosvenor Gallery confirms the opinion expressed in my work that no part of them was touched by Rubens' own hand. Formerly in the collection of Edward Gray, Esq.

ALBERT CUYP.—A landscape with rocks on the right, and more in the centre a rising ground with trees, and a flock of sheep reposing ; a cow and a shepherd. On the left a misty distance, with a ruin and a piece of still water with three cows rising from it. In the foreground are three shepherds, and a shepherdess who is speaking to a peasant on the right of the trees. Between the trees and the rocks are another flock of sheep and some figures. On wood, 1 ft. 7½ in. high, 2 ft. 5 in. wide. We see in this picture the union of truth, transparency, and a treatment of admirable body, with that felicity of composition for which this master is particularly esteemed.

VANDYCK.—A male portrait in middle life, with moustache and pointed beard, and white collar. Bust picture. On wood, 1 ft. 7½ in. high, 2 ft. 5 in. wide. This fine picture unites a spirited and animated conception with an unusual warmth of tone, approaching Rembrandt. The head is of admirable body ; the dress only slightly treated.

JAN VAN DER HEYDEN.—View of a village lying partly on rising ground. On the left in the foreground is a fine tree. On the right are various trees which skirt a plain. Two horsemen advancing through a gateway, and other figures, are by the hand of ADRIAN VAN DE VELDE. Signed. On wood, 1 ft. 9 in. high, 2 ft. 4½ in. wide. This picture, which is unusually large for the master, belongs to his warmest and most harmonious works. The execution of the details is, as usual, most minute.

TITIAN.—The portrait of the painter with his mistress, who wears a furred garment over a red and yellow striped dress. She is pointing to herself, while Titian lays his hand on her person. In the foreground is a skull. The background is dark. Figures more than half-length. On canvas, 2 ft. 11½ in. high, 2 ft. 7½ in. wide. The situation of the lady and the presence of the skull intend to express the contrast between life and death. This picture, of which there is an etching by Vandyck, is treated, especially the female figure, in a broad and masterly tone. The head of Titian is tamer and flatter, and indicates the hand of a scholar.

Teniers.—St. Peter delivered from prison. The whole foreground represents a guard-room. On the right are two soldiers
and a peasant playing cards; a peasant stands looking on.   In
the middle distance are four other peasants. On the left, armour,
weapons, a drum, a trumpet, a red dress, and on the wall a sword
and two pistols. In the background, lighted by the glory, is the
figure of Peter, with the angel delivering him. Signed. On
wood, 2 ft. high, 2 ft. 10 in. wide. Of admirable keeping, and
carefully executed in warm flesh tones.

Rubens.—The Emperor Charles V. enthroned beneath a canopy
in a stately apartment, is conferring commercial privileges on the
town of Antwerp. A kneeling figure supported by Minerva is
receiving the document. In the foreground on each side are a
large number of official personages and guards. On wood, 1 ft.
9 in. high, 4 ft. 1 in. wide. Of great skill of arrangement, admirable in keeping, and of broad and masterly treatment.

Claude Lorraine.—The Adoration of the Golden Calf, in a
large and rich landscape. On the right hand are large trees
extending to the middle distance. On the left are huge masses
of rock ; near them are trees, which unite in the centre with the
above-mentioned trees. In the foreground is seen the calf, very
small, upon a stout pillar partially twisted, and adorned above with
reliefs ; Aaron is pointing to it. On the altar is a sacrifice burning.
Around are a multitude of Israelitish men and women ; some of
them kneeling in adoration. Others are dancing. The background
consists of a hilly distance of beautiful lines, with Moses and an
angel upon a rock. On canvas, 3 ft. 9 in. high, 4 ft. 10$\frac{1}{4}$ in. wide.
This picture, painted 1659 for M. Goly, agrees in the leading
feature with that painted five years earlier for Carlo Cavillo, and
now in the Grosvenor Gallery. It differs, however, in many respects ;
for instance, in the circumstance of there being no water in the
background, and in its being considerably smaller. It was formerly
in the possession of Sir R. Child. The keeping of this fine picture
is somewhat disturbed by the over-bright figures.

Jacob Ruysdael.—A mill on the left in the centre of a stream
which is dashing impetuously along. On the right a wall with
high trees above it ; and further behind a tower. A hill in the
distance. The sky is covered with rainy clouds. On canvas, 2 ft.
10 in. high, 3 ft. 11$\frac{1}{2}$ in. wide. The general gloomy effect of this

broadly and finely treated picture is somewhat relieved by a gleam of sun which falls on the water and the mill.

TENIERS.—The Seven Works of Mercy. In the representation of this subject the painter has adhered to his usual peasant life. The composition is rich ; the feeding of the hungry, the clothing of the naked, and the giving drink to the thirsty, being made the prominent works. Signed. On wood, 2 ft. 3¼ in. high, 3 ft. 11½ in. wide. Five pictures of this subject are known by Teniers, the finest of which is that in the collection of Baron Steengracht at the Hague. Two others, very admirable, are in the Louvre and in the collection of Lord Ashburton. This example is less luminous in tone; but the colouring is warm, and the execution minute. Formerly in Sir Thos. Baring's collection.

JEAN BAPTISTE GREUZE.—Upon an easel. A young girl in a white dress, with a straw hat with flowers in it hanging on her left arm, is plucking the petals from a white flower in order to tell her fortune. On canvas, of oval form, 2 ft. 2¾ in. high, 1 ft. 11¾ in. wide. The serious expression with which she is performing this important operation is very becoming to the pretty face. The execution is in a solid body, and of very delicate and transparent tone.

An enamel portrait of Flaxman in this room is a good and careful work by the well-known W. ESSEX.

LUCA DELLA ROBBIA.—A moderately raised relief in terracotta with coloured glazings representing the Virgin with the Child on her lap, who with the left hand is drawing a stalk of lilies at the foot of the Virgin towards him, while with the right he is also grasping at it. Of admirable style, attractive motive, pleasing forms, and careful execution.

BACK DRAWING-ROOM.

This apartment is adorned with water-colour drawings by eminent English artists.

PROUT.—View of the Doge's palace, of the Piazetta, and of the Zecca, taken from the canal close to the Riva de Schiavoni. 2 ft. 5½ in. high, 3 ft. 5 in. wide. This is one of the best specimens I know of the master, for the great power of foreground peculiar to him, is here combined with singular transparency, and an unusual delicacy of gradation in the various distances.

COPLEY FIELDING.—A stormy sea with a vessel in danger of

being wrecked. 3 ft. 0¾ in. high, 3 ft. 3¾ in. wide.   The large size of this picture, the truth of the waves, and the effect of the dark masses of clouds, render this one of the best productions of this well-known master.

TURNER.—Mountains round a lake, crowned with fine buildings. On the left a wooded hill, and a tree before it.   The whole scene floats in a warm sunny glow.   2 ft. 2½ in. high, 3 ft. 8½ in. wide. Of masterly treatment, and conceived in a Claude-like taste.

PICTURES BELONGING TO SIR CHARLES EASTLAKE, P.R.A.

Vol. II. p. 263.

ANDREA MANTEGNA.—The Virgin is supporting with both hands the Child, who stands entirely undraped on her lap.   He holds the thumb of her left hand with his right, and has his right arm round her neck.   She is looking at him with earnest love and adoration, while he, taken almost in front, and with his head slightly inclined to one side, is looking thoughtfully straight before him.   On the right, seen quite in front, is Joseph, represented as a bald-headed old man ; on the left Elizabeth, of about the same age, with a grey cloth over her head, arm, and shoulders.   Before her is St. John the Baptist as a child, pointing with the right hand to Christ, while he looks at the spectator and directs his attention to the motto " Ecce Agnus Dei."   The dress of the Virgin is a vermilion red ; her mantle a dull green watered stuff : the background dark.   In body-colour, on cloth.   Small life-sized figures. About 3 ft. high, 2 ft. 4 in. wide.   But rarely did this great master attain such a combination of beauty and softness of form, with the purest and most elevated feeling, as in the head of the Virgin. This, with the masterly drawing and modelling of the Child, and the delicate rendering of reflected lights and cast shadows, suffices to prove that the execution of this admirably preserved picture belongs to his ripest time, and can hardly be assigned to an earlier period than 1500.   The saints on each side are more realistic, but of earnest and dignified conception.   I entirely agree with Sir Charles Eastlake in believing this to be the picture mentioned by Ridolfi, in his ' Life of Mantegna,' vol. i. p. 72, where he says, —" Il Signor Bernardo Giunti, gentilhuomo Fiorentino, invaghito della pittura, conserva del Mantegna una Madonna col Bambino in seno, e due Santi a lato, con San Giovanni, in mezze figure, delle eccellenti opere sue."

GIOVANNI BELLINI.—A large landscape, with a thick wood in the middle distance extending towards the left; through the stems is seen a bright light; in the background are buildings, and hills behind. In the foreground is the death of Peter Martyr, who is seen on the right, pierced by a murderer in chain armour, while another pursues his fleeing companion more in the centre. On the border of the wood, undisturbed by this tragedy, are some figures occupied felling trees. On a scroll on the left is the name " Joannes Bellinus." On wood. If the cultivated lover of art takes pleasure in tracing in every great masterpiece one link of that chain which each painter receives from his predecessors and transmits to those coming after him, he will especially trace it here. That the painter's chief object in this picture was the thorough rendering of the landscape is obvious; nor need we wonder at this fact when we consider the antecedents of his father and master Jacobo Bellini, on which the remarkable book of which we have given a description, in the British Museum, throws additional light. At the same time the high degree of development which this landscape displays is well calculated to excite our admiration. The trees not only show an extraordinary detail in every portion—stems, branches, and foliage—but they also form a mass which impresses the spectator with the idea of a thick wood. The distance also already falls back from the eye in a certain degree. In this landscape we recognise the type of the landscapes of the scholars of Giovanni Bellini, and not only of those who like Cima da Conegliano adhered strictly to his forms of art, but even of the founders of the golden age of Giorgione and Titian; for it is evident that this picture served as model for the wood in the celebrated landscape in the Camuccini collection, now in the possession of the Duke of Northumberland. It is remarkable that, while the proportions of the figures hewing wood are slender in treatment, those in the foreground are rather short. The motives are very animated. In excellent preservation.

CIMA DA CONEGLIANO.—1. St. Sebastian, with only a cloth round his loins, standing in a niche, transfixed with two arrows, and with his hands tied behind him. The portrait-like head is dignified in expression.   The figure is unusually slender, refined, and of graceful action.   The modelling is very careful, in a full and warm tone.

2. St. Mark.   Companion to the above, and also standing in a niche.   Dressed in red tunic and blue mantle, holding his Gospel in his left hand, and in the right hand, which hangs by his side, a pen. The head is of dignified character, the drapery of pure taste.   Both are on wood.

PIETRO DEGLI INGANNATI.—The Child seated on the lap of the Virgin, giving the benediction to St. Catherine, who stands on the left with a palm-branch in her left hand, her right upon the wheel.   Opposite to her is St. Joseph.   Behind him and the Virgin is a green curtain, behind St. Catherine a landscape. Judging from the mild and pleasing character of the heads, and from the only slight development of the forms of the Child, I am inclined to ascribe this picture to this little-known scholar of Giovanni Bellini.   The warm colours are harmoniously arranged. The features and right hand of St. Catherine are of beautiful form. On wood.

PALMA VECCHIO.—The Child seated on the Virgin's lap, in the act of caressing St. Joseph, who kneels before him.   Behind St. Joseph is the donor, standing with folded hands.   On the left of the Virgin, seated, is the Magdalen, holding the box of ointment in her left hand, her right hand inclined towards her breast.   Next to her is St. Francis kneeling.   The background, landscape.   Whole-length figures, the size of life.   On canvas.   About 8 ft. square. Pleasing in the heads, warm in the flesh-tones, and harmonious in the rest of the colouring,   The less strict treatment shows the later time of the master.

DOMENICO GHIRLANDAJO.—The Virgin, with downcast eyes, is supporting with her right hand the right leg of the Child, who is standing on the right, on a parapet covered with a carpet. With her left hand she holds a slight gauze veil, which passes in front of the Child.   The background is a landscape.   Her head expresses a decorous, modest, and maidenly character—that of the Child the innocence of infancy.   The full forms of his body, the legs of which are, however, too short, are carefully modelled, and the colouring clear and blooming.   Above terminating in a semi-circle.   On wood.   About 4 ft. high, 2 ft. 4 in. wide.

Cosimo Tura, called Il Cosmé.—The Virgin seated on a richly-adorned throne below an arch with two pilasters, supporting with her left hand the head of the Child, who has fallen asleep with the music of six angels. Of four of these angels—two and two on each side of the throne—the two standing behind are playing on small violins, the two kneeling in front on the lute, the one on the right accompanying with his voice. Two other angels are below, the one playing on an organ of very peculiar form at the foot of the throne, while the other blows the bellows with his left hand. A sky of a fine blue forms the background. On wood; about 10 ft. high, 4 ft. wide. This is an unusually good work by this master, who is rare even in Italy, and who introduced the style taught by Squarcione in Padua into his native city, Ferrara. This form of art is especially recognisable in the Renaissance taste which prevails in the architectural portions and in the puffy folds of the drapery Both in the heads and in the other nude portions a decidedly realistic feeling is seen. The colouring is incomparably clearer and warmer than in other pictures by the master. Finally, the preservation is of rare excellence.

ADDITIONS TO THE WORKS OF ART BELONGING TO C. SACKVILLE BALE, ESQ.,

71, Cambridge Terrace, Edgeware Road.

Vol. II. p. 329.

This gentleman, with the highly cultivated feeling for art which I have already described, has, during the last four years, added to the various departments of his collection with as much success as zeal. I must limit myself to the description of the most important objects.

Considering the extreme rarity of antique pictures beyond Naples and its vicinity, I may first mention a small circle of about 8 or 9 inches in diameter, representing the half-length figure of a triton holding with the right hand a young sea-bull of greenish colour by a red bridle, and in the left a reed wand. The water is very well indicated; the ground is black. The motives are very animated, the flesh of dark brown tone, the treatment light, broad, and decorative, and the preservation good. This picture was formerly in the well-known collection of Dr. Meade, and is described in 'Turnbull's Ancient Paintings.'

BENOZZO GOZZOLI.—The Virgin and Child enthroned, with nine angels. This beautiful little picture, already described as belonging to Miss Rogers (vol. ii. p. 267), was purchased by Mr. Bale at the sale of the Rogers collection.

ADRIAN OSTADE.—A lawyer reading in his room. Less brilliant in colour than other pictures of this kind by the master, but highly attractive in decision of drawing and delicacy of chiaroscuro.

Mr. Bale has also greatly enriched his collection of admirable drawings.

SANDRO BOTTICELLI.—Study for his picture of the Calumny of Apelles in the Gallery of the Uffizj at Florence, comprehending the figure of the judge, the figure next him, and that of the female who is dragging Innocence by the hair. Spiritedly drawn with the pen; the shadows in Indian ink, and the light heightened with white.

LORENZO DI CREDI.—A female head of moderate size. Charming in feeling, and lightly and delicately drawn on coloured paper with a silver point.

PARMIGIANINO.—1. Heads of children of uncommon beauty, in red chalk.

2. Study of trees in sepia, with the pen and brush. Very spirited.

TITIAN.—1. A grand landscape, with the chain of Alps at Friuli. Of broad and masterly drawing with the reed-pen in bistre.

2. A landscape. Very broadly treated with the pen and bistre.

3. A landscape, with a shepherd in the foreground; in the background the chain of Alps and a town. Very poetical and masterly; with the reed-pen and Indian ink.

4. A head. Broad and masterly; with the pen.

5. Study of a donkey, in chalk. Of the utmost truth. From the Ottley collection.

VANDYCK.—1. The Mocking of Christ. This is not the same composition engraved by Bolswert. In Indian ink and sepia, with pen and brush. From the collection of Plos van Amstel. Very spirited.

2. Venus and Adonis. In sepia. Good.

3. A study of armour. In sepia, with pen and brush. Of masterly and careful execution.

ALBERT CUYP.—1. On the left a wood; in the distance a piece of water. Of broad and masterly drawing in chalk, and washed in with sepia.

2. Study of a cow in sunshine. Masterly. In Indian ink.

3. A shepherd boy. Similar in treatment and value to the foregoing.

BACKHUYSEN.—An agitated sea, with a sailing-boat. Broad and masterly. In Indian ink.

BERGHEM.—1, 2, 3. In the foreground a man on horseback, with cattle in sunshine. In the centre a piece of water, in the background a hill. Signed. Of great effect, and spiritedly drawn in bistre. The two other drawings by this master belong to his choicest specimens.

"A. RENESSE, *f*. 1669."—This is the inscription on a portrait of a boy of great truth of conception, and delicate but masterly drawing, in black and red chalk, in the taste of Rembrandt. This is the first specimen I have seen of this painter, although he is far more entitled to a place in the dictionary of artists than many who figure in it.

JANET.—A male portrait. Of very pronounced character, and of masterly drawing, in his usual style, with black and red chalk.

REMBRANDT.—1. The Annunciation. Cleverly composed, and of great effect. Carefully executed in bistre.

2. A girl looking out of a window. Very pleasing, and of masterly execution, with the pen and brush, in Indian ink and bistre.

3. A sheet with various subjects, among which a child crying is remarkable. Broad and vigorous, with pen and bistre.

4. A landscape, with water in the foreground, on the banks of which are houses. In Indian ink and bistre, and so carefully executed that it has the effect of a picture.

5. A distant view. Lightly and spiritedly thrown on the paper with sepia.

LENAIN.—Various figures. Of animated conception, and powerfully drawn in sepia.

ADRIAN VAN DE VELDE.—A shepherd, shepherdess, and horsemen under a tree. Signed, and dated 1667. The chiaroscuro of the general effect excellent, and the details rendered in black chalk with much feeling.

Jan Steen.—A peasant looking into a drinking-vessel, which he is holding aloft; also a woman and a man. Signed. Slightly but very spiritedly drawn with pen and brush in sepia. Drawings by this painter seldom occur.

Jan van Huysum.—1. A duck. Carefully and spiritedly drawn in the freshest water-colours. Formerly in the Verstolk Collection. A present from Mr. Hawkins of Bicknor.

2. Study of a poppy, two convolvuluses, and a rose. Highly masterly; also in water-colour.

3. Flowers in a jar. A study. In Indian ink. Broad and spirited.

4. Tulips, in water-colour. Masterly.

Artus van der Neer.—View of a canal. Picturesque and broad, in black chalk.

Jan van Goyen.—A sea-coast. Signed, and dated 1649. Of pure feeling for nature, and broad and spirited.

Backhuysen.—View of the coast of Scheveningen, after the departure of the fleet of William of Orange. Many figures are introduced. Spiritedly executed in Indian ink.

Schotel.—A sea view, with a fresh wind. The waves of great truth. The execution in Indian ink is very careful.

Albert Durer.—1. Study of buttercups, trefoil, &c., in water-colour. On parchment. Of singular truth, and marvellous execution of detail.

2. A bird. In similar style. Very broadly treated. Dated 1509, and with the earliest form of his monogram. A proof that even at this late period he occasionally employed it.

3. A large beetle. In the same style, and also admirable.

The following miniature portraits I found the most remarkable :—

Holbein.—Portrait of the Princess Mary, afterwards Catholic Queen Mary, as a young girl. From the Rogers collection. Of rare delicacy.

Isaac Oliver.—Portrait of Lord Southampton, in black dress and white collar. An oval, about $1\frac{1}{2}$ in. high, and $1\frac{2}{12}$ in. across. Inscribed with the monogram of the artist and 1623. Very careful. How highly the miniatures of remarkable personages by celebrated artists are still prized is proved by the sum (50*l.*) which Mr. Bale gave for this work.

Among the antiquities the following objects most struck me :—

An Egyptian idol, about $2\frac{1}{2}$ in. high, of earthenware. Thousands of this class occur, but the delicacy with which the head in this instance is executed, and the fine turquoise blue colour, are qualities seldom seen, and which sufficiently explain the sum of 20*l.* given for it.

A golden circle, probably the setting of a brooch. The pattern shows a delicacy of taste, and the workmanship a completeness, such as I have scarcely seen in the antique. At the same time this specimen is in perfect preservation. From the Rogers collection.

An antique necklace of great beauty, from the De Bruges collection.

Two rings with glass enamel; one of them with a fine piece of aventurine. These are very remarkable.

Of the mediæval and later period the following objects struck me as most worthy of note :—

A mediæval ring, from the De Bruges collection, of considerable breadth; in design, enamels, and filigree work the finest specimen I have seen of this kind. It contains a small case for relics or an amulet.

The Crucifixion, with the Virgin and St. John, on a small Limoges enamel, by Pierre Rexmon, set as a little altarpiece. Of uncommon refinement of heads, showing the influence of German art, and particularly harmonious in effect of colour.

The profile of a young man in relief, in the Pappenheim slatestone, now employed for lithography. On the reverse the date "Ao 1658," and the initials G. P., probably those of the artist. The conception is fresh and animated, and the execution excellent. From the Woodburn collection.

A very beautiful example of the so rare "petition-crown of Thomas Simon," executed in order to show King Charles II. that native artists were capable of sinking the dies for his Majesty's coin—a service in which foreigners were employed. The royal head, crowned with laurel, is very flatly treated; the flesh parts, hair, and drapery, very softly worked in the dotted manner. The reverse contains in the centre a circle, and St. George on horseback, very small, with the inscription around, "Honny soit," &c. ; three armorial bearings and a harp are in four compartments, and between each the cipher x, and the inscription, "Magnæ Bri. Fr. et Hib. Rex. 1663." For this crown Mr. Bale paid the sum of 154*l*.

Another great rarity is a large gold medal, with the true and animated portrait of General Monk on the obverse, and his name, titles, and dignities in Latin on the reverse.

Finally, I must call attention to two vessels with lids of Japan lacquered ware, which show great beauty and originality of ornamentation.

SIR JOHN SOANE'S COLLECTION.
Vol. II. p. 320.

Through the kindness of Mr. Bealey, keeper of the Soane Museum, I was enabled, in 1854, to devote a careful examination to the MSS. with miniatures it contains. They are of Italian, French, and Netherlandish origin. As the Italian are of the most importance, I take them first, and also in chronological order.

The Vulgate. Large octavo. Written in two columns, in a very small and beautiful minuscule letter ; judging from the character of the accompanying cotemporary pictures, about 1250. The Days of the Creation are in two stripes. The pictures in the initials are exceedingly small. The Trinity is represented in the Italian form—the Almighty holding the Saviour on the Cross, the Holy Ghost, as a dove, hovering between them. A larger, but unfortunately ruined picture, represents the Root of Jesse. The motives of these pictures are very animated and speaking, the proportions generally very short, the execution, with black outlines, simple but very precise. Combatants are represented in chain armour. The grounds consist of burnished gold. The ornamentation which proceeds from the stripes with the Days of the Creation has a particular Italian character. The forms of the initials are in gold ; the fillings out, of a dark red and dark blue with simple flourishes, are very tasteful. Single figures in prayer also occur here and there, probably introduced by the proprietor of the MS. in the second half of the 15th century, and by a very skilful hand. He is thus probably represented himself, immediately at the beginning, in the garb of a knight. Two weapons below doubtless refer also to him. On the page with the Root of Jesse is a kneeling monk, with a weapon below, who is particularly remarkable.

Prayer-book. Small octavo. In two columns, in a large and powerful minuscule letter, written on fine parchment on 433 leaves, the twenty-four of the unornamented calendar included. This book contains the Office of the Virgin, the Office for the Dead, for the Cross, for the Holy Ghost, the Seven Penitential Psalms, and the Psalmi graduales. The cover in itself deserves notice. It is adorned on both sides, in the centre, corners, and clasps, with very tasteful decorations on red silk, of silver gilt, with fine filigree work and *nielli*. On a small plate in a circle in the centre of the upper side is the Virgin with the Child, in tolerably good workmanship. On the lower side, in similar shape, the I. H. S., and on the clasps the words " Dominus tecum " and " Ave gratia plena," all in niello-work. The pictures in this volume are ascribed, in the first place, to the hand of Girolamo dai Libri, who is, in the second place, stated to be the son of Francesco dai Libri, instead of exactly the reverse. They do not, however, correspond with the authentic works of either of these painters, but bear rather a Florentine character, in the manner of the well-known Attavante, and may have been executed about 1480. Of this kind are especially the rich and tasteful decorations which ornament the borders of both the first pages before the Office for the Dead and the Penitential Psalms. Also the more simple border ornamentation which sometimes occurs has quite a Florentine aspect. The same may be said of a portion of the pictures, namely, of the twelve figures on the first two pages, and of the Virgin and Child on the second. Although these exhibit a skilful hand, they are surpassed by another, by whom the Annunciation, David cutting off the head of Goliah, with a pretty landscape, and David as a tender youth with Goliah's head, were executed. Particularly characteristic is the picture of Christ's Entry into Jerusalem, in which two female figures kneeling in the foreground are the principal objects; and on the page opposite the half-length figure of a skeleton, through which a serpent is twisting, in the attitude of prayer; as also below, the Fall, symbolically represented, in a circle.

But by far the most celebrated manuscript here preserved is the

Commentary on St. Paul's Epistles by the Patriarch of Aquileja and Cardinal, Marino Grimani, nephew to the well-known Cardinal Domenico Grimani, and decorated by his commission with miniatures by Don Giulio Clovio. Large folio, one column, beautifully written on the finest parchment, in a still somewhat Gothic minuscule letter. As the border had somewhat suffered, a new border has, with great skill, been so joined on in parchment as to form one with the old original. The superb cover is probably of the same period as the above described restoration, and is of green velvet. The high reputation of Don Giulio is here far more justified in the arabesques and pictures of this work, which belong to his earlier time, than in most of the examples of his art which I have seen in different European collections. The execution in this instance must be assigned to a period between 1527 and 1546 ; for in the title-page Marino Grimani is already designated as Cardinal—an appointment bestowed on him by Pope Clement VII. in 1527—while he died in 1546. The following circumstances, however, render it highly probable that Don Giulio executed these miniatures in 1531 and 32, which, as he was born in 1498, makes him at that time 33 or 34 years of age. Vasari tells us, namely, that in consequence of a vow formed when in the hands of the Spaniards, by whom he was taken prisoner at the sack of Rome by the army of Charles V., in 1527, Don Giulio Clovio entered the monastery of S. Ruffino in Mantua, where he remained three years ; but that having, in a journey to another monastery of the order, broken his leg, and received very unskilful treatment in the Abbey of Candiana in the Paduan territory, his case came to the knowledge of Cardinal Grimani, who was a great admirer of his art, and who therefore obtained permission of the pope to take him into his service and cure him of his accident. Being restored to health, and having laid aside his monastic robe, he proceeded to Perugia, where the Cardinal resided as Legate, and executed for him four pictures in an Office of the Virgin, and also " in uno Epistolario tre storie grandiose di San Paolo Apostolo." That this is the MS. so designated appears not only from an inscription I will give further on, and from the circumstance of the subject being identical, but also from the fact that Vasari adds that one of the three large pictures had recently been sent to Spain. At this time indeed there is but *one* large picture left in the work, which proves that a second must also

at some time have been abstracted. Having thus supplied all the
information at my command as regards the painter, the patron, and
the time and place of the execution of this work, I proceed to a
nearer description of the miniatures themselves. The border
immediately on the first page is in the style of the Raphaelesque
arabesques, and is distinguished for delicacy of taste, and great
elegance and refinement of execution. On the broad side border
are seen masks, cameos, small landscapes, satyrs, children, &c.,
in gay succession. A head of Minerva especially, in a circle,
executed in colour, is of the highest finish. On the narrow border
appear beautiful birds, among which a cock is conspicuous, as
also three satyr masks, and, quite below, a very successful
old woman with a spindle, probably meant for one of the Fates.
Finally, the lower border consists of an extensive landscape, with
three shepherds conversing in the foreground. This is somewhat
cold and crude in tone. At the place where the initial letter
usually occurs, is seen instead, in brown heightened with gold, a
man in a contemplative position, excellent in motive, drawing, and
drapery. At the beginning of the Preface to the Commentary on
the Epistle to the Romans is a very beautiful C, in similar style,
with two male figures in the spaces, one of whom is pointing to the
superscription. The outer border is decorated with golden arabesques of the rarest elegance, in the centre of which, in an oval, is
an onyx cameo with a fight of horsemen, admirably imitated. The
superscription preceding the Commentary itself is in golden capitals
on a dark-green ground, and makes a splendid effect. The leaf
opposite contains by way of title-page the Conversion of St. Paul, in
which Don Giulio Clovio has entirely adhered to Raphael's cartoon
of the same subject. The two figures only, with St. Paul's horse,
are here rendered smaller, and placed more in the background.
The whole landscape also is altered. This picture is of wonderful
finish : the border also is very richly ornamented. Above, in the
centre, in brown and gold, in a horizontal oval, is the Trinity—the
First and the Second Persons enthroned, with secular crowns on their
heads, holding one sceptre in the centre between them ; above them
hovers the Holy Ghost in the form of a dove, of unusually large size.
At the sides are youthful angels blowing their trumpets. Next to
this oval are splendid weapons, armour, &c. In the upper angles
are two figures freely copied from Michael Angelo's figures in

chiaroscuro in the Sistine Chapel, and here executed in beautiful and warm colouring. One of them is holding armour and shield as a kind of trophy. Below this one, on the narrow side, is St. Paul, represented as a statue of bronze gilt, and again weapons, particularly a shield with the head of Medusa. Also above, on the broad side, are weapons, and directly below, in an oval, St. Paul preaching at Athens, in somewhat too crude colouring. At the end is the figure of Peace, lightly attired in a green chlamys, and in the act of setting fire with a torch to weapons at her feet. This figure, the fine profile of which plainly shows the scholar of Giulio Romano, is in every respect, in grace of motive, beauty of forms, charm of colouring, and marvellous delicacy of modelling, one of the most successful efforts of this painter. As a companion, on the narrow side, is a boy carrying a suit of armour. In the centre of the lower border are four others, two of them holding a circle, in which is represented the Stoning of St. Stephen, a rich coloured picture conceived by the painter himself, but rather exaggerated in some of the motives. Near the boy holding the armour is the following highly important inscription in golden capitals :—" Marino Grimani Car. et Legato Perusino, Patrono suo Julius Crovata pingebat." The last word but one shows the painter to be a native of Croatia. On the following page, on the upper border, in a horizontal oval, in brown and gold, is the Cardinal, seen at his writing-table in eager discourse with two standing men ; another figure of excellent motive in the background. On each side of the oval are two white doves and a scroll with the word " Simplices." Finally, at both the corners are again figures holding weapons, taken from Michael Angelo. On the broad side border, above, in a circle, is the portrait of the Cardinal in colours, still tolerably youthful, with delicate clever features and a long brown beard. This is a perfect marvel in the union of truth, animation, and tenderness of execution, and incomparably the best portrait by Giulio Clovio I know. The figure of Mars below this, leaning on his shield, in gorgeous armour, is also masterly, but does not equal the figure of Peace before-mentioned. On the narrow side, in an upright oval, in brown and gold, is an elderly man with a staff in his right hand, a vessel in the left, with the inscription " Pastoris munus." Below him again, weapons and a boy carrying armour. On the lower border are two frightful dragons of gay colours ; in the centre a circle with a landscape of very tender gradation, with six charming children occupied around the coat of arms of the Cardinal ; four of them supporting it, while an angel holds the Cardinal's hat above. Below the arms, and between the dragons, a scroll with the word " Prudentes," which, with the word " Simplices " above-mentioned, was evidently the motto of the Cardinal, signifying the text "·Be ye wise as serpents and gentle as doves." This superb MS. was bought from the Duke of Buckingham, father of the present Duke, with some other MSS., various intaglios, and some engravings by Lucas van Leyden, for the sum of 2000*l*. Independent also of the beauty of the miniatures, this work possesses a two-fold interest. It shows, firstly, how the inventions of the greatest geniuses, such as Raphael and Michael Angelo, were adopted in the subordinate branches of the art, and set forth with the highest exercise of technical skill ; and, secondly, it proves the taste for classical reminiscences to have been so deeply rooted that even in a work of religious import, by a high ecclesiastic, he authorised the mixture of mythological and scriptural representations in its decoration.

I now proceed to the MSS. with French miniatures. The second volume of the well-known French translation of the History of the Jews by Josephus, beginning at the 16th book. Folio, in two columns, in a strong minuscule letter, and at the heading of each book (the last and 27th excepted) adorned with a large miniature, in which three different hands may be distinguished. The first hand, by whom the picture preceding the 16th book was executed, is that of a careful and skilful miniature-painter, but one of inferior rank. The second hand, to whom the picture preceding the 17th book belongs, is more powerful in colour, and bolder and broader in treatment. The third, which is the author of the picture preceding the 19th book, is by far the best. The heads are animated, the motives speaking, the colouring warm, and the execution care̶ ful. By this hand is also the picture representing the Roman camp before Jerusalem, entirely in the forms proper to the period of the painter. Among the tents, that belonging to Titus is distinguished by being rose-coloured. The execution is in every part peculiarly careful, as seen in the hems of the dresses, in the weapons, and in the buildings, which are heightened with gold. The borders of all the pictures are quite in the French taste, with single flowers and tendrils on a pale gold ground. The initials are small, but graceful.

The arms of the House of Lancaster, p. 1a, show that this book was executed for a member of that family. From the style of the miniatures, the date 1470-80 may be assigned to this work, which may therefore possibly have been executed for Henry VII. before he ascended the throne.

Prayer-book, small octavo, written in one column, with a small minuscule letter, and richly bound in red velvet worked in gold. This contains a number of very delicate miniatures, agreeing so strikingly with those in the celebrated Hours of Anne of Bretagne, that they may be assigned to a somewhat earlier period of the same painter. The stage of development, and the style of the very commonplace sloping stripes which form the border ornaments, point to 1480 as the most probable period of execution. Of the four Evangelists, each on a separate page at the commencement of the Gospel, St. Mark is the most remarkable. He is represented as an old man writing, of portrait-like character. In the picture of the Annunciation the angel is of great delicacy ; also the Virgin in the Presentation, and in Glory. The heads of Christ and of Pilate are distinguished by originality and refinement.

Prayer-book. Octavo. Part is failing at the beginning. It is written on fine parchment, and contains pleasing border decorations of flowers and fruits, like those mentioned in a former MS., and which ornament many French and Netherlandish MSS. from 1480 to 1530. The pictures themselves, some of which are in chiaroscuro, are of very inferior value. The work belongs without doubt to the North of France, and to the termination of the 15th century.

I proceed finally to the MSS. with Dutch miniatures.

Prayer-book. Wide octavo, written in Dutch in one column, in a vigorous minuscule letter. This is a work of second-rate order. The two first pictures—the Annunciation, and the Virgin and Child in the initial—alone deserve notice. The heads of the Virgin are of pretty round forms, and delicate in feeling. The borders of these two pages are also rich and careful, like those of the two last mentioned MSS., though not of great refinement. Many of the other borders still display the olden style, with rich flourishes drawn with the pen, golden knosps, and the gay, acanthus-like tendrils. Upon the whole the date may be assigned to about 1490.

A Latin Missal, bound in red velvet. Large octavo, written in one column, in a strong minuscule letter, on fine parchment, with

very wide borders. It contains 356 pages, and is a very rich and
splendid volume. In the beginning is an inscription, both in Italian
and German, stating that this book was presented by Wolfgang
Wilhelm, Pfalzgraf of the Rhine, to Johanna, Duchess of Villenosa,
his mother. This is a fresh proof of the influence which the style of
art proper to the French miniature-painters exercised even upon the
Dutch artists, for both the technical process and the combination of
colours show the French manner. Nay, even the mode of conception
is frequently so alike that one would be inclined to ascribe these
miniatures to French artists, if the following reasons did not decide
them to be of Dutch origin. The tendency is throughout realistic;
the proportions of the figures very short. In the Calendar, such
saints as Lievin, Quentin, Lambert, Medardus, Gildardus, Gudula,
point to Belgium, and Wolfgang, Christine, Columban, and Kuni-
gunde to Germany. From these facts, and from the style of the
pictures, I should conclude that this work was executed, both text
and pictures, in Holland. The Calendar, which occupies 12 pages,
is one of the richest I know; the text of each page being framed in
the following manner. Above, in colours, upon a blue field, is the
sign of the Zodiac; below, occupying the whole width, and carefully finished, the appropriate occupation of the month. On the
wide border, in brown and gold, are events from Bible history; on
the narrower border, two saints as statues, in the same style. Thus
on the page dedicated to January the wide border contains the
Presentation, the Adoration of the Kings, and the Conversion of
St. Paul. Of the various miniature-painters engaged in the decoration of this work, the author of the pictures in the Calendar
may be considered the most frenchified. In the essentials of the
art he is weak, the compositions are tasteless, the motives tame, the
heads spiritless, and the drawing insignificant; while, on the other
hand, the colouring is lively, and the execution very skilful and
careful. By his hand are the majority of the other pictures; for
instance, the Visit of the Queen of Sheba to Solomon. Among the
other painters, some are far superior. I may mention at once the first
picture, representing Christ in Glory, and occupying a whole page.
Here the old mosaic type, though somewhat softened, is adhered to,
while the execution, in colours of unusual force, is very careful.
Christ on the Mount of Olives, and Christ betrayed by Judas, are
both, as in the French school, treated as night-pieces. Judging

from the architecture, and from the whole style of art, particularly
as seen in the already developed aërial perspective, the period of
this MS. can scarcely be pronounced to be earlier than 1520.   For
beauty of feeling and tenderness of harmony the Visitation, and
the Virgin and Child adored by St. Augustin, may be considered
the best pictures; for elevation of expression, the Mater Dolorata
supported by St. John, and the Seven Sacraments.   The Dutch
character is most strongly seen in the Adoration of the Kings, in
which the colouring is very powerful, and the expression of space,
the house, and the landscape, all of admirable delicacy.   The same
may be observed in other backgrounds.   Here and there the
arrangements of the objects are borrowed from the Biblia Pau-
perum ; as, for example, the Annunciation, and Gideon before the
Fleece, to which an angel is pointing, in a very beautiful landscape.
The very rich decorations of the borders, in the same taste as those
of the foregoing MS., are in point of delicacy almost of the first
order.   The preservation of the whole is all that can be desired.
This missal was purchased in 1821 at the sale of Edward Knight,
Esq., by the Duke of Buckingham.

LETTER III.

Lord Overstone's collection — Lord Caledon's pictures — Dowager Lady Waldegrave's pictures — Mr. Gladstone's pictures — Two Gaspar Poussins
belonging to the Hoare family — Mr. St. John Mildmay's collection — Mr.
Robarts's collection — Artus van der Neer belonging to Lord Shaftesbury
— Mr. Davenport Bromley's collection — Lord Wensleydale's pictures —
Mr. Edward Cheney's collection — Rev. Mr. Townshend's collection —
Earl Stanhope's pictures — Mr. Cornwall Legh's pictures — Mr. Mar-
shall's pictures — Mr. William Russell's collection — Mr. Beresford Hope's
collection — Mr. Field's collection — Manuscript belonging to Mr. Boxall
— Mr. Tulloch's collection — Mr. Henderson's collection — Collection of
late Mr. James — Objects of art belonging to Mr. Felix Slade.

LORD OVERSTONE'S COLLECTION,

2, Carlton Gardens.

This choice collection contains more especially a series of chefs-
d'œuvre of the Dutch school, proceeding, in great measure, from
the well-known gallery of Baron Verstolk at the Hague. Lord
Overstone also possesses admirable specimens of the Italian,
Spanish, French, and English schools, which are seen to great
advantage in the fine apartments of his London residence.

THE LIBRARY.

Peter de Hooghe.—View of the back court of a house,
having an open door at the end of it, with an ascent of two steps
to enter a garden. Near the centre of the court is seated a
gentleman about to enjoy his tankard and pipe, with which a
woman standing before him has provided him. He has invited
her to take a glass, which she is in the act of drinking. At the
same time a child is crossing the court with a pot of embers in her
hand. On canvas. 2 ft. 4 in. high, 1 ft. 11 in. wide. This
master, who is the painter of sunlight *par excellence*, appears in
this beautiful picture in the highest perfection of his powers.
Although treated upon the whole on a scale of cool harmony, yet
he has happily avoided all monotony by the introduction of the
red petticoat of the woman, which is repeated in delicate gradations
in the different planes of distance by the window shutter and by

the red tiles. The chiaroscuro of the view beyond, with the steps and trees, is admirable. Formerly in the collection of Mr. Wells of Redleaf.

TENIERS.—1. An alchemist in his laboratory, seated before his hearth blowing the fire beneath a crucible. In the background are two other alchemists. 1 ft. 6½ in. high, 1 ft. 1½ in. wide. Of masterly treatment, and of the utmost delicacy of the cool tones which pervade the whole picture. Formerly in the possession of Baron James Rothschild of Paris.

REMBRANDT.—1. A landscape exhibiting an extensive view over the flat country of Holland. A river, commencing from the foreground, winds through the scene and is lost in the distance; in the foreground, on the left, are cottages surrounded by trees, and farther back a windmill under the deep shadow of dark rainy clouds, with which the sky is covered. A few clouds and the horizon are dimly lighted by a gleam of sunshine, which falls also on a sandy hill; a loftier hill is in the distance. The solitude of the scene is only disturbed by a few figures. One figure is standing before the nearest cottage, another stands in the doorway, and in the river in front are some men in a boat. The scene is enriched in its different planes of distance by a multitude of details—trees, bushes, meadows, &c. On canvas. 4 ft. 3½ in. high, 5 ft. 5 in. wide. Of the twenty landscapes, or thereabouts, which are known to be by the hand of Rembrandt, this is far the largest, and at the same time one of the finest examples. The spectator scarcely knows whether most to admire the poetic feeling of a melancholy grandeur whicn pervades this picture, or the masterly execution with which it is expressed. The transparency with which every portion, and even the deepest shadow, is rendered, shows Rembrandt to be the greatest master in chiaroscuro of the whole Netherlandish school; at the same time the treatment is as marrowy as it is juicy—as broad as it is careful. This landscape doubtless served as model to Philip de Koningk and Ruysdael in those pictures in which they have expressed the peculiar charm of a widely-extended flat distance. In 1825 it was in the collection of Count de Vence at Paris. Engraved by De Marcenay.

ISAAC VAN OSTADE.—1. View of a country inn, at which a gentleman has just arrived and dismounted from a grey cob horse; his back is turned towards the spectator, and he appears to

be giving his orders to a man who stands before him with a can in
his hand; a trough, with hay in it, is placed before his horse.
The hostess is at the door taking up a child, which has clung to
her knees as if frightened.   A peasant sits at the other side of the
door filling his pipe.   At the end of the house, and leading to an
adjoining cottage, is a flight of stone steps with two children at the
foot; a woman sitting at her spinning-wheel, and a man standing
at her side, are at the top of the steps.   A pig, a dog, and some
fowls are near some rude buildings or sheds on the opposite side.
In front is a basket lying on its side.   The steeple of a church
rises above the second cottage, and some trees are at the end of
the buildings.   Signed and dated 1649.   On canvas.   2 ft. 6 in.
wide, 2 ft. high.   The composition is very picturesque, and at the
same time rich in details.   The light, which falls with singular
power and transparency on the grey cob, is delicately repeated in
the middle distance on the clouds, and further back on the bright
horizon.   The tone is very powerful and warm, and all the forms
given with great decision.   In 1825 this beautiful picture was in
the possession of Prince Galitzin at Paris, afterwards in that of
Mr. Wells of Redleaf.

TENIERS.—2. The interior of a tavern with a young peasant
man seated at a table, a pipe in his left hand, a glass raised
jovially in his right.   At the same table is an old peasant, also
seated.   Four other figures are in the room.   On wood.   1 ft.
1 in. high, by 1 ft. 5½ in. wide.   Carefully and spiritedly carried
out in his cool harmony of colour.

DINING-ROOM.

DOMENICHINO.—1. A landscape with grand towers on a piece
of water, on which is a boat with three figures.   Three others are
busy fishing, and three more are in the middle distance.   On the
left is a large tree.   Hills in the background.   On wood.   1ft. 6 in.
high, by 2 ft. 6½ in. wide.   Although a genuine picture by the
master, the composition is not remarkable, and it is somewhat
heavy in colouring and poor in treatment.

LUDOLPH BACKHUYSEN.—1. A stormy sea, with a boat in the
foreground; two larger vessels in the middle distance, and other
in the remote background; a coast on the right hand.   On canvas.
2 ft. 1½ in. high, by 2 ft. 9 in. wide.   The agitated waves are

expressed with great mastery, and the execution is most careful in the delicate cool tones of his best time.

Jacob Ruysdael.—1. A landscape with rising ground on the left hand overgrown with trees; a road leads over it, with a woman and child in the foreground. On the right is a piece of dark water, and beyond it a hill. The sky is kept tolerably light. Signed with the initials. On canvas. 1 ft. 7 in. high, 2 ft. 1 in. wide. Of the earlier time of the master, and of singular truth. The trees are especially admirable. The execution is highly careful. Formerly in the collection of Edward Gray, Esq.

Willem van de Velde.—1. A calm sea, with a coast near, and another coast in the distance. On the water are two principal groups of vessels, and several single vessels of different sizes, some of which are filled with troops. On canvas. 2 ft. 1½ in. high, 3 ft. 6½ in. wide. A rich picture, of masterly carrying out in a clear cool tone. The reflection of the objects in the water is particularly admirable. Formerly in the Van der Pol collection in Rotterdam.

Clarkson Stanfield.—1. A rocky Italian valley, with houses and a bridge. Macaroni-mills at Amalfi. On canvas. 2 ft. 6 in. high, 2 ft. 1 in. wide. Sunny and clear in the keeping, and carefully executed.

Philip Wouvermans. — A fierce battle of horsemen and infantry. The principal group in the centre of the foreground consists of a man on a grey horse aiming at a trumpeter on a brown horse, who, in default of any other instrument, is defending himself with his trumpet. Another figure is between them on the ground. Near them is a horseman firing a pistol at a foot soldier, who is in the act of piercing his rearing brown horse with a lance. More towards the left is a standard-bearer galloping away in fear of the pistol. On canvas. 2 ft. 1 in. high, 2 ft. 8 in. wide. This picture is one of the chefs-d'œuvre of the second period of the master. The composition, though so animated, is very distinct, the single motives very momentary and true, the expression of the heads most forcible, the figures and horses of unusual size, and the execution of every part very careful. It reminds the spectator in many respects of the well-known battle-piece in the collection of M. van Loon in Amsterdam. Formerly in the collection of the King of Holland.

BERNARDO BELLOTTO.—View of the Piazza of St. Mark. On canvas. 2 ft. 2½ in. high, 4 ft. 4 in. wide. A rich and careful, and, for him, transparent picture.

CLARKSON STANFIELD.—2. A sunny court between rocks and trees, with two figures. A companion to the other Stanfield. Kitchen of the inn at Amalfi. On canvas. 2 ft. 6 in. high, 2 ft. 1 in. wide. Of admirable keeping, great clearness, and careful execution.

ARTUS VAN DER NEER.—1. A Dutch village on a canal surrounded with trees, on a bright moonlight night. In the foreground are two hewers of wood at their occupation. In the middle distance some fishermen. Signed. On canvas. 2 ft. 1½ in. high, 2 ft. 7 in. wide. The effect of moonlight is here rendered with admirable skill in every portion. The treatment is highly solid and free, proving that this picture belongs to his later time.

JAN HACKAERT.—A view of the woods at the Hague, traversed by a road, with a party of men on horse and on foot. Figures by ADRIAN VAN DE VELDE. 2 ft. 3 in. high, 2 ft. wide. The cool obscurity of a forest, with a few gleams of sunlight falling on the lofty-stemmed trees, is admirably expressed. The delicacy of the aërial perspective is particularly remarkable. All the details are of great truth of nature, and the treatment both free and careful. Formerly in the collection of Baron Verstolk at the Hague.

ARTUS VAN DER NEER.—2. Moonlight view of the principal street of a Dutch village, with the church and richly-wooded ground. In front, seated upon a felled tree, is a man in conversation with a woman; more on the right three other figures. In the middle distance are five cows. In the distance a man and woman are seen walking. Signed. On canvas. 2 ft. 4 in. high, 2 ft. 8½ in. wide. The composition of this picture is very attractive, and the effect of the moonlight is all that can be desired for truth. The style of the careful execution indicates the middle period of the master.

THOMAS STOTHARD.—1. Jacob's Dream. In the foreground is the sleeping patriarch; behind him, in a glow of light, is the heavenly ladder, on which are six angels. On canvas, 4 ft. 1 in. high, 3 ft. 3 in. wide. One of the most distinguished pictures by this genial and versatile master. The action of Jacob's sleep is of great truth, and the angels are noble and refined both in form and movement. The colouring of Jacob also is unusually powerful and clear; that of the angels delicately graduated. The keeping of the whole is very harmonious, and the details careful.

JACOB RUYSDAEL.—2. A landscape, with a waterfall of moderate volume in the foreground. In the middle distance is a house reflected in the still water above the fall, with a group of trees. On the right is a wood before a hill, which extends in perspective lines to the background. Some clouds are lighted with unusual warmth for him. Signed. 2 ft. 3 in. high, 1 ft. 8½ in. wide. A picture of pleasing composition and very careful finish, of the middle period of the master.

JAN BOTH.—1. A landscape, with a chain of hills stretching from the foreground on the left deep into the picture. On the right are some trees. On a road in the foreground are two laden mules, with their driver and a dog. On a mountain-path are other figures and cattle. On canvas. 2 ft. ½ in. high, 2 ft. 7 in. wide. Of great charm of composition and careful carrying out.

LORD OVERSTONE'S PRIVATE ROOM.

REMBRANDT.—2. An aged lady, styled "The Artist's Grandmother," having the appearance of being upwards of eighty years of age, of a thin and withered countenance, seen in front. She has on a black velvet cap, which descends in front in a point on the forehead, and wears a full broad white ruff, and a plain black gown, which is fastened in front. The background is dark. Inscribed and dated 1660. On canvas. 2 ft. 8 in. high, 2 ft. 1 in. wide. Arched in form. The extraordinary truth of life, the decision of forms, the depth and transparency of the golden tone, and the certainty and breadth of the spirited treatment, assign to this picture a distinguished place among the portraits by Rembrandt. Formerly in the collection of Lord Charles Townshend, and later in that of Baron Verstolk.

JAN WYNANTS. — 1. A landscape, exhibiting a country diversified with hill and dale and clusters of trees. Upon a winding road, over a hill on the right, is a sportsman approaching, followed by his dog. The opposite side is composed of a clayey hill, surmounted by a few light trees and bushes, and fenced in at the side by wooden rails; some open country and a wood complete the composition. Figures by ADRIAN VAN DE VELDE. 1 ft. 3 in.

high, 1 ft. 7 in. wide. A cool morning effect is most truthfully rendered in this fine picture of the master's middle period. The aërial perspective is of unusual delicacy, the execution of the details highly careful.

SIR AUGUSTUS CALCOTT.—1. View of the river Maas by Rotterdam, with several large and small vessels, in morning light. On canvas. 1 ft. 6½ in. high, 2 ft. 4 in. wide. This picture is of admirable effect and uncommon transparency, and shows the successful study of Cuyp.

2. The Pool on the Thames, with several vessels. On canvas. 10 in. high, 1 ft. 8 in. wide. Broadly and sketchily treated, but full of spirit.

SMALL DRAWING-ROOM.

GUIDO RENI.—1. The infant Jesus asleep upon a couch of a reddish colour, the Virgin gazing tenderly upon him. On canvas. 2 ft. 1 in. high, 2 ft. 6½ in. wide. Oval in the width. An excellent example of this composition, which occurs frequently with unimportant deviations, another of which, also excellent, is in the Grosvenor Gallery. There the Virgin is entirely in shadow, and the Child in a subdued light; here both are in full bright light. The expression of maternal joy is very tender, the sleep of the infant very natural, and the modelling of the nude of masterly execution in a delicate silvery tone.

ADAM PYNACKER.—A landscape, with a piece of water dividing two eminences, and a bridge over it. In the foreground two boats and a cart with oxen, in which are a woman and other figures, and a barrel. The bright morning sun is clearly reflected in the still water. View on the Tiber. On canvas. 2 ft. 6 in. high, 2 ft. 1 in. wide. Of great effect and very careful execution, but somewhat cold in the shadows. Formerly in the collection of Baron Verstolk.

ADRIAN VAN DE VELDE.—In the foreground is a ford with a herd of seven cows, six sheep, and a goat—a herdswoman driving a white cow. In the middle-ground are a horseman and a man on foot. On the left, rising ground with trees; on the right, a hilly distance. Signed and dated 1665. On canvas. 1 ft. 9½ in. high, 1 ft. 10½ in. wide. Rich and tasteful in composition, delicate in drawing, harmonious in effect, and soft and careful in execution, though without degenerating into that over-smoothness which characterises his later pictures.

JAN STEEN.—1. An alchemist seated at his stove is about to commit to the fatal crucible the last gulden belonging to his wife, who stands weeping behind him. Between them is a man reading a receipt aloud to the woman, and endeavouring to inspire her with confidence in the result. Behind her is a boy of sorrowful expression, holding a clarionet. In the background is a coarse reddish man calling aloud something which a thin pale man in profile is dictating to him. On the chimney is a label with the words " Theophrastus Payeselsus."* Signed and dated 1668. On canvas. 2 ft. 5½ in. high, 2 ft. 6 in. wide. The tale is admirably told, and the separate figures capitally characterised, without, as occasionally with him, falling into caricature. The colouring, with the exception of the powerfully-coloured woman, is rather dim ; the treatment singularly spirited and broad, and at the same time careful.

JAN VAN DE CAPELLA.—A quiet sea, with coast in the fore-ground and on the left hand ; in the centre some small vessels ; on the right a small man-of-war, firing off a gun ; in the distance other vessels ; the clouds brightly lighted on the left. On wood. 1 ft. 7 in. high, 1 ft. 11 in. wide. This picture is in all respects— for example, in the reflections on the water—of such delicacy and transparency, and at the same time so picturesquely composed and carefully finished, that it belongs to the best works known to me of the master.

WILLEM VAN DE VELDE.—A marine view in perfect calm weather. On the left three fishing smacks lying at anchor ; beyond these a sloop, and on the opposite side another smack in front of a frigate. Other vessels and small craft are perceptible in the dis-tance. The blue sky is broken by a few light grey clouds. On canvas. 1 ft. 6 in. high, 1 ft. 11 in. wide. This picture sufficiently shows us how justly the master was renowned for his calm seas, for the transparency of the reflections of every object is quite astonish-ing. The execution also is throughout as careful as it is spirited. Formerly in the collection of Baron Verstolk.

DOMENICHINO.—2. The Assumption of the Magdalen. She is borne upward by infant angels, and accompanied by two youthful

* Sic.

angels. Three cherubim are also in the air. Below on the right is a wooded hill; on the left the sea. On canvas. 5 ft. 4 in. high, 3 ft. 11½ in. wide. This picture is finely composed, of noble and feeling heads, of delicate drawing, and careful modelling of every part. In colouring, however, it is one of those specimens of the master which are heavy and brick-like in the flesh tones. Formerly in the Palazzo Caprara at Bologna. (See Buchanan's 'Memoirs of Painting,' vol. ii. p. 159.)

JAN BOTH.—1. A landscape, with rocks on the right, partially overgrown with trees, from which a waterfall is dashing; on the left a hilly distance. In very warm light. On wood. 1 ft. high, 1 ft. 3½ in. wide. An enchanting little picture. The beautiful composition is here combined with singular depth and transparency of the warm colouring, with great delicacy of aërial perspective, and a very finished execution of marrowy touch. Formerly in the collection of Casimir Perrier.

ALBERT CUYP.—A flat country, with a shepherdess in a red petticoat standing quite in the foreground. Near her a sheep standing, and a sheep and goat reposing; in the middle distance three other figures. Signed. On wood. 1 ft. 4 in. high, 1 ft. 2½ in. wide. Very striking in the effect of the powerful colour and warm lighting, and at the same time more carefully executed than usual in his admirable impasto. Of the middle period of the master.

WILLIAM VAN MIERIS.—A woman selling chesnuts and apples in a window, and a boy about to conclude a bargain with her; between them a man; on the sill of the window hangs a string of onions; in the background is a basket with fruit. On wood. 1 ft. 3½ in. high, 1 ft. 1½ in. wide. Of careful execution in every respect, but somewhat cold and heavy in the over-red flesh tones.

CORNELIUS DUSART.—A peasant family—father, mother, and two boys—loitering at the door of a house, under a porch of vine-leaves. Before them is a hawker offering his goods; behind, in the village, two girls. Signed and dated 1680. On wood. 1 ft. 5½ in. high, 1 ft. 2½ in. wide. In this little picture Dusart approaches very near to Adrian Ostade, his master. The heads are very animated, and not, as often the case, caricatured; the keeping, which is cool for him, is delicate and clear; the execution very careful.

ARTUS VAN DER NEER.—3. The moon casting her silver light

over a frozen Dutch canal, with villages on each shore.   Numerous
figures on the ice.   Signed.   1 ft. 6 in. high, 2 ft. 3 in. wide.
Admirable in general effect, but hard in the details, showing
the earlier time of the master.   At the same time the treatment is
slight, and the wood is seen through in the foreground.

Isaac van Ostade. — 2.   A peasant on horseback before a
cart, with two other horses; near them are three trees bare of
leaf.   Signed.   On wood.   1 ft. $3\frac{1}{2}$ in. high, 1 ft. $8\frac{1}{2}$ in. wide.
Carefully executed in an admirable impasto, and of very powerful
colouring.

Jan Both.—2.   A chain of rocks stretches from the right deep
into the centre of the picture; from them flows a stream, over
which a bridge leads into the background; in the centre of the
foreground is a light tree; on the left two similar trees, and a
peasant on a cart drawn by oxen.   11 in. high, 1 ft. 4 in. wide.
One of the prettiest little pictures by the master, both in composition and warm, mild harmony, as well as in the delicacy of
gradation and beauty of execution.

Hobbema.—1.   A landscape with trees on the right, and a village
in the background, with a light sunny cloud over it.   A man and
woman on a road in the foreground.   On wood. $10\frac{1}{2}$ in. high,
1 ft. 4 in. wide.   Of singular power, freshness and transparency, evidently painted under the influence of his contemporary
Ruysdael.

Artus van der Neer.—4.   A very wide Dutch canal, frozen
over, with a village on its banks, on a clear sunny winter's day.
On the ice are various figures on a small scale.   Signed and
dated 1643.   On wood.   1 ft. 8 in. high, 2 ft. 2 in. wide.   This
picture is very attractive for the general brightness, admirable
treatment, and delicate aërial perspective, which leads the eye
deep into the scene.   The date shows it to have been executed in
the painter's thirtieth year.   The wood itself is here left in the
shadows in the foreground.

Teniers.—3 and 4.   Two small landscapes in a box, representing
country people before their homes: on one of them is a dancing
couple.   On wood.   Each $6\frac{1}{2}$ in. high, $9\frac{1}{2}$ in. wide.   Of tender
and spirited execution in a light, broken tone.

Thomas Stothard.—2-13.   Twelve small pictures illustrating
the 'Pilgrim's Progress;' of oval form.   Each 6 in. high, $7\frac{1}{2}$ in.

wide. These are slightly treated works, some of them only in chiaroscuro, but clever in composition, and graceful in motive.

MURILLO.—The Virgin in Glory, in a robe of deep crimson, and mantle of deep blue, holding the Child on her arm. The head is surrounded by a warm glow; otherwise the background is dark. On canvas. 3 ft. 4 in. high, 2 ft. 6½ in. wide. This is the piece which was cut by a French officer out of a large picture formerly belonging to Marshal Soult; a repetition of which, on a small scale, by the hand of the master, is in Lady Overstone's Morning Room. The Virgin is, for Murillo, of unusual elevation of features, and also unusually serious in expression; at the same time it is finished with singular care in his warmest and most dazzling golden tones.

CLAUDE LORRAINE.—The Enchanted Castle. A noble edifice, in the Roman style, rises on the extreme verge of a rock in the centre of the middle distance, with the sea flowing at its base. The space from the castle to the foreground presents broken ground overgrown with bushes, amongst which are a few young trees. The view extends hence on the left, over rising ground to the distant hills. On the right rises a beautiful group of trees of various kinds from a bank. A female figure (styled, in the index of the Liber Veritatis, Psyche) is seated in a contemplative attitude on the left of the foreground. Besides this figure there are a stag and a doe grazing, and a doe leaping. On canvas. 2 ft. 10 in. high, 5 ft. 0½ in. wide. The highly poetic impression produced by this picture corresponds entirely with the name given to it. In the cool keeping we feel the fresh morning breeze. The gradation is as delicate as the execution is free and light. It was painted in 1664 for the Conestabile Colonna, and passed successively through the hands of Messrs. Davenant, Chauncey, de Calonne, Walsh Porter, and Wells, till it reached those of the present owner.

CARLO DOLCE.—The Virgin, with her eyes cast up, and a torch in her raised right hand, is holding the Infant on her lap. On wood. 3 ft. 1 in. high, 2 ft. 7 in. wide—with blunted corners. This picture is favourably distinguished from many by the master, both by the composition, the noble feeling, and conscientious execution of every part. The head of the Virgin is of beautiful form, and the strong foreshortening of the Child very well drawn. The modelling of all the flesh parts is also excellent.

HOBBEMA.—2. On the right a mill, with the falling mill-stream faintly reflected on the surface of the dark water below. In the middle distance are houses surrounded with trees, before which are a gentleman and lady; in the centre a group of trees; on the left a view on to a field with sheaves of corn and a sunny village. The sky is lightly covered with grey and silvery clouds. On canvas. 3 ft. 0½ in. high, 4 ft. 2½ in. wide. The contrast of the dark foreground with the light sunny distance is as striking as it is pleasing, and one of the finest effects I know by the master. The sky is of the rarest transparency; the execution singularly careful. Formerly in the collection of Baron Verstolk.

JACOB RUYSDAEL.—3. A Waterfall. A mountainous country, divided on the right by a chasm, through which issues a rapid stream, which falls in masses of white foam amongst large rocks, and flows gurgling in eddies along the foreground, impeded in its course by two rocks. The water is bounded by a high hill, on the summit of which stands a lonely house; the roofs of several cottages are visible among a thick wood which clothes the ridge of the hill. Another cottage is on the left, and a broken line of bushes extends along the declivity of the hill, on which the painter and an attendant are seated. A church is seen in the distance, and blue hills on the horizon. The clear sky is partially covered with light clouds. Signed. On canvas. 3 ft. 6 in. high, 4 ft. 11 in. wide. This picture is in every respect one of the finest known to me of the master. The whole shows a true and profound feeling for nature. The water is of the most admirable animation, with the utmost breadth and softness of execution. The individuality of every portion is more marked, and the number of details more numerous, than in any other picture on so large a scale by Ruysdael that has come before me. Formerly in the collection of Baron Verstolk.

MURILLO.—2. The Virgin holding the Child on her lap, who is in the liveliest action. Whole-length figures, life-size. On canvas. 5 ft. high, 3 ft. 7 in. wide. In this picture also the head of the Virgin is of unusual elevation of character for the master, but somewhat hard in the shadows. The hands are admirably drawn. The Child on the other hand is quite realistic, and of the utmost softness, transparency, and delicacy in the modelling of the figure. The keeping of the whole is very beautiful. Formerly in the Palazzo Santo Jago at Madrid, and afterwards in the possession of Lord Berwick. (See Buchanan's Materials, &c., vol. II., pp. 221 and 234.)

JACOB RUYSDAEL. — 4. On the right a wooded height with a view in the open distance, with a road on which are two men in conversation; more in front are four sheep; in the foreground are felled trees; on the left, in front, is a piece of still water; behind, a hill. Sunny clouds are in the sky. On canvas. 3 ft. 6 in. high, 4 ft. 2½ in. wide. A pleasing composition of the earlier time of the master. The execution careful, but the tone somewhat heavy. The sky shows the influence of Hobbema.

GUIDO RENI. — 2. A Sibyl, youthfully conceived; a stout white band on her brown hair, and otherwise attired in white. Pointing with her left hand to herself. The background dark. Half-length. On canvas. 2 ft. 8½ in. high, 2 ft. 1 in. wide. What an immense difference between Michael Angelo's conception of the ancient Sibyl as a noble prophetess, and the pretty, amiable young girl before us! The painting, however, in a clear, silvery tone, is masterly.

SALVATOR ROSA.—A mountainous landscape, with a high rock on the left, and old and lofty trees on the right; in the middle distance a piece of still water, with the figures of the youthful Tobit with the fish, and the angel giving him instructions. On canvas. 2 ft. 4½ in. high, 3 ft. 4 in. wide. A warm lighting of great transparency and a very careful finish are combined for once in this fine picture with the poetic composition proper to the master. The figures also, especially the angel, are very graceful.

TITIAN.—The sketch for the large picture of the Last Supper, in the Museum at Madrid, which Titian executed for Philip II. of Spain. The scene is taking place in a space with pillars (two of which towards the left are partially twisted), and with an arch in the centre, through which a landscape is seen; above is a lamp by which all the objects are brightly lighted. Our Saviour has just spoken the words, "One of you will betray me," the Disciples are in the greatest excitement, and St. John has sunk down with grief by the Saviour's side. Under the table is a dog gnawing a bone; before the table are a large basket and a metal vessel of water from which a dove is drinking. On canvas. 2 ft. 5½ in. high, 3 ft. 4½ in. wide. The whole conception is as spirited as it is original; the treatment of singular mastery and breadth, and so slight that the red ground shines through in many places. Formerly in the possession of Benjamin West.

Not far from this was the following picture on a chair :—

ADRIAN VAN OSTADE.—Still life. On a board laid over a barrel are two fish; two more are on an earthen dish; in a tub leaning against the wall are earthenware with a woollen cloth; a pump, a net, and other objects are close by. A vine is above. A bright light falls through a window with two broken panes on these objects. On wood. 1 ft. 5½ in. high, 1 ft. 2 in. wide. This picture is a striking specimen of the fact that true art depends not so much on the object as on the manner in which it is represented; for by dint of picturesqueness of arrangement, masterly distribution, warmth of lighting, extraordinary truth of detail, and breadth and softness of touch, these highly uninteresting objects form a very attractive whole.

On an easel opposite the last-described picture were the two following :—

TENIERS.—5. A pretty young woman seated, with a glass of wine in her hand, listening to the gallantry of an old peasant, who sits by her side, with his right hand on her shoulder, while at the same time his elderly wife is watching their movements from an opening above. Upon the door of the opening is a little owl of very serious expression. Signed. On wood. 1 ft. high, 9 in. wide. A little gem ! The heads are treated in his clearest and brightest golden tones; otherwise a cool harmony predominates. In the dress of the young woman, especially, who wears a grey petticoat, a light grey jacket, and a blueish apron, the colours are combined with the utmost delicacy. The execution is of very solid impasto, and of rare finish. Formerly in the collection of Edward Gray, Esq.

JAN STEEN.—2. A representation of the Dutch proverb, " As the old people sung, so pipe also the young "—a composition of sixteen figures. Seated in the centre is a stout woman with an immoderately fat baby at a table; opposite is an organman; an old woman is singing; a boy blowing the bagpipe; more in the background is a man playing the violin; an old man is flourishing a rummer glass; below is a little girl with a jug, and a boy pretending to play upon a tobacco-pipe; and a dog. A crown hangs from the ceiling, on which are the first words of the proverb, "SOO DOVDE." Signed. On wood. 1 ft. 5 in. high, 1 ft. 11 in. wide. The peculiar humour of the master appears in full measure in some of these figures, especially in the organman; on the other hand, the vulgarity is here and there too exaggerated, especially in the fat baby. In point of solid and careful execution, however, this picture is a first-rate specimen of his art. Formerly in the collection of Baron Verstolk.

SMALL ROOM ADJOINING THE SMALL DRAWING-ROOM.

EDDIS.—1. A gipsy woman, with dark hair and black eyes, seated, and pointing with her right hand to her left, while she looks at the spectator as if to challenge him to have his fortune told; next her a little girl, who has drawn the large red headgear of the woman also over her head. A landscape background. On canvas. 4 ft. 6 in. high, 3 ft. 2 in. wide. Oval form. The character of the gipsy is well and livelily expressed, the colouring powerful and clear, and the execution careful.

LANCE.—Fruit, in a golden vessel upon a table. Landscape background. On canvas. Circular picture. 1 ft. 11½ in. in diameter. Very true to nature in form and colour, the latter of great power. The execution careful.

LADY OVERSTONE'S MORNING ROOM.

ANNIBALE CARRACCI. — The dead Christ lamented by the Magdalen. On slate. 1 ft. 2 in. high, 10 in. wide. Noble in forms, and fine in the position of the Christ. The Magdalen recalls the celebrated picture of the Three Maries at Castle Howard, and is warm in feeling. Of careful execution.

MURILLO.—3. The Virgin in Glory, in white dress and blue mantle. Five angels below, one of whom bears a palm, and another a lily. On canvas. 1 ft. 3 in. high, 10½ in. wide. A charming little picture in his silvery tones, and of light and spirited but careful treatment. Formerly in the Brackenbury collection.

4. Head of Christ, crowned with thorns, upon the Sudarium. On wood. 1 ft. 8 in. high, 1 ft. 3 in. wide. Although the mode

of conception entirely differs from the old type, and has something
portrait-like in character, yet it is highly attractive for the
nobility of feeling, the clear, juicy, and earnest tone of the colouring, and the careful execution.   Formerly in the possession of
Richard Ford, Esq.

5. The Virgin in Glory, holding the Infant on her arm.   She is
dressed here in a dark-red robe and deep blue mantle: twelve
angels around her.   On canvas.   1 ft. 3 in. high, 11 in. wide.
This is the sketch I mentioned above, to the great picture
formerly in the Soult collection.   The harmony of the execution
is, however, warm, though in some parts, especially in the head of
the Virgin, too hard.

QUENTIN MATSYS.—Christ and John the Baptist as children,
undraped, seated upon a green carpet, and kissing each other;
behind them a red curtain.   On wood.   9 in. high, 11½ in. wide.
Attractive in motive, pure in feeling, clear in colouring, and
careful in finish.

Venetian School, perhaps Savoldo, scholar of Titian.—A young
nun of pretty features, with a dark violet cloth round her head,
which falls down on each side, and a white cloth covering the chin
and part of the cheeks: with her right hand she grasps the white
cloth.   The background sky.   On canvas.   1 ft. 0½ in. high, 11½ in.
wide.   A pleasing picture, good in the keeping, and large and
spirited in the treatment.

EDDIS.—2. Naomi, Ruth, and Orpah.   On canvas.   4 ft. 3½
in. high, 5 ft. wide.   To the knees.   Pure and elevated in the
feeling of the heads, carefully drawn, and executed in a transparent tone.

MISS LOYD'S ROOM.

LUDOLPH BACKHUYSEN. — 2. An agitated sea; in the foreground a boat; on the right a large vessel foreshortened in full
sail; a gleam of sunlight falls on the foremost waves.   On wood.
1 ft. high, 1 ft. 3½ in. wide.   Of the finest quality, truthful, clear,
and very careful.

JAN WYNANTS.—2. A landscape.   On the left a tree which is
almost dead; quite in the foreground a piece of water; near this
a shepherd and a small flock of sheep driven inwards.   Figures by
ADRIAN VAN DE VELDE.   Trees in the background; the clouds

lighted by the sun. On canvas. 1 ft. 2 in. high, 1 ft. 1½ in. wide. Admirably treated in a cool morning tone, and of the finest rendering of the details even in the distance.

GREUZE.—A young girl in red corsage and white sleeves, feeding a very small bird, which is perched on the door of its cage. Canvas pasted on wood. 8¾ in. high, 7¼ in. wide. A sweet little picture, delicately executed in a very broken and subdued tone of colour.

JACOB RUYSDAEL.—5. Two windmills on a canal; on the right in front are trees and a bridge, on which is a man; the background is overshadowed by clouds, while a distant cloud is illumined by the sun. On wood. 1 ft. 0½ in. high, 1 ft. 2 in. wide. A charming little picture of intense feeling for nature and masterly treatment. The reflections in the water are especially successsful.

JACOB VAN DER ULFT.—A landscape with lofty-stemmed trees, behind them houses with a wall, before which is a group of men resting; in the foreground a piece of water with a rider on a grey horse, holding a restive brown horse by the bridle; bathing figures are in the water. 7 in. high, 9 in. wide. Very attractive, both for the picturesque composition and the excellent and careful painting.

MURILLO.—6. The Virgin showing the sleeping Child to St. Joseph, who is adoring; at the foot of the Child is the little St. John. On wood. 8 in. high, 8½ in. wide. The sleeping Child is very true, and also very soft and clear in colour. The head of the Virgin has suffered by cleaning, and St. Joseph and the Baptist have been so overpainted as to lose all spirit.

WATTEAU.—A party of gentlemen and ladies in a garden; on the left are two ladies loitering by a fountain adorned with sculptures; on the right a gentleman with a mandolin and a lady have stretched themselves on the ground; a little girl is with them; behind them a lady and gentleman standing in conversation; in the middle distance are various couples reposing, and one standing. On wood. 8 in. high, 10½ in. wide. Very picturesquely arranged, of clear and decided lighting, and of rare precision in the miniature-like execution.

PICTURES NOT YET PLACED.

WILLEM VAN DE VELDE.—3. The sea with a fresh breeze; on the right a fishing-boat, in which are two men, with white sail;

near them a skiff; also a sailing-boat with four men, and further back a three-masted vessel; in the far distance another vessel. Dark shadows fall from the clouds on one side of the water; other clouds are illumined by the sun. Signed. On wood. 1 ft. 2 in. high, 1 ft. 4½ in. wide. An admirable picture of the best time of the master.

REMBRANDT.—3. The Woman taken in Adultery. A composition of eleven figures. Christ is pointing to the legible Dutch inscription on the ground. On wood. 11½ in. high, 10½ in. wide. A slight sketch, but admirable in composition and lighting.

PETER NEEFS.—View of the Interior of Antwerp Cathedral, with numerous figures. Signed. On canvas. 1 ft. 11½ in. high, 3 ft. 7 in. wide. Carefully executed in a silvery tone with great delicacy of aërial perspective.

PARMIGIANINO.— The Virgin seated on the ground with the Child standing before her, who is impetuously caressed by the infant St. John; behind St. John is the Magdalen seen in profile, with the box of ointment. A landscape background. On canvas. 2 ft. 1 in. high, 1 ft. 9 in. wide. This composition occasionally occurs by the master, and is very attractive from the motive of the children, and the beautiful head of the Magdalen. This example is broad and almost slight in treatment, but spirited.

LORENZO DI CREDI.—Coronation of the Virgin, a small but fine picture, from the collection of the late Mr. Rogers.

COLLECTION OF PICTURES BELONGING TO LORD CALEDON,
5, CARLTON HOUSE TERRACE.

This collection contains valuable pictures of the Italian, Spanish, French, and Netherlandish Schools.

DINING-ROOM.

JAN WEENIX.—A dead hare and pheasant, fruit, and a live spaniel. Too empty in proportion to its large size, and very dark.

GIOVANNI BELLINI (?).—The Virgin seated in the open air, with the Child on her lap, who is holding a white cup. On the right is Joseph leaning; on the left St. John. Two partridges also appear, such as the early Venetians often introduced. This picture does not appear to me of sufficient importance for Bellini, but it is of warm and transparent flesh tones, and in composition as well as heads a pleasing work of his school.

Guercino.—St. Sebastian reclining against a tree. This picture, which is careful, and of very dark shadows, shows in conception and treatment the influence of Michael Angelo da Caravaggio.

Michael Mireveldt. — 1 and 2. A male and a female portrait. To the knees. Excellent pictures of his best time. Very animated, true, clear, and unusually soft.

Lucas van Uden.—1. A large landscape, with an extended distance, in the taste of his master Rubens; on the right a carriage with three grey horses harnessed. This fine picture is now in a very darkened state.

LIBRARY.

Heinrick van Steinwyck the Elder. — 1. Still life. A portrait, books, &c. Tastefully arranged, and true and careful in detail.

Lucas van Uden.—2. A small landscape; on the right a wood, on the left distance. Warm and careful.

Bassano, and, as it appears to me, Leandro.—A numerous train of cattle; perhaps the Exodus of the Israelites from Egypt. Of very transparent colouring.

Decker.—A large landscape; on the right, in the foreground, a water-mill. Of good composition, but, upon the whole, somewhat dark.

Le Nain.—1. A French peasant family. Very scattered in arrangement, but animated in detail.

De Heem (?).—A fruit-piece, grapes, &c. A good picture, but rather to be ascribed to Pierson.

Lucas van Uden. — 3. A landscape, with a very striking group of trees in the centre; the sky warmly lighted. Very attractive.

Rembrandt.—1. A portrait. Looks promising, but hangs in too dark a place to admit of an opinion.

Salvator Rosa.—1. The sea-god Glaucus seeking in vain to overpower Scylla. The same composition of which there is an etching by the master. Though in a very dark place, the picture appears to me a genuine and careful work.

2. Sea-coast, with rocky shore. One of his pictures with a disagreeable red tone.

Dobson.—Portrait of an Officer with a pistol. Half-length. Approaching Vandyck in animation of conception and execution.

Dirk van Delen. — A Church; with figures by Geritz van Herp.

Palamedes Palamedess. — Soldiers in an interior. Picturesquely arranged, and carefully executed.

Le Nain.—2. A woman seated, three children, and a beggar. A good picture.

Jacob van Artois.—1 and 2. Two landscapes by this clever but often scenic master; the one with a distance belonging to his very good pictures.

ANTE-ROOM.

Innocenzo da Imola.—An Altarpiece, with the Marriage of the Virgin, with only the Magdalen, and another female Saint, beside the priest. The head of the Virgin, as usual with this painter, is taken from Raphael. A good and careful picture.

Salvator Rosa.—3. The composition of a knight bound to a tree, on which is a Crucifix, which he etched. A very black specimen of this oft-occurring picture.

Artus van der Neer.—View of a canal with houses; on the right, in front, a shepherd, four cows, and fishermen, in warm, clear lighting. Of delicate keeping and careful execution.

Karel Dujardin.—On the left, in the foreground, the stem of a tree; near it an ox and a sheep in a piece of water, through which a woman is passing; in the background a lofty rocky hill. Prettily composed and cleverly treated, but the middle distance rather heavy in tone.

Jan van der Heyden.—View of a town. A gate in the centre is particularly striking. The pretty figures are by Eglon van der Neer. Of a monotonous and somewhat heavy brown tone.

Karel Rutharts.—1 and 2. Two hunting pieces. Pretty little pictures by this not common master.

Teniers.—1. A landscape; on the left high hills with buildings and a stream at their feet; on the right an eminence with two shepherds. Of beautiful and warm lighting, but somewhat heavy in tone.

PETER NEEFS.—Interior of a church. One of his brownly toned pictures.

HEINRICK VAN STEINWYCK THE ELDER.—Interior of a church. Clear and delicate in tone.

WOUVERMANS.—In the centre of the foreground a grey horse, almost entirely in half shadow. Next it a woman, and a man on the ground ; on the right a rising ground, on which is a tree. An upright picture, of very powerful colour, in his first manner.

CANALETTO.—1. View of the Capitol from the Forum. Powerful and warm in tone, and very careful.

2. The companion. View from Rome. This is much poorer in composition, and heavier in tone.

REMBRANDT (?).—2. Portrait of a young man. A picture of merit, but too tame for him, and rather to be considered as the work of JAN LIEVENS.

TENIERS.—2. Interior of a peasant house. In the foreground, on the left, a maid employed in peeling onions ; next her domestic utensils, a melon, and a dead duck ; in the background three peasants at a table, and a fourth going out of the door. Of very powerful effect, but somewhat brown in tone.

REMBRANDT.—3. His own portrait. By way of exception the broader side of the face is in full light here, and of a very yellow tone. This picture hangs too high, however, for an opinion.

DRAWING-ROOM.

ADAM PYNACKER.—A landscape. Two peasants and a dog before a building. This picture is in so dirty and unsightly a condition that I only assign it to this master by way of supposition.

GUIDO RENI.—St. Matthew the Evangelist reading. A careful picture.

GUIDO CAGNACCI.—Cleopatra. The elevated forms and expression show the influence of Guido. Particularly warm and clear in colour, and careful in execution.

MURILLO.—1. The Virgin in Glory. Her eyes humbly cast down,—in a white robe and blue mantle. Numerous angels' heads above ; on the left a group of angels. Below, a larger number of angelic figures, one of them bearing a lily, another a palm-branch. An altarpiece. Form and expression of the Virgin's head delicate.

2. Portrait of a man in an oval, of very brown colour, but too high and darkly hung for an opinion.

3. The companion picture. Portrait of a lady of pretty features, and in a rich dress. This hangs more favourably. It is of very transparent colouring, but, in my opinion, too empty in the forms and too smooth in touch for Murillo. It shows, however, a good Spanish painter, but one unknown to me.

WILLEM VAN DE VELDE.—The Sea-shore at Scheveningen, with numerous spirited figures by the hand of ADRIAN VAN DE VELDE. Signed, and dated 1659. It is much to be regretted that this light and masterly-treated picture—one of those very few occasions on which both these great masters united their powers—should have suffered, both as a whole, and especially in some of the figures, by over cleaning.

VANDYCK.—Portrait of the Marchesa Spinola in a red dress. Next to her a little daughter in blue. The background grey, with a curtain. Whole-length figures, life size. An admirable picture of his Genoese time. The delicate head of the lady is beautifully blended in a golden tone; that of the child of great animation.

NICOLAS POUSSIN.—1. A large landscape. On the right, in the foreground, is a large antique sarcophagus, with the Rape of Proserpine, a subject often seen on sarcophagi. At the foot of this, seated on the ground, are a man, a woman, and a child. Behind are the ruins of a temple, with lofty trees; on the left the ruins of a grand building, with a flight of steps down to a piece of water, on the other shore of which are a tower and hills. How truly this poetic landscape is conceived in a purely antique taste is proved by some of the landscapes discovered in Pompeii, in which remains of architecture form a principal feature. The colouring is also particularly powerful and clear, and the carefully-treated figures very warm.

JAN BOTH.—On the right, rocks with a waterfall. In the centre of the foreground a tree, and, more on the left, upon a road, two drivers with loaded mules. Quite on the left, another tree. His very warm tone here degenerates into a disagreeable red.

ALESSANDRO ALLORI.—Portrait of a young man of noble features, a letter in his right hand, his left placed against his hip; of spirited conception, and careful execution in a somewhat grey tone.

NICOLAS POUSSIN.—2. The Virgin with the Child standing on her lap in the vicinity of ruins. The Child is looking down at the little adoring St. John. Behind the last-named is St. Elizabeth seated. On the left, turning away from the spectator, is St. Joseph reading. The background architecture and sky. This small cabinet picture, which is known by an early engraving, is, it is true, secular in expression, but finely composed, and very carefully executed in a clear colour.

The Fall of Phaëton, purporting to be by Rubens, is a copy; also the Triumph of Silenus, attributed to Guido, but too empty in the heads and heavy in colour for that master.

PICTURES BELONGING TO THE DOWAGER LADY WALDEGRAVE, CARLTON HOUSE GARDENS.

SIR JOSHUA REYNOLDS.—1. Portrait of three Ladies Waldegrave in one group. This in every respect is one of the most remarkable works of the master. The delicate conception of female youth and beauty is here combined with a decided delineation of individual character, an admirable keeping undisturbed by the three white dresses, a more than usually pronounced development of forms, and a colouring as warm as it is bright and transparent. The execution also is, what we rarely see with Sir Joshua, equal in all parts, extending, for instance, to the admirably painted table, round which the three sisters are seated.

2, 3, and 4. The portrait of a brother of these ladies, that of a Duchess of Gloucester, and of Sir Robert Walpole, belong also to his good works.

DOMENICHINO.—Portrait of Cardinal Barberini. Of noble and animated conception, careful execution and clear colouring.

PICTURES BELONGING TO WILLIAM GLADSTONE, ESQ., M.P., 11, CARLTON HOUSE TERRACE.

Among the pictures I remarked in Mr. Gladstone's house the following deserve to be more generally known:—

Lucas Cranach. — The Entombment. Of great truth of feeling, and powerful and clear colour. The size moderate.

Joachim Patenier.—The Virgin and Child seated in a landscape. A female saint on each side, also seated. Delicate and elevated in character of heads, and carefully carried out in detail.

Spanish School.—A saint with two monks walking on the water, and approaching the shore, where several figures await them. Whole length, life size. From the collection of Louis Philippe. Of great animation of motives and heads. Now much defaced by dirt.

Richard Wilson.—A landscape, which, for size, beauty of composition, powerful effect, and careful rendering, may be considered one of his chief works.

Dyce.—A female head of rare beauty of form and purity of feeling, and also very carefully executed.

Through the unfailing kindness of Sir Charles Anderson, I obtained the sight of two large landscapes by Gaspar Poussin, which in every respect belong to the most important works of this master. These are the property of the Hoare family, generally resident at Wavendon House, Buckinghamshire. The pictures, however, at the time of my inspection, were at No. 7 a, St. James's Square, the residence of Mrs. Howe.

1. On the right is a spreading wood; on the left a hilly distance. In front are two sportsmen, whose antique chlamys forms a singular contrast to the guns which they carry. The one is loading his weapon, the other figure is seated. Three dogs are also in the picture, and another sportsman is seen upon a road. About 5 ft. 6 in. high, 7 ft. wide. This picture is not only grand in feeling, and poetical in the lines and forms of the clouds, but it is particularly transparent for the master, and broadly but carefully treated in an admirable impasto.

2. On the right is a rising ground with cattle descending from it, and stately trees. On the left a hill of very gradual elevation; more on the left trees again. Between these trees and the hill lies the Campagna of Rome, the horizontal lines of which are broken by the fine forms of Mount Soracte. In the middle of the fore-

ground is Eurydice bitten by the asp, with female companions, and Orpheus reposing. This picture has the same fine qualities as its companion. Both are in admirable preservation.

COLLECTION OF PICTURES BELONGING TO HUMPHREY
ST. JOHN MILDMAY, ESQ.,
No. 46, BERKELEY SQUARE.

The strength of this collection, which is moderate in number, but valuable in quality, consists in pictures of the Dutch school, formerly in the well-known gallery of Baron Verstolk at the Hague. Lord Overstone, Mr. Thomas Baring, and the father of the present youthful possessor, were the three chief purchasers of that collection.

DRAWING-ROOM.

JAN WYNANTS.—On a high road, leading through a hilly and richly-wooded country, with a piece of water, is a horseman attacked by two robbers on foot, while a third is firing after another traveller who is escaping. In the foreground is the stump of a dead tree and various plants. Signed, and dated 1668. 2 ft. 3 in. high, 2 ft. 10 in. wide. On canvas. Very happy in composition, and particularly attractive for the spirited figures, which are by the hand of WOUVERMANS. The picture is also carefully carried out, though, like all the later works of the master, rather grey in general tone.

JACOB RUYSDAEL.—1. View of the Coast of Scheveningen. On the left is the wide extent of successive downs, on the furthest of which is a gleam of sun. Behind it rises the pointed tower of the village. On the right is the expanse of sea, only broken by two fishing-boats. On the coast are numerous figures, of which three ladies, one of them holding a fan, and a group of three men, are conspicuous. On canvas. Signed. 1 ft. 9 in. high, 2 ft. 2 in. wide. This picture, which, when in the Choiseul Gallery, was engraved by Le Bas, is one of the most refined examples of this often-treated subject by the master. The subdued sunshine, the breakers, and the sky, are of marvellous truth, softness, and mastery.

2. The companion picture. View of the sea-coast, with the

town of Muyden in the distance. On the right a succession of lofty sand downs, and a road skirting along them, on which are an officer and two ladies with a page. In the centre and on the right, in the shallows of the water, are several shrimp-fishers and others. On the coast a boat with two sailors, in the distance some fishing-boats. The dark rent clouds which overshadow this side are of singular power. The cold and melancholy impression of a northern nature is given with enchanting truth.

PHILIP WOUVERMANS.—A combat of horsemen and foot on each side, a windmill on fire in the vicinity, and a village with a little stream; a man on a bay horse on the edge of the stream, who has just fired his piece at an opponent on a piebald horse, who is falling, is particularly conspicuous. Here and there are groups of combatants. On wood. 1 ft. 9½ in. high, 2 ft. 7¾ in. wide. Of very powerful effect, though partially somewhat dark. Highly momentary in action, and very carefully executed in his second manner.

JAN STEEN.—A candlelight scene. A large apartment, with a party of five persons on the left. One of them, a young lady, who is playing cards with a gentleman, is taking counsel with a stout gentleman standing behind her. Opposite is a merry fellow with a card in his hand, and a man smoking his pipe standing. A youth is entering with a light; two others, seen above him, also with lights, are on the landing-place. On the other side is a party of seven persons, for whom a woman is opening oysters. On wood. 1 ft. 4½ in. high, 1 ft. 9½ in. wide. Among the night pieces by Jan Steen this picture may well carry off the prize. Though not actually painted in competition with Gerard Dow's celebrated night-piece in the Gallery of Amsterdam, as Mr. Smith believes, yet, both in the skill and truth with which the gradations of six various kinds of light are here introduced, and the well-balanced composition, it invites a comparison with that picture. In the impasto of the careful execution it is also excellent.

WILLEM ROMEYN. — A mountainous landscape, with cattle reposing on the left, and other cattle advancing upon a road on the right. Another specimen of a masterpiece by a painter of secondary rank. Very pleasing in composition, clear, though cool and dark in tone, and solid in execution.

KAREL DUJARDIN.—In the foreground of a bare rocky country,

with a reed fence running through it, are a sheep and a lamb. On the right sits a man in a sheepskin jacket with red sleeves, occupied in darning a stocking. On wood. 10 in. high, $13\frac{1}{2}$ in. wide. Both composition and lighting express the delicately picturesque feeling of the master. The sheep, which is in sunshine, is particularly admirable. The tone, which is generally heavy, does not equal the execution in excellence.

WILLEM VAN DE VELDE.—A quiet sea. On the right, in the middle distance, is a large strongly foreshortened vessel, and in the distance another discharging a gun. On the left, in the foreground, not far from a strip of land, is a boat with a dark sail, seen on the broadside, and behind, another with a white sail. On the extreme left a skiff with two figures. The sky is moderately cloudy. On wood. About 1 ft. high, 2 ft. 3 in. wide. The effect of the dark boat and sail is striking, while the clearness of the water, and the delicacy in the gradations of aërial perspective, combine to render this an exquisite picture.

PHILIP WOUVERMANS.—2. A landscape. On the right, in the foreground, is a piece of water, with a bridge over it. A house, with a tree behind. On the left is a party of sportsmen with falcons, among whom the figure of a lady upon a grey horse is conspicuous. In the distance are hills. On copper. A small but highly refined and charming picture of cool effect.

MINDERHOUT HOBBEMA.—View of a lock, with quays and adjacent buildings of the Haarlem Sluice at Amsterdam. In a canal enclosed within the walls of the sluice are two boats, with a man in each. Behind the gate of the sluice, in the centre, is a drawbridge, over which the masts of ships are seen. On the one hand is a group of trees, on the other houses with trees before them, and, rising far above, the Herring-packers' tower. Two figures on the quay, near a large basket, are conspicuous. On canvas. 2 ft. $6\frac{1}{2}$ in. high, 3 ft. 2 in. wide. This is a very interesting production for the admirers of this master. The composition is in the taste of Van der Heyden, and the effect produced by the contrast between the deep and transparent chiaroscuro of most of the objects, and the warm sunny light, is of wonderful charm. The execution is also unusually careful.

JOHANN LINGELBACH.—1. Horsemen halting before a smithy. On the right a woman, man, and child. On wood. Prettily composed, and of a delicacy of execution almost equal to Wouvermans, though darker and heavier in tone.

Nicholas Berghem.—View of a hilly country, with a broad road and a pool of water in the foreground. On the left a shepherdess in a yellow corsage and blue apron, carrying a lamb under her arm, and a boy with a stick driving a red cow. Four goats, a sheep, a dog, and a fifth goat, are on their left. On the other side, in the middle distance, is a similar group, and, on a turn of the road, two horsemen. On canvas. 1 ft. 11½ in. high, 1 ft. 7 in. wide. The composition is of great beauty, the rendering of the animals very delicate. One of the most attractive pictures of the best time of the master, and of marvellous preservation.

Adrian van de Velde.—In the centre of the foreground is a red cow lying behind a brown one. More on the left, and behind, is a dark cow standing and bellowing. On the right, between two willows, are a man and woman before another dark cow. Next to the first-mentioned animals are a sheep and two lambs reposing. On the left, a hilly distance. Very happily composed, warm in tone, delicately felt, and carefully finished. Of the middle and best time of the master.

Van de Capella.—A calm sea. On the right, seen in perspective gradation, are several boats. On the left, foreshortened, a man-of-war, and, seen on the broadside, a manned barge. The sky is slightly cloudy. Both the barge and the sky approach Cuyp in power of tone, the other portions resemble Willem van de Velde in clearness and delicacy.

Domenichino.—This is the only picture of the Italian school in this apartment. A small landscape. On the right is a large tree. A boat upon a stream is approaching. The distant hills are warmly lighted. Of poetical feeling, and very powerful colouring.

DINING-ROOM.

Ludolf Backhuysen.—A sea-coast, with slightly agitated water. On the shore, in the foreground, are fishes and fishermen. Quite on the right a gentleman, lady, and greyhound. Behind them a pier and some boats. In the middle distance, on the right, is a large vessel foreshortened, and quite on the right two sailing-boats. In the distance is a large ship under sail. Another coast is seen on the horizon. The sky is light on the right, and dark on the left side. A large and careful picture of the good time of the master.

JOHANN LINGELBACH.—2. View of a hilly sea-coast. In the foreground are two horsemen on a brown and a grey horse. Beside them a man on foot. A good picture.

ANTOINE WATTEAU.—In a free space, surrounded by wood, are a couple dancing a minuet. On the right three musicians, on the left a party of five ladies and four gentlemen looking on. Five of the party are recumbent. Very happily composed, of striking effect of light, and rendered throughout, including the trees, with as much spirit as care.

JOSEPH VERNET.—1 and 2. Of these two large pictures, the view of the port of Genoa particularly pleased me.

THE LIBRARY.

GUERCINO.—Christ and the Woman of Samaria. Between the figures, in the landscape background, are buildings. A very remarkable specimen of the master, from the gallery of the Duke of Lucca. Figures half-length. The expression of the Saviour, who is speaking, is very animated, also that of attention in the woman. The tone is warm, golden, and clear, the execution very careful.

LEANDRO BASSANO.—1. Christ visiting Martha and Mary. He is advancing from a gateway into an open space, and is greeted by the two sisters. Of animated motives, and very powerful colouring. The landscape particularly successful.

2. The companion picture. The Adoration of the Kings. The composition is limited to the merely needful figures. The glow of colouring is astonishing, while the flesh parts, especially of the Child, are over red.

COLLECTION BELONGING TO ABRAHAM ROBARTS, ESQ., HILL STREET, BERKELEY SQUARE.

Considering the number and excellence of the collections of the Dutch school gathered together in England, it is no small compliment to the one before us to say that it occupies a distinguished place among them. Nor is this collection wanting in single specimens of merit of the Flemish, French, and Spanish schools. The pictures are tastefully arranged in the admirably kept apartments, and I had the advantage of being allowed to examine them without interruption. I was also indebted to the kindness of Mrs. Robarts for information on some particulars.

THE DRAWING-ROOM.

Cuyp.—1. View of the river Maas towards evening, with slightly clouded sky, and perfect calm. On the right a large barge manned with soldiers, into which an officer is stepping from a boat. On the left other barges, leading the eye in lines of perspective towards the centre. Immediately in the front, in two small boats, are ladies and gentlemen besides rowers, and quite on the left a village with a pointed tower. This signed picture, which is of considerable size, is of the same period as the well-known views on the Maas in Lord Brownlow's collection (formerly Sir Abraham Hume's) and in the Bridgewater Gallery, and approaches these in beauty. The warm and clear reflections of every object in the evening light are admirable, and the execution broad and masterly in a full body.

2. View of the town of Dort, with the church with its well-known blunt tower in the centre. Round about are six windmills. On the left, in the foreground, is a narrow piece of water, with three cows on its further shore, one of whom is drinking. A yellow cow reposing approaches Adrian van de Velde in delicacy. On the right, on the bank nearest to us, and next some beautifully painted large-leaved plants, is a shepherd recumbent with six sheep. Quite on the right are two horsemen on a brown and a gray horse. Next the latter a woman with a basket on her head, and a boy. The sky is cloudy, and over this and every other object is diffused a warm and powerful evening light. By means of this picture, which is as novel as it is beautiful in composition, and of considerable size, I became acquainted with a new phase of this great master. The keeping is excellent; the execution as careful as it is spirited, and the impasto solid.

Jacob Ruysdael.—In the foreground is a waterfall divided by impeding rocks into two parts. In the middle distance are two slightly overgrown eminences, between which runs the water. On the eminence on the left is a shepherd with his flock. The rocks and some of the clouds are lighted with the warm afternoon sun. The composition is very attractive, the treatment broad and spirited, and the water especially rendered in a masterly manner.

TENIERS.—In the foreground on the right, round a table, are six peasants smoking and drinking. On the left is a woman bringing a plate of food, and a jug from the cellar. In the background are four other peasants before a fire. Signed. On wood. In the very decided lighting of the foreground the white jacket of one of the peasants is particularly conspicuous. The background is kept in a dark but transparent chiaroscuro. This picture approaches Adrian Ostade in warmth and depth of tone, and is also of very solid treatment.

RUBENS.—The Virgin holding with her right hand the Child, who is standing on her lap, and whose right hand is on her left breast, while her left hand touches his left foot. Some architecture is in the dark background. To the knees. On wood. 3 ft. 3 in. high, 2 ft. 7½ in. wide. Although a picture of great merit, this is not comparable in transparency and solidity with the same composition in the collection of Mr. Edmund Foster (see vol. ii. p. 451), and is, as Mr. Smith observes in his Catalogue, vol. ix. p. 299, probably only retouched by Rubens.

BACKHUYSEN.—A somewhat agitated sea. In the middle a large vessel. In the left, in the distance, a harbour with many other ships. Some shadows of clouds on the water are happily varied by a ray of light. Transparent in tone, careful in execution, and of the best time of the master.

VAN DER HEYDEN.—View of a Dutch town, with a canal through the whole breadth of the foreground. Its clear waters reflect a bridge in the middle distance, and a barge of masterly foreshortening on the shore on the right. In the background, illumined by the sun, is a church with a tower-like cupola. Some figures and two swans are introduced by the hand of ADRIAN VAN DE VELDE. Signed. Almost quadrangular in form, attractive in composition, of unusual warmth and power of chiaroscuro, and of far broader and more solid treatment than usual. A first-rate picture.

PYNACKER.—In the foreground is a barge laden with wares, putting over a stream. On the opposite side is a chain of rocks which recede in the picture; the foremost crowned with a fortress.

The cool, clear morning light, and the reflections in the water, are masterly, the execution very careful, and the whole very admirable.

CORNELIS DUSART.—1. Nine-pin players eating and drinking in a village. A rich and very happily arranged composition. Bright clouds are in the sky. The painter here approaches his master, Adrian Ostade, in power and transparency.

JAN STEEN.—An officer sitting in a tavern, with a girl on his knee. A mechanic, with a cap and bare chest, a glass in his hand, is looking at the group. A woman and two men are at a table on which is ham and bread. On a bench close by is a beer-glass, a cloth, a clay pipe, and some shrimps. Behind, in the doorway, are a boy and two men talking with a man outside the window. Signed. On wood. 1 ft. 2¾ in. high, 1 ft. 7 in. wide. For admirably rendered chiaroscuro, and broad, spirited, and very careful execution, this belongs to the best works of the master.

JAN and ANDREAS BOTH.—In the foreground on the right are two lofty trees; at their feet a woman on a mule, with two loaded mules following; next her a man on foot. Hills extend from the middle ground into the distance. More on the left are some trees; and further still on the left a piece of still water. A moderately large picture, of unusually powerful and yet transparent colouring. The treatment somewhat broader than usual.

GONZALES COQUES.—A lady in a blue dress and white lace, playing the lute, seated; next her a man in black, his right hand on his hip. Quite on the left a table with a red cloth. In the background pillars and a curtain, and on the right a bit of sky. Of unusual delicacy and mastery of execution, approaching Metzu.

HOBBEMA.—View of a village. On the right in the foreground are large trees; rather more towards the centre and more behind some houses, whence issue a party in a carriage with two horses, who are addressed by two beggars. In the centre the distance is closed by trees and houses. On the left, in the deep shadows of trees, is a cottage. A very remarkable picture, the composition displaying more taste than usual. The rendering of the light, which falls directly on the centre of the objects in foreground, middle distance, and background, and also silvers the clouds, is particularly fortunate. The portions in shadow are also unusually juicy and clear. Form and size are very pleasing.

Van Slingelandt.—At an open window with the sun shining on it is a maidservant occupied baking something in a vessel, and speaking to a little girl who is about to bake a cake. In point of composition, warmth of tone, and softness of treatment, this belongs to the most attractive pictures of the master.

THE BACK DRAWING-ROOM.

Nicholas Berghem.—On the left are stately rocks receding into the extreme right. In the foreground a piece of water with an ox, a cow, and some sheep being driven through. Behind them a woman on a mule, and other figures on foot. On wood. Solidly executed in the cool blueish tones of his later time.

Jan Wynants.—In the foreground on the right is a nearly dead tree, behind which is a wood. In the centre, in the distance, is a hill. On the left in the middle distance, trees and a village. A horseman on a road, with other figures and animals, are introduced by Lingelbach. Of agreeable composition and careful carrying out.

Adrian van de Velde.—Portrait of a stately man, in a yellowish brown dress, worked with gold, white falling collar and broad-brimmed hat; upon a black horse. Next him a dog. Cows are seen in the landscape, which terminates in hills. The sky is slightly clouded. Signed and dated 1658. Oval. About 8 in. high, 6 in. wide. Very delicately conceived, and of masterly though miniature-like execution in a very harmonious tone.

Van de Capella.—A quiet piece of water animated by two groups of foreshortened ships. One of the finest pictures of the master, approaching Cuyp in solidity of execution and transparency of tone.

David van Tol.—A woman selling fish and vegetables. On the parapet a relievo. Very clever, and quite in the taste of his master, Gerard Dow.

Nicolas Maas.—An old woman seated, taken quite in front, and reading the Bible in her lap through a glass which she holds in her right hand. Before her a spinning-wheel. Upon a chair is a red cushion. Very pleasing in feeling, and approaching Rembrandt in power and glow of colouring.

Willem Mieris.—A woman selling vegetables and game, bargaining with a young man for two partridges, and pointing to a piece of beef in a basket. She is surrounded with cauliflowers, carrots, and small birds. On the window-sill is a relievo of children. On wood. 1 ft. 3 in. high, 1 ft. wide. Executed with his usual finish, but unusually pleasing. The tone is cool.

GREUZE.—A little girl hugging a very small spaniel, with a blue ribbon in her brown hair. The background grey. The childlike feeling is very charming, and the picture carefully executed in a warm and powerful tone.

ADRIAN VAN OSTADE.—1. A lawyer seated in his room, reading papers. Writing materials on a table; a library behind. In point of truth, transparency of sunny effect, and masterly execution, this is a particularly choice specimen of a subject for which the master had a great predilection.

CUYP.—3. Five cows standing on the shores of the river Maas, partly in the water. Dark clouds overshadow the picture, which is illumined by a soft evening light. Of the best time of the painter. Of deep feeling for nature, and solid execution.

ADRIAN VAN OSTADE.—2. An old woman in a blue dress, a white kerchief round her head, standing with her spindle in the door, the upper half of which is open. Above is a rather thinly growing vine. Signed. The head, which is unusually large for him, is carefully finished in a warm brownish tone, and in admirable body.

CLAUDE LORRAINE.—A seaport, with several vessels. On the right, in the middle distance, are hills receding deep into the picture. In front, on the shore, are eight female figures. The sky is slightly clouded; the horizon mild and warm. The broad treatment, and the somewhat gloomy and heavy tone of every part, excepting the sky, identify this large picture as one of the later works of the master.

CUYP.—4. Cows near the river Maas; four standing and two reposing. On the right the river is seen outspread; on the left the commencement of rising ground. A pendant to the former, and resembling it in lighting, and also in solidity of execution. It surpasses it, however, in beauty of composition.

ADRIAN VAN OSTADE.—3. A man with a jug in a door. Pendant to the foregoing, and still superior to it in transparency of golden tone.

VANDYCK.—Bust picture of a man in black dress, with white

M 2

collar. Refined in feeling, and executed in the yellowish luminous flesh-tones of his latest Netherlandish time.

MURILLO.—A roguish, laughing boy, with a hat and feathers, pointing to the spectator. Very animatedly conceived and painted in a solid and glowing tone approaching Rembrandt.

CORNELIS DUSART.—2. A hand organ-player amusing a peasant family with his music. Happily composed and carefully finished in an harmonious but somewhat cooler tone than usual.

PHILIP WOUVERMANS.—A farrier's-shop, at which the driver of a post-waggon and others have halted with their steeds. Among them is a gentleman on a roan horse, the off forefoot of which the farrier is examining, while one of his workmen stands behind him ready to assist. A woman with a child is at the door of the house, near which is a man holding a bay horse. A grey and a bay horse stand together in the foreground, to the left of which are a woman and two travellers reposing. The distant country is a little hilly and hazy. Signed. On wood. 1 ft. 2½ in. high, 1 ft. 6½ in. wide. Although the general effect is somewhat dark, yet the tones are throughout clear, the composition rich and picturesque, and the execution very solid in his second manner.

DINING-ROOM.

WILLEM VAN DE VELDE.—A calm sea. On the right a small ship of war, with a strongly manned boat approaching it from the centre. On the left, foreshortened, another man-of-war. Here and there are various vessels. A few light sunny clouds in the sky. The foremost vessels are of great power, their reflections of singular transparency, and the gradation of aërial perspective into the background of the utmost delicacy. In every respect one of the finest works of the master. About 2 ft. 8 in. high, 3 ft. 8 in. wide.

FERDINAND BOL.—Portrait of a young man in hat and feather, and a red coat, looking at the spectator with folded hands. In front a parapet, the background architecture. True and living in conception, and approaching Rembrandt in power and clearness.

ANOTHER ROOM.

ISAAC VAN OSTADE.—On the left, intersected by the frame, is a house, with a flight of lofty steps leading up to the door. Above, before the door, a figure, and upon the steps two more. Below, in front of the steps, a hunting party resting, among whom a lady in a red dress is conspicuous. Two dogs are also by, with a keeper. On the left is a horseman coming up a hill; in the distance another hill. Very originally composed, and of unusual and almost Rembrandt-like depth of chiaroscuro. In solidity of treatment also this picture approaches the specimen of the master in the late Sir Robert Peel's possession.

ALDERT VAN EVERDINGEN.—An agitated sea, enlivened with sailing vessels and smaller craft. In the distance the shore, with a three-masted vessel lying on it. Gleams of sunshine break the shadow on the waters, and illumine some clouds with a warm light. Even in this unusual subject the great master is recognisable. The tone reminds us of Simon de Vlieger, whom, however, he does not equal in the truthful delineation of the waves.

MICHAEL VAN MUSCHER.—In a room with a high light is a family, with the man looking at himself in the glass. In a further room are two other figures. A very successful picture by this less known master, who in effect and in colouring stands halfway between Peter de Hooghe and Nicolas Maas.

SIMON DE VLIEGER.—View of the river Maas. In front is a strand on which are fishermen. Not far from them are three fishing-boats; further off two vessels of war, each of which is firing a gun. The admirable linear and aërial perspective, the mild glow of the lighting, the transparency of the reflections, the truth of the water, and the solid treatment, all render this picture one of the finest by the master.

LUDOLPH BACKHUYSEN.—A slightly agitated sea, with various vessels, among which a sailing-boat with a broad white flag, in strong foreshortening, is particularly conspicuous. A delicate and picturesque alternation of gleams of light with shadows of clouds varies the surface of the water. An excellent picture of the best time of the master.

JAN WYNANTS.—A large landscape of his late hard and crude time, with which a hunting party introduced by LINGELBACH well corresponds.

B. C. KOEKOEK.—A very meritorious daylight landscape by this popular but very unequal master of the modern Dutch school.

PICTURE BY ARTUS VAN DER NEER,

IN POSSESSION OF LORD SHAFTESBURY, 24, GROSVENOR SQUARE.

This, perhaps the largest existing picture by the master, adorns the dining-room of this nobleman's residence. It represents a Dutch canal, with the houses, some of them of considerable size, on each bank. On all these objects the moon is shedding its peaceful light. In the centre, towards the foreground, is a large boat lying at the shore, on which is seen the well-known monogram of the painter. On the extreme left, at a fence before a house, is a sportsman, offering a dead hare to its inmates ; not far off are two sporting dogs. The other bank of the canal is also variously animated with figures, among others by a man and a child. In the centre of the middle distance is a light bridge. This picture, which belongs to the later time of the master, is of extraordinary effect and power. Notwithstanding the broad and free treatment, it is carefully executed in every part, which is especially evident in the details of the foreground.

PICTURES BELONGING TO DAVENPORT BROMLEY, ESQ.,

32, GROSVENOR STREET.

This gentleman has in the last few years increased his collection by various fortunate acquisitions, which I had the pleasure to see in his London house. To these are also added the fine LEONARDO DA VINCI mentioned in my 'Treasures of Art,' and since then acknowledged as a work of the great master by Rio, in his work on Leonardo da Vinci and his school ; and the Venus by SANDRO BOTTICELLI.

DUCCIO DI BUONINSEGNA.—1. The Crucifixion; a very rich composition, full of the most elevated and animated motives, and showing in every portion the most delicate execution. Considering the extreme rarity of this great Italian painter in the Byzantine style, this is a very important acquisition. From the de Bammeville collection.

2. An Episcopal Saint with two scrolls in his hand, and in robes of gold brocade. Above, in a circle, is a saint. I am decidedly

of opinion that this is a portion of an altar-picture by the same master.

Pesello Peselli.—The Virgin, with the Child held before her by an angel, and grasping with his left hand the little finger of his mother's right hand. Between Mother and Child the head of another angel. Behind the group a wall, with stiff trees seen above it. From the collection of the Earl of Orford.

Giovan Antonio Sogliani.—To this master I am most inclined to attribute a Virgin and Child of great completeness of rendering in every part, especially in the modelling of the forms of the Child. The character of the heads, the style of the folds in the drapery, the combination of colours, are all evidences of the best time of this master.

Sandro Botticelli.—Venus. Full-length figure. A different picture to that mentioned above. Attractive in motive, and of delicate forms.

Antonio Pollajuolo.—A female portrait in profile. From the collection of the late Miss Rogers. My numerous studies since the year 1835 confirm my belief that this is a work by that master. See vol. ii. p. 269.

Jacobo Pacchiarotto.—The Virgin with the Child on her arm, who with his right hand is reaching down a cross. The background landscape. Almost to the knees. The style of elevated feeling, the delicate character of the heads, the very decided forms, and the warm colouring, all indicate this rare master, who is little seen beyond his native city of Siena. The arms of the Medici on the old frame prove it to have been once in the possession of that family.

Ambrogio di Fossano, called Il Borgognone.—An altar-piece. The Virgin and Child on the throne with four angels. On the right St. John the Baptist, on the left St. John the Evangelist, represented aged, as in early art, and with the eagle by his side. In the character of the heads this picture differs, and certainly not advantageously, from most of the works of this master, and is also more slightly treated. In all other respects, however, it agrees so entirely with him that I find it difficult to give any other name to it.

Palma Vecchio.—An allegorical representation. An undraped youth kneeling, and seen in profile, has his hand on the shoulder of a draped girl, who, looking at him, is drawing his attention to a half-length figure appearing in the air. On the left at her feet is Cupid standing, bow in hand, his quiver on the ground. The background a hilly landscape, with warm evening light. This kind of subject was, as is known, first treated by Giorgione, and his influence is distinctly seen in the noble head and golden flesh-tones of the youth. On the other hand, the head of the girl is that of a model from whom Palma Vecchio frequently painted, while her golden-coloured drapery, which covers one of the legs of the youth, and the character of the landscape, are entirely in his customary style. An excellent picture.

ANDREA SCHIAVONE.—The Birth of the Virgin; a rich composition, full of spirited, lively, and graceful motives, and of excellent taste in the draperies. Overcleaning has unfortunately rendered the colours too cold.

PICTURES IN POSSESSION OF LORD WENSLEYDALE,
PARK STREET.

FRANCESCO ALBANI.—The Expulsion of Adam and Eve from Paradise. In the clouds is the Almighty, accompanied by two little angels, and in the act of commanding a larger angel who is descending with a sword. Adam is turning away his head with shame, Eve raising her hands as if in entreaty. Figures about a third life-size. Lord Wensleydale possesses the whole correspondence relative to the production of this picture, which has been also recently published by Gualandi. From this it appears that the painter received the commission for this work in 1647 from one Cesare Leopardi, a friend of art residing at Osimo, a little place not far from Loretto, through the medium of Berlingiero Gessi, the writer, and that it was finished in the beginning of July, 1649. When we reflect that Albani was then in his 71st year we shall share in some degree the admiration which the picture excited among his contemporaries; for though the composition is not very happy, the motives are speaking, the head of Eve pleasing, the flesh part very carefully modelled from nature, and of very warm colouring. The preservation is excellent. I agree with Gualandi that the price of 70 scudi, considering the esteem in which Albani was held, was very small. The last letter from Albani to his patron, dated 9th October, 1649, is very characteristic of the period. The expressions in which he thanks him for his approbation are very cringing, and his compliments exceedingly far fetched.

Barnaba da Modena.—A picture about 2 ft. 3 in. high, 1 ft. 9 in. wide, in four compartments, two and two, each containing a picture.

1. The Coronation of the Virgin, with Christ placing the crown on her head with both hands, according to the manner of Giotto. Around are numerous angels, some supporting the canopy, some adoring, others playing on musical instruments. Five kneeling angels, namely, are seen below, full-length figures, one playing the organ, another the lute, a third the violin, while the fourth is beating the kettle-drums which are suspended on the back of the fifth. The drapery of Christ and the Virgin are strictly Byzantine, with narrow folds executed in gold.

2. The Trinity: the First Person is represented as an old man with a grey beard, the draperies of the same character as in the preceding picture, holding before him the already dead and very meagre figure of Christ upon the cross, in a blue mandorla. At the terminations of the mandorla are the attributes of the four Evangelists, in the following arrangement:—The eagle above on the right; on the left, instead of the angel of St. Matthew, an old bearded man, as frequently seen on the earlier monuments; below, the lion, and on the left the bull; all with large glories. Next the last are the Virgin and St. John the Baptist, in speaking gestures, and of elevated expression.

3. The Virgin enthroned, with the Child upon her lap, draped, and in the act of benediction. Behind her a red curtain with gold pattern, upheld by two beautiful angels. In the golden glory of the Virgin, in capital letters, are the words, " Ave gratia plena." Below, very small, the donor kneeling, with his wife in a red dress, and presented by St. Catherine, who is very beautiful.

4. The Crucifixion, a very rich composition. The dead Christ is conceived in the Byzantine style. Two angels are carrying the soul of the repentant thief, in the form of a little child, to heaven in a cloth; two demons are seizing that of the unrepentant thief out of his mouth. The group of the women and St. John surrounding the fainting Virgin is very fine. At the cross is the

Magdalen; below the cross, in fine action, is a figure seated. The group of the guards consists of four seated and three standing figures. Behind the cross are three priests and six horsemen.

The picture is also accompanied by a predella with the bust-pictures of the twelve apostles.

This work bears the inscription " Barnabas de Mutina, pinxit, 1374." This is very important, as showing that this rare master— whose pictures in the Frankfort and Berlin galleries, inscribed 1368 and 1369, are executed somewhat coarsely in the strict Byzantine manner — was afterwards strongly influenced by the school of Giotto, and evidently by Giusto Padovano. For we find here a similar form of heads, the same pale flesh tones, and the same kind of careful modelling as in the small altarpiece by Giusto Padovano in the collection of His Royal Highness Prince Albert. At the same time this picture shows that he was obviously the teacher of his countryman Tomaso da Modena, as may be proved by a comparison with the signed pictures by the latter, both in Vienna and Prague. The preservation is excellent.

GUIDO RENI.—His well-known Fortuna. The copies of this work are numerous. The transparent colouring and careful finish of this picture, however, incline me to believe it a repetition by his school.

BALTHASAR DENNER ?—To this master are ascribed the portraits of an old man and woman. Judging from the weaker modelling and cold colouring, they appear to me rather the work of his rival SEIBOLD, who is often mistaken for him.

JAN VAN GOYEN.—A small but very pleasing landscape, remarkable for feeling for nature, transparency of tone, and a finish rarely seen in this master.

MR. EDWARD CHENEY'S COLLECTION,
4, AUDLEY SQUARE.

This gentleman belongs to that class of the lovers of art who are guided by a general taste for the beautiful. Although, therefore, pictures constitute the chief contents of his collection, yet delicate specimens of sculpture in metal and ivory, and various ecclesiastical and secular objects, are scattered around. Some drawings by the older masters are also worthy of attention. The pictures were chiefly collected during a residence of several years at Venice, and belong therefore principally to that school. Some Spanish masters, however, are also among them.

TITIAN.—1. A Repose in Egypt. The Virgin, seated on the ground, is holding the Child, who is in lively action, on her lap; his right arm is held by Joseph, who is kneeling before him. The figures are about three-quarters the size of life; the proportions of the picture about $2\frac{1}{2}$ ft. high by $3\frac{1}{2}$ wide. The Virgin is of unusually elevated character for the master; the tone of the whole very harmonious and warm. Joseph especially is of a glowing colour which recalls Giorgione. The effect of the landscape, with a perfectly luminous horizon, is excellent. The picture is obviously of the middle period of the master.

ANDREA SCHIAVONE.—7. Seven small pictures of oval form, formerly the decoration of a harpsichord. The centre piece represents Apollo surrounded with a glory, and holding an arrow in his hand. In the smaller pictures are eleven more of the gods, kneeling and sitting. These little specimens are spiritedly composed, and lightly and broadly executed in a warm tone of singular juiciness and depth.

BONIFAZIO.—The Destruction of Pharaoh, and Moses striking the Rock—a sketch of rare animation of motives, and great juiciness of golden tone.

TINTORETTO.—1. Portrait of a Procurator of St. Mark, half-length, of broad and masterly execution, in the reddish golden tone which is peculiar to him.

ANDREA SCHIAVONE.—8. The Exposure of the Infant Moses; of very animated, and in some respects graceful motives, showing the painter's study of Parmigianino.

GUARDI.—1 and 2. Two pretty views of Venice, one of them with a balloon.

PIETRO LONGHI.—A party in a room. A spirited sketch by this painter, who is little known out of Venice, and who might be appropriately termed the Venetian Watteau. Many of his pictures express a state of society which reminds one of Goldoni's comedies.

LICINIO REGILLO, called IL PORDENONE.—Copy of the Belvedere Apollo, to the knees; of great warmth of tone, but has suffered injury.

TITIAN.—2. Portrait of an aged Doge in his robes of office. Although this picture is still attractive in point of truth and animation of conception, yet over-cleaning has destroyed the charm of the colouring.

3. Portrait of a Venetian General, in armour, decorated with gold, almost to the knees; of animated conception and glowing colouring. The hardness of the forms, especially of the eyelids, is doubtless owing to restoration.

PARIS BORDONE.—Portrait of a stately lady, of considerable *embonpoint*, in a purple dress. Judging from conception and treatment, I am inclined rather to attribute this to PAUL VERONESE.

TINTORETTO.—2. Portrait of a Venetian Admiral in armour. The background a view of the sea. To the knees. Very spiritedly composed, and executed in a tone of flesh unusually pale for him.

GENTILE BELLINI.—Portrait of a Doge in his robes of office, the surface being gilt, and the folds painted in upon them with brown lake. The character of the individual is here seized with great decision. The tone of the flesh is, however, pale.

BONIFAZIO.—2. The Virgin nursing the Child; at the sides two adoring angels. Particularly beautiful and graceful in motives, and not inferior to Titian in power of colour.

A picture attributed to GIOVANNI BELLINI appears to me too weak for him, especially in the drawing of the eyes and hands, and has also suffered.

ANDREA SCHIAVONE.—9, 10, and 11. A small picture in three compartments. In the centre the Sacrifice of Isaac, with Judith, a noble figure, on one side, and David on the other. Of singular power and harmony of colouring.

TIEPOLO.—1. Christ sleeping in the storm, with the frightened disciples awakening him. Almost too dramatically conceived, and of an unusual power of colouring for the painter.

ANDREA SCHIAVONE.—12. A landscape with a youthful figure, probably meant for Cupid, shooting at some girls. A charming little picture.

BONIFAZIO.—3. The Baptism of Christ, with three adoring angels. Companion to the former, and not less charming.

THE LIBRARY.

ZURBARAN.—1. A monk praying, in white dress of his order, before him a book and a skull. Of elevated feeling and very careful execution.

COLVIN SMITH.—Portrait of Sir Walter Scott, painted 1816. The trueheartedness of the expression is very animated.

MATEO CEREZO.—The Virgin holding the Child on her lap, who is stretching out his hand to the adoring Joseph. Form and colouring show the successful study of Vandyck—the hands especially indicate his influence. From the collection of Louis Philippe.

TITIAN.—4. Christ before Pilate, with two other figures. To the knees. All betokens the later time of the master. The forms are almost too powerful, the colouring less transparent, and the treatment in its breadth approaching a decorative character.

TINTORETTO.—3. Three saints; one of his numerous slight and decorative works.

LEANDRO BASSANO.—1. Portrait of a Dominican. Of great animation.

ZURBARAN.—2. A monk with a crucifix. Companion to the above, and of similar merit.

TIEPOLO.—20. A collection of sketches for ceilings (nineteen in number), executed for churches in Venice, and among others for that of the church of the Jesuits. Some of them very spirited.

A cabinet contains many little gems of art. I was especially struck with a small antique head in marble, of most attractive expression and good workmanship; also with a small bust of Cromwell in touchstone. Among various medals in bronze I remarked one of a knight with a broadly turned-up hat, with the inscription 1527; animated in conception and of excellent workmanship. Next in order I may mention another smaller medal with a man in a cap; and a third, the heads of which are, singular to say, represented in a three-quarter view. These are very remarkable works.

Another cabinet close by displays good bronzes of the Cinquecento time:—a Cupid bound; a female figure with that of a man under her feet, quite in the style of John of Bologna; and two of those door-knockers from Venetian palaces on which true art has so energetically set her seal. The one with Neptune in the centre, and two writhing dolphins at his side, is as happily conceived as it is capitally executed. The same may be said of another from the Grimani Palace, formed of two dolphins only.

I may also mention the following objects in the same cabinet :— A Crucifix of considerable size, of the 14th century, with a very rich foot, in the most elegant Italian Gothic. The figure of the Christ is however weak. The whole upper half of the Crucifix never originally belonged to it.

A very graceful little iron casket, richly and delicately inlaid with gold.

A metal dish of oriental workmanship, very tastefully ornamented with enamels and inlaid work.

A portion of an ivory relievo of the 14th century, representing the Virgin and Child and two angels, and showing the decided influence of the school of Giovanni Pisani.

A censer of the 14th century; a ciborium of the 15th: both Italian, and both of great elegance of form.

A statuette of St. Gregory from the church of that saint at Venice. This is a remarkable example of painted and partially gilt Italian sculpture. On his drapery are paintings of saints. At the sides are four black little figures of monks receiving two books from St. Gregory.

Among various specimens of majolica, I was particularly struck by one with the Visitation, and a plate with Cupid shooting. Both these subjects are of great beauty.

Mr. Cheney also favoured me with the sight of two seals of cardinals, which decidedly belong to the most remarkable things of this kind. Both have the form of a mandorla, or almond-shaped glory. The one, according to the inscription, is that of Cardinal Ippolito de' Medici. In the centre is the Adoration with six shepherds ; and also, by a strange symbolical conception, St. Lawrence in the centre, with St. Peter and St. Paul at his side. The Almighty appears above. Below are the arms of the Medici, over which are two angels holding the Cardinal's cap. As the gridiron of St. Lawrence and other portions are failing, I entirely agree with Mr. Cheney that this is the model of the metal coat-of-arms now in the collection of the Grand Duke of Tuscany, and there erroneously assigned to Benvenuto Cellini, for it breathes altogether the feeling of Raphael's time, and is executed with the utmost spirit and care.

DINING-ROOM.

MORETTO (?).—Portrait of an old and very bald man, in black dress with white collar. A Maltese cross hangs by a ribbon very low on his chest. His right hand rests on a book, in the left he holds a glove. The background is brown. Almost to the knees. Very animated in conception, the style of which, as also the yellowish warm and transparent tone, indicate rather Moretto's scholar, GIOVANNI BATTISTA MORONI.

LEANDRO BASSANO.—2. Portrait of an old man with white collar. Both hands on the arms of the chair in which he is seated. Next him a table on which is a book. The background is grey. Almost to the knees. Animatedly conceived, and spiritedly and broadly though carefully executed in a reddish gold tone.

FRANCESCO DOMENICI.—His own portrait, much larger than life. The hair hangs in rich quantity low on each side of the head, which is covered with a black cap : his dress is of a dark purple red, with large full sleeves of a yellow colour. On the left, in the background, is the marble statue of a Venus, without head and one arm, in a niche ; on the right a view of buildings. Half-length figure. In a circle, in the centre of which is a dog, is the following inscription, " Franc. Domenic se pinxit 1530." The fine features of the face are grandly conceived in the taste of Giorgione ; also the warm glow of the colour and the keeping show a successful aim at the imitation of that master. The hands only, which hold some object, are empty in form, and of weak drawing.

FRANCESCO BASSANO.—Portrait of an old man in black dress, his right hand on a table covered with a purple cloth ; next him, on the left, a setter dog. The background dark. Almost to the knees. The animated conception is here combined with a broad and careful execution, in a cool reddish but transparent tone.

TINTORETTO.—4. A Procurator of St. Mark, seated, in his crimson robes. Through the window is seen a landscape with a piece of water and a tower. The head is cleverly executed in a clear somewhat reddish golden tone ; the hands, as is often the case with this master, are somewhat slightly treated.

COLLECTION OF REV. MR. CHAUNCEY HARE TOWNSHEND.

I feel it to be especially my duty to draw the attention of English lovers of art to the collection of Mr. Townshend, which not only contains many remarkable specimens both of the earlier and modern English school, but is also interspersed with admirable works by the best painters of Belgium, Holland, Germany, and Switzerland, which are comparatively seldom met with in England. These have a most satisfactory effect in the light and handsome apartments in which they are placed.

DINING-ROOM.

COLLINS.—A small landscape. Very attractive in feeling, and in the cool harmony of tone.

VERBOEKHOVEN.— 1. An ass and two sheep in a plain. The truth of the animals, and the admirable aërial perspective, place this little picture among the best by this unequal master. Signed.

MÜLLER.—A little girl, with a sick lamb, is seated by a well; two goats reposing by her. The background a hilly distance. Signed and dated 1835. The feeling in the girl is very pleasing; the animals are true to nature; the lighting is happy; the colouring clear, and the treatment careful, and of fine impasto.

ROTHMANN.—The Bay of Aulis: a small repetition of the large picture in the Pinacothek of modern art at Munich. Few painters have rendered this classic scenery so suggestive of thought to every instructed mind with such poetic feeling as Rothmann. The effect of this small picture, which is represented in the warmest lighting, is of great beauty. On the other hand, in the attempt to render the style of historical landscape, the painter has here as elsewhere treated the trees in a too general and conventional manner.

SCHELFHOUT.—A winter landscape, with a mill, and a frozen canal, animated with skaters. Signed and dated 1846. This picture is a laudable specimen of that picturesqueness of conception, truth of every part, and careful execution, which, in my opinion, place this already aged painter at the head of the modern Dutch school.

VERBOEKHOVEN.—2. An Inn, with a woman giving drink

to a traveller ; and with a horseman on a grey horse, a brown cow feeding, and hens and chickens. Signed and dated 1845. Tastefully composed ; of decided lighting, and uncommon delicacy of carrying out.

DANBY. — "The Upas-tree : " a picture of very large proportions. Monstrous rocks shut in the Valley of Death, in the midst of which stands the fatal tree, of moderate size ; its bare stem, with a pine-like head, spreading poison in the atmosphere. Around are numerous skeletons, and other victims in various stages of corruption : one living man is covering his face with his hands in despair at his approaching fate : a bird infected by the air is falling dead. This picture combines a gloomily poetic conception of this frightful subject with a very careful execution of detail, but has much darkened on account of defective technical treatment ; in a few years more it will hardly be visible.

HOGUET.—A landscape, in which a windmill and a cornrick are most conspicuous. Signed. This is superior to many pictures by this Berlin painter in softness and transparency of colouring, and excellence of keeping.

JOHANN KIRNER (born in Baden, but belonging to the Munich school).—A scene from the Roman Revolution of 1848 ; a troop of boys, with a girl among them, are shouting for Pius IX. and the Constitution. Signed and dated 1848. Animated and interesting in motives and heads, but the landscape background weak.

CHRISTIAN MORGENSTERN (a native of Hamburgh, but also of the Munich school).—A plain with water : alps in the background. Signed and dated 1847. True in conception, of great effect of lighting, and carefully executed.

ZWENGAUER.—A still, clear lake with a boat, and the warmest evening light reflected in it   These are the favourite subjects of this artist, who resides at Schleissheim near Munich. The peaceful feeling of a fine summer's evening is most happily expressed ; the effect is clear and true, and the execution conscientious.

VAN HOVE.— A maidservant, in a front room, listening to a domestic concert between a gentleman and lady in a back apartment. Like most specimens of this favourite Dutch painter, this picture is skilfully treated in the taste of Peter de Hooghe. The three figures, however, are insufficient to give interest to the large size of the work.

STANFIELD.— A rocky sea-coast with a town. In front a vessel on the rough water ; the sun is just breaking through clouds. In point of attractiveness of composition, exemplary keeping, and well-felt and careful execution, this picture belongs to the most successful specimens of this eminent painter.

EDWARD HILDEBRANDT. — Rainy weather. A grey and a black horse indistinctly reflected in a piece of still water with willows. Signed and dated 1848. Simple as this subject is, the truth of observation and delicacy of keeping with which it is carried out render it very attractive.

EDWARD SCHLEICH.—A landscape, taken from the scenery around Munich, where the painter resides. The time is dawn, with stags returning to a wood. Signed. This picture shows great feeling for nature and truth of effect ; the distance alone is somewhat heavy in tone.

NEUREUTHER.—I was delighted to find here a rich water-colour drawing by this artist, whose masterly etchings are so well known to all friends of art. The subject is the chief scene from Baron Zedlitz's poem of ' *Das Wald Fräulein*,' treated in his spirited and original manner. Signed.

In a light corridor, decorated with fine flowers, which leads from the dining-room, are placed the following pictures :—

MULREADY.—A richly wooded landscape, with a piece of still and transparent water ; on the shore an angler ; to the right is a view over a sunny distance. This picture, about 1 ft. 6 in. high, by 1 ft. 11 in. wide, has a singular charm. The whole is imbued with the most refined feeling for nature, and notwithstanding the close individuality of detail, viz. in the trees, the keeping is admirably preserved, and the colour equally powerful, true, and transparent.

NICAISE DE KEYSER.—An old man engaged in study, of good motive and effect of light, but rather too decorative in treatment for this small scale of size.

ALBERT ZIMMERMANN (a native of Dresden, but resident in Munich).—An extensive plain with alps in the distance. The true freshness of morning, and the delicate aërial perspective, render this a particularly attractive specimen of the master.

DRAWING-ROOM.

Claude Lorraine.—On the right are large trees, with goats and sheep feeding near; in the centre are two shepherds, one of them seated and blowing a pipe, the other standing; on the left three cows, and a distance with lofty hills. A pleasing composition with a marvellously luminous atmosphere. The juicy colouring and the careful details of the execution assign this to the early period of the master. This picture, which is dark in itself, loses much of its effect by the unfavourable place it occupies·

Raphael (?). — An old repetition of the *Belle Jardinière*, painted on wood, and the size of the original in the Louvre. Although of very careful execution, the following reasons show it to be not only not by the great master himself, but rather a copy by some excellent Netherlandish painter. The forms of the children are too full, at the same time empty and deficient in the higher refinement of feeling; the tone of the flesh is in general too cold, assuming a rosy tint in the cheeks, and a too decided bluish colour in the shadows. The same cold tone predominates in the landscape, in which are seen those obelisks and pyramids which those Netherlandish painters who imitated the Italian forms of art first introduced. Finally, we here observe that smooth and melting treatment which is characteristic of the Netherlanders of the 16th century. In spite of all these circumstances, however, the picture is very attractive.

Gonzales Coques.—To this master I am inclined to attribute the portraits of Charles I. and Queen Henrietta Maria, who is handing him a wreath of laurel. The figures are obviously taken from portraits by Vandyck, and are about half the size of life; the colouring is clear, the execution soft and delicate.

Solomon Ruysdael. — View of a Dutch canal. A good specimen of this master, whose works are attractive for their true feeling for nature.

Willem van de Velde.—In the foreground a sea-coast, with a boat with two men, and a larger fishing-boat with a sail lighted by the sun and reflected in the water. Further, in the distance, is a large vessel. A charming variety of effect is here produced by the shifting sunbeams and shadows of clouds. Very carefully painted on wood.

N 2

ADRIAN VAN DE VELDE.—A rocky landscape with huntsmen. This rather dark picture, of an unusually tall form, is of the later period of the master, and very attractive.

PALAMEDES PALAMEDESS.—A courtyard with many figures, among which a trumpeter in the act of blowing his instrument, and a woman with a child on her arm, are conspicuous. For picturesque composition and careful carrying out, this is a good specimen of the painter.

TENIERS.—A large landscape, with tall rocks on the right, and a shepherd, a bagpipe-player, two cows, eight sheep, and two pigs, on the left at the foot of some wooded rising ground ; in the centre a river. The beautiful management of the light, the general transparency, and the unusual carefulness of execution in so large a landscape by the master, render this an admirable picture.

ADRIAN OSTADE.—Three peasants in an interior ; one of them asleep. In tone of colour and softness of touch this pretty picture recalls Adrian Brouwer.

Finally, I may mention the wooden frame of a mirror, richly carved with grapes, poppies, laurel, ivy, and maize, of masterly execution. This is a splendid example of GIBBONS, who executed similar works in Hampton Court Palace.

STAIRCASE.

RUBENS.—The Triumph of Saul, who is seen in a car in the middle distance ; more in the foreground is David with the head of Goliah ; behind are trophies of arms and weapons of the time of the painter, and the virgins praising David ; on the right, in the foreground, is a woman with a child, quite in the same motive as the group in the Elevation of the Cross in the cathedral at Antwerp. This sketch, which is painted on wood, about 2 ft. 4 in. high, by 3 ft. wide, is one of the most spirited specimens of the master. Judging from the style of representation and from the character of the spirited horses, I should adjudge it to the period of the celebrated fight with the Amazons in the Gallery at Munich.

CALAME.—An Alpine scene with a deep ravine ; mountains covered with snow on the right, and with a bold outline of rock on the left, are bathed in the glow of the evening sun ; in front is a grand tree. Of great transparency of colouring, carefulness of execution, and of splendid effect.

THE LIBRARY.

CARLO DOLCE.—The Virgin holding the standing Child. This appears to be a careful and genuine picture, but it hangs too high and in too dark a place for any positive opinion.

PICTURES BELONGING TO EARL STANHOPE.

VELASQUEZ.—Portrait of a stately man in black dress, with black hair and beard. The background dark. More than half-length. The conception exhibits in a conspicuous degree the *grandezza* peculiar to Velasquez, and the execution, in a warm brown tone, like that of his own portrait in the Uffizj at Florence and in Bridgewater House, is broad, marrowy, and spirited. This portrait has been by some erroneously supposed to be that of the Count-Duke Olivarez; the features of that individual, however, were very different, and far plainer and coarser than those here represented. Formerly in the collection of Count Lecchi at Brescia, and purchased thence by Lord Stanhope—then Lord Mahon—in 1846.

TITIAN.—Portrait of Philip II. of Spain in his younger days. The great refinement of conception, bright golden tone, equality and care of execution, and admirable preservation, render this one of the best of the portraits of this monarch by Titian. Bought by Lord Mahon in 1844 at the sale of Mr. Harman's collection.

These two pictures hang as companions in the library of Lord Stanhope's town residence.

PICTURES BELONGING TO G. CORNWALL LEGH, ESQ.,
EATON PLACE.

The majority of these pictures belong to the Italian school. As time did not permit me to take my notes in presence of the pictures, this description necessarily lacks that correctness which it is always my desire to attain.

BERNARDINO LUINI.—The Virgin and Child, with another person. The Child is standing before the mother. A picture of agreeable composition and animated heads, of careful finish and good preservation.

Jacopo Pacchiarotto.—The Virgin and Child, and other figures. A genuine and attractive picture by this master, who is seldom seen out of his native city Siena.

Francesco Francia.—A female saint in a landscape. Whole-length figure on a small scale. Graceful in motive, and elevated in expression, and of tasteful drapery and powerful colouring.

Giacomo Francia (son of the foregoing).—A Holy Family. Happily composed, pleasing in the heads, of delicate tone of colour, and carefully executed.

Giulio Francia.—A Holy Family. Judging from the little attractiveness of the heads, and the coldness of the colouring, I am inclined to consider this the work of the less-gifted nephew of Francesco Francia.

Lorenzo Costa.—The Annunciation. A miniature picture in oil, of very agreeable motives, warm colouring, and delicate rendering of the rich architecture and landscape background.

Raphael (?).—The Virgin and Child. Decidedly not by Raphael, but by some less-gifted scholar of Perugino. Perhaps an earlier and weaker work by Spagna.

Luca Longhi.—St. Catherine. Very lovely and graceful, but of the time when this chief painter of Ravenna had become feebler both in feeling and colouring.

Timoteo della Vite.—Christ on the Mount of Olives. A miniature of unusual size and great beauty, executed on parchment. Of elevated invention, excellent drawing, and very careful but not slavish execution.

Salvator Rosa.—A small landscape. A piece of still water in the foreground, with delicately executed figures. On the sides and behind are trees, and a wall of rock. The execution is carried very far, though somewhat uniform in the foliage.

The following pictures of the Dutch school were striking:—

Teniers.—A landscape, with some figures. Genuine, but not of high merit.

Philip Wouvermans.—Horsemen in an open landscape. A beautiful picture, of powerful colouring.

Minderhout Hobbema (?).—A landscape signed with the name of this painter, with powerful trees and a blueish distance.

It appears to me to be rather a dark but genuine picture by RUYSDAEL.

KAREL DUJARDIN.—Portrait of William of Orange, called the Silent, with another figure on horseback. This picture hangs so unfavourably, that I should not have mentioned it, but that it appears to me a good work. If really by Karel Dujardin, which appears to me a little doubtful, it cannot represent the above-named Prince, who was murdered in 1584, while Karel Dujardin was only born in 1635.

PICTURES BELONGING TO WILLIAM MARSHALL, ESQ., 85, EATON SQUARE.

Although small in number, the choice of these pictures evinces a very correct taste in art.

SITTING-ROOM.

CLAUDE LORRAINE.—A small picture of almost quadrangular form, with an expanse of water, and a bridge. Too dry and sunken in condition to admit of a more decided opinion.

F. R. LEE.—A landscape, in which an avenue, foreshortened, is a principal feature. In the foreground are a grey and two brown horses. Of great truth of form and colour, admirable aërial perspective, and careful finish.

Portrait of a young man with a flower in his hand. In feeling and execution this shows much affinity to Holbein; it is however by another hand unknown to me.

DINING-ROOM.

MURILLO.—His own portrait, in a black dress, and with hands. This picture, with which I was well acquainted in the Standish collection, formerly in the Louvre, is animated in conception, and equable, solid, and masterly in carrying out. It is remarkable how much more his features express the realistic, rather than the religious and sentimental side of his genius.

Some pictures of the Dutch school in this room look promising, but hang too high to be justly estimated.

FRONT DRAWING-ROOM.

Sir Augustus Calcott.—The Tomb of Cicero, with an extended view over the sea. This picture is as happy in the choice of the point of view, as it is delicate in gradation and careful in execution.

Collins.—1. Three children by some water. Very naïve in feeling and of good keeping.

2. Three children afraid of a beggar, who is seated before them. One of the finest works by this painter, who seldom attained such force and transparency. Here all surrounding portions—a house, a wooden paling, and a wood—display the same equable finish.

3 and 4. These are also good specimens of the master; so that I could mention no other collection in which he may be studied so favourably.

Turner.—A large picture, belonging to those examples of his later time which in my brief summary of the characteristics of that marvellous painter I have denominated as souls of pictures without bodies. In order to admire such as these, the spectator must have been led by the magician step by step to this extreme. A fresh and unprepared eye, however, can never relish them.

The head of a female saint, apparently St. Catherine, shows, in the style of refined expression and tenderness of colour, much affinity to Correggio.

BACK DRAWING-ROOM.

Sir David Wilkie.—The well-known picture of Napoleon and Pope Pius VII., which I saw in the studio of the painter in 1835. Of the small number of historical pictures by this master, this is by far the most important. The subject, it is true, is very difficult to treat as a picture. At the same time he has quite succeeded in bringing forward the contrast between the quiet firmness of the Pope, against which even the iron will of so terrible a despot can prevail nothing. I was glad to find that the colours had not changed, which is a result seldom found in a modern picture.

Sir Charles Eastlake.—Two sisters, a blonde and a brunette. The former, whose figure displays great beauty of form, holding a book. The whole is imbued with refined and elevated feeling, the tone of colour very happy, and the execution thoroughly conscientious.

Sir Augustus Calcott.—A young girl, her head in chiaroscuro. Of pleasing feeling, graceful motive, and skilful composition.

━━━━━━━━━

PICTURES AND OBJECTS OF ART BELONGING TO
WILLIAM RUSSELL, ESQ.,

38, Chesham Place.

In addition to a collection of pictures of the earlier as well as of the modern English school, Mr. Russell possesses a numerous collection of drawings of various periods and schools. He has also gathered together the richest collection existing of those coloured woodcuts known to connoisseurs as "*chiaroscuros.*"

I proceed first to notice those pictures and drawings which appeared to me the most remarkable, in the order they occupy in the different rooms.

DRAWING-ROOM.

Rubens.—The Conversion of St. Paul. This is altogether a different composition from that known by Bolswert's engraving,—the picture of which is in the possession of Mr. Miles, of Leigh Court,—and one of less fortunate arrangement. It is however a very spirited sketch.

Giorgio Vasari.—A very careful and transparently coloured repetition of the picture of the Italian poets, Dante, Petrarch, and Boccaccio, G. Cavalcanti, Ficino, and Poliziano, at Florence, on a smaller scale.

Vandyck.—St. Rock entreating the assistance of Christ for the figures smitten with the plague, who are seen at the lower part of the sketch. Above is the Saviour descending at his prayer. Very spirited.

Bartolommeo Schidone.—Cupid seated on the ground. Of animated conception, and of powerful and clear colouring.

Sir Edwin Landseer.—Portrait of a brown dog, with a white hare, some ptarmigan, and a black-cock dead beside him. The

dog is very fine and of the utmost animation, and the white fur of
the hare is admirably given. The same may be said of the
plumage of the birds.

ANDREA SCHIAVONE.—The Judgment of Paris. The motive
is unusually graceful. The full forms of the goddesses are, however, rather terrestrial. The picture is very attractive for its
golden colouring and careful execution.

PIETRO FRANCESCO MOLA.—Landscape with Hagar and Ishmael in the Desert, the angel standing by. The figures are particularly warm and powerful in colour for him. The darkening of
the poetic landscape has however sacrificed some of its charm.

THE LIBRARY.

STOTHARD.—I was greatly interested in examining seven pictures in chiaroscuro, by this inventive and spirited painter, distributed partly in this room and on the staircase. The figures are
half the size of life, and illustrate Froissart's and Monstrelet's
chronicles of the wars of the English and French in the 14th and
15th centuries. These are all of great vivacity, and some so happily composed that it would well answer to bring them before the
public in the form of lithographs or woodcuts.

JOACHIM PATENIER.—The Virgin giving the breast to the
Infant Christ. She is seated in a landscape with pointed rocks
and a view of the sea. An admirable work of the latest and best
time of the master. The head of the Virgin is of rare tenderness;
the Child also of freer action than usual, and of pretty and full
forms.

LUCAS DE HEERE (?).—One of the most delicate specimens of
those pictures of graceful young girls, of the tenderest execution,
but of a cool scale of colour, which occasionally occur under the
name of this master. The costume, however, which belongs to
about the middle of the 16th century, shows that the picture could
not have been executed by a master not born until 1534. The
girl is represented holding a book with miniatures in her hand.
Next her stands a covered cup. The background is green.

FRANCESCO DOMENICI.—The same portrait which I saw and
have described in the possession of Mr. Edward Cheney. Its
unfavourable position between two windows allowed me to form
no correct estimate of its merits.

DRAWINGS.

CORREGGIO.—1. The Virgin holding the Child with both arms. In red chalk. As refined in feeling as it is soft and broad in execution. From the collection of Richard Cosway.

2. An angel, with an original and happy turn of the head, but rather too full in the forms. Executed with brush and chalk in a warm and delicate tone.

RAPHAEL.—1. The group of the Pope borne in a litter, which occurs in the fresco of the Heliodorus in the Vatican. A slight but free drawing in black chalk, the draperies in red chalk. Although, from the fact of this drawing being squared, it appears to have been intended to be copied on a larger scale, yet certain variations from the fresco, such as the introduction of a bishop and a boy, show that it was an earlier and unexecuted sketch.

David severing the head of Goliah: a composition well known by Marc Antonio's engraving. This large drawing, which is carefully executed in bistre, heightened with white, is more probably by GIULIO ROMANO.

MICHAEL ANGELO.—An undraped male figure, apparently intended as a canon of proportion, very broadly and spiritedly drawn with the pen.

RAPHAEL.—2. The Virgin with the Child and St. Elizabeth, purporting to be a fragment of the cartoon of the well-known Holy Family in Naples, executed by the master for Leonello da Carpi. The head of the Virgin is certainly very spirited, and the whole drawing of broad and masterly execution in black chalk; at the same time the cartoon, as well as the picture of this Holy Family, both a portion of the Farnese inheritance, is known to be preserved in the Museo Borbonico at Naples. As both these cartoons have suffered, and as I have not seen the one in Naples for sixteen years, I refrain from any opinion.

3. Lucretia about to stab herself. Essentially the same composition as that engraved by Marc Antonio, but with the head very different. About one and a half times as large as the engraving. Originally, as the left arm evidences, admirably drawn in black chalk, but since gone over with the pen by an inferior hand.

VANDYCK.—1. Samson and Dalilah. Broad and masterly,

and at the same time very carefully drawn in sepia, with the colours of the draperies indicated in broken tones.

A male portrait with black cap. In black chalk. Judging from the style of feeling, I am disposed to assign this to FRANCESCO FRANCIA.

A female saint, with a palm-branch in her right hand, and a book in her left. On blue paper. The lights given with delicate strokes of white, and the shadows in dark blue. The character of the noble head, the graceful motive, the tastefulness of the drapery, and the style of masterly treatment, are most indicative of FRA FILIPPO LIPPI.

SIR DAVID WILKIE.—Study of the head of Columbus for his well-known picture. Very interesting.

JAN VAN HUYSUM.—Several mounted sheets of a series, containing 160 drawings of flowers and fruit, preserved in a portfolio. Executed in water-colours, with a refined feeling for the picturesque, and uncommon vigour, and in very bright colours.

GREUZE.—A mother and two boys, the latter quarrelling for a spoonful of porridge. The conception is very animated, the lighting sunny, and the execution in Indian ink fresh and light.

SIR JOSHUA REYNOLDS.—Una kneeling by the Lion. In sepia. The head of Una is very tender; the rest, and especially the landscape background, very broadly treated. Drawings by this master are very scarce.

VANDYCK.—2. Queen Henrietta Maria, with her child on her lap. A slight but very clever study for the portrait. In black and red chalk.

ALBERT DURER.—A pretty woman, with a very elaborate head-dress. Slightly and spiritedly drawn with the brush in Indian ink, with tender indications of the colours. With the monogram, and the date 1500 in the master's handwriting, and the following words:—"Ein . . . . . as man zur Kirchen goat." I could not decipher the failing words.

HANS HOLBEIN.—The Ascension. A rich composition for a painted window, enclosed in a tracery of late Gothic taste. Executed with a broad pen, and slightly washed in Indian ink. On the border are festoons of fruit. Although only a tracing of the original drawing, it is very important as a specimen of Holbein. The free, but admirably balanced composition—the intellectual heads—the beautiful motives and pure taste of the draperies, show him to have reached the highest pinnacle of the developed art of the cinquecento.

REMBRANDT.—An undraped figure reposing. Signed. Very spiritedly drawn in bistre.

NICHOLAS POUSSIN.—1. Christ giving the Keys to Peter. An admirable study in sepia for the well-known picture in the Louvre.

Death of Germanicus. An excellent drawing in bistre for the well-known picture.

Besides these Mr. Russell possesses a large number of drawings in portfolios, which unfortunately I had no time to inspect.

Nor do the limits of this work allow me space for the description of the different specimens of woodcuts called *chiaroscuros*. I must therefore content myself with stating that I here saw various impressions of the rarest Italian works of this class, by HUGO DA CARPI, ANDREANI, BOLDRINI, CORIOLANO, GHANDRINI, I. N. DA VICENZA, and A. DA TRENTO. The same may be said of the Germans—ALBERT DURER and others.

Finally I may remark that both the Library and the Dining-room contain pictures of great excellence. In the last-named room is an admirable painting of a dead lion, by SIR EDWIN LANDSEER. Here also I had not the time to take the necessary notes.

OBJECTS OF ART IN THE HOUSE OF A. J. BERESFORD HOPE, ESQ.,

1, CONNAUGHT PLACE.

Mr. Beresford Hope belongs to that yet limited number of collectors in England whose taste for art embraces a very universal standard. At the same time this gentleman is especially interested in ecclesiastical art, which he has himself promoted by employing Mr. Dyce to execute frescoes in the new church in Margaret Street, London. The mediæval objects of art collected with this tendency are kept in a small apartment which has the appearance of a chapel, being partly disposed on the walls and partly under a glass case on a table. I take the pictures, however, first in order.

EARLY GERMAN, TOWARDS 1400.—Small altarpiece with wings. In the centre, above, under a Gothic canopy, are Christ and the Virgin; below, Christ supported by angels, but here represented alive. On each side are four saints. On the wings, in two rows, above, are ten saints; below, the four Latin Fathers. On the outer side, above, the Adoration of the Kings; below, numerous saints. Upon a projection, two saints within, and the Annunciation without. A gold ground. This is the most delicate and beautiful specimen of a miniature in tempera executed on wood I have yet seen of early German art of this period. The animated and already individual heads express a fine feeling, the execution is very tender, and the deep brown tone of the whole shows the use of the amber varnish.

JAN VAN EYCK.—The Virgin standing, and holding the Child on her arm. She is dressed in a scarlet mantle, and inclines her head to the Child, whose action seems as if he was going to embrace her. The background is formed of a Gothic chapel of rich architecture, and decorated with sculpture. Above is the inscription, " Domus Dei est, et porta cœli;" below, " Ipsa est quam preparavit Domus filio Dni (short for Domini) mei." On wood. 1 ft. 8¾ in. high, 11 in. wide. This admirably preserved picture, which I had already seen in the collection of the King of Holland, displays in full measure the solidity of execution of this master. At the same time there is every evidence of its being an early picture by him. The folds of the drapery still retain that purity of taste which he acquired from his master and brother Hubert van Eyck, and which he afterwards exchanged for sharp and arbitrary breaks; while the unskilfully foreshortened mouth, and the too large nose of the Virgin, show his own still deficient practice.

SCHOOL OF FRA FILIPPO LIPPI.—The Adoration of the Kings. A rich composition, in the form of a long and lofty predella. The forms are very animated, the heads delicate, while the over-long and twisted neck of the kneeling king is as unaccountable as it is objectionable.

I proceed next to the sculpture.

A large altarpiece with wings, carved in wood, from a church at Ypres, in Belgium, the Crucifixion in the centre, with the events before and after it represented in other compartments, with

rich Gothic accessories.   This is the work of a very able master
of the end of the 15th century.   The motives are speaking, the
forms slender, the drapery of good taste.   Considerable portions
of the original over-painting are preserved.

A crucifix in wood, with some pretty angels around.   This was
executed between 1530-40, and displays elevated feeling, good
drawing, and excellent execution.

Among the ecclesiastical utensils and other small objects of art
I noticed the following :—

The pedestal of a candelabrum in the Romanesque style, which,
judging from the pure and simple form, cannot be assigned to a
period later than the year 1000.

Two bishops' croziers of brass gilt, and with enamels, are interesting specimens of the 12th century, and, I believe, of German
workmanship.   In the one the fight of the archangel Michael with
the dragon is represented.

A graceful crozier of Italian Gothic taste, of about 1400, in
which pictures of the 16th century are inserted.

A censer of beautiful form, and very tasteful Romanesque
decorations in bronze gilt, and with enamels, which, however, have
in great part fallen out.

Some Russian casts in metal, in the form of triptychs, of very
flat relief and of blunt forms, the grounds in enamel, are remarkable for various representations of early Byzantine tradition.
One of them, with St. Nicholas, on a wing, might, as respects form
of art and character of writing, belong to the 15th century.

In another room, in two glass cases, are kept many little articles
remarkable for art or beauty of material.   By far the most
important is a ewer of sardonyx, mounted in gold enamelled, and
enriched with precious stones.   A stately dragon, harnessed by
Cupid, forms the handle.   The foot is of particular elegance.
Taste and workmanship agree so entirely with authentic examples of BENVENUTO CELLINI, that I cannot hesitate to ascribe
this object to him.   It formed a part of the crown jewels of
France before the first revolution, and was fully described in the
inventory made by decree of the National Assembly in 1791.
No. 410.

DRAWING-ROOM.

SCHOOL OF TITIAN.—Peter drawing his net at the command of Christ. Several disciples present. A picture that looks promising, but is seen in such an unfavourable light that I could form no more decided opinion.

HONDEKOETER.—Two subjects of fowls of considerable size.

ARTUS VAN DER NEER.—A small moonlight landscape, which hangs in a very dark place.

Among the splendid objects of furniture two cabinets with fruits in Florentine *pietra dura* are remarkable.

Of the books preserved in a large glass case the folio edition of Shakspeare, and manuscripts with Italian, French, English, and Dutch miniatures, are to be seen among other rarities.

LIBRARY.

MURILLO.—The head of Christ, of uncommon power of colour, perfectly agreeing in feature with that belonging to Lord Overstone.

PICTURES BELONGING TO G. FIELD, ESQ.

These admirable Netherlandish pictures were exhibited in 1856 in one of the public apartments in Marlborough House. I am not, however, able to say where they are usually placed.

TENIERS.—1. Four peasants seated at a table on the right in the foreground, two of them playing cards. Another is standing near. Above is a woman looking down from an aperture. Behind, at a fireplace, are two more peasants and a woman and a man leaving the apartment. On the left in front are all kinds of implements, a tub, a broom, &c., and a dog. Signed. On wood. The foremost group is very spiritedly treated in a bright golden tone ; the heads of unusual animation. Decidedly executed between 1640 and 1650, which was the best time of the master. The rest is more sketchily treated.

2. A small landscape with three peasants and a dog ; behind is a village in sunshine. Signed with the monogram. Of admirable effect.

Adrian van Ostade.—Country people playing at ninepins. A composition of nine figures. In front, upon a bench, a peasant, and on the ground two cocks preparing to fight. Signed, and dated 1655. The last figure, however, I am not quite certain of. On wood. This masterpiece is very interesting, as showing that he at one time sought to imitate the manner of his brother Isaac, both in composition and power of tone. The heads, however, are throughout impressed with his own character.

2. An interior, with a peasant seated in the foreground on the right, lighting his pipe at a chafing-dish. On the left is another holding his pipe. In the background, on the left, are a man and woman. Signed, and dated 1673. Very animated heads, and of masterly treatment, though the second peasant is particularly vulgar in character, and over red in colouring.

Philip Wouvermans.—1. A landscape. On the right a large piece of water with a boat and three men, and in the distance peasant houses with willows. On the left are trees, figures bathing, and a wooden bridge. Quite on the right, in front of a house, are a horseman and a girl. The sky is very dark on the left, but towards the right a cloud is lighted by the sun. Signed. The tone is dark and cool, but clear, and the whole picture, which is carefully painted in the second manner of the master, has a peculiar charm.

2. A fierce conflict between horse and foot. Two horsemen riding through a brook, one of them firing off a pistol, and a foot soldier in the midst, cutting at an officer with his sabre, are conspicuous. Signed. The composition, the very rapid action, the careful and spirited treatment in the earlier style of his second manner, and, finally, the size of the picture, render this one of the choicest specimens of the master. The hilly background is alone somewhat uncertain in execution.

Jan Mienze Molenaer.—A winter landscape. On the left side is a perspective of step-like buildings, slightly covered with snow, and a windmill deep in the picture. Before the foremost house is a peasant. On the right a frozen canal, with a man buckling on his skates. The sky is clear and reddish towards the horizon. Signed. This picture confirms my assertion that the painters of a secondary class occasionally showed themselves equal to the first. This picture, for instance, is not inferior to Ruysdael in depth of feeling for nature, in clearness of tone, and mastery of treatment.

ADRIAN VAN DE VELDE.—A wood with dark-cast shadows. Below a large tree are seen a cow, a ram, and a sheep reposing. In the middle distance are two cows standing. Quite on the right is another fine tree. The flat horizon is kept very light. Signed, and dated 1668. This is the most successful representation of a wood I know by the master. It is remarkable for power, depth, and transparency, and has a peculiarly poetical charm.

NICHOLAS BERGHEM.—On the left, in front, is a girl milking a goat, and a little dog who is trying to drink the milk. In the centre is an old shepherd stooping over a sheep. On the right a young man leaning against an ass. In the middle distance is a monument, in the distance hills. Signed. A warmly-toned and careful picture of his later time, the harmony being only disturbed by the too gaudy yellow and blue of the woman's dress.

MINDERHOUT HOBBEMA.—On the right a wood, and a man on a grey horse on a road ; also a pedestrian and a dog. A piece of water winding through at different distances is seen in several reaches. On the foremost are two ducks, and on the shore a dog drinking. On the shore of the last reach is an angler. In the centre of the middle distance are houses in sunshine, while the whole left side lies in profound but clear shadow. Not only signed but dated 1667, which is unusual. In every respect, composition, power, transparency, and mastery of treatment (for instance the light reflections in the various surfaces of water), one of his most beautiful and attractive works.

JACOB RUYSDAEL.—1. On the left a stately watermill, with trees. The sky mostly covered with grey clouds, the water glittering in the sun. On canvas, and of considerable size. Very original, and of rare power of colouring and masterly breadth of treatment.

2. Some houses with trees near them, one of them in sunshine, with smoke proceeding from a chimney. Next to it, towards the centre, oaks and other trees. On the left, in the middle distance, another house with a tree. The foreground is covered with bushes and weeds. Signed. This fine picture, the light clouds in which remind us of Hobbema, recalls, in the style of its marrowy and yet careful treatment, the view of the castle of Bentheim in the possession of Mr. Walter of Bearwood.

3. In the foreground, on the left, a small lake. In the middle distance is a ruin with a tree, on the right a small wood. Between these is a road on which are a man and a boy.· A portion of the road, and a cloud in the otherwise grey sky, are in sunshine. Inscribed with the monogram. Very attractive in composition, and, notwithstanding the general dark tone, very transparent.

JAN WYNANTS.—On the left a sand-hill, on which are a shepherd and shepherdess, and their flock. On the right, on a hill, are two trees. In the foreground is a horseman addressed by beggars. In the distance are buildings, with a wood. Inscribed with the monogram. Soft, warm, clear, and harmonious, and of very tender execution. The figures by the hand of LINGELBACH,

ADAM PYNACKER.—On the left are two lofty light trees, on the right a rock with a waterfall, and thence hills, one before the other, stretching in perspective lines into the background, which they terminate. In the foreground are two horsemen in gallop, a man, and a dog. A warm evening light enters on the left side. Of an upright form. Tastefully composed, clear in tone, and careful in treatment.

ARTUS VAN DER NEER.—1. A moonlight scene. The moon unusually high, and shining upon a canal, thus forming a striking contrast to the dark shadows, and to a fire in front of a house, which is also reflected in the water. In the foreground are two anglers. In the sky are numerous heavy clouds. This picture, which is of considerable size, is, notwithstanding the prevailing darkness, admirable in point of generally carried out transparency. On the expanse of water are steel-blue tones of charming effect.

2. A sunset upon a canal, with a village on the right bank. Quite on the left, in the middle distance, a windmill. In front, in the centre, a man, and, more on the right, three cows. Dark clouds are in the sky. Signed. The striking contrast of the light and warm sunshine on the left, with the deep but transparent masses of cloud opposite, the Rembrandt-like energy of tone, and the spirited and careful treatment, render this small picture of the best period of the master in the highest degree attractive.

3. A winter landscape. A broad frozen canal, enlivened with skaters and a sledge. The glow of the sun, hidden with reddish clouds, is reflected upon the ice. Inscribed with the monogram. The general tone is somewhat reddish, the half-lights of masterly

execution, and the aërial perspective very delicate. The treatment shows his somewhat earlier time.

WILLEM VAN DE VELDE.—A calm sea. Quite in the foreground is a narrow shore, on which stand three men. On the left is a small skiff, and further back three fishing-boats. More on the right, in the distance, is a large vessel. Silvery clouds are in the sky. The foremost three boats are kept dark, all the rest floats in an atmosphere of charming transparency.

VAN DER HEYDEN.—On the left, in front of a wall, is a cross. On the right a wall, and in the middle distance a house. In the centre, towards the foreground, are a gentleman and lady walking, accompanied by a servant, and addressed for alms by a pilgrim and a boy. Further back are another man and woman, and a dog drinking from a fountain. The sky is only slightly clouded. Of pretty composition, and, though somewhat dark, yet of clear and harmonious tone. The figures are by ADRIAN VAN DE VELDE.

GREUZE.—A golden-haired boy in white dress, with a black breast-piece, his head inclined towards the right. The background grey. Charming in feeling, warm and clear in colouring, and solid in execution.

MANUSCRIPT OF THE SPECULUM HUMANÆ SALVATIONIS,
WITH ITALIAN MINIATURES, IN POSSESSION OF
WILLIAM BOXALL, ESQ., A.R.A.,

14, WELBECK STREET.

This MS., which is on parchment, in a small oblong folio, contains twenty-five sheets, painted on each side—each page with two pictures—and is a fresh example of the frequent occurrence in Italy of this work, which probably originated with the Benedictines.* Unfortunately this specimen is very defective, inasmuch as the whole cycle of illustrations amounts to 192. Nor do those which are here preserved follow in their proper course. Above each picture are the contents given in Latin in abbreviations, the lower part being often mutilated by the cutting away of one stripe. The pictures proceed from an excellent painter of the Tuscan school, probably a Florentine, and quite correspond with the types of art

* See p. 310, vol. i., of 'Treasures of Art.'

which prevailed in the second half of the 14th century. The outlines are lightly and softly rendered with the point of the brush in
Indian ink, and the flesh parts coloured; but all the rest are more
or less carefully executed with light shading, the artistic value
corresponding with the degree of care. In many heads, however, a
feeling for beauty and purity of expression is rendered with so little
labour as to merit admiration. The same may be said of many
motives of a speaking, and sometimes of an elevated character.
Violent motives are however but lame, and the expression of tor-
mented people too quiet. The proportions are slender, the intention of the drapery pure in taste, but often too little carried out.
Rocks and trees are still given in the typical forms which Byzantine types had transmitted, and the golden glories of sainted persons
often cover the faces of figures standing next them. I must content
myself with noticing a number of the most remarkable illustrations.
In the first picture, the Wise and Foolish Virgins, one of the
latter—the second from the centre—is of uncommon beauty. In
the second picture, the Feast of Belshazzar, the youthfully conceived figure of Daniel is an admirable specimen of drapery. The
third picture, representing Satan, is quite in the taste of Orgagna
in the Campo Santo. The figure of Christ on the Mount of Olives,
No. 13, is highly noble and dignified; the same also in the picture
of the Betrayal; and in No. 18, the Crucifixion, where the Saviour
is dying. In the picture of the Mater Dolorosa, besides the usual
sword which is piercing her breast, her hands and feet, in order to
increase the expression of sorrow, are represented as transfixed
with daggers; this is new to me. The next picture is the Presentation in the Temple, containing only the figures of the Virgin,
the Child, and the High Priest; here the figures are conceived
quite in the manner of statues, with the motives and heads
of all three equally excellent. Joseph Sleeping, No. 21, is in
point of truth and beauty of motive one of the most successful in
the whole book. Admirable is the expression of surprise in the
Seven Learned Men, No. 22, whom the youthful Christ is teaching in the Temple. The figure and expression of Christ in the
next picture after that—the Bearing of the Cross—are very fine. In
the Descent from the Cross, No. 25, the chief motive quite agrees
with Duccio's conception in the picture in the cathedral at Siena.
The figures of the women in the Visitation, No. 30, are attractive

both for the statuesque grandeur of their forms, and the expression of deep pathos in their heads. In the Adoration of the Kings, No. 31, the Virgin is of marvellous beauty, and the Child of full forms. The Virgin also in the Presentation in the Temple, No. 32, has a fine profile of mild expression. As a composition, the same subject, No. 39, is still finer. The outstretched action of the arms in both Virgin and Child is as noble as it is speaking. To the most successful composition of the series belongs, however, the Flight into Egypt. The motive of the Child, who is caressing his mother as he sits on the ass, is very heartfelt; also that of Joseph looking round as he leads the ass. As a specimen of the lameness of very energetic scenes, I may mention No. 53, David, who, represented larger than Goliath, is cutting off his head. Excellent, on the other hand, is the penitent David, No. 58, who, enthroned and much agitated, is taking off his crown. No. 67 is very characteristic of the modes of conception peculiar to the Roman Church. The Virgin is seen standing, with Pope, Cardinals, &c., in supplication around her, and the inscription, " Beata Virgo Maria est nostra defensatrix et pacificatrix." No. 70, Naomi and the two other women ; the expression of grief in action and physiognomy is very intense. The same may be said of the Entombment, No. 71, where the expression of the Virgin and another woman, accompanied by three other women, is heartrending. In the Crucifixion, a rich composition, No. 75, the dying Saviour is dignifiedly conceived. The representation of David's wife Michal, No. 75, who, from a wall, is turning the beautiful youth below, who is playing the harp, into ridicule in the presence of two women, is graceful and original. In the picture of Joseph cast into a well by his brethren, No. 77, the well itself is remarkable as being represented in the form of a beautiful antique fountain. Equally original and fine is the conception of the three Children in the Fiery Furnace, No. 80 ; the furnace being represented as a stately building, with an angel shielding them with a large robe. Among the most successful figures is that of Jacob, No. 88, who is weeping at the sight of Joseph's coat. Finally I may mention a representation of an ostrich, No. 90, feeding her young, who are looking out of a vessel of beautiful form, with a snake. The ostrich is depicted like a bird of prey, and the snake writhed around is so large that it would easily squeeze the ostrich to death.

PICTURES BELONGING TO JAMES TULLOCH, ESQ., F.R.S., &c.,
16, Montague Place, Russell Square.

The number of pictures gathered together by this zealous collector hardly amounts to less than a hundred. They belong chiefly to the Netherlandish school, with a few specimens of the Italian, French, German, and English schools. Much as there is worthy of note among them, the limits of this work only permit of my dwelling more particularly upon a few. Through Mr. Tulloch's kindness I was enabled to obtain the measurements of these, which, considering the immense accumulation of pictures in England, is of the greatest importance for the prevention of mistakes.

Philip Wouvermans.—A smithy, with travellers and horses. Before the building is a tree and a vine-arbour; beneath these a man and a woman on a brown horse. A grey horse is being shod; before the animal is an officer. Further in the picture are other horses in a foreshortened position, and a man engaged about a saddle. Two dogs and fowls are also seen; more figures are in the middle distance. The sky is covered with dark clouds, the distance only is bluish. Upon wood, 1 ft. 2 in. high, 1 ft. 4 in. wide. Signed. This picture is in the second manner of the master, and is remarkable for its tasteful and rich composition, for the great power of the colouring, for the singular transparency even in the darkest shadows, and finally for its solid and careful execution.

Salvator Rosa.—A rocky sea-coast in Calabria, with various boats and numerous figures; 1 ft. 5 in. high, 2 ft. 4 in. wide. This picture is not only very rich in details, and of singular beauty of atmosphere, but is superior to many by the master in point of transparency and careful execution.

Willem van de Velde.—A calm sea. The shore quite in the foreground, with a small skiff and a larger fishing-boat; 2 ft. ½ in. wide, 5 ft. 5¼ in. high. A warm sunny light is rendered with masterly skill. Also the aërial perspective is of rare beauty. This charming picture is of the best time of the master.

Sebastian Bourdon.—Christ with the Samaritan woman at the well. 1 ft. 10½ in. high, 1 ft. 4½ in. wide. Of elevated conception, especially the woman. The tone of colour harmonious and warm.

Teniers.—Three peasants by a fire; one standing, the others

seated, and one of them filling his pipe. Further within is a fourth engaged in some domestic occupation. 1 ft. 2½ in. high, 10½ in. wide. The warm and sunny effect is very harmonious, and the touch most spirited and broad.

SCHALCKEN.—A maidservant by candlelight. 11¼ in. high, 8¾ in. wide. A genuine and good picture, though, as is general with this master, very empty and prosaic in feeling.

ARNOLD HOUBRAKEN.—The Shame of Calisto. 1 ft. 5½ in. high, 1 ft. 10½ in. wide. Signed. I should hesitate to mention this picture were it not characteristic of the peculiar æsthetic standard of the painter, who is well known as one of the most distinguished writers upon the Netherlandish school. His pictures are also very rare. In the over-smooth and delicate treatment of this rich composition we see the tendency of Adrian van der Werff, to whom this picture approaches very near. Houbraken, however, is far inferior in the taste of his drawing, his proportions being shorter and his forms more clumsy.

HENDRIK ROCKES, called ZORG.—1 and 2. Peasants at table eating and singing: companion pieces, each 10 in. high by 10 in. wide. These are very good specimens of the master, who, possessing the incomparable technical powers of his school, occasionally approaches very near to its highest masters.

ABRAHAM BEGYN.—View of Trieste, with various vessels and numerous figures, but a ruin with four pillars in the harbour is probably the invention of the painter. 2 ft. 1 in. high, 2 ft. 4½ in. wide. Signed. This master, who is upon the whole of a second-rate order, appears to great advantage in this warm, clear, and careful picture, which reminds us of similar subjects by Jan Baptiste Weenix.

CUYP.—A little girl with a shepherd's crook is feeding two sheep. Inscribed, "Maria Strick van Scharlaaken Regneer's Dogter, geboren den 13ten Oktober 1646, en overleeden den 15ten Juni 1669." 2 ft. 8 in. high, 2 ft. 0¾ in. wide. This little head is almost the size of life, and is of the most charming naïveté, warmth, transparency, and truth of colouring.

RUBENS.—The apotheosis of a hero crowned by Fame and Pallas. A composition of 6 figures for a ceiling. Upon wood. 2 ft. 1 in. high, 1 ft. 7 in. wide. Of very clever motives, and broad and masterly treatment.

WYNANTS.—A landscape. 9¾ in. high, 11½ in. wide. A pretty little picture.

JAN BREUGHEL.—A Dutch canal, with houses, ships, and figures. 8 in. high, 10 in. wide. Careful, and of particular transparency.

DE BYERS.—View of a Dutch canal. Signed and dated 1758. 11 in. high, 1 ft. wide. This painter, who is totally unknown to me, is a clever imitator of the manner of Jan van der Heyden, and another instance of the large number of able painters which Holland produced so late as in the 18th century.

PHILIP ROOS, called ROSA DI TIVOLI (?).—A landscape, with cattle and an old castle. 1 ft. 1 in. high, 1 ft. 7 in. wide. If this picture be by the master, it must belong to his earlier time, when he followed the steps of his uncle Heinrich Roos in point of clearness of colouring and tenderness of execution.

WATTEAU.—A " fête champêtre," with three ladies and a gentleman in a landscape. 1 ft. 8½ in. high, 2 ft. 5 in. wide. The figures are attractive, but the colouring somewhat heavy and dark.

CHRISTIAN GEORGE SCHÜTZ.—An alpine landscape near Lauterburg, in the canton of Berne, with a waterfall. In the background the chain of high Alps covered with snow. 1 ft. ¾ in. wide, 1 ft. 4 in. high. This painter flourished about the middle of the 18th century, and from his numerous views of the Rhine was known in Germany by the name of " *Rhein-Schütz.*" I should not, however, have mentioned him, but that the picture before us is not only a specimen of the careful execution usual with him, but shows a power and clearness of colouring which places him on a par with those good masters of the Dutch school who treated similar subjects, namely, with Herrmann Saftleven.

JAMES BARRY.—Pandora in the Assembly of Gods. Hebe presenting nectar to Jupiter. A sketch for his great picture for the Society of Arts, executed at Rome in brown chiaroscuro. 1 ft. 6 in. high, 2 ft. 3½ in. wide. The pleasing forms and motives render this an attractive picture.

PAUL VERONESE (?).—In the foreground is a buffet; in the middle distance a party at a meal. A page is setting on a dish. 4 ft. 11 in. high, 7 ft. wide. Full of life, and of masterly and careful execution. Judging, however, from expression of heads, colouring, and treatment, I am rather inclined to attribute this to TINTORETTO.

PAUL BRIL.—A rocky landscape with a waterfall, with a hunting-party. 3 ft. 5 in. high, 5 ft. 6 in. wide. A poetic picture, rich in detail, and broadly treated, of the later and best time of the master.

SIMON DE VLIEGER.—A rough sea, with several vessels. 1 ft. 5½ in. high by 1 ft. 10 in. wide. A poetic picture, with rich details, and of broad treatment, of the later and best time of the master.

CASPAR NETSCHER.—The Shame of Calisto. 1 ft. 8½ in. high, 1 ft. 5½ in. wide. Of his later time, when his colouring was somewhat pale and crude.

COLLECTION OF WORKS OF ART BELONGING TO
MR. HENDERSON,

3, MONTAGUE STREET, RUSSELL SQUARE.

The collection of Mr. Henderson affords another of those examples so frequently occurring in England, where the individual taste of the collector is seen strongly impressed upon the works of art in his possession. It consists chiefly of water-colour drawings of the modern English school, of oil-paintings in which the Netherlandish school predominates, and of specimens of earthenware, of which majolica forms the principal portion. The special taste of the collector is however indicated by the fact that the water-colour and other drawings are mostly by the hands of Cattermole and David Cox, and the pictures chiefly cabinet paintings of the smallest size, and in this respect not likely to lose the good opinion of those who consider the quality more than the quantity of a work of art.

I proceed first to notice the water-colour and other drawings. Nowhere have I hitherto seen so many specimens of Cattermole, who, as regards subjects where the human figure is introduced, may be considered the head of the English water-colour school. They decorate the walls of Mr. Henderson's own room. The distinctness with which the subject is rendered, even when of the artist's own invention ; the delicate feeling for the picturesque with which the figures are arranged in the space; the frequently admirable character of the heads and forms; the finely balanced harmony of colour, alternately of the warm and cold scale; the happy arrangement of his architectural backgrounds; and finally his free and spirited execution, render his works highly attractive, and justify the great popularity they enjoy in England. I describe these drawings by the names attached to them by the artist.

"The Quarrel." A knight just risen from play is in the act of drawing his sword. His antagonist, still seated, has already drawn his dagger. A monk takes advantage of the excitement to seize the hand of a girl carrying a jug. The motives very animated, and the keeping excellent.

"The Warning." Figures of knights before a fireplace. A girl, presenting a bottle, is whispering to one of them to the effect that guests, probably of an unwelcome kind, are at the door. With the exception of the bright form of the girl the group is treated in a serious and dark spirit, admirably exemplifying the gloomy chivalrous feeling so often conspicuous in Walter Scott's novels.

"The Conspirators of Holyrood." The dismal nature of this subject is very well expressed in this masterly composition of seventeen figures, one of whom is writing, while others are whispering together, and others, farther back, are seen at the window.

"Venice." Beneath the arch of a bridge is seen a boat, five men, and baggage, a shadow being cast on half the group. To the right, on the shore, are several figures; to the left two more. Through the bridge in the distance is seen Venice in sunshine. This very sketchily-treated picture shows in every part, by the contrast of light and sunny colours with deep and transparent shadows, by the clearness of the water, and the warm and powerful keeping, how entirely such subjects are adapted to Cattermole's powers.

"Christ Preaching." The arrangement here shows much resemblance to that of the cartoon of the Death of Ananias. In the centre, upon an elevated stage, are seen Christ and the Apostles, and in the foreground the hearers. The mass of light is here very powerful; the colouring of the different planes of distance which are graduated with great delicacy, is very transparent, the architecture of a warm tone, and the execution, for him, very careful.

"The Betrayer Betrayed." A knight of powerful frame is

lying upon a couch, with a girl weeping at the foot, whom he appears to be reproaching for having accused him as her betrayer. Several figures in armour are seen entering, one of whom is reading aloud the order of arrest, while another, with drawn sword, lays his hand on the culprit. The light which falls through the window on the head of the bed is very decided; the characters of the different figures very speaking; and the harmony of the broken colours, which incline to the cool scale, quite charming.

"The Festival of the Monastery." Figures of monks upon steps are seen receiving a procession of men, with some women and boys, who are approaching with bare heads in rows of three and four, side by side. Another procession is seen moving in the middle distance. On the right, in the foreground, is a cardinal seated. The distinctness of this rich composition, the successful foreshortening of the figures side by side, the admirable gradation of light seen through the window, and the delicate balance of colour, all render this drawing highly attractive.

"The Knotty Point." In a Gothic room, illumined with a sunny beam of light, are seen monks seated and standing, consulting authorities. The construction of the whole composition is particularly happy, the motives very speaking, and the keeping, in a bright chiaroscuro, masterly.

"Pilgrims at the Gate of the Monastery." In the centre, in the doorway, are two monks, the elder of whom is speaking to two pilgrims, and pointing to the interior of the building. On the left is a pilgrim seated, to whom meat and drink are being served from a window. On the right is a monk seated teaching some boys. In the middle and far distance are other figures. This drawing is animated in the motives, and of admirable keeping in the cool harmony, which only finds a well-chosen balance in some red draperies.

"The Baron's Chapel." A Gothic apartment, with a priest reading aloud from a folio volume to the baron and his lady, who are seated opposite to him, with numerous other figures seated and standing. The motives excellent, and colouring and keeping of masterly carrying out.

"Columbus at the Convent of La Rabida." A prior and his monks are seated and standing round a table, and listening, with an attention which is admirably expressed, to the narrative of

Columbus, who is seated behind the table. The keeping is masterly. These figures, which are unusually large, are broadly sketched in upon a rough pasteboard with very coarse surface.

" The Refectory : relieving the Poor." In the centre are two monks giving food to a young girl and three children. On each side, some more in front, some more behind, are monks at table conversing. On the left is an old man with a bowl of soup in his lap, and a figure carrying a piece of roasted meat. The manner in which the figures are disposed in the space shows great artistic skill, and the keeping, which is throughout in cool and broken colours, is admirable. Also on pasteboard.

" Reading the Fathers." Two priests are seen before a desk, with a folio volume on it. Behind, enthroned, is a prelate in violet dress. Among the other hearers are three seated figures. Masterly in every respect. On pasteboard.

" The Cardinal's Study." A cardinal of gloomy expression is being read to by a priest. Three other persons are also listening. Of bright lighting, and admirably carried out in colour.

A landscape. The chief object here is a rocky fortress, with a little stream at its foot. The trees are too conventional in form, but colouring and effect are masterly.

A landscape. A piece of still water in the foreground, with aquatic plants upon it, in flower. Behind are some trees, on the left buildings. The sky is bright. Of great power and transparency.

Next to these water-colour drawings I may mention a number of drawings executed in charcoal, and broadly and freely treated with the assistance of the stump.

" The Baron's Chapel." The baron, seated in the midst, is listening to his chaplain reading from the desk. Other figures are around, seated and standing. A bright light enters by the window. Of admirable arrangement and effect.

" Pilgrims at Vespers." The scene is laid in a chapel of an early Gothic style. A light chiaroscuro tone is finely carried out with the stump.

" A Prior instructing his Monks." The prior is seated in the midst on a raised seat, and pointing to a book in his lap. On the left are monks seated ; on the right, standing. The composition, both as a whole and in its separate motives, is very successful.

The following landscapes show how skilfully **Mr. Cattermole** has applied the use of charcoal even in this line.

" The Falls of the Thummel, in Scotland." In the foreground is seen the dark, falling mass of water. Beyond the stream is a hill of gloomy aspect. Through the heavy clouds are seen a few gleams of light. The expression of melancholy horror is very strikingly rendered. I must add, however, that the foam of the water is too woolly in effect.

" The Moonlight March." In the foreground are cavalry passing a piece of water ; beyond are a ruin and some trees. The feeling of night is admirably expressed.

The landscapes and sea-pieces by David Cox comprise a period of about thirty years. The generally fortunate point of view, the beauty and variety of the skies, the clear colouring, the delicacy of the aërial perspective, and the spirited, though often only sketchy treatment, render these drawings a rich feast to the lover of art.

I now proceed to consider the pictures in oil.

DINING-ROOM.

Peter Tyssens.—Bacchus surrounded by children, in the taste of Rubens, though colder and heavier in colour. The landscape by Artois, and the fruit by Snyders. I mention this picture especially as a remarkable specimen of the manner in which three painters of such distinct style contrived so to work together as to produce an harmonious and very attractive whole.

Melchior Hondekoeter.—A family of fowls and a peacock contrast strangely with a landscape of classic character with ruins. The details are admirable, but the tone of the whole, as was frequent with this master, somewhat heavy.

Hendrik Rockes, called Zorg.—1. A man and his wife at breakfast, caressing each other. Transparent, delicate, and careful.

2. A man and his wife playing at cards. An old man is present. The companion to the foregoing, and less transparent.

Willem van Aelst.—1. A partridge on a table. Signed, and dated 1674.

2. The companion. Peaches, grapes, nuts, &c., upon a table. Both these pictures display the taste and high finish of the master.

Clarkson Stanfield.—An agitated sea. On the left is a

pier; in the centre a vessel with a sail. The waves are very rough. A masterly specimen of this well-known master.

In this apartment, among various objects of valuable earthenware, are some particularly choice Apostles' jugs.

DRAWING-ROOM.

JAN WYNANTS.—1. On the right is a hill with trees; in the middle distance is a piece of water; in the distance rising ground. More on the left is a road with figures by LINGELBACH. Signed, and dated 1670. Of pleasing composition and careful execution, though, like most of his later pictures, somewhat heavy in tone.

SOLOMON RUYSDAEL.—View of a Dutch village. Of very picturesque conception in the taste of Waterloo's etchings, and of unusual warmth of colouring.

NICHOLAS BERGHEM.—In the foreground is a piece of still water, through which a white cow, other cattle, and a cart are passing. Of great truth of detail; the sky very transparent; the general tone, however, rather dark.

EGBERT VAN DER POEL.—A view of the town of Breda, with two Gothic towers, after the fire. The sky is clouded, with a gleam of sun. Signed, and dated 12 October 1654. One of the best pictures I know by the master; transparent and beautiful in effect, and far more delicate in detail than usual.

VAN DE CAPELLA.—A winter landscape, with a frozen canal. Signed, and dated 1653. This is quite a new aspect of this great marine painter, who shows equal eminence in this line. A profound feeling for nature is here combined with delicate drawing and an astonishing truthfulness in every part—as, for instance, the effect of the frosty fog, the shadows of the clouds, and the surface of the ice.

HENDRIK ROCKES, called ZORG.—3. An aged alchemist with spectacles is watching by a sunny window some process going on in a caldron, beneath which a lad is blowing the fire with the bellows. Signed, and dated 1643. This is another instance of what I have advanced, viz. that painters of a secondary class occasionally equal in their best works those of the highest order. Here the truth of the heads, the power and clearness of the colouring, and the tenderness of execution impart a great charm to this picture.

CORNELIS BEGA.—A peasant woman is seen within a house door, into which a girl with a basket is entering. An evening light pervades the picture, which displays a clearness, force, and warmth, and so masterly a chiaroscuro as is seldom seen in the cool-toned works of this pupil of Adrian van Ostade.

FRANCESCO GUARDI.—1. In this picture water forms so principal a feature that it may rank as a marine-piece. Of peculiar charm in the transparent and steel-blue tones characteristic of him.

JOSEPH VAN CRAESBEKE.—A woman making pancakes. A boy and two children are by the stove. Many accessories occupy the space—a cupboard, a tablecloth in sunshine, &c. Signed. Works by this painter, who was a pupil of Brouwer, are seldom seen, and, in my opinion, he is far too little esteemed. Here the animation of the forms and heads—that of the woman painted in a transparent golden tone approaching A. van Ostade—is combined with admirable keeping and solid and spirited treatment.

RICHARD WILSON.—View of Funchal in Madeira. A very spirited sketch.

ADAM PYNACKER.—A landscape, animated by a hunting party with falcons. Of great delicacy of atmosphere, and very pleasing in composition. The general tone, however, cold.

ARTUS VAN DER NEER.—A sea-coast, with a windmill on the left. Signed. The silvery tone and delicacy of aërial perspective give this picture a peculiar charm.

JAN VAN GOYEN.—View of a Dutch canal. Of the utmost truth, and, at the same time, of greater force, transparency, and warmth of colouring than usual.

JAN VAN OS THE YOUNGER.—In the foreground are fruits; more behind is a vase with some flowers. Both in composition and execution this master is a successful follower of Jan van Huysum.

ABRAHAM STORK.—A sea-coast, with a pier. Signed. Very careful, and unusually transparent for the master.

A male portrait, in rich armour and a standing ruff, is so excellent in conception and colouring that, though I cannot decide as to the master, I cannot pass it over in silence.

The same remark applies to a clever portrait of a young man with a plaited collar, which, in my opinion, is erroneously assigned to Velasquez.

Joseph Vernet.—View of a stream, surrounded with hills. Particularly delicate and careful for him.

Frans de Paula Ferg.—Landscape, with hills in the background. A vehicle with two horses is the principal object. One of the best pictures by this second-rate painter known to me. Seldom does he display such transparency and freshness of colour.

Albert Cuyp.—1. View of the river Maas. On the shore nearest the spectator are three cows and a herdsman, two boys, and a boat with two men. On the stream are vessels, and, opposite, a flat shore. Of warm tone, especially in the sky; and the execution as solid as the feeling for nature is profound.

Jan Wouvermans.—Landscape, with animals. This picture, which recalls the taste of Wynants, is powerful and clear in colouring, and delicate in rendering.

Adrian van Ostade.—An interior, with a peasant in a state of great hilarity. Very transparent, warm, and harmonious.

Adrian van de Velde.—Cattle upon a meadow, which is only diversified by a willow. In the distance a village. Delicate in feeling and tender in treatment.

Willem van de Velde.—An agitated sea. Admirable. The tone shows the influence of Simon de Vlieger.

Teniers.—A peasant with a glass and a jug. Behind him a monkey. Of spirited treatment, but somewhat heavy in colouring.

Jan Mienze Molenaer.—A winter landscape, with men and animals upon the ice. Of unusual softness and harmony of colour for him, and of great delicacy of treatment.

Jan Wynants.—2. A very small landscape of his best time. Of forcible colour, sunny lighting, and spirited treatment.

3. Landscape, with his favourite sand-hill in the warmest sunshine, and animated by a horseman and animals. A picture of the finest quality.

Cornelius Poelemburg.—St. Peter. Very delicate and tender.

Jan Huchtenburg.—Landscape, with horses and horsemen. A rich and careful picture.

Jan Wynants.—4. On the right are trees; on the left a sand-hill, with hills rising behind. A man and a woman on horseback, four dogs, and a man seated, are admirably introduced by Philip Wouvermans. Warm in tone and delicate in carrying out.

PHILIP WOUVERMANS.—A flat country, with a man on a grey horse, and a dog on the left next a tree, and in the centre a road, with a woman and a child. More on the right is a piece of still water, with a wooden bridge across it in the middle distance, on which is a pedestrian. An admirable picture in his first manner, the sunlight upon the grey horse and the water forming a striking and picturesque contrast to the darkly-clouded sky.

FRANCESCO GUARDI.—2, 3, 4, and 5. Four small views of Venice, all of the same size. Harmonious and careful, and of great charm.

A male portrait in an oval, in black dress, with white falling collar. The ground a curtain of broken green. Delicately conceived, and warm and soft in colouring. I cannot, however, pronounce upon the master with certainty.

CANALETTO.—1. View of the Church of S. Francesco della Vigna. Very careful, transparent, and warm.

BERNARDO BELLOTTO.—View of a narrow canal in Venice, with a bridge in the middle distance; various figures in the foreground. Very picturesquely conceived, unusual in tone, and of careful execution.

SIR JOSHUA REYNOLDS.—Portrait of Mrs. Abingdon in the costume of a page. Of oval form. Delicate in feeling and colour.

ALBERT CUYP.—2. A richly-wooded landscape with cattle, in evening light. Little indication of decided colouring is seen here; the keeping is misty, and the tone delicate.

FRANCESCO GUARDI.—6. A piece of water in the foreground, with ruins behind. A small picture of great charm.

ARTUS VAN DER NEER.—The evening sun, breaking through clouds, spreads its glowing beams over a broad canal, diversified with boats, and with houses on each side. This picture rivals Rembrandt in poetry of feeling, glow of colour, and solidity of impasto.

JAN VAN DER HEYDEN.—On the left is a summer-house and a wall, on the right a garden, with a building in the distance with trees before it. At one of the garden-beds is a woman stooping, and a man. The sky is very transparent. Signed. This beautiful little picture is especially attractive for delicacy and harmony of chiaroscuro.

CANALETTO.—2. View of the Church of S. Pietro di Castello. On the left a bridge, admirably foreshortened. In warmth of sunshiny effect and solid impasto this picture displays no common excellence.

3. View of the Canale Regio. The reflection of the sunlit houses upon the clear water on the left side is marvellously fine, and forms a charming contrast with the buildings on the right side in half shadow, and with those further off in the centre, which are entirely in shadow. A worthy companion to the foregoing.

FRANCESCO GUARDI.—7. View of the Dogana and Church of the Salute. The point of view is very happily chosen here. The rendering of the broken reflections of the sunlit buildings in the steel-blue water, with which the sky is in admirable keeping, has an effect of peculiar charm.

8. View of the Church of S. Giorgio Maggiore, so taken as to make the building appear as if on a separate island. The large mass of still water shows great delicacy of greenish-blue tones. Companion to the above.

9. On the left side is St. Mark's Cathedral foreshortened; directly opposite the spectator is the clock-tower, and on the right a portion of the Procuratie. Of the utmost force, depth, softness and clearness of tone.

FREDERIC MOUCHERON.—A pleasing landscape, recalling Pynacker in conception and tone.

JAN VAN DER MEER DE JONGE.—On the left are a ram, a sheep, and a lamb reposing, and two cows standing. Signed. Warmer and clearer in tone than usual, and very careful.

ABRAHAM BEGYN.—A landscape in the style of Jan Both, with figures and animals in the taste of Berghem. Delicate and careful, but somewhat heavy in tone.

PHILIP DE KONINGK.—An extended view. A sand-hill with figures and cattle on the right, on the left in the foreground a bleaching-ground, and in the distance a stream. The sky is slightly clouded. This little picture is not only admirable as a whole for composition, lighting, power, and transparency of colour, but it is very attractive for the delicacy with which the details are carried out, and for the variety in the tone of the trees, some of which are treated in the cool colours seen in Hobbema.

JACOB RUYSDAEL.—View of the town of Haarlem and the surrounding country. Among the pictures I know of this subject by the master, this one deserves particular attention. The deep but transparent chiaroscuro, which is only broken by a ray of sun, is rendered with masterly power, while the sea, seen in the extreme distance in the shifting sunlight, is expressed with great delicacy. The clouds are of unusual softness, and the execution, though careful, free.

JAN WYNANTS.—5. A hilly landscape. On the right, before a rising ground, is a cow in deep, warm, half shadow; in the centre a piece of water, with a grey and a brown horse. The gradation of light in this little piece, of which the grey horse forms the principal focus, is particularly worthy of admiration.

VAN DE CAPELLA.—A calm sea with boats, with portions of the coast on each side. On the left, in front, are two fishermen drawing a net; more in the centre, three others similarly occupied. This valuable little picture, with its cool harmony, is an exception to the generally warm colouring of the master. His usual mastery is however seen in the result; for the reflection in the steel-blue surface of the water is of the utmost refinement, and the slightly clouded sky of the tenderest atmospheric effect.

ADRIAN VAN DE VELDE.—View of a Dutch canal. On the right is a small portion of the bank, with a brown horse and a goat standing, and two sheep reposing. Beyond the canal on the left, in the middle distance, is a village with trees; and by the shore two sailing-boats and a little skiff, which cast their reflections in the perfectly calm water. The sky is blue, with the exception of a few sunlit clouds. This little picture is a striking proof that very high art can be compressed within a very small space, for we have here combined that refined feeling for nature and tender harmony of broken colours which together exemplify the high perfection attained by this great school.

LUDOLF BACKHUYSEN.—An agitated sea, two large boats forming the chief mass. On the right, in the distance, is a large vessel. On the horizon is seen a coast, on which a gleam of light falls. In the sky are grey and soft clouds. This picture is remarkable for transparency of tone, beauty of lighting, and delicacy of carrying out.

FRANCESCO GUARDI.—10. View of the Church of S. Francesca della Vigna at Venice. To enhance the effect, the tower is represented higher than it really is. The lighting is unusually cheerful and sunny for the master, and the reflections in the water and the aërial perspective admirable.

Albert Cuyp.—2. Portrait of a young lady in a black dress, with white cap and collar. The ground is brown. The animated conception harmonises with the soft and masterly treatment.

Among the different miniatures I may mention a very finished portrait by Petitot of Madame de Grignon, the well-known daughter of Madame de Sévigné, to whom she addressed her letters. It is framed in tortoiseshell, and forms the lid of a gold snuffbox.

In various cabinets are collected 90 plates of very choice majolica. Among them are six of especial beauty, signed with the name of Maestro Giorgio, some of them lustre plates, and one adorned with the admirably-drawn Triumph of Galatea after Raphael. Five very fine examples of those plates executed by the Arabians in the course of the 15th and beginning of the 16th century are also here. These plates especially belong to Malaga and the island of Majorca, and are distinguished for their rich ornamentation in a metallic oxide which has the brilliancy of gold, and makes a splendid effect.

Next to these may be mentioned a number of small filigree silver vessels of transparent construction—plates, circular dishes with lids, for betel-nuts, a flask intended for rose-water, and other silver articles in which coffee-cups can be held; all in delicate taste and of marvellously rich workmanship.

Five specimens of Persian porcelain ware, known to be as peculiar as they are rare, are also here.

My opinion of Chinese work in bronze was also much raised by the sight of a large vase with silver decorations inlaid, and small dishes with feet, on which plants were admirably imitated. Mr. Henderson also possesses a whole set of beautiful Oriental bronzes, with rich inlaid work.

PICTURES AND OBJECTS OF ART BELONGING TO
MRS. ANDREW JAMES.

This collection, to which I procured access through the kindness of my friend Mr. Carpenter, was formed by the late Andrew James, Esq., a corn-dealer, and gives laudable evidence of the taste and discrimination of that gentleman. Although the strength of the collection consists in a rich and choice series of drawings by Rembrandt, Watteau, and other masters, it includes also a small number of good cabinet pictures. I take these first in order.

JACOB RUYSDAEL.—On the left is a small cottage, from the chimney of which issues a slender wreath of smoke. Before the cottage is a small pool of water. The background is a flat country. The scene lies partially in a deep but clear chiaroscuro, partially in a reflected evening light. Signed. The feeling of a still peaceful evening, with scenery of a modest and domestic character, is here expressed in a remarkable degree. At the same time the effect is admirable, and the execution masterly.

WATTEAU.—1. A peep into a simple and happy *ménage.* The grandmother is seated at a spindle ; the wife—her daughter apparently—is sewing a dress; a great girl is holding a pretty kitten on her arm, at which a little dog is barking ; while a little boy lies reposing in great comfort. In this unusual subject Watteau appears to great advantage. The general effect is pleasingly domestic ; the heads are very animated, the keeping excellent, and the sketchy treatment is very clever.

2 and 3. Two small but attractive pictures, with gentlemen and ladies in the open air. In one of them is a very pretty girl seen in profile, and a couple turning from the spectator. The other picture is conspicuous for power and transparency of colour.

FRANK HALS.—Portrait of a young man. Small, but very spirited, and of masterly treatment.

STOTHARD.—1. Héloise. A recumbent figure. The features are noble, and of very tender execution.

2. A girl, accompanied by a female friend, is having her fortune told by an old woman. In the background is her lover listening. Charming in feeling ; the heads pretty, the colouring transparent, and of unusual carefulness of finish.

3 and 4, two small pictures, are also meritorious, but sketchy.

ISABEY.—A crowd of children going to school, watched by an old Abbé, probably the teacher. A slight but very clever sketch.

DRAWINGS.

ALBERT DURER.—A masterly pen-drawing, with dragons and other ornaments, apparently designed for a goldsmith. Inscribed with monogram, and dated 1503.

REMBRANDT.—I know of no collection, either public or private, which contains a series of admirable drawings by this master so illustrative of his various classes of subjects—sacred, *genre*, portrait, and landscape. Most of these proceed from the collections of Sir Joshua Reynolds and Sir Thomas Lawrence. The latter are marked with the initials of Mr. Esdaile, who, as is well known, purchased all the Rembrandt drawings of the Lawrence collection from Mr. Woodburn. I must content myself with noticing some of the most remarkable of each class of subject.

The Sacrifice of Abraham. Very slight, but very spirited; a totally different composition from the well-known etching.

Hagar and Ishmael. Of extraordinary depth of feeling.

The Death of Absalom.

The Departure of the youthful Tobias.

The youthful Christ teaching in the Temple.

The Raising of Jairus' Daughter.

Christ washing the Disciples' feet.

The Prodigal Son.

A skeleton upon a horse-skeleton, with a legbone as a bâton, is a frightful but clever reminiscence of those forms of thought which gave rise to the Dance of Death in the middle ages.

An old woman making pancakes. Executed in bistre, and approaching a picture in power of effect.

Singing children, with a large star. It was thus that they perambulated Amsterdam in the time of Rembrandt on the three days of the Epiphany.

An old woman looking out of a window.

Four musicians.

A man with broad-brimmed hat, and of roguish expression. Whole-length figure.

A woman sleeping.

A boy sleeping. Very spirited, but so broad and slight that at most it could not have occupied more than five minutes in execution.

Several sleeping children.

His own portrait.

Several landscapes, one of which, with a windmill, is remarkable. A sea-piece, and an architectural drawing for a gate at Amsterdam.

Some specimens of the school of Rembrandt are also worthy of note, viz. a landscape by GOVAERT FLINCK, with an expanse of water and an extensive plain in the distance, displaying a most delicate feeling for nature and a masterly use of the pen. Also a landscape by ROLANDT ROGMAN, and one by VAN BORSUM.

ADRIAN OSTADE.—A framed water-colour drawing of a party of peasants before a house. Signed. This is one of the finest specimens of the kind I have seen, being not only spirited in the heads, and very picturesque in the rich composition, but differing from his usual somewhat crudely coloured drawings in a harmony of colouring and power of chiaroscuro which approach his oil pictures.

ANTOINE WATTEAU.—For all who have closely studied the pictures of this clever painter, this collection of his drawings is in a high degree instructive and interesting. It contains a large number of studies from nature for his pictures, chiefly on grey paper, executed in red, black, and white chalks, with great breadth and mastery, and with the utmost animation of conception. Generally speaking, the same model supplies at least two views. A rich series of heads on a larger scale is also executed in the same style. A sheet with a young man; another with an old man playing the flute, in two views; and a third with young girls in different positions, are remarkably fine. A large number of other drawings as beautiful, according to Mr. Carpenter's assurance, as the above, I had not time even to look at.

Admirable specimens of the modern English school are also to be seen in this collection. Two framed drawings by TURNER display great refinement of feeling, combined with a broad and masterly but careful execution. I was especially interested by one of them—the view of some castle which played a part in Cromwell's time.

I was next attracted by a set of large drawings of the finest scenery of Italy—for instance, of Capri—by COUSINS. The poetic conception, the harmonious colouring, the admirable keeping, the tenderness with which the atmosphere is rendered, and the masterly and broad keeping, impart to these drawings a great charm.

The variety of tastes which distinguished the late Mr. James are seen to great advantage in the following objects:—

A small terra-cotta vessel of the unusual shape of a wine-glass, of very depressed form, supported on a large foot. On the upper depressed part of the vessel are combats, chiefly between two figures—black, on a yellow ground. These figures, in point of variety, animation, and beauty of motive, as well as excellence of drawing, belong to the finest creations I know of the kind, and prove that this archaic style was still adopted, even when art had attained its highest development. This terra-cotta was purchased at Mr. William Hope's sale in Paris.

A small statuette, in terra-cotta, of a Victory, seated, with extended wings, on which the original blue colour is still in great measure preserved. This is very original and graceful in motive, and the drapery in good style.

A flask of the crimson glass invented by the German Kunkel combines with the deep crimson colour great elegance of form and setting.

Finally, a cabinet contains a choice of very delicate Sèvres, among which I may particularly mention two vases of the fine Dubarry blue, and some other pieces of a charming crimson.

In the hands of Mrs. James all these treasures are preserved with more than common reverence.

OBJECTS OF ART BELONGING TO FELIX SLADE, ESQ.

I was introduced to this gentleman by the kindness of Mr. Carpenter. The various contents of his collection evince equal knowledge and taste. They may be divided into three heads:—objects of glass; early engravings; and rare, and principally illustrated books. I was not able to inspect the engravings, which, in the opinion of one so qualified to judge as Mr. Carpenter, are remarkable for beauty of impression; nor, on account of their great number and interest, can I give more than a superficial account of the other works of art; for in spite of every facility that a long visit and the kind guidance of Mr. Slade himself afforded me, I was unable to take any immediate notes. Such however is the importance of this collection, that I feel it my duty towards all those interested in objects of art and rare books to call their attention to it.

OBJECTS OF ART IN GLASS.

EGYPTIAN.—A small staff, in the form of a pillar, with a very elegant capital.   Of the utmost rarity.

GRECO-ROMAN.—Two armlets of a fine azure colour, with gold ends.   Though acquainted with most of the existing specimens of the kind, these beautiful armlets are new to me.

Two earrings, in which the blue of the turquoise is very happily imitated.   Of very elegant form.

A necklace of very peculiar style.

Various little vessels of very pretty form and colour.

MEDIÆVAL AND MODERN GLASS (principally of Venetian manufacture, also German, Dutch, and English).—These objects display a variety of forms, an elegance and artistic beauty of pattern, a charm of refinement in the combination of colours, and an excellence of preservation, such as I have never seen in this degree before.   These attractions are further set off by the taste with which these treasures are arranged in the different compartments of two cabinets, one of which is especially rich.   This is the work of Mr. Nichols, a friend of Mr. Slade, who also possesses a fine collection of objects in glass.   The value and charm of the chiefly illustrated incunabula, of the works decorated with woodcuts, and of other rare books belonging to the various nations remarkable for such, which abound here in number and surpassing beauty, is further increased by the bindings in which they are preserved, many of which are veritable works of art.   Some of these are the production of celebrated early workers in this line.   The majority, however, are by the best English and French bookbinders of our time.   The first place for richness and splendour must be assigned to the binding of the engravings of Turner's ' Views in England and Scotland,' which, in the great Paris Exhibition of 1855, was distinguished with a first-class medal.   Unwillingly was I compelled to let one beautiful volume after another merely pass through my hands.   In order to particularise something out of this true *embarras de richesses*, I may mention the very rare first edition of Holbein's ' Dance of Death;' the first and second editions of the Bible, with the fine woodcuts by Petit Bernard ; and finally a superb specimen of the first edition of the ' Hypnerotomachia' of Poliphilus.

Mr. Slade has also recently made the acquisition of some coloured Greek terra-cotta vases of remarkable beauty. The following three are from the collection of the late Mr. Rogers :—

A vase, black, with a yellow compartment of moderate size, on which, in black, are two combatants about to fight with their lances. These have an animation and elevation which show a true Homeric feeling, and are delicate in drawing.

A black vase, with yellow figures. Silenus seated with the cantharus : opposite to him a female figure in a hovering position, offering him a lion with one hand, and holding a serpent in the other. This recalls the well-known representation of Thetis resisting Peleus. Of good style and careful drawing.

A tazza, with yellow figures on a black ground—youthful forms of bacchanalian race, and chiefly satyrs. These are partly in attitudes of repose, partly in lively action. The full and beautiful forms, the admirable drawing, and the marvellous truth and grace of the motives display the best period of Greek art.

Of two remarkably fine Lecythi, or small vessels containing ointment, from the Durand collection, I am unable even so much as to describe the subjects.

LETTER IV.

Collection of pictures in Kensington Palace belonging to His Royal Highness the Prince Consort — Byzantine, Early Russian, Italian, German schools, &c. — Ancient coins and pictures belonging to General Fox — Earl of Harrington's collection — Mr. Nichols's pictures — Crystal Palace — MSS. and works of art belonging to His Royal Highness the Duke d'Aumale — Pictures in Sion House — Lord Jersey's collection, Osterley Park.

COLLECTION OF PICTURES IN KENSINGTON PALACE, BELONGING TO H.R.H. THE PRINCE CONSORT.

THIS collection was formed by Prince Ludwig Wallerstein, and came into the possession of the Prince Consort by purchase. The large altar-picture by Matthew Grunewald has been the only addition made to it, having been purchased by the Prince at the sale of Lord Orford's pictures. No other collection in England presents such a union of Byzantine, Russian, Italian, German, and Netherlandish works of the 14th, 15th, and first half of the 16th centuries; and it is on this account in a high degree interesting and instructive. The numbers attached to each picture refer to a catalogue of this collection which I compiled for H.R.H.

BYZANTINE SCHOOL.

4. The Sudarium, with the legend of King Abgarus.—On cedar. Size, including a gilt border, 1 ft. $3\frac{1}{2}$ in. by 1 ft. $1\frac{3}{4}$ in. This picture is very remarkable, as the only complete representation of the legend of King Abgarus of Edessa, by which a different origin is assigned to the story of the Sudarium or " vera Icon " from that current among the Western nations as the legend of St. Veronica. The interesting and animated motives prove this to be a repetition of a good early original, while the repetition itself, judging from the fused execution of the flesh, the thinness of the hair, and the taste of the ornaments above the upper and lower inscription, can hardly be ascribed to an earlier period than 1550. The early character of the letters proves nothing, as letters of the same form occur in Byzantine pictures bearing inscribed

dates of the 17th century. An example of this kind inscribed Emanuel Tzane and 1640 is in the Berlin Museum (No. 1056). According to Lanzi, this was a Greek priest who lived in Venice, and he mentions several pictures by him similarly inscribed.

7. The Nativity.—Very small full-length figures. On cedar. 9½ in. by 5¼ in. The conception of this picture indicates a very early and good original. The actions of the kings, who are calling each other's attention to the star, are particularly excellent. The figures in the clouds and the two old men with Joseph are new to me, nor can I account for them. The tame execution corresponds technically, in many respects, with the above-mentioned picture by Emanuel Tzane, in the Berlin Museum, and probably belongs also to the 17th century.

EARLY RUSSIAN SCHOOL.

9. The Monastery of Solowetzk, on the White Sea.—On wood. 11 in. by 9 in. A Russian picture of unusually good style of heads, especially that of the Virgin; and, judging from the character of the writing, about the 14th century. It is particularly interesting on account of the richness of the architecture.

ITALIAN SCHOOL.

11. The Adoration of the Kings, between rocks. Triptych.— Full-length figures. On wood. Centre piece, 1 ft. 7 in. by 9½ in. ; each wing 1 ft. 7 in. by 3¾ in. Of good motives and full forms, admirable in style of drapery, and powerful in colour. The treatment, however, especially of the heads, is somewhat rude. The outsides of the wings or doors have much suffered.

13. Justus of Padua.—Small triptych on wood, in tempera. Full-length figures. The skies throughout golden. 1 ft. 5½ in. by 8½ in. ; each wing 1 ft. 6 in. by 4½ in.

In the Central Compartment. Coronation of the Virgin.

The Left Wing. The Annunciation.

Lower Compartment of the Left Wing. The Nativity.

The Right Wing, Lower Compartment. The Crucifixion.

Upper Compartments of the Outside. On the left, the Expulsion of Joachim from the Temple.

Lower Compartment to the Left. The meeting of Joachim and Anna at the Beautiful Gate.

Lower still is the Presentation of the Virgin in the Temple.
Lower Compartment to the Right.   The Birth of the Virgin.
Beneath this.   The Marriage of the Virgin.

An admirable production in conception and execution, and most delicately finished. The date 1367 is on the pedestal, and on the back is inscribed "Justus pinxit in Archa." The word "Archa" most probably means Arqua, famous as Petrarch's dwelling-place. This picture is the only example I know which exhibits this admirable master as a tempera painter. In point of composition, beauty, and truth of some highly dramatic motives, noble style of drapery, and delicate completion, he represents the highest artistic development of his time. In all these respects, too, he shows so close an affinity with Taddeo Gaddi, Giotto's principal scholar—witness the frescoes by Taddeo in the Baroncelli and Bandini Chapels in the Church of S. Croce, at Florence, —as to induce the belief of his having been a scholar of that master.* Only in his pale flesh tones do we remark a decided difference. He is particularly important in the history of art as assisting to throw light on Aldighiero da Zevio and Jacobo d'Avanzo, the admirable Paduan painters, whose frescoes have been illustrated in a work by Ernst Förster.

16. SANO DI PIETRO.—Virgin and Child. On wood. 1 ft. 10 in. by 1 ft. 3 in. A picture attractive in motive, and pleasing in the heads of the Child and the Angels. The works of this generally-speaking mediocre master are rightly cited as specimens of the decline of the Sienese school, which, having attained great excellence in the 13th and 14th centuries, was outstripped by the Florentine school in the 15th; a circumstance which agrees also with the decline of the political importance of Siena at that time.

UMBRIAN SCHOOL, AND SCHOOL OF ROMAGNA.

17. NICCOLO ALUNNO.—Virgin and Child. Niccolo Alunno, an excellent master of the Umbrian school, was first suggested by Rumohr as the probable teacher of Pietro Perugino. Judging

---

* This conclusion gains in probability from a notice by Zani reporting him to be a Florentine by birth, and a son of Gio. Menabuoi, and that he received the name of Padovano merely from his long residence in Padua. (See ' Menabuoi,' Zani's Encyclopedia, parte 1ᵐᵃ, vol. xiii.; also the ' Annotazioni ' in the same vol., p. 470, No. 45.) Vasari attributes to him all the frescoes in the chapel of St. John the Baptist, in the chapel of St. Luke, in the church of St. Antonio, and also those in the chapel degli Eremitani, all in Padua. See the Florence edition of 1832-38, part 1, p. 429.

from a dated and inscribed picture on the high altar of the church of La Bastia (a small place not far from Assisi), with which it corresponds, I consider this picture to be by the hand of the master named above. The head of the Virgin especially is very noble. M. Hartzen, however, the well known critic on art, is inclined to attribute this picture to Pinturicchio.

18. BERNARDINO BETTI, called PINTURICCHIO.—Virgin and Child. On wood. 1 ft. 10 in. by 1 ft. 3½ in. Of the earliest and best time of the master; beautiful in composition and delicate and noble in feeling.

19. MARCO PALMEZZANO DA FORLÌ.—Judith. Figures rather more than half-length. On wood. 2 ft. 8¾ in. by 1 ft. 11¼ in. This is decidedly the work of this secondary master of the school of Romagna, who, though somewhat dry, was careful in execution.

LATE FLORENTINE SCHOOL.

20. ANGELO BRONZINO.—Portrait of Cosmo I., Grand Duke of Tuscany. On wood. 8 in. by 6½ in. Among the numerous portraits of this prince by the master, this takes a very distinguished place for the unusual warmth and softness of the colouring, combined with his usual truth and careful rendering.

GERMAN SCHOOL.

COLOGNE AND LOWER RHENISH SCHOOLS OF THE 15TH CENTURY.

22. STEPHEN LOTHENER (flourished in Cologne, 1442-1451).— St. Catherine of Alexandria, St. Matthew and St. John the Evangelists. Full-length figures. On a gold background. 2 ft. 3 in. by 1 ft. 11 in. This fine picture agrees so entirely in the noble character of the heads, in drawing, cast of drapery, and style of colour, with the well-known picture in the Cologne Cathedral, that it may be decidedly assigned to the same painter. It appears, however, to have been earlier executed. The above-given name "Stephen Lothener" was only ascertained some years ago, and is due to the researches of M. Merlo in the archives of Cologne. Albert Durer, in his Journal in the Netherlands, says that he gave the keeper of the Town House Chapel at Cologne two silver pennies to see Master Stephen's pictures. In examining the old registers of the place, M. Merlo discovered that, between the years 1442 and 1451, one Stephen Lothener was twice elected, as a distin-

guished painter, to fill the office of Councillor among his brethren of the same guild. The Cathedral picture, therefore, being the same as was formerly in the chapel of the Town House, there is no doubt that the Master Stephen mentioned by Albert Durer is the painter of the same, and identical with Stephen Lothener. We thus also arrive at the knowledge that this picture was painted towards 1450, and not, as has been generally supposed, in 1410.*

23. The MASTER of the LIEVERSBERG PASSION (flourished in Cologne, 1466-70).—The Presentation in the Temple. Full-length figures. On wood. 3 ft. 7 in. by 2 ft. 9½ in. The companion to this picture, representing the Marriage of the Virgin, exists in the Royal Gallery at Munich. Researches in Meckenen, a small town in Westphalia, have proved that no painter of the name of Israel van Meckenen, originally given to this picture, ever existed, but that the well-known goldsmith and engraver Israel van Meckeln is alone traceable there. The name, therefore, of Israel van Meckenen as the painter of this picture and of many others, as given by the Boisserées, is perfectly untenable. Most of the pictures by this master having been discovered in Cologne, or in the adjacent country, for instance in the church of Linz on the Rhine, he is generally assumed to have been a Cologne painter, who introduced there the realistic feeling of the Van Eyck school, and flourished about 1460-70, which is evident from inscribed pictures. As his principal work, the Passion, in eight compartments, was formerly in the possession of the late M. Lieversberg of Cologne, he is usually designated as above. The picture here belongs to his best works.

24. Portrait of a lady of the name of Hoferin. (The name being inscribed at the top of the picture.) On wood. 1 ft. 9 in. by 1 ft. 3½ in. Animatedly conceived, and very carefully executed. Portraits by German painters of the 15th century are rare.

LOWER RHENISH SCHOOL.

26. Virgin and Child. Half-length figures. On fine linen. 1 ft. 2½ in. by 10½ in. The very round forms indicate the Lower Rhenish school, while the whole conception and the style of the gold ground show the marked influence of the old Dutch school.

---

* See notice of M. Merlo's work, by Sotzmann, in the Kunstblatt of 1853, p. 31.

The feeling is delicate, the motive and expression of the Child very animated. The colours have doubtless much faded with time. The execution, especially of the hair, is very careful. Towards 1500.

27. The Holy Family. Full-length figures. On fine linen. 1 ft. 4½ in. by 1 ft. A noble and refined sentiment pervades this picture, especially the figure of the Virgin. The motive of Joseph with the Child is very peculiar. The flowers on the border are treated quite in that taste which prevailed first in the Netherlands, after 1480, in Prayer Books, and which, by the end of the century, had partially spread through Germany.

30. MARTIN SCHONGAUER (died 1488.* Scholar of Roger van der Weyden the elder).—Virgin and Child. Full-length figures. On wood. 11 in. by 8¾ in. This valuable little picture agrees so entirely in character of the heads, and in drawing and style of drapery, with the well-known engravings by this master, and in colouring and treatment with his *only* authenticated pictures at Colmar—one representing the Virgin within an enclosure of roses being in the church of that place, and two wings of another altar-piece in the library—that it may be unquestionably considered as the work of Martin Schongauer's hand. It is, therefore, one of the finest and most remarkable in this collection, and not only the only known picture by the master in England, but, with the exception of those at Colmar, in Europe.

31. Crucifixion. Full-length figures. On wood. 7 in. by 7 in. The composition, expression of heads, warmth of colour, and careful and masterly execution of this little picture, indicate an admirable artist.

SCHOOL OF VAN EYCK.

32. HANS MEMLING.†—Virgin and Child. Half-length figures. On wood. 1 ft. 4 in. by 11 in. This picture is of the later and better time of Memling, scholar of Roger van der Weyden the elder (usually called Roger of Bruges), the best scholar of Jan van Eyck. It agrees most with the Virgin and Child in the Hos-

---

* See my remarks on Ernst Förster's History of German Art, Kunstblatt of 1854, p. 186.
† Usually, but erroneously, called HEMLING. The grounds for believing the name to have been Memling are stated in my remarks on Förster's work in the Kunstblatt of 1854, p. 177.

pital of St. John at Bruges, a picture executed for Nevenhoven the younger, and dated 1487.

NETHERLANDISH SCHOOL, about 1480.   Most resembling GOSWIN VAN DER
WEYDEN.

34. Coronation of the Virgin.   Triptych.   Full-length figures. On wood.   Principal picture, 3 ft. 5 in. by 2 ft. 2 in. ; each wing, 3 ft. 5½ in. by 11 in.   This picture is of the utmost interest from the whole style of the conception, the great richness of the figures, and the position which it occupies in the progress of the Van Eyck school.   While it quite retains the fulness of individuality (namely, in the heads, and especially in the male heads) which is charac- teristic of this school, and also possesses much of that solidity and mastery of treatment, particularly of the draperies, which distin- guish Memling, we remark something already prosaic in the ex- pressions, a departure from the feeling for beauty, especially in the tame and little attractive female heads, and finally a cold green tone in the flesh.   The authentic picture by Goswin van der Weyden, son of the younger Roger, which this work recalls, is in the Museum at Brussels, and represents a Coronation of the Virgin.

35. GERHART VAN DER MEERE [?] (scholar of Hubert van Eyck).—Virgin and Child.   More than half-length figures.   On wood.   8 in. by 6 in.   As no authentic work by Margaret van Eyck is known at all, the name formerly given to this beautiful little picture is quite arbitrary.   It agrees most, in character of heads and in colouring, with a work by Gerhart van der Meere, scholar of Hubert van Eyck, in the church of St. Bavon at Ghent.

36. ROGIER VAN DER WEYDEN the younger (died 1529. Scho- lar of his father, Rogier van der Weyden the elder).—1. Depo- sition from the Cross.   More than half-length figures.   2 ft. 6½ in. by 1 ft. 8 in.   This picture agrees so entirely with the Deposition from the Cross in the Museum at Berlin (No. 534), which Van Mander certifies as the work of Rogier van der Weyden the younger, that I cannot hesitate to ascribe it to him.   The great glow of colour and the solidity of execution bespeak, however, an earlier time of the master; to which period also, according to Passavant (see Christliche Kunst in Spanien, p. 134-137), two other examples of the same Deposition, now in Spain, may be assigned,

the one (obviously the earliest) in the church of S. Lorenzo in the Escurial, the other in the Royal Gallery at Madrid.

2. Ecce Homo. Half-length figures. On wood, gilt ground. 1 ft. 2½ in. by 11 in.

3. Mater Dolorosa. On wood, gilt ground. 1 ft. 2½ in. by 11 in.

Two excellent pictures by the master ; the Virgin of noble and earnest feeling. Both warm and transparent in colour, and of the earlier time of the master.

38. JAN GOSSAERT, called MABUSE.—Portrait of an Ecclesiastic. Half-length. Formerly ascribed to Memling, but the aërial perspective of the background is far too developed for him. The supposition, too, that this fine portrait, the beauty of which I fully recognise, is that of Van der Rüst, the Carmelite, who received Memling when wounded after the battle of Nancy, is unfounded ; the story itself standing on very insecure foundation. On the other hand, both conception and colouring agree with the portraits by Mabuse, belonging to the time when he executed those of the King and Queen of Scotland, now at Hampton Court.

39. A MASTER related to the earlier time of Mabuse.—The Virgin and Child in a Garden. Full-length figures. On wood. 1 ft. 1½ in. by 10½ in. Happily composed, noble in the full forms, of good expression, and of very careful execution.

GERMAN SCHOOL OF THE 16TH AND 17TH CENTURIES.

SCHOOLS OF FRANCONIA AND UPPER SAXONY.

40. HANS VON CULMBACH.—Portrait of a young man. Half-length. On wood. 1 ft. 8 in. by 1 ft. 2 in. This good portrait belongs assuredly to the school of Albert Durer. It recalls Hans von Culmbach more than any other painter.

SWABIAN SCHOOL.

42. HANS BURCKMAIR.—The Adoration of the Infant Christ. Full-length figures. On wood. 3 ft. 9 in. by 2 ft. 2 in. A good picture by this principal painter of the Augsburg school, about 1520, in his decidedly realistic manner; thus the shepherds are the best part. Of great power and depth of colour.

43. MARTIN SCHAFNER, of Ulm (flourished 1499-1535).—

The Infant Christ learning to walk. Full-length figures. On wood. 1 ft. 10½ in. by 1 ft. 6 in. The mildness in the head of the Virgin, the original motive, which is very animated in the Child, the tender colour of the flesh, and the careful execution, render this picture very attractive. The four principal pictures by this rare master, representing events from the Life of the Virgin, are in the Munich Gallery.

45. MASTER UNKNOWN, with a monogram composed of M and O, and the date 1530.—A portrait. Half-length. On wood. 1 ft. 9½ in. by 1 ft. 7½ in. This delicate picture, which has, however, suffered in the flesh tones, has many of the characteristics of Martin Schafner. I could not succeed in making out the meaning of the monogram.

SCHOOL OF COLOGNE.

36. A COLOGNE MASTER, supposed to be of the name of Cristoph, flourished 1510-30. — St. Peter and St. Dorothea. Full-length figures. The three companion-pictures to this work of art are now in the Pinacothek at Munich. On wood. 4 ft. 2 in. by 2 ft. 4½ in. The name of Lucas van Leyden, given originally by the Boisserées to the painter of this picture, is quite arbitrary; inasmuch as it agrees in no respect either with the numerous engravings, nor yet with the rare paintings by that master. Almost all the pictures known of the painter before us were formerly in churches in Cologne, so that he may be assumed to have belonged to that city. The name of Cristoph is said to have been connected with one of the pictures, whence the name now given to all. I am convinced that he must have formed himself upon Quentin Matsys, whom he quite equals in minute and masterly detail of execution, though he falls far short of him in feeling for beauty and refinement, as seen in his monotonous female heads, and in his ugly hands.

NETHERLANDISH SCHOOL OF THE 16TH CENTURY.

52. Virgin and Child in a garden. Full-length figures. On wood. 2 ft. by 1 ft. 8 in. Delicate and sweet in feeling, the modelling tenderly blended in a cool subdued flesh-tone. The landscape also very careful.

53. BERNARDIN VAN ORLEY (BAREND VAN BRUSSELS).—

1. Christ and Mary Magdalen. " Lord, if thou hadst been here, my brother had not died." Full-length figures. On wood. 2 ft. 6 in. by 2 ft. 6 in. The Christ of great power of colour; the female heads of noble character, though somewhat monotonous, the draperies admirably modelled in a deep juicy tone, and the whole execution uncommonly careful. This picture belongs to his middle and best time.

54.—2. The Holy Family near a fountain. Full-length figures. On wood. 2 ft. 8½ in. by 2 ft. 1 in. A careful picture of his later time ; pleasing in the head of the Virgin, but cold and crude in colour.

55.—3. Portrait of a woman. On wood. 10 in. by 7 in. Very delicate in feeling, the execution fused and delicate, and of the utmost detail in the hair.

56.—4. Virgin and Child, with two Saints. Full-length figures. On wood. 1 ft. 8 in. by 1 ft. 2½ in. A careful picture of the earlier time of the master, the head of the Child especially pretty.

57. JOACHIM PATENIER of Dinant.—1. The Magdalen. Figure more than half-length. On wood. 1 ft. 8½ in. by 1 ft. 2 in. Particularly pleasing in the forms and careful in the execution. The heavy flesh-tones show his later time.

58.—2. St. Christopher. Full-length figures. On wood. 1 ft. 10 in. by 10 in. Of the middle time of the master ; in some parts the landscape has suffered.

59.—3. St. John in the Island of Patmos. Full-length figure. On wood. 1 ft. 2½ in. by 9½ in. A picture of the later time of the master, feeble in character, drawing, and colour, though interesting in the details.

60.—4. The Crucifixion. Full-length figures. On wood. 2 ft. 11½ in. by 1 ft. 11 in. The fine feeling in the soft folds of the Virgin's drapery, and other figures, show that this was painted under Italian influence in the latest time of the master, of which it is by far the finest specimen I know. He appears here to great advantage as the earliest Netherlandish landscape-painter. The group of trees in the centre announces, in point of chiaroscuro and truth, the coming of Ruysdael.

61. JAN VAN HEEMSEN. The monogram of the painter, HH, and the date 1534, are inscribed on the top of pillar.—The

Adoration of the Kings.   Figures nearly full-length.   On wood.
3 ft. 2½ in. by 2 ft. 2½ in.   Of noble character of heads, considering
the master, but, as usual with him, hard in the outlines, and heavy
and gaudy in the colouring.   The execution careful.

64. JAN MABUSE. — 1.   A girl writing.   Half-length.   On
wood.   11 in. by 9 in.   Very attractive for the naïve feeling and
admirable foreshortening of the inclined head.   The hands have
the short and thick fingers peculiar to Mabuse in his portraits—
for instance, the children of Henry the Seventh at Hampton
Court.

65.—2. Madonna and Child, in a Landscape.   Full-length
figures.   On wood.   Diameter, 2 ft. 8 in.   The head of the Virgin
is very noble, the landscape of very careful execution.   The cold
tone in the whole picture bespeaks the later time of the master.

66. JAN MOSTAERT [?].—A Pietà.   Full-length figures.   On
wood.   11 in. by 8½ in.   The whole style of art here shows a
later period than Hugo van der Goes, to whom this picture was
formerly attributed, and approaches more to the character of Jan
Mostaert, who longest retained the feeling of the Van Eyck school.
The head of the Virgin is noble in the expression, that of the
Christ less agreeable and not true, from the stiff manner in which
it stands erect and unsupported.   The execution is very careful.

68. HERRY DE BLES, called CIVETTA.—1. Mount Calvary.
Full-length figures.   On wood.   3 ft. 1½ in. by 2 ft. 2½ in.   Unusually noble in the heads, rich in detail, and careful in execution.
The pervading heavy and grey tone bespeaks the middle time
of the master.

69.—2. The Adoration of the Kings.   Triptych.   Full-length
figures.   On wood.   Size of centre picture, 3 ft. 5 in. by 2 ft.
3 in. ; each wing, 3 ft. 5 in. by 1 ft.   Well composed and carefully executed, but rather feeble in drawing and tame in the
expression of the heads.   The middle time of the master.

70.—3. The Deposition from the Cross.   Triptych.   Full-length
figures.   On wood.   The centre picture, 2 ft. 10½ in. by 1 ft.
10½ in. ; each wing, 2 ft. 5 in. by 9 in.

78. MATTHEW GRUNEWALD (flourished about 1480-1520).—
The Virgin with the Child in Glory, surrounded by Angels.
A triptych.   Whole-length figures, about three-quarter-life size.
Centre picture.   The Virgin in the middle standing on the

crescent, in which is a large face, and holding the Infant on her
right arm, while she gives him a bunch of grapes with the left
hand, of which the Child is about to break off a grape. Her golden
hair flows down on each side. In the air are two angels holding an
imperial crown over her head. On the right is St. Catherine standing and holding with her right hand the hilt of a sword, and with
her left the wheel, both the instruments of her martyrdom. On
her left is St. Barbara holding an open book with her left hand.
Behind her is the tower, in a window of which is her attribute the
chalice.

Right wing. St. Nicolas of Bari, in episcopal robes, holding
with both hands a large book, on which the three purses are somewhat indistinctly represented as round substances.

Left wing. St. George. In full armour of the period of the
painter, standing on the dragon. His right hand holds a lance
with a banner—his left is on the hilt of a sword. The blue colour
on the wings is modern.

Right wing, outer side. St. James the elder. The pilgrim's
staff in his hands, the scallop-shell on his hat, and at his side four
staffs crossed two and two. Next him is another saint holding a
long staff terminating in a cross in both hands, and in the left
hand his cap also.

Left wing, outer side. St. Erasmus in episcopal robes and crook.
In his left hand a book. Against his left arm leans the instrument with which his bowels were torn out; also the bowels themselves in regular red stripes.

This is one of the most remarkable of the now very rare works
of this great master, who lived in Aschaffenburg, and was probably
born there. That scarcely anything is known of him is a striking
proof of the very meagre materials existing of the earlier art-
history of Germany. Mr. Passavant and myself have each recognised in this painter the master of Lucas Cranach, whom, however, he far surpasses in feeling for beauty, and taste, and particularly in drawing, though inferior to Lucas Cranach's later works
in transparency of colouring. The heads of both the female
saints are elevated in form and dignified in expression—those of
SS. Nicolas and George of very true and portrait-like conception.
The draperies show a far purer taste than even most of Albert
Durer's works. The colouring, finally, is of great power and clear-

ness. The outer sides are by the hand of a skilful assistant. The
outlines are harder, the colouring greyer, the modelling inferior,
but the characters of the heads, which are correctly drawn, are
very good.

Besides these the Prince Consort has recently purchased some
frescoes from the Sacchetti Palace, at Brescia, by LATTANZIO
GAMBARA, representing scenes from the combats of the Centaurs
and Lapithæ, &c. These frescoes are worthy of note, as belonging
to a comparatively late period, and yet displaying in essential
respects, such as feeling for beauty, energy of conception, solid
treatment, and full colouring, the manner of the great Italian
fresco-painters of the first half of the 16th century.

ANCIENT COINS AND PICTURES IN THE POSSESSION OF
GENERAL FOX,
KENSINGTON.

Among my most agreeable reminiscences of England is that
of a Sunday spent beneath the hospitable roof of this gentleman.
General and Lady Mary Fox reside in a house within a garden
which adjoins the beautiful grounds of Holland House.   Nothing
can exceed the comfort and picturesque arrangement of the interior,
which is decorated with paintings and objects of art, nor the beauty
and admirable order of the garden, all of which appeared to the
best advantage on a bright sunny day.   Here also I found my
esteemed friend Mr. Burgon, the great numismatic connoisseur,
who kindly directed my attention at once to the finest and most
important specimens in a collection of Greek coins amounting to
above 7000 in number.   Although acquainted with the most
remarkable coins in the great collections of Munich, Vienna, Paris,
and the British Museum, I nevertheless found various examples
here which were either new to me, or which I had not previously
seen in such perfect preservation.   Above all, I must notice two
coins of the city of Thurii with the head of Pallas on the obverse.
Even in the earlier one the ideal of this goddess is seen developed
with great purity of form, while in the head of the other, which
belongs to the finest period of Grecian art, I do not hesitate to
recognise that representation of the goddess which, of all that has

descended to us, gives us the worthiest idea of Phidias' conception of the same, as rendered in his chryselephantine statue. The high relief in which this coin is executed has afforded the artist the means of an unusual degree of carrying out. The conception combines an astonishing grandeur with the purest beauty, and the highest perfection of plastic style with rich accessories of the most elevated taste; to all of which is superadded a preservation which leaves nothing to be desired. In comparison with this, I must own that even the beautiful head of the Arethusa on the tetradrachm of Syracuse takes a secondary place. Upon the helmet Mr. Burgon has discovered a minute V, the monogram of the artist. In comparison with this it was very interesting to remark the Pallas upon an Athenian coin in which the more purely feminine ideal and the mild and tender character are more worked out, which probably followed the conception of Phidias, whose statue bore the name of Kallimorphos. A head of Alexander upon a tetradrachm of Lysimachus approaches in beauty the head of the same monarch on the same coin in the British Museum, vol. i. p. 92. A coin of the city of Pytheus inscribed Θεοδοτος εποιησε, with a head of Apollo taken in front, and with broad, soft forms, on the obverse, is a unique specimen. It is one of the two known Greek coins with the name of the artist at length. As General Fox, who treated me with the confidence of an old friend, remarked the interest with which this coin inspired me, he offered me what I should never have ventured to request, but which I most thankfully accepted, viz. an impression of it. It would involve me too far were I to attempt to describe the number of important coins, partly in the archaic and partly in the finest style of Greek art, which I found here. I will only remark that this collection also contains the well-known small electron coins from Asia Minor, which, in the great deficiency of large specimens of authentic sculpture, are of the greatest significance in the history of the Ionic school. Some of these are very beautiful.

Among the pictures that are distributed in the various apartments I found also much that interested me. In the library, which is decorated with a series of portraits, is that of Garrick by SIR JOSHUA REYNOLDS, which is as spirited in conception as it is warm and true in colouring, and careful in execution. A female portrait also, in profile, by the same, in Lady Mary's charming room, is, however faded, still very attractive. Some early Italian pictures of the 14th century serve to show the extensive range of General Fox's taste. In the hall are two dignified figures, half-lengths, probably intended for Prophets, of the School of Giotto. Two other good pictures of the same school had been recently acquired from the Rev. Mr. Sandford. I also observed a small picture by the Sienese master Sano di Pietro. The history of Susannah also, upon a *cassone* (chest), is remarkable; it is probably by Dello. A Spanish painter, who is here represented by scenes in the taste of Watteau, and of great elegance, painted on what was originally the panels of a coach, is new to me.

Finally, this visit gave me the agreeable opportunity of making the acquaintance of Mr. Waddington, the well-known collector of coins, who usually resides in Paris.

PICTURES BELONGING TO THE EARL OF HARRINGTON,
Harrington House, Kensington.

These pictures, which are distributed in the different apartments of a large house, created no favourable impression by their general appearance. The cause for this consists partly in their neglected condition, and partly in the way in which good pictures are mixed up with others of an inferior kind, and originals with copies. Although giving the pictures according to the apartments in which they hang, I subjoin the numbers in all cases where they are appended, so that in case of any change of place it may be easier to identify them.

THE HALL.

Sir Peter Lely.—Portrait of King Charles the Second, seated, in rich dress. Warmly coloured, and of careful execution.

THE LIBRARY.

Jan Messys. — The Virgin with the standing Child. The head of the Virgin elevated; in other respects also a particularly good example of this often repeated picture. I don't know what master's name is given to it here.

Canaletti.—1 and 2. Views of less-known portions of Venice. Clear and careful.

THE DINING-ROOM.

PARMIGIANINO.—Ganymede carried off by the Eagle. Not fortunate in composition, but clear, warm, and powerful. Here attributed to Annibale Carracci. Another example of this picture is in the Dresden Gallery.

THE SALOON.

This name is given to a stately hall with a gallery around.

VANDYCK.—1. Portrait of Charles the First, standing, in an unusual dress, his right hand on his hip, and holding out the left hand. The background architecture and landscape. Full-length figure, life-size. Of warm and clear colouring and careful execution. Painted about 1636.

2. Portrait of Queen Henrietta, in white silk dress, her right hand leaning on a table covered with a green cloth, her left lightly holding her dress. The background similar in character to the foregoing. Not inferior in point of art to the companion picture.

A picture representing the Continence of Scipio is here erroneously ascribed to Vandyck. I don't know how far it agrees with the picture of that subject, also attributed to Vandyck, which was engraved by Miller, in the collection of the Duke of Argyle. In colouring and treatment it most recalls THEODOR BOYERMANS, a master who painted much in Antwerp.

The Woman taken in Adultery, called Rubens, is an early copy of the fine picture in the Miles collection at Leigh Court.

THE PICTURE-GALLERY.

JAN BREUGHEL.—(No. 69.) A high-road, with carts and horsemen. Particularly warm, clear, and transparent in colour.

JOB BERKHEYDEN.— 1 (No. 143). Two horsemen have pulled up before a tavern with a vine hanging over the entrance. A third has dismounted. Near them are a woman and dogs. Signed. Pleasingly composed, and as careful as it is powerful in colour, though somewhat heavy.

2 (No. 112). Of similar merit, but cruder in colouring.

CUYP. — 1 (No. 134). Two horsemen before a house, one of whom has dismounted from his grey horse. Next them a man and two dogs. Of his first period, when his colouring was heavy and his flesh-tones red.

2. The companion. A similar composition of similar style.

Sir Joshua Reynolds.—1. Portrait of the Honble. Francis Stanhope, as a child, standing in a landscape, dressed in white silk, with hat and feathers. This picture is warmly coloured, but leaves the mind cold.

2. Portrait of the Honble. Lincoln Stanhope, also in white silk, but seated, and pointing to a drawing in his left hand. A charming child, spiritedly rendered in a delicate tone, analogous to Greuze.

3. Portrait of the Honble. Leicester Stanhope, now Lord Harrington, as a child, with a drum. The background landscape. The head is pretty ; the arms have unfortunately suffered.

4. Portrait of the Honble. Fitzroy Stanhope, also in a landscape, playing with a large dog. Of great power and clearness of colour.

5 (No. 31). Portrait of a woman, seated, with pretty features, holding a little girl before her, dressed, like herself, in white silk. At her right side is another girl. The background a landscape of warm tone. To the knees. Very animatedly conceived, and warmly coloured. The little girl with the hat and feathers is the most attractive.

Teniers. — 1 (No. 161). The interior of a tavern, with an old and a young peasant playing cards. The latter is showing two aces. An old man with a jug of beer, a young man, and further behind a third figure with a beer-glass (very sketchily treated), are looking on. In the background are three other persons before a chimney. Signed. Spiritedly thrown on the canvas in a brownish tone.

Philip Wouvermans.—A man on a grey horse, and a lady, are stopping before a smithy, within which a brown horse is being shod. Besides these are several other figures, fowls, and two pigs lying down. Behind the smithy are ruins. In the distance an airy mountain. On wood. Almost miniature-like in execution, but of cool, and, in the foreground, of dark colouring.

Teniers.—2 (No. 158). In the foreground are nine figures playing with ninepins. Further behind are houses. The distance is illumined with a gleam of sunshine. On wood. Signed. In a very brown but clear tone, and spiritedly painted.

Cornelis Poelemburg.—(No. 93.) The Baptism of Christ.

A rich composition of careful execution. Disfigured by having been enlarged all round.

Lucas van Leyden.—To this rare master I attribute a small altarpiece with wings. The centre picture contains the Virgin seated in a landscape, and giving a pink to the Child. On a tree behind her is an owl and several other birds. On the right wing is St. Anna approaching ; on the left wing is a saint kneeling, with an immense head of hair, and holding a shepherd's crook. A later inscription on the frame informs us that this figure represents St. Gratianus. Of very solid carrying out. Now much disfigured by dirt.

Constantin Netscher. — 1 and 2. To this son of Gaspar Netscher I attribute two small whole-length portraits, on wood, which an inscription of later date on the frame assigns to the Chevalier van der Werff. The first (No. 118) represents, according to a contemporary inscription, Anne Hyde, Countess of Clarendon ; the second (No. 119) la Duchesse de Chevreux, represented as a young lady in pink dress, with two greyhounds. These pictures appear to me not smooth enough in treatment for Van der Werff.

Willem van de Velde. — 1 (No. 71). A quiet sea, with various boats and a small man-of-war, whence a cannon is being fired. Sky and water have a reddish light. The reflections of the vessels in the water are admirable, and the whole of great power.

2 (No. 90). A slightly agitated sea. On the right a fleet of men-of-war receding in perspective in the distance ; on the left, and more in the foreground, a vessel whence a gun is being fired. Quite in front is a pier, and two sailors launching a boat. The delicate clouds are tenderly lighted. Companion to the foregoing, but far finer. The smoke from the gun is of the greatest truth.

Job Berkheyden.—(No. 30.) To this master I attribute a pleasing little picture in the taste of Wouvermans.

Vandyck.—3 (No. 31). The Virgin seated and looking tenderly at the Child, who sits naked on her lap, and is also looking at her, and stretching his right hand towards her. The head of the Virgin is unusually noble, the execution careful, in a warm, but not exactly clear tone. The modelling of the Child is very fine. I saw another example of this picture in 1835, in the collection of Sir Thomas Hope.   I do not venture, however, after so long an interval, to enter into a comparison of the two.

APOLLO DRAWING-ROOM.

Vandyck.—4 (No. 131). The Virgin seated, and contemplating the Child, who is leaning against her partly uncovered breast. The ground is dark.   On wood.   The same picture perhaps which was engraved by Lorenzi, and mentioned in Smith's Catalogue as No. 429.   Both the forms and the somewhat sorrowful expression of the Virgin are very noble, and the modelling in a powerful brownish tone of admirable body.

Salvator Rosa.—1 and 2. Two small pictures of horsemen fighting.   Spirited and sketchy, with very dark shadows.

Jan van Goyen.—A landscape, with grand trees in the foreground, under which four figures are loitering. Signed, and dated 1632.   An unusual composition for the master.   Broad, slight, but of masterly handling.

Canaletti.—1 and 2. Two views of Venice. Small and pleasing pictures.

DRAWING-ROOM.

Vandyck (?).—Portrait of a daughter of Charles the First. This hangs in too high and dark a place for any opinion.

Zurbaran.—(No. 2.) I am most reminded of this master in a picture of St. Anthony of Padua reading, with two books next him on one side, and a lily on the other.   The strongly foreshortened head is noble in form and feeling, the execution is masterly.

Teniers.—(No. 72.) An organman with a dog by a string, and a woman with a warming-pan, in a village.   Signed.   Broadly treated in a heavy brown tone.

Marco Oggione.—(No. 79.) I am inclined to attribute to this master a small early copy on wood of Leonardo da Vinci's Madonna del Lago, known by Longhi's engraving.   The head of the Virgin is elevated, and of great power and colour; the two children are less successful.

Quirinus Breklenkamp.—(No. 139.) A mother and daughter in earnest conversation—the father listening.   It is a pity that this picture, which is pleasing in composition, and particularly warm in colour, should be so much sunk.

Philip Wouvermans.—(No. 167.) To this master and to his

first period I attribute a picture with a man standing by a grey horse, and a woman with a child sitting on the ground. A warm evening light makes a good effect.

CONSTANTIN NETSCHER.—(No. 83.) Portrait of a young girl in rose-coloured hat, holding roses. Animatedly conceived, and, in the dress especially, of broad and soft treatment.

STOTHARD.—(No. 13.) A very prettily composed Centaur family appears to me to be by this master. In the foreground is a female Centaur nursing her young one; at her feet is another; behind her, foreshortened, is the male. Of powerful colouring.

COLLECTION OF PICTURES BELONGING TO R. P. NICHOLS, ESQ., 25, MAIDA HILL WEST, PADDINGTON.

Mr. Nichols belongs to that class of collectors in England who, while animated by an ardent love for art, show no exclusiveness of taste. This gentleman possesses examples of the most various schools and epochs. I must confine myself to the notice of the most remarkable.

DINING-ROOM.

GIROLAMO DA SANTA CROCE.—King David seated in the open air and playing the harp, which is here represented as a kind of guitar. This picture has been ascribed to different masters. I recognised it, however, as the work of this scholar of Giovanni Bellini, who brought his master's manner into repute in his native city of Bergamo. Though realistic in form, the elevated feeling in the head renders it very attractive; the effect of the general warmth and mildness of the harmony is also very beautiful, and every portion—hands, drapery, and landscape background—are rendered with great detail and care. A life-size figure like this by the master is but rarely seen.

FRANCESCO FRANCIA.—Portrait of a man in youthful years. This picture is attractive both in feeling and colour, but hangs too high for an adequate opinion of its merits, the more so as it is covered with a glass.

GUIDO RENI.—The penitent Magdalen. A stately example of this often-treated subject by the master. Beautiful in forms, and of a decided silvery tone, but somewhat cold in feeling.

PHILIP WOUVERMANS.—A large picture, with a group of horsemen as the principal object. An admirable work in his second manner.

2. A picture in his first manner. Genuine and fine.

3. A landscape, still in the taste of his master Wynants, with but few figures of men and animals. Of great delicacy of keeping, and pure feeling for nature.

SCHOOL OF TITIAN.—Holy Family in a landscape. Very pleasing in composition, and of warm and harmonious colouring.

DRAWING-ROOM.

RUBENS.— A sketch of tolerable size for one of his Ascensions of the Virgin; if I remember right, for the picture on the high altar in the cathedral of Antwerp. Very spirited, and of a warm and very harmonious tone. The bright golden tone of the angels is particularly charming. As Rubens frequently committed the execution of these pictures in great measure to his scholars, to whom such sketches served as the model by which they worked, they are often observed to be carried out with a degree of detail hardly compatible with the idea of a sketch. This is the case here, though the covering of a glass prevented my forming a closer opinion of the treatment of the brush.

MURILLO.—His favourite representation of the Immaculate Conception, treated in cool tones. The head is noble, and worthy of the master; but the very commonplace forms of the angels, and still more the somewhat heavy tone, indicate the co-operation of his scholars.

GUIDO RENI.—St. Lucy. Half-length. Very attractive in forms and in the feeling of the head, as well as in the tenderly-warm and harmonious tone.

ZURBARAN.—A large and careful sketch for one of his principal pictures in Seville. Above are a saint and the four Fathers of the Church. Below are other saints. Admirably composed, powerful in colour, and of spirited treatment.

ADRIAN VAN DE VELDE.—A rich and somewhat large picture, only distinguished from the fine picture in the Grosvenor Gallery (vol. ii. p. 168) by a few additions.

CARLO DOLCE.—St. Anthony adoring the Infant Christ, who is appearing to him. Less insipidly sweet in feeling than usual with the master, and of fine and transparent colouring.

SASSOFERRATO.—The Virgin and Child. Copy of the well-known Camuccini Raphael now in the collection of the Duke of Northumberland—with this difference, that the painter has rendered the figures the size of life, and introduced St. Joseph with some success. Very pleasing, unusually warm in tone, and very careful.

THE HALL.

VANDYKE.—Study of a grey horse, about half life-size. Very spirited.

PIETRO DE MOYA.—Portrait of a Priest. This shows how the painter studied Vandyck, and, after him, Velasquez. Animated and careful.

A FEW NOTICES ON THE CRYSTAL PALACE AT SYDENHAM, CONSIDERED AS A MUSEUM OF ART.

After all that has been written about this magnificent undertaking, it would be superfluous, no less than presumptuous, for me to offer an opinion upon it in any detail. Still less can I attempt to describe the infinite number of works of art there united. To do this, as the various catalogues prove, would occupy several volumes.

Considering, however, the title assumed by my work, there is no doubt that to omit that treasury contained within these glass walls would not only be unjustifiable, but might be interpreted as a want of appreciation on my part of its real importance. Under these circumstances I have thought it better to offer at all events a few general observations. These will principally refer to the necessary conditions of the undertaking; to the effect, peculiar only to this locality, produced by the objects of art on the minds of the general observer, the amateur, and the connoisseur; and finally to a few points regarding the best possible way of exhibiting the works of all ages and all nations which appear to me to be of importance for the completion of the great plan. The collections of natural history and manufactures, as not belonging to my department, must, however, be passed over in silence.

Our age has been reproached, and not unjustly, for an absence as compared to other periods, of an architectural style peculiar to itself, and for executing buildings in the mere eclectic adaptation of the Greek, the Roman, the Norman, the Gothic, and the Renaissance styles, or in the imitation of the tastelessness of the Rococo, or even in the arbitrary combination of various orders of architecture in one. The Crystal Palace, however, affords a brilliant proof that our time has not only fulfilled the task assigned to it, but fulfilled it in a thoroughly new and original manner. It is at once obvious that none of the styles already mentioned could have answered for the purpose here attained. The object was to roof over a space of an extent compared with which St. Peter's at Rome appears moderate, and further to roof it over at so airy an height that considerable erections should find space within it. It was necessary, also, that the contents destined for exhibition should be surrounded with ample light; and above all it was indispensable to insure to a building of such colossal dimensions a corresponding stability of material. These conditions could only be accomplished by the combination of the most solid material—iron, with the most fragile substance—glass. The idea of this union on so extended a scale, which originated in the mind of Sir Joseph Paxton, is, however, entirely new, and belongs exclusively to our time. Having, therefore, as is known to have been the case with *all* forms of architecture, first fulfilled the practical objects of its existence, the style is found to develop new and peculiar beauties of its own. The sense of lightness and boldness combined with strength is suggested by this style as by none other preceding it. The alternation of straight and flowing lines affords the eye the charm of variety, while in this respect the palace of Sydenham, by arching the roof of the naves and side aisles as well as the great transept, far exceeds its predecessor in Hyde Park. The proportions are also far more happily balanced, and the whole appearance more harmonious. If it must be granted that this particular architecture of the 19th century is totally deficient in monumental effect, it possesses, on the other hand, the element of the marvellous and fairylike in the highest degree. It is remarkable also that this very element has proceeded solely from the soberest calculations of engineering knowledge—reminding one of a piece of music by Beethoven—the result apparently of an unfettered fancy, and yet based in reality upon a mathematical combination. Independent, however, of Paxton, who gave the original idea, and of the great engineers who carried it out, it must be remembered that England is the only country which offers the conditions essential to the accomplishment of such an undertaking. Here alone, namely, can be found private individuals of that largeness of mind which leads them to unite for a common purpose, and at the same time of that indispensable and extraordinary wealth which shrinks not from obstacles which in other countries would be looked upon as insurmountable. In the case of the Crystal Palace the everlasting honour of having first gathered together a number of individuals willing to carry the idea into execution belongs to Joseph Leech. For the command, also, of the three great classes of contents—the works of art of all periods of time and of all people of the globe; the productions of nature from the time of the antediluvian animals; and the creations of industry most characteristic of our age—for the command of these no other nation is so favourably situated as the English. As respects works of art, their love of travel and adventure gives them the most complete knowledge of all that is most remarkable, and their world-extended commerce the readiest means of obtaining all they desire to possess; while, as concerns the department of manufactures, England itself offers them all that is most perfect, and in the richest abundance.

But to turn to that which most concerns this work, viz. the department of art. I may first remark that, whether for the unlearned, the amateur, or the connoisseur, the Crystal Palace in this respect offers a combination of means of information and enjoyment such as has never been hitherto presented to the world. It is distinguished from all previous exhibitions of art by the circumstance that a considerable number of architectural structures are here seen in their original size; and, as those who are acquainted with some well-known building only by means of drawings will acknowledge, the real size in this case is far more important for a right conception of the effect of architecture than either for that of painting or sculpture. While, therefore, various of the Courts, such as the Pompeian and the Alhambra, are in this respect strikingly successful, it is to be regretted that Egyptian architecture, the great distinction of which is its colossal dimen-

sions, should not rather have been represented by a few of the
largest columns from the temple of Carnac than by the more
extensive court on a small scale which is here seen.   It stands to
reason that, considering the number and extent of specimens of
architecture existing, only a few single examples could, at best,
be given here.   By the ceaseless labours, however, of the directors
of the Crystal Palace, every possible means for the study of this
art by means of representation has been afforded ; and in the year
1856 a collection of photographs of the most remarkable ecclesiastical and secular edifices were placed in the building.

As regards the art of sculpture, which, by means of casts, may
be seen in a form differing, if carefully executed, from the original
only in point of material, the fundamental idea has admitted of
the nearest approach to perfection in point of realisation.   At the
same time neither expense nor trouble have been spared in order
to attain this end.   While, therefore, those who are unacquainted
with the originals may find here a boundless field of enjoyment
and instruction, the connoisseur also benefits in no ordinary
degree.   As is well known to all who have been engaged in such
studies, there is nothing which so much assists the formation of the
judgment as regards works of art as the comparison of a large
number equally of the most different and of the most allied
examples.   Thus, for instance, the relation of the art of sculpture
to that of architecture, under the protection of which it was first
fostered and developed, as exemplified by the three distinct
periods of art—that of early Egypt, Greece, and Italy in the
time of Bernini—is here brought to view in the most striking
manner.   In Egypt, where the mother retained the daughter at
all times in strict and rigid dependence, sculpture never attained
a free and separate development, but continued throughout—as a
glance at the seated colossi and at the Egyptian reliefs suffices to
prove—to show an architectonic character.   In Greece the relation of the one to the other appears in the happiest medium.
Here the mother is seen granting the daughter sufficient liberty
to assert her being and speak her own tongue, at the same
time confining her so far within limits that sculpture can never
be said to have forgotten her origin.   From this happy com-
promise has resulted the *plastic* style, properly speaking.   For the
arrangement of the sculptures of the Parthenon consequent on

the form of the pediment, that of the reliefs in the metopes, and of the well-known Panathenaic Procession along the building, offer the most convincing testimony of the instrumentality of architecture in developing the three principal forms of sculpture—the round, alto, and basso relievo. Finally, in the time of Bernini, sculpture, having forgotten her descent, threw off all allegiance to architecture, and wandered at will. For this breach of filial piety she was severely punished, the penalty being the loss of her own proper laws of style, and the adoption in their stead of those of painting, which were totally at variance with her conditions. A proof of this is seen in Bernini's Pietà from the crypt of the Capella Corsini, in the church of S. Giovanni in Laterano. As regards, also, the comparison between nearly-allied forms of sculpture, the spectator will find the numerous representations of the same idea as expressed by Greek sculptors highly important. And this gives me the opportunity of remarking one of the greatest characteristics in the art of this marvellously gifted people; for while, on the one hand, the delicacy of their feeling led them never essentially to depart from that form of representation which had been once pronounced the most fitted to the end proposed, they, on the other hand, by no means lapsed into habits of slavish repetition. Thus they will be always found adopting delicate modifications suggested by the peculiarities of the local legend, or by the individuality of the artist, &c., and yet always within the bounds of the established ideal. This reveals to us not only the means by which the high development of the various types was attained, but also the secret of the length of time that art maintained this elevation. And here I need only refer the reader to the various conceptions of the ideal of the Venus, exemplified by the various statues of the goddess here brought together, and of which the Venus of Milo and of the Capitol, and the Venus de' Medici, are peculiarly characteristic. And the same remark extends even to the portrait busts, as a comparison of the three busts of Homer will show. All three agree in the chief characteristics attributed to the father of poetry, and yet each exhibits an original and in many respects different development. Also, as regards the chief works of Christian sculpture we have direct means of comparison, as, for instance, between the colossal equestrian statues in bronze of the two celebrated condottieri, Gatta-

melata and Coleoni, the first and earlier by Donatello, before
the church of S. Antonio at Padua, the second and later by
Verocchio, before the church of SS. Giovanni e Paolo at Venice.
While we recognise in the more quiet and restrained conception
of Donatello a certain influence of the antique, the more realistic
invention of Verocchio gives us the impetuous force of the period
of Coleoni.

At present the great scheme of the Crystal Palace has effected
but little in the exhibition of the art of painting. But here
serious impediments arise. For, in order to give the public
the same advantages in painting as in sculpture, copies of the
finest works of all periods and schools, the size of the originals, would be requisite. This, however, would demand a far
greater outlay than in the case of plaster casts, without at the
same time affording the same satisfactory result. The directors
of the Palace, well aware of this deficiency, have therefore
endeavoured to supply it temporarily by the exhibition of a
number of water-coloured copies. But, independent of the small-
ness of scale as compared with the originals, these drawings bear
too much the impress of the individuality of the copyist, otherwise
a very skilful artist. Far more satisfactory is the copy of the
ceiling of the Stanza della Segnatura, by Raphael, which gives a
good representation of the monumental painting of the Italian
school at the period of its highest excellence. A series of tapestries from the cartoons of Raphael, and various copies from some
of the chief works of Rubens arranged as transparencies, are well
adapted to the purpose in view. An exhibition of the paintings of
the different nations of our own time, which was opened in 1855,
contains also many good specimens, and is well calculated to give a
general idea of modern art.

Finally, as appertaining to the department of art, I may mention the tasteful basins and fountains, with the banks of exquisite
shrubs and flowers, the creepers and pendent flower-beds, which
decorate the interior of the palace, while of the gardens and
waterworks outside the building I can only say that they are
conceived and carried out with a grandeur of design which has no
parallel in the world. At the same time the distant and extensive
view over a richly-wooded country, which stretches from the gar-

dens and seems to carry them up to the horizon, alone richly repays the journey from London.

It is of the greatest importance to society in general that an undertaking which offers not only the richest means of artistic education—in which, as I can testify by my repeated visits to this country, the English people are making slow but sure progress—but the highest forms of intellectual amusement, should not be allowed to fail for want of support. And if the increasing intelligence and true public spirit of the nation at large be chiefly requisite for this purpose, the directors of the palace, on the other hand, will remember that much depends, also, on the ability, energy, and prudence with which the affairs of the company are administered. And that both these and every other agency may combine to effect so desirable an end as the permanent success of the Crystal Palace, must be the wish of every one to whom the good of mankind and the promotion of the arts are dear.

WORKS OF ART BELONGING TO HIS ROYAL HIGHNESS THE DUKE OF AUMALE,

AT ORLEANS HOUSE, TWICKENHAM.

At this charming seat in the neighbourhood of London, the Duke d'Aumale, whose rare attainments and ardent love of literature and art are so well known, has collected a perfect treasury of manuscripts, rare editions, oil pictures, paintings on glass, majolica and glass vessels, and even some specimens of interesting sculpture. A portion of these objects belong to the Condé inheritance. On occasion of my visit to England in 1854, his Royal Highness did me the honour to invite me to a breakfast *en famille*, after which he proceeded, in the kindest way, to do the honours of his collection. A similar opportunity in 1856 enabled me to inspect his later and considerable acquisitions, including the collection of the late Duke of Salerno, various contributions from the Bernal sale, and some new MSS. with miniatures. Of these I can only mention the most important.

An Evangeliarium. In large octavo. On the upper side of the binding, in ivory, is the Crucifixion in the centre, and the four signs of the Evangelists in the corners. Judging from the form

of the heads and the thick and crooked noses, these reliefs belong
to the 9th century, while the figures in copper-gilt, between the
centre and the corners, are attributable to the 12th century.
The miniatures of the four Evangelists show much affinity, both
in types and also in the light broken colours, to those manuscripts
executed at Bamberg, at the end of the 10th century, by order of
the Emperor Henry II., and which are now preserved partly in the
court library at Munich, and partly still at Bamberg. These,
however, have an earlier appearance, which is further confirmed by
the character of the beautiful initials, and by the purple-coloured
pages. Judging from both these evidences, the date of this MS.
may be assigned to about 850. The mention of Saint Ludger,
patron of Münster, at the beginning, indicates that it was executed
in a Westphalian convent, and I was assured by the Duke that
the MS. was obtained from that quarter.

By far the most important acquisition of this kind made by the
Duke since 1854 is a Prayer-book, of a moderate folio size, on
strong but very smooth parchment, written in two columns, in a
very large minuscule letter, and with a very wide border. Portrait and coat-of-arms testify this to have been executed for Duke
Jean de Berry, brother of King Charles V. of France, an ardent
patron of miniature-painting, on which he lavished princely sums.
Further, it appears highly probable that this is the same which in
the year 1416 (as may be gathered from the valuation attached to
each MS.) was mentioned in a catalogue compiled after the death
of the Duke in that year, the original of which in parchment is
preserved in the library of St. Genofeva at Paris, in the following
words :—" Très grandes, très belles et riches heures, très notable-
ment illuminées et historiées de grandes histoires de la main de
Jacquevrart de Hodin et autres ouvriers de Monseigneur," &c.
It is said further to contain " les heures de Notre Dame, les sept
psaumes, les heures de la croix et du Saint Esprit, de la passion,
et du Saint Esprit encore, et l'office des Morts." * The beauty
also of the unusually large miniatures, which surpasses not only
every other MS. belonging to this Duke I have hitherto seen, but
every MS. adorned with French miniatures of that time with
which I am acquainted, agrees with this supposition. The same

* Barrois (Bibliothèque protopographique) gives a slight mention of this MS.,
No. 586, p. 99.

may be said of the contents of the text, of which, at my request, his Royal Highness gave me a precise abstract in his own hand.* From this it appears that in the Mass of the Holy Sacrament—leaf 188—a leaf is wanting. The death of the Duke de Berry interrupted the completion of the artistic ornamentation—both pictures as well as border decorations—and with the exception of the picture in the Calendar belonging to the month of December, which appears to me rather earlier, was not finished until the latter half of the 15th century, by a miniature-painter of that school which produced the well-known Heures of Anne of Bretagne. The researches of the Duke d'Aumale, of which he kindly gave me the benefit, give the following explanation :—Bonne de Berry, daughter of Duke Jean de Berry, had, by her first marriage, with Amadeus VII. Count of Savoy, a daughter, by name Jeanne de Savoye, who, in 1407, married John Jacob Palæologus, Count of Aquasana, son of Theodore Palæologus, Marquis of Monferrat. Now the lower border of one of these later miniatures contains the arms of Monferrat and Savoy, and the representation of a prince and princess kneeling on the edge. Hence it is manifest that to these personages may be attributed the completion of the artistic ornamentation of this MS. which had descended to them by inheritance. The Duke has even succeeded in determining with great probability the name of the painter of these later miniatures. Lanzi mentions, namely, the existence of a French painter — Nicolas Robert by name — who was employed from 1473 to 1477 at the Court of Savoy. The fact of the above-mentioned Jeanne de Savoye having died as early as 1460 proves nothing, since it is only by mere chance that the name of this painter has been preserved at this somewhat later date. Having thus given the historical facts connected with this valuable MS., which was purchased by the Duke in Genoa, I now proceed

---

* In my 'Kunstwerke und Künstler in Paris,' p. 339, I have been betrayed into an error by following the supposition of Count Auguste de Bastard, to the effect that the Prayer-book " MSS. latins, No. 919," in the Imperial Library at Paris, is the same mentioned in the old catalogue as above. It is true the expression " grandes histoires " is far less applicable to the Paris MS., which contains *only* smaller pictures, than to that belonging to the Duke d'Aumale, in which are many pictures occupying a whole page. And if the text includes more and especially smaller paragraphs than are mentioned in the list of the old catalogue, we must remember that, in forming an inventory and estimate, only such notification of the chief portions are given as suffice to identify the manuscript. The very high estimate also, namely, of 4000 *livres Tournois*, applies far more to the work before us than to that in the Louvre, which is by no means so rich in point of art.

to describe its contents and artistic worth. Immediately at the beginning we find each month of the calendar preceded by a picture occupying a whole page. Over each picture are three jointed stripes enclosing a semicircular arch : the space within the arch is azure, and upon it, for each month, the figure of a deity, also in blue. Thus in January we have the figure of Apollo represented as an old long-bearded man, on a vehicle constructed in the form of the period, like a cart with a tent upon it, holding the golden rays of the sun in both hands. Attached to the vehicle are two winged horses in gallop. The nearest stripe, which is white, is each time intended to indicate the change of the moon and the number of the days of each month. In January, however, and in some of the other months, the necessary text is failing. The next stripe above, which is blue, contains each time two signs of the Zodiac ; for instance, in January, Capricorn and Aquarius ; in February, Aquarius and Pisces ; in March, Pisces and Aries, and so on. The uppermost stripe, which is again white, is finally appropriated for the indication of the days which each of these signs govern : these indications, however, are often absent. These little pictures, blue upon blue, are by another hand than that which executed the large pictures. All the pictures, large and small, bear evidence of French artists, sometimes partaking more of the Netherlandish, sometimes more of the Italian influence, and finally adhering to the peculiar French style of art. Of the larger pictures I must content myself with the particular description of only one : I select that belonging to January as the richest and most remarkable. The occupation of the month is here represented by the picture of the Duke of Savoy at a ceremonious dinner : this personage is seen seated at a table spread with a white table-cloth with a lozenge-shaped pattern of the greatest delicacy, and dressed in a robe of azure gold brocade lined with fur, and with a fur cap. His face is thoroughly individual and very animated ; he is conversing with a prelate who is his only companion. The meats are served up on the richly stored table in gold and silver dishes ; one large dish especially, in the form of a ship with two beaks, and very well executed in brown, and heightened with brush gold, is very remarkable. On the point of one of the beaks is a bear, and on the other a swan. These two—ours—cygne—pronounced together express the name Oursine (or little she bear), which the Duke had bestowed on his second wife,* Jeanne de Boulogne et d'Auvergne, and occur often in other Prayer-books belonging to this personage.   In the vessel itself are several gold plates.   Three very richly attired young seigneurs are waiting upon the Duke; a kneeling servant, half in grey, half in red livery, lengthways, is occupied cutting a piece of meat from a joint for a white greyhound: on the right is the buffet with splendid gold vessels, which, strange to say, at this early period (at latest 1416), display no longer Gothic, but very delicate forms of the Renaissance—a striking proof how early, at least in the form of utensils, this taste was introduced into France.   Before the buffet is a young seigneur who is reaching two vessels to a servant in the same livery as above described, and holding wine-jug and cups of gold.   Behind the Duke is a chest about 3 ft. high, and covered with a cloth of blue, golden brocade; behind this again is the seneschal, a very animated portrait, his bâton of office on his right shoulder, dressed in a fine red coat with gold crowns on it, and a golden collar and tassels, who is pronouncing the words in golden letters before him, "Aproche, aproche," to four superbly dressed seigneurs, the two foremost of whom, with their raised and averted hands, well express that awe in the presence of the Duke which restrains their steps.   On the other side, behind the Duke, is architecture, with a mantelpiece, the fire of which is only slightly indicated above a screen of delicate basket-work, fastened to a wooden pole; above this is a red canopy, in which, in three circles, are the arms of the Duke, golden lilies on a blue field, and, with the significance explained above, two bears and seven swans; in the background is a view in the open air; in the centre two troops of cavalry with lances, about to begin a combat or a tournament; on the right a third troop issuing from the gate of a town; on the left a fourth with only the points of the helmets, the banners, and the lances seen above the mantelpiece.   In the admirable painter of this masterly picture we recognise in a high degree the influence of the highly developed realistic tendency of Netherlandish art, on which subject I have expressed myself at length in my notice of the miniatures of Jean de Bruges,† exe-

---

* Particulars may be found in a notice of a Prayer-Book belonging to the same Duke in the library of the old Dukes of Burgundy by the librarian of the same, M. Marchal, in vol. xi. No. 6, of the Bulletins of the Royal Academy of Brussels.
   † See 'Deutsches Kunstblatt' of 1852, No. 30, p. 248.

cuted in 1371, in the Prayer-book of King Charles V., now in the
Westreenen Library at the Hague. The Duke de Berry, as is
well known, was brother to King Charles V., so that we may conclude with certainty that the miniature-painter attached to the
Duke took these miniatures by Jean de Bruges as his model.
The very individual heads are finely modelled in a broken tone of
a delicate brown, the proportions are slender, the motives speaking
and easy, and the hands of good action and elegant, though with
meagre fingers. The rendering also of the space is extraordinary
for the time, and the execution in delicate strokes and of good
impasto unites softness and certainty of touch. The trees have
still the conventional pointed form which was adopted in 1360.
Both the insipidity of the greens and the dulness of the surface
bespeak decidedly a French artist, and in all probability we have
here the hand of the above-mentioned Jacquevrart or Hodin,
though it is not in our power to identify it as one or the other
with certainty.

The illustration of February is particularly admirable as a
representation of a winter landscape, with town and hills in the
distance, under deep snow, and with the idea of winter thoroughly
carried out. Thus in the foreground is the section of a house,
with a girl and two young men within warming themselves at a
stove; in a pen with a roof are seen sheep; the beehives are
snowed over; a man is felling a tree, and another is driving an
ass. The picture for March is also another landscape, in which
the cool and delicate general tone admirably represents the first
outbreak of spring. A fortress of very picturesque look is in the
distance, with a golden dragon flying over it in the air. This I
agree with his Royal Highness in believing to be the town of
Lusignan, and the dragon the beautiful Melusina, who was so
transformed. The scene is still leafless, but is enlivened by shepherd and flock, by vinedressers pruning their vines, and by country
people ploughing and sowing seed. The picture for April is by
another artist, inferior to the first in the drawing, but surpassing
him in freshness of colour, in the landscape, and in freedom of
treatment. The heads of the figures, which consist of four ladies,
two of them seated, plucking flowers, and two standing with two
gentlemen, are too small, emptier in the otherwise pretty forms,
and colder in tone. The folds in the drapery in the seated women

are broad and soft.   The green of the trees is very fresh and full.
A piece of water, rendered with silver, is tenderly toned off with
grey.   Behind is a castle.   The picture of May, by the same
hand, shows us the stately manner in which the higher classes
celebrated this joyous month in the middle ages.   In front of a
wood decked with the fresh green of spring, behind which a town
is seen, appears a procession of richly dressed figures on horseback,
the ladies with wreaths of foliage, and the gentlemen with garlands round their necks of the same, led by five musicians, trum-
peters, &c., also mounted.   The impression of festivity, gladness,
and freshness produced by this picture is admirable.   In the
representation of June, a landscape of cool and tender effect, with
a very picturesque view of a town in the background, the first
hand reappears.   In the figures of two elegant girls making hay
in the foreground, while three men are mowing in the middle distance, his mastery of the human figure is again evident.   The girl
with a white veil has a delicate profile.   July is again by the
second hand, displaying a landscape with a fortress surrounded
with moats, which are executed in silver.   In the middle distance
are two men with sickles, cutting corn.   In the foreground are
shepherd and shepherdess with a flock of sheep.   By the same
hand is also the picture of August, with a lady, and two gentlemen with ladies riding pillion behind them, going a hunting with
falcons.   In the river, which is rendered in silver, are figures
bathing.   In the background is harvest going on, and a fortress.
The effect of the whole is charming, and of very delicate general
tone.   September, instead of as usual October, is typified by a
very grandly represented vintage.   In the landscape, which is much
made out, is a Gothic fortress.   The figures here are somewhat
rude, this being in most cases the characteristic of a later hand
engaged in this work, probably shortly before the year 1460, and
of which this is the first specimen.   With October, however, the
first hand returns to the scene.   We see here the sowing and
harrowing of the winter's seed, the crows and ravens which follow
the fresh furrows being very animatedly given.   Behind a silver
tower is a large fortress, which displays the middle ages in their full
stateliness.   Some walks in front of the walls are given with great
delicacy.   November shows the pigs being fattened with acorns in
the open air.   This is by the later hand ; the free and careful

treatment of the trees deserves particular mention. The proportions of the figures are, however, somewhat short. The picture
for December represents a boar-hunt. The extraordinary freedom
of the motives of the dogs and huntsmen attacking the boar, and
the treatment of the forest, and of the castle seen above it,
bespeaks an artist of later date certainly than the Duke de Berry,
but probably earlier than the painter who flourished towards 1460.
To one familiar with old MSS. with miniatures of this kind, it is
no matter of surprise that, if not completed in the time of the
original patron, which was often the case, pictures by later hands
should be found sometimes in the middle, sometimes at the end
of the book. For when the text was completely written the
different spaces of it were intrusted to various artists, and then, if
from any reason they did not finish their task, or did not even
begin it, the sheets were after a certain time returned to be bound
up with the rest of the book. But the singular thing here is that,
while the pictures of three of the months are by later hands, the
artistic decorations of the calendar are almost throughout contemporary with the text, so that I am tempted to think that the
three original pictures must have been in some way spoiled, and
replaced by others of a later time. All the remaining decoration
of the calendar is also very rich. The ornamentation of the letters
K and L at the beginning of each month, as well as that of the
borders, which throughout the whole MS. display the period of the
Duke de Berry, and which consist in part of the old-fashioned
golden knobs and small leaves, and in part of already finely
coloured leaf-work, show great pomp of colour and much elegance.
In the writing of the text of the calendar, gold, crimson, and azure
are alone used. At the end of the calendar, leaf 14b, is a large
mandorla, with two youthful and very delicately coloured male
figures back to back, so that the one is seen quite in front, the
other quite from behind, and therefore but little visible. On the
front figure are the indications of several constellations. The
ground is of a delicate blue, with little golden clouds. Around,
in twelve azure margins, are the twelve signs of the zodiac.
Below are Sagittarius, Gemini, and Aquarius, small figures, with
fine heads, free and graceful motives, and in excellent drawing.
In this picture a third painter, coeval with the Duke de Berry,
appears for the first time, of a decidedly idealistic tendency, and

in that respect appertaining still to the older time. This is the same hand which executed the Prophets and Apostles in a Psalter belonging to the Duke de Berry (Supplement, franc. 2015 of the Imperial Library, Paris), and several miniatures in a Prayer-book, also the property of the same royal individual, and who is most probably the master mentioned in the old catalogue as Maître André Beauneveu.* The next leaf, 17a, showing the Apocalyptic Vision of St. John in the Isle of Patmos, is also by the same hand. The kneeling Evangelist is remarkable for the good foreshortening of the head, for the very animated motive, and for the conformity to style observable in the broad and soft folds of the drapery. The figure of the Almighty enthroned in the sky is also characterised by great dignity, and by the deep tone of the purple markings in the golden robe. Finally, the figures of the four-and-twenty elders, seated on two benches, surprise us with the variety of the heads and the liveliness of the motives. Next St. John is the eagle holding the ink and the case for his pen. With leaf 19b, the Martyrdom of St. Mark, appears the fourth artist contemporary with the Duke de Berry, who displays a strong Italian influence. The expression of the saint is very fine. He is being strangled in a dalmatic of the richest azure and gold brocade. The keeping of the whole is cool. By this very admirable painter, probably either the Hodin or the Jaquevrart before mentioned, is the last picture, the Duke and his suite, in the already alluded to Prayer-book (Lavallière 15), which in my admiration I erroneously ascribed to an Italian master. Leaf 25b, the Garden of Eden, is one of the most attractive pictures by the third hand. In the centre of a circle in gold is the Fountain of the Water of Life, of very fine Gothic form. Within the circle are the following subjects:—1. The Almighty, represented as an old man with a white beard in an azure mantle, of excellent taste, is bestowing Eve upon Adam. 2. Eve at the tree of knowledge being tempted by the serpent, the upper part of which is in the form of a woman. 3. Eve kneeling and presenting the apple to Adam. 4. Both are being expelled by a seraph from a golden gate of fine Gothic form. The rivers which surround the garden of Eden are indicated in blue. By the same hand are also the four following pictures:—Leaf 27b.

* See 'Kunstwerke und Künstler in Paris,' pp. 335 and 337.

King David, a very noble figure in admirable drapery of a light
violet colour, is adoring the Almighty in the clouds. Opposite
him are Moors. The ground here, as often, is still the chessboard
pattern.—Leaf 28a. Two Apostles preaching from the pulpit;
the one whose audience are black is doubtless St. Philip. The
audience are of admirable motives.—Leaf 38b. The Visitation.
The Virgin is a grand figure of very pure style of drapery, fine
features, and elevated expression. The rocks in the landscape
have still the old conventional Byzantine form.—Leaf 44b. The
Nativity. The Virgin has a beautiful profile.—Leaf 51b. The
Procession of the Three Kings, who are gathered together by a
small and elegant Gothic tower. Here the first hand again
appears.—Leaf 52a. The Adoration of the Kings is already conceived in the style of Raphael's tapestries in the Vatican. This
is by the third hand. Behind the Virgin are beautiful maidens.
The numerous male figures with their turbans, and other accessories,
as for instance a tame panther led by a string, have a decided
Oriental character.—Leaf 54b. The Presentation in the Temple
is of singular refinement in the head of the Virgin, and also of
great power of colour. A male figure also on the left of the foreground surprises us with the beauty of his white drapery. The
Gothic architecture, of a light grey tone, is of singular elegance,
and the landscape rich and beautiful.—Leaf 59b. The Coronation
of the Virgin, a rich and fine composition, is by the third hand.
The Virgin is seen in profile. Christ has a golden crown on, and
three golden angels hold three other crowns above his head, while
a blue angel holds one over the head of the Virgin. Next this
last angel are others like him in the sky, playing on musical instruments. On the left, in adoration, are Apostles; below, saints.
—Leaf 63b. The Fall of the Angels is very peculiarly conceived.
In the sky are seen the golden seats empty which they occupied.
The angels themselves are in blue robes, and have not yet for-
feited their beautiful forms. By the third hand.—Leaf 107a. In
the representation of hell are many motives new to me. Satan
seated on a gridiron is holding a bundle of the condemned in each
hand, while he ejects from his mouth many others in a stream of
fire high into the air. These little figures are surprising for their
free and lively motives. Finally, the fire under the gridiron, containing many condemned, is kindled by four bellows worked by

demons : this is by the second hand.   Leaf 141b. Christ and St. Peter ; the first a very noble figure, with the band of guards lying as if dead on the ground : by the third hand.   Leaf 142a. Judas and his troop, with Christ captive, before the door of the high priest, at which one of the guards is knocking with a battle-axe.   This subject is seldom met with.   Considering also the period, this picture deserves perhaps most admiration for the chiaroscuro in the representation of Night, with golden stars in the sky.   The armour, which is of the time of the painter, is admirably executed in silver : by the fourth hand.   By the same hand are the three following :—Leaf 143a. The Flagellation, which is rather lame. —Leaf 145b. The Betrayal of Christ, one of the finest pictures in the book.   The head of the guard next Christ is very animated, and the foremost of the two naked thieves, who are already conducted out of the city gate, is very delicate in drawing.   And finally, leaf 146a. Christ bearing his Cross, in which the head of the Saviour turning round is very noble, and the condition of the crowd, in the very rich but not crowded composition, admirably expressed. —Leaf 152a. The Crucifixion, by the third hand, is the earliest instance I know of its representation as a night-piece, the time being chosen when darkness overspreads the scene.   In this rich composition, which includes the two thieves, the looking up of the masses of people to the cross is very well expressed.   As respects single figures I may mention the elevation of motive and expression which characterise the Saviour, the Virgin, and the Centurion.—Leaf 155b. The Descent from the Cross.   This is by the second hand.   The group of the body with the three figures engaged in lowering it is as true as it is fine in invention.   The conception of the Virgin, who is standing upright, has something grand ; the other women, on the other hand, look too cheerful. The figure of Joseph of Arimathea, standing below, in a turban, is obviously the portrait of a Jew of noble character of head.— Leaf 160b. The Temptation, by the second hand, is treated quite as a landscape.   The small figure of Christ standing on a rock is, however, noble.   The demon next him is hovering in the air.— Leaf 165a. Christ expelling evil spirits, by the second hand, is very dignified in conception.   The face of the possessed man is fine, and the expression of astonishment in the bystanders admirable.—Leaf 167b. The Feeding of the Four Thousand, by the

same hand. The robe of Christ is of a grand simplicity, the expressive heads very individual, and the power of colouring extraordinary. The same may be said of leaf 170b, the Raising of
Lazarus, by the same painter. As regards the nude, the motive,
and the expression of the fine head of Lazarus and that of the
Virgin, who is gazing at her son, this is quite a little marvel.—
Leaf 152b. Palm Sunday. Here the first hand is seen again.
Christ and the Apostles are very dignified, the ass and the colt
very true. to nature, the astonishment in the heads of the Jews
very animated, and all the heads executed with particular care.—
Leaf 192. The Finding and Adoration of the true Cross, in pre-
sence of St. Helena, the Emperor Constantine, and four blacks.
This is a masterly work of the second hand. The golden statues
of Moses and of two prophets on a building are of excellent style.
To the same painter belongs, finally, leaf 194, a view of Mont St.
Michel in Normandy, with the combat between the Archangel
Michael and the dragon, who is already wounded, with sunken
head, in the sky. Boats lying dry on the strand show that it is
the time of ebb. In the border are heads in circles, executed with
uncommon beauty. As the importance of a picture consists in
the artistic skill and not in the size, and as these not only
represent the highest artistic excellence of their time, but, in
default of large pictures, are the chief specimens of the extraordinary development of the French art of this period, about 1416,
I have purposely entered into a somewhat circumstantial description of them. Judging from these pictures, we may conclude,
firstly, that the French painters, while they did not surpass the
Italian of the same time in elevation of moral conception and in
style of drapery, were far superior to them in mastery of the
means of representation, in the carrying out of portraits, and the
treatment of space with a certain richness of detail. In this
respect all will agree with me who compare the *earlier* works of
Fiesole, born 1387, which are the best which the Italians have to
show, with these contemporary pictures. Secondly, the French
painters approached in excellence to the later qualities of the
Netherlandish school, and excelled them in their earlier merits.
At about this time Hubert van Eyck must be considered to have
attained the climax of his art, while his brother John van Eyck
had begun his career. Thirdly, these pictures perfectly explain

the appearance of so great a painter as Jean Fouquet * immediately after the middle of the 15th century. The artists who executed these pictures were obviously his predecessors. To an Italian painter, however, and it is well known that the Duke de Berry employed several, I am disposed to attribute numerous little heads in initials, of very noble forms and expression, and tender execution—for instance, one in leaf 27a. As regards the supposed pictures by the hand of a later master, Nicolas Robert, I content myself with observing that the number of the same, in pictures occupying a whole page, in vignettes, and in initials, is very considerable. As we have seen already in the Calendar, they occur in the course of the MS. alternately with the earlier pictures. Finally I may remark that this relic is in wonderful preservation.

A manuscript of the 'Miroir Historiale de Gille Gracien,' a large folio in two columns, dated 1463, and written in a large and full minuscule letter. This contains a considerable number of miniatures by an artist of tolerable skill, showing in the heads, as well as in the whole form of art, that style which had flourished both in France and in the Netherlands from about 1360, and proving that in some instances that style was still practised after the realistic tendency of art had obtained in France in the person of Jean Fouquet, and had been fully developed in the Netherlands by the scholars of Hubert van Eyck.

Next to these I was most attracted by the third part of Julius Cæsar's Commentaries, the first part of which I had already seen in 1835, in the library of the British Museum, and critically noticed in the first edition of this work. The part in the Duke d'Aumale's possession contains miniatures by Godefroy, all inscribed with the letter G and 1520, and on leaf 52 with the name of the master full length. These miniatures differ from those in the first part, inasmuch as the artist has here endeavoured to imitate the German School, and namely Albert Durer.†

Another MS., of which I no longer remember the contents, displays pretty miniatures of the school of Jean Fouquet, and very beautiful initials.

---

* See 'Kunstwerke und Künstler in Paris,' p. 371 and further.
† The second part of this work is in the Library at Paris. Count Delaborde, in his 'Renaissance des Arts à la Cour de France,' vol. i. p. 899, was the first, as far as I am aware, to notice this work. I have never seen it myself.

A large folio in two columns, of the first half of the 15th century, containing romances of the legendary times of the Round Table—Tristram, Lancelot of the Lake, &c.—is adorned with very good miniatures, considering this class of book.

An example of the length of time that caligraphists and miniature-painters continued to contribute to the decoration of books, even when the invention of printing and of the arts of wood-cutting and engraving had very much curtailed their number, is afforded in a charming little book in small octavo, entitled ' Heures de nostre Dame escrites à la main, MDCXXXXVII, par N. Jarry Parisien.' He was the most celebrated caligraphist of his time, and in truth a more elegant and equable text can hardly be seen. The miniatures also, which somewhat recall Pierre Mignard, are of the utmost tenderness in forms and execution, though certainly affected in motives, *fade* in expression, and insipid in colour. I can only mention the two little angels holding the title—the portrait of the patron of the volume, a gentleman of very frivolous appearance—the picture of Moses—of the Virgin and Child—and of David playing the harp.

As regards Block-books, I may mention a copy I saw here of the Life of John the Baptist, the plates of which are neither pasted together nor illuminated; they are restored, however, in some parts. It was formerly in the possession of Messrs. Payne and Foss.

Among the fine Aldine editions in the best preservation included in the library, I particularly remarked a Virgil, and the Metamorphoses of Ovid, on parchment. Both these and other rare French and German incunabula exercise, even outwardly in their bindings —some of which are old, while others are modern—a spell over the imagination of the beholder, of which the uninitiated can form no conception.

I now proceed to the pictures.

ITALIAN SCHOOL.

SANDRO BOTTICELLI.—The Virgin looking down on the Child, who is sitting on her lap, and taking a rose from a basket an angel is reaching to her. This picture, which is particularly attractive for the fine feeling in the head of the Virgin, belongs to the earlier time of the master, and distinctly shows the influence of his master Fra Filippo Lippi. It is of unusual power of colouring.

BERNARDINO LUINI.—The Virgin and Joseph kneeling and adoring the Child. A simple but good composition; the head of the Virgin very noble, the colouring particularly powerful, the execution throughout careful.

LUCA LONGHI.—The Virgin and Child enthroned, with an angel at their feet playing on the lute. On the right St. Francis, on the left St. Anthony of Padua; quite below, as bust pictures, the donor and his wife. This is the best picture I know by the so-called Raphael of Ravenna. The heads are serious and noble, the angel of great beauty, the portraits true and animated, the colouring warm, and the execution in a good impasto and very careful.

JULIO ROMANO.—A female portrait. Of great animation and very powerful colouring. The position of one hand is, however, not happy.

PRIMATICCIO.—Portrait of the Cardinal de Châtillon. Signed and dated 1548. Æt. 31. The portraits by this master are so rare, that this is an important specimen. The conception is earnest and noble, the drawing strict, the colouring warm, and the execution solid.

SCIPIO GAETANO.—1. A male portrait. Another master not often seen out of Italy, who unites animated conception with powerful colouring.

2. Portrait of an old man of somewhat Jewish appearance. Smaller than the foregoing. Of a warmth and depth of colour approaching Rembrandt.

ANNIBALE CARRACCI.—The figure of Venus sleeping, larger than life, and surrounded by numerous amorini. A landscape background. This picture has the character of monumental art, recalling the grand forms, graceful motives, and deep colouring of the best frescoes of this master in the Farnese Palace at Rome. This, and the four separate figures of amorini, the bold but graceful foreshortenings of which show the happy influence of Correggio, doubtless originally formed the decoration of a room.

Two other allegorical figures also, Aurora and the winged figure of Night, with Sleep and Death in her arms, of very earnest character and powerful colouring, may probably have belonged to the same series.

GUIDO RENI.—"La Madonna della Pace." This is the title of a picture representing the Madonna enthroned, with the Child in the act of benediction in her lap, and angels around. The composition is well balanced, the heads very pretty, the colouring bright, warm, and clear, and the execution careful.

LIONELLO SPADA.—Christ with two guards, one of whom is pressing the crown of thorns on to his head. This picture is remarkable for good drawing, animated motives, powerful colouring, and broad and marrowy painting.

SASSOFERRATO.—The Virgin and Child, with Joseph adoring. A composition differing from his usual type, noble and refined in the heads, and conscientious in carrying out.

SALVATOR ROSA.—The collection of the Prince of Salerno was very rich in this master. I select the most important. 1. Daniel in the Lions' Den. 2. His deliverance from the same. These two pictures show in a high degree the wild and poetic feeling of the painter, and have an extraordinary power of effect. 3. A rocky landscape with St. Jerome. 4. The companion to the last —a similar composition with a monk praying. These are grand in treatment, and the last of especial clearness.

SPANISH SCHOOL.

MURILLO.—St. Joseph dressed in white, with the infant Christ, also in a white garment. An attractive little picture of clear effect.

NETHERLANDISH SCHOOL.

The Entombment. A picture by a Netherlandish artist of the 16th century, in imitation of the Italian school. The motives more original than pleasing, and the outlines somewhat hard. The head of the fainting Virgin is however very noble, and the execution careful. This picture was here erroneously ascribed to Daniel da Volterra.

GERHARD HONTHORST.—Christ with the Disciples at Emmaus by candle-light. He has taken advantage of the opportunity to produce a striking effect.

VANDYCK.—1. Portrait of the Count de Berg. Differently conceived to the picture in Windsor. Very animated, and almost Titianesque in glow and clearness of colouring.

2. A female portrait in a black-and-white dress. To the knees. Of uncommon elegance of conception and tenderness of colouring, and very remarkable as showing in every part the influence of his contemporary Velasquez.

Philippe de Champagne.—1. Portrait of Cardinal Mazarin, taken in front. Very animated, and carefully carried out in a clear colouring.

2. Portrait of La Mère Catherine Agnès Arnauld, of the Port Royal Convent : the same who is represented in prayer in the well-known picture in the Louvre. An admirable drawing.

Jean Clouet.—Portrait of Leonora, sister of Charles V. and second wife to Francis I. Compared with two pictures of this Princess by the master at Hampton Court (vol. ii. p. 363), and in the possession of M. de Minutoli in Silesia, this is too hard, and may rather be supposed to be an old copy. From the Bernal collection.

François Clouet.—1. Portrait of the Queen of Charles IX., an Austrian Princess. Very careful, but somewhat smoothly executed. From the Bernal collection.

2 and 3. King Henry II. and his son the Duke d'Alençon on horseback. Two miniatures of the most delicate execution. Knowing no authentic miniatures by this painter, I cannot pronounce with certainty as to the correctness of this title. From the Bernal collection.

Portrait of Jeanne d'Albret, a careful Limoges enamel, almost life-size. A great rarity.

Leopold Robert.—A Neapolitan woman with a boy upon the ruins of a house overthrown by an earthquake. A beautiful picture. This frightful scene is rendered with much feeling in the heads, and with great mastery of execution.

Nicolas Poussin.—The Murder of the Innocents, a composition of few figures. This otherwise good and genuine picture is rendered somewhat unattractive by the action of one of the murderers, who is treading on a dead child.

Hyacinthe Rigaud.—The youthful Louis XV. in his coronation robes. Whole-length figure, life-size. One of those pictures of stately pomp which this painter so well understood to represent.

Largillière.—A male portrait, both in conception and in

clear and warm colouring one of the best specimens of this excellent master. One of the hands is worthy of Vandyck.

AUBRY.—1 and 2. A fox and a wolf hunt. In point of animation and careful execution these are very choice pictures by this remarkable animal-painter.

MELCHIOR HONDEKOETER.—A very fine picture of fowls, in which a turkey-cock plays a conspicuous part.

The following specimens of glass-painting struck me as most remarkable :—

The Duke de Montmorenci, with four sons still in boyhood and all kneeling, under the protection of St. John the Evangelist. Opposite them is the Duchess with three daughters in the same position, and accompanied by another patron saint. These portraits, which are about half the size of life, and carefully executed in a monochrome of brown, belong, and especially those of the Duke and his sons, which are best preserved, to the best examples of this kind, of the first half of the 16th century, with which I am acquainted. Judging from the style of conception, the cartoons for this picture may have proceeded from the hand of Jean Clouet. The robes of state are admirably executed. This painter was less versed in the representation of saints ; the St. John here is borrowed from Raphael's cartoon of Peter and John healing the lame man at the Beautiful Gate of the Temple, while the other, which is his own conception, is not successful. These glass paintings are from the château of Ecouen.

A rich series of glass paintings represents the subject of Cupid and Psyche, well known to all lovers of art by the engravings of the Master of the Dice. The figures are about nine inches high, and are given with a truth and an excellence of expression and drawing which merit the utmost admiration. Whether, as here considered, these are the work of Bernard of Palissy I am not able to say, as I know nothing authentic by him in this class of art.

I must also mention two admirable portraits in enamel by PETITOT, representing the Queen of Louis XIV. and the Grand Condé. The conception of this latter is particularly animated.

The following appeared to me the most interesting specimens in sculpture :—

The busts of the Great Condé and Turenne, by COUSTOU. Spirited and careful works in marble.

The head of Henry IV. in coloured wax, probably executed from the cast taken after death. I never saw a portrait of this monarch in which the features show such benevolence and amiability of character as here. The conception is animated and the workmanship careful.

A number of square tiles of glazed earthenware with paintings were interesting to me in the history of art. They are in the style of majolica, and decorate two walls of a room. Their original derivation, which was Rouen, and also the evident influence of the school of Fontainebleau, show that they were executed in France. Though mediocre in point of art, yet they serve to show that the long residence of Girolamo della Robbia in France, and the application of the class of art which bears his family name in decorating the château called Madrid, erected by Francis I. in the neighbourhood of Paris, had founded a manufactory of the same in France.

A rich collection of vessels in glass is here preserved in a case. A large beaker presents one of the finest examples both in form and taste of decoration that I know of the kind. Nor can I leave unnoticed some specimens of majolica richly ornamented in oxydised metal, which has the effect of gold, and are called "Moorish dishes."

Two breastplates in armour, with figures and ornaments, belong in taste, refinement, and mastery to the maturity of the cinquecento period.

Finally I must mention a large cabinet in buhl, which in point of wealth and beauty of decoration far exceeds the usual standard of the finest specimens of this stately class of furniture.

PICTURES AT SION HOUSE,

SEAT OF THE DUKE OF NORTHUMBERLAND.

The princely splendour of the mansion, with its various decorations, of which I will only instance a series of marble statues, after the finest antiques—the beauty of the garden and conservatories, containing the finest flowers and rarest shrubs and trees, and the admirable order in which all are kept up, render Sion House one of those residences so characteristic of England, which every cultivated traveller will most desire to see. I only regret that the accumulation of those materials to which this work is especially dedicated, compels me to leave every other source of beauty and interest unnoticed. The pictures, properly speaking, constitute no gallery, but are many of them, including some of great excellence, distributed in parts of the building not usually seen by visitors. The kindness of the Duchess, however, procured me admission to them.*

THE DRAWING-ROOM.

SIR PETER LELY.—Portraits of Charles I. and his son James Duke of York. A good copy from a fine picture by Vandyck.

THE DINING-ROOM.

JAMES BARRY.—Portrait of the first Duke of Northumberland. Animated and careful.

SIR JOSHUA REYNOLDS.—Portrait of the first Duchess, in full state. Unusually hard and heavy in colouring for him.

MIREVELDT.—Portrait of Prince Henry Frederick of Orange, spirited, clear, and careful.

SIR JOSHUA REYNOLDS.—Portrait of Queen Charlotte, in purple mantle of state lined with ermine, taken in profile in the act of walking. A landscape background. Whole-length figure, life-size. Of animated conception and very careful completion.

SIR THOMAS LAWRENCE.—Portrait of the last Duke of Northumberland, in black dress with white sleeves, and hat with white feathers. The background a crimson curtain and dark sky. Half-length. Of great animation, and carefully executed in transparent colouring. The way in which the hands are cut off is, however, tasteless.

THE ANTE-DINING-ROOM.

SIR EDWIN LANDSEER.—Deer-stalking. Masterly, and of the utmost truth.

JAMES WARD.—1. Portrait of the horse ridden by Buonaparte at the battle of Marengo.

---

* In 1856 I had the honour to be the Duke's guest at Sion House, and had thus the opportunity of studying the various works of art with greater leisure, and of completing and correcting my former notes.

2. Also, as a companion to the above, the brown charger, Copenhagen, on which Wellington rode at Waterloo. Both of these pictures are true in conception, and broadly painted in a powerful tone.

Snyders.—A wild-boar hunt. A fortunate composition, of the greatest truth of detail, with the full transparency of his colouring, and his broad and spirited touch.

The following pictures, which hang in two corridors and in smaller rooms, I singled out among a large number, as the most worthy of note. Some meritorious works, however, remain unnoticed.

Albert Durer.—Portrait of his father, Albert Durer the goldsmith, in a black cap, and orange-coloured fur garment. With the following inscription: " 1497, albrecht thvrer der elter vnd alt 70 jor." On wood. Although this portrait very nearly agrees with that presented by the city of Nuremberg to Charles I.—with another picture, the portrait of himself, sold at the sale of Charles I.'s collection, for 100*l.*, and now in the Uffizj at Florence—yet I cannot consider it to be a copy of that picture. It differs in many respects: the ground of the Florence picture is green—this is dark: the date of the Florence picture is 1498—of this 1497: the execution of the Florence picture is careful—of this slight; though at the same time so spirited and clear, that I can attribute it to no other hand but that of Albert Durer. It was also considered to be by this master when in the collection of the Earl of Arundel, where Hollar engraved it in 1644.

Hans Schäuffelein.—Portrait of a man with a white beard, in black dress, and a black cap on his head; in his hand a watch of that oval form called Nuremberg eggs. The background consists of lofty hills, with the sea and an island. Judging from this background, I am inclined to consider this a portrait of the well-known navigator and geographer, Martin Behaim, who in his old days visited his native city, Nuremberg, for a considerable period. The island is probably that of Fayal, discovered by himself. The truth of the conception, the very careful treatment, and the somewhat brown tone of the flesh, remind me, of all the Nuremberg painters of that period, most of the above-named.

Jan Schoreel.—Two wings of an altarpiece, with the Presentation in the Temple, and the Raising of Lazarus. Good specimens of this very rare master.

BERNARDIN VAN ORLEY.—Mary Magdalen. Unfortunately much rubbed.

GAROFALO.—John the Baptist in a landscape, pointing to a lamb as the symbol of Christ. A delicate specimen of the master.

SALVATOR ROSA.—A rocky landscape with water, and figures of banditti. Cleverly composed, and carefully executed in a warm clear tone.

GASPAR POUSSIN.—1 and 2. Two landscapes, both poetically conceived and spiritedly executed, but rather dark.

CORNELIUS SACHTLEVEN.—An interior, with a mother, two children, and goats. A careful and transparent specimen of this master, who is not often seen in England.

TENIERS.—Landscape, with shepherd and flock. Very original in effect of light, and of great transparency.

LUCA GIORDANO.—1 and 2. Venus and Cupid, and a shepherd wiping the foot of a shepherdess. Two attractive pictures.

PALAMEDES STEVENS.—A party in a room. A delicate picture, which has, however, suffered.

DAVID VINCKEBOOM.—A fair. Bold and clever. Erroneously attributed to Jerome Bosch.

JAN VAN DER MEER DE JONGE.—A shepherdess with sheep, and a child. A good picture by this favourite sheep-painter.

GYSSELS.—Dead game. Tastefully composed, and an admirable specimen of that delicate execution peculiar to him.

JAN BOTH.—A rocky landscape, with water. Of upright and narrow form. Delicately carried out in a warm and clear tone.

JAN BAPTISTE WEENIX.—A boy. Animated, careful, and of good colour.

PETER BREUGHEL THE YOUNGER, called HELL BREUGHEL.—A kitchen.

VAN UDEN.—Trees on the left, and a house, before which are the figures of the Hermits SS. Paul and Anthony, painted by Titian. The landscape is very poetical; the figures spirited.

PIETER DE LAAR, called BAMBOCCIO.—Stately Roman ruins, with a party on horseback and on foot. Well composed, and carefully executed in a powerful but clear tone.

Judocus de Momper.—Landscape.   Of particularly careful finish for him.

Cornelius Sachtleven.—Interior of a peasant house, with a woman, a girl, a boy, a cow, three goats resting, and fowls.

Evert van Aelst.—A breakfast; well arranged and careful.

Roland Savery.—Landscape with animals, erroneously entitled Jan Breughel.

Cornelius Bega.—Peasants in a room, erroneously called Brouwer.

David Vinckeboom.—Landscape, with the flight into Egypt, erroneously called Jan Breughel.

Hans Holbein.—1. Portrait of Edward VI., as a child; in red dress and barett. Whole-length figure. In delicacy of feeling for nature, great transparency of colour, and careful carrying out, this is one of the finest portraits by Holbein of this prince that I know. It is here attributed to Mabuse, who died, however, in 1532, five years before the birth of Edward VI.

2. Portrait of the Protector Duke of Somerset, with a somewhat long and brown but thin beard; in a black dress with white collar and black cap; holding a medallion in his right hand with St. George and the Dragon. The background blueish. A small picture, of very animated conception; the hands very elegant in form and position, and the execution very finished.

Mark Gerard.—Portrait of Queen Elizabeth in middle age, with black dress and high white ruff. Bust picture. Of individual conception, moderate drawing, and pale colouring.

Pietro Torregiano.—Bust of Henry VII., executed in a dark stone, and inscribed MDIX. The forms are very strongly rendered, and an expression of pain pervades the whole face, especially the open mouth.

OSTERLEY PARK.

Seat of Lord Jersey, near Hounslow, Middlesex.

Having had the honour of meeting Lady Jersey at Ravensworth Castle, on occasion of a visit there in the company of my late friend Mr. Anderson of Coxlodge Hall, near Newcastle, I was indebted to her Ladyship for the advantage of a few lines to the housekeeper at Osterley. Accordingly I proceeded to visit that place, where I enjoyed the opportunity of inspecting the works of art with the utmost ease and liberty.

The following specimens of sculpture first attracted my attention in the entrance hall :—

Torso of a Pallas, in Parian marble. Originally of tolerably good workmanship, but now defaced by retouches and restorations.

Torso of another female figure—to which I can give no name—also in Parian marble, and of good workmanship, but in no better preservation than the foregoing.

The staircase next commands attention. The ceiling represents the apotheosis of some prince, by RUBENS. Here not only the invention, as in the ceiling-pictures in Whitehall, but the execution also is by the great master. The colouring is of marvellous power and transparency, and the keeping admirably balanced.

THE DINING-ROOM.

The paintings which decorate these walls—dated 1767—proceed from the hand of ANDREA ZUCCHI, pupil of Amigoni, born in Venice, 1726. Though one of the last scions of this great school, and displaying that superficiality and slightness which might be expected, yet the merits of a good keeping and a skilful management of the brush are still observable.

THE GALLERY.

GASPAR POUSSIN.—1. An extensive view. Three figures in the foreground. The linear perspective is admirable, and the feeling elevated, but the execution is rather decorative in character.

SALVATOR ROSA.—1. A landscape, with Tobit and the angel. Finely composed, of moderate size, and of very powerful effect.

2. A sea-shore, with Apollo speaking to the Sibyl, who kneels before him. The motive of these figures, which are about one-fourth the size of life, is unusually good, the colouring clear and delicate, and the execution remarkably careful.

CLAUDE LORRAINE.—1. Morning. A bridge in front, with trees behind it. On the left is a woman asleep under a kind of tent, two goats butting at each other, two shepherds, and a flock of sheep. On the right a drove of cattle; behind these rising ground, with light trees and a temple. In the background water, and delicately executed hills. This picture belongs to the finest specimens of the master's best time, but has unfortunately lost much of its original beauty by considerable restorations.

2. Evening. The companion to the above. On the left in the foreground are trees and a temple. More in the centre a shepherdess leaning against a white cow, talking to a shepherd, with their flocks around. In the middle distance, on the right, a bridge; behind this a village and hills, and finally the sea, with a glowing sun—its full light subdued by the surrounding vapour—reflected in the water. Signed "Claudio Romæ, 1656." In point of composition, and the warm clear evening light in which every object is steeped, this is a work of the first order.

NICOLAS POUSSIN.—A landscape with Silenus sleeping, and a nymph rubbing him with mulberries. Eighteen amorini and a follower of Pan animate the scene; some are fluttering in the trees, others dancing, and some sleeping. Two satyrs are looking on. Behind a large rock, before which are trees, is a hilly distance. In the middle distance is water. About 4 ft. high by 5 ft. wide. This picture is of the same period as that of Nymphs and Satyrs dancing, in the National Gallery, and is just as poetic in composition, as clear in colouring, and as careful in execution. It is in very good preservation.

PALMA GIOVANE.—The Entombment. A very good picture by this second-rate master, evidently executed under the influence of Tintoretto. Here erroneously attributed to Palma Vecchio.

GUIDO RENI.—The Virgin seated, and holding the Infant on her lap. The heads have not only the elevation of form proper to Guido, but also a greater warmth of feeling than is usual with him. The execution is also very careful, so that I consider this picture one of the best specimens of the master I have met with in England.

VANDYCK.—Portrait of Lord Strafford, as General. Full-length figure, life-size, in complete armour. The head is of decided and animated forms, but the hands are slight, and the treatment of all the rest of an almost decorative breadth.

GASPAR POUSSIN.—2. A rocky landscape with rich vegetation. In the centre a view of the plain of the Campagna. In the foreground are two figures conversing—one standing, the other seated. Highly poetic in feeling, with a far more powerful and warm green than usual, and with much attractive detail.

3. Companion to the above. In the distance a blueish chain of rocks. In front two nymphs conversing. This picture is distinguished by the same admirable qualities as the last.

HOLBEIN (?).—Portrait of Sir Thomas Gresham, the well-known founder of the London Exchange. I cannot decide as to the truth of the portrait, but I can certainly pronounce Holbein not to have been the author of the picture. As far as the height at which it hangs allowed me to judge, I conceive it to be Italian in origin, and of the Lombard school.

DOMENICHINO.—A male portrait. Bust-size. This looks promising, but hangs too high.

SALVATOR ROSA.—3. Jonas ejected by the whale. Of wild and fantastic conception. Dark in colouring and of decorative treatment.

MICHAEL ANGELO CARAVAGGIO.—Abel seated, and holding a flute. Next him a donkey and a sheep. A good specimen of the master. The colouring particularly powerful. The sheep alone is somewhat stiff.

RUBENS.—Portrait of George Villiers, first Duke of Buckingham, on a brown horse. On the right, in a corner, Neptune and Amphitrite. Fame in the air before the Duke, with a wreath; next him a boy genius, and other allegorical figures. In the background the sea with ships. Full-length figures, the size of life. About 9 ft. high by 10 ft. wide. This picture is one of the most stately in the portrait line by the master I know. Indeed the head of the Duke is so spirited and animated in conception, the colouring so powerful and clear, and the execution of such delicacy, that the great master's desire to produce his best for the patron who had purchased his collections of art is very obvious. The same feeling evidently led him to execute the allegorical figures with his own hand. To JORDAENS, however, he intrusted the Neptune and Amphitrite, and the landscape background to some inferior painter of his school.

THE DRAWING-ROOM.

GASPAR POUSSIN.—4 and 5. Two good landscapes, here placed above the doors.

S<small>ALVATOR</small> R<small>OSA</small>.—4 and 5. Two very poetic and carefully executed landscapes by this master also decorate two other doors.

J<small>ACOB</small> R<small>UYSDAEL</small>.—A large landscape, with a magnificent beech-tree, and a piece of water with aquatic flowers, conspicuous in the foreground. On the left a peep through trees. On the right a distant view. The figures which animate the landscape appear to be by B<small>ERGHEM</small>. This broad and finely-treated picture hangs over the mantel-piece, and is much sunk and darkened by long neglect. About 4½ ft. high by 6 ft. wide.

Two pictures of Jacob and Rachel, and David anointed by Samuel, are here erroneously ascribed to Titian. They are pleasing pictures of the later realistic Florentine school of colourists, and recall in many respects the works of G<small>IOVANNI</small> B<small>ILIVERT</small>.

TAPESTRY DRAWING-ROOM.

In this apartment are some well-executed Gobelin tapestries of the last century.

BREAKFAST-ROOM.

S<small>IR</small> J<small>OSHUA</small> R<small>EYNOLDS</small>.—1. Portrait of Mrs. Child, grandmother of Lady Jersey. Half-length, in an oval form. The beauty of the lady, and the easy way in which she rests on her right hand—the harmonious colouring of her dress, which consists of some light shot material, and the very careful modelling in a transparent tone, combine to render this picture attractive in a high degree.

2. Portrait of Mr. Child, husband of the foregoing lady, in the dress of a sportsman. Full-length, life-size. This is also very animatedly composed, but it is harder in the forms and crude in colouring.

S<small>ALVATOR</small> R<small>OSA</small>.—6. An upright landscape with a grand tree and several figures.

THE LIBRARY.

This room is also painted by Z<small>UCCHI</small> in the same way as the staircase abovementioned.

Among the books are various curiosities, which the civil housekeeper allowed my companion, Mr. Murray, of Albemarle Street, and myself, to inspect in great comfort.

By far the most important is a Breviary, in 8vo., according to the Roman ritual, on fine parchment, beautifully written in minuscule letters of Gothic character, in two columns. Strange to say, no calendar occurs in this work. Both as regards the border decorations, consisting of single flowers and fruits, and the miniatures themselves, it presents a first-rate specimen of the ripest time of the French miniature school, viz. towards the end of the 15th century. The artistic ornamentation is also very rich. On the first page appears King David enthroned; before him the prophet Nathan and five other individuals. The favourite vein of humour is also not wanting, for a monkey has caught a cat by the tail. The folds of the drapery are of very good style, and also the landscape background of delicate rendering. The letters I. G. below the figure of an ecclesiastic kneeling refer probably to him, as the patron of the work, and recur afterwards frequently.

" LA BIBLE DES POETES."—This is the title of a French translation of Ovid's Metamorphoses, printed in folio. The frontispiece miniature, which occupies a whole page, as well as the others, are mechanical works of that school of French miniature-painting which attained its height in the well-known 'Heures' of Anne of Bretagne in the Louvre.

Here we also saw some printed works by CAXTON.

LETTER V.

Sir Culling Eardley's collection, Belvedere — Collection of Rev. John Fuller Russell, Greenhithe — Mr. Foster's collection, Clewer Manor — Mr. Sanders' collection, Taplow House — Mr. Walter's collection, Bearwood — Objects of art at Aldermaston — Mr. Morrison's pictures, Basildon Park.

COLLECTION OF PICTURES BELONGING TO SIR CULLING EARDLEY, BART.,

BELVEDERE, NEAR ERITH.

This is one of the most pleasing country seats I have seen in England, which is no small praise in a land which surpasses all others in the number and beauty of its country residences. The park is extensive, and varied with undulating ground and fine trees, but the peculiar charm of Belvedere consists in the view over the Thames, with the full traffic of vessels passing to and fro below the great capital. The contrast between this solitude of refreshing verdure, and the world's great thoroughfares seen from it, is very striking and poetical. The society of Sir Culling and his family, and the interesting nature of the pictures, some of which are of a high class, and many very remarkable, only made me the more regret that my time did not permit me to avail myself of the hospitality with which I was pressed to stay longer.

The pictures comprise the Italian, Spanish, French, Netherlandish, and English schools. I take them in the order in which they are arranged in the different rooms :—

THE DRAWING-ROOM.

MURILLO.—1. The Assumption of the Virgin : the Madonna, a noble and graceful figure in a white dress, finely relieved by her dark blue mantle, is soaring upwards upon a crescent, with her eyes fixed in ecstasy above. Although the individuality of the features indicates realistic taste, yet the head is of great purity and unusual elevation of character. Four cherubim are near the crescent, and four angels on the right, one of whom holds a palm,

another an olive-branch, a third roses, and the fourth another
flower; on the left, above, are two more angels, one holding up
a lily.   About 10 ft. high, 8 ft. wide.   This picture is one of the
most admirable of Murillo's many representations of this subject.
The effect is striking and peculiar for this reason, that the Virgin's
figure, which is kept in a delicate silvery tone, is seen in contrast
to the warm but very broken tones of the surrounding glory,
while the angels, in a clear, subdued, and delicately warm colour,
partially resembling peach-blossom, form an agreeable transition
between the two.   At the same time the execution is very careful,
and the white robes and intense blue of the mantle are modelled
with masterly power.

2. The Flight into Egypt.   The Virgin, seated on an ass, is
looking tenderly upon the sleeping Infant, while Joseph holds his
staff with the left hand over his shoulder, and guides the animal
with the right.   The sky of the landscape background is dark.
About 8 ft. high, 6 ft. wide.   This picture is quite an exception
to the usual style of the master, and is particularly characteristic
of the whole tendency of the Spanish school; for the very individual heads of the Virgin and Joseph show affinity in the elevation of expression to the Italian school, while the ass is treated
with the vigour and circumstantial truth of the Netherlandish
masters.   The forms are decided, but soft, and rendered in a warm
and clear tone.   The head of the Child is a model of truth of
nature.

JAN WEENIX.—Dead animals, comprising a white fox, a wolf,
and some wild ducks; near them is seated a large dog in the act
of barking; in the air is a wild duck flying.   The landscape is of
a darker tone; the dog is of great animation, and the other
animals of rare truth.   The treatment is throughout masterly.

VANDYCK.—1. A family picture : the mother in a black silk
dress, with a full white ruff, is holding a very well-fed baby on her
lap, which is looking round at the father, seated by, and taken
almost full front.   The background consists of a red curtain and a
dark landscape.   This fine picture was probably executed soon
after the return of Vandyck from Italy.   The somewhat heavy,
reddish-brown tone in the head of the Child, and the hands of the
man, as also the colour and treatment of the curtain, recall his
works undertaken in Genoa, while the very animated heads of

both the parents, and the luminous yellow tone in which they are painted, bear witness to the manner of Rubens, to which he continued to adhere for a time after his return to the Netherlands. The head of the woman has a pleasing domestic expression; that of the man is admirably foreshortened. The mistake of supposing these portraits to represent the painter Snyders and his wife and child proceeds probably from the fact that the two ladies are somewhat alike. But the portrait of Snyders in Castle Howard proves him to have differed entirely from the portrait here.

Luca Giordano.—Christ teaching in the Temple. Although a very good specimen of the master's realistic tendency, yet, compared with most of the pictures in this apartment, it appears to little advantage.

Vandyck.—2. A noble lady with four children, said to be the Duchess of Buckingham. She is dressed in white above, and in some dark colour in the lower part of her dress, and is holding a naked infant on her lap. Before her stands a little fair girl in black dress and white apron, looking full at the spectator with her large dark eyes, her right hand on her mother's lap. Next, and partly behind the little girl, is a grown-up sister, also in black, and behind her a great boy. The background consists of a splendid curtain suspended from a column with caryatides, and of a landscape. This fine picture has also been attributed to Rubens; but, in my opinion, is decidedly a work of Vandyck's earlier time, when he painted the family of Sir Balthasar Gerbier, in Windsor Castle, where it also passed under the name of Rubens.* The style of conception, and the clear light tone in the manner of Rubens, agree entirely with that picture, and even the same motive of the charming little girl, looking at the spectator, occurs in the Windsor picture.

Paolo Farinato.—The Marriage at Cana. The cold, reddish flesh tones and the whole treatment of this picture incline me to pronounce this a good work of this scholar of Paul Veronese. It is here attributed to Paul Veronese himself. Figures about half life-size.

Teniers.—1. One of the various existing representations of the gallery of the Archduke Leopold of Austria, with the figures of that prince and of Teniers himself, who, as is well known, was

* See vol. ii. p. 437.

the keeper of the collection : he is here seen pointing out a drawing to the notice of the Archduke. Judging from the heavy tone and lame execution, however, this is only an old copy.

2. The same may be said of the companion picture, where Teniers is seen in the same gallery painting an old woman : this is, however, the best of the two.

THE BILLIARD-ROOM.

PALMA VECCHIO.—Marriage of St. Catherine. The Child, in animated action, on the lap of the Virgin, is about to place the ring on the finger of the Saint, who is looking fervently up to him ; she is seen in profile, with a palm in her hand ; on the left is Joseph with a staff ; the background consists of a hilly landscape, with shadows of clouds. This picture is as attractive in composition as in its powerful golden tones ; the less decision of the forms, and the broader treatment, as compared with most pictures by the master, indicate his later time. On wood. About 3 ft. high, by 4 ft. wide.

GASPAR POUSSIN.—1 and 2. These are of his larger class of works ; one of which, although finely composed, is rather dark ; the other has four figures in the foreground, with mountains in the distance, the noble forms of which give a peculiar charm to the picture.

LUDOLPH BACKHUYSEN.—A sea-piece, which belongs to his better works.

SNYDERS. — Two blue earthen vessels, one of them containing crabs : a jug, dead birds, and light-coloured grapes. Admirably carried out in a clear, silvery tone.

ROGIER VAN DER WEYDEN THE YOUNGER.—The Entombment. Joseph of Arimathea is holding the back of the Saviour's head with his left hand, and with the right seems to urge the utmost care in the treatment of the sacred body. Nicodemus sustains the body under the knees in order to place it in the sepulchre. St. John, next to him, is holding the winding-sheet with his right hand, and with his left the left hand of the Saviour ; next to him is the Virgin, with very noble features, the hands folded, looking at her son with the expression of the intensest sorrow ; between her and Joseph of Arimathea are the heads of two other afflicted women ; in the dark background is seen the ladder up to the cross. The composition is so crowded that, though the half-length figures described are about three-fourths the size of life, the picture is not more than 4 ft. high, by 3 ft. wide. The meagreness of the limbs of Christ, and the very great warmth of the colouring, vividly recall the manner of his father Rogier van der Weyden the elder, and thus indicate the early time of the son. The truth and depth of feeling proper to this master are here combined with a more elevated form of heads; the execution is very solid. The tears of the women and of St. John are admirably painted.

SCHOOL OF BERNARDINO LUINI.—St. Catherine, with an open book in her hand, is looking down upon it; at her sides are two angels—the one on the right leaning on the wheel. The heads are of that Leonardesque type which Luini followed; but the somewhat empty forms and the heavy shadows forbid my ascribing this otherwise pleasing picture to him.

PIETRO DELLA VECCHIA.—Three Italian peasant-lads playing cards. Of very animated conception, but the tone particularly heavy and brown. Erroneously ascribed to Domenico Feti.

JAN BREUGHEL.—1. A landscape, apparently representing the Garden of Eden, for wild beasts and the tamer animals are depicted together. The presence of some shepherds, however, is rather a contradiction. In the representation of the panthers and lions the creations of Rubens have been borrowed; for the latter especially the picture of Daniel in the Lions' Den in Hamilton Palace. On wood. The colouring is as powerful and luminous as the execution is finished.

2. Landscape, with numerous animals, fruits, and flowers. Allegorical figures relating to science—for instance, astronomy—and to wine and music, are by the hand of JOHANN ROTHENHAMMER. This combined work is most successful.

NETHERLANDISH SCHOOL — TOWARDS 1500.—The Stem of Jesse. Below, in the centre, seated on a marble throne, is St. Anna, holding in her right hand a page of an open and admirably drawn book. On the parapet of the throne are two child angels, the one playing the double flute, the other the violoncello. At the feet of St. Anna is the Virgin, seated, in a blue dress, holding with both hands the infant Christ, in whose little hand is a wreath of coral; on the right is the donor, a youthful figure in a black fur

dress, kneeling; behind him, in canonicals, with red gloves and a
staff, is Aaron; on the left, also kneeling, is the female donor, an
elderly woman; behind her is David playing on the harp; from
behind the throne rises the stem of Jesse upon a gold ground,
forming thirteen branches, each with a flower terminating in a half-
length figure—eleven male and two female: from the names
written by them, not all now legible, it appears that these represent prophets, apostles, and saints. Quite at top, in the centre, is
the Virgin with the Child to whom a Saint (perhaps Joseph) is
reaching a book; on the Virgin's right is the First Person of the
Trinity, with the papal crown on his head, and in the left hand
the globe. On wood. About 3 ft. high, 2 ft. 6 in. wide. With
the exception of a crack which goes through two of the heads, in
good preservation. This is the finest work I have seen by that
unknown master who painted the Baptism of Christ in the collection of the Academy at Bruges—there wrongly ascribed to Memling. We thus see this subject of the stem of Jesse, which was
so popular in the middle ages, here once more repeated towards
the termination of that period, with some arbitrary alterations, it
is true, but with the purest and most elevated religious feeling;
at the same time the heads, though somewhat similar in character,
display a degree of beauty, and the hands and cast of the drapery
a knowledge, which is quite astonishing. The head of St. John
the Evangelist, one of the half-length figures, is especially of the
rarest delicacy; although the colouring of the flesh and drapery is
cool, yet a refined harmony pervades the whole picture: the
superiority of the drawing, and the greater delicacy with which
every portion is rendered, prove that this picture was executed
somewhat later than that in Bruges.

PETER NEEFS.—1 and 2. Interiors of a church, both pretty
pictures; one of them is seen by torchlight.

ADAM PYNACKER.—A Dutch scene, with a canal. A purer
feeling for nature, and a warmer and more transparent colouring,
are here displayed than is usual with the master.

THE LIBRARY.

CLAUDE LORRAINE.—Fine buildings occupy the left of the foreground; in the centre are stately trees, while other trees occupy
the whole space of the picture on the right upwards; between

these two masses of trees lies the view of a plain with a lake; figures are in the foreground, among which those of two women are particularly remarkable; the sky is warmly lighted. This grand picture, about 6 ft. high, by 8 ft. wide, is of the later time of the master.

BENJAMIN WEST.—Portrait of Lord Eardley, grandfather of Sir Culling. The figure is standing with the right hand upon his side, the left on a table. To the knees. Signed, and dated 1764. This picture is therefore the more remarkable as having been executed in West's 26th year. The composition is easy, the head true to nature, and the colouring transparent.

SIR JOSHUA REYNOLDS.—1. Portrait of the wife of the above in a blue dress. Bust picture. The delicate profile has an agreeable expression; the tender colouring is very transparent, and the execution careful.

2. Portrait of Sir John Eardley Wilmot, Lord Chief Justice, in a grey coat. The conception very true and simple, and the treatment careful.

REMBRANDT.—1. Portrait of a man in a black dress, and in a black broad-brimmed hat and white collar, from which two strings depend. Signed, and dated 1667. Of glowing colour, and, like most of his later pictures, of very broad treatment. The hands, especially the right, are only sketched.

JAN VAN HEMESSEN.—The parable of the Unjust Steward. This is an unusually good picture by this commonplace and tasteless painter; the heads are less vulgar; the colouring of great power; the execution hard as usual, but careful.

REMBRANDT.—2. The picture of an old man with a strange smile; a cap of a light colour on his head; his dress dark, with a brown-yellow collar. This is so like himself that one is tempted to think it is his own portrait. It is the *ne plus ultra* of coarse, bold, and decorative treatment.

ANTE-ROOM TO DINING-ROOM.

RÖTING, a painter of the Düsseldorf school.—Portrait of Sir Culling Eardley. To the knees. Very animated and like. Signed and dated 1855.

LEANDRO BASSANO.—1 and 2. Two pictures, one representing a vintage, the other a smithy, symbolical doubtless of summer and winter. These belong to the better works of the master. The backgrounds only are, as generally with him, too dark.

THE DINING-ROOM.

This large apartment is decorated by thirteen pictures by ANGELICA KAUFFMANN, let into the walls, and which, by their pleasing composition and cheerful colouring, have an agreeable effect.

CANALETTO.—1 and 2. Views of Venice, one of them representing the Doge's palace, with the festival of the Bucentaur. Good specimens of the master.

FRANZ POURBUS THE YOUNGER.—Portrait of a man with his son. To the knees. Natural, warm, and well finished.

LAURENT DE LA HIRE.—Belisarius receiving alms from a woman. A careful and well-coloured picture by the painter.

THE GALLERY.

SIR JOSHUA REYNOLDS.—3. Portrait of Lady Say and Sele, with a boy, afterwards Colonel Eardley. The lady is seated, in a white dress, with a black hat and feathers on her head, and another on her lap. The boy is standing, with a walking-stick in his right hand. The background is a landscape. An attractive picture, of great animation and transparency.

GAINSBOROUGH.—Portrait of Lord Gage. Of great merit.

SIR CULLING EARDLEY'S PRIVATE ROOM.

PHILIP WOUVERMANS.—1. Interior of a court, with a stone gateway in the background. On the left is a group consisting of a grey horse held by a boy, a gentleman, and a groom. In the centre a rider galloping along on a piebald horse. On the right two horses with a groom. Quite in the foreground is a man next the overturned base of a column. Above the wall of the court are seen two light trees, with clouds illuminated by the sun. A very delicate picture of his second manner, the effect of which is injured by the darkening of the foreground.

2. The companion to the above. Also the interior of a court, with a portion of an open gateway. On the wall is a field-piece, and three figures are next trees. On the left, in the foreground, is a brown horse tied up, and a grey horse held by a groom. In

the centre is a gentleman on a piebald horse galloping round upon a rein. By the post is a groom and two figures looking on. The sky resembles that of the companion picture, with the same merits and quality.

Artus van der Neer.—A wide canal frozen, with villages on the bank, and with a sledge, skaiters, and other persons upon it. In the foreground, towards the left, are some leafless trees. The delicate aërial perspective, and the mild warm tone, especially of the sky, render this picture very attractive. The treatment shows the early time of the master.

Gaspar Poussin.—3. A landscape. In the foreground, on the left, are lofty trees ; more on the right, by a piece of water, two figures ; beyond, two other figures, with one in a boat. In the middle distance are buildings of a noble and simple form ; in the background hills, the highest of which is lighted by the sun. One of those rare works by the master which, in addition to a poetical composition and careful execution, possess a warm and clear colouring.

Rubens.—A sketch for one of the triumphal arches erected from his designs to honour the entrance of the Infant Ferdinand. The often repeated allegory of Time bringing Truth to light is here treated by Rubens, in his dramatic-fantastic taste, as the old dragon of the Apocalypse, with demons and possessed men lying on the ground, while the faithful, in adoration, are partly kneeling upon them. The treatment is very decorative, and the tone unusually heavy.

Jan van Goyen.—1. Sea-piece ; spiritedly executed, but belonging in colour to his pale ashen-tinted works.

Willem van de Velde.—A calm sea. On the right, quite in the foreground, on the shore, is a boat with three figures. Two fishermen are standing in the water. In the centre are two fishing-boats and a skiff. On the right, in the distance, is a large vessel, whence a gun is fired. Of remarkable delicacy, but the red tone of the clouds not favourable.

Jan van Goyen.—2. View of a Dutch canal. Unusually clear and powerful for him.

School of Rembrandt.—A king and a priest in a building, looking at books. Attributed to Rembrandt, but too feeble for him.

THE STAIRCASE.

POMPEO BATTONI.—Portraits of Lord Eardley and his tutor. Full-length figures, life-size. Next them a dog. This picture is a proof that this master was well adapted for this class of painting. The arrangement is happy, the heads animated, and the whole carefully executed in a fresh colouring.

ADDITIONS TO THE COLLECTION OF THE REV. JOHN FULLER RUSSELL,

NOW OF GREENHITHE, KENT.

(Vol. II. p. 461.)

This gentleman has, since 1854, added so many valuable pictures to his collection that I can do no less than mention them.

ITALIAN SCHOOL.

DON SILVESTRO CAMALDOLESE.—1. Death and glorification of the Virgin. A miniature on vellum. Described in my ' Art and Artists in England,' vol. ii. p. 129, English translation. From Mr. Young Ottley's collection.

2. A royal saint; half-length; crowned, and vested in a superb cope, with six smaller half-length figures of saints. A miniature on vellum. From the collections of Mr. Young Ottley and Mr. Rogers. Of great beauty.

TADDEO DI BARTOLO.—A Diptych. On the right wing is represented the Crucifixion, with the Virgin and St. John on either hand, the cross being embraced by the Magdalen. On the left wing the Virgin and Child enthroned, between St. James the Greater and St. John the Baptist and two angels. In tempera, on gold ground. In the upper portion of the frame, which is enriched with jewels, are two circular compartments with the Annunciation. Half-length figures. An interesting work by this rare and important master of the early Sienese school.

AMBROGIO BORGOGNONE.—The dead Christ mourned by infant angels. In oil, on panel. The meagre forms of the Christ indicate the earlier time of the master. The angels, however, fully display the childlike and touching expression so characteristic of him.

SCHOOL OF GIOTTO, about 1370.—Marriage of the Virgin. In tempera, on panel.

UGOLINO DA SIENA.—1. The Resurrection. Forming the seventh of the predella pictures of his great picture in the church of the S. Croce at Florence. In tempera, gold ground, on panel.

2. Two angels. Tempera, gold ground, on panel.

NETHERLANDISH AND GERMAN SCHOOLS.

HANS MEMLING.—A Diptych. On the right the Crucifixion, a rich composition, with Jerusalem in the distance. On the left wing Jeanne de France, wife of John II., Duke of Bourbon (born 1426, married 1450, died 1482), a beautiful person, still in youthful years, kneeling before a *prie dieu*, on which is a blue covering with fleurs-de-lys. Before her an angel, wearing an alb, bears a shield emblazoned with her arms. Behind her is John the Baptist. In the sky are the Virgin and Child, who is giving the benediction, surrounded by a rainbow, and enthroned on the Crescent. Above the Child hovers the Dove. At the top of the picture is the Almighty, conventionally represented as "the Ancient of Days," wearing a triple crown and crimson robe, and giving the benediction with his right hand. Background, landscape and sky. On panel. A small and very beautiful picture by the master, executed like a miniature, recalling in many respects his master, Rogier van der Weyden the elder. Of uncommon preservation.

QUENTIN MATSYS.—The Virgin and Child, on panel, in the earlier manner of the master, and therefore redder and heavier in tone than his later pictures.

EARLY FLEMISH SCHOOL, about 1430.—St. Jerome, sitting at a reading-desk, with cardinal's hat and robe, within a Gothic chamber, is turning towards a lion, who holds up his right paw, and seems to solicit attention. In the background are two windows partly open, with shutters, and two shelves on which are vessels, plates, books, &c. Forming a sort of frame to the above scene is a stone arch supported by pillars of pointed architecture, with statues of saints beneath canopies on their capitals. The head of St. Jerome is surrounded by a gilt nimbus. On panel. An excellent and interesting work by a contemporary of the Van Eycks, painted in the manner of the old school of Cologne, which prevailed independently of Cologne from 1350 to 1430 in all the countries of Europe, excepting Italy, and which also, still later, when the realistic manner in art was introduced by the Van Eycks, was adhered to by many painters until 1470.

SCHOOL OF ROGIER VAN DER WEYDEN THE ELDER.—The Virgin and Child. Similar to the figures of the Virgin and Child in the large picture of St. Luke taking the portrait of the Virgin in the gallery at Munich, though incomparably less delicate in rendering. I take this opportunity to observe that a picture representing the Saviour taking leave of his Mother—mentioned vol. ii. p. 462—is by a mistake in printing ascribed to Albert Durer. It is the work of his scholar ALBRECHT ALTDORFER.

My last visit to this hospitable gentleman gave me also the leisure to examine several works contained in his library, and not hitherto mentioned.

A very beautiful copy of the first edition of the Hypnerotomachia of Poliphilus, with the well-known woodcuts, published in 1499 by Aldus of Venice.

The very rare English incunabula, entitled 'Speculum Christiani,' an octavo volume, with the following inscription at the end : " Iste libellus impressa est in opulentissima Civitate Londoniæ per me Wilhelmum de Machlinia ad instantiam nec non expensas Henrici Frankenbergh Mercatoris offenb."

The first edition of Matthew Parker's work, 'de Antiquitate Ecclesiæ Britannicæ,' MDLXXII. A folio volume printed by John Day. A woodcut of allegorical import, which adorns the title-page, shows in the motives of the figures, some of which are very beautiful, the influence of Holbein's art. The execution is very simple, and only of very moderate artistic merit.

Three of the first editions of Shakspeare's plays : the Midsummer Night's Dream, 1600 ; Macbeth, 1608 ; and the Merry Wives of Windsor, 1619. For an enthusiastic admirer of this great searcher of the heights and depths of the human mind there is something indescribably touching in seeing the modest form in which he first appeared, and I took these volumes into my hands with a poetic feeling scarcely inferior in devotion to that with which a believer touches the relics of a saint.

ADDITIONS TO THE COLLECTION OF EDMUND FOSTER, ESQ.,
CLEWER MANOR, NEAR WINDSOR.

(Vol. II. p. 451.)

In the additions which this gentleman has made since 1854 to his small collection he has not been faithless to his old motto, " Few and good." I was struck by the following :—

MURILLO.—The Assumption of the Virgin, who is seen enthroned on clouds, her eyes cast upwards and her hands folded ; she is wrapped in a dress of silvery white and a blue mantle, and is borne on high accompanied by nine angels. Above, on each side, are three cherubim ; below is her tomb, with the twelve Apostles, among whom St. John, quite on the left, is very remarkable, and two holy women. The motives of the Virgin and of the Apostles are speaking and of elevated character, the composition in the limited space very rich, the contrast between the cool ethereal harmony of the upper half, and the warm and powerful colouring of the lower half, especially on the right side, is very happy. The execution is careful, though broad and spirited. Among the small pictures by the master this takes a very distinguished place.

JACOB RUYSDAEL.—A watermill and a house built of tiles and wood on the left. Between them is the mill-dam, whence the water rushes and flows in a foaming stream the whole length of the foreground. On the right are light bushes and water-plants. In the middle distance a man and a white dog. In front two large stones, bushes, and reeds. Signed, and dated 1653. On wood. 1 ft. 10½ in. high, 3 ft. 3 in. wide. This picture, which is one of the most original and beautiful works of the master, was formerly in the possession of Casimir Perrier, and afterwards in the hands of Mr. Brown, the picture-dealer, where I saw it some years ago. The freshness and energy, freedom and spirit of the handling, the fine lighting with the house half in sunshine, and the, for him, unusually lighted-up clouds which recall Hobbema, give this picture a particular character in the eyes of those who understand the master.

JAN BOTH.—On the left a high rock, and near it a tree. A small waterfall is seen between large masses of rock. On the right are three step-like hills receding one behind the other. On the road next the foremost hill is a woman on a mule, and

a man with a loaded mule behind him.   In the distance are two
loaded donkeys being driven up.   3 ft. 6 in. high, 3 ft. 4 in. wide.
This picture was formerly No. 78 of the first cabinet of the excellent Ducal Gallery of Brunswick at Saltzthalum.   It is in every
respect a capital work by the master.   The composition is very
fortunate, the chiaroscuro in the foreground of great transparency,
the warm lighting not overdone, and the execution throughout
equally solid.

JAN WEENIX.—A dead hare, two partridges, and other birds.
On the right is a building in the style of a temple.   This is a picture of very picturesque arrangement, of grander extent than his
usual works of this kind, of exemplary keeping, and, with all his
usual finish, of powerful tone.

ALBERT CUYP.—A view on the Rhine.   On the right is a rising
ground with a town, and on a projecting tongue of land a church-
yard, trees, and buildings.   In the foreground is a beech, on the
left a cow standing and another reposing, with the herdsman sitting
by.   In the distance, in the most delicate rendering, the other
shore of the stream.   Some clouds are in the sky.   On wood.
1 ft. 10 in. high, 2 ft. 6 in. wide.   This is a picture of the finest
quality, and quite in the manner and of the time of Mr. Holford's
well-known view on the Maas.

MURILLO.—The Virgin seated, showing the Infant, who is
sleeping in her lap, to Joseph.   At the feet of the Virgin, in adoration, is the little St. John.   The background consists of trees on
the right, and dark sky on the left.   Figures fully the size of life,
and to the knees.   About 5 ft. high by 4 ft. wide.   The Virgin is
unusually elevated in character for him, and, with the Child, is
admirably modelled in a transparent silvery tone.   St. John and
Joseph on the other hand are treated in a powerful reddish tone.
The carrying out of the purple robe of the Virgin is very careful;
the blue of her mantle very dark.   This capital picture was formerly in the Harvey collection.

PHILIP WOUVERMANS.—A small landscape, much in the taste
of his master Wynants, animated with figures.   Quite a little gem
in delicacy of tone and execution.

COLLECTION OF PICTURES BELONGING TO JOSEPH SANDERS,
ESQ., AT HIS SEAT, TAPLOW HOUSE, NEAR MAIDENHEAD.

Having the advantage of knowing a large number of so-called
" pleasure-grounds" both in England and Scotland, I may venture
to express the opinion that both in tastefulness of situation, looking
as they do upon the pretty neighbourhood of Maidenhead, and also
for the excellent manner in which they are kept, the grounds
belonging to this charming and hospitable seat are among the
finest I have seen. The interior of the house is also decorated
with that best ornament, a collection of pictures, containing much
that is valuable, and some specimens that are highly remarkable, of
the Italian, Flemish, Dutch, and English schools.

THE DRAWING-ROOM.

BERGHEM.—Merrymaking. Peasants in an interior. A couple
are dancing to the music of a hurdygurdy and a fiddle, the musicians placed in an elevated position. Two other couples (one of
them making love) are seated at a table. A cat is setting up her
back at a dog. Painted in chiaroscuro, and signed. This is a
very successful attempt on the part of this gifted painter to imitate
the style of Adrian van Ostade, though the heads, both of the
figures and animals, show his own manner.

JAN WYNANTS.—1. Landscape with a road, quite on the left
towards the foreground, on which are a woman, a boy, and a dog.
The road is cut off by a piece of water, which terminates in hills.
On wood. Signed, and dated 1674. Of careful rendering, but
somewhat heavy and dark in colour.

CORNELIS POELEMBERG.—A hilly landscape with ruins. In the
foreground towards the right is a Riposo. Very tender and
harmonious.

E. VAN DER POEL.—A fire. Of striking effect and marrowy
execution.

ADAM PYNACKER.—A hilly landscape, with a storm raging.
In the foreground, on the right, by a piece of water, are two
frightened cows, a herdsman, and a dog. With the exception of
the warm sky, cold in tone, but of excellent keeping, and very
carefully carried out.

JAN WYNANTS.—2. A hilly landscape, with his favourite sand-hill with a tree on the right. A grey horse drawing a cart, with a man and a woman on the left, and a woman, a boy, and a dog more in front, are introduced by LINGELBACH. Signed. On canvas pasted on wood. Attractive both for composition and careful finish. The heavy tone shows the later time of the master.

ABRAHAM STORCK.—A calm. On the right is a pier, with figures, and a fishing boat. So choice a work of the master as to approach Willem van de Velde in delicacy of touch and clearness of tone.

GAINSBOROUGH.—A mountainous landscape. In the centre of the foreground washwomen by a dark piece of water. In power and clearness of the warm light and dark masses of shadow this charming picture approaches Philip de Koningck.

GIORGIONE (?).—The Virgin seated on the ground and holding the Child on her arm. On the right is Joseph, on the left, kneeling in adoration, is an aged saint, and a youthful saint in profile. Two other figures also, resembling shepherds, are approaching in prayer. The background a landscape. On wood. The deep glow of colour, the feeling in the head, and the beauty of the youthful saint account for the title above given ; the outlines, however, are too hard for Giorgione, and the colouring too dense. On the other hand, most of the heads and the landscape bespeak the hand of DOSSO DOSSI, of whom this may be considered a remarkable specimen.

GOVAERT FLINCK.—Bust-picture of an aged Rabbi. Animated, warm, and careful.

RICHARD WILSON.—Landscape, with buildings, and a piece of water, over which is a bridge. In front, on the right, is a boat. The great transparency and admirable impasto show the happy influence of Cuyp.

NASMYTH.—A landscape with an extensive distance. Of good invention and careful rendering.

JAN VICTORS.—View of a village, in the taste of Van Goyen. On the right are various figures, rather large. With his usual truth, but warmer in tone.

ROMNEY.—Portrait of a young man leaning on his right hand. Animated, of good colouring, and of broad and spirited treatment.

BERNARDO STROZZI.—The bust-picture of a Magdalen, obviously a portrait, appears to me to be by this painter. It is of masterly painting, in warm and clear colouring.

BONIFAZIO (?).—The Virgin and Child, St. Joseph, and a female saint, perhaps St. Dorothea, with roses. This small picture, which looks very promising, is hung too high.

DINING-ROOM.

JACOB RUYSDAEL.—On the right, in the foreground, is a waterfall, in the background mountains. On the left on a hill is a house between two fir-trees and other trees. A piece of water and the clouds are illumined with a sunbeam. The poetic composition of this beautiful picture shows the influence of Everdingen. It is very powerful and fresh in effect and colour, and broad and spirited in treatment.

ARTUS VAN DER NEER.—A Dutch town with gables, with a canal in the centre, seen by the light of the moon, which is tolerably high, and partly concealed by a light tree. On the right, in the foreground, are a man and woman in conversation. Warm and transparent, and of broad and masterly treatment in his latest manner.

BERGHEM. — 2. A hilly landscape with warm morning light. Quite on the right is a building on a hill after the fashion of the Temple of the Sibyl at Tivoli, and below, in the foreground, in deep chiaroscuro, a shepherd with two cows and two sheep. On the left, in the background, dark hills.

WALKER.—Portrait of an ancestor of Mr. Sanders—an adherent of Cromwell — in armour. Of true conception and capital execution.

FREDERICK MOUCHERON.—A landscape, with a lofty pillar on the right side; on the left, in the distance, a hill. A good example of the master, and rendered further valuable by figures by ADRIAN VAN DE VELDE.

MARCANTONIO FRANCESCHINI.—The Birth of Adonis. An excellent picture by the master, in which he approaches very near Albano.

CARLO MARATTI.—The Virgin holding the Child, who is caressing her. Very pleasing, of warm tone, and careful execution.

KAREL DUJARDIN.—A hilly landscape with a shepherd and shepherdess, a naked boy, an ass, and four sheep passing a ford.

This pretty picture, which was formerly in Count Pourtalis' collection in Paris, has unfortunately much suffered.

ANDREA SCHIAVONE.—Christ, accompanied by five Disciples, speaking to a woman on the right side of the picture, next a pillar of the Temple. The background landscape. Figures about two-thirds life-size. Powerful in colour, and more carefully finished than usual.

ALDERT VAN EVERDINGEN.—A piece of water is rushing down by a rock, on which is a peasant-house surrounded with trees. The sky is quite clear. Of great freshness of nature and power of tone, and of broad and masterly handling. An upright picture.

SALVATOR ROSA.—A hilly landscape with water on the left. Two trees are seen in front with their stems crossing each other ; on the right, next the stump of a tree, are four figures, one of them fishing. Happily composed, and of powerful but dark tone. The execution careful.

TITIAN.—The Magdalen. The same composition which occurs so frequently on a larger and smaller scale, painted originally for the Duke of Mantua, and of which the master doubtless made several repetitions. Of these this may be considered one of the best both in animation of conception and depth of feeling, in the transparency of the deep golden tones, and in the full and spirited execution. This is the most important picture of the collection.

ADRIAN VAN DE VELDE.—On the right, in the middle distance, is a hill overgrown with trees. Before it a brown cow drinking at a piece of water. In the foreground, in the centre, a woman washing her feet; next her two cows reposing, the one seen in front, the other behind ; and three sheep, one of them walking. A hilly distance. Signed. A charming picture of the middle time of the master. Pleasing in composition, harmonious in the clear and mildly warm tone, and of delicate rendering of detail.

JAN BOTH.—On the left trees, and a rocky cavern, with a piece of water before it at which two grey horses are being watered ; near them a brown horse and three men. On the right, by a rising ground, are two trees with crossing stems. In the distance water and very tenderly indicated hills. In the foreground a rock. Particularly powerful and warm in tone.

SIR JOSHUA REYNOLDS.—His own portrait, before his journey to Rome, and therefore in youthful years. Mahlstick and palette are in his left hand; the right hand is held over his eyes as if to sharpen his sight, so that his eyes are overshadowed by it.   The very animated and original conception, the transparent colour and careful handling, are already characteristic of this gifted painter.

GIULIO ROMANO (?).—Portrait of Bramante, the celebrated architect, in black dress and cap. In warmth of colouring, solidity, and impasto, and mode of treatment, especially of the shirt, this spirited picture so much resembles those portraits by Raphael in the Doria Palace at Rome, of Andrea Novagero and Agostino Beazzano (commonly but arbitrarily called Bartolo and Baldo), that I am much inclined to assign it to the hand of Raphael, especially in the principal portions. It is also quite probable that he would have executed the portrait of a master of kindred feeling, whom he so much respected.

BILLIARD-ROOM.

THOMAS FORD.—A girl standing at a toilette-table, looking over her shoulder at the spectator. Of pretty and original motive, delicate keeping, rich and tasteful accessories, and broad but careful treatment. Signed, and dated 1848.

COLLECTION OF PICTURES BELONGING TO MR. WALTER,
AT HIS SEAT, BEARWOOD, NEAR READING.

In 1856, through the kind intervention of Mr. Edmund Foster, my long entertained wish to inspect this collection was gratified. It consists chiefly of choice pictures of the Dutch school of the 17th century. Though the owner was on the Continent, I was nevertheless permitted to examine the pictures in the company of Messrs. Foster and Sanders. Unfortunately the lighting was in great measure obscured by violent rain.   I proceed to describe the pictures in the order in which they are distributed in the rooms.

DRAWING-ROOM.

PAUL POTTER.—On an eminence in the centre of the fore-ground lies a beautiful cow of light colour with yellow spots, the animal being seen in her whole length. Next her is a blackish cow in a foreshortened view seen from behind. Behind her is a bull standing. On the left is the old stem of a tree and a wooden fence. Some light clouds are in the sky. On wood. 1 ft. 5½ in. high, 1 ft. 3 in. wide. Signed, and dated 1647. Great as were my anticipations regarding this celebrated picture, they were, which is rarely the case, surpassed. Without seeing the picture no idea can be formed of the plastic rendering of the forms; and while, at a certain distance, the effect of the animals is that of life itself, the carefulness of the execution, though always rendered with a fat brush, is such—for instance in the ear of the light-coloured cow—that the delusion of reality is increased on the closest inspection. What a painter was this, who, at twenty-two years of age, had already attained such perfection! At an earlier period this masterwork belonged to the well-known Braamcamp and Smeth van Alpen collections. In 1823 it was obtained at the sale of Mr. Watson Taylor's pictures for the price of 1210 guineas. It was purchased, with the rest of the collection at Bearwood, with the exception of a few pictures, by the father of the present proprietor, the late Mr. John Walter.

NICHOLAS BERGHEM.—A landscape. On the right is a woman on a grey horse, and other figures and animals. Behind are blue mountains. On the left, in the middle distance, is a tree with another group of figures and animals passing a ford near it. The general tone is of a heavy blue. A careful picture of his later time.

KAREL DUJARDIN.—On the right the arches of a building, and three boys bathing; on the left, in the foreground, a laden mule, a woman on a horse, and sheep, and in the background hills. The sky, which is unusual for him, is of a very warm tone. On canvas. In point of composition, keeping, and carrying out, a picture of the first class.

PETER DE HOOGHE.—A Dutch garden with flowers and the marble statue of a boy, with nine ninepins placed in the foreground. A lady is speaking to a young man opposite to her; another, turned from the spectator, to two gentlemen in the middle distance, one of whom is seated. Behind the last figure is a house. The sky is of warm tone. On canvas. An upright picture. This is an unusual specimen of the master, the landscape being the principal part, and the figures kept small. The whole makes a very peaceful impression, though the verdure of the garden is somewhat too heavy, by which the keeping is rather disturbed. On the other hand, the figures are of great animation, of very transparent tone, and very delicately executed.

JAN WYNANTS.—A landscape with trees and buildings. In front, in the centre, is a piece of water ; on the right, on a small eminence, thinly clothed trees. In the distance hills. On wood. Of great truth, and as solidly as delicately executed. Only rather dull in tone.

JAN BOTH.—On the left rising ground, with trees of light foliage before it. In the centre of the middle distance a piece of water ; in the foreground another piece, with two men standing by it. On the right, in the distance, are hills receding one behind the other. On canvas. Of tolerably large size and very warm in tone, though somewhat trivial in treatment, especially of the trees.

ADAM PYNACKER.—Landscape with a stream, with boats upon it. Rich in details and very careful, but the colour very cold.

SASSOFERRATO.—The Virgin and Child. She has a rose in her left hand. Half-length. The well-known pleasing character of this master is here combined with an unusual warm colour and a careful execution.

GONZALES COCQUES.—A family-group of six persons, in a landscape. On wood. In every respect—arrangement, animation of heads, warmth and clearness of tone, spirited and careful execution—this is one of the finest works of this rare and charming master.

NICHOLAS BERGHEM. — A winter landscape. On the right buildings, before which are men and horses—among the latter a grey horse, On the left a small stair. In the distance a windmill. This large picture displays singular truth in every portion, with a delicate harmony in the warm lighting.

ISAAC VAN OSTADE.—1. A peasant-house, with a door such as is seen in stables, on the lower half of which a man is leaning. Before it is a woman with her child. Opposite to her stands a sportsman. On wood. Upright. Of masterly handling and of great power of colour.

ADRIAN VAN OSTADE.—1. A party in an interior. A large picture for him, but placed too high for me to form any opinion of it on so dark a day.

ADRIAN VAN DE VELDE.—Two sheep by the stem of a tree. Signed. Small, delicate, and harmonious.

DINING-ROOM.

JACOB RUYSDAEL.—View of the Castle of the Counts of Bentheim on the Lower Rhine. Although two fine pictures by the master, of which this castle is the subject—the one at Dresden, the other in the Van Brienen collection at Amsterdam—are already known to me, yet both are far surpassed, in size as well as in masterly treatment, by this one. I think it highly probable, therefore, that Mr. Walter's picture was, as tradition avers, painted as a commission for Count Bentheim himself. Like the stag-hunt at Dresden, and the large picture, with figures by Berghem, in the Louvre, it belongs to the chefs-d'œuvre of the master. Although less attractive in composition than those, and upon the whole of somewhat darker effect, it surpasses them in the union of admirable keeping, great richness of details, and in solid and spirited carrying out. It is also in a state of rare preservation. The acquisition of this picture, which only took place in 1856, shows that Mr. Walter intends to continue the collection upon the same elevated standard, and with the same choice taste, by which his father was guided.

PHILIP WOUVERMANS. — A sea-shore with numerous figures. A large picture, but of a cold, grey, and heavy tone. Signed.

ADRIAN VAN OSTADE.—2. The Adoration of the Shepherds. Signed, and dated 1669. Although rendered with his usual peasant physiognomies, the heads are of the utmost refinement. The tone, with the exception of the somewhat heavy background, is golden and clear, and the execution spirited and careful.

HOBBEMA.—In the foreground a piece of water, into which a woman is dragging a cow. On the right a small rising ground with trees. In the middle distance a village. On the left, towards the centre, lofty trees. Signed. This large picture, which proceeds from the collection of Lady Hampden, was originally of great beauty, but the present heavy, dark tone of the foreground and trees greatly injures the keeping. A discreet cleaning and fresh varnish would much assist this.

JAN STEEN.—The Marriage at Cana. The subject is degraded to the level of his sphere of art, but the picture is rich and careful. The background only has somewhat darkened.

ISAAC VAN OSTADE.—2. Peasants passing a ford on foot and on horseback. On the right, over the water, is a hill, on the left houses, in the centre a tree. In the foreground a woman seated, with a child. On wood. This moderately large picture is very remarkable for clear and glowing colouring and marrowy execution.

FREDERIC MOUCHERON.—A landscape. Well composed, and carefully executed, but cold in tone.

MIDDLE DRAWING-ROOM.

TERBURG.—A girl pouring out something from a jug into a glass for a gentleman who is filling his pipe. An old woman is by. A delicate but very sunken picture, standing greatly in need of restoration.

FRANCESCO ALBANO.—Christ appearing to the Magdalen. A very pretty picture.

TENIERS.—Two peasants in an interior, one holding a jug. A small picture of warm tone, and spirited and careful handling.

JAN VAN DER HEYDEN.—1. Landscape, with a town in the middle distance, with figures by ADRIAN VAN DE VELDE. Warm and clear in colour, and refined in carrying out.

1. The companion-picture, with buildings in the centre. In the background, on the left, blue hills. Of the same excellence.

FRANS MIERIS.—Portrait of a young painter holding a palette, and leaning with his right arm on a parapet. In the background an easel. Signed, and dated 1667. Very animated and highly finished.

HEINRICH VON VLIET.—Interior of a church. Of masterly perspective, tone, and treatment.

NICOLAS MAAS.—Portrait of an old woman seated in an armchair, in black cap and dress, with spectacles in her right hand and a book in her left. Very animated, and finely painted in a warm and transparent tone, and with a broad and soft brush.

THE HALL.

JAN BAPTISTA WEENIX.—A seaport, with buildings, and colonnade of pillars, beneath which gentlemen and ladies are walking. In front a man sleeping, and two dogs. A rich picture, clear in colour, and careful in execution.

Abraham Mignon.—A fruit-piece. Rich and careful, but cold in tone.

Johann George Plazer.—1 and 2.   Two pictures richly finished, but, as usual with him, crude and mannered.

OBJECTS OF ART AT ALDERMASTON,

(near Reading,)

Seat of Higford Burr, Esq.

A visit of two days at Aldermaston, in the company of Lord Lovelace, Sir Gardner Wilkinson, and Mr. Layard, has left me very agreeable reminiscences.   I here became acquainted with that energy which had led to the excavations at Nineveh under a totally new aspect.   A tour undertaken by Mr. Layard in Italy during the winter of 1855 convinced him that many of the frescoes of the great masters of the 14th and 15th centuries were hastening to destruction ; and deeply imbued with a sense of their importance, he boldly resolved to preserve at all events their outlines, by means of tracings, for posterity.   As the greater part of these frescoes are on arched ceilings, or very high walls, scaffoldings were in most cases requisite for the purpose.   To take tracings of ceiling pictures at all is a work of great exertion and inconvenience.   Not only had such principal difficulties to be overcome, but all those minor impediments, such as the obtaining proper materials, and the securing means of safe transport, which in Italy are attended with so much trouble, and finally that also of total inexperience in this kind of employment.   All these the Nineveh energy succeeded in conquering, and I had the gratification of inspecting a series of tracings from works which were not in all instances known to myself.   It was interesting to me also to observe that, as the tracings advanced, Mr. Layard's power of rendering the forms considerably improved.   The absence of the general effect and colouring of these compositions was happily supplied by a set of drawings of great carefulness and delicate feeling executed by Mrs. Burr, our accomplished hostess.   I must content myself with noticing a few of the most remarkable works thus brought before us :—

OF THE FOURTEENTH CENTURY.

GIOTTO.—His frescoes in the church at Assisi, and his Last Supper in the refectory of S. Croce at Florence.

SIMONE MEMMI.—Some of the best preserved figures in the Palazzo del Governo at Siena.

AMBROGIO LORENZETTI.—The finest figures in the large hall of the same building.

TADDEO DI BARTOLO.—Various figures from the chapel of the same building.

NICCOLO DI PIETRO.—The finest frescoes from the Chapter-house of the Convent of S. Francesco at Pisa.

CENNINO DI DREA CENNINI.—Of this painter, known by his work on painting, no authentic work had hitherto been known. Mr. Layard, however, discovered one in a church in the small town of S. Geminiano: it represents the Virgin and Child enthroned, with Saints around. He appears here, however, as a master of very inferior order.

OF THE FIFTEENTH CENTURY.

BENOZZO GOZZOLI.—The most important figures of his early frescoes in the church of S. Agostino at S. Geminiano.

PIETRO DELLA FRANCESCA.—Remarkably fine heads from his frescoes in the choir chapel of the church of S. Francesco at Arezzo.

CENNO DI SER CENNI.—The Adoration of the true Cross in the church at Volterra—a rich and peculiar composition; and the Death of St. Anthony the Hermit, with fine groups of adoring women at the sides. This painter, who is quite unknown to me, shows himself to be an important master.

PIETRO PERUGINO.—The Martyrdom of St. Sebastian, in a convent in a small place called Panicale. This picture, which, according to Passavant, was painted in 1505 *al secco* upon the walls, proves what admirable works this master occasionally executed even at so late a period. The Saint, both in motive and form, is one of the most beautiful undraped figures he produced; also the animated actions of the four archers are treated with great freedom.

PINTURICCHIO.—Various portions of the frescoes in the chapel of S. Maria Maggiore at Spello.   The Annunciation is especially remarkable.

OF THE SIXTEENTH CENTURY.

VINCENZO DI S. GEMINIANO.—From a private house in S. Geminiano.   The Virgin and Child enthroned, and single figures of Saints.   Pictures by this scholar of Raphael are, as is well known, extremely rare.   He appears here very graceful in his motives.

I was further agreeably surprised by a considerable collection of large water-colour drawings of much artistic feeling, carefully executed by Mrs. Burr.   These comprise the finest and most interesting scenes and buildings in Egypt, Palestine, Asia Minor, Constantinople, Greece, Italy, Spain, Switzerland, and England, all drawn from nature.

Finally, we were allowed to inspect a number of clever and animated sketches by Sir Gardner Wilkinson, taken during his travels in Egypt, Greece, Malta, and other countries.   More especially was I interested by a church of great antiquity in the Byzantine style in Upper Egypt.

COLLECTION OF PICTURES, SCULPTURES, AND OTHER WORKS
OF ART AT BASILDON PARK,

SEAT OF JAMES MORRISON, ESQ.

THE FRONT HALL.

On the left of the entrance is a Roman relic in the form of a quadrangular altar of Carrara marble.   At the two front angles are female figures holding garlands of laurel on each side, which are confined at the other angles with rams' heads with Jupiter Ammon horns.   Upon the four corners are eagles.   In front, in a small relief, is the death of Opheltes, son of Lycurgus King of Nemea, obviously taken from the same original which served as the model for the large and beautiful relief in the Palazzo Spada at Rome.   Opheltes is seen encircled by the serpent; his nurse, Hypsipyle, is standing by, and one of the seven heroes of Thebes is combating the animal.   The workmanship is late Roman. From the Strawberry Hill collection.   Upon this altar is a cinerary urn of beautiful form, decorated with grapes and vine-leaves, flatly treated.

THE HALL.

Turner.—1. A landscape. On the right two beautiful groups of trees, between which is a view of a mighty Roman ruin, with arched roof, and other trees seen above. In the centre a fine stream which leads the eye deep into the landscape, and in whose clear surface all objects are reflected. On the shore in the distance lies a city outstretched, behind which various chains of hills close the horizon. Before the centre group of trees is an altar with a lyre upon it, which a female figure is crowning, whilst others are dancing. Other figures, one of them with a harp, are by an antique fountain in the form of a sarcophagus. On the left side, blowing a pipe, is a shepherd, with a little flock. On canvas, 5 ft. 6 in. high, 10 ft. wide.

This picture, which is composed in the taste of Claude, belongs, in point of conception, beauty of effect, power and clearness of colouring, and careful and spirited execution, to the chefs-d'œuvre of this great master.

THE OCTAGON.

This apartment, which is very pretty in proportion, is richly decorated with a series of pictures by the most distinguished modern English painters.

William Hilton.—That scene from Milton's Comus where Una is bound by the spells of Comus and his train, which is the favourite subject of many English painters. Una is seen seated in the greatest terror in the centre, while Comus, a youth of great beauty, holds up a goblet of wine before her. Besides him are other bacchanal figures, striking the cymbals in wild action. In the background are her brothers hastening to her rescue, one of them in the act of drawing his sword. On canvas, 4 ft. 1 in. high, 7 ft. 9½ in. wide. Animated and speaking in motives, graceful in actions, beautiful and characteristic in forms, with a happy arrangement of the light as it falls on the principal group. Clear and powerful in colouring, and carefully painted in a solid body.

Sir Charles Eastlake. — The flight of Francesco Carrara, Duke of Padua, with his Duchess, Taddea d'Este, from Giovanni

Galeazzo Visconti, the tyrant of Milan. The Duke is looking anxiously back and supporting his wife, who is seated on a mule, and much exhausted with fatigue. On canvas. 4 ft. 4 in. high, 3 ft. 11 in. wide. Animated in the noble heads, speaking in motives, tender and harmonious in colouring, and of equally careful finish in every part. This is the original, properly speaking, of the picture in the Vernon Gallery, and obviously superior to it.

TURNER.—2. A landscape. Trees in the foreground on the right side, before which are three figures conversing over a Corinthian capital. Near them a shepherd and shepherdess, with some sheep. Further on another flock, most of them reposing. In the middle distance a piece of clear water, with buildings and trees lying beyond reflected in it. Two fishermen in a boat on the water. Signed. On canvas. 3 ft. high, 3 ft. 11 in. wide. This enchanting picture combines in happily balanced proportions great beauty of conception with the transparent colouring of a warm evening light, and an equable carefulness of execution.

CONSTABLE.—A richly-wooded landscape. On canvas. 4 ft. 8 in. high, 3 ft. 11 in. wide. Of that truth of nature, transparency of colouring, and careful finish, which so favourably distinguish the works of this master.

COLLINS.—The fisherman's farewell to his family. He is kissing his youngest child, while the eldest boy is carrying bread, lights, and a lantern for the night-watch. Besides these is a woman with a baby, and another with a girl leaning against her in talk with a countryman. Above the water is the crescent of the moon partly overshadowed. On the left, behind the cottage, high rocks and clouds illumined by the evening sun. Signed and dated 1826. On canvas. 2 ft. 8 in. high, 3 ft. 6 in. wide. Very attractive in motives, of good keeping and careful execution. Well known by the engraving.

WEBSTER.—A sick girl in a chair, with a medical man feeling her pulse. Her mother is occupied at the fireplace. A maidservant is dropping medicine into a spoon. A younger sister is looking on, and a brother at the window is appropriating some oranges. On wood. 1 ft. 7 in. high, 1 ft. 11¼ in. wide. Greatly recalling Wilkie in the humour and admirable character of the heads. Of excellent keeping, clear colouring, and equally carried out and solid execution.

HOGARTH.—The picture called the Punch Club, generally known to connoisseurs by his etching. Showing, in a most lively way, the various effects of the genial beverage. On canvas. 2 ft. 3 in. high, 2 ft. 11 in. wide. This work does not quite answer the expectations formed from the etching; for, though very clever, it is of somewhat too cold a red in the flesh-tones, and rather gaudy. It has also darkened in some parts.

PICKERSGILL.—Portrait of the celebrated naturalist Alexander von Humboldt. He is seated in full dress, with the star and the broad band of the order of the Red Eagle. One hand rests on a map. To the knees. On canvas. 4 ft. 8 in. high, 3 ft. 7 in. wide. This portrait unites a faithful likeness with a lively conception, a clear colouring, and a careful execution.

WILSON.—The view of some particular locality, richly wooded and hilly, with a piece of water, and a country house near it. On canvas. Of great truth, and carefully painted in a clear silvery tone.

ALEXANDER NASMYTH.—A landscape with a stately oak and a piece of water in the foreground and a hilly distance. On wood. 1 ft. 7 in. high, 2 ft. 1 in. wide. True in the details, and of careful execution in a cool tone.

SIR DAVID WILKIE.—A young girl confessing to a priest. In the foreground are two girls from the Campagna, in a crouching position. Opposite them, kneeling, three countrymen on a pilgrimage, and a little girl. Signed and dated Rome, 1827. On canvas. 1 ft. 6 in. high, 1 ft. 2½ in. wide. Very happily composed, of speaking motives, bright and harmonious in colour, and light and spirited in treatment.

STANFIELD.—An Italian sea-coast, with country people and two shepherds and their flock in the foreground. In the middle distance a small town. In the background a fortress with picturesque towers and walls. On canvas. 2 ft. 10 in. high, 4 ft. 1 in. wide. The point of view is very happily chosen, and the cool fresh morning light expressed in delicate gradations. The whole effect very attractive.

HILTON.—Penelope recognising Ulysses. She is hastening to his arms, whilst he looks joyfully down upon her. Telemachus is on one side of him, Euryclea and five maidens at her side. On canvas. 3 ft. 3 in. high, 4 ft. ½ in. wide. The principal group is conceived much in the spirit of the poet. The forms of the greatest purity, the expression touching, the colouring clear and harmonious, and the execution careful.

WARD.—A girl milking a cow at the entrance of a stall. A landscape, in the taste of Rubens, forms the background. Every object is warmly lighted by the evening sun. On wood. 3 ft. 7 in. high, 4 ft. 8 in. wide. Of great truth of nature, transparent in colour, and carefully painted.

THE LIBRARY.

The objects of art that adorn this room are few, but very remarkable.

NICOLAS POUSSIN.—A bacchanal. On the right a nymph beating a tambourine. Next her another nymph about to convert a ram into a riding-horse, and at the same time crowning the terminal statue of Pan, whose face is coloured with the juice of the grape. A boy is reaching a garland to her in a basket. In front is a drunken attendant of Pan, supported by a satyr. In the centre is a nymph holding Pan—who is lying on the ground —by the horns, and keeping him off. Next her, but further back, is another nymph bearing along the head of a young deer. Finally, on the left, riding on a goat, is a nymph caressed by a satyr, and taking grapes and flowers from a basket which a kneeling satyr presents to her on his head. Another satyr, behind, is blowing the *tuba*. Some trees are in the middle distance ; behind, a hilly landscape with a warmly-lighted horizon. On canvas. 4 ft. 4 in. high, 4 ft. 9 in. wide. In point of richness of composition, beauty of forms, ingenious motives, graceful move- ments, power and clearness of colouring, and equally carried out execution in a good impasto, this picture belongs to the finest specimens of the master, and is at the same time admirably pre- served. It is obviously of the same period as the celebrated bacchanalian dance in the National Gallery. Formerly in the collection of Lord Ashburnham.

REMBRANDT.—A female portrait, which passes for that of his daughter. She is seated in an armchair, and dressed in white with a furred robe. The background is dark. To the knees. On canvas. 3 ft. 9 in. high, 2 ft. 9 in. wide. Very transparent in colouring, and of broad and masterly treatment.

Rubens.—The Virgin holding the Infant, who is seated on a white cushion on her lap. She is looking down lovingly at an angel who is presenting a basket of fruit, particularly grapes, to the Child. On the right is St. Joseph, looking on. Behind the figures is a stone wall and a curtain. On the left a landscape with trees, with clouds illumined by the evening light. To the knees. On canvas. 3 ft. 11 in. high, 5 ft. 4 in. wide. The composition is very attractive, the characters unusually noble for Rubens. The execution in a powerful and transparent golden tone is very careful. The picture is in excellent preservation. Formerly in the collection of Sir Simon Clarke.

Parmigianino.—Cupid borne aloft by two other amorini. On wood. 8¼ in. high, 6½ in. wide. Of pleasing motives and light and spirited execution. The flesh-tones very cool for him. Formerly in the Palazzo Barberini at Rome.

The bronze statue of a Mænade. The figure is in wild action, throwing her head back and tossing the right arm upwards, while she supports herself with the left hand on the edge of a large tambourine that touches the ground. The light drapery has fallen from the upper part of the person, and covers only the lower. In the inside of the tambourine is the fawn's hide. Only one leg of it, on which she holds her thumb, hangs over towards the front. About two-thirds the size of life. This is a very puzzling work. The invention is so bold, so beautiful, and so original, the expression of inspiration so admirable, as to remind us of a Greek artist of the best period. On the other hand, the short proportions, the very short and thick throat, the treatment of the falling hair and of the folds of the drapery, both of which are devoid of style, are evidences which give this statue a very modern look.

The front part of the bookcase consists of a beautiful brown marble with shells, which is framed in a black marble.

PINK DRAWING-ROOM.

Leonardo da Vinci.—A half-length female figure—a wreath of flowers in her hair—looking at the spectator ; the head somewhat turned to the right with a pleasing expression. She is holding a bunch of flowers in her right hand before her left shoulder, while with the left hand she grasps her garment, which only covers the lower left portion of her person. In the dark background some leaves are traceable. On wood. 2 ft. 2 in. high, 1 ft. 8½ in. wide. This picture is under glass. The features of the face show that type of beauty belonging to Leonardo da Vinci which was so frequently repeated. In this instance, however, they exhibit such refinement of form, such a charm of gracefulness, and such delicacy of *sfumato*, that I am inclined to attribute this head really to the hand of Leonardo himself. Other portions, on the other hand, are too full and too empty for him, and visibly indicate the hand of a scholar, most probably that of Bernardino Luini. This highly attractive picture was formerly in the possession of Sir Thomas Baring, at Stratton.

Over the mantelpiece is a relief by the celebrated sculptor FRANÇOIS DU QUESNOY, called, from his native country, IL FIAMINGO.—It is in ivory, and represents ten bacchanalian children playing with each other and with two goats. The motives are very animated. The full forms recall Rubens, and the execution is very careful. The background is of ebony. Under a glass.

A circular vessel of rock crystal with deeply cut figures, which, to judge from their character, are by the hand of ANDREA BELLI, though called Andrea Vicentino. Three figures are represented, separated by small light trees. The one is a youthful male form, with his right hand terminating in a laurel-branch ; the second a man in armour with a lyre ; the third, and by far the most beautiful, a Venus with bow and arrow. The setting, in silver gilt, especially the lid, shows a later time, and is of inferior workmanship.

OAK-ROOM.

This apartment contains, within a moderate space, a rich series of fine old pictures—the greater part of the Netherlandish school—with some of the French, and some of the German school.

TENIERS.—1. An old woman, behind the chair of a doctor, anxiously expecting his verdict upon the contents of a bottle which he is attentively considering. On a table with a green cloth before him are books, an hourglass, inkstand, and globe. On another table bottles with medicine. In an opening in the roof is a man attentively looking on. On the right, through an open door, is seen the tower of Antwerp Cathedral. Signed. On wood. 1 ft. 2¾ in. high, 1 ft. 11½ in. wide. Very animatedly conceived and luminous in the harmonious colours. The flesh-tones very brown. The execution of the accessories *alla prima* is broad and masterly.

GASPAR POUSSIN.—1. A landscape. In the foreground a shepherd with his dog and four goats. Near them some trees of scanty foliage. Lofty hills in the distance. On canvas. 1 ft. 9¾ in. high, 1 ft. 4¾ in. wide. The influence of Titian is seen in the composition of this picture. The forms are more decided, the colour more insipid, and the treatment more careful than usual.

WATTEAU.—1. A group of three ladies and two gentlemen extended on the ground listening to the guitar of Pierrot, who stands in the centre. Behind him a pedestal with a vase. An indistinct distance forms the background. On canvas. 1 ft. 5¼ in. high, 1 ft. 2½ in. wide. Of very happy arrangement, lightly and clearly treated with a charming harmony of silvery tones.

DUJARDIN.—1. A brown cow is reposing in the foreground before a wooden fence, behind which is a grey horse foreshortened. Next him is a sheep. Further back, and turned from the spectator, is a shepherdess with a spindle, and two sheep resting. In the middle distance are hills. In the background are high rocky mountains, which, with the clouds, are warmly lighted. Signed. On canvas. 11¼ in. high, 1 ft. 2 in. wide. This picture possesses all the most esteemed qualities of the master,—picturesque composition, truth of character, and delicacy of drawing; above all, a general clearness and lightness of tone, and solid careful execution—and all these in an unusual degree.

ARTUS VAN DER NEER.—A frozen canal, with villages on its banks. Numerous figures on the ice making merry. Signed. On canvas. 1 ft. 7¾ in. high, 2 ft. 5 in. wide. Of that perfect transparency of a mild, warm tone for which the pictures of this master are so esteemed, and of admirable aërial perspective; at the same time somewhat slight in treatment.

HOBBEMA.—On the right hand a cottage, with a group of trees of rich foliage before it, the largest of which casts its shadow over the whole foreground. Under the same, on a road, are a

woman and two men in conversation, and a third about to leave
them.   In the centre of the foreground a small pond and a high
road leading to the middle distance, where another house surrounded with trees is remarkable.   On each side of this are views,
also terminating with trees, with gleams of sunshine, which also
illumine the clouds.   On canvas.   3 ft. 1 in. high, 4 ft. 3 in. wide.
The effect of this picture is equally powerful and transparent, the
middle distance is particularly rich in those cool, silvery tones
peculiar to the master, while at the same time the details are
finished with the utmost care.   This masterpiece was formerly in
the collection of Ed. Gray, Esq.

GASPAR POUSSIN.—2. A landscape. The foreground closed on
the right by lofty trees.   A stately building rises in the middle
distance.   The background consists of mountains of beautiful
form gleaming in the evening sun ; one of them resembles Mount
Soracte. On canvas. 3 ft. high, 4 ft. wide. The highly poetic
feeling of the master is here united with an unusual carefulness of
execution and a greater transparency than is common with the
majority of his pictures.

ADRIAN VAN DE VELDE.—A landscape with rising ground in
the centre of the middle distance, with ruins on the right and
trees on the left.   In the centre of the foreground is a woman on
a grey horse, indistinctly reflected in the dark water from which
he is drinking.   Next the grey horse is a cow of pale colour with
a white head, and a dog.   On the left, resting under a tree, is a ·
shepherd, and a woman speaking with him.   Next them a goat
and two sheep reposing, another standing.   Signed, and dated
1669.   On wood.   1 ft. 2½ in. high, 1 ft. 4½ in. wide.   Of very
happy composition, and carefully executed in a particularly mild
and harmonious tone, unusual at this late period of the master.
It is also in excellent preservation.

GUERCINO.—St. Sebastian pierced with arrows, and lying on
the ground in strong foreshortening.   Two angels are with him—
one of them floating in the air and pointing to him, the other at
the left holding an arrow he has drawn from him.   On copper.
1 ft. 4½ in. high, 1 ft. 1 in. wide.   Of unusually noble character
for him, both in the heads and forms, and painted *con amore* in a
deep, juicy, and warm tone.

TENIERS. —2. The interior of a stable, with a brown and dark-

coloured cow, and a cowboy with a sheep. Near the door sits an
aged peasant-woman with reel and spindle. Next her is her husband, a spade in one hand, pointing to the open door with his right
hand, and speaking to her. Near the woman are a grey cat and
a pig. Through the door a small piece of landscape is visible.
Signed. On wood. 1 ft. $2\frac{1}{4}$ in. high, 1 ft. $2\frac{1}{2}$ in. wide. Judging
from the bright golden tone of the flesh, the clearness and harmony
of the colours, and the equally free and careful treatment, this
picture must have been painted between 1640 and 1650, the best
time of the master.

DUJARDIN.—2. The farrier's shop. A piebald horse is being shod
on the left hind foot, which a man in his shirt-sleeves is holding.
Behind the piebald is a brown horse, which is being driven back-
ward by a rider on a grey horse. In the middle distance is another
house and a wall. In the distance a hill. A light cloud is
illumined by the sun. Signed. On canvas. 1 ft. 8 in. high,
1 ft. 4 in. wide. A careful picture, and one of warm colouring
for him. Formerly in the collection of Ed. Gray, Esq.

GYSSELS.—Dead game—a swan, a small roe, a hare, and small
birds, and a heron hanging down from a pedestal. A dark landscape with ruins, and a large vase, forms the background. On
copper. 1 ft. 3 in. high, 1 ft. 7 in. wide. This picture shows in
the highest degree the indescribably minute execution and the
softness and delicacy in the rendering of fur and plumage for
which this master is so much esteemed.

VANDYCK.—1. Portrait of Charles I. in armour. At his left
hand a table with red cloth and a helmet upon it, on which he
is leaning by his elbow, so that the hand hangs down. In the
right hand he has a staff. Half-length figure. On canvas.
3 ft. $6\frac{1}{2}$ in. high, 2 ft. $8\frac{1}{2}$ in. wide. The well-known features of
this king are here carefully rendered in a warm tone and good
impasto.

BACKHUYSEN.—A slightly agitated sea with several boats in the
foreground ; a man-of-war in the middle distance. On canvas.
1 ft. 5 in. high, 1 ft. 9 in. wide. This picture belongs to the
middle and best period of the master, and shows the whole delicacy of his touch, and cool harmony of his keeping. Formerly in
the collection of the Duchess de Berri.

JAN BOTH.—1. On the right, in the foreground, is a stream

dashing down between rocks and trees. In the middle distance are seen delicate trees against the sky. Upon a road are three laden mules with their drivers, and further back a man with a dog. In the middle distance is a piece of water with a village upon it. The horizon is bounded by hills. Signed. 2 ft. 1 in. high, 2 ft. 9 in. wide. Finely composed, and clearly and carefully executed in a mild warm tone. Formerly in the collection of Mr. Beckford.

PYNACKER.—A landscape with ruins on the left. The morning light falls through an opening in the ruins. In the background is a bluish hill. In the foreground is a shepherd with a cow and sheep. Signed. On canvas. 2 ft. 2½ in. high, 1 ft. 9 in. wide. The composition is pleasing, the colouring, for him, particularly clear, and the execution careful.

VANDYCK.—2. Portraits of two ladies, seated. The one on the right is dressed in white, with wide reddish sleeves, pointing with her left hand to the other, who is dressed in black, with white under sleeves, and is holding up an orange-branch in her right hand and a rose in her left. The background is formed of a wall on the right and a landscape on the left. To the knees. On canvas. 3 ft. 3½ in. high, 5 ft. 6 in. wide. This picture is remarkable for warmth and clearness of tone and for careful and melting execution. Judging from these qualities, it may have been painted about 1635. Formerly at Strawberry Hill.

PAUL POTTER.—Before a stately stone house is a group of three large trees—near them five more, leading into the picture. Under the first is a cow reposing, and towards the other a cow standing. Quite in the foreground, to the left, is a sheep standing and two lying. In the interior of the house are a man and woman. Behind the trees are a coach and two horses and a footman, who are relieved against a sandy rising ground illumined by the sun. In a meadow are two sheep. The sky is partially covered with rain-clouds. Signed, and dated 1652. On wood. 1 ft. 6¼ in. high, 1 ft. 2½ in. wide. One of the finest landscapes known to me by the master. Seldom did he paint large trees with so much truth. The pure truth of nature, the highly careful finish, and the great transparency in every part, render this picture very attractive. Formerly in the Poullain collection, and engraved in that gallery. Afterwards in the possession of Mr. Jeremiah Harman.

ADRIAN VAN OSTADE.—A room in a tavern, after dinner. At the window is the woman of the house with a child and six peasants. More in the centre a peasant standing and drinking, and opposite to him a man and a woman sitting on a bench. At the fireplace are a boy and maid cleaning pots and pans. On the right is a man pouring beer from a jug into another vessel, and a child on a chair. On the left in front a boy playing with a dog. Signed, and dated 1669. On wood. 1 ft. $3\frac{3}{4}$ in. high, $11\frac{3}{4}$ in. wide. The chiaroscuro in this fine picture is of singular depth and clearness. The small figures are painted like a miniature, and are yet freely executed. Formerly in the collection of Ed. Gray, Esq.

WATTEAU.—2. In front a gentleman playing the guitar. Next to him a lady with a rose in her right hand, and a little girl and dog. In the foreground a loving pair, and a gentleman with a shepherd's staff. The scene is laid in a landscape, in which is an urn on a pedestal. On wood. 1 ft. 4 in. high, 1 ft. $0\frac{1}{2}$ in. wide. This carefully executed picture is one of the master's rather gaudy works.

SIR JOSHUA REYNOLDS.—His own portrait in youthful years. On canvas. 2 ft. high, 2 ft. $6\frac{1}{4}$ in. wide. Animated, but inferior to the portraits of Sir Joshua by himself in the untruthful and sulphury tone.

JAN BOTH.—2. A waterfall dashing between mighty rocks. On the left three figures under a tree. Hills in the distance. On wood. 1 ft. 9 in. high, 2 ft. 1 in. wide. Attractive in composition, and carefully executed in a powerful, warm tone.

GASPAR POUSSIN.—3. A wooded hill with stately buildings. Blue hills behind. Two persons conversing in the foreground. On canvas. 2 ft. $3\frac{1}{2}$ in. high, 1 ft. $7\frac{1}{2}$ in. wide. Of beautiful lines and poetic feeling, the colouring transparent, and execution careful.

SCHOOL-ROOM.

HARLOW.—The painter has chosen the passage from the fourth scene of the second act of Shakspeare's Henry the Eighth. In the foreground is Queen Catherine of Arragon, holding her well-known address to the judges, Cardinals Wolsey and Campeggio, in the matter of her divorce from the King. The latter, seated at a table, is evidently excited by her words. In the background is Henry VIII. seated on a raised throne. Numerous figures beside. On wood. 5 ft. 3 in. high, 7 ft. 2 in. wide. The composition is good, the motives and the expression of the heads speaking and true, the keeping—the whole background being kept in half-shadow—excellent, the colouring powerful and clear, and finally the execution broad but careful.

GREUZE.—Study for the head of the father who is blessing the bridal pair, in the well-known picture in the Louvre. Above the size of life, and of masterly drawing in red and black chalk.

LETTER VI.

COLLECTION OF PICTURES BELONGING TO THE REV. MR. HEATH, VICAR OF ENFIELD.

MR. HEATH belongs to that small class of English connoisseurs who, while possessing a true taste for all that is beautiful in art, are especially devoted to the acquisition of pictures of the early Netherlandish and German schools. His small collection is not only remarkable for the value of the pictures, but for the admirable effect of the high light in the hall of his house containing these treasures. I proceed to notice those which appeared to me the most important.

HANS MEMLING. — A small altarpiece with wings. In the centre, under the cross, is the body of the Saviour lamented by the Virgin and disciples. The body is lying on a white cloth, the head and upper part supported by St. John, who is clad in a vermilion mantle and coat. Behind the body is the Virgin in a light blue dress and white veil, her hands clasped. Quite on the left is the Magdalen kneeling in superb attire, her dress being of dark violet lined with grey fur, with a yellow petticoat with a broad trimming of the same fur. The sleeves are of the finest crimson. She is clasping her hands above her head with a passionate gesture. At the head of Christ, on the ground, are the crown of thorns and the nails. The landscape is hilly, with a truly luminous horizon; some light and numerous roundish trees, and rocks, are on the right, at the foot of which Joseph of Arimathea with spices, Nicodemus, and two holy women are walking. On the right wing is St. James the Greater with a long brown beard, in a purple coat, and grey mantle with green lining, reading a book ; the pilgrim's staff with the scrip attached to it leaning against his shoulder. In the landscape, which is of similar character to that just described, is a town. On the left wing is St. Christopher, his right hand high upon the staff on which he supports himself, the left hand upon his hip, thus expressing in a lively manner the weight of the Child, who is of great beauty, and is bestowing the benediction upon him. The landscape is a continuation of that in the centre, only that the stream has rocks on each side. The centre picture 2 ft. high, 1 ft. 8 in. wide. The body of the Saviour is meagre and stiff. The grief of the women is very intense and elevated, that of St. John of very earnest and dignified expression ; the tears are truthfully rendered, and the colouring of astonishing force and power. This picture, which, with the exception of a few retouches in the head of Christ, is well preserved, is one of the finest examples of the master. It represents the same stage of development as that of the Marriage of St. Catherine in the Hospital of St. John at Bruges. In the heads it shows much affinity with that of the Pietà in the same building. Great closeness of observation is displayed in the reflection of St. Christopher's red mantle in the water, especially where the movement has given rise to circles.

QUENTIN MATSYS.—The head of the sorrowing Virgin, which is turned with rather a lively action towards the left side. I am inclined to consider this beautiful picture the fragment of a Pietà. Features and expression agree remarkably with the large picture by the master in the museum at Antwerp, proving that this fragment belongs to that maturest time of the master in which depth of expression stands on the same level with his delicate rendering.

SCHOOL OF ROGIER VAN DER WEYDEN THE ELDER.—Altarpiece, with wings. Centre picture, the Descent from the Cross. The motives show much affinity with the principal picture by Rogier van der Weyden the younger, three examples of which exist, two in Madrid, and one in Berlin. The general character of the composition is however different, and most of the heads are ruder and more feeble. On the inner side of the wings on the right hand is the Finding of the True Cross, which is identified by the recovery of a dead man touched by it. On the left, in the background, is the Emperor Constantine, who, according to the

legend, when riding in imperial robes upon a grey horse, in order
to bring the cross to Constantinople, found the gate, which is here
decorated with red stars, closed against him.   In consequence of
this, as is here represented in the foreground, he returned with the
cross humbly on foot, in a penitential garb, and was received at the
open gate by the bishop, surrounded by priests.   Courtiers similarly
attired are following, the foremost bearing the crown.   On the
outer side, on the left wing, is the infant Christ, to whom
Augustus, the Emperor of the West, at the order of the Sibyl, is
paying adoration; on the left wing is Christ appearing in the sky
within the star adored by the three kings from the East.   Both
these pictures agree entirely with two by Rogier van der Weyden
the elder in the Berlin Museum (No. 535), though different in the
heads, and incomparably less refined; thus affording a new proof
of what I have elsewhere stated, that the inventions of this great
master were looked upon as the types for various subjects.
Although all three pictures are decidedly by the same hand,
they could scarcely have belonged together originally, the wings
being shorter than the centre picture, and too wide for it.

HUGO VAN DER GOES.—The Virgin, dressed in a gold and
black brocade, is seated beneath a canopy on a stone bench, which
is overgrown with grass and weeds.   The Child is on her lap, and
is stretching his right hand for a flower which she is in the act of
plucking.   On each side is a view of a landscape with water.
About 10 in. high, 8 in. wide.   The head of the Virgin approaches
the excellence of Memling; the Child, on the other hand, is too
weak and hard; and the picture corresponds in all respects, more
especially in the style of the very solid treatment, with the only
authenticated picture by Hugo van der Goes in the small church
of S. Maria Nuova, at Florence.

GERHARDT VAN DER MEERE (?).—1. The Virgin enthroned,
with the Child on her lap, who is clasping a book which lies on
the left arm of the throne.   On both sides of the background are a
garden and a town.   About 1 ft. 10 in. high, 1 ft. 4 in. wide.   The
flesh tones are pale, the folds of the drapery in very good taste,
and the general effect light.   The background is executed *con amore*.

THE SAME (?).—2. The Virgin looking down at the Child on
her lap, who is looking around with lively expression and grasping
her bosom, which is covered with her robe.   The background a

landscape. The heads are noble, earnest, and peculiar; the execution is solid.

SCHOOL OF THE BROTHERS VAN EYCK, ABOUT 1470.—The Infant swathed in bands is lying on the ground, adored by the kneeling Virgin, who is depicted almost in front, and by three youthful angels also kneeling; three others are floating in the air under the roof of the house. On the left is Joseph in a red dress, and three shepherds looking in. The Virgin and the three angels are of elevated motives and expression, the draperies, though sharp in character, are well understood, the colouring pale, and the treatment showing the well-known excellence of the school. This is a very small picture.

SCHOOL OF VAN EYCK, ABOUT 1480.—The Virgin is seen seated in the open air, on a stone bench with grass, plucking a flower for the Child. In the sky is the Almighty. The background contains buildings, and next to them a garden in which three girls are walking. The heads are ugly; the red and blue draperies of uncommon power, depth, and clearness; the flesh tones are also of great transparency. The very original background contains many pretty details—a peacock, swans, &c. All the technical parts show the school in its highest development.

JAN MABUSE (?).—The Virgin and Joseph adoring the new-born Child. In the air are two angels, in the distance two shepherds. The composition is good, and the colouring powerful. I consider this little picture to be the work of BERNARD VAN ORLEY.

JAN MOSTAERT.—The Entombment. The Virgin and three other Maries are looking after the body of the Saviour, which Joseph of Arimathea and Nicodemus are bearing away to the sepulchre. The heads are noble and refined, the proportions short, the colouring of great depth, and the execution excellent. The size is moderate.

JOACHIM PATENIER.—The Virgin lamenting over the body of the Saviour on her lap; St. John is standing at the head. In the distance is St. Andrew with his cross, and adoring spectators. A small picture of noble heads and admirable execution. Unfortunately the Christ is much retouched.

HERRI DE BLES, CALLED CIVETTA.—The Virgin with a rose in her right hand is holding the Child upon her lap, who has a bird in his right hand. In the sky are two angels holding a crown over her head. A very finished landscape forms the background. The Child is too full in the forms; the heads of the angels elevated in character, the flesh tones are reddish, and the whole of great power and of very successful execution.

FLEMISH SCHOOL, TIME OF QUENTIN MATSYS.—Portrait of an old woman. Very animatedly conceived, and of masterly rendering.

LOWER RHENISH SCHOOL, ABOUT 1500.—A small altarpiece with wings—the Adoration of the Kings, two of which are on the wings. However tasteless many of the heads, the artistic development is otherwise so advanced, and the miniature-like execution so solid, that it would be well worth while ascertaining the name of the master. A picture by the same hand, the Death of the Virgin, is in the Berlin Museum, No. 552.

MARTIN SCHAFNER.—The wing of an altarpiece. On the inner side is the Marriage of the Virgin, on the outer side the Magdalen with the box of ointment. This is a successful figure, upon a patterned ground. Of the earlier time of the master, of tolerably warm flesh tones, and of very good taste in the draperies.

HANS BURKMAIR.—St. Natalitia, as it appears from an inscription, represented seated. In the background are buildings of antique Roman taste. Of the later time of the master, and of miniature-like finish.

EARLY ITALIAN SCHOOL.

The only specimen of this school is by NICCOLO ALUNNO. This rare master, however, is too important for me to omit noticing this example. The subject is a kneeling saint in a hilly landscape recommending a supplicating family—father, mother, and children —to the Almighty, who appears in the sky. The heads and gestures display the energy of religious feeling peculiar to the master; the forms are also carefully modelled, though of a certain hardness. The brownish tone of the colouring is rather heavy.

THE LATER DUTCH SCHOOL.

GABRIEL METZU.—A fishwoman, who is holding up a fish to a lady standing on the steps of a house, whence a girl, with a plate in her hand, is coming. A dog is also on the steps. Signed. On wood. 11¼ in. high, 9½ in. wide. Formerly in the Gaignat collection. Of clever and broad treatment, in his warm, golden, and transparent tone.

ARY DE VOYS.—A youth by a window-sill, accompanying his voice with the violin. Of great delicacy.

KAREL DUJARDIN.—1. On the left is a shepherdess with her child, and a dog seated on his haunches. The small flock consists of three sheep, two of which are reposing and one standing, and one reposing cow. Behind are a house and a tree. On the right in the background a hilly country. Signed. Of pleasing composition and clever treatment.

2. Landscape with ruins, in the warm evening light. In the foreground on the left is a sheep being milked, and on the right a woman on an ass, with another accompanying her. Of very beautiful effect, rich in numerous details, and solid in execution, though in many respects unlike the master.

ALBERT CUYP.—A landscape with two horsemen, the one on a grey, the other on a brown horse. On wood. Very powerful in effect.

JAN ASSELYN.—Landscape with buildings; in the centre a grey horse. On canvas, and of tolerable size. This is one of his remarkable and solidly carried out pictures.

JACOB RUYSDAEL.—A dark landscape, with an old oak, a striking object, in the centre. On a dark piece of water are two swans and four cygnets. On the right, in the middle distance, is a wood, on the left a hilly distance. On canvas. Of great feeling for nature, and very careful rendering.

Of the later Flemish school is a darkly-treated but poetical landscape by TENIERS.

Nor is the French school quite unrepresented. A poor family about to take their humble meal, by LENAIN, bears witness to the truth of feeling which rendered this master so popular. It is also very carefully finished.

COLLECTION OF PICTURES BELONGING TO LORD ENFIELD,

WROTHAM PARK.

I obtained the permission to visit this collection through the kind intervention of Mr. Anthony, who was engaged in the restoration of some of the pictures. I found his Lordship on the point of starting for London, but he kindly introduced me to one of his daughters, and I the more enjoyed the undisturbed study of his treasures, inasmuch as they greatly exceeded my expectations.

FIRST DRAWING-ROOM.

ANNIBALE CARRACCI.—A landscape with a large piece of water, with a boat in the foreground and three figures in it, one of whom is in the act of punting. On the right are some trees ; on the left, in the distance, a mountain. Of unusual clearness, especially of the sky, which has light clouds. It is a pity that this little picture is placed far too high over a door.

GIULIO ROMANO.—Holy Family. The Infant stands leaning between the knees of the Madonna, and is giving an open book to the little St. John, who is adoring him. Behind them, completing the group, is St. Joseph seated. On the left, in the landscape, is a female saint approaching with a basket in her left hand. On wood. About 2 ft. 6 in. high, 2 ft. wide. This picture belongs in every way to the best works of the master. The Virgin is very noble in conception ; the Child resembles that in Mr. Munro's picture, attributed to Raphael, but which I have imputed to Giulio Romano. Joseph is of dignified and powerful character. The female saint in the landscape has quite the motive of the Virgin in the Visitation by Raphael in the Madrid Gallery—a picture also in great part by Giulio Romano. The modelling of the whole work is in a deep brown tone, and very careful.

WILLEM VAN DE VELDE.—A calm sea. In the centre, in the foreground, a larger and smaller boat. On the left another small boat with three figures and three baskets. On the right, in the distance, a man-of-war. Along the whole horizon a slender line of coast. Light and sunny clouds in the sky. Wood. About 1 ft. 3 in. high, by 1 ft. 6 in. wide. Signed. The reflection in the water of the warm tones of the vessel is wonderful, and forms a charming contrast to the prevailing silvery colour.

DOMENICHINO (?).—The Shame of Calisto. A very dramatic composition of nine figures, about the same size as that of Diana and her Nymphs in the Borghese Gallery in Rome. I here neither recognise the style, drawing, nor even colouring of Domenichino, while the very speaking motives, the thorough modelling, the noble character of the heads, and the general conception of the forms, incline me to ascribe the picture to AGOSTINO CARRACCI.

ARTUS VAN DER NEER.—View of a broad canal in moonlight, with several boats, one containing four figures. On the shore two fishermen drawing a large net. Wood. About 11 in. high, by 1 ft. 3 in. wide. Signed. The execution is unusually careful, and the effect of the moonlight almost too clear and warm. This picture is of the earlier time of the master.

NICOLAS BERGHEM.—A large and hilly landscape. In the foreground a shepherdess with a basket of vegetables walking before a little flock of five sheep and some warm and transparently-coloured cows. In the centre is a figure on a grey horse, with another figure on foot. Wood. About 1 ft. 6 in. high, by 1 ft. 10 in. wide. Signed. The cool tones of the hills contrast strikingly with the warm colouring of the foreground and sky. This is a particularly rich and careful picture of the later time of the master.

KAREL DUJARDIN.—A boy in red mantle and cap playing a fiddle, and beating time with his right foot, is making a little white dog dance. Next him a peasant-boy on an ass, and another dog. Behind him, all in half-shadow, a man and a girl, and in the doorway of a house an old woman with a child. In the middle distance a wall. Sunny clouds in the sky. Wood. Effect and composition very attractive, but the colouring somewhat heavy, and the treatment rather broad and slight.

MURILLO.—1. Repose in Egypt. In the centre is the Virgin adoring the Child, who looks up to her from her lap. On the left Joseph holding the ass, and also adoring. On the ground, between the Virgin and Joseph, a gourd bottle, a straw hat, and a bundle. On the right two angels of somewhat similar character of head standing in adoration. Above in the air are two charming infantine angels, and a third employed in hanging a red curtain between two trees as a screen. In the background are mountains. About 8 ft. square; the figures about three quarters the size of life. This is in every respect a remarkable work of the master. The rich composition is well balanced; the expression of the Virgin's head touching, that of Joseph unusually noble. The colouring of the flesh is also in his fine transparent golden tones, the effect harmonious, and the execution throughout careful.

Fra Bartolommeo (?).—The Virgin nursing the Child, who is seated on her right knee, and looking down, with his hand on the back of the kneeling and adoring Baptist. Figures life-size. The motive, the head, and the drapery of the Virgin show in a stronger degree the influence of Michael Angelo than I ever before remarked in the works of Fra Bartolommeo. The forms of the Child also are too clumsy and heavy, and the flesh too red a brown for him. The head of the Virgin, however, is elevated, and the whole picture indicates an excellent master, who reminds me most of Pontormo.

Abel Grimmer fecit 1608.—This is the inscription on an interior of a saloon quite in the taste of Van Bassen. Some figures in conversation, and a couple dancing to the music of violin and lute, are entirely in the manner of Franz Franck. Wood. About 1 ft. 8 in. high, 2 ft. wide. This master is entirely unknown to me, and, though hard in the outlines, his observation of perspective and his clean and precise execution entitle him to be rescued from oblivion.

Verboom.—A wood, with a house in it. On the left some buildings belonging to a village. Composition and lighting are picturesque; the colouring transparent, especially in the sky; and the execution careful.

Velasquez.—View of a stately château in a garden. The picture is enlivened with various figures, among which an ecclesiastic in a litter drawn by two horses, with a horseman and a gentleman on foot in the foreground, are conspicuous. To the left on a shore is a fine vessel, with water and hills behind it. In the garden, in front of trees, are two bronze undraped statues on pedestals. Light warm clouds in the sky. Canvas. About 2 ft. 2 in. high, by 2 ft. 8 in. wide. This picture is spiritedly and broadly painted in a clear tone, which, in the litter above mentioned, approaches the force of Rembrandt. Considering how seldom the genuine works of Velasquez are found out of Spain, it is highly interesting and valuable. No doubt the scene represents a place well known in the painter's time.

Nicolas Poussin.—A landscape with a calm lake in the middle distance. In the foreground, seated among pedestals and grand bases of columns, is an old man with a sheet of paper upon his lap, which an angel, standing next him, takes hold of. More in the distance is a rising ground, with a village and a fortress, and further back a chain of hills.   Canvas.   About 4 ft. high, by 5 ft. wide.   Of much grandeur and poetry of invention, and astonishing beauty in the lighting of the clouds.

TENIERS.—Interior of a village alehouse.   In front are three peasants seated at a table.   The young peasant is looking upwards and blowing the smoke from his pipe ; the old one, in his shirt-sleeves, is lighting his pipe ; while the third, between the two former, is filling his.   Behind, next the fireplace, are two peasants playing cards, and before the fireplace three more. Above is a small window, through which an old woman is looking. On wood.   About 1 ft. 2 in. high, 1 ft. 8 in. wide.   This picture was decidedly painted between 1640 and 1650, and therefore in the best time of the master, and may be considered as one of his choicest specimens.   The composition is very picturesque, the keeping of the silvery tones, skilfully broken by a red cap on the back of a chair, admirable ; the colouring very fine, and the execution as spirited as it is careful.

VANDYCK.—A family picture.   Thomas Wentworth, Duke of Cleveland, represented standing, in a black silk dress with white collar, the left hand upon his hip, the right holding a medal with a red ribbon round his neck.   Next him is another man in armour, further on the duchess seated, in white satin, and next her a younger lady in blue silk caressing a spaniel.   The background consists of architecture, hangings, and landscape.   To the knees. The head of the duke, which is very spirited in conception, and transparent and true in colour, is by far the best, and will be doubtless found to agree with the portrait of the same personage in Lord Verulam's possession.   On the other hand, the head of the other male figure is the weakest in the picture, and is also so heavy and dull in tone, that it is impossible to attribute it to Vandyck.   The weakness of tone renders also the female figures doubtful.

HOBBEMA (?).—Various cottages among trees.   Upon a road four oxen and a shepherd.   Although this landscape, which is of considerable size, is quite in the taste of Hobbema, yet the trees, as well as the sky, bear more the stamp of RUYSDAEL, 1.   The general tone also appears too heavy for Hobbema.   The high position of the picture, however, prevented me from arriving at any certainty.

PETER DE HOOGHE.—The courtyard of a wine-house, with two figures seated under a vine, one of them smoking, the other holding a jug of wine. Next them is a female servant about to empty a glass of wine, to which one of them appears to have treated her. At an open court door, through which a canal is seen, is a girl with a little dog. Above the vine are the branches of trees. In the left of the foreground are a barrel and a kettle. Signed and dated 1658. The clear sunny tone and the very harmonious colouring render this picture exceedingly attractive.

MICHAEL ANGELO DA CARRAVAGGIO. — The Unbelieving Thomas. To the knees. The heads appear to me too noble, and the treatment not sufficiently energetic, for this painter. The picture has in every way a greater affinity to RIBERA.

JAN BOTH (?).—On the right trees with lofty trunks, between them a road with figures and animals. To the left a piece of water, with rocks rising behind. A warm tone pervades the sky. Both conception and treatment incline me to attribute this fine picture rather to JAN HACKERT.

JACOB RUYSDAEL.—2. A hilly landscape clothed with trees, with a waterfall of moderate dimensions divided into two parts. This picture, which is somewhat large, and of very pronounced greens and careful execution, hangs, unfortunately, in a dark and high position.

SECOND DRAWING-ROOM.

TITIAN (?).—The Virgin holding the Child on her lap, to whom the little St. John, supported by Elizabeth, is presenting the scroll with Ecce Agnus Dei. Quite on the right is St. Joseph; on the left an aged saint, probably St. Matthew, pointing to a book which an angel holds before him. Above the figures are ruins, with a hilly distance and a warm horizon. Whole-length figures, almost life-size. Judging from the character of the heads, the somewhat empty and undecided forms of the children, and the general tone of colour, I am inclined to consider this as a late work of PALMA VECCHIO.

PARMIGIANINO.—A male portrait in a black furred coat, a cap on his head, and a casket in his left hand. A coin lies before him. Half-length. In the landscape background is a very well painted piece of sculpture. This picture displays great energy, uncommon decision of forms, and a masterly modelling in a powerful reddish brown tone.

Giorgione (?).—Portrait of a pretty woman, taken quite in front, in a red dress and white sleeves. A dark background. Almost to the knees. The conception and style of the powerful and very transparent colouring show this to be a fine work by Paris Bordone.

Paul Bril.—A hilly landscape, with a waterfall in the middle distance, seen through a cavern. In the foreground the figures of Diana and her nymphs bathing, and surprised by Actæon, by the hand of Annibale Carracci. This highly poetic landscape belongs to the finest specimens of the master. The figures by Carracci are also very spirited.

Rubens.—Christ bearing his Cross. Half-length. However warm and clear the colouring, it does not reconcile us to the expressionless head and awkward arm.

Domenichino.—A landscape with high rocky hills. To the left a waterfall. In the middle distance is a grand rock with its base watered by a stream, the opposite shore of which is bordered by rocks. In the foreground is Diana with her nymphs hunting. In the sky two charming little amorini. In comprehensiveness of subject, grandeur of forms, and noble and poetic feeling, one of the chefs-d'œuvre of the master in this line.

Jan Both.—Trees on the left, with rocks rising behind. In front travellers with asses. In the middle distance a waterfall, on the left rising ground. In the background misty hills. This picture, which is almost quadrangular in form, is of admirable effect, and also attractive from its numerous details.

Murillo.—2. St. Joseph with a lily in his left hand, his right holding the boy Christ, who is walking beside him. Angels and angels' heads in the sky. Whole-length figures, life-size. An elevated expression of melancholy pervades the heads. The execution also is very careful in a silvery tone.

Guido Reni.—The Magdalen looking upwards. To the knees. An especially fine specimen of this frequently-recurring subject by the master. The beautiful features are here, as usual, borrowed from the head of one of Niobe's daughters. The colouring is very transparent, and the modelling careful.

THE LIBRARY.

Vandyck.—Portrait of Lord Strafford. A bust picture. This agrees throughout with the picture in Wentworth House belonging to Lord Fitzwilliam, and looks promising, though it hangs in too dark a place for any decided opinion.

Canaletto.—View of the Piazzetta at Venice. A picture full of details, and of admirable effect and careful execution.

MISS ENFIELD'S ROOM.

Jan Both.—A very attractive landscape.

Bonifazio.—The Virgin and Child in glory, with the little St. John. In this finely effective picture the master has successfully aimed to approach Titian.

Dirk van Bergen.—Different kinds of cattle in a landscape. A particularly transparent and careful picture, in which he comes near to his master, Adrian van de Velde.

THE STAIRCASE.

Some pleasing pictures by Angelica Kauffmann, among which one from the history of Coriolanus is conspicuous.

Van de Capella.—A calm sea, with numerous vessels. A man-of-war in the foreground is especially remarkable. This is a large picture of great warmth and purity of tone and masterly execution. It had no certain place at the time of my visit.

COLLECTION OF PICTURES BELONGING TO SIR THOMAS SEBRIGHT,

AT HIS SEAT, BEECHWOOD, SEVEN MILES FROM THE STATION, BOXMOOR.

I had the good fortune to be accompanied to this place by Sir Coutts Lindsay and Mr. Chambers. The stately brick mansion contains many pleasing apartments. A large hall in the centre, lighted from above, with a gallery at the height of the first story communicating with the rooms, has a very imposing character. The collection consists of pictures of the Italian, Spanish, French, and Netherlandish schools, comprising many of considerable interest in point of art, and some of great value.

THE LARGE CENTRE HALL.

GUIDO RENI.—St. Jerome, a crucifix in his left hand, a stone in his right. A dark background. Half-length figure in an oval. Of warm and clear colouring, and of masterly execution in his broadest touch.

GUERCINO.—The Virgin holding the Child on her lap, who is turning over the leaves of a book she holds in her hand. The ground dark. Almost to the knees. The heads are unusually noble in character, and carefully modelled in a bright tone. This picture belongs to the most attractive specimens of his light manner.

LEANDRO BASSANO.—Portrait of a man standing, with black hair and beard, and a black dress trimmed with brown fur. His right hand is hanging at his side, his left placed on the arm of a chair. The ground is dark. Almost to the knees. Very animated, of marrowy execution, and modelled in a brown but somewhat heavy flesh tone.

LEONARDO DA VINCI (?).—The Virgin, seated in a landscape, holding with her right arm the Child, who is seated next her on her mantle, holding up a cross with both hands. The movement of her left hand expresses her astonishment at this action of the Child. This composition, which, in my opinion, is decidedly attributable to Leonardo, is repeated in various pictures bearing his name, and differing from each other in their landscape backgrounds, none of which, however, that I have seen, are by the hand of the master. They differ also greatly in artistic merit—that in the gallery at Munich, purchased by King Louis of Bavaria for a considerable sum, is the weakest example of the subject I know ; that in the collection of Count Harrach of Vienna the finest. The one before us may be placed between the two. It is far better drawn than the first, and agrees in the fine warm colouring with the last-mentioned. I am not, however, able to indicate by name the skilful scholar or follower of Leonardo to whom it may be assigned.

GIORGIONE (?).—Christ sinking under the weight of the Cross in the foreground. The fainting Virgin is supported by the holy women. Farther behind is the Crucifixion, the Magdalen embracing the Cross, the Virgin and St. John on each side. The background is Jerusalem. Small figures. Although this picture hangs too high for me to decide as to the master, yet, from the tone of the landscape, it is evidently not by Giorgione, but, from the combination of the very glowing colours, appears rather a good work of the Ferrarese school.

VANDYCK.—1. The figure of Christ, clothed only in a white robe round the lower part of the person, is showing the wounds on his hands to the unbelieving Thomas, who is stooping down. Next the latter is St. Peter and another apostle. The ground is dark. Almost to the knees. The figure of Christ is remarkable for unusual elevation of forms and expression, and for the coolness of colouring, which also extends to the figure of St. Peter. The keeping is as masterly as the carrying out is refined.

FRANZ SNYDERS.—A very spirited, true, and powerfully-coloured study for the upper part of the two panthers in the gallery at Munich, where these animals are pursuing a doe. The motive by which the foremost animal is snarling at the other because he does not want him to have any share of the booty is not so apparent here.

PIER DI COSIMO.—1 and 2. This rare master is here represented by two compositions of bacchanalian subjects, which, according to Vasari, he executed for Giovanni Vespucci. One of them is unfinished. They are full of strange and original inventions, and are carefully executed in a warm tone.

GASPAR POUSSIN.—1 and 2. Two landscapes in body colours. Of great charm, both of composition and colouring, though in the latter respect almost too lively. The one has the figures of two men combating an animal, the other is animated by the story of Hercules shooting at the centaur.

RAPHAEL (?).—A landscape, with St. Jerome on the right, who, with a stone in his left hand, is doing penance before a small crucifix fastened high upon a tree; his right hand is raised. On the right, before a cave, are Christ and St. John, as children, conversing. In the background mountains and a piece of water. About 2 ft. high by 1 ft. 3 in. wide. The figures are too unintelligent, the colouring too heavy, and the treatment of the trees too mechanical for Raphael. It is, however, a good picture of the time, reminding me most of TIMOTEO VITI.

SALVATOR ROSA.—1. A dark landscape with heavy clouds. On a slab of rock are three warriors, one of them in armour and on a brown horse. Spiritedly composed, and of powerful effect.

2. A landscape with clear sky. On the right the stems of trees leaning towards each other. On a rock are three figures, one of them kneeling. Companion to the foregoing, though somewhat inferior in merit.

CORREGGIO (?).—An unfinished picture, representing an unintelligible allegory. In the centre, only drawn on a flesh-coloured ground, is a female form, with a female angel about to place a crown on her head. Next to the woman, and also only in outline, is an animal, most probably a lamb. On the right is another female figure seated on a lion-skin, looking at the first-named woman, with her face turned from the spectator, and seen in profile —her left hand on the hilt of a sword. On the left is a third female figure, with an instrument for writing in her right hand, and pointing into the picture with her left. Before her, with his back turned, is a boy, who, looking at the spectator, also points into the picture. On wood. This picture, which is executed in oil, agrees in style of composition, in forms, motives, and heads, with both the body-coloured pictures now exhibited in the department of the drawings in the Louvre. The finished portions are also of masterly modelling, though in some parts—for instance, the figure on the left— too heavy and untransparent for Correggio. This interesting but enigmatical picture was formerly in the Altieri Palace at Rome, and afterwards in the possession of Sir David Wilkie.

VANDYCK.—2. Standing portrait of Charles I. in black dress with white collar and large silver star. His glove in his left hand, his right hand on the brim of his hat, which lies on a table covered with a cloth. On the right is a curtain. The ground is dark. Among the numerous pictures of Charles I. by the painter, this one occupies a distinguished place. The bright golden tone, and the soft, broad, but careful treatment, indicate the earlier part of his English period, about 1634--35.

SIR THOMAS SEBRIGHT'S ROOM.

MURILLO.—The Virgin, life-size, in white robe and blue mantle, the head turned up towards the left side, her hands folded on her breast, borne upwards by six angels. Rays of silver light surround her head, the sky being also kept cool. The tender warm flesh-tones form a charming contrast. The expression of the head is very sentimental, the effect of the whole highly ethereal and delicate, and the treatment as light as it is spirited.

ANDREA DEL SARTO (?).—Portrait of a young man in black dress, and with a black hat—his right hand on his hip, his left holding by his girdle. The ground green. Almost to the knees. Of serious and elevated conception, and masterly drawing, and admirably modelled in a broken flesh-tone. The general style, however, and especially the somewhat heavy colouring, are indica-tive rather of FRANCIABIGIO, the fellow-labourer with Andrea del Sarto.

GIORGIONE (?).—Portrait of a man of powerful and decided physiognomy, in armour, holding a spear in his left hand. The circumstance of his hand being too large, and the whole feeling of the picture, are opposed to the probability of its being by Giorgione. It is, however, by some very skilful master of the Venetian school.

ANNIBALE CARRACCI.—The Virgin holding the Child on her lap, who has an apple in his left hand. On the right, by a cradle, is St. John; on the left St. Joseph, pointing to a book. A land-scape background. A powerfully and clearly coloured and care-fully carried out specimen of this well-known composition.

BOURGUIGNON.—A subject of horsemen, of unusual warmth and transparency, and also very powerful.

SALVATOR ROSA.—3. A male head, bound round with a kind of cloth. Powerful, but very dark.

PARMIGIANINO.—St. John the Baptist, as a bust picture, of colossal proportions. The ground dark. Of fine forms and spirited treatment, but very dark in the shadows.

DINING-ROOM.

RUBENS.—A male portrait, in an outlandish dress. The right hand supported on a staff, with the left hand holding a gold chain. A key at the girdle. Almost to the knees. Very animated, and the head admirably treated in a golden tone.

LEONARDO DA VINCI (?).—The Battle of the Standard, known to all lovers of art by Edelinck's engraving from the famous car-toon executed for the republic of Florence. The figures about a third life-size. On wood. Although in a very darkened and dirty condition, yet it is evident that the forms are too empty and too little understood to justify the master's name. Also in an historical sense, it is highly improbable that the over-occupied Leonardo should have had time to execute this picture. As an early representation in colour of this group, however, it has a certain interest.

DRAWING-ROOM.

WILLEM VAN DE VELDE.—A calm sea. Among the vessels which enliven the surface, one in the middle-distance, somewhat towards the left, is remarkable. Warm and clear in tone, and of masterly treatment.

The Adoration of the Kings, a rich circular composition, with numerous portrait-like figures, is here arbitrarily assigned to Giovanni Santi. But all who, like myself, are acquainted with the authentic pictures of this master in Italy and elsewhere, will feel that conception and character of heads, as well as the hard outlines and very dark general tone, are at variance with the father of Raphael. Judging from all these characteristics, and also from the treatment of the gold, especially in the drapery of the kneeling king, I am inclined to believe this to be a remarkable picture of the early Spanish school. The head of a youth in profile is of great beauty.

THE GALLERY IN THE GREAT HALL.

SIR JOSHUA REYNOLDS.—Portraits of Mr. Croft and his wife. Almost to the knees. This is one of his pictures which unite an animated conception with a very solid execution. The portrait of the lady is also very attractive for her beautiful features.

LADY SEBRIGHT'S BED-ROOM.

CORNELIS HUYSMAN.—1 and 2. Two landscapes. Belonging in composition and execution to his better works.

The library also contains numerous rare old engravings and MSS. with miniatures. Among the first I may name the very rare first edition of the Book of Common Prayer. Among the MSS. is one which, in Sir Thomas Sebright's opinion, was executed for Leo X., and in mine for Clement VII. It is adorned with careful miniatures, erroneously attributed to Giulio Clovio, who flourished later. Also a prayer-book of French miniatures of moderate artistic value, executed about 1460.

The visitor to Beechwood will also be struck by the rich furniture, and by the number of noble trees. The largest cedar of Lebanon I have yet seen in England is here.

ADDITIONS TO THE COLLECTION OF THE DUKE OF BEDFORD,

AT WOBURN ABBEY.

(Vol. III. p. 464.)

I had long entertained the wish to give a more complete account of the pictures at Woburn Abbey, which, though described in my work entitled ' Art and Artists in England' in 1838, were then seen under very unfavourable circumstances. Through the kind intervention of Mr. William Russell, this visit was accomplished in 1856, and, by order of the Duke, I was allowed to inspect the collection at perfect leisure, being assisted in my researches by a very civil housekeeper. As some alteration has taken place in the arrangement since 1835, I proceed to notice them according to the apartments they occupy, merely naming those I have described before, or at best adding a short remark.

NORTH CORRIDOR.

HANS HOLBEIN.—Portrait of John Russell. This looks promising, but hangs too high for a closer opinion.

DANIEL MYTENS.—Portrait of the first Earl of Portland. A dignified individuality is here very truly conceived, and carefully executed in warm and powerful colouring.

GAINSBOROUGH.—1. Portrait of the first Duke of Bedford. Of refined and animated conception, and well carried out on a cool scale of colour.

SIR JOSHUA REYNOLDS.—1. Portrait of the Marquis of Tavistock. Bust picture. Of great refinement, but pale in colour.

PRINCE ALBERT'S SITTING-ROOM.

GAINSBOROUGH.—2 and 3. Two fine landscapes, with cattle.

SIR AUGUSTUS CALCOTT (see p. 466).—View of the Scheldt. An admirable picture of his best time.

PRINCE ALBERT'S DRESSING-ROOM.

A series of portraits by SIR JOSHUA REYNOLDS, among which that of the Lady Caroline Russell, to the knees, is distinguished for beauty and elegance.

THE QUEEN'S BED-ROOM.

COLLINS.—A sale of fish upon the shore (p. 466). Of good keeping, animated figures, and careful treatment.

SIR JOHN HAYTER.—Trial of Lord William Russell. Well known by the admirable engraving, and not so able as that would lead us to expect.

SIR EDWIN LANDSEER.—1. Stag-hunt. In this large and rich picture I am inclined to recognise the influence of Rubens.

THE QUEEN'S DRESSING-ROOM.

BONNINGTON.—View of a sea-coast in France. Of luminous transparency.

LESLIE.—Lady Jane Grey refusing the offer of the Crown. The composition not so fortunate as usual, and the colouring weak, but the heads refined and full of expression.

SIR CHARLES EASTLAKE.—Pilgrims in sight of Rome (p. 466).

PAUL POTTER (?).—Landscape with cattle. Though placed too high for an opinion, I can at all events decide it not to be by that master. The style of conception corresponds more with CUYP, 1.

SIR EDWIN LANDSEER.—2. Stags in the park at Woburn. Happily composed, and the heads of the animals very animated, but the colouring cold, and the treatment rather scenic.

THE QUEEN'S SITTING-ROOM.

CLAUDE LORRAINE.—View of the Castle of St. Angelo, with the bridge over the Tiber. By this more favourable light I perceived that my former opinion of this large and fine picture was unfounded. It offers an unusual combination of warmth, power, and clearness of tone.

GASPAR POUSSIN.—1. Large landscape, with two persons conversing in the foreground. The composition in his most elevated style, and also clearer in colour than the darkness in which I viewed it before had led me to believe.

WILSON.—View of Haddon Hall. Very picturesque in effect, and of careful handling, but somewhat dark in colour.

GASPAR POUSSIN.—2. On the left are high hills, on the right an extensive distance with water. In the middle distance is also water. The sky, which is unusual with this master, is almost without clouds. A worthy companion in every way to the preceding picture.

ALBERT CUYP.—2. View of the Rhine, with the town of Nymwegen. In the foreground, on the near shore, a shepherd boy and girl, and four cows; the town on the other side. A large picture of his best time. The mild prevailing light is of great transparency, and the reflections in the water of marvellous truth.

THE SALOON.

ANNIBALE CARRACCI.—Christ appearing to the Magdalen. Figures about three-fourths life-size. A remarkable picture. The expression of the Magdalen particularly true and noble; the landscape background fine, and the keeping excellent.

SIR JOSHUA REYNOLDS.—Portrait of the Marchioness of Tavistock. Whole-length, life-size. She is standing, crowning a statue. Behind, on the right, is a mulatto woman. The background landscape. The fine features of the lady are rendered with great animation and refinement; at the same time the colouring is warm and transparent, and the effect of the whole enchanting.

VELASQUEZ.—Portrait of Admiral Pareja. Whole-length, life-size. The stern dignity of the individual is very animatedly expressed. The execution of the flesh tones in a deep brown tone is very spirited.

MURILLO.—The large picture with the angels (p. 465).

NICOLAS POUSSIN (?).—A highly poetical landscape with luminous horizon. In the centre a piece of still water. Conception and handling incline me to consider this a fine work by GASPAR POUSSIN, 3.

RUBENS.—1. Abel dead (p. 465).

GASPAR POUSSIN.—4. A sea view. On the left a chain of hills receding one behind the other. Pictures by this master in which the sea is the principal subject are seldom met with. This equally bears witness, however, to the grandeur of his mode of conception. Unfortunately it has darkened in some parts.

REMBRANDT.—1. Joseph interpreting the chief Baker's and Butler's dreams. To the knees. The heads very speaking and animated, the tone of the flesh clear but subdued, and the deep chiaroscuro of the whole of masterly rendering.

BENEDETTO CASTIGLIONE.—The Departure of the Israelites from Egypt. A rich composition, but much darkened.

GUERCINO.—1. Samson.

DINING-ROOM.

A series of stately portraits by VANDYCK gives this room a most imposing appearance.

VANDYCK.—1. Portrait of Francis Russell, 4th Earl of Bedford. Dated 1636 (p. 464).

3. Anne Carr, wife of William Earl of Bedford (p. 464).

4. Charles I. Whole-length, life-size. Too empty and feeble for Vandyck, and only an early copy.

5. Lady Herbert, in a white silk dress. Full-length, life-size. But little attractive, and too heavy and dull for the master.

6. Aubertus Miraeus (p. 464). Solidly painted in a golden tone, at the period when he sojourned in the Netherlands, after his return from Italy.

7. Henrietta Maria, queen of Charles I. (?) The features differ so much from those of this well-known personage, that I am inclined to consider it the portrait of another woman. The picture itself is very doubtful.

8. Percy, Earl of Northumberland, Lord High Admiral. In the background, on the left, is the sea, with ships. This personage is often seen, purporting to be by the hand of Vandyck. The portrait before us is heavy and dark in tone.

9. The Duchess of Orleans, daughter of Charles I. Of great delicacy and transparency, but doubtless another lady, as dates prove that Vandyck could not have painted her at this age.

SMALL BREAKFAST-ROOM.

VANDYCK.—10. The Earl of Bristol, and the 5th Earl of Bedford. Whole-lengths, life-size. The flesh tones a decided brown. The hands beautiful, but the treatment of the drapery very scenic.

11. Portrait of Anne Carr, Countess of Bedford. To the knees. Far less fine than the portrait in the dining-room. The forms are empty.

12. Christ with the globe. The features more pleasing than dignified, and the forms rather empty.

REMBRANDT.—2. An aged Rabbi (p. 464).

SALVATOR ROSA.—Diogenes. A bust picture. Of great energy of forms and colour.

SIR JOSHUA REYNOLDS.—A third picture of the Marchioness of Tavistock. Half-length. Of great charm.

THE LIBRARY.

Although I was able this time to inspect at leisure the interesting series of portraits of painters and other distinguished individuals which adorn this apartment, yet many of them hang both too high and in too dark positions to permit of any certain verdict.

PHILIP DE CHAMPAGNE.—Portrait of Colbert the minister. True and careful.

LANFRANCO.—His own portrait. Very animatedly conceived, and of brown and powerful tone.

VANDYCK.—13. Portraits of Daniel Mytens and his wife (p. 464).

RUBENS.—2. His own portrait. The features so unlike his, that doubtless another person must be here represented. Otherwise a fine picture of clear colour.

VANDYCK.—14. A male portrait. Very warm and powerful.

JOHANN KUPETZSKY.—His own portrait. True, powerful in tone, and careful.

TITIAN.—1. His own portrait. The features are unlike his known portraits. The picture hangs also in a high and dark position.

SIR GODFREY KNELLER.—His own portrait, still youthful. Of animated conception, and carefully carried out in a clear colour.

MICHAEL MIREVELDT.—His own portrait. True, warm, clear, and careful.

REMBRANDT.—3. His own portrait in middle-age. He holds one hand before his breast. Warm and clear in colouring, and of very energetic treatment (p. 465).

GIACOMO BASSANO.—His own portrait. Animated, warm, and broadly treated.

TITIAN (?).—2. Portrait of the celebrated anatomist Vesalius. Conception, colouring, and treatment lead me to consider it rather a good picture by TINTORETTO, 1.

TENIERS.—His own portrait. A successful imitation of Vandyck in conception, colouring, and breadth of treatment.

VANDYCK.—15. Portrait of M. de Mallery. This specimen of an often-repeated picture is somewhat heavy in tone of colour.

FRANZ HALS.—His own portrait. Highly animated, and spiritedly sketched in a powerful tone.

HOGARTH.—His own portrait. The bold, decided character is very truly expressed.

MURILLO.—His own portrait. More yellowish in the flesh tones than the other portraits of the master known to me. Otherwise of very promising appearance, but hung too high for me to judge.

TINTORETTO.—2. His own portrait, still in youthful years. The features of the face appear much nobler than in the portrait which represents him an aged man. Almost to the knees. Admirably coloured, and very carefully executed.

JAN STEEN.—His own portrait. Holding palette and brush. Very animated, and of spirited handling.

SIR JOSHUA REYNOLDS.—His own portrait. Of feebler character than those known to me, but too high for an opinion.

GUERCINO.—2. His own portrait, in already advanced years. True and powerfully coloured.

LEANDRO BASSANO.—His own portrait. Powerfully painted in a strong red tone.

CARLO CAGLIARI.—Portrait of his father, Paul Veronese, in profile. To the knees. The noble features are admirably conceived.

REMBRANDT.—4. Portrait of Gerard Dow. Both master and sitter appear to me doubtful.

ALBERT CUYP.—3. His own portrait. I feel here the same doubt I expressed before (p. 465).

CAVALIERE D' ARPINO.—His own portrait. I have the features of this painter too little before me to judge whether this picture, which represents a stately individuality, of very warm colouring, be really his portrait.

SIR JOSHUA REYNOLDS.—The portraits of Goldsmith and Garrick. These do not belong to his most remarkable works.

VANDYCK.—16. His own portrait. The features differ entirely from his authentic portraits, but it is a good picture. The great height allows of no judgment.

IN A CORRIDOR.

VANDYCK.—17. A male portrait, representing, if I rightly understood the housekeeper, a Herr Jan van Ufer. Of refined conception, and carefully rendered.

SIR ANTHONY MORE.—1. Portrait of Catholic Queen Mary. Very true and careful.

2 and 3. Portraits of the same and her husband Philip II. of
Spain. Whole-length figures on a small scale. Genuine and
delicate pictures, of which, in my very imperfect view of them in
1835, I wrongly conceived a doubt.

I remark in conclusion, that a picture by TENIERS, two by
CUYP, and one by PAUL POTTER (pp. 465 and 466) were erroneously introduced here. They belong to the Duke of Bedford's
town residence, where they were described by me (vol. ii. p. 285).

Unavoidable circumstances prevented my visiting, on this occasion, Coleworth House, the seat of Hollingsworth Magniac, Esq.,
in the neighbourhood of Woburn, which contains a rich and
beautiful collection of articles of virtù.

OBJECTS OF ART AT KNOLE PARK,
SEAT OF EARL AMHERST, NEAR SEVENOAKS, KENT.

An expedition from London to the county of Kent, chiefly for
the purpose of visiting Knole Park, was combined with various
circumstances which render the remembrance of it particularly
agreeable. The company of my friend Mr. Murray, the meeting
with other distinguished and amiable characters, the charming
scenery of the county with its grandly wooded hills in the full
vigour of summer verdure, and finally the interesting nature of
the objects of art, formed attractions of no common kind. The
finely undulated character of the park also, with its noble beeches
and fresh lawns, gives to Knole Park a very prominent place
among English seats. The rambling house belongs to the small
number of residences of which considerable portions date from
the 15th and 16th centuries, and which have preserved also specimens of old domestic furniture. Among the numerous pictures
distributed through the apartments are many of interest and some
of value.

THE HALL.

An antique marble statue of Demosthenes, the size of life and
of good workmanship, forms the principal ornament of this apartment. It is in excellent preservation, only the hands and portions
of the feet being new. My friend Mr. George Scharf has given a

careful description of it accompanied with a good illustration. The walls are appropriately decorated with family pictures.

BALL-ROOM.

GAINSBOROUGH.—Portrait of Lord George Germain, seated. To the knees. Of very animated conception, particularly clear colouring, and careful execution.

VANDYCK.—1. A male portrait in armour and red dress. Unusually red in the flesh-tones, otherwise painted with great mastery.

SIR JOSHUA REYNOLDS.—1. Portrait of the third Earl of Dorset. One of his inferior works.

LADY'S ROOM.

This apartment is not generally shown to visitors, and a natural consideration for the venerable Lord Amherst, who received us with kindness, and led us himself into the room, forbade our remaining long in it, so that I can only observe that a picture by WOUVERMANS (1) appeared upon a cursory view to be genuine; and a female portrait, to the knees, by SIR ANTHONY MORE, an animated and carefully finished picture.

CARTOON GALLERY.

DOBSON. — Portrait of the Earl of Albemarle with a page. Background a pillar and landscape. Of lively conception, and carefully treated in a powerful, warm, and clear tone of colour.

SIR THOMAS LAWRENCE.—Portrait of King George IV. Whole length, life size. Somewhat artificial in arrangement, but of good colouring, and carefully executed for him.

THE CRIMSON DRAWING-ROOM.

DOMENICHINO.—A Sibyl. Very like the celebrated picture from Stowe, now in possession of the Marquis of Hertford, and, judging from the clear colouring and careful making out, probably an early repetition. Too highly hung for any more precise opinion.

SIR JOSHUA REYNOLDS.—2. The well-known picture of Count Ugolino which I formerly saw and described in the Exhibition of the British Institution. (Vol. ii. p. 334.)

HANS HOLBEIN.—Portrait of King Henry VIII. As usual taken quite in front, and almost to the knees. The ground blue. Careful, and in a warmer tone than usual.

PHILIP WOUVERMANS.—2. A man on a grey horse, with a woman and child, a man and two dogs before him. On the left a building with ivy growing upon it. The sky of a reddish warm tone. A good picture of his second manner.

LODOVICO MAZZOLINO.—Adoration of the Kings. A pleasing picture. The architecture and the sky, however, rather too sharply cleaned.

SIR JOSHUA REYNOLDS.—3. Portrait of Madame Bucalli, a celebrated dancer of his time, taking off her mask. A somewhat hard picture in forms and colour for him.

TENIERS.—1. Country-people drinking, dancing, and making merry in front of a house. This picture is attractive for its lively action, delicate and cool tones, and spirited treatment. The landscape is a principal feature.

GAROFALO.—Judith, with a sword in her right hand, triumphantly holding up the head of Holofernes in her left. On the right, next her, is her maid, pointing to heaven with her right hand. In the background the tent of Holofernes. The expression of each head noble, and the Judith of slender and beautiful form and graceful action. The tone of the flesh is delicately broken. The careful execution broad and free.

VANDYCK.—2. Frances Countess of Dorset, with brown hair, in a white silk dress, holding her veil with her right hand, and pointing forwards with her left. On the left, in the background, is a rock, on the right a view. Full-length, life-size. Of great elegance.

SIR PETER LELY.—Portrait of the Duke of Cleveland, hung as a pendant to the foregoing. In animated arrangement and powerful colouring one of his good works.

TENIERS.—2. A guard-room. In the foreground armour and weapons, on the right a soldier, on the left five more playing with dice. In the middle distance before a fire-place three others. In the background is the angel delivering St. Peter from prison. On copper, with rounded corners. An excellent picture in his cool tones, and of admirable impasto.

JAN MIEL.—A family of beggars among ruins. Genuine, but of moderate merit.

z 2

SIR JOSHUA REYNOLDS.—4. The picture known by the name of Robinetta. A girl dressed in white, of agreeable features, and with chesnut-brown hair, seated by a bird's cage, and feeding the bird, which is on her right shoulder, with her head turned towards it. The background a landscape. To the knees. Of very pleasing feeling, and of solid and spirited treatment in warm and clear colouring.

5. The Fortune-teller. A laughing young girl seated, and with her right hand held out by a brown-haired youth with a red cap to a gipsy who is telling her fortune. The background of landscape character. The heads very animated, the colouring of great warmth, and the treatment careful.

6. Portrait of a popular singer, by name Schindlerin. In an oval. The ground grey. The expression very sentimental, the execution of great mastery.

NICOLAS BERGHEM.—On the left in the foreground lofty trees, with three oxen and an ass. To the right hills receding into the distance. In the centre a man on an ass, pedestrians, and a dog. Of pleasing composition and of spirited and careful treatment in a warm, vigorous, and clear tone.

PIETRO PERUGINO (?).—This erroneous name is borne by an early and somewhat enlarged copy—true in the fine heads, but cold in tone—of the small Raphael of his Peruginesque time, in the Museum at Berlin, No. 149, representing the Virgin and Child, with SS. Jerome and Francis on each side.

SIR JOSHUA REYNOLDS.—7. The child Samuel, looking upwards, his right hand raised in prayer. Half-length. A very pleasing example in clearness of colouring, and careful treatment, of this often repeated subject, for which Sir Joshua made use of a very beautiful boy as a model.

ANDREA DEL SARTO (?).—The Virgin and Child and St. John. A good picture of his school, warm and clear in the flesh-tones.

DINING-ROOM.

This apartment is adorned in a rare and interesting manner by very good portraits of great artists of various walks—composers, painters, players, and also distinguished literati. The following attracted my attention. By SIR JOSHUA REYNOLDS are :—

8. The well-known actress Mrs. Abingdon, in a white dress,

standing next a pedestal, on which she is leaning with her right hand, and holding a mask in her left, which is hanging at her side. On the left a statue. The background of landscape character. Whole-length, life-size. Her features, though not beautiful, are animated and significant in expression. The execution of the flesh very spirited, and as true as it is warm and clear.

9. Portrait of Goldsmith, in profile. An honest face. Of very lively conception.

10. Portrait of Garrick. Very characteristic. The clasped hands are admirable. The unusually red tone of flesh was perhaps a peculiarity in him.

11. The well-known composer Sacchini. An intellectual face. Broadly treated with a certain ostentation of freedom, and with less truth of tone than usual.

12. Dr. Johnson, in profile. The head highly characteristic and animated, but the hands neglected.

13. His own portrait, holding a paper in his right hand. Among the various portraits of himself, this is remarkable for warm and clear colouring, and careful carrying out.

DENNER.—Portrait of Handel, in an oval. Very truly conceived and carefully carried out in delicate colour.

DOBSON.—His own portrait, seated, with one hand on a skull. A powerful man. Of clever arrangement and careful finish.

On our return to Sevenoaks we had the unexpected pleasure of meeting Lord and Lady Stanhope on horseback, about to pay Lord Amherst a visit. A kind invitation to dinner at their seat in the neighbourhood it was not in our power to accept.

PICTURES BELONGING TO HUMPHREY MILDMAY, ESQ.,

AT HIS SEAT, SHOREHAM PLACE, NEAR SEVENOAKS.

In compliance with an invitation from Mrs. Mildmay, we drove from Knole Park to Shoreham Place. A clear trout-stream, shaded by fine trees, and the fresh verdure of the undulating grounds, give the house, which is new, spacious, and comfortable, a very attractive position. The pictures which decorate the walls of the library form part of the collection which I had already described in Mr. Mildmay's London residence, and are so remarkable that I am glad thus to complete my notices.

JAN BOTH.—On the left a waterfall streaming down a rock—a road with figures—and on the right an extensive distance. From the Verstolk collection. A fine composition, of considerable size, and executed in a subdued warm tone of good impasto.

ISAAC VAN OSTADE.—A large landscape, the chief feature being a village enlivened with various figures. Too highly placed for a closer inspection. The general tone, however, appeared to be rather heavy.

JAN VAN DER HEYDEN.—A very attractive and signed picture, of somewhat broader and freer treatment than customary with him.

PETER DE HOOGHE.—The interior of a room, with the foreground in deep shadow. On the left a woman holding bread in her left hand, and next her a child praying. The motives very pleasing. In general effect this belongs to the darker pictures of the master. From the Verstolk collection.

ARTUS VAN DER NEER.—A small but charming landscape by daylight.

JAN HACKERT.—A large landscape, very attractive for the clear colouring and masterly and careful rendering.

FRANZ SNYDERS.—1 and 2. These companion-pictures hang in another room. They represent a combat between wolves and dogs, and bears and dogs. They are, however, somewhat overladen in composition, and in many parts less free and intelligent in treatment than usual.

PICTURES AT GATTON PARK,
SEAT OF THE COUNTESS OF WARWICK.

This country-house, which is distant two miles from the town of Reigate, and twenty miles from London, is the recent erection of the late Lord Monson. It is a building of great splendour, in the Italian style. A domed apartment, in which not only the flooring but the lower portion of the walls consists of marble, is particularly remarkable, while the late Lord is entitled to no small credit in having applied painting of a monumental character to the upper portion of the walls. Four large compartments have been decorated by the English painter Severn with four female figures, symbolical of virtues; Prudence being represented by Esther, Resolution by Eleanor, Queen of Edward I., Patience by Penelope; the fourth has escaped my recollection. Below these pictures are the same qualities typified by infant genii. As regards invention, individual motives, and transparency of colour, these compositions possess much merit; in point of drawing, however, they are not so successful, while a certain emptiness in the forms exhibits the deficiency of an earnest completion in the details.

The chapel is also very splendidly adorned, and several rooms contain a moderate number of more or less valuable pictures.

By far the most important object in the house, and the real cause of my visit, in which I was accompanied by my friends Sir Charles Eastlake and Mr. Passavant, is the Holy Family, by Leonardo da Vinci, known to all lovers of art throughout Europe by Forster's masterly engraving, and the more important as being the chief work we possess of the somewhat earlier time of the great master. The whole style of the modelling, and the yellowish, brownish colouring of the flesh, recall on the one hand his master, Andrea Verrocchio, and on the other his fellow scholar Lorenzo di Credi. Although in the infant Christ and the little St. John those indications of numerous little folds occur in the flesh which are peculiar to those masters, yet the forms are incomparably more refined and better understood, and the shadows, with much greater transparency, far more intense. The head of the Virgin does not yet display the well-known type of the female heads of his later time, the oval of the face being rounder, and the cheeks more filled out. The expression of maternal feeling is of great warmth and fervency. A peaceful joy pervades the features of the infant Christ. In the draperies, especially in the red robe of the Virgin, local colours are used in great force; her blue mantle is lined with green. The execution of the nude is of melting tenderness, and the hair so careful that the single hairs are expressed. The preservation of this gem, which the late Lord Monson purchased of Mr. Woodburn for 4000*l.*, is, upon the whole, excellent, only the lower part of Zachariah's beard betrays, in its broad treatment and absence of understanding, the hand of a restorer.

SEBASTIAN DEL PIOMBO.—A stately male portrait belongs to those later works of the master which have so much darkened with time as only to present the shadow of what they originally were.

GUIDO RENI. — The Virgin and Child. Transparent and delicate.

An old copy of Raphael's own portrait, executed, according to Mr. Passavant (an opinion which appears to me highly probable), for his friend Francesco Francia. It is best known by Paul Pontin's engraving.

In a small room next this are a set of landscapes attributed to CLAUDE LORRAINE, and engraved as such in an Italian work which lies here open. They made, however, no favourable impression on me.

Among various pictures hanging in a corridor, in a very unfavourable light, I was struck by the uncommon truth and extraordinary power of colouring in the subject of a boy and girl playing cards. This picture vividly recalls the masterly portrait of an old woman by Nicolas Maas in the assembly rooms of Felix Meritis at Amsterdam.

A male portrait also, by DOBSON, which approaches Vandyck in merit, and a saint with the infant Christ by GUIDO, which is carefully painted in his light but warm tones, deserve careful notice.

ADDITIONS TO THE COLLECTION BELONGING TO EARL COWPER,

AT PANSHANGER.

(Vol. III. p. 7.)

A pleasant sojourn of a few days in the charming country residence of my friend Mr. Bellenden Ker enabled me, under his kind auspices, once more to visit Panshanger, and the splendid collection of pictures which are seen to such advantage there. I was thus able to renew, and in one instance to improve upon, my former impressions, also to see pictures which I had omitted to notice, or which have been added since, and others which had been inaccessible to me on my first visit. This was the case with many of those in the drawing-room.

The bust picture of an oval form (see p. 12, vol. iii.) there attributed to Andrea del Sarto I am now persuaded is a work by

PONTORMO in his latter time, when his forms were soft and undecided.

The pictures I had before omitted are the following :—

PERUGINO (?).—A male portrait, with a landscape background. Judging from the feeling, the colouring, the form of the hands— that of the left, held before the person, being particularly beautiful—I venture to pronounce this an admirable work by FRANCESCO FRANCIA.

DANIEL DA VOLTERRA.—An example of Michael Angelo's often-repeated Pietà, with two angels supporting the arms of the dead Saviour as he lies in the lap of the Virgin. The expression of the Virgin's head is, in point of depth and energy, worthy of his grand model. The other portions are, however, by no means equal to this.

PAUL VERONESE.—The Virgin enthroned, a book in her right hand, holding with her left the Child standing on her lap. A cherub holds her veil. Next her is Joseph ; on the base of the throne is the little St. John. Below, on the left, are St. Francis and a female saint with a palm ; on the right a cardinal. The angel holding the veil is by no means a happy motive in the composition. The warm colouring, the softness of the forms, and the careful painting, render this picture very attractive.

The following pictures in the gallery were altogether new to me :—

CORREGGIO.—The Ecce Homo—an unfinished work on wood. 1 ft. high, 9 in. wide. The head is fortunately quite completed, and shows a combination of elevation and refinement of form, a depth of feeling, warmth and beauty of colouring, and, finally, a vigour of treatment, which render it worthy of the great name it bears. In the management of the tones it recalls the Correggios in the National Gallery. Besides the head, a portion of red drapery is all that is finished. The rest, like the ground, is white. The frame, also, with its rich and elegant decoration of eight children, with festoons of fruit and flowers between, deserves mention. This picture was purchased by the late Lord Cowper from Prince Talleyrand.

THORBURN.—Portrait of Lady Melbourne, full-length—a work displaying in the fullest extent the peculiar elegance of conception and execution of this well-known miniature-painter, as well as his great power and clearness of colouring.

THE DRAWING-ROOM.

Teniers.—Interior of an oil-mill, with a single figure. Of admirable transparency of chiaroscuro and masterly execution.

Rubens.—Sketch of an altarpiece. A pope and emperor in the centre are worshipping a saint, unknown to me by name, who appears above, and to whom the sick below are brought to be healed. The dramatic conception is full of fire, and the treatment most spirited.

Gaspar Poussin.—1 and 2. Two small landscapes, rather dark, but highly poetical in composition.

Jan Both.—A landscape, with a waterfall between high rocks. The composition, powerful colouring, and careful execution, render this large picture very agreeable.

Adam Pynacker.—Landscape, with rocks and a waterfall on the left, and on the right an extended distance. On wood. About 1 ft. 2 in. high, by 1 ft. 10 in. wide. The warmth of the tone and the delicacy of the whole work class this among the best pictures of this unequal master.

Here are also various pictures by Sir Joshua Reynolds, the following the most remarkable :—

Three children of Lord Melbourne in the open air. One of them the subsequently well-known Premier. Of great animation.

A little girl warming herself. Very pretty.

Finally I must mention a youthful portrait of the present Lady Palmerston by Hoppner. The composition, with her hat in one hand, is easy and tasteful, and the beautiful features are rendered with refinement and animation.

LETTER VII.

Collection of pictures belonging to Vernon Harcourt, Esq., Nuneham Park —
Additions to collection at Longford Castle, seat of Lord Folkestone —
Pictures belonging to General Buckley, Newhall — Collection of pictures
belonging to the Earl of Normanton, Somerley — Collection belonging to
Sir Wm. Knighton, Blendworth Lodge — Collection belonging to E. G.
Bankes, Esq., Kingston Lacy.

COLLECTION OF PICTURES AT NUNEHAM PARK,

NEAR ABINGDON ROAD, NOT FAR FROM OXFORD, THE SEAT OF VERNON
HARCOURT, ESQ.

(Vol. III. p. 134.)

NUNEHAM PARK occupies a distinguished place among English
country seats. The position of the house, with the ground sloping
from it on one side, has been most judiciously chosen. The flower-
beds next the house are beautifully laid out, richly filled, and
excellently kept. The pleasure-grounds, with a view of Oxford,
and picturesque groups of trees, have a charming effect. The
apartments in which the pictures are distributed are of agreeable
proportions, and several of them stately in size. The pictures
consist chiefly of the Netherlandish, French, and English schools,
including also specimens of Italian, Spanish, and German masters.
Many of them are of value, and some of remarkable merit.
Although the proprietor was not at home, a letter from him to
a very civil housekeeper secured me the uninterrupted use of my
time. I take the pictures in the order in which they are
arranged.

THE ANTE-ROOM.

F. DECKER.—A stately landscape, with buildings and trees
behind. A piece of water close by reflects a warm evening sky.
An unusually good specimen of this scholar of Ruysdael.

VANDYCK.—Portrait of Queen Henrietta Maria in a white silk
dress, on which her left hand is resting; her right hand holds
roses. To the knees. Next her is a table on which is the crown;
in the background is a red curtain. Though the picture hangs

rather high, it is easy to distinguish that the head is of warm colour and delicate rendering. The accessories are however very scenically treated, and doubtless the work of a scholar.

SIR JOSHUA REYNOLDS.—1. A female portrait—perhaps the Duchess of Gloucester—whole-length, though on a small scale. Leaning on her right hand, she is looking upwards. A pleasing landscape forms the background. The conception is refined and animated, the colouring harmonious, and the execution careful.

SIR GODFREY KNELLER. — Portrait of Pope, and signed " A. Pope." He is in a loose dress with a red cap, in a reflective position, his right hand on his forehead, and his elbow on a bust of Homer. One of the best portraits of this eminent individual with which I am acquainted. The delicate and shrewd features are very animatedly caught and carefully modelled in warm and delicate colouring. As I have since understood from the proprietor, this picture belongs to the drawing-room.

FRANZ SNYDERS.—Dogs and dead game in a landscape. Of masterly treatment, and carried out with unusual care in his clear tones.

DINING-ROOM.

GAINSBOROUGH.—Portrait of the Countess Spencer; a bust picture with hands, in an almost masculine dress. Of oval form. Very animatedly conceived, but somewhat slightly treated, particularly the landscape background.

SIR JOSHUA REYNOLDS.—2. A schoolboy carrying a large book with both hands. The earnest expression is well suited to the young face. The colouring as powerful and harmonious as the treatment is broad and careful.

SEBASTIAN BOURDON.—To this scholar of Nicolas Poussin I am inclined to attribute a Holy Family in the open air, with the St. Joseph kneeling, and presenting a flower to the Child. A picture of transparent colouring and careful execution.

SIR JOSHUA REYNOLDS.—3. Portraits of two Lords Harcourt, brothers, with the wife of the elder, aunt to the present owner of Nuneham. The one in ermine robe is seated, the lady opposite him the same ; the other brother, an officer, is represented standing. Whole-length, life-size. In the background are pillars, a curtain, and sky. A first-rate specimen of the master, combining animated conception with a throughout clear and forcible tone, and a marrowy execution.

Murillo (?).—Boy with fruit before him, bitten in the finger by a lizard. The fright of the boy is well expressed, and the powerfully-toned execution very careful; but the treatment of the fruit and of a glass with flowers is too sharp and metallic for Murillo.

Sir Joshua Reynolds.—4. A good example of the often-repeated infant Samuel kneeling, with his right hand raised, looking up at a light in the sky.

Rubens.—The landscape known by the name of " la Charrette embourbée," and engraved by Bolswert. In the foreground is a cart with one wheel sunk, and the driver propping up the vehicle to prevent its overturn. The master has here represented the transition from night to dawn with a hand as bold as it is successful. While the moon is still seen reflected in the water on the left, the morning light is already seen on the right, especially on the stems of trees. The aërial perspective, and the delicate silvery tone which pervades the whole, and which is only balanced by the red cap and reddish legs of the driver, and by a fire more behind, by which two figures are lying, are admirable, and the treatment light and spirited.

THE BILLIARD-ROOM.

Sir Joshua Reynolds.—5. Portrait of Granville Leveson Gower, Marquis of Stafford. Of good motive and expression, but somewhat faded.

6. Portrait of Mary Countess of Harcourt, seated in the open air. The conception easy and animated, but the treatment too scenical and slight.

THE DRAWING-ROOM.

On the walls of this agreeably-proportioned apartment, which are hung with crimson silk, the pictures have a beautiful effect.

Nicolas Poussin.—1. Moses striking the Rock. This composition, which entirely differs from the master's well-known version of the subject, consists of figures about half the size of life, and has unfortunately much darkened. It hangs also in far too high and dark a place. Nevertheless I was able to do justice to the fine motives and to the unusual truth of nature in the heads. It is about 6 ft. high and 8 ft. wide, and is one of the very large pictures by the master.

WILLEM VAN DE VELDE.—The Embarkation of Charles II. at Scheveningen. A large picture, more remarkable for its subject than its beauty, as the numerous sails repeat the same lines too often.

NICOLAS POUSSIN.—2. A landscape of about the same size as the preceding picture by him, with Venus and Mars. Numerous amorini are playing with his weapons, two of them carrying his shield, and one sharpening an arrow. The somewhat stout forms of the Venus, the treatment and tone of colouring, bear witness to a somewhat early period. Unfortunately the picture has darkened, and is now much sunk.

JAN BOTH.—A large landscape with stately trees before hills on the left. In the background a high mountain.

TITIAN (?).—St. Margaret. Decidedly only a school copy. The original is said to be in Madrid.

RUBENS and TENIERS (?).—Landscape with figures and animals. The landscape is decidedly by VAN UDEN—very pleasing, and broadly treated for him. The figures, I am inclined to think, really by RUBENS.

JACOB RUYSDAEL.—1. Landscape with a small waterfall in the foreground. A specimen of his pure feeling for nature, and very careful in execution, though, now at all events, very dark.

ARTUS VAN DER NEER. — A remarkably fine work of the master.

FRANCESCO GRIMALDI, called IL BOLOGNESE.—A landscape, about 10 ft. high by 8 ft. wide, of poetic composition, with figures almost the size of life by ANNIBALE CARRACCI—two sportsmen in a boat, and one climbing a tree. One of the most important pictures I know by the master.

GASPAR POUSSIN.—A hilly landscape — in the foreground a figure reposing, and another angling. Finely invented and carefully painted, but somewhat dark.

BERGHEM.—A genuine, but very much darkened picture.

CLAUDE LORRAINE.—A landscape with a cool reddish sky, and bluish hills. Genuine, but too much darkened to be agreeable.

MURILLO (?).—Two beggar-boys in a landscape. This hangs

too high for any decision. If by the master, the motives and heads belong to his least fortunate efforts.

JAN ASSELYN.—A very large landscape, with a broken bridge, and buildings. In the foreground, on the shore, figures and bales of goods. An important work, but placed too high.

JACOB RUYSDAEL.—2. Landscape with a waterfall in the foreground, and a house in the middle distance with a red roof. On the left, more behind, is a hill crowned with buildings. About 4 ft. high, 5 ft. 6 in. wide. Both composition and treatment show the influence of Everdingen. Somewhat darkened.

GASPAR POUSSIN (?).—Landscapes—companion-pictures—attributed to this master, but I am inclined to think them rather by the hand of his great relative NICOLAS POUSSIN, 3 and 4. Not only the compositions are in his style, but the forms of the hills evince his greater decision. Above all, however, the spirited figures enlivening the landscape show his brush. The picture with the rocky hills in the background with buildings is the most attractive. In the foreground are three figures on the left and a dog—on the shores of a piece of water are races between a grey and a black horse, with numerous spectators expressing the liveliest interest.

A Flight into Egypt, with the Virgin on an ass, and two pretty angels accompanying, is a pleasing picture of powerful and clear tone, and of considerable size. As far as the high and dark position it occupies would allow me to judge, I am inclined to believe it a work by ALESSANDRO VERONESE, called L'ORBETTO.

THE LIBRARY.

SOFONISBA ANGUSCIOLA.—Her own portrait, still very youthful. Delicate, charming, and clear. A small picture.

FRANCESCO ALBANI.—Holy Family in a landscape. A pleasing little picture of clear colouring.

The wings of an altarpiece of the old Swabian school, with Cornelius, the papal saint, with a horn of consecrated oil in his right hand, and the episcopal staff with the double cross in his left, and St. Catherine and her wheel, and the king who caused her martyrdom under her feet. This good picture reminds me most of the earlier time of MARTIN SCHAFFNER of Ulm.

Among the portraits above the bookcases is one of dark appearance, apparently an important head, between two oval pictures, which promises well, but is too high and in too dark a place to warrant an opinion.

GALLERY.

HONDEKOETER. — Fowls. A good composition, careful and clear and forcible in colour.

NORTH GALLERY.

NICOLAS POUSSIN.—5. Landscape, with a circular tower in the centre. Very poetic in feeling, and of fine lighting and careful execution. I know not to what master it is here attributed.

The following pictures, which I saw in Mr. Vernon Harcourt's town residence, in Carlton Gardens, belong also to the collection at Nuneham.

GENTILE BELLINI.—Portrait of a Doge. But little attractive.

SIR JOSHUA REYNOLDS.—1 and 2. Portrait of Simon Earl of Harcourt, and portrait of the father of the same. Both good works of the master.

Finally I must mention a silver censer which is remarkable for the taste of the design, and for the admirable execution of the perforated work. It is an old family possession.

WINCHESTER—ADDITIONAL.

(Vol. III. p. 135.)

Through the kindness of the Rev. H. W. Gunner I obtained permission in 1856 to inspect the MS. of a Vulgate in the library of Winchester Cathedral, which had been long known to me by reputation as one of the chief specimens of early English miniature-painting. It consists of three folio volumes written in two columns on parchment in a strong minuscule letter, and contains a considerable number of larger and smaller initials. Most of the pictures are in the larger initials, but occasional vignettes also occur. At the beginning is St. Jerome in an initial letter. It is remarkable that the large " I " at the head of the book of Genesis does not, as is usually the case, contain the seven days of the Creation, but represents, first, the birth of Eve, whom the Almighty is upraising from the sleeping figure of Adam—and, last, Christ as Judge of the world. In some of the larger initials the fantastic element is seen in various forms of dragon-life. Two dragons, for instance, are seen enfolding a man, while a third is trying to rescue him. These representations are in the fillings out of the letters, while the body of the letter is occupied with decorations in the Romanesque taste, which are alike remarkable for beauty of forms, delicate gradations of harmonious colour, and the utmost precision of execution. The same may be said of the smaller initials, which consist only of ornamentation of this class. Unfortunately many initials have been cut out. The figures are of very tall proportions—often dignified in expression —the folds of drapery narrow, according to the style of Romanesque sculpture, the colour beautiful, and the ground of burnished gold with dots. Many of the pictures are only half finished ; others, especially in the third volume, only drawn out, but with great care. I cannot agree in the opinion of those who consider the artistic decorations of this MS. to be the work of different periods, but am inclined to pronounce it, judging from forms and execution, entirely the work of the first half of the 12th century. This Vulgate reminds me forcibly of another in a larger form in the library of S. Geneviève at Paris, the writer of which styles himself "Manerius scriptor cantuariensis." This latter, however, belongs to the first half of the 13th century.*

ADDITIONS TO THE COLLECTION AT LONGFORD CASTLE,

SEAT OF LORD FOLKESTONE.

(Vol. III. p. 138.)

Having experienced the mortification of being driven through this important collection on the occasion of my stay in England in 1835, I was the more rejoiced to repeat my visit in the company of my kind friend Mr. Danby Seymour. To the intervention of this gentleman I owed a most polite reception on the part of Lord Folkestone, eldest son of the Earl of Radnor, who allowed me to inspect the pictures in undisturbed freedom and comfort. I am, therefore, fortunately enabled to complete my report of some of the pictures I only noticed slightly before, and to add the description of many that are new to me. Of the 208 pictures contained in a

* See 'Kunstwerke und Künstler in Paris,' p. 288.

catalogue printed in 1849, with the names of the master and a short description, I can only give the more important, distinguishing the most remarkable of these by an asterisk, and retaining the number of each picture, so as to facilitate the researches of those who may follow in my steps. Others of less value I have also mentioned, where it was necessary to correct the name of the master. Owing to long neglect, however, many are not seen to fair advantage.

GAINSBOROUGH.—(5.) 1. Anne, wife of James second Earl of Radnor. A good picture.

MICHAEL MIREVELDT.—(14.) 1. An animated and careful male portrait, I am inclined to think of a Prince of Orange.

JUDOCUS DE MOMPER.—(15.) A landscape. Poetically composed, and of free and spirited handling.

TENIERS. — (16.) Return from the Chace. Here ascribed to Teniers the elder, but in my opinion one of the earlier works of the son, and, with the exception of a somewhat too dark tone of landscape, very attractive.

FRANZ DE PAULA FERG.—(17 and 19.) Two landscapes—companion-pictures. The last, especially, a good work.

JOHANN LINGELBACH.—Strolling fortune-tellers. Very good ; in the taste of Wouvermans.

REMBRANDT.—(20.) A male portrait, but not his own, though here so called. Finely painted in a clear golden tone. A bust picture.

* SALVATOR ROSA.—(22.) Seaports with vessels. This occupies a distinguished place among the works of the master, for happy composition, unusual warmth of tone, and spirited treatment. It is also of considerable size.

* WILLEM VAN DE VELDE.—(23.) A slightly-agitated sea, with several vessels by a pier. On wood. 1 ft. 3 in. high by 1 ft. 6 in. wide. A picture of the most delicate quality.

RUBENS (?).—A male portrait. I am inclined to consider this a good work by an Italian master.

FRANZ HALS.—1 and 2. Small circular portraits of an old man and woman, without numbers. Such slight but spirited little specimens of this great master are justly esteemed by the connoisseur.

TENIERS.—(25.) Peasants making merry in the open air. The heads, though in a somewhat heavy brown tone, are spirited, and the sunny landscape very pleasing.

SIR JOSHUA REYNOLDS.—1. James second Earl of Radnor as a boy. Very animated; the dress of cool colours. The landscape background very dark.

*RUBENS.—(28.) 1. Cupids occupied with harvest. One is mowing, and two others shearing the corn with sickles. One is lifting it up, another carrying it away, a third tying it in sheaves. Two have common wings; two butterflies' wings; two are without wings. The landscape is by VAN UDEN, 1. On wood. About 2 ft. high by 2 ft. 8 in. wide. One of the great master's most original and attractive inventions. The motives charming, and spiritedly and carefully executed in a bright tone. The landscape is also very pretty.

*JACOB RUYSDAEL.—(29.) A moonlight landscape, of considerable size. This beautiful picture proves the great master to have been also equal to this class of subject. But the rarer such works, the more is it to be lamented that the sunken state of this one should so deface its merits.

JAN WYNANTS.—(33.) A large and fine landscape. (See vol. iii. p. 141.)

GASPAR POUSSIN.—(35.) 1. A landscape, which looks promising, but is too dark, and also hangs in too dark a place.

(37.) 2. View of the falls at Tivoli. A fine and careful picture of upright form.

MICHAEL MIREVELDT.—(43.) 2. Portrait of a Prince of Orange. True, transparent, and careful.

*HANS HOLBEIN.—(40.) 1. Portrait of Sir Anthony Denny, in a peculiar kind of armour. Next him his helmet; and behind him a tree, on which his musket hangs. On the tree the following inscription:—Ætatis XLII. MDL., and a monogram. Head, hair, and hands are masterly, and point decidedly to the hand of Holbein. I am also inclined to interpret the monogram as "Holbein fecit." It is here attributed to Lucas de Heere; but independent of the fact of its being far too good a work for him, it must be remembered that this painter was only 16 years of age in 1550.

VANDYCK (?).—(41.) Portrait of David Ryckaert. Copy of the picture in the Dresden Gallery.

ALBERT DURER (?).—(44.) Civetta. (See vol. iii. p. 140.) I will only add that SS. John the Baptist and Evangelist are on the wings, and both very successful figures.

ALBERT DURER (?).—(51 and 50.) The Annunciation, and the Adoration of the Kings. By a good master of the Netherlandish school of about 1520.

CARLO MARATTI (?).—(54.) The Holy Family. A very successful work by PIETRO DA CORTONA.

JOHANN ROTHENHAMMER.—(56.) The Descent from the Cross. A very choice picture by the master.

LODOVICO CARRACCI.—(58.) The Holy Family. Well composed, and fine in feeling. It has unfortunately much darkened.

CORNELIS JANSEN.—(60.) His own portrait. Animatedly conceived, clear in colour, and soft in touch.

JAN BREUGHEL.—(61.) A landscape. Unusually good.

*RUBENS.—(62.) 2. Diana and her Nymphs. (See vol. ii. p. 141.) On wood. A very spirited sketch for the picture in the Dresden Gallery, of which there is another example in Northumberland House.

VELVET BREUGHEL (?).—(65.) Flower-piece. Decidedly by VAN KESSEL.

HOLBEIN (?).—Portraits of Calvin (66), Œcolampadius (71), and Beza (70). These are too coarse for him.

WYNANTS.—(75.) A landscape in his ordinary style, warm and clear in tone, and adorned with figures of a sportsman and three dogs by ADRIAN VAN DE VELDE. (See vol. iii. p. 142.)

HANS HOLBEIN.—(76.) 2. Portrait of Erasmus, mentioned vol. iii. p. 139, and alone worth a pilgrimage to Longford Castle. Seldom has a painter so fully succeeded in bringing to view the whole character of so original a mind as in this instance. In the mouth and small eyes may be seen the unspeakable studies of a long life, to which the painter has drawn attention by the inscription upon the gilt edges of a book bound in red, and elegantly decorated, on which Erasmus is leaning, and which runs thus :—ΗΡΑΚΛΕΟΙ ΠΟΝΟΙ Erasmi Rodero. i.e. the Herculæan labours of Erasmus of Rotterdam. The face also expresses the sagacity and knowledge of life gained by long experience. Beneath the black cap are seen scanty white locks. According to the custom of the time he is richly attired; his dress consisting of a coat bordered with brown fur, and a dress lined with black fur, with a large violet cape with a broad projecting border of black fur. The accessories also are rich. The head is relieved by a green curtain fastened to an iron

rod.   On his right is a pilaster in a very elegant Renaissance taste.
Although the masterly and careful execution extends to every
portion—the brown fur, for example, is wonderfully painted, and
the admirably foreshortened hands of the most individual character
—yet the face, which is rendered in bright golden tones, surpasses
everything else in delicacy of modelling.   All combines to show
that the painter here tried to do his best, while a Latin inscription
proves that he himself was satisfied with the result.   This inscription is placed next the date MDXXIII, and, though not wholly
legible, we can trace the following :—" Ille ego Joannes Holbein
non favie   .   .   .   minius erit, quam mihi."   The preservation
leaves nothing to be desired.

*THE SAME.—(80.) 3. Portrait of Peter Ægydius, also men-
tioned before (vol. iii. p. 139). He is represented in a black cap and
a brown fur dress, seated behind a desk, with his right hand on a
book, on which is the inscription ANTIBAPBAROS, meaning, without
doubt, *antibarbaros.*   In his left hand is a letter inscribed, " Viro
literatissimo Petro Egidio, amico carissimo," &c.   Upon the table
is a hour-glass, and on the wall two shelves.   On the lower shelf
are four books and a metal vessel, on the upper also books, almost
all with titles.   This portrait is also in a bright golden tone, and
as animated in conception as it is delicate in individuality.   It is,
however, less thoroughly carried out in detail than the preceding.

CARLO DOLCE.—(95.) 1. His own portrait.   (See vol. iii. p.
140.)

LUCAS DE HEERE (?).—A female portrait, almost to the knees ;
in my opinion rightly named Mary Stuart ; at all events, the
features agree with those in the drawing by Janet in the imperial
collection of engravings and drawings at Paris.   She wears a cap
richly trimmed with pearls and precious stones, and a dress of a
patterned stuff in dark violet, with white bodice and sleeves.
The ground is dark.   A silvery tone prevails in the flesh.   By a
good master, though I do not venture to determine his name.

JAN DAVID DE HEEM.—(99.) Fruit, a tankard, and flowers.
The background landscape.   Signed and dated 1645.   Light and
clear in colour, and of masterly rendering.

DROGSLODT.—(101.) Peasants in a scuffle.   Signed with the
name of this inferior master, but here erroneously assigned to
Teniers.

Jan van Uden.—(102.) 2. A somewhat crude landscape.

Pietro Francesco Mola.—(103.) A landscape. Apparently genuine, but too high for any opinion.

Jean Mabuse.—The children of Henry VII.—Prince Arthur, Prince Henry, and Princess Margaret. Of the various cotemporary repetitions of this picture, this specimen, which was in the collection of Charles I., approaches nearest to the original at Hampton Court, and proceeds no doubt from the master's hand.

*Murillo.—(107.) Ruth and Naomi. A small picture. Decidedly realistic in conception, and of great force of colour. Now very dark.

Jan van Ravesteyn.—(111.) A Prince of Orange. Animated, transparent, and careful.

Jan Mostaert.—(113.) A male portrait, with landscape background, erroneously stated to be that of Thomas Duke of Norfolk, and painted by Holbein. I believe it to be a good picture by Mostaert.

Federigo Zucchero.—(116.) Portrait of Queen Elizabeth. On wood. One of the genuine and good portraits of this queen by the master.

Caspar Netscher.—(117.) A female portrait, called Queen Mary. Signed, and dated 1680. Doubtless the wife of William III. A delicate picture in a silvery tone.

Guido Reni.—(118.) The Magdalen. See vol. iii. p. 140.

Samuel de Koningk.—(119.) Nathan and David. Here called Rembrandt, but in my opinion a good specimen of the master named.

*Claude Lorraine.—1. (120.) Sunrise. An allegorical representation of the dawn of the Roman Empire (see vol. iii. p. 140). A splendid picture, though somewhat heavier in tone than its companion.

Sebastian del Piombo (?).—(122.) St. Sebastian bound. The figure agrees entirely with that in a picture in the Dresden Gallery, and both indicate a composition by Michael Angelo. Treatment, colouring, and background differ, however, in every respect, and point rather to the Netherlandish master Hans van Hemessen. Only the rapidity with which I was compelled to view this collection on a former visit can excuse my having allowed the name of Sebastian del Piombo to pass unquestioned (see vol. iii. p. 140).

*Nicolas Poussin.—(123.) 1. The Adoration of the Golden Calf (see vol. iii. p. 141).

Correggio (?).—(124.) Venus disarming Love. On the left a follower of Pan. The oft-recurring composition; but too feeble in the modelling, and too monotonous and heavy in the colouring, which has an affinity to Luca Cambiasi.

*Nicolas Poussin.—(125). 2. The Exodus of the Israelites (see vol. iii. p. 141).

*Guido Reni.—(126.) Jupiter and Europa. The original of the frequent repetitions. The head spirited, and the whole picture executed in a warm and transparent tone.

*Hans Holbein.—(127.) 4. As regards this fine work, I can only add to what I have already said (vol. iii. p. 139), that the statement of its being dated is erroneous. Mr. Danby Seymour and I examined the whole picture in the closest manner, and found no trace of a date. We discovered, however, that the age of the learned man is 25. His companion is supposed to be Sir Thomas Wyatt, one of the most learned and accomplished men of his time. I am indebted to a letter from Lord Folkestone for this information.

*Claude Lorraine.—2. (128.) Sunset. Allegorical representation of the decline of the Roman Empire (see vol. iii. p. 140). In charm of mild and warm lighting this picture belongs to the best time of the master. The same feeling is here incomparably expressed which Goethe has breathed forth in his well-known poem ' The Wanderer.'

*Carlo Dolce.—(129.) 2. Christ crowned with Thorns. Of deeper feeling and nobler forms than usual, and with the solemn tone of the fine colours quite in harmony with the subject.

Pietro da Cortona.—(132.) Joseph's Dream. An unusually good picture for him.

*Velasquez.—(131.) 1. Adrian Pulido Pareja. Whole-length figure, life-size, tanned by a southern sun, and with jet black hair; in his right hand the admiral's bâton, in his left his hat. The dress of black velvet, with sleeves of a flowered white satin, and a falling collar of white lace. As regards its artistic merit, see vol. iii. p. 141.

*Titian.—(133.) Portrait of a man, apparently a general. Whole-length, standing figure, life-size : in black dress, with sleeves of chain armour ; next him his helmet, at which he is looking, and a portion of the stem of a laurel. The background buildings and sky. A masterly work. (See vol. iii. p. 140.)

*Vandyck.—(135.) 1. Portrait of Gaston Duke of Orleans. With a breastplate ; in his right hand the bâton, the left on his hip. Whole-length standing figure. In the background a curtain. Very animated, of great elegance of motive, and spirited treatment.

Raphael (?).—(136.) A female portrait. I must adhere to my already expressed opinion that this fine picture is by the hand of Sebastian del Piombo. (See vol. iii. p. 140.)

Rubens (?).—(137.) Portrait of his son. In my opinion a very warmly coloured picture of the earlier period of Vandyck, 2.

Titian (?).—(138.) A male portrait, called Cæsar Borgia, Duke of Valentinois. Inscribed " Anno æt. suæ xxxx." Judging from conception and colouring, an admirable portrait by Giacomo Bassano.

*Hans Holbein.—(140.) 5. A male portrait in a black dress lined with fur, called Luther. This name, which I disputed on my first visit (vol. iii. p. 139), is now marked in the catalogue as doubtful. The whole intention of the picture shows that a remarkable naturalist, and perhaps traveller, is here portrayed. With his right hand he is pointing to a globe upon his lap, on which the four seasons are indicated by four stripes one above another, and with a tablet with a lion's head above, on which is the following Latin inscription :—" Lux tenebris rursus luci tenebre (sic) fugienti succedunt, stabilis res tibi nulla manet." The head is somewhat above life-size, and the noble features express an earnest enthusiasm. Judging from the grandly-conceived forms, from the transparency of the still warm tone, and the breadth of treatment, I am inclined to assign this fine portrait to about the year 1538.

Lodovico Carracci (?).—(141.) The Holy Family, arranged according to the motive of Raphael's Madonna della Sedia, but with St. John adoring on the opposite side. In feeling for colour the picture recalls Sebastian del Piombo ; nevertheless I am inclined to think it the work of a good but somewhat later master of the Venetian school.

HOLBEIN (?).—(142.) Portrait of Lady Carey. Too feeble for the master, but a pretty picture in itself.

CORNELIS POELEMBERG.—(143.) Landscape with figures bathing. Pleasing.

TINTORETTO (?). — (144.) A male portrait with the date MDXXXX. On wood. A good picture by another hand.

*GIORGIONE (?).—(145.) Portrait of the celebrated Violante, daughter of Palma Vecchio, most arbitrarily designated as Titian's mistress. Dated 1540. In my former description I stated this to be an early repetition; I now believe it to be a very beautiful picture by PARIS BORDONE.

TITIAN (?).—(146.) Portrait of a sculptor, with his right hand on a bust. A fine work by TINTORETTO.

*VELASQUEZ.—(147.) 2. Portrait of Juan de Pareja, called the Slave of Velasquez, in dark green coat with white falling collar. Of highly animated conception, and broad and masterly painting.

CORNELIS JANSEN.—(148.) Mr. Taylor, Master of the Revels to Charles I. A good and transparent picture.

TERBURG (?).—(150.) A family picture. A good work in the style of De Keyser.

HENDRIK VAN AVERKAMP, called "DE STOMME VAN CAMPEN." —(151.) A winter piece. Good specimen of the master.

GIACOMO BASSANO.—The Four Seasons (156, 159, 161, 163). Genuine and good pictures.

F. H. MANS.—(160.) View of a Dutch Canal. Signed and dated 1675. A good picture by this inferior master, here attributed to a painter of the name of Van Cleve, unknown to me.

KATWICK.—This to me unknown name is inscribed on a small landscape painted on wood, and without a number. The excellent keeping in a silvery tone, allied to Wouvermans, shows no common hand.

RUBENS (?).—(165.) Portrait of a woman. This is a delicate picture in the style and of the time of Caspar Netscher, but hangs too high to admit of an opinion.

SIR PETER LELY.—(169.) His own portrait. Animated and careful.

MICHAEL MIREVELDT.—(170.) 3. Sir Peter Young. 79 years old. Animated, clear, and careful.

BOURGUIGNON.—(171.) A battle-piece. A good work of the master.

SIR JOSHUA REYNOLDS.—(172.) 2. Lady Tilney Long. Refined and elegant.

RUBENS (?).—(173.) The Duke of Alva on horseback. Only a picture of the school.

*RUBENS (?).—(176.) Portrait of Mary of Medicis, wife of Henry IV. of France. A delicate picture by VANDYCK, 3, in which, however, the hands are so rubbed that they look quite white.

LODOVICO CARRACCI.—(178.) A Charity. Fine in feeling, well composed, and carefully executed.

*VANDYCK.—(182.) 4. Portrait of the Countess of Chesterfield. Whole-length figure. One of his less thoroughly-rendered works.

*VANDYCK.—(183.) 5. Portrait of the Countess of Monmouth. In the same style as the foregoing.

*HENRICK VAN VLIET.—(186.) Interior of a church. Signed and dated 1669. In point of truth of aërial and linear perspective, and in power of colour and broad soft treatment, a work of the first class. Here most arbitrarily entitled Van Cleef.

VAN SOMER.—(187.) Louis Stuart, Duke of Richmond and Lennox. This hangs in a dark place, but appears to be genuine.

GAINSBOROUGH.—(190.) 2. Honourable W. H. Bouverie. 1773. Animated, and of harmonious colouring.

3. Honourable Edward Bouverie. 1773. Of similar merit.

SIR JOSHUA REYNOLDS.—(205.) 3. Anne Countess of Radnor. 1786. To the knees. Of great elegance.

This collection is not only the first in England as regards Holbein, but, considering the master-works of other schools, and also the large number of valuable pictures it contains, generally speaking, it may justly be considered one of the most important in the country. At the same time it would greatly gain in effect by the discreet cleaning and varnishing of many a work now seen to disadvantage.

PICTURES IN THE POSSESSION OF GENERAL BUCKLEY,

NEWHALL.

On our road from Longford Castle to Somerley, my kind cicerone, Mr. Danby Seymour, stopped at Newhall, about a mile from

Longford, the residence of General Buckley, son-in-law of Lord Radnor. The number of pictures distributed in the different apartments is considerable, and the majority of them attractive. In our hurried visit, the following left the most lively impression on my mind.

ADRIAN VAN DE VELDE.—Cattle in a landscape. A delicate picture of the later time of the master.

WILLEM VAN DE VELDE.—A good sea-piece.

CLAUDE LORRAINE.—A rather large landscape. Of fine composition and effect of colour.

JACOB DE HEUSCH.—A large landscape, with grand rocks, much in the taste of Jan Both, and one of the painter's best works.

COLLECTION OF PICTURES BELONGING TO THE EARL OF NORMANTON,

SOMERLEY, NEAR RINGWOOD, HAMPSHIRE.

As early as 1851 Lord Normanton favoured me with an invitation to Somerley, which I was unfortunately unable to accept. I was therefore the more glad to repair my omission in 1854, when I visited Somerley from Longford Castle. Lord Normanton had returned from London the day before, and gave Mr. Danby Seymour and myself a most kind reception. The house is finely situated on an eminence, and commands distant and pleasing views, enlivened by a small stream. The close vicinity of stately trees is very peculiar and striking. The circumstance also of all the principal apartments being on the ground floor corresponds with the character of a villa. But my chief pleasure and surprise was the stately picture gallery, which the Earl had only recently completed after a plan of his own. The proportions of the gallery are not only fine, and the gold decorations rich and tasteful, but the lighting from above is so happily calculated that every picture receives a clear and gentle light, while the reflections which so much disturb the enjoyment of the similarly lighted Bridgewater Gallery are quite avoided. This end is attained more especially by the fact that the light falls only from each side of the roof, the whole length of the centre being kept dark. The large number of pictures which adorn the walls are also worthy of the apartment, including fine works of the Italian, Spanish, French, and English schools. No master, however, is so well represented, either in number or quality, as Sir Joshua Reynolds, so that it may boldly be asserted that no one who has not seen this gallery can judge of the powers of the great English master in their whole extent. I give the pictures in the order in which they hang.

VANDYCK.—1. The Princess Mary, daughter of Charles I., whole-length standing figure in a light blue dress, carried out in a delicate cool tone.

INNOCENZO DA IMOLA.—The Virgin and Child and St. John, with SS. Jerome and Francis. A particularly attractive picture, especially in the beautiful head of the Virgin, and also warm in colour, and careful in execution.

SIR JOSHUA REYNOLDS.—1. Sketch for the Adoration of the Shepherds, which, as one of his most noted historical compositions, is the more to be valued from the fact of the picture having been destroyed by a fire at Belvoir Castle.

ARTUS VAN DER NEER.—1. A Rhine view in Guelders, taken by evening light. On the right, in front, are several cows. Signed. Of rare force of colour, and carried out with great delicacy.

SALVATOR ROSA.—1. An impetuous fight : of the same large size as that in the Louvre. Spiritedly composed, but much darkened.

BERGHEM.—A landscape with cattle in the foreground. Poetically conceived, but dark, and the trees differing in form and treatment from his usual style.

WILLEM VAN DE VELDE.—1. A calm sea. In front a coast, with a pier. Signed. On canvas. Of rare delicacy of tone and execution.

HANS HOLBEIN.—Portrait of Lady Jane Grey. Half-length figure, seated. Why the, it is true, young and pretty lady here represented is so named, I cannot say. The letter D introduced in her dress, and supposed to allude to her name, as the wife of Lord Dudley, is not sufficient basis for such an appellation. All those qualities, however, proper to Holbein's later period—his elevation and delicacy of conception, freedom of motive, beauty of form, and masterly modelling in a cool local tone—are seen here. When I saw the picture in Lord Normanton's house in London, in 1835, it was most arbitrarily attributed to Luca Penni.

Jan Both.—A waterfall between rocks. In the foreground on the right are three figures. Signed. The water is here treated in the cool tones of Pynacker; but the colouring otherwise very powerful, and the execution careful.

Backhuysen.—An agitated sea. In front a boat; in the background two large vessels. Of that delicate steel-blue tone, and of that tender touch, peculiar to his best pictures.

Correggio (?).—The Virgin and Child, and St. John. Only a tolerable picture of his school.

Bernhard van Orley.—Portrait of a woman. Animated and careful.

Willem van de Velde.—2. A fresh breeze. On the right in the foreground are two fishing-boats; on the left in the middle distance, a large vessel. The sky is partially clouded. A sunbeam lightens up the foremost waves. Signed. In every respect of the finest quality.

Rubens (?).—Four couple, accompanied by amorini, are conversing and feasting with wine and music in a garden. This large picture is the pleasing work of a scholar of Rubens, in my opinion most probably Cornelis Schut.

Gaspar Poussin.—A mountainous landscape, with a piece of dark water in the foreground, and a waterfall on the left. Above one of the hills in the distance is a bright cloud. A spirited work.

Richard Wilson.—A landscape, with water in the middle distance. On the left of the foreground a tree, on the right a hill. Attractive in composition, transparent and warm in colouring, and carefully executed.

Cornelis Poelemberg and Willem de Heusch.—Two pretty and careful little landscapes, the figures painted by Poelemberg.

Murillo.—1. A very spirited sketch for his well-known picture in Seville, Moses striking the Rock.

Teniers.—1. A landscape with stormy weather. In the foreground three peasants, in the middle distance a castle. Signed. A delicate picture.

2. The companion picture, with figures angling, and a castle situated on the water. The silvery tones are beautifully carried out.

3. One of those pictures by Teniers representing a picture-

gallery. Here he has painted himself at the easel. A figure kneeling is looking at a small picture, another is standing behind. Signed. Carefully executed in a delicate and cool tone, which is only disturbed by the somewhat gaudy imitations of pictures by Rubens and other colourists.

JAN WYNANTS.—A landscape, with a house, and tree next it in the middle distance on the right, and behind it a warm light. On the left a tender distance. Signed. A very delicate picture.

CARLO MARATTI.—The Child next the Virgin, and looking up to her while he points to a book. The background landscape. An unusually pleasing picture by the master, with lovely heads, powerful and clear colouring, and of careful execution.

PINTURICCHIO.—The Virgin holding the Child on her arm. The background landscape. Of the earlier and best time of the master. The head of the Virgin is elevated and refined. Unfortunately stippled over in many parts.

TITIAN.—Venus and Adonis. The same composition as the picture in the National Gallery. The colour clearer and the execution more careful. The landscape very beautiful.

CLAUDE LORRAINE.—1. A landscape with light and lofty trees on the left, in the middle distance a piece of water with a bridge across it. Behind, on the left, a hill and a castle. Closing the foreground on the left some trees. A skiff upon the water. An admirable work of the middle and best time of the master. Very powerful in the foreground, the trees of warm tone, the distance of rare delicacy.

ADRIAN VAN DIEST.—1 and 2. Two landscapes : one of them representing a storm ; the other containing a misty distance. Two very poetical and successful pictures by this clever but unequal painter, who was born at the Hague, and whose works are to be seen almost only in England.

WOUVERMANS.—A landscape, with a sand-hill, lighted by the sun, on which are some figures. Two others are in a piece of water on the left in the foreground. In the distance are houses. On wood. Of uncommon warmth and power, great delicacy of touch, and luminous transparency of sky.

DOMENICHINO.—A landscape of circular form, about 9 inches in diameter, with Tobit and the Angel. On wood. Of great transparency and delicacy.

ARTUS VAN DER NEER.—2. A moonlight landscape. On wood. 8 in. high, 1 ft. wide. Very poetical and of rare power and warmth.

PARMIGIANINO.—The Marriage of St. Catherine. The Child is looking at the Virgin, a slender figure, seen in profile. St. Catherine is also in profile. In the foreground on the left is the powerful old head of a male saint; in a window two other aged heads. One of the most beautiful pictures I know by the master. The head of the Child is of rare beauty, and the motive graceful, without, as is generally the case with Parmigianino, being too artificial. The drawing is delicate, the colouring blooming and yet harmonious, and the execution very careful in a good impasto.

PAUL BRIL.—A small landscape; but one of his most delicate works.

ALBERT CUYP.—Moonlight on a piece of water. In front, on the left, trees; behind, a rock and a fortress. Very poetical in feeling, the effect of light admirable, and the execution careful.

MURILLO.—2. Four angels, life size. Formerly in a convent at Seville. Pleasing in forms, delicately shaded off in fine colouring, and carefully painted.

ARTUS VAN DER NEER.—3. The soft light of the moon, half hid behind clouds, is seen over a wide expanse of water. In the foreground are two men; on the left a boat. Signed. Differing from his usual moonlight compositions. The colouring as warm as it is clear, the treatment broad.

CANALETTO.—View of the Doge's Palace, and the Riva dei Schiavoni. Of the finest harmony of powerful and transparent colouring.

GUIDO RENI.—A young female figure, perhaps a Flora, with a light reddish drapery, leaning with the right hand upon a pedestal, on which are flowers, a rose-branch in her left hand. On a smaller pedestal is a vase with flowers. In the background blue mountains. In the beautiful head is seen, in the fullest extent, the charm peculiar to Guido; the motive is also very graceful, and the execution careful in a bright warm tone.

In this apartment is a very tasteful mantel-piece in marble, with two female figures holding festoons of fruit at the corners.

MURILLO.—3. A slave with a basket of flowers. Almost to the

knees. Very animated in conception, carefully drawn, and finely modelled in a cool reddish tone.

SALVATOR ROSA.—2. A landscape, with a tree on the left of the foreground, and on the right in the middle distance lofty wooded hills. In front, upon a rock, three men. Poetically composed, and of spirited rendering in rare force of colour.

CLAUDE LORRAINE.—2. A seaport. The morning sun is shining on a series of magnificent buildings on the right. On the left are numerous vessels and a tower. A shadow is cast on the water from a ship. On another vessel are St. Ursula and her companions. Here and there are numerous other figures. Among the pictures of this class by the master, this takes a prominent position for richness of composition, power, and transparency of foreground, tenderly graduated airy distance, and mild and warm tone of sky.

PIETRO DA CORTONA.—The Marriage of St. Catherine. Of pleasing composition; the Child very charming. The colouring is here very clear, and the treatment unusually careful.

H. KOECKOCK.—A storm, with a stranding boat. Signed H. K. 1842. In every respect one of the most successful pictures of this unequal master, and bearing comparison with the following pictures.

VAN DE CAPELLA.—A stream with both banks seen, in perfectly calm weather. In front on the shore is a numerously manned boat; further off other vessels. Vapoury clouds in the sky. The clearness and truth of the reflections are of marvellous charm.

PATRICK NASMYTH.—A landscape in the taste of Ruysdael; of pure feeling for nature, clear in colouring, and careful in carrying out.

RUYSDAEL.—1. On the right and left are houses; in the centre of the middle distance a small wood with a view into the distance. In the foreground on a road are a man and woman. Signed. Of the best time of the master. Very powerful in colouring, and carefully carried out in every part.

SIR JOSHUA REYNOLDS.—2. The Virgin and Child, St. John, and Joseph in a landscape. Judiciously arranged and warmly coloured, but little corresponding with the character of a Holy Family.

PANNINI.—View of the interior of the Pantheon, with numerous figures. A true masterpiece in delicacy of chiaroscuro and aërial perspective.

MURILLO.—4. The infant Christ sleeping on a white cloth. The ground dark. Of realistic conception, but of the utmost truth and delicacy of gradation. Certain transition tones in grey are charming.

RUYSDAEL.—2. Quite in the foreground is the fall of a stream. On the left a wooded hill with a water-mill, houses, and a church. On the right, more in front, is a tree, with a shepherd seated near it with his dog. The sun is lighting the clouds and the hills with a silvery tone. On wood. Also of the best time of the master, and carried out in detail *con amore*.

LESUEUR.—The Annunciation. The figures about ¾ life-size. Seldom is such an important work of the master met with out of France. Great tenderness of feeling is here combined with delicate and noble forms and charming execution.

BONNINGTON.—A flat country, with a piece of water with cows standing. Of very picturesque charm, warmly lighted, and of clear and powerful colouring.

CLAUDE LORRAINE.—3. On the right a tree and buildings; on the left a stem of a tree and a piece of water, over which is a bridge. Behind are hills. Of his earlier time; powerful in colour and careful in execution.

ETTY.—A sleeping child. Above, other children and angels. The first-mentioned figure is good, the others too hard.

CORREGGIO (?).—A fine old copy from the ' Vierge au panier' in the National Gallery.

HOGARTH.—Portraits of two girls with their little sister and a boy; also a cat and a bullfinch. A very interesting picture by the master, great transparency being combined with the animation peculiar to him. The execution is also very careful.

SIR THOMAS LAWRENCE.—1. Portrait of Lord Normanton. To the knees. Of lively conception, and of far more solid and equal execution than usual.

GREUZE.—1, 2, 3, and 4. Four pictures of his favourite subject, young girls. All genuine and attractive. The one with her finger on her lip, from the collection of Lord Charles Townshend, is of the greatest charm; next in merit to this is the one with a lamb.

UWINS.—A procession of Italian peasant-women. Graceful in

the heads and motives, transparent in colouring, and careful in treatment.

MORLAND.—A flat country, with a piece of water, with a horse rising from it. In truth of feeling, harmony of colour, and careful execution one of the best pictures of this careless master.

CRESWICK.—Girl crossing the brook. Delicately and clearly carried out in a silvery tone. A birch is particularly successful.

SIR JOSHUA REYNOLDS.—3. A gipsy telling a girl's fortune from her hand. The girl is laughing, but a young man appears to disapprove of the prophecy. The background landscape. Of great power of colour, but the young man too hard.

4. Una kneeling in a white dress, the lioness resting beside her. The background a midnight sky. Una is very tender and lovely, and the whole picture highly poetical.

5. Portrait of Henry Earl of Pembroke. Taken quite in front, in uniform. A bust picture. The features of this handsome man are delicately rendered, and the painting careful.

6. Portrait of Mr. Garrick. A delicate and warmly coloured little head. The dress and other accessories are only laid in.

Seven allegorical figures, life-size, models for the painted glass in the chapel of New College, Oxford. The window itself is very unsatisfactory, but there is no doubt that these figures are the most important works executed by Sir Joshua out of the field of portrait-painting. Though the figures are not near equal to the heads in point of finish, yet as designs they are very distinguished.

8. Justice and Mercy. A noble figure with beautiful features, in a light violet dress. The left arm, with which she holds the scales, is of very graceful action. The colouring powerful and clear.

9. Temperance pouring a liquid from one vessel into another. Her profile, with long dark eyelashes, is very charming, but too portrait-like.

10. Charity. Of maidenly and mild character, with a child round her neck, and two older children at her feet; the boy with a charming head. The power and warmth of the transparent colouring is extraordinary.

11. Faith. Standing on a pedestal, holding the cross with her

left hand and pointing upwards with the right. A noble feeling pervades the head,—the right arm is rather too stout.

12. Hope. Dressed in green, taken in profile, and looking upwards. The head well expresses the character of Hope, and the action of the uplifted hands is very speaking.

13. Prudence. Dressed in white, and looking in a glass. In her right hand she holds an arrow with a serpent twisted round it. Her profile is of rare beauty.

14. Fortitude. Taken quite in front and with a helmet, dressed in white, with a brown mantle. The noble features are powerful, but still delicate and feminine. Of extraordinary power of colouring.

15. Portrait of Lady Hamilton. Pointing with her right hand to her mouth. Of great charm.

16. A little girl in a white dress, in a go-cart. This shows in full measure that delightful character which this master imparted to his portraits of children, and is also in his warm and transparent colouring.

17. His own portrait, holding a drawing-book. Still in youthful years. Animated, soft, and warm, but somewhat emptier than the portraits which he afterwards painted of himself.

18. A little girl hugging a white kitten with reddish spots, which is winking its eyes with great satisfaction. Most charming in the Correggio-like flesh-tones.

19. Portraits of two sisters, both young and attractive, especially the one in profile.

20. Portrait of Mrs. Inchbald, the popular writer, in a black dress, with white scarf, in profile, leaning on her right hand, looking out of the picture with an earnest expression. In her left hand a letter. Conceived with great delicacy, especially the fine eyes, and spiritedly painted in very harmonious and clear colouring.

21. Lady Pembroke. The features of this lady are of a beauty such as nature too seldom shows us, and the pleasure with which the master rendered them is obvious in the clear colouring and unusual finish.

22. The infant Samuel kneeling in prayer, illuminated by a ray which falls upon him out of the surrounding darkness. Both in the beauty of head, in the reddish warm colouring, and the

very careful execution, this is the finest example I know of this picture.

23. Portrait of Miss Gwyn. Whole-length, in yellow dress. With the exception of the mouth, which is rather out of drawing, of great charm.

24. A little girl standing; next her a dog. The background of landscape character. Very childlike and naïve.

25. Portrait of Nelson. A bust picture. The painter has here lavished all his powers. The conception is as animated as it is noble, the colouring very powerful, and the rendering of the forms very decided and throughout solid.

In addition to these, Lord Normanton has since acquired another admirable picture by Sir Joshua, in London, but which, owing to untoward circumstances, I was not able to see.

GAINSBOROUGH.—1. Portrait of Pitt, still very young, standing, in a brown coat. Next him a table, on which is an inkstand. Behind him a deep crimson curtain. The delicate and shrewd features, of very earnest expression, are of masterly rendering. The left hand is also of great beauty. One of the finest pictures I know by the master, and certainly the most successful portrait of this celebrated statesman. Purchased from Lord Radnor.

SIMPSON (a scholar of Sir Joshua Reynolds unknown to me).— Portrait of the Duke of Wellington, taken in front. Among the many likenesses of the Duke I have seen, this one is conspicuous for characteristic conception, warm colouring, and careful execution.

CASPAR NETSCHER.—Portrait of William III. as Prince of Orange. Whole-length figure, half-life size, standing, in armour. His right hand holds the bâton of command, his left is on his helmet. A fight is going on in the background. Very characteristically conceived, and carefully painted. From an inscription on the back, it appears that this was the picture sent to the Princess Mary in England, though at a later period sent back to Holland, as a present to the head of the house of Hope.

ROMNEY.—Portrait of Lady Hamilton. Of great charm.

Among the rich furniture of the gallery, partly purchased by Lord Normanton, at the Watson Taylor sale, is a rich cabinet of *pietre dure* in relief, and a table of petrified wood, which belonged to Henrietta Maria, and later to Maria Theresa. The name of the Viennese artist who executed the rich setting of a later period is upon it.

LIBRARY.

Gainsborough.—2. Portrait of the mother of Lord Normanton. An elderly lady, in black dress. Delicate and animated.

3. Portrait of Pitt, drawn in black chalk on a brownish paper, the cheeks only touched with red. Upon the whole, of masterly drawing, especially the eyes and mouth, but the right nostril rather too strongly foreshortened for the view of the face.

Sir David Wilkie.—The sketch for the picture of the Will in the Gallery of Modern Paintings at Munich. Very spirited, and more powerful in keeping than the picture.

Guardi.—1 and 2. Two Venetian views of rare transparency.

In another room is a portrait of the late Lady Normanton, whole-length figure, life-size, by Sir Thomas Lawrence, 2. The background is of a landscape character. With her right hand she lightly touches a pedestal. The fine features of this lady, who was a blonde, gave the painter an excellent opportunity of exhibiting his power of gradation in the flesh-tones. In other respects, also, the picture shows in a high degree the elegance of conception peculiar to him.

DINING-ROOM.

Rubens.—A lioness writhing in death with open jaws. Life-size. Of the utmost truth and mastery, and corresponding in colouring and treatment with the picture of Daniel in the Lions' Den, at Hamilton Palace.

Finally, I here found a very successful work by Byström, the Swedish sculptor — the statue of a girl about to bathe. The simple and pure motive is borrowed from an antique statue of a nymph, formerly in Rome, now at Tegel, the seat of the late minister Humboldt, in the vicinity of Berlin. The delicate rendering in marble, however, is the work of Byström.

COLLECTION BELONGING TO SIR WILLIAM KNIGHTON, BART.,

Blendworth Lodge, Hampshire.

When last in Hampshire I was unacquainted with the existence of this collection, and therefore am not able to speak of it from personal inspection. I feel it, however, my duty to call the attention of the English connoisseur to it, the more so as the father of the present Baronet founded the collection at a time when his attendance on George IV. gave him the opportunity of purchasing good works of art. The pictures, which amount to between 80 and 100 in number, are placed in a gallery, lighted from above, 45 ft. in length by 25 ft. broad. The English school, including Northcote, Gainsborough, Benjamin West, Sir Joshua Reynolds, Sir Thomas Lawrence, and above all Wilkie, is reported to be admirably represented. Among the fifteen pictures by Wilkie is the "Spanish Mother." Of the older masters, the names of Luini, Titian, Bissolo, Tintoretto, Murillo, Velasquez, Albert Durer, Rubens, Rembrandt, Isaac Ostade, Teniers, Wm. Van de Velde, Gaspar Poussin, Ruysdael, Hobbema, Wouvermans, have been mentioned to me.

Drawings by Wilkie, Turner, Prout, and the old masters, and engravings by Albert Durer, further enrich the collection.

I have also been told of interesting pictures, especially a series by

Luca Giordano, at Uppark in the same county, seat of Lady Featherstonhaugh, and of a collection at Stansted Park, seat of the late Charles Dixon, Esq.

COLLECTION OF PICTURES BELONGING TO E. G. BANKES, ESQ.,
KINGSTON LACY.

Under the kind auspices of Mr. Danby Seymour, I proceeded to Kingston Lacy, arrangements having been made that, even in the absence of the owner, the unrestricted inspection of the highly remarkable collection, which comprises chefs-d'œuvre of the Italian and Spanish schools, should be granted to us. The house is very stately. A flight of marble steps conducts to the upper rooms; the doors also have marble panels; beautiful vases of valuable marbles are distributed here and there, and the frames of some of the pictures are skilfully carved in wood. The Italian and Spanish pictures were collected with great discrimination and success by the late W. J. Bankes, Esq., while those of the Netherlandish and English schools have been long in the family, many of them as long as they have been painted. I give the pictures according to the rooms they occupy.

THE GRAND SALOON.

Rubens.—1. Portrait of the Marchesa Brigitta Spinola, as bride of Doge Doria, in a splendid dress of white silk, with a large ruff, and rich ornaments of pearl and precious stones, seated in an armchair. The background architecture. Signed, " Petr. Paulus Rubens pinxit 1606." About 9 ft. high, 5 ft. wide. For one like myself, who have written upon the life and works of Rubens, this picture, painted in his 29th year, is of the utmost interest. The head is delicately conceived, the execution not yet of the freedom and breadth of his later pictures, but still melting, in the style of his master Otto Venius. The general keeping, also, of the picture is dark, contrasting curiously with his later luminous and light works.

2. The companion to the above. The portrait of the Marchesa Maria, Princess Grimaldi, in similar costume and arrangement, but with the addition of a hideous dwarf, who is drawing a red curtain from between pillars, and letting in a ray of sun. The head is here still more delicate, the effect of the whole incomparably more clear and luminous, and pointing more directly to his later period. The curtain alone still recalls Otto Venius in colour and treatment. Both were purchased by the late Mr. Bankes, in Genoa, from the Grimaldi Palace.

Vandyck.—Richard Weston, Earl of Pembroke, Lord High Treasurer of Charles I. In black dress, with the right arm leaning on a pedestal, a letter in his hand. A long staff of office is in his left hand. In the background is a curtain and pillar. The head is very delicate, and also the right hand, but the accessories are scenically treated. To all appearance painted about 1638.

The other five pictures here attributed to Vandyck—the portraits of Charles I., Henrietta Maria, the often-repeated composition of their three children, those of Sir John Balace and his wife, a Miss Bankes—I did not see properly, nor, must I own, did my glance at them give me any opinion of their value.

Frans Snyders.—1 and 2. Companion pictures. A horse torn by wolves, and a bull fighting with dogs. These are pic-

tures of considerable size and astonishing animation of dramatic
motive, though more scenical in treatment than his more delicately
rendered works. These were carried by the French from Spain
to Paris, and are reported to have been copied at the Gobelins
manufactory by order of Napoleon. After the peace, however,
they were restored to the hands of their owner, the Marchese
Altamira, were sent to London, and, together with the hereafter
to be mentioned portrait of Philip IV., by Velasquez, were sold
for 100*l.*

A large and beautiful wreath of fruits and flowers, with four
children in the centre, painted by a scholar of Rubens after one of
that master's known compositions.

RAPHAEL.—The Virgin standing, and bending down sidewards,
with her right hand raised, to the Child, who is seated before her
on part of an entablature, and looking round at her in lively action,
while, at the same time, he points to St. John. This latter is kneeling, quite in the corner of the picture, holding the cross with both
hands. In the background, on the right, are ruins; on the left a
steep hill with buildings on it. In the centre, more in the distance, is the view of a town with a church with a cupola and two
towers. On wood. About 2 ft. 8 in. high, 1 ft. 10 in. wide. On
the back is the initial of Charles I. and the crown. The composition is beautiful, and also the head of the Virgin, which has a
striking resemblance to the so-called Madonna del Passeggio, of
which there are many examples, the best of which, though not the
original, is in the Bridgewater gallery. The motive also of the
Virgin recalls that picture. The finest part of the work before us
is, however, the expression of the Child, which is truly worthy of
Raphael. But though disposed to give the fullest belief to the circumstances detailed by the family as authorising the name of the
great master, viz. that the picture passed for a Raphael in the
Escurial, that during the war with France it was sent away and
hidden in a wine-barrel, and then smuggled over to England—
though disposed to believe all this, yet I cannot convince myself
that it is really by Raphael's hand. Those who have compared the
works of the great master ever so superficially will agree with me
that, judging from the perfectly developed type of the cinquecento,
and the brown-red flesh-tones, this picture could only belong to his
later time; for this, however, the drawing is too unequal. The

shoulder of the St. John is even very feeble. On the other hand, everything combines to show us that this is a fine work by Giulio Romano. We here find the same strong markings of the roundish joints, the same hardness of outline, the same style of flesh-tones and very fused character of execution, and the same making-out of the plants of the foreground. The fact also of the picture's having borne the name of Raphael in the collection of Charles I. is very doubtful, as it does not appear in Vanderdoort's catalogue, which mentions the works of Raphael in that collection.* The preservation of the picture is excellent.

Giorgione.—The Judgment of Solomon. An unfinished picture of about 8 ft. high by 12 ft. wide, with ten figures the size of life. From the Marescalchi collection in Bologna. The painter has conceived the scene in a Roman sense, with a prætor or emperor sitting in judgment. In the centre of a stately apartment is King Solomon seated on a lofty throne within an apsis-shaped tribunal. On his left is an elderly judge of noble figure in a dark dress and vermilion toga. On his right a young man in a crouching position, and on the upper step of the throne another, the fine motive of whom recalls one of the lictors in Raphael's cartoon of St. Paul striking Elymas the sorcerer with blindness. Next the old judge, but more in front, is the pretended mother, a figure of great elegance, with fine features and noble expression. At her side is a young man pointing to the place where the master intended to introduce the living child. This is distinctly apparent by the motive of the executioner close by, a naked figure of slender proportion and dark-brown colour, with his right hand raised, obviously about to fulfil the sentence, though the sword is still wanting. On the king's right is the real mother, also a noble figure, in a robe of juicy green and a mantle of broken red almost slipped down, pointing with her outstretched and delicate hand towards the child, meaning that she would rather surrender it to the other woman than sacrifice its life. Behind her is another young woman. Further back a warrior and an old man. On each side of the tribunal is a foreshortened arcade of white marble pillars. This picture is incomparably the most important of the whole collection. Among the very few works,

---

* Judging from the subject alone, it might truly be the picture mentioned by me, vol. ii. p. 475, but the addition "whole-length figures, *half life-size*," does not correspond, and agrees far better with the Alba Madonna now at Petersburg.

generally speaking, of this great master, who occupies in the Venetian school the same position as Leonardo da Vinci in the
Florentine, that before us exhibits the most important composition.
The delicate feeling for style which is evinced in the balance of the
composition shows us also how thoroughly fitted he was for such a
task.   The freedom of the motives, and the development of forms,
point to his last period.   I have no doubt that the completion of
this picture was hindered by his early death.   The very circumstance, however, of its being unfinished, renders the picture on
technical grounds the more interesting.   It is evident that the
whole under painting was laid in a broken brown tone, and that,
while he availed himself of this groundwork for his shadows, the
modelling in local colours was confined only to the lights and half-
lights, and executed also in cool tones ; his own warm glow of
colour being produced by the operation of glazings.   The general
effect is already, it is true, harmonious, but almost throughout
subdued.

TITIAN.—1. Portrait of the Marchese di Savorgnano, from the
Marescalchi collection at Bologna.   Very elevated in conception,
and of masterly and careful execution in bright golden tones.   This
picture was not at Kingston Lacy at the time of my visit, but I
saw it in the British Institution in 1856.

2. Venus, surrounded with a quantity of jewellery, called " Omnia
Vanitas."   This picture also was not there.   Mr. Nugent Bankes,
whom I saw in Berlin in April, 1857, and to whom I am indebted
for various particulars concerning this collection, was of opinion that
this picture proceeded from the Orleans gallery ; but as I do not
find it in an old catalogue of that gallery, I am rather inclined to
trust the account given me at Kingston Lacy of its having been
purchased from the Marescalchi collection.

SALVATOR ROSA.—Portrait of Mr. Altham, first-cousin to Sir
Ralph Bankes, in the character of a hermit, with a Death's head and
an inscription referring to the vanity of the world.   Whole-length
figure, life-size.   The head is very careful, but the prosaic nature
of the features corresponds ill with the style of conception.

MASSIMO STANZIONI. — Portrait of a Mr. Bankes, painted in
Naples.   An excellent work by this capital master, who is rarely
seen out of Naples.

SEBASTIAN BOURDON. — 1. The Judgment of Midas.   Life-sized figures. Of fortunate composition in the style of his model Nicolas Poussin.

2. Europa and the Bull. The companion to the above, but not so happy in invention.

SIR JOSHUA REYNOLDS.—Portrait of Mr. Woodley—a family-picture. Half-length figure in an oval. The head, which is almost in profile, is charming, the rest is only slightly treated.

SIR GODFREY KNELLER.—A woman with a child. This is said to be an admirable picture by him, but I did not see it.

SIR THOMAS LAWRENCE.—1 and 2. Two portraits. The one of Miss Ridley he himself considered one of his best. I did not see either of them.

JAN MABUSE.—The Virgin and Child. Very small. Not seen by me.

GREUZE.—A sleeping girl. Reported as beautiful, but not seen by me.

DINING-ROOM.

TINTORETTO.—Apollo and the Muses, a ceiling picture from the Grimani palace at Venice. The composition feeble. Apollo, for instance, is unsuccessful, but the scenically treated execution is good. This picture, with two ceiling pictures by BONIFAZIO, recently purchased in Venice, is destined to ornament the ceiling of the library.

GUIDO RENI.—A ceiling picture in fresco. The Dawn, in the form of a strongly foreshortened descending Genius, is pointing with two staffs which he holds in his crossed hands to Day and Night, whom he is sending forth to begin their course. Day, a powerful youth, in red garment, and diffusing a warm light around, is soaring to the one side; Night, a beautiful female form, lightly attired in a blue mantle of stars, and surrounded with darkness, to the other side: both are looking back. From the Zampieri palace at Bologna. Both these colossal figures are of great power of colour, and obviously designed to be seen at a considerable height. The whole invention has something studied.

DRAWING-ROOM.

BERGHEM.—A very hilly landscape, with high rocks rising on the one side, before which are two fine trees. Between these is a

pathway leading to a cavern, and on the pathway are cows, a flock
of sheep, and a shepherd drinking water from a stream out of
his hat. On the other side is a high road, with a man and two
women, one of whom is on a mule, with two cows, a laden ass,
and numerous sheep approaching. Behind these, across a piece
of shallow water, are the ruins of several arches, and further still a
mountainous country. Signed, and dated 1665. About 7 ft. high,
5 ft. wide. On canvas. This stately picture, which is one of the
largest Berghem ever painted, was a commission given him, through
Sir Peter Lely, by Sir Ralph Bankes, for the price, including the
frame, as the painter's receipt, still preserved by the family, testifies,
of about 30*l.* This grand composition, taken in a warm evening
light, must be very effective. When I saw the picture, however, it
was very darkened and dry. The treatment is broad.

THE LIBRARY.

SIR PETER LELY.—1, 2, 3, 4, 5, and 6. Portraits of Sir Ralph
Bankes, Mr. Stafford, Lady Middleton, Mr. Gilly, Lady Jenkinson,
and Miss Bankes. These portraits, which were all painted for
the Bankes family, belong to that class of his pictures in which,
both in conception as well as careful and spirited execution, he
sought to approach his model Vandyck. Sir Joshua Reynolds
greatly admired these pictures.

ROMNEY.—Portrait of Mrs. Bankes, whole-length figure, life-size.
A beautiful woman. In comparison with Lely, however, this picture appears very empty and cold.

I mention here four pictures by ANNIBALE CARRACCI, representing the four elements by four scenes from Ovid. For instance,
Earth by the fable of Hercules and Antæus. I did not, however,
see them.

THE SPANISH ROOM.

This name is given to a very rich and tastefully adorned apartment, from the circumstance of its containing the Spanish pictures
belonging to this collection. The walls are covered with a leather
tapestry, which is one of the most beautiful of the kind I have seen.
The whole surface is gilt, with flowers and pattern introduced, the
spaces of which are painted with a red varnish, through which the
gold, shining like foil, has a superb effect. The painted ceiling,

which is divided by rich golden festoons of fruit into different compartments, came from the Contarini palace in Venice. The larger and centre compartment, of quadrangular form, contains the Apotheosis of an aged saint by PAUL VERONESE. Around are Jupiter, Neptune, Juno, and, as it appeared to me, Apollo. This picture is of great power and clearness of colouring, and of spirited and careful treatment. The pretty amorini with doves and fruit in two friezes at the sides show another, but also a very skilful hand. In the arabesques, in various small compartments, may be traced the always salutary influence of Giovanni da Udine, who, as is well known, returned later from Rome to Venice. The whole ceiling is a fine example of the later cinquecento taste in Venice.

MURILLO.—1. An angel, seated on a cube-shaped stone, is holding a cardinal's hat over himself, so that his face is thrown into shadow. This is charming in head and motive, and of a warmth and transparency of chiaroscuro which recalls Titian. It was doubtless cut out of a larger picture, and was found in Spain on the back of a dead French soldier, in his knapsack.

VELASQUEZ.—1. The picture known by the name of " Las Meniñas " in the Royal Gallery at Madrid. The Bankes family believe this to be a sketch for that work ; Mr. Stirling, however, pronounces it a fine copy, and says that the sketch, at the commencement of this century, was in the possession of the statesman Jovellanos. As I have not seen the large picture in Madrid, any description on my part would be unbecoming. At the same time I must confess that the very spirited and free treatment, the delicate silver tone, and the clear and deep chiaroscuro, did not give me the impression of a copy, and of a copy of very diminished proportions. May it not be possible that this picture, which was purchased long after the commencement of the century by the late Mr. J. W. Bankes, is the very sketch mentioned by Mr. Stirling?

2. Portrait of a Cardinal. Very animated and masterly, but one of those pictures in which the painter was carried away by his off-hand freedom into a broad and scenical treatment.

LUIS DE MORALES, called EL DEVINO.—Christ bound to the pillar. From the convent of Atocha at Madrid. The expression of sorrow is noble and intense, the fused treatment very finished.

RIBALTA.—The Virgin holding the Child before her, who is in

animated action. Two angels playing on musical instruments are also present. I am not able to judge as to the correctness of the name. The conception is worldly in character, and the colouring crude.

ZURBARAN.—S. Justa with a pitcher. Whole-length figure. Easy in motive, and of excellent keeping—the head more pleasing than important.

MURILLO.—2. St. Augustin, seated at a table, a pen in his right hand, looking up in inspiration in a strongly twisted position, and listening as if he heard a voice from above. Whole-length figure, life-size. The very animated head is of thoroughly realistic conception, but noble in feeling; the tone of the flesh golden. Accessories, such as books, are executed with a truth of nature rivalling the Netherlandish painters. This admirable picture was formerly in the possession of Philip Duke of Savoy.

HYACINTH HIERONYMUS DE ESPINOSA.—Portrait of Francisco Vives de Canamas de Faura, a Valentian noble, his right hand on the head of a fine dog. Whole-length figure, life-size. The correctness of the name I leave unquestioned. The conception has something stern and melancholy; the drawing is thorough, and treatment very broad.

ALONSO CANO.—A child sleeping on a white couch surrounded with a red curtain. Of great truth of form and colour, and of masterly painting.

MURILLO (?).—Two beggar-boys, one of them eating a bunch of grapes, the other a melon. Early copy of the picture in the gallery at Munich.

VELASQUEZ.—3. Portrait of Philip IV. in black dress, holding a paper in his right hand. Whole-length figure, life-size. The head is very carefully painted in a bright golden tone, and also the hands, especially the right, which is a model of truth in form and colour. This picture, which was painted for the first Marquis of Leganes, was afterwards in the collection of Count Altamira.

MURILLO.—3. St. Rosa in a white dress, with black mantle and veil both in one, receiving on her knees a rose from the infant Christ, who is seated before her on a basket. On the right is a ray of light from heaven; on the left, in the background, houses. Whole-length figures, life-size. In the expression of the Child, who is looking up, there is a sorrowful yearning, while the noble features of the saint express true humility. The execution in a clear reddish tone is very careful. The hands are in admirable drawing and action. Formerly in the collection of the Marchese Diogma at Granada.

PEDRO ORRENTE.—1 and 2. Two pictures of frieze-like form, one representing Moses before the burning bush, the other David killing the lion. These are conceived in a landscape form, and are lightly and sketchily treated. I am not acquainted with the master.

I know no other collection in England containing so many valuable pictures of the Spanish school.

LETTER VIII.

Pictures belonging to H. D. Seymour, Esq., Knoyle House — Pictures belonging to Lord Heytesbury, Heytesbury — Pictures belonging to Joseph Everett, Esq., Heytesbury — Pictures at Wardour Castle, seat of Lord Arundel of Wardour — Collection at Corsham Court, seat of Lord Methuen — Ruins of Glastonbury Abbey — Objects of art in and around Birmingham — Hawthorn House — Edgbaston — Endwood Court — Manufactories — Lichfield Cathedral — Collection of sculptures and pictures at Marbury Hall — Water-colour drawings belonging to —— Cooke, Esq., Manchester — Collection of pictures belonging to Samuel Ashton, Esq., near Manchester — Collection of pictures belonging to John Chapman, Esq., near Manchester — Pictures belonging to Jacob Fletcher, Esq., near Liverpool — Collection of pictures at Holker Hall, seat of Earl of Burlington — Collection of pictures belonging to Rev. Thos. Staniforth, at Storrs, Windermere.

PICTURES BELONGING TO MR. SEYMOUR,

AT KNOYLE HOUSE, NEAR HINDON, WILTSHIRE.

FROM Kingston I proceeded, under the escort of Mr. Danby Seymour, to visit Mrs. Seymour, his mother, at Knoyle House, where I spent a few days of great interest and enjoyment, and of the finest weather, partly in the hospitable circle of the family, and partly in excursions in the neighbourhood, for the purpose of examining works of art, to which my kind host obtained admission for me. In Knoyle House I found a small number of well-chosen pictures, chiefly of the Netherlandish school, for which I was unprepared.

JAN BOTH.—A landscape. In the centre of the foreground are two trees, beneath which is a traveller resting, and a laden ass. On the right rises a rocky and wooded ground. On the left is a horizontal hill. On wood. About 3 ft. high, 4 ft. wide. The composition is peculiar, the colouring of a clear and mildly warm tone, and the execution careful.

ADRIAN VAN DE VELDE.—A landscape with cattle. In the centre, in warm lighting, is a brown cow and some sheep reposing. Under a tree are shepherd and shepherdess, resting and conversing. The background richly wooded and hilly. Signed and dated

1669. Of delicate feeling, and carefully executed, though, upon the whole, somewhat dark.

ALBERT CUYP.—A sportsman watching for game upon his knees, and with a fowling-piece. Of the second period of the master, animatedly conceived and of warm and clear colouring.

JOSEPH VERNET.—View of a sea-coast, with rocks in the foreground; near the rocks figures bathing. Of the good time of the master.

MELCHIOR HONDEKOETER.—A white hen, in the open air, of the utmost truth and mastery of painting. This I am inclined to attribute to his earlier time, when his colouring was the most transparent.

WILLEM VAN DE VELDE.—A calm sea, with various vessels, most of them manned. On the left a coast. The sky is slightly clouded. The figures by ADRIAN VAN DE VELDE. A beautiful picture, of powerful tone and mildly warm lighting. It is very dry, however, and wants varnish.

JAN VAN DER HEYDEN.—A house among trees; a shepherd with his flock, and a horseman talking to a pedestrian upon a road which passes the house. Some sheep within a fence. On the left, in the foreground, a piece of water. The figures and animals are by ADRIAN VAN DE VELDE. A charming picture, of warm tone, and of the greatest delicacy of execution.

BERNARDIN VAN ORLEY.—The Virgin and Joseph adoring the newborn Child. A very pleasing little picture.

ALESSANDRO TURCHI, called L'ORBETTO.—A Pietà, painted, as usual with him, on stone.

PAUL POTTER (?).—A cow's head. Over life-size. In truth of conception and masterly and broad treatment, worthy of the master; but the landscape background is not of the same character.

The following pictures belong to a younger brother of the family, Mr. Alfred Seymour:—

LUIS DE MORALES.—The Child, seated on the lap of the Virgin, has with his right hand so placed a reel as to form a cross. The inspiration with which he regards this shows that he is ready to fulfil his awful destiny. Tears are rolling down the cheeks of the Virgin at the sight. Of elevated feeling, and very carefully executed in a tender melting tone. Another example of this picture is in the Berlin Gallery.

GASPAR POUSSIN.—An agreeable landscape.

JACOB RUYSDAEL.—A waterfall.   Genuine, but of that class of his pictures which, by the crudeness of some portions, and the darkness of others, make no pleasant impression.

PICTURES BELONGING TO LORD HEYTESBURY,

HEYTESBURY, WILTSHIRE.

I made the acquaintance of this accomplished and amiable nobleman with the more pleasure, from his knowledge of my late friend William von Humboldt.   He assured me that no particular plan had guided him in the formation of his collection, but that he had purchased whatever attracted his taste in the different countries where his career as diplomatist had led him.   He thus succeeded in acquiring a number of valuable works of the Italian, Spanish, French, and Netherlandish schools, among which, as I shall have occasion to show, are a few very remarkable specimens of the Spanish school.   I notice the pictures in the order which they occupied in the apartments.

DRAWING-ROOM.

PAUL VERONESE.—1. The Baptism of Christ.   Of landscape conception, and with only three figures.   The heads elevated, and the colouring powerful.

2. The Finding of Moses.   A small, upright picture.   In his cool tone, and, considering the number of pictures of this subject by the master, of little importance.

TENIERS.—1. An old peasant caressing a girl, and watched by his old wife.   Slightly but spiritedly treated in his scale of cool harmony.

LUCA GIORDANO.—King Philip II. inspecting the plan of the Escurial.   A rich composition, conceived as a landscape.   This is a carefully executed sketch for the large picture on the staircase of the Escurial.

THE COLOGNE MASTER OF THE WELL-KNOWN DEATH OF THE VIRGIN IN THE MUNICH GALLERY (there erroneously called Schoreel).—Descent from the Cross, taken from the celebrated picture by Rogier van de Weyden the younger, of which three examples exist, two of which are in Madrid, the third in the Berlin Museum. Only the figure on the ladder, and the expressions of some of the heads, are altered. The figures are about a third the size of life, and instead of the gilt ground a landscape is introduced. The execution in his luminous colours is very finished.

VELASQUEZ.—The sketch for his well-known picture "los Borrachos," in the gallery at Madrid. Here, instead of nine figures there are only six. The kneeling figure, who in the large picture is almost nude, is here dressed. Signed and dated 1624. Of admirable expression in the coarse reality of the powerful peasants' heads, and spiritedly but by no means sketchily executed in a warm tone.

TENIERS.—2. Interior of a guard-house. In the foreground a soldier trying to drum. A good picture treated like the foregoing, to which it forms a companion.

CARLO DOLCE.—His often repeated Madonna in profile, with the sky-blue drapery thrown over her head. The size of life, and of particular delicacy.

JUAN JUANNES.—Christ with the crown of thorns, and eyes red with weeping. A good copy of the often-recurring Ecce Homo by Rogier van der Weyden the younger, and so faithful that even the stippled gold ground is imitated. While we have here a new proof of the strong influence which the school of Van Eyck exercised upon the early Spanish painters, it is the more surprising that, instead of Rogier's Mater Dolorosa, generally the companion to the Ecce Homo, we have here one of portrait-like but noble character, of pale tone and intense and moving expression, quite of his own invention. The face is turned strongly to one side, the execution delicate and melting, and the ground the same as in the picture of the Christ. I do not venture to discuss the correctness of the name assigned, but I must own that this is one of the best specimens of the early Spanish school I have seen.

BERNARDINO LUINI.—The Baptism of Christ. About $3\frac{1}{2}$ ft. high and 2 ft. wide. Among the comparatively few pictures on a small scale by the master, this is the most beautiful I know. The Christ is of very graceful motive, of noble type of head, and of refined expression. The compassion expressed in the head of the Baptist is of a peculiar and prophetic character. A spirit of gentle humility characterises the heads of the two angels, who are holding the drapery of Christ on their shoulders. In the careful execution is particularly seen the *sfumato* peculiar to his master, Leonardo da Vinci. The landscape background is so delicately carried out, that I consider it to be by the hand of BERNAZZANO, who, it is well known, often executed this portion for the scholars of Leonardo.

BARTOLOMMEO SCHIDONE.—The Virgin holding the Child, St. John adoring. On the other side Joseph.* Of powerful colouring and careful execution. The same picture with figures life-size is in the gallery at Naples.

RAPHAEL (?).—The well-known Holy Family originally executed for Leonello da Carpi, in the gallery at Naples. An early and careful copy, somewhat hard in forms and dark in colour.

TENIERS.—3. A landscape, with few objects but peasants' houses. On the right, in the foreground, some peasants. Of great freshness and transparency.

4. The companion. Interior of a peasant's house, with seven persons on the left at a table. Of charming painting in a delicate silvery tone.

5. A landscape, with a large rocky cavern. St. Anthony in the foreground. One of his brownly toned pictures.

MURILLO.—St. John and the Lamb. In a silvery tone. This has unfortunately much suffered.

ZURBARAN.—1 and 2. Two pictures of saints. Whole-length, life-size, with landscape background. Of serious and dignified conception, admirable drawing, and masterly painting.

TENIERS.—6. A landscape with water, on which are towers and a bridge. Signed and dated 1646. Of delicate keeping, in a cool tone.

7. The companion picture. A landscape of similar character. A cow being milked in the foreground. Similarly inscribed, and of similar merit.

MURILLO.—2. The picture known in Spain as "las Gallegas" (Gallician girls). Two girls at a window: one of them, with common features, leaning on her right hand, is looking at the spectator with rather a bold expression, while the other and older one, with rather a cunning look, is hiding her face. Of very animated conception, of admirable drawing in every part, especially the hands, and careful carrying out in a somewhat grey tone for him.   Purchased in 1823 from the family of Count Altamira.

GUERCINO.—The Magdalen seated.   To the knees.   Of unusual nobility of form and expression for him, and carefully rendered in his warm brown tone.

JAN VAN EYCK.—St. Francis receiving the Stigmata.   Throughout of portrait-like character, though delicate in feature, and very earnest in expression.   The saint is kneeling before a mass of rock.   The crucifix, which appears in the sky, has not, as usual, six, but only four wings.   In front of the saint, his face covered with his hands, in a dark cowl, is the lay brother.   In the rocky landscape, which terminates at the horizon with snow mountains, are seen various small figures, and a skiff on a piece of water.   On wood.   8 in. high, 6 in. wide.   In the treatment of the equally delicate, solid, and miniature-like execution, this little picture agrees entirely with the beautiful altarpiece by Jan van Eyck in the Dresden Gallery, surpassing it, however, in the depth of the warm brown tone, which, with the exception of the wings of the Archangel Michael, has been lost to the Dresden picture by overcleaning.   This finely-preserved little gem was formerly assigned to Albert Durer, under which name Lord Heytesbury purchased it of a medical man in Lisbon.   It was probably executed by Jan van Eyck at Lisbon, during the time he passed there, when accompanying the mission from Duke Philip the Good of Burgundy, to request the hand of the Princess Isabella in 1428-29.

ANTE-ROOM.

GASPAR POUSSIN.—A fine landscape with grand hills, the foremost of which are in shadow, and those behind illumined by a sunbeam.

ZURBARAN.—3. St. Francis, standing in a dark space.   The expression of ecstasy is lively.   This picture is part of a set with the former.

4. A saint, with a skull.   Of great power of effect.   Also part of the same set.

DINING-ROOM.

Alonso Cano.—The Magdalen repentant. Half-length. Of true feeling. Unusually grey in the shadows for him.

Giulio Romano.—Marriage of St. Catherine. Well composed and of pleasing motive and forms. Also of spirited and careful execution, but hard in the outlines and dark in colouring.

Murillo.—The Virgin showing St. Joseph the Child sleeping on her lap. In front the little St. John adoring. A repetition of the fine picture I have described in Mr. Foster's collection, and the sketch for which I have also mentioned as belonging to Lord Overstone.

Nicolas Poussin.—1. A view of Ponte Molle, conceived with taste and of delicate keeping.

Claude Lorraine.—1 and 2. Two small landscapes, of a horizontal oval, both with a piece of water. These are delicate and clearly-coloured works of his best time.

Salvator Rosa.—Portrait of a man, evidently a well-known person, and whom I have remarked in other pictures. Of animated conception, but too grey in the colouring.

Nicolas Poussin.—2. Herminia on a piebald horse, seeking refuge with the shepherds. Finely composed, and Herminia of noble profile. The landscape background also excellent. The conspicuous spots of the horse, however, rather disturb the keeping.

Zurbaran.—5. The infant Christ on an ass, with Joseph and St. John. Coarsely realistic in conception, but the heads animated and of masterly treatment.

Carlo Cignani.—A Charity. A very pleasing picture.

Domenichino.—A landscape, in which buildings play a principal part, with John preaching, and his hearers. On wood. A picture of rich detail and animated execution.

A boy carried along by other boys in the character of a King. A work of charming humour, and recalling Velasquez both in that respect and in its spirited treatment.

PICTURES BELONGING TO JOSEPH EVERETT, ESQ.,

HEYTESBURY.

I was not a little surprised to find in the small house close to Lord Heytesbury's seat, belonging to this gentleman, some pictures which would take an honourable place even in the largest gallery.

PAUL POTTER.—On the left is a fence, with two brown cows feeding, and two reposing near it. Behind these, standing, is a young ox. On the right, in the middle distance, is another cow feeding, and three sheep. Signed and dated 1650. 2 ft. 1 in. high, 2 ft. 4 in. wide. This picture, which is of pleasing composition, is of masterly painting in a powerful tone, at the same time of broader execution than usual in proportion with the larger scale.

ISAAC VAN OSTADE.—The horses belonging to a well-filled vehicle being fed before a village tavern situated between trees. A horseman on a foreshortened grey horse is taking some beer. The background has a view of the village. A fortunate and rich composition, in a deep glowing tone, and of solid impasto.

JAN STEEN.—A man and his wife seated in a bower of vines before a house ; they have dined, and the dessert is on the table. While the woman is nodding the man has taken a book, and a maid is about to clear the table. The background is a landscape. The liveliness and characteristic point of the representation, the transparency of the colouring, and the equable and careful execution place this among the choicest works of the master.

BALTHASAR DENNER.—The portrait of an old woman who was frequently painted by him. Signed and dated 1726. His well-known minutia of execution is here united with a transparency not always his characteristic.

The following pictures also deserve mention :—

TENIERS.—Peasants fighting after cards. Spirited.

VAN DER HELST.—Portrait of a little girl in a blue frock. A bust-picture with hands. Executed in the more broken but delicate tones of the later time of this great master.

UECHTERFELD.—A domestic scene. A girl singing at the piano, another standing by her. More in the background are man and wife, and a dog. The agreeableness of the composition, the cool but harmonious colouring and careful painting, render this a charming picture by this second-rate master.

SASSOFERRATO.—A copy of the fine picture by Andrea Solario in the gallery of Count Schönborn at Pommersfelden, not far from Bamberg, and of which there are many copies. In the foreground are flowers.

PICTURES AT WARDOUR CASTLE,

SEAT OF LORD ARUNDEL OF WARDOUR, WILTSHIRE.

To Mr. Danby Seymour and his acquaintance with Lord Arundel
I am also indebted for the convenient inspection of these works of
art. The house, which is of considerable size, though with remarkably small doors, contains some very stately apartments, and a
sumptuous chapel of large dimensions. Among the numerous pictures I can only select those which are most remarkable.

LARGE DRAWING-ROOM.

JOSEPH VERNET.—1 and 2. Two pictures, one of them a tem-
pest on a sea-coast, the other a calm sea by moonlight. These are
distinguished for careful execution as well as poetic invention.

HOBBEMA (?).—A landscape with a wooded height, on which
are the houses and church of a village. Too highly hung over a
mirror to admit of an opinion, but at that distance I am much
more inclined to believe it a good work by RUYSDAEL.

SASSOFERRATO.—1. The Virgin with the sleeping Child. A
delicately painted but rather coldly coloured example of this so
frequently recurring picture.

2. The Virgin affectionately contemplating the sleeping Child.
A very pretty copy of the well-known and often repeated com-
position by Guido Reni, one of which is in the collection of the
Marquis of Westminster, another in that of Lord Overstone.

REMBRANDT.—A landscape, with a grey horse conspicuous.
This doubtless once fine picture has much suffered, and especially
in the background.

DRAWING-ROOM.

SIR JOSHUA REYNOLDS.—Portrait of a lady. Of refined conception and clever treatment, but unfortunately faded.

GERARD DOW.—The blind Tobias groping with his little dog
to meet his son. In the doorway is the angel. The room contains all kinds of furniture. On wood, 3 ft. 6 in. high, 4 ft. 4 in.
wide. This, the largest known picture by the master, is without
doubt the same mentioned by Lebrun in his work 'Les Peintres
Flamands,' as having been in the Bramcamp collection, and
thence sent to England. It was obviously painted at a time when

he had not long left his master Rembrandt. It is drawn with peculiar care—the bare feet, for instance, are of unusual delicacy for him—and carried out in a very harmonious tone.

GASPAR POUSSIN.—1 and 2. Two landscapes with high mountains and a waterfall. Finely composed, and sustained in his delicate, cool tone.

TENIERS.—A very large and somewhat scenically treated landscape.

SALVATOR ROSA.—1 and 2. Two landscapes with large trees, with banditti.

SALOON.

RIBERA.—A Pietà. Unusually elevated in character for him, but much injured with cleaning.

MICHAEL ANGELO DA CARAVAGGIO.—A shepherd with a dog and ass in a landscape. Of great truth and masterly painting.

VELASQUEZ.—A male head. Spirited.

GUIDO RENI.—A youthful little head. Of masterly rendering in a warm tone.

BILLIARD-ROOM.

PALMA GIOVANE.—An executioner about to behead the kneeling figure of Pope Sixtus. More happy in composition than usual, warmer in tone, and more solid in treatment. The headsman especially is a fine figure.

THE CHAPEL.

CASPAR DE CRAYER.—An Assumption. This is on one of the side walls. Though of worldly character of expression, yet it approaches Rubens in power and warmth of colour.

Here also is a beautiful relief in marble, representing the Virgin, the Child, and the little St. John, which, judging from conception and style of development, may be of the school of BEGARELLI of Modena. A very beautiful antique sarcophagus of verd antique, with a porphyry lid, vessels of Oriental alabaster, and small columns at the altar, of the same material, are highly worthy of remark.

From the castle we drove through the fine park to the ruins of the old castle, about a mile off, the stately walls and towers of

which, showing the forms of the Gothic style of the 14th and 15th
centuries, rear themselves upon a considerable eminence. In the
interior is a doorway in the Renaissance taste. Shady avenues
and grand cedars combine with these ruins in producing a most
picturesque effect, and the numerous visitors, disregarding the
rainy weather, proved the admiration in which this scenery is
held.

COLLECTION AT CORSHAM COURT, NEAR CHIPPENHAM,

SEAT OF LORD METHUEN.

Having seen some of the principal pictures formerly at Corsham
Court in the hands of other owners, I erroneously concluded that
the whole collection had been disposed of, and therefore suppressed
all mention of it in my 'Treasures of Art in Great Britain.' I
now find that Lord Methuen is still the possessor of the following
pictures:—

JAN VAN EYCK (?).—The Virgin and Child enthroned. On the
right a female saint, here called St. Anna, giving a pear to the
Virgin; on the left Joseph with a book; before him St. Catherine
seated. On wood. About 2 ft. 8 in. high, 2 ft. 2 in. wide. A very
beautiful picture by some Netherlandish painter, who partially
imitated the Italian manner, after the beginning of the 16th century,
and about sixty years after the death of Jan van Eyck.

ADAM ELZHEIMER.—1. St. Paul on the Island of Melita
dropping the Snake into the Fire. A small rich picture, in which
the tendency to the fantastic, the art of lighting, and the conscientious solidity of execution belonging to this rare master, are
seen in a great degree.

ALBERT DURER (?).—The Adoration of the Shepherds. An
early picture by LUCAS VAN LEYDEN, somewhat poor in composition, but in tone and careful treatment recalling the Last
Judgment by this master in the Hôtel de Ville at Leyden.

GIORGIONE (?).—Portrait of Scanderbeg, half-length figure.
An admirable picture by HOLBEIN, painted in his yellowish brown
tones in the first years of his sojourn in England. The colour is
unfortunately flaking off.

MICHAEL ANGELO (?).—Ganymede borne aloft by the angel.
A very careful and good specimen of this bold and frequently-

repeated composition, but as little the work of Michael Angelo as any other repetition I have seen.

CARLO DOLCE.—1. Christ blessing the Elements—a picture greatly admired here, corresponding throughout with the well-known picture by the same master in the Dresden Gallery, but inferior to that in execution and transparency.

BOURGUIGNON.—A landscape, with robbers. Very spirited, and of great warmth of tone.

MABUSE.—An early but moderate copy of the children of Henry VII. These frequent early repetitions prove how popular the admirable original must have been.

CARLO DOLCE.—2. The Magdalen in the Pharisee's house washing the feet of Christ. This composition, with figures life-size, entirely departs from the usual manner of the master, and is said to have been executed from a drawing by Cigoli. The painting is, nevertheless, very melting and finished; the shadows have darkened.

LIONELLO SPADA.—David with the Head of Goliah. A careful and warmly-coloured picture by this rare master, who succeeded in combining the power and truth of Michael Angelo da Caravaggio with the more dignified conception of the Carracci.

GUIDO RENI (?).—The Baptism of Christ. This appears to me rather a good picture by his scholar SIMONE OF PESARO.

RUBENS.—The spirited wolf-hunt which I saw at Lord Ashburton's; somewhat smaller, but throughout of so solid and masterly an execution, and such depth and power of colour, that, excepting Rubens, no one but Snyders could have worked upon the animals.

VANDYCK.—1. The Betrayal of Christ. Judas is about to embrace the Saviour, who is surrounded by the crowd of guards, one of whom carries a torch. This picture, which is about 9 ft. high and 7 ft. wide, belongs to the earlier time of the master. In the luminous warm colouring it still recalls Rubens, and is of extraordinary effect. It appears to be the companion to the Crowning with Thorns in the Berlin Museum, No. 770.

LESUEUR. — Pope Clement blessing St. Dionysius. Figures life-size. With the depth and purity of feeling which distinguishes Lesueur before all other French painters is here combined in this fine picture an unusual power of colouring and careful treatment.

CARLO CIGNANI.—The Madonna and Child. Very lovely and

attractive. In cabinet pictures of modest pretensions the painters of this time are seen to most advantage.

GUERCINO.—Christ and the Samaritan woman at the well. Painted in his clear warm manner, but empty in the heads.

ADAM ELZHEIMER.—2. The Death of Procris. The figures less fortunate than the tenderly-treated landscape. The effect of damp has spread a darkening crust over it.

CARLO DOLCE.—3. A guardian angel with a boy pointing upwards to a beam of light. A very elegant little miniature in oil.

PIETRO DA CORTONA.—The Virgin in glory adored by several saints. About 4 ft. high, 2 ft. 6 in. wide. In point of feeling, lighting, power, and clearness of colour and careful execution, a first-rate picture by the master.

VANDYCK.—2. James Stuart, Duke of Richmond and Lennox, with light curling hair falling on his shoulders, his right hand on the head of a greyhound, the left on his hip. Whole-length, life-size, in an elegant black silk dress. This picture possesses in a high degree that aristocratic, light, and easy style of representation so peculiar to Vandyck. One of the hands is, however, feebler than usual with him.

The above-mentioned pictures are all part of the original collection of Corsham Court, to which are now added the following important works inherited by Lord Methuen from the late Rev. John Sandford, who collected them during a residence of many years at Florence. I give them in the order and with the numbers of the catalogue which accompanies them.

No. 2. PINTURICCHIO (?).—The Dismissal of Hagar. Although I could only see this picture through a glass, and in a feeble light, yet I am convinced that it is not by the hand of Pinturicchio, but most probably a good picture by UBERTINI.

No. 7. NICOLAS POUSSIN.—A landscape, with the blind giant Orion meeting the rising sun, in order to regain his sight. A picture of the loftiest poetry of sentiment, of the time and in the style of the landscape with Diogenes in the Louvre. Painted in 1658 for M. Passart, later in the possession of Sir Joshua Reynolds, who purchased it from the collection of the French minister Calonne. Mr. Sandford brought this picture to England in 1820.

No. 8. ANDREA DEL SARTO.—Portrait of a man. Of masterly

execution, but not, as here stated, his own portrait. From the Ricci collection in Florence.

No. 9. GUIDO RENI.—Portrait of his patron, Paul V. From the Casa Torrigiani in Florence. Spiritedly conceived, and of masterly treatment.

No. 13. GIOTTO (?).—A small altar with wings. Interesting in parts, but only a picture of the school.

No. 15. SEBASTIAN DEL PIOMBO.—Portrait of Francesco Albizzi. This picture, which is mentioned by Vasari, has quite the grand conception of his later time, but also the pale and unattractive colouring of that period.

No. 17. TINTORETTO.—Portrait of a Procurator of St. Mark's, said to be of the Pesaro family. Cleverly composed, and warmly coloured, but somewhat loose in treatment.

No. 18. JUSTUS SUSTERMANS.—Portrait of Galileo. From the Pandolfini family, for whom it was painted. Of lively conception and broad treatment.

No. 23. A replica of Raphael's Madonna dell' Impannata. The subdued light in which this was placed, and the glass over it, rendered a close inspection impossible. At all events it is a fine picture, of careful execution and uncommon force of colour.

No. 24. A good cotemporary replica of the picture, by LUINI, in the Sciarra Colonna Palace at Rome, known by the title of " Modesty and Vanity."

No. 25. DANIEL DA VOLTERRA.—A Mater Dolorosa. The pale features very noble in character, and of deep sentiment.

No. 28. GENTILE DA FABRIANO. — The Coronation of the Virgin. A careful work of his earlier time.

No. 29. FIESOLE.—Death of the Virgin. Formerly the altar-piece of a chapel near Leghorn. In richness of composition, and variety of the most refined and beautiful heads, this is one of the most admirable works I know of the master, and at the same time in marvellous preservation.

No. 30. FRA BARTOLOMMEO.—The Virgin and Child. This picture looks very promising, but in the absence of light, and with the glass over it, I venture no decided opinion.

No. 31 and 32. UBERTINI, called IL BACCHIACCA. — The History of Joseph. From the Gaddi collection. In point of rich-ness of invention, happy motives, power of colouring, and solidity of painting, these are two of his best works, and also in excellent preservation.

No. 33. DOMENICHINO.—St. Catherine. From the Colonna collection in Rome. Unusually grand in conception, and broad and masterly in treatment.

No. 34. RIDOLFO GHIRLANDAJO.—The Virgin and Child, with the little St. John. A charming picture by this painter, who was the friend of Raphael.

No. 36. LODOVICO CARRACCI.—The Annunciation. I never before saw this master in so small and miniature-like a form. The little picture displays, however, great depth of sentiment in the heads, and uncommon finish.

No. 39. PONTORMO.—1. The Virgin with the Child and St. John. In expression and tone of colour nearly allied to his master, Andrea del Sarto.

No. 40. FRA FILIPPO LIPPI.—The Annunciation, with an animated portrait of the donor. According to Vasari, painted by order of Jacopo Bellucci for the church of S. Jacopo at Pistoja. Of very original motive, the angel presenting a lily with both hands to the Virgin. The heads noble, and the execution very careful.

No. 36 and 37.*—2 and 3. An angel and the Magdalen. Careful works by FRA FILIPPO LIPPI.

No. 40. GIOVANNI DI SAN GIOVANNI.—The Virgin, the Child, and St. John, in fresco. A particularly fine picture by the master, of the time of the decline of the school, in which Andrea del Sarto was evidently his model.

No. 42 and 43. SALVATOR ROSA.—Two landscapes of rich and remarkable composition, although in many respects somewhat dark.

No. 44. PONTORMO.—2. His own portrait. Of spirited conception, and admirably executed in clear and harmonious colouring.

No. 45. GUIDO RENI (?).—The Virgin and Child. She is of great elevation of character, but the Child unusually realistic. The colouring is of great depth and power, allied to Carlo Dolce.

No. 47. GUERCINO.—The infant Christ bearing the cross. At his feet the globe. Of original conception, and carefully executed in his transparent manner.

No. 48. CLAUDE LORRAINE.—A small landscape, with St. John

---

* The Numbers 36 to 40 occur twice over in the Catalogue.

in the desert. Painted on tin, with a notice at the back of his having painted this picture for a friend in acknowledgment of some service. The composition pleasing, and execution careful.

No. 49. DANIEL DA VOLTERRA.—Study for his celebrated fresco at Rome. Very spirited, and with essential differences of design. A picture on the back of this, the Crucifixion, is of elevated composition and admirable execution.

No. 50. LAVINIA FONTANA.—SS. Cecilia and Sebastian. A delicate little picture by this gifted lady.

GRANACCI.—The Annunciation. Formerly on the altar of the convent of S. Apollonia. A genuine but somewhat gaudy picture.

No. 52. LORENZO DI CREDI.—The Virgin, the Child, and angels. A genuine and in many parts pleasing picture.

No. 53. CORREGGIO (?).—The Fall of Phaëton. Although the height at which this picture was placed, the bad light, and the glass over it, allowed of no decision, yet the motives are so fine, and so much in the spirit of the master, that I cannot omit to mention it.

No. 55. CORREGGIO.—Cartoon of an angel in the Cupola at Parma. From the Casa Pandolfini. So graceful in motive, and so soft and grand in the forms, that I am not inclined to question the name given.

ALBANO.—Landscape, with Salmacis and Hermaphrodite. A fine picture.

RUINS OF GLASTONBURY ABBEY.

The ceremony of opening a railway gave occasion to Mr. Danby Seymour's family to remove to Glastonbury, whither all their hospitably-entertained guests, including myself, accompanied them. Mr. Danby Seymour is proprietor of an estate at Glastonbury which includes the ruins of the celebrated abbey, once the burial-place of the Anglo-Saxon kings. Though most of the party were in open carriages, yet the occasional heavy showers that fell did not disturb the general gaiety. On arriving at the pretty and spacious home that awaited us, the party was joined by Mr. Crawford, known as the founder of the now flourishing town of Singapore. The whole ceremony, attended by numerous persons who dined in tents, was as novel as it was interesting to me. The ruins of the abbey church, which are seen from the back of the house, are of great extent, but with considerable gaps. The best preserved part is the chapel dedicated to St. Joseph, which lay in front of the west side of the church, and was probably connected with it by a building on the same side. This chapel is a beautiful specimen of the circular arch, called in England the Norman style, and on the Continent the Romanesque. The whole formation of the building, in which the pointed arch already occasionally occurs (though some Gothic windows in the façade are evidently of later introduction), bears evidence to the close of the 12th century. The proportions of the building are very fine; a doorway in the façade, and another on the northern side, are richly decorated with admirably-executed ornaments. Among those on the latter are a number of small, now almost obliterated sculptures, which in the outer chamfer represent fantastic animals and comic groups; but in the inner display ecclesiastical subjects. They are both of very sharp workmanship. Both in the mouldings and in the framework of the windows—two on the north side, and four on the south side— occurs the zigzag ornament, the favourite feature of mediæval English buildings, in forms of application as rich as they are peculiar. Two capitals, also, now preserved on the mantelpiece in the hall of the dwelling-house, show, though injured, forms of great originality and excellent treatment. The arched roof of the interior has fallen in. The flat-arched roof of the crypt is, however, by means of strong bracings, still preserved. Some fragments of statues of the 12th century, still kept there, are unfortunately quite without form. Here also, gushing from beneath a rich decoration, are seen the clear waters of a spring which was formerly held sacred. The whole building, partially covered with ivy, has a very picturesque effect.

However defective the remains of the church may be, they suffice to show its original extent, and give a distinct idea of plan and style. This was without question one of the largest churches in England, having five aisles, the centre one at least double the width of the others. Of these the two outer aisles terminated behind the transept, while the two others continued through the choir. Round the middle aisle and the transept—an occurrence of the utmost rarity—ran three galleries, one over the other. The windows in the interior were enframed by arches in the wall. The choir and transept were raised about eight steps.   Judging from the isolated architectural forms, the church constituted a transition from the Norman to the Gothic style.   While the pointed arch was chiefly employed, many portions, and most of the ornaments, are in the Norman style.   Only two massive pillars, where the transept transects the nave (the most considerable of the present remains), show, both in their capitals and clustered columns, the entirely developed character of the Gothic style.   The workmanship of the ornaments in the church is excellent.

Below the above-mentioned chapel of St. Joseph is the kitchen of the abbey, built in Henry VIII.'s time.   It forms a considerable octagon, terminating in an airy cupola surmounted by a lantern, and is both internally and externally of good proportions.   On alternate walls are four fireplaces.   The statue of a bishop let into the wall is very interesting.   Judging from the form of the mitre and the style of drapery, it may belong to the 12th century.   Nor can I omit to mention a barn 100 feet long, also in the Gothic style, which belonged to the abbey, and which partakes of the monumental character formerly extended even to such buildings.   The walls, of immense thickness, rise to a considerable height.   The very narrow windows have the form of loopholes, though terminating in a trefoil at each end.   In order to show its association with a religious institution, the barn has on each side one of the signs of an evangelist.   The wooden ridge of the roof is of pretty and artistic form.

The day after the railway ceremony I returned as far on the way to Knoyle House as Longleat, the magnificent seat of the Marquis of Bath, where I took leave of this most amiable family, to whom I had been indebted for days rich equally in enjoyment and information, and turned my steps northward.

OBJECTS OF ART IN AND AROUND BIRMINGHAM.

The good star which had presided, with few exceptions, over my various excursions in England, was more especially in the ascendant during my visit to Birmingham.   I was so fortunate as to meet with my former friend Mr. Horsley the painter, who had taken up his residence for a time in Birmingham.   I was not only indebted to him for the most hospitable welcome in his own house, but, with the help of a charming little pony-carriage, he drove me to all the known proprietors of pictures in the vicinity, and procured me the means of seeing the Town-hall and the more important factories in the most agreeable manner. All this, which I should otherwise not have attempted at all, or which would have cost me much time, was further accomplished by Mr. Horsley's kind assistance and arrangement in a day and a half.

The lofty situation of Birmingham not only renders it healthy, but its broad streets and cleanly-built brick houses give it a far more agreeable aspect than that assumed by most manufacturing towns. The Town-hall, also, is one of the most stately edifices in England. It is built in the form of a grand Corinthian temple, of very good proportions, and with a basement-story in the rustico style. The chief apartment consists of a colossal saloon, sufficient to accommodate 4000 persons, in which there is a large organ : a concert of good music takes place here every Monday, the admission to which is only three-pence. Every philanthropist must hail with pleasure an arrangement which thus renders a noble and intellectual enjoyment accessible to the working classes. At the same time the manufacturers have shown a truly humane and Christian feeling by the way in which, by means of churches, schools, reading-rooms, and medical institutions, they have provided for the wants, spiritual and bodily, of their workmen. The manufacturers themselves reside in comfortable villas, surrounded with gardens, in the neighbourhood. I was kindly taken by Mr. Horsley to the following houses, containing pictures of the modern English school, of which I can only particularise the more important :—

HAWTHORN HOUSE, HANDSWORTH ; RESIDENCE OF
EDWIN BULLOCK, ESQ.

SIR CHARLES EASTLAKE.—Ruth sleeping at the feet of Boaz. This is one of the most remarkable works by Sir Charles Eastlake. The heads are fine in form, and of refined and elevated character, the whole carried out in most harmonious keeping.

COLLINS.—A morning-landscape, with very attractive figures. A chef-d'œuvre of the master in point of composition, clearness of colouring, and careful finish.

Here are also good specimens of LESLIE, ETTY, CONSTABLE, MÜLLER, LINNELL, and DAVID COX.

On the staircase are a landscape by RUYSDAEL, and fowls by HONDEKOETER.

EDGBASTON ; —— BIRCH, ESQ.

LESLIE.—Christ with Martha and Mary. This picture showed me the master in a new and also favourable light. The conception is dignified, and the heads of Christ and the Magdalen of delicate feeling.

CONSTABLE.—1. A large landscape. The masterly hand with which nature is here represented in form, colouring, and aerial effect, renders this one of his most important works.

2. Another landscape—slight, but spirited in treatment, and recalling Titian.

MACLISE.—1. Robin Hood and his band. Full of spirited and original motives.

2. A banquet after a masquerade. One of his largest pictures, abounding in the most original inventions, but cold in the flesh-tones.

ETTY.—Head of a young girl. Charming.

EDGBASTON ; JOSEPH GILLOTT, ESQ.

This gentleman, who is the principal inventor of the manufacture of steel pens, is a zealous lover of art. His pictures, which are choice and numerous, are placed in a gallery lighted from above, which he has built for them.

ETTY.—1. The Rape of Proserpine. A moderately large picture. Spirited, of very dramatic conception, graceful motives, and great beauty of female forms.

2. The three Graces. Also of charming motives and beautiful forms.

3. A girl bathing, and looking upwards. Of rare charm of expression.

4. Venus Anadyomene. Life-size. Painted from a model of great beauty of feature, and carefully modelled in every part.

I know of no other collection in England which shows this master to such advantage.

MACLISE.—The Sleeping Princess and her Court. One of his richest and most peculiar compositions.

STANFIELD.—1 and 2. Two admirable sea-pieces.

LINNELL.—A very successful landscape.

Good specimens of MÜLLER and DAVID COX are also here.

On the following day Mr. Gillott had the kindness to show me over his manufactory, and also his town-house, in which I saw the following Dutch pictures of the 17th century :—

ALBERT CUYP.—A large landscape. Two cows in the foreground ; the black one foreshortened. Also a herd-boy. In his second manner and of great power.

ISAAC OSTADE.—A landscape of great size for him, with several figures. In so dry and unsightly a condition as to admit of no further opinion.

Two pictures by RUYSDAEL, one by HOBBEMA, a sea-piece by WILLEM VAN DE VELDE, a large sea-piece by ABRAHAM STORCK, and other earlier pictures which belong to Mr. Gillott, were not then in his house.

ENDWOOD COURT ; —— SHARPE, ESQ.

MÜLLER. — 1. Figures praying in the desert. Very spirited and original.

2. A fine landscape.

And some other pictures.

Early that morning I had visited a large glass-manufactory under the guidance of the proprietor, Mr. James Chance. I here obtained some idea of the immense quantities in which this material is produced, and which are requisite for the supply of such a building as the Crystal Palace at Sydenham.

In the Messrs. Elkington's show-rooms also I saw much that was interesting, of which I may mention a large dish offered as a prize for the Warwick races, with an admirable copy of a Pompeian picture in the centre. Also some vases with the Apotheosis of Homer, and the Centaur family, taken from the silver vessels in the Museo Borbonico.

In Winfield brass-works I found a number of objects, especially among the chandeliers and bedsteads, of great beauty of form. The same may be said of Jennings's *papier-maché* factory. The excellence of the workmanship, and the elegance which pervaded all these establishments, filled me with astonishment.

LICHFIELD CATHEDRAL.

Of all the ecclesiastical buildings in England in the Gothic style, this cathedral, which is executed in a fine red sandstone, gives most the impression of the perfect completion of every part. This may especially be said of the three towers, one of which stands at the junction of transept and nave, and the other two at the façade. All three are finished up to the point of the spire. The façade, which has been recently renewed, and unfortunately only in plaster, has, upon the whole, a fine and rich appearance. Considered in detail, however, the seated figures in the gallery are too extravagant in action. Although of moderate size, the interior, with its three aisles and harmonious proportions, has a fine and imposing effect. The general architectural forms, the richness of the clustered columns, the beautiful and elaborate capitals, &c., are all evidences of the earliest and finest period of Gothic art, about the middle of the 13th century. Only the horizontal forms somewhat disturb the effect of the columns which transect them. The two side aisles are half the width and half the height of the centre aisle. The Lady Chapel, of somewhat later erection, though still of very beautiful character, and of the width of the centre aisle, forms the choir. The rich canopies of the stalls are most elaborately wrought in stone. Many of the windows of the choir are filled with painted glass of Netherlandish origin of the first half of the 16th century, representing scenes from the life of Christ and the Virgin, and especially the Passion. I found on them the dates 1534 and 1539. The scenes with architectural backgrounds, in the taste of the Renaissance, correspond with the mannered style of art which at that time prevailed in the Netherlands. The best of them are the portraits, which are true and animated. Some painted glass of modern insertion is very gaudy.

As regards monumental sculpture, I may mention a few statues of bishops of the first half of the 13th century, which are good in style, though of moderate execution. Also the monument to two young girls by Chantrey, of pleasing invention and careful workmanship.

The Chapterhouse, which is constructed in the form of a sexagon, is of very pleasing proportions. The same may be said of the Library above it, which I visited for the purpose of inspecting an Evangeliarium with Irish miniatures. It is in large quarto, approaching the size of a folio. The pictures of the four Evangelists are of that barbarous caligraphic character on which I have already commented. Various initials, on the other hand, are of peculiar beauty of invention, and of that artistic workmanship peculiar, at that early time, to the Irish. By far the most important object is a page entirely covered with ornamentation, and which, in distribution of space, beauty of pattern and colours, and precision of execution, may be compared to the finest specimens I have seen. Much of it, however, is defaced by the wear and tear the volume has undergone.

The gentleman who has the superintendence of the Library showed me the utmost possible attention.

COLLECTION OF SCULPTURE AND PICTURES AT MARBURY HALL,

SEAT OF THE LATE SMITH BARRY, ESQ., NEAR NORTHWICK, FIVE MILES FROM THE RAILWAY STATION, HARTFORD, CHESHIRE.

These objects of art are preserved in a red-brick mansion of no imposing effect externally, but containing handsome apartments, and commanding a beautiful view of the park, which is of considerable extent. On the left is a fine expanse of water. Having been favoured by the kindness of the late lamented owner with a letter to the housekeeper, I was enabled to examine the collection with the utmost leisure and comfort; being further assisted by a printed catalogue, enumerating above 21 statues, 19 busts, 6 reliefs, 10 stone vases, and 9 altars—all antique;—and above 326 pictures.

A colossal male statue, holding a globe in the right hand, is kept in an outhouse. The unfavourable lighting only enabled me to perceive that the proportions were heavy, the forms hard, and the whole joined together in many pieces.

THE HALL.

A vase about 3 ft. high, of the finest porphyry. The form beautiful, and the lid antique.

A very large marble vase, on the surface of which, in very high relief, is represented a marriage—figures about 2 ft. high. The bride appears, as in the Aldobrandini painting, enveloped in a veil, with the exception of her face, and very bashful. A stately female figure next to her points to the bridegroom — a noble figure, wearing the Phrygian cap,—who is drawn along by Cupid. Three Muses are also present; two of them, Terpsichore and Euterpe, accompanying the scene with the music of the lyre and flute, while Polyhymnia, who is represented with exactly the same motive as in the Apotheosis of Homer on the relief in the British Museum, is singing the bridal song. The free and beautiful motives show a Greek origin, while the moderate character of the Roman workmanship would assign the execution of the vase to about the 2nd century. Formerly in the Colombaro Palace at Naples, and purchased by the well-known Mr. Jenkins, who in my opinion not only undertook the restoration of heads, arms, and other portions, but changed the original form from the mouth of a fountain into that of a vase. The supposition that this scene represents the mystical introduction of Adonis to Venus, or to Proserpine, appears to me quite arbitrary. How far the following inscription, LOC H.S.P.S GRAECEI AE PF. RVFA POMPON. DIANAE, may assist to solve the question, I cannot determine.

In a glass case, near this vase, is a small collection of antiquities, statuettes, small painted terracotta vases, glass vessels, lamps, &c. Many of these objects are pleasing, but some are modern.

Among the altars of quadrangular form are some of agreeable and rich decoration.

A colossal statue of Antinous, represented as Vertumnus. In the upper part of the drapery which covers the lower part of his person he holds the fruits of the earth as an attribute of his godhead. This statue has a bad light between two windows, yet I saw enough to convince me that the workmanship is good, but that the head does not belong to it. The statue was discovered in the Baths of Hadrian, in 1771, by Gavin Hamilton.

The statue of Jupiter Stator enthroned, 6 ft. 9 in. high. The ideal character of the deity is here well conceived, and the execution in good style, but far from being carried out in detail. The nose, part of the eyebrows, a small piece of the under lip, portions of the drapery, and the great toe of the left foot are new. Formerly in the Villa d'Este, Tivoli.

Statue of Venus Victrix. Life-size, clad in drapery of very delicate material, which leaves both arms and the left breast bare.

Of good character and beautiful motive, but of moderate workmanship. The tip of the nose, the right hand, and part of the arm are modern. The left hand is wanting. Excavated by Gavin Hamilton at Torre Columbaro.

Statue of a Bacchante, draped, with the exception of the right side of the upper part of the person. Above the fillet, which is unusually low upon the forehead, is a wreath of massive flowers. The expression of the charming head is very characteristic, the motive pretty and original, and the execution, especially of head and drapery, careful and conformable to the laws of style. This statue stands on a circular altar, which is prettily decorated with three genii holding festoons of fruits, and with a shield and a tragic mask.

The torso also of a powerful male figure, though much injured, deserves mention for its good workmanship.

Among the busts are some Roman emperors of tolerable execution.

The mantelpiece in the hall is of that fine green English marble which nearly resembles verde antique.

THE LIBRARY.

VANDYCK.—1. The Virgin holding the standing Child on a parapet, St. John looking earnestly up at him, and holding up the scroll with the "Ecce Agnus Dei." The background a curtain and landscape. This is one of the best of the frequently recurring examples of this composition. The head of the Virgin is elevated, and that of the Child charming, and the execution in a warm tone, resembling Titian, is of great solidity. Over the fireplace.

BONIFAZIO.—1. The Marriage of St. Catherine, with St. John and the lamb. The background a landscape in the taste of Titian. The head of the Virgin is noble, and the general colouring of the picture fine. It hangs too high for any further opinion.

Two other Holy Families, of the same period of the Venetian school, as far as I could judge in the unfavourable places they occupy, are creditable but less important works.

ANTE-ROOM.

LEANDRO BASSANO.—A woman on a horse receiving a child from another woman; another child is on the ground. Sheep are in the background. A good work.

JAN LIEVENS.—Job in his misery. A capital work in the taste of Rembrandt, though far less powerful in colouring.

SALVATOR ROSA.—1. A picture erroneously called Christ on the Mount of Olives, but in my opinion representing the angel announcing the birth of Samson to his parents. The figures are disagreeable, and the colouring a heavy brown.

2. The Raising of Lazarus—the companion picture, and still more disagreeable.

CANALETTO.—An unusual view of the Grand Canal, Venice. Very clear in colouring, and carefully carried out in detail.

BELTRAFFIO.—An altarpiece. In the centre the Virgin, with folded hands, adoring the Child seated on her lap. Before her the donatrix, an old woman, whom the Child is blessing, and who is presented by St. John the Evangelist, who holds a large chalice. Between him and the Virgin are two male saints, the one with his eyes raised, and the other folding his hands and looking down on the Child. Behind the Virgin are two more saints, the foremost of whom resembles the saint looking down in the picture by Leonardo da Vinci at Gatton Park, while the other has a gloomy aspect. On wood, about 5 ft. high and 5 ft. wide. This picture is here called a Perugino, a title which a very superficial knowledge of the Italian schools of the 15th century suffices to set aside. Those better instructed will at once perceive this to be one of the rare works of Beltraffio, the admirable scholar of Leonardo da Vinci. The remarkably beautiful Child is modelled quite in the same way as that in the master's chef-d'œuvre in the Louvre; the other sacred personages have also the same decided realistic character as in that picture. The greater hardness of outlines, and the use of gold in the borders of the draperies and in the glories, indicate, however, a somewhat earlier period. The modelling, in an admirable impasto, is throughout excellent, and the preservation, upon the whole, good. After the above-mentioned picture in the Louvre, this is the most important work by Beltraffio I know, and also the most remarkable picture in this collection.

LODOVICO CARRACCI.—St. Francis praying before the crucifix, in lively action. This appears to be a genuine picture, but hangs too high and in too dark a place for me to decide.

TITIAN (?).—A good school copy of his Peter Martyr on a smaller scale.

VELASQUEZ.—Cupid in the open air, with small dead birds; next him two ducks. In the foreground cabbages and a melon. The Cupid decidedly realistic. Judging from the somewhat heavy brownish tone, and manner of the very spirited painting, this picture probably belongs to his early time.

ZURBARAN (?).—St. Elizabeth in a rich dress of the time of Vandyck, in her left hand a sceptre, in her right a coin. In the distance is a beggar. The portrait of some lady of the time of an excellent, but to me unknown, Spanish painter.

BONIFAZIO.—2. Susannah and the Elders. Very originally conceived and spiritedly painted in his warm colouring.

DINING-ROOM.

ZURBARAN (?).—St. Stephen pointing to a stone lying on a book. Whole-length figure, life-size. Rather too hard in outline, and too cool in flesh-tones, for this master, but by some good Spanish painter.

MICHAEL ANGELO DA CARAVAGGIO (?).—Christ and the Doctors in the Temple. The Christ is of too elevated a character, and the painting too tame, for him. The picture is, however, by an excellent master.

GUIDO RENI.—1. The Holy Family. St. John is presenting two doves. Very pleasing, but not further advanced than a spirited under-painting.

LE SUEUR.—A Holy Family; a rich, pleasing, and carefully executed composition. The character of the Virgin, however, is unusually worldly for him.

GUERCINO.—The dying Tancred lamented by Herminia. Well composed, but one of those pictures by the master in which his flesh has a disagreeable greenish colour.

GUIDO RENI.—2. The Virgin holding the swathed Child. The heads pretty, and coloured with unusual animation for him.

PAOLO FARINATO.—To this follower of Paul Veronese I attribute a Virgin and Child and four saints, to which no name is here given. It is also a good specimen of the painter.

PIETRO DELLA VECCHIA.—A girl singing, accompanied by a man on the guitar. A good picture by this imitator of Giorgione, here erroneously called a Frank Hals.

TINTORETTO.—St. Catherine. Whole-length, life-size. Slight, of very spirited painting. Erroneously called Paul Veronese.

Titian (?).—A large dog. True and masterly, but, judging from the tone and character of the landscape, decidedly by Giacomo Bassano, 1.

Paris Bordone.—1. The Virgin and Child surrounded with the little Baptist and five saints in a large landscape. Of great charm of warm colouring, but otherwise somewhat slightly treated.

2. Venus, Mars, and Cupid. One of his pictures with hard outlines.

WAITING-ROOM.

Annibale Carracci. — The cartoon for the fresco in the Farnese Palace, with Silenus on the ass, and the powerful figure of the satyr blowing the horn.

APARTMENTS UP-STAIRS—MRS. SMITH BARRY'S BOUDOIR.

Vandyck.—2. The Virgin in glory. Numerous saints above and below. Admirably composed, of spirited motives, delicate colouring and keeping, and with some portions carefully executed.

Rubens.—Three amorini occupied with harvest. One is mowing with a scythe, another cutting with a sickle, the third carrying the corn. The motives agree with three corresponding figures in a picture at Longford Castle, of which this appears to me the sketchy but most spirited first design.

Guido Reni.—3. A careful, and, for him, warmly-coloured sketch for his Murder of the Innocents in the gallery at Bologna.

Gaspar Poussin.—A beautiful landscape with a waterfall. The paint is flaking off, so that the picture requires immediate attention.

MRS. SMITH BARRY'S BED-ROOM.

Rubens.—1, 2, 3, 4, 5, and 6. Six sketches for pictures from the life of Achilles. All six are very spirited, but two especially, Achilles being bathed in the Styx, and Vulcan presenting the armour, are, besides that, carefully executed in powerful colouring.

Lo Spagna.—The Magdalen with the box of ointment. Small half-length figure. Of very elevated feeling and delicate execution. The glory and the border of the robe are in gold. I am not aware what name is here given to this little picture.

School of Ferrara.—The Adoration of the Kings. A good

picture by that cotemporary of Mazzolino who is characterised by a very red tone of flesh, but whose name I have not yet discovered.

TIEPOLO.—1 and 2. The Sacrifice of Iphigenia. Delicate in tone and of spirited and sketchy treatment. The subject of the companion picture was not clear to me, but it is of similar merit.

VANDYCK.—3. Portrait of Sir William Temple looking round. Of great animation.

GIROLAMO DA SANTA CROCE. — The Crucifixion. A small picture, full of beautiful motives and heads, and very carefully executed in a warm tone. The motive of the fainting Virgin is taken from the Borghese Entombment by Raphael. I know not what name the picture here bears.

MR. SMITH BARRY'S DRESSING-ROOM.

A family in the open air, in the taste of GONZALES COQUES, but too highly hung for any further opinion.

GASPAR POUSSIN.—1. A landscape of circular form. This promises well, but is hung in too high and dark a position.

A PASSAGE.

A male portrait, whole-length, life-size, in the open air. This looks like a slight but spirited work by PAUL VERONESE.

PORTRAIT PASSAGE.

Portrait of a Venetian admiral in armour. The background a view of the sea, with a galley. To the knees. Very animatedly conceived, and of masterly painting in a warm tone. The position too dark for me to decide the master, but recalling Tintoretto.

GERARD HONTHORST.—1 and 2. Christ on the Mount of Olives, and being mocked. The conception coarsely realistic, but the execution, in a warm tone, careful.

ANOTHER PASSAGE.

GIACOMO BASSANO. — 2. A saint adoring the Virgin, who appears to him in glory upon the crescent. Of more elevated conception than usual, and of masterly painting.

ANOTHER PASSAGE.

CORNELIS JANSEN (?).—A male portrait with a hand holding a glove. This appears to me a delicate picture by MORONI.

Nicolas Poussin.—1. A landscape of very poetical composition, clear colouring, and careful execution. In the foreground an angler, two figures drawing water, and four other figures in the middle distance.

A BED-ROOM.

Salvator Rosa.—1 and 2. Two fine landscapes with rocks upon water.

Pynacker (?).—A landscape of great depth of colour, and kept in chiaroscuro, with the exception of shepherds reposing in the foreground.

ANOTHER APARTMENT, CLOSE TO LAST BED-ROOM.

Gaspar Poussin (?). — 2. A landscape. Too unfavourably hung over the door.

Nicolas Poussin.—2. A very poetic landscape, with buildings in the centre, and lofty hills in the background.

Leandro Bassano.—A Holy Family in a landscape, with the little St. John adoring. A good picture.

A Last Supper, figures life-size, of very decorative but skilful handling, reminded me in many respects of Palma Giovane.

SERVANTS' HALL PASSAGE.

Il Cavaliere Liberi.—The Virgin and Child, who is embraced by an angel. Also three other angels. A good work.

Gerard Honthorst.—3. Christ before Pilate by candlelight.

4. Peter delivered from prison by the angel. Both good pictures. Another example of the last is in the Berlin Museum.

Besides these there are many pictures placed in dark passages, or one over the other, among which probably are some of merit. It was not possible, however, for me to see them.

WATER-COLOUR DRAWINGS IN POSSESSION OF —— COOKE, ESQ.

MANCHESTER.

This gentleman has a choice collection of water-colour drawings by the first masters in this line. As he was not present, and no catalogue in existence, I have given the names merely to the best of my judgment. Mistakes may thus have occurred for which I beg the indulgence of the reader, since I do not profess to have the same knowledge of this class of art as of the old masters, or of the oil-painters of the English school.

DRAWING-ROOM.

GOODALL.—1. The harvest waggon. Of rich and happy composition, warm and clear in colouring, and of masterly treatment. Dated 1853.

TOPHAM.—1. A mother drinking with her child in a hilly country. The heads pleasing, the effect of sunny warmth, and the handling broad and masterly.

GOODALL.—2. The erection of the Maypole. A rich composition, full of happy motives, and of clear and beautiful keeping.

W. WYLDE.—1 and 2. View of St. Paul's from the Thames, and another view of the banks of the Thames. These drawings are of powerful but dark effect.

TOPHAM.—2. A mother stooping backwards, and her child. The motives good, and effect transparent and charming.

HERBERT.—Marino Falieri, in his robes as doge, holding up his clenched right hand in lively action. Next him his daughter. Dated 1839. Of lively and energetic conception.

TURNER.—View of Windsor Castle. Judging from the happy choice of point of view, from the extraordinary effect produced, and the clever treatment, I am inclined to attribute this drawing to the hand of Turner.

W. WYLDE.—3. A hilly landscape of considerable size. True to nature, clear, and careful.

TOPHAM.—3. A gipsy woman telling a girl's fortune from her hand. Of excellent motive and expression, and of deep harmonious effect. Dated 1853.

CATTERMOLE.—Lady Macbeth putting the daggers in Duncan's bed-room. Her terrible beauty is quite conceived in the spirit of the great dramatist, while the way in which she looks towards the bed finely expresses her wish to do the act herself. The keeping is masterly.

DINING-ROOM.

CATTERMOLE.—A large landscape, with trees and ruins, in the vicinity of which a horse is being watered. A painter is drawing from a girl. Here also the keeping is admirable, though in many respects the treatment too decorative.

HUNT.—A young girl seated. Of astonishing power of colour. Other good drawings by this artist are also here.

T. S. COOPER.—A cow standing and two sheep reposing. True and powerful.

COPLEY FIELDING.—A calm. On the right a coast, on the left ships. One of his masterly productions, and very large.

W. WYLDE.—4. Turks reposing. Very picturesque, and of rare force of colour.

5. A couple dancing. Either Italian or Spanish. Graceful, of great power, and careful execution.

LOUIS HAGHE.—Monks giving drink to pilgrims. A large drawing of very artistic arrangement, astonishing power, and excellent keeping.

MACLISE.—The hand kiss. Very careful, powerful, and of singular truth for him.

SIR EDWIN LANDSEER.—Heads of two greyhounds in profile. Of extraordinary truth and broad and masterly treatment.

COLLECTION OF PICTURES BELONGING TO
SAMUEL ASHTON, ESQ.,
NEAR MANCHESTER.

Besides several admirable paintings and water-colour drawings of the English school, this gentleman possesses some pleasing specimens of the modern French school.

SMALL ROOM UP-STAIRS.—WATER-COLOUR DRAWINGS.

CATTERMOLE.—1 and 2. Two admirable drawings.

HUNT.—A kitchen. Of extraordinary truth.

FRED. TAYLER.—A lady and gentleman with falcons. Very animated, and of clear luminous effect.

CRESWICK.—A landscape of upright form. On the right, in the foreground, is a woman seated with a child, and a young man. On the left a woman and child standing. Happily composed, and of sunny effect.

T. S. COOPER.—A flock of sheep with twisted horns. Dated 1843. Masterly.

LOUIS HAGHE.—Interior of a Belgian hôtel de ville, with monks bringing a case before the judge. Of fortunate composition and admirable keeping. The heads well individualised, the colouring of great power, and the touch masterly.

SIR DAVID WILKIE.—Tam O'Shanter. Of animated conception, and carefully drawn in a cool and harmonious tone.

STAIRCASE.

E. COOKE.—A fresh breeze. A boat in the foreground. True and sunny.

CONSTABLE.—A very large landscape, with a rainbow, and figures crossing a ford in a boat. The background the cathedral of Salisbury. One of his chief works. Of great truth of detail and general effect, which is of extraordinary power. A faithful picture of English nature.

HERBERT.—Baptism of King Ethelred. Well composed, and of capital expression. The forms, however, harder than usual.

ARY SCHEFFER.—1. Christ lamented by the three Maries—a composition well known by means of Keller's admirable engraving. The feeling as intense and beautiful as the modelling is flat and the colouring pale.

THE LIBRARY.

MÜLLER.—A landscape, with the cathedral of Salisbury in the background ; a troop of soldiers with baggage-waggon in the foreground. A rainbow is in the sky, and the landscape is glistening with moisture. Signed and dated 1845. Of the rarest truth and astonishing force of effect.

THE DRAWING-ROOM.

EGG.—Henrietta Maria.

ELMORE.—The origin of the Guelfs and Ghibellines. Of great merit.

SIR AUGUSTUS CALCOTT.—A sea-piece, with an airiness of effect like Cuyp. Delicate and true.

TURNER.—Trees on a piece of water. In the style of Hobbema. Of airy warmth, but somewhat indistinct.

ELMORE.—Hotspur and the Fop. Somewhat crude and hard.

DINING-ROOM.

FICHEL.—A family concert. Rich and delicate.

PLASSAN.—A party of the time of Louis XIV. A young abbé speaking to a lady ; an officer present. Delicate and masterly.

POOLE.—A girl surprised bathing. Of graceful motive, clear colouring, and careful execution.

STANFIELD.—View of a port. Dated 1846. One of his capital pictures.

COLLINS.—View of a sea-shore. Powerful and transparent.

WEBSTER.—A concert. A pretty and diminished repetition of his large picture.

ARY SCHEFFER. — 2, 3, 4, and 5. Small but careful and attractive repetitions of his pictures from Faust. Four in one frame.

T. S. COOPER.—Three cows. True, powerful, and clear.

COLLECTION OF PICTURES BELONGING TO
JOHN CHAPMAN, ESQ.,
IN THE VICINITY OF MANCHESTER.

Much taste and knowledge has been exercised in the selection of these pictures of the English and earlier Dutch schools.

DINING-ROOM.

SIR DAVID WILKIE.—The Rent-Day. It is superfluous to say a word as to the subject of a picture so well known to the public by means of Raimbach's excellent engraving. All I need say, therefore, is that, as regards refinement of motive, individuality of expression, clearness and power of colouring, and solid execution and rendering of forms, this picture, painted in 1809, is the finest I know by the master. He received for it from Lord Mulgrave the modest sum of 150*l.* I believe that the present possessor paid about 2000*l.* for it. On wood.

MULREADY.—The travelling Druggist. He is weighing out rhubarb for a sick child, whom the mother, seen in the upper half of an open door, holds on her arm. In the corner is a dog and a birdcage. Very animated in the heads, and carried out with great harmony and care in a full and powerful colour. Dated

1827. On wood, and of the (for the master) unusual size of about 3 ft. high and 2½ ft. wide.

SIR CHARLES EASTLAKE.—A girl with a dove, called Irene. Elevated in feeling, and delicately carried out in very harmonious colouring.

STANFIELD. — A fresh breeze. Dated 1848. In truth and clearness of the water, general effect, and execution, this is one of his best pictures.

PAYNE.—1. View of the Doge's Palace, Venice. Of uncommon transparency, and very solid treatment. The reflections in the water are admirably given.

2. A view of the Grand Canal surpasses the first in the same qualities.

LINNELL.—Landscape with cattle. A cow being milked. With another the operation is over, and a girl is carrying away a pail of milk. The other figures are a boy, a girl with a child on her arm, and a calf. Also numerous cocks and hens. Signed, and dated 1829. One of the best of his pictures I know. Every part, especially the cattle, well executed, and the effect powerful and sunny.

T. S. COOPER.—A cow grazing, a goat, and two sheep ; a small picture, but attractive for its truth and solid rendering.

SIR EDWIN LANDSEER.—1. A black dog, the size of life, watching packages. In the distance are tired posthorses. Signed, and dated 1821, and therefore painted in his 19th year. The truth, extraordinary power, and careful execution in a good impasto, show how early the powers of this painter were developed.

ADRIAN VAN DE VELDE.—The coast at Scheveningen. On the right a church-tower. Various figures enliven the strand, the breakers on which show that the tide is coming in. A picturesque variety is produced by the warm sunshine and by the shadows of clouds. Signed, and dated 1665. Among the pictures of this class by Adrian van de Velde this is the largest and finest I know.

SIR E. LANDSEER.—2. Portrait of a dog looking up. Of wonderful truth.

JAN STEEN.—Merrymaking. Full of droll ideas, and animated, but not one of his delicately painted pictures.

SIR E. LANDSEER.—3. Three dogs watching a ferret, who is unearthing a weasel. Another ferret in a cage with an iron grating. Of the most delicate observation of nature, especially the white dog, and of masterly carrying out in a very clear and forcible tone.

LEE.—Two sportsmen, with hares and pheasants. Also a grey horse. Powerful and careful.

WEBSTER.—Recruiting. A large and rich picture. A young fellow who has enlisted during intoxication is seen before a house, with a tree next it, with his mother and sweetheart remonstrating. Full also of delicate and true motives in other respects, and for warmth and power of colouring and admirable keeping the most important picture I know by him. Signed.

CRESWICK.—A small landscape, with a water-mill. Sunny and delicate.

CRESWICK and COOPER.—Cattle at the foot of a large tree. Picturesque, powerful, and clear. Of the best time of both painters.

REDGRAVE.—Landscape, with a brick house on the right, and a wood on the left. True, forcible, and careful.

TENIERS. — A young peasant smoking. On the left an old man coming in. Solidly executed in a warm and clear tone.

DRAWING-ROOM.

SIR AUGUSTUS CALCOTT.—A sea-coast in the taste of Claude. Well composed and drawn, but cool and heavy in tone.

MACLISE.—1 and 2. The departure and return of Moses—from the Vicar of Wakefield. Of great humour and far more truth than usual, and solidly executed with good keeping.

WEBSTER.—2. A sick child at a meal, with a girl and boy begging for some of the food. Dated 1837. Very truthful in motive and expression, and also clear in colour and refined in execution.

3. Three children at a peep-show. One of them kneeling and looking in. Of similar merit as the foregoing.

HERBERT.—Lear banishing Cordelia. The same composition as in the fresco in the Houses of Parliament. Animated and careful.

TURNER.—1. Fishmarket on the shore. Of harmonious colouring and solid execution.

2. A landscape in which he has borrowed the lovely scenery of Sicily. High mountains of fine lines and a waterfall, with the

Rape of Proserpine very cleverly introduced. The whole conception is grand, the lighting and warm evening sky splendid, and the execution very fine.

PICTURES IN POSSESSION OF JACOB FLETCHER, ESQ.,

ALLERTON, NEAR LIVERPOOL.

These pictures are few but choice. Mr. Fletcher was unfortunately so ill that I had not the pleasure of seeing him. His brother, however, did the honours of the collection with the utmost kindness.

MURILLO.—The Assumption of the Virgin; an altarpiece. She is soaring upwards in very lively action, her left hand raised, and looking up to the left side. The hair is black, and contrasts very decidedly with the pale flesh tones. Over her white dress is a blue mantle. In the yellow-ochre glory are various cherubim, around her feet six angels, one of whom is in deep shadow. Below, by the sarcophagus, are seven apostles, most of them looking up, others down. In the tomb is a white rose. Formerly in the church of the Capuchin Convent at Genoa. The Virgin is entirely taken from a pretty model. The angels are warmly and clearly coloured, without partaking of the peach-blossom tint. Among the apostles, who are very harmoniously coloured in a powerful tone, the one in profile, quite on the right, is a noble head.

TITIAN.—The Virgin as Mater Dolorosa, with folded hands. The ground dark. Half-length. Signed. Formerly in the Borghese Gallery, Rome. Of the frequently-occurring examples of this composition this is one of the best. The expression is intense and noble, of a full but subdued and warm colour. The hands especially expressive in action, and excellently coloured.

PAOLO VERONESE.—1. A little picture, called the Triumph of Truth, representing a woman of very graceful motive, with Hercules with the club next her, and Cupid. The background is landscape. The same picture, with figures life-size, called Hercules and Wisdom, passed from the Orleans collection into that of Mr. Hope; and Mr. Fletcher knows of two repetitions in the collections of Lord Bute and Lord Ribblesdale. This is of extraordinary brilliancy of colour.

2. The repentant Magdalen.   Whole-length, life-size, admirably relieved against the landscape background.   Her golden hair harmonises with her green dress, which she holds with her left hand, while her right is turned towards her chest.   On the right, in a corner, is an angel pointing upwards.   On the left, on a rising ground, is a book, with a Death's head, and above it a bush.   In the beautiful blue sky are some white clouds.   Seldom is this master so large and noble in his forms, and so profound in expression.

JAN BOTH.—On the right is a hill, with a chain of hills extending from it into the background, the last of them very airy. In the centre are trees.   In the foreground a woman on a donkey, and a man next them.   Well composed, and of careful painting, but somewhat too red in the warm tone.

RACHEL RUYSCH.—Beautiful flowers in a dark vessel, and a large rummer glass.   Signed.   Of unusual force and clearness.

PANNINI.—A good architectural piece.

COLLECTION OF PICTURES AT HOLKER HALL,

SEAT OF THE EARL OF BURLINGTON, LANCASHIRE.

I was indebted to the kindness of the Countess of Hardwicke for an introduction to Lord Burlington, who received me most politely. The collection, which consists of a series of fine landscapes such as only the largest galleries can show, was formed in the latter part of the last century by Sir William Lowther, and, together with Holker Hall, passed into the Burlington family by inheritance.

I take the pictures according to the apartments in which they are distributed.

ANTE-ROOM.

CLAUDE LORRAINE.—1. The largest picture in an upright form I know by the master.   On the right is a stately tree, which rises almost up to the edge of the picture.   On the left a wood, with a palm-tree.   In the centre is a piece of water with a boat and two figures.   In the middle distance is a small waterfall.   More in the background a bridge; behind which, in a plain, lies a town outspread, while a lofty hill rises on the horizon.   At the foot of the large tree in the foreground is a Repose in Egypt, and I believe by the hand of Sassoferrato. The Virgin is holding the Child on her lap; an angel is presenting flowers, another folding its hands. On the left is Joseph, reading. This picture occurs in the Liber Veritatis, No. 88. No. 47 also presents a very similar composition. About 8 ft. high, 5 ft. wide. The tenderly warm horizon, and the clear atmosphere with silvery clouds, show that the time is morning. The whole style of the treatment, which is very broad, and the warm tone of the green, indicate the middle time of the master. The distance is of extraordinary charm. In the foreground, however, the over-blue drapery of the Virgin somewhat disturbs the harmony.

2. On the left a large tree, at the foot of which is Argus conversing with Mercury. Near them is Io in form of a cow, and other cattle. In the centre a dark mass of trees. On the right, in the foreground, a piece of water, and another in the middle distance. Behind, are lightly undulating hills. In the sky are reddish clouds. In the trees too much of a reddish-brown colour prevails. This picture has so much darkened as to be little enjoyable, and is also darkly hung.

3. The companion of the foregoing. On the right are three Corinthian columns, with entablature. Behind and beside them, more towards the centre, are trees. On the left, quite in front, are stems of trees. In the centre a small piece of water, clear as silver, with a small town, with walls, upon it. The distance terminates in tender blue hills. In the foreground is a shepherd, almost undraped, blowing the bagpipe. Behind him are goats. In the middle distance is another shepherd, who stands out dark against the water, and is driving his flock behind the ruins and among the trees. A charming composition, with very transparent distance, but unfortunately darkened in the foreground. Of a somewhat later, but still excellent time of the master.

Frederick Moucheron.—A particularly good landscape.

Tintoretto.—Clever portrait of a man in black dress. A bust picture with hands. The ground dark.

Sir Joshua Reynolds.—Portrait of Sir William Lowther. Of refined conception.

Hobbema.—1. View of a village. On the left a dark piece of water, more on the right a large tree.

2. The companion picture. On the right a rising ground with trees; on the left a broad plain with villages. A distant meadow is lighted by the sun. Both these pictures—1 ft. 9½ in. high, 1 ft. 3½ in. wide—are of rare warmth, freshness, and power. The last approaches Rembrandt in depth of colour.

PYNACKER.—A landscape, with a dark piece of water. On the left of the foreground a shepherd and cattle. Of very powerful colouring and solidly carried out.

BOURGUIGNON.—1 and 2. Two clever landscapes.

WOUVERMANS.—1. On the right a tree and a tent. A soldier close by, making love to a *vivandière*, and a seated dog. Two horsemen on a brown horse and a grey. In the distance a sportsman. On wood. A beautiful and transparent picture in his second manner.

2. A hilly landscape, in which two horses are being watered, one of which, a grey horse, is restive. Two figures are bathing. This appears to be a genuine and good work, but it is much sunk.

DRAWING-ROOM.

HANS MEMLING.—St. Christopher baptized by the infant Christ on his shoulders. Almost the same picture as in a wing of the small altarpiece at Munich, only smaller, and, as a single piece, of broader and better form. The saint is also differently represented. Of marvellous power of colouring. The landscape truly luminous, and the execution of singular delicacy. Excellently preserved. Most arbitrarily entitled Albert Durer.

CLAUDE LORRAINE.—4. One of his largest pictures, about 7 ft. high by 9 ft. wide. No. 126 of the Liber Veritatis. On the right, on a rising ground, a temple to Apollo; next it, overshadowed by trees, Apollo and the Muses. In the foreground the Castalian spring, which poets are approaching, with swans floating on it, and deer drinking from its waters. On the right, in the foreground, a very large river-god. In the middle distance a piece of water, and the distance of great tenderness. Of great grandeur and coolness of effect, and of thoroughly careful execution.

IL CIGOLI.—St. Francis. The head of much feeling, and warm and soft. The rest very dark.

RUBENS.—A landscape. On the left trees, through which the

warm evening sun is shining. Quite in the foreground two sportsmen, one of them shooting a bird. On the right a herd of cows, two women milking them, a third with a milkpail on her head. Quite on the left the view of a meadow. On wood. About 4 ft. high, 5½ ft. wide. As respects the deep feeling for nature and the poetry of the warm lighting, this is one of the finest landscapes of the master, though at this time rather dry and sunk.

JOSEPH VERNET.—1 and 2. Two good sea-pieces. The storm is particularly remarkable.

JACOB RUYSDAEL.—1. On the left an eminence with trees; next it a road. On the left a wood. The sky is grey. Though very dark, this little landscape is remarkable for feeling for nature and clever handling.

HOBBEMA.—3. On the right a group of trees, behind them a house. In the middle of the foreground a road, with some figures. On the left, in the middle distance, a village. In the centre brushwood. The sky somewhat cloudy. On wood. About 3 ft. high, 4 ft. wide. A picture of the first class in point of composition as well as size. Powerful, warm, and clear in tone, and as carefully as it is spiritedly executed.

VAN DE CAPELLA.—A calm sea. On the right, in the foreground, some boats. On the left is seen the coast retreating in perspective, and a boat with five men. Warm and clear in tone. A charming picture.

CANALETTO.—View of the Piazzetta. It hangs in too dark a place for any opinion, and looks more like GUARDI.

JAN BREUGHEL.—A large bunch of flowers in a vessel. Genuine and excellent.

WILLEM VAN DE VELDE.—A quiet sea. On the left a large vessel, from which a gun is being fired. On the right the shore, with a boat in which are two men, and another, about which three men are occupied. A beautiful picture of very warm colouring.

CORNELIS POELEMBURG.—A landscape with the youthful Tobit and the angel. This appears a good picture, but hangs too high.

GASPAR POUSSIN.—A landscape with a lofty hill in the centre. On the right in the foreground a dark piece of water, with two figures and a dog approaching. Fine in composition, but somewhat dark.

Verboom.—A landscape with buildings on a piece of water. Of sunny transparency, and very careful.

DINING-ROOM.

Vandyck.—Portrait of a young man in black dress, almost to the knees. On the right a pedestal, on the left a landscape. Of animated conception, clear colouring, and masterly painting.

Jacob Ruysdael.—2 and 3. Two landscapes which look very promising, but are too high for an opinion.

Bourguignon.—3 and 4. Two good pictures with horsemen.

Jacob Ruysdael.—4. On the left in the foreground is a cottage and trees, among them a willow. Quite in front a piece of water. On the right in some brushwood are two men and a boy. Light clouds in the sky. In the centre of the background is a windmill. A picture of the best time of the master, and of very solid carrying out.

Peter Neefs.—1 and 2. Interior of a church by day, and by candlelight. Two good, signed pictures.

Zuccharelli.—1 and 2. Two pleasing and, for him, particularly careful landscapes.

Pieter van Bloemen.—A cattle-piece. Good.

Teniers.—Interior of a peasant's house, with two peasants playing cards; two others are looking on, and two more are by the hearth in the background. Among the accessories a dog and a pitcher are particularly remarkable. A good picture, but somewhat brown in tone.

ANTE-ROOM.

Jacob Ruysdael.—5. View of an extensive level country, lit up by occasional gleams of sun. A delicate little picture, almost quadrangular in form.

Jacob de Heusch.—A landscape of capital and solid painting, but hung too high.

Buchtenschild.—1 and 2. These two sea-pieces by this maser, who is quite unknown to me, are allied to Ruysdael in conception, and also show great merit in execution.

Giacomo Bassano.—Christ on the Mount of Olives. This promises much, but hangs in too dark and high a position.

A BED-ROOM.

GAINSBOROUGH.—Portrait of the Earl of Burlington, father of the present; next him a little dog with pointed nose. The background landscape. Of animated conception, and delicately executed in a somewhat cold colouring of the head.

VAN SOMERS.—Elizabeth Wriothesley, daughter of the Earl of Southampton, with a large parrot. True, careful, and clear.

SCHIDONE.—Cupid. A pretty picture.

ROLAND SAVERY.—Daniel in the Lions' Den. An excellent work.

SCHOOL-ROOM.

J. W. STAP.—This is the signature of a master quite unknown to me, representing an old man reading, and a boy warming his hands. Judging from the whole style of art, from the truthfulness of conception, clear colouring, and solid execution, this picture may have been executed between 1530-40.

In this room is a very rich chimneypiece of fine wood carving.

LIBRARY.

This stately apartment contains the fine chimneypiece of about 1490, executed by the Lombardi family, who produced so many excellent works in Venice.

I was also favoured with the sight of some folios of drawings, among which are some of value. More especially I may call attention to two pen-drawings of THE SCHOOL OF THE VAN EYCKS.

COLLECTION OF PICTURES BELONGING TO THE REV. THOMAS STANIFORTH,

At Storrs, on Lake Windermere, four miles from the Station of the same name.

This collection, formed by the late Mr. Bolton, contains several first-rate pictures, and many of merit. They are seen in the roomy apartments of a house which commands beautiful views of the lake.

DINING-ROOM.

GUERCINO.—Lot and his Daughters. In the background the burning cities. Solidly executed in a clear tone, and one of the best specimens of a subject he so often repeated. Generally known by the engraving by R. Morghen.

A good early copy of Quentin Matsys' Misers, in Windsor Castle.

LIBRARY.

MURILLO.—Joseph giving the Child to the Virgin. The carpenter's bench is in the room. Whole-length figures, life-size. This realistically treated picture is very attractive for warmth and truth, especially in the head of the Virgin. Joseph's drapery also is of very good style, and the careful execution of a warm tone and good impasto. Engraved by Boydell. By far the best picture in the collection.

ANTE-ROOM.

A sea-piece. A gun is being fired from a ship. This picture looks very much like WILLEM VAN DE VELDE, but hangs too high for any opinion.

JAN ASSELYN.—Ruins, with a sportsman with a red jacket. A careful and pleasing picture of delicate tone.

GABRIEL METZU.—An apothecary with a book in a window-recess. A solid picture in his brownish tone.

A delicate female portrait recalls CASPAR NETSCHER, but is also hung too high for an opinion.

DRAWING-ROOM.

JAN BAPTISTE WEENIX.—A landscape, with John of Bologna's well-known group of the Rape of the Sabines introduced. Among the figures that of a seller of game is conspicuous. A good picture of the master, and of powerful colour.

GIOVANNI PEDRINI.—The Virgin and Child—the latter in act of benediction. The Virgin has something refined, the Child is feeble.

TENIERS.—1, 2, 3, and 4. The Seasons, in imitation of Bassano. Four small pictures of powerful effect.

CARLO DOLCE.—A male saint with a palm-branch. The ground blue. Very dark in the shadow. The saint is wrongly called St. Joseph.

CLAUDE LORRAINE.—On the left a dark piece of water, through which cows are driven, trees and a hill. On the right three figures, another piece of water, and a hilly distance. Reddish clouds in the sky. Formerly in the possession of Sir Joshua Reynolds, later in that of Mr. Hart Davis. Although these circumstances are evidences of its originality, yet the picture is now so darkened that it would be difficult to form any opinion.

There are also two remarkable busts of Pitt and Canning—the first good ; the second, by CHANTREY, admirable.

BILLIARD-ROOM.

JAN STEEN.—A party in the open air. In the centre a youth in a black dress playing the fiddle, and looking at an old ballad-singer, who, with a great basket on his back, is holding a sheet of music in his left hand. On his left arm is a staff with an iron crook. Next him, seated on the ground, is a girl holding a bowl, and next her a black poodle. Opposite the old man are two boys, one of whom, leaning on a pail, is listening with open mouth, whilst the other boy, his arms folded, is looking at the singer. Finally, a woman with a child on her arm on the ground. On the left a house surrounded with light trees; on the right a hilly distance. On canvas. About 3 ft. high, 5 ft. wide. One of the finest works of the master. Of admirable humour and character, and the warm effect of the evening sun capitally rendered in a solid impasto. Also in excellent preservation.

A large cabinet contains a rich collection of porcelain, with specimens of all the different manufactories.

The pleasure-grounds and hothouses are well worth a visit.

LETTER IX.

Objects of art in Edinburgh — Archæological Society — the Antiquarian Museum — Pictures, &c., belonging to Lord Murray — Pictures belonging to James Gibson Craig, Esq. — Works of art belonging to Mr. Playfair — Gainsborough belonging to Robert Graham, Esq. — Gainsborough belonging to Major Mair — Collection of pictures at Dalkeith Palace — Collection at Gosford, seat of Lord Wemyss — Pictures at Marchmont House, seat of Sir Hugh Hume Campbell — Collection at Broom Hall, seat of Lord Elgin — Objects of art at Rossie Priory, seat of Lord Kinnaird — Objects of art at Keir, seat of William Stirling, Esq. — Collection at Dunmore Park — M'Lellan Gallery, Glasgow — Collection at Bothwell Castle.

ADDITIONS TO THE OBJECTS OF ART IN EDINBURGH.

(Vol. III. p. 266.)

An invitation to attend the meeting of the Archæological Society in Edinburgh, in 1856, led me to visit this beautiful city for the second time, when the impression it made upon me was quite as great as at first, a sure sign that its beauties are of no ordinary kind. Meanwhile a grand and appropriate museum has been raised on the mound behind the Royal Institution for the reception of objects of art, in the apartments of which, lighted from above, the temporary but rich and interesting Archæological Exhibition was held.

As respects pictures, one important acquisition has been made in a specimen of that great and rare master LICINIO REGILLO, called IL PORDENONE, the rival of Titian. It is a picture of considerable size, representing the Adoration of the Kings, and was formerly in Edinburgh, in the collection of Lord Eldin. It agrees in composition, and in most other respects, with a picture of the same subject in Burleigh House, in which I first identified this master, and is in excellent preservation.

THE ANTIQUARIAN MUSEUM.

Mr. James Gibson Craig was the first to call my attention to this institution. I found a large room, and an ante-room, containing a considerable collection of early Scotch and Roman, and also some specimens of Grecian, Egyptian, and Indian antiquities, among which is much that is worthy of notice, and some objects even of great beauty. Another apartment contains a small library; and a fourth, portraits of the Stuart dynasty, and the remains of an early picture by a Scotch master, which is so remarkable that I must describe it more closely. It represents the Child surrounded with golden rays, and lying on a part of the robe of the Virgin; her figure is destroyed. The Child is pointing to himself. Inscribed "Opus Felicis de Scotia, 1488." Figures about half life-size, and painted on wood on a *gesso* ground. Considering the early period, it is a creditable production. The full forms of the body are well modelled, and of good drawing for the time, the colouring deep, and the treatment solid.

PICTURES AND OBJECTS OF ART IN POSSESSION OF LORD MURRAY,

GREAT STUART STREET, EDINBURGH.

DRAWING-ROOM.

GREUZE.—1. A young girl lamenting, with closed eyes, the death of the canary-bird which lies before her on its cage. Very truthful and delicate in feeling, and of very careful painting.

2. A schoolboy saying his lesson over to himself, and closing the book with his hand. Of very delicate feeling for nature in expression, and of excellent execution.

3. Sketch for the charming picture in the Louvre of the girl holding flowers. Slight, but clever.

4. A young girl of charming features and expression, and as powerful as transparent in colour.

WATTEAU.—1. A party in the open air. A man in an oriental dress, and a girl, are dancing a minuet. An excellent picture, of vigorous and warm colouring, and spiritedly treated.

2. A girl trying to blow a little windmill, which a boy holds before her, into motion; the boy is laughing at her eagerness. The background landscape. Very delightful, true, and spirited.

PATER.—1. Ladies and gentlemen; some of them in very easy attitudes. Very delicate and harmonious in keeping.

2. A small, but pretty picture.

Lord Murray has also inherited a number of antique objects of art which the late General Ramsay collected in Rome. Some fine things are among them, of which I describe a few more closely.

The flat relief of a horseman, with the chlamys and the petasus. About 1 ft. 2 in. high, 1 ft. 8 in. wide.

Also a fragment of a horse, and of a man holding it, of Pentelic marble. These are treated in the style of the Procession on the Parthenon, and are of rare beauty.

The head of Bacchus, with the fig-branch. *Mezzo rilievo.* In terracotta. Very noble in character, and of broad and careful workmanship.

A Bacchante in bronze, with a wreath of vine-leaves, lightly draped, and with the skin of the roe. Two bunches of grapes at the sides. A relief showing a very peculiar conception of the character, and of a soft workmanship truly conformable to style.

Bronze statuette of a Venus, on its original pedestal, holding her hair in her raised left hand, and in the right a golden *patera.* She is decorated with a golden armlet, and gold rings round her ankles. At her feet is Cupid, holding in his left hand a looking-glass, in his right, as it appeared to me, the apple, the prize of beauty won by his mother. The figure of Venus is about 4 in. high, the pedestal 2 in. high. Although the workmanship is tolerably good, yet the chief interest consists in the motives and gold ornaments.

A bronze vase of the kind called *prefericulum,* with the head of a youth, about ⅔ life-size, of singular delicacy and beauty of features. The treatment of the hair with little prominence is antiquated.

Athys, or Adonis, a small head of terracotta. The very delicate and soft execution corresponds with the effeminate character.

A marble bust of Julius Cæsar. The nose is unusually thick, and the forms very prominent. If this bust be antique, it is probably not earlier than towards the end of the 2nd century after Christ.

PICTURES IN THE POSSESSION OF JAMES GIBSON CRAIG, ESQ.

EDINBURGH.

I was indebted to Mr. James Gibson Craig for the kindest welcome in Edinburgh, and had the privilege of spending a very happy week under his roof. Our mornings were spent in visiting the collections of pictures in the vicinity of this picturesque city, and the evenings in society of the most agreeable kind, consisting partly of the fellow citizens of my kind host, and partly of the strangers whom the Archæological Meeting had drawn together. Mr. Gibson Craig possesses a large and admirable library, and some pictures, both curious and beautiful, which I proceed to describe.

UNKNOWN.—Portrait of King Richard III., in a black dress and black cap, in the act of drawing off a ring from a finger of his right hand. The ground crimson. A bust picture, about ¾ life-size. Of very frivolous character, and of moderate value as a work of art.

HANS SCHAÜFELEIN.—To this painter I attribute the picture of a girl in a black dress with brown trimming, and a gold chain about her neck, her hands folded. The conception is animated, the colouring pale.

FEDERIGO ZUCCHERO.—1. Portrait of Sir Walter Raleigh, almost to the knees. In very elegant costume, with white sleeves and breeches, and a black doublet richly adorned with pearls and embroidery. The decided character of the individual is excellently conceived, the tone of the flesh a reddish warm. The execution is particularly careful. This portrait is expressly mentioned in the Life of this remarkable man by Oldey, vol. i. p. 145 of the London edition of 1736.

2. The Portrait of Sir Walter Raleigh's wife. Though the companion to the foregoing picture, and also mentioned in the same work, it is so far feebler in drawing and execution, that it must be by another painter.

GIORGIONE.—A small landscape. In the brown but very warm and clearly treated landscape are seen, in the centre, the three thick boughs of a dead tree. On a road close by is a man, and further off, and only slightly indicated, another figure. In the middle distance are two trees; more in the background a group of buildings, forming a very picturesque line; and on the horizon blue mountains. In the sky are light silvery clouds. On wood. About 6 in. high, 8 in. wide. So cleverly composed, and executed with so broad and masterly a hand, that it is not unworthy of the great name.

BOUCHER.—Portrait of Madame de Pompadour, in a white silk

dress, a small book on her lap. She is seated in a garden. Very pretty.

SIR GODFREY KNELLER.—Portrait of the celebrated Duchess of Marlborough, still in youthful years. Beautiful and supercilious. Very finished.

PANNINI.—A rich and picturesque combination of early Roman ruins. A large picture of very powerful keeping and solid execution.

HOGARTH.—Portrait of a lady in profile, almost to the knees, in a yellow silk dress, with white gloves, and a fan in her right hand. The ground dark. One of his best portraits, the animated conception being combined with warmth and clearness of tone, and an execution equally spirited, broad, and careful.

SIR HENRY RAEBURN.—1. Portrait of a lady. Half-length figure. Delicate in conception and tone. The head of careful painting.

2. A male portrait. Of animated conception. Carefully carried out in a clear tone allied to Rembrandt.

SIR DAVID WILKIE.—Two girls standing and listening to a Highlander playing the bagpipe. Next him his dog. From a poem by Burns. Signed and dated 1823. On wood. About 1 ft. high, 1 ft. 5 in. wide. In full daylight, and of masterly carrying out. The head of one of the girls of exquisite chiaroscuro. The landscape background of the utmost transparency. Purchased by the present owner for 400*l*.

THOMSON OF DUDDINGSTONE.—1. View of the Castle of Dunbar. Well put together, and of delicate gradation of colour.

2. A small landscape, of much merit.

M'CULLOCH.—Mountains and a sunny plain, seen in happy contrast. Of broad and masterly execution.

Also a water-colour drawing by ALLAN, called the "Scotch Hogarth," representing a young man reproved in kirk for frail conduct. Full of characteristic and humorous features. -Signed and dated 1792.

Finally, I must mention a small model of Michael Angelo's Moses in terracotta, about 1 ft. 6 in. high, which was purchased in Rome in 1802, by the well-known Mr. James Irvine, for the late John Clerk, Esq., and afterwards came into the possession of Lord Eldin. The workmanship is intelligent and careful.

WORKS OF ART BELONGING TO MR. PLAYFAIR, THE ARCHITECT.

This gentleman is the architect of a portion of the stately University building, of the imposing mass called Donaldson's Hospital, and of several other Edinburgh edifices.

DRAWING-ROOM.

SIR HENRY RAEBURN.—Portrait of Playfair the metaphysician, uncle of the architect. To the knees, seated. Of very animated conception, admirable keeping, and carefully rendered in a powerful tone.

THOMSON OF DUDDINGSTONE.—A dark sea in the foreground, in the distance grand rocks. A large picture of very poetical conception and good keeping; but, owing to a defective technical knowledge, much cracked.

DAVID ROBERTS.—A very happily-chosen and admirably-executed view of Donaldson's Hospital.

THE HALL.

CHANTREY.—Bust of Playfair the metaphysician, in marble. Of animated conception, with all the wrinkles and other details of the skin carried out with great minutiæ, but also great mastery.

I was indebted to my kind host Mr. James Gibson Craig for the admission to two families, in each of which I saw an admirable portrait by GAINSBOROUGH.

The one is in the possesssion of Mr. Robert Graham of Balgowan, and represents the Honourable Mrs. Graham, wife of General Graham, afterwards Lord Lynedoch, and daughter of Lord Cathcart. Full-length figure, life-size, standing. In the beautiful and delicate features appears an air of youthful disdain. The face is admirably modelled, and of clear and delicate colour. The beautiful hands are also finely painted and set in action. The clear and cool tone prevailing in her dress contrasts well with the vigorous crimson of the lower part of the figure. The background is of a landscape character, the keeping admirable. A study from nature for this picture, reported to be of the highest beauty, was unfortunately not visible. The circumstance of this lady's having died in the freshest bloom of her youth gives this picture an additional interest.

The other Gainsborough portrait, belonging to Mrs. Mair, wife of Major Mair, represents her grandmother, Mrs. Siddons, at the age of twenty-five. She is taken seated. The fine and noble features of the most intellectual expression are seen greatly to their advantage in profile. The motive of the hands is easy, and they are well painted. The cool colours of the dress are well relieved against a crimson curtain. The flesh-tones are unusually warm for him, and the execution throughout solid and careful. To the knees.

COLLECTION OF PICTURES AT DALKEITH PALACE,
SEAT OF THE DUKE OF BUCCLEUCH, NEAR EDINBURGH.

This time I succeeded in visiting Dalkeith Palace, and am thus enabled to describe its contents from personal observation, whereas the notice given in vol. iii. p. 313, was only an extract from Black's Guide through Scotland.

ENTRANCE HALL.

SIR DAVID WILKIE. — Portrait of George IV. More than half-length. Of animated conception and great power of colour.

MARBLE HALL.

CLAUDE LORRAINE.—1. Quite on the left a circular temple with Doric columns, with groups of trees next it. In the middle distance, almost in the centre, a bridge. On the right a view of the sea, with the island of Capri on the horizon. Behind the temple a chain of hills retreating into the distance. Under the trees the Apostle Philip and the Eunuch. A rich and beautiful composition of the middle time of the master. Now somewhat sunk.

CAMPBELL.—Marble statue of the Duke of Wellington. Very like, and of careful workmanship.

STAIRCASE.

HOLBEIN.—Sir Nicholas Carew, master of the horse to Henry VIII., in armour. A curtain behind. More than half-length. Of very animated conception, and masterly carrying out in every part, especially the hands, in a warm tone and in powerful colour.

Titian (?).—The fragment of a burnt picture. The Duke of Parma as a child. Although of great merit, yet the great name given to it appears to me questionable.

BREAKFAST-ROOM.

Guardi (?).—The chief views of Venice. Judging from tone and treatment I am more inclined to attribute these pictures to the hand of Bernardo Bellotto.

Pannini.—1 and 2. The Baths of Titus, and Roman ruins. Two large pictures, the second especially admirable.

The torso of an antique female statue, of Parian marble, of good workmanship, especially of the drapery. The head is modern. This is remarkable, as having been found in England.

GALLERY.

Gainsborough.—1 and 2. Portraits of the Duke and Duchess of Montague. Both seated—whole-length figures, life-size. Of very true and refined conception, and carefully executed in his cool tones.

Sir Joshua Reynolds.—1. Elizabeth Duchess of Buccleuch, with her daughter. Whole-length, life-size. Of very attractive composition, and as warm as transparent in colour.

The other pictures preserved here, by Sir Joshua, belong also to his most remarkable works, especially a boy leaning, in a landscape, with a dog next him. 2.

Claude Lorraine.—2. A landscape of fine composition, with a sea-view in sunny lighting. Of extraordinary depth of tone and solid treatment.

Ruysdael.—A wooded landscape, of great power.

Wouvermans. — A stag-hunt. A remarkable work of the master.

Wynants.—A landscape of great truth of nature.

Vandyck.—1. A whole-length male portrait. The head very refined.

Rembrandt.—A female portrait, taken in front, and almost to the knees. Of marvellous power and transparency and careful finish.

Joseph Vernet.—A very good landscape.

Andrea del Sarto (?).—An altarpiece. Six saints, two of whom are kneeling in adoration of the somewhat small crucifix appearing in the clouds. The composition is fine, and decidedly belongs to the master. Also some of the heads are beautiful, for instance that of the kneeling saint on the left. The fact, however, that many portions are heavy and dark, and that the picture is painted on canvas, leads me to believe it an excellent school-copy.

In another room is a picture by VANDYCK, 2. representing two youths. Of warm tone and careful execution.

SMALL ROOM.

SALVATOR ROSA.—A landscape of very poetic composition, but now much darkened.

DRAWING-ROOM.

CANALETTO.—1, 2, 3, 4, 5, and 6. Six views of Venice, painted for the Buccleuch family. In size, transparency, power of colour, and careful finish, they belong to his best works.

7. A view of Montague House, Whitehall, is very interesting.

COLLECTION OF PICTURES AT GOSFORD HOUSE,

SEAT OF THE EARL OF WEMYSS.

I had the advantage, accompanied by Mr. Gibson Craig, to be received by Lady Wemyss, who took me over the principal apartments, which contain a large number of pictures. I was indebted to Lord Elcho, son of the Earl of Wemyss, for calling my attention to this collection.

SMALL ROOM NEXT THE DRAWING-ROOM.

JACOB RUYSDAEL.—1 and 2. View of the plain and town of Harlem. Two rather small pictures of equal size and almost quadrangular form. The one represents a house in the foreground, with a sunlit bleaching-ground, and more on the left, in the middle distance, the town with the church. The sky, covered with dark clouds, is of peculiar beauty. The other has a piece of water quite in front, and rather on the right, in the middle distance, a wood, above which the tower of the town appears. In the background is a very bright ray of sun, which, with a sunny cloud seen behind a dark one, produces an effect as charming as it is striking. Both pictures belong to his very refined works.

ADRIAN VAN DER WERFF.—Lot and his Daughters. A delicate repetition of the picture in the Museum at Berlin, on a smaller scale.

HOGARTH.—The picture from the Harlot's Progress where she is upsetting the tea-table; known by the engraving. One of his coarser works.

ARTOIS.—A large and admirable landscape.

QUENTIN MATSYS (?).—An old school copy of the Misers.

DRAWING-ROOM.

TENIERS.—In the foreground, on the right, seated at a table, are a young man smoking, and an old one filling his pipe. On the left, in the distance, is a woman with a beer-glass. Signed. A small work by the master.

TENIERS THE ELDER.—A rocky landscape. St. Anthony before a cave. Well composed, but very brown.

CLAUDE LORRAINE.—The same composition I have described in the picture at Dalkeith Palace. This one, however, left a more favourable impression on my mind. The sky is particularly clear and beautiful, with a mild warm tone towards the horizon.

NICOLAS POUSSIN.—The Baptism of Christ. The scene is laid quite on the right of the picture. The heads, which are almost all seen in profile, are of much expression. The whole treatment and the greenish tone of the flesh show the earlier time of the master.

MURILLO (?).—The Infant Christ, as the Good Shepherd, with the shepherd's crook in his left hand; his right hand laid on the head of one of the three sheep next him. On the right foliage, on the left a flock of sheep and hills. Tenderly sentimental in expression, and delicate and clear in colour, but not sufficiently decided and rich in the touch of the brush.

WILLEM VAN DE VELDE.—A slightly agitated sea. On the right, in the shadow of a cloud, is a two-masted vessel; on the left, in the middle distance, a three-masted vessel in sail. Quite on the right are more vessels and dark clouds. A large picture of peaceful effect and very careful execution.

VELASQUEZ.—Portrait of a man of middle age, in black dress with white collar. Holding a paper in his right hand and his dress with the left. The ground of one tone. Of refined and lively conception, and spiritedly painted in a cool reddish tone.

HEINRICH MOMMERS.—A hunting party halting on a hill. A very good picture by this less-known master, erroneously called Wouvermans.

DAVID RYCKAERT.—A party of peasants in the open air. A moderately large and a good picture.

ARTUS VAN DER NEER.—Moonlight. The moon is rather high in the sky. Of powerful effect, but too brown in colour.

JAN VAN GOYEN.—1 and 2. Remarkably fine views of Dutch canals.

PERUGINO.—The Virgin seated, and holding the Child on her lap—on the left the little St. John adoring. The background landscape. This once beautiful picture has been much defaced by cleanings and retouches.

ANDREA SACCHI.—Portrait of a Pope, with a moustache, his right hand raised. The ground dark. Very animatedly given.

GIULIO ROMANO.—A triumphal procession. A fragment. The heads of great energy, and motives very animated—a prisoner is being struck. These are the redeeming qualities of a hard and crude picture.

JAN VAN DER HEYDEN.—On the left, in the foreground, is a white cow; behind, a house, a tree, and a bush. On the right a canal with a woman washing, and two men walking. Also other figures and a dog. With the exception of the cow and the delicate and clear sky, of very heavy tone, and unusually broad in treatment. At the same time a genuine and good picture by the master.

DAVID VAN TOL.—A hermit. A careful copy from his model Gerard Dow.

BERGHEM (?).—On the right, before a wooded height, is a figure on a mule, with an ass and another man in a red jacket. Very attractive and clear, but placed too high for me to judge.

SCHOOL OF LEONARDO DA VINCI.—A female head, delicately modelled in the well-known type of the school, but very pale; the drapery the same.

SIR PETER LELY.—Portrait of a woman, holding her drapery towards her with her left hand. The ground dark. A delicate conception is here combined with clear colouring and soft treatment.

JACOB RUYSDAEL.—3. A winter landscape. On the left a hill,

on which are trees and a house, all snowed over. These are illumined by sunshine, which contrasts strongly with the dark clouds. Very picturesque and clever. Almost a quadrangular picture.

PETER NEEFS.—Interior of a church by candlelight. Appears to be good, but hangs too high for me to decide.

SALVATOR ROSA.—On the right a lofty rock with trees; in the middle distance a piece of water; behind, mountains. Four figures in the foreground. A remarkably fine composition, but now, with the exception of the warm sky, much sunk.

STAIRCASE.

JACOB RUYSDAEL.—4. A canal stretches from the foreground to the background of the picture; ruins, with arches, on the right shore; on the left, two willows and two small boats, with a man in one of them. In the middle distance a fisherman. Some of the clouds grey, others illumined by the sun. On canvas. A very original and fine picture by the master, and of singular power and depth of cool tone. The light reflections in the water are admirable.

MELCHIOR HONDEKOETER.—On the right a black and brown hen with four chickens; also a duck and other fowls. Of great power and breadth of treatment.

HANS MEMLING.—Head of a youthful Saint with an arrow in his hand; perhaps St. Sebastian. The background a column and landscape. A fragment, I am inclined to think, of a larger picture. Refined in feeling, and carefully carried out in the warm brownish tones of his latest pictures.

A good portrait of Descartes.

DINING-ROOM.

HOBBEMA.—On the right, in the foreground, a piece of water, with a cow, a man and woman, and a goat, on its bank. Further back a peasant's house. On the left a wood in sunshine. The sky especially clear and sunny. In point of size, warmth of tone, and truth of detail, one of the most important works of the master.

RUBENS (?).—Vertumnus and Pomona. A good school picture, most probably by JORDAENS.

JANSEN VAN CEULEN.—1 and 2. The small portraits of an old

man and a young girl.   Of animated conception and careful treatment, and less pale in tone than usual.

GIORGIONE (?).—Portrait of a man, with a landscape background.   A fine picture, but conception, treatment, and cool tone of landscape far more in the style of his imitator, FRANCESCO DOMENICI.

JORDAENS.—The proverb " As the fathers sung, so whistle the sons."   Size and richness of composition, solid execution, and power of colour, render this one of the best examples of a subject so often treated by him.

SNYDERS.—1. A stag-hunt.   A very good picture.

2. A kitchen subject.   Also good, but the two figures too feeble for Rubens, to whom they are assigned.

3. Another subject of the same class, with a lobster and a dish of strawberries.

CARLO MARATTI.—The Virgin and Child.   Very pleasing.

Other good works may be among the remaining pictures, but they hang in positions too dark and unfavourable for me to form any opinion.

PICTURES AT MARCHMONT HOUSE,

SEAT OF SIR HUGH HUME CAMPBELL, BERWICKSHIRE.

Although I have not visited Marchmont House, I am, with the exception of a few, acquainted with the following pictures, which include a choice selection of the Dutch masters.

CUYP.—Philip baptizing the Eunuch.   The view exhibits a hilly and highly luxuriant country, under the aspect of a bright sunny afternoon.   The eunuch is accompanied by several attendants. The carriage is drawn by two white horses.   On canvas.   3 ft. 7 in. high, 5 ft. 4 in. wide.   This is one of the finest specimens of the master.   It is finished with great care, and the aërial perspective and brilliancy of the sunshine are quite surprising.

RUYSDAEL.—1. A forest scene.   In the foreground masses of rock, through which a broad brook falls in gentle cascades.   Over the rocky bank are fallen a silvery beech and an oak.   Further back are lofty trees of various kinds.   More in the distance a man in a red jacket, a woman, and some sheep.   On canvas.   3 ft. 2 in.

high, 3 ft. 11 in. wide. Poetical in feeling, and the various tints of the foliage, the detail of the herbage, the rocks, and the water exquisitely rendered.

2. A group of trees, the stems of which are reflected in the water, which occupies the principal part of the foreground. Two fallen trees are on the left, and behind them two cows, some sheep, a man, and a dog. In the distance is a church-tower and some cottages. Canvas. 3 ft. 2 in. high, 3 ft. 11 in. wide. Fine, and very uncommon in the composition, brilliant in effect, and successful in the rendering of the varieties of the foliage.

3. The Cottage. Canvas. 10 in. high, 13 in. wide. Of great freshness, and painted with much vigour.

JAN WYNANTS.—1. On the right a fine oak, with herbage at its base, behind it a grove of trees. On the left a river and mountains. On a road, by LINGELBACH, a man conversing with a woman on horseback, a child, and a dog, and near them a man fishing. Canvas. 3 ft. high, 3 ft. 10 in. wide. A fine specimen of the master, in his free, broad manner.

2. A woman driving a flock of sheep through an archway. Figures and animals by ADRIAN VAN DE VELDE. Canvas. 1 ft. 2 in. high, 1 ft. 5 in. wide. An uncommon and very successful composition, excellent in the rendering of the freshness of the morning light, and highly finished by both masters.

TENIERS.—1. A Corps de Garde. Soldiers gambling. A man with a yellow coat is turned with his back to the spectator. On the left a drum, a hat and feather. On the right armour and a red cloak. Copper. 1 ft. 7 in. high, 2 ft. 1 in. wide. Very fine in keeping, and spirited in touch.

2. The Temptation of St. Anthony. Panel. 1 ft. 5 in. high, 1 ft. 9 in. wide. An unusually good specimen of a subject he treated so often. Painted with surprising dexterity and freedom.

JAN STEEN.—1. Peasants regaling at a country inn. A couple are dancing to the music of a bagpipe. Panel. 2 ft. 2 in. high, 2 ft. wide. A first-rate picture by the master, combining with all his humour a clearness and brilliancy approaching Adrian van Ostade, and at the same time highly finished.

2. A gentleman presenting a lady with an oyster. Panel. About 1 ft. 3 in. high, 1 ft. wide. Very highly finished.

WILLEM MIERIS.—The Death of Cleopatra. Her attendants

behind her in various attitudes of grief. Signed, and dated 1688. Panel. 1 ft. 1 in. high, 1 ft. 6 in. wide. A fine specimen of this master's best time.

WILLEM VAN DE VELDE.—1. Ships in distress.

2. View from the shore, looking out seaward, during a light breeze. Panel. 4¾ in. high, 9¼ in. wide. Masterly little pictures.

BACKHUYSEN.—A view of the Dutch coast, represented under the effect of a fresh breeze. On the right, near the front, is a coaster. Ahead of her is a row-boat full of figures. On the opposite side is a yacht in full sail. A low line of coast is seen beyond her, and two ships of war in the distance. A heavy cloud throws a shadow over the rolling sea. Canvas. 2 ft. 5 in. high, 3 ft. 3 in. wide. A beautiful work.

RUBENS.—Sketch for part of the ceiling at Whitehall—Minerva with her Ægis repelling the harpies of War and Discord from the throne of James I. Panel. 2 ft. 3 in. high, 2 ft. 9 in. wide. Very vigorous and brilliant, and an interesting example of his principle of loading the high lights and keeping the shadows thin and transparent.

VANDYCK.—Portrait of Don Livio Odescalchi, in a black dress and full white ruff. His right hand rests on a gorget, his left holds his sword below the hilt. Canvas. About 4 ft. 2 in. high, 3 ft. 4 in. wide. An admirable work, in the master's Genoese manner.

COLLECTION OF PICTURES BELONGING TO LORD ELGIN,

BROOM HALL.

Other pictures besides those here mentioned may be at Broom Hall, which I did not visit, having seen the following pictures at Glasgow, in one of the rooms of the McLellan Gallery, to whose care Lord Elgin had committed them, so that they might be generally seen. I was indebted for the knowledge of them to Lady Matilda Maxwell, the sister of Lord Elgin, with whom I spent some very agreeable days at Pollock, Sir John Maxwell's delightful seat, in the neighbourhood of Glasgow, and who was so kind as to show them to me herself.

LEONARDO DA VINCI (?).—St. Sebastian, taken as a tender youth, an arrow in his hand, with fair hair falling on his shoulders, a fillet round his forehead, and a red dress with black collar and large sleeves. The ground dark. A bust picture. The fine features are rendered with great delicacy and decision of forms. The feeling, however, and the style of the reddish flesh tones and treatment, show rather the hand of ANTONIO BELTRAFFIO, one of Leonardo's best and rarest scholars.

SEBASTIAN DEL PIOMBO.—A female portrait with both hands. In one hand she holds an object, which, at the height at which the picture was hung, I could not distinguish. The ground is dark. The fine features are very nobly conceived, and the execution, in the broken tone of his later period, is careful.

ANDREA DEL SARTO (?).—The Holy Family. This composition often occurs. I consider this to be an early copy.

MORETTO OF BRESCIA. — An aged smith, with hammer and tongs at the anvil. Behind him is the hearth. Life-size. Executed with great truth in a delicate silvery tone. In my opinion, erroneously ascribed to GIOVANNI BATTISTA MORONI, his scholar.

ANNIBALE CARRACCI.—St. Francis contemplating a crucifix. Of unusual depth of expression, and of broad and masterly carrying out.

SCHIDONE.—John the Baptist sleeping. Large life-size. To the knees. A careful, warm, and masterly rendering of a fine model.

SALVATOR ROSA.—A warrior in armour looking round. Spirited and lively, but dark.

VELASQUEZ.—The Conde Duca Olivarez on a white horse, looking round, so that he is almost seen in profile. A smoke is ascending from the slightly-rendered landscape. Half life-size. Of great life and elevation of conception, admirable in keeping, and broad and masterly in execution.

ADAM ELZHEIMER.—In the foreground St. Peter, whom the angel is delivering from prison. Behind are three guards sleeping round a fire. An excellent picture by this very rare master, of astonishing force of effect, and solid and delicate carrying out.

A girl reading. A picture of great charm and delicate finish, by that, to me, unknown Netherlandish painter who alternately goes by the name of MABUSE (as here) and LUCAS DE HEERE. Both appellations are alike wrong.

JOSEPH VERNET.—The effect of a storm upon a coast. Admirably composed, but rather cold and gaudy in colour.

OBJECTS OF ART AT ROSSIE PRIORY,

SEAT OF LORD KINNAIRD, NEAR INCHTURE, SEVEN MILES FROM DUNDEE.

Provided with a letter from Lady Ruthven, who takes a true interest in matters of art, I succeeded in obtaining admission even in the absence of Lord Kinnaird. As no catalogue of the pictures exists, I was left to my own judgment as to their proper titles. I also found here some specimens of sculpture, antique and modern, of value, and a large collection of antiquities.

DINING-ROOM.

Portrait of a man in black dress, drawing back a red curtain with his right hand, and holding a paper in his left. A remarkable work by some excellent Italian master whom I am not able to name.

GAINSBOROUGH.—Portrait of a man in a simple brownish dress, his hat in his left hand. The background landscape. Of natural and unpretending composition, and delicately executed in a cool tone.

VANDYCK.—Portrait of a lady in black silk dress with white collar, with a child on her lap. A red curtain forms the background. The head of the mother is very transparent, that of the child duller in tone. Painted in his Genoese manner.

VANDYCK (?).—A boy, dressed in white, leaning with his right hand on the arm of a red chair. Whole length. A good picture, but questionable whether by Vandyck.

ANTE-ROOM.

THOMAS CAMPBELL.—A shepherd boy seated, with the Phrygian cap; perhaps intended for Ganymede. He is looking upwards, while he holds the tie of the sandal of his right foot. Signed, and dated " Romæ, 1821." Of pleasing character, and carefully executed in marble.

RUDOLPH SCHADOW. — A Discobolus. Signed, and dated "Romæ, 1821." Of animated and pleasing action, and carefully carried out.

An antique torso of a youth. Of Parian marble. The workmanship moderate.

DRAWING-ROOM.

GUIDO RENI.—The repentant Magdalen. Half-length figure. Her right hand upon her chest, her left holding a skull. Of elevated feeling, and tenderly executed in a broken and harmonious tone.

LEONARDO DA VINCI (?).—A specimen of that picture of a beautiful woman, known by the name of *La Columbine*, once in the collection of the King of Holland. A fine picture, in a warm tone, and carefully executed, by one of Leonardo's scholars.

FRANCESCO FRANCIA.—The Virgin holding the sleeping Child, who is lying on a cushion on a parapet, holding a goldfinch in his left hand. The background landscape. The figures half life-size. A very pretty picture of his later time.

BERNARDINO REGILLO.—A female figure behind a parapet, the head turned to the right, holding an open book in her left hand. On the left are two men, the one drawing the attention of the other to something. The background architecture, with a distant view. The woman and one of the men are very elevated in expression. The whole is very attractive.

• SCHOOL OF FRA BARTOLOMMEO.—The Virgin with the Child on her lap, pointing with the forefinger of the left hand to its mouth, and with its right hand between the leaves of a book. The background architecture. On the right a view of the distance. Of remarkable glow of colour, and pleasing though somewhat empty heads.

SASSOFERRATO.—The Virgin with the sleeping Child. In point of refinement of heads, and warmth of colouring, this is a particularly fine example of this frequently occurring composition.

LODOVICO CARRACCI.—1. St. Francis in ecstacy, with closed eyes, supported by two angels. A small picture, of elevated expression and careful finish.

PAUL VERONESE.—On the right an altar, at which a male saint with a palm-branch is standing, while a kneeling woman is presented by a female saint, also with a palm. On the left is an acolyte boy with a candle in his right hand and a censer in his left. In the foreground a dog. Although executed in his grey tones, this picture is very pleasing in point of composition, character of heads, and careful execution.

School of Leonardo da Vinci.—Portrait of a woman with a costly fillet across her forehead, and a rich dress; a book in her left hand, a feather fan in her right. The ground dark. In front a parapet. The shadows of this beautiful picture are deep, and the lights yellowish, and every part is thoroughly carried out.

Lodovico Carracci.—2. The repentant Magdalen, in a landscape. Full-length figure. Of noble head and graceful motive, and tenderly warm in colour.

Schidone.—The Holy Family, with Joseph, with white bushy hair, in profile. Figures the size of life. A powerful and careful specimen of a composition he often repeated.

Andrea del Sarto.—Portrait of a man, with moustachio and beard, large black cap, green coat, and grey mantle. His left hand on the hilt of a dagger, a glove in his right. The ground dark. Almost to the knees. On wood. One of his finest portraits. Of great elevation of conception and delicate drawing, and throughout admirably rendered.

Michael Angelo (?).—The well-known composition of the Crucifixion. A delicate little picture, probably executed by Marcello Venusti.

Titian.—A female portrait; arms and chest bare; the left side partially draped with a skin. Very animated, and of warm transparent colouring.

Rubens.—Portrait of a man in black dress and white collar; a broad-brimmed hat on his head, and holding his dress with his right hand. The background a curtain, and a very beautiful landscape of warm tone. Almost to the knees. Of great freshness of conception, and recalling in breadth and spirit of treatment the man with the falcon in the Royal collection.

Rembrandt.—Portrait of a man with a white cloth round his head, in a dark-coloured dress, and holding a book with both hands. Half-length figure, rather above life-size. Signed and dated 1661. Taken in fuller lighting than usual, and most spiritedly treated with the broad touch of his later time.

LIBRARY.

ANDREA SOLARIO.—To this master I am inclined to ascribe an altarpiece representing a Pietà, in a composition of eight figures, life-size. The motives are excellent; the sorrow expressed in the noble heads is intense and true, and the colouring of great warmth and clearness. It is the most important work I know by this master.

TINTORETTO.—The Conversion of St. Paul. Spiritedly but strangely and sketchily treated.

SIR JOSHUA REYNOLDS.—A good repetition of the Banished Lord in the National Gallery.

In a small room is an altar-picture representing the Virgin enthroned, with SS. Rock and Sebastian at her sides. Inscribed " Cola de Amatricio Faciebat 1522." This is a feeble straggler of an earlier period.

Other pictures also, among those distributed in the house, may be of value. A Pietà on the staircase, with several of the motives from Annibale Carracci's well-known picture in Lord Carlisle's possession, looks promising, but is hung, like many of the others, in too high and dark a place.

THE GALLERY.

This apartment, which is of considerable length, contains a number of busts, with vases and small sculptures upon tables. Among the latter is a pretty torso of a Venus, in marble. A series of large pieces of a mosaic from Pompeii are interesting, especially two sea-gods of considerable size, with heads of great energy, careful workmanship, and powerful colouring.

The windows command a charming view of the bay, and the hills beyond.

OBJECTS OF ART AT KEIR,
SEAT OF WILLIAM STIRLING, ESQ., M.P., NEAR STIRLING.

Although the owner of Keir, the well-known author of ' Annals of Spanish,' Painters was not at home, yet he had kindly taken steps to ensure every facility for inspecting the contents of the house to Mr. James Gibson Craig and myself. The grand situation of this residence, with the beautifully laid out and kept pleasure-grounds, and the magnificent view over the Carse of Stirling, with the town and castle-rock, and the Abbey Craig, would alone amply reward the traveller.

BILLIARD-ROOM.

MURILLO.—An altarpiece. The Virgin looking down on the Child she holds on her lap, who is pointing with the left hand to her. On the left, at her feet, is the little St. John standing, with a bird in his right hand, which he is showing to the infant Christ; in his left hand the cross. The background architecture. This picture was formerly in the church of the Convent de la Madre de Dios, at Seville, in which Murillo's daughter took the veil. The heads are decidedly realistic in character, but pleasing. The execution careful, in a subdued but very harmonious tone.

ZURBARAN.—SS. Justa and Ruffina. About half life-size. Spiritedly treated in a delicate and cool tone.

RUBENS.—1. Philip IV. King of Spain. A bust picture. In a black dress with embroidery. The background a red curtain. Animated, warm, and clear in colour; soft and masterly in treatment.

CASPAR DE CRAYER.—Don Ferdinando, the Cardinal Infant, brother of Philip IV., in the dress of a cardinal. On the right of the background landscape; on the left a curtain. Of refined and animated conception; the clear blonde complexion of great transparency, and the keeping harmonious.

GOYA.—1, 2, 3, and 4. Four light sketches of boys playing. Many of the motives good, but the colouring heavy.

STAIRCASE.

MORALES.—The Virgin lamenting over the body of Christ. A bust picture with hands. Particularly warm in colouring for him. Hung in a dark position.

CARENNO.—A male portrait, in black dress. A letter in his right hand. A bust picture. The ground dark. Of lively conception and clear and warm colour.

SOFONISBA ANGUSCIOLA.—Portrait of herself at an easel, painting the Virgin and Child. On wood. Delicately conceived, clear in colour, and very careful.

PANTOJA.—1. Margaret of Austria, wife of Philip III. of

Spain, in very rich attire. Her right hand on the arm of a chair; a handkerchief in her left. The background a curtain. Full-length, life-size. Of very true invention, and far softer in execution than other pictures I know by him.

2. Another Princess. Companion to the above. In black, with rouged cheeks. Otherwise of similar conception and merit.

ZURBARAN.—2. The Virgin with a crown on her head, her hands crossed. Around her a circle of reddish cherub heads. Of portrait-like forms, but elevated feeling, with warm colouring and careful finish.

RUBENS.—2. Portrait of his first wife, Catherine Brandt, in a black and red dress. Spiritedly and broadly drawn in chalk.

TOBAR.—Portrait of his master, Murillo. Quite different from the pictures that master painted of himself, of melancholy character and pale colouring.

IVAN DE LAS ROCLAS.—Portrait of a monk. Of great truth.

ZURBARAN.—3. Marriage of St. Catherine, in the garb of a nun. Christ not represented as usual as a Child, but in manhood. Next to him the Virgin. All upon clouds. The heads are weak; the folds of the drapery very large; the colouring subdued, but harmonious.

JUAN FERNANDEZ NAVARRETE, called EL MUDO.—His own portrait, quite in front, and only the head given. The ground dark. Of very peculiar and genuine Spanish character. The flesh tones yellow, the eyes and hair very black. From the Soult collection.

ALONSO CANO.—The painted statue of the Virgin, about $2\frac{1}{2}$ ft. high, standing on the crescent. At her feet five cherubim heads. This was the first opportunity I had had of seeing a work of this class. The colouring of the noble and refined head is very tender, and the execution of the whole very careful. The cherubim are pretty, but monotonous. The general effect very attractive.

CORRIDOR.

TERBURG (?).—Portrait of Cinq Mars, in an oval. The head of a miniature-like fineness. The treatment, however, of the ruff, appears to me too hard and minute for the master.

WALKER.—Portrait of Cromwell. This picture hangs in a dark position, but appears to be a good work of the master.

RUSSIAN SCHOOL.—A small altarpiece with several small pictures of unusual finish. The proportions of the figures very long.

PHILIP HACKERT.—1 and 2. Landscapes with cattle. Good specimens of the master. Signed and dated 1799.

ALBANO.—The Child sleeping on a cushion, on the bosom of the Virgin, who is holding an open book. Two adoring angels are near them. A horizontal oval. On copper. Very pleasing, of warm tone and soft forms.

ANDREA PREVITALI.—Three men, and a woman with a lute in the centre. The man in armour on the right has a red cap on, and a halberd in his right hand; the one on the left, in black, is stooping his head, which is taken almost in front. The background a wall, with festoons of fruit above. Half-length figures, larger than life. The whole composition is in the taste of Giorgione, and the very noble head of the second figure approaches that painter also in character. Judging, however, from the paler tone in the head of the woman, and a certain emptiness in the forms, I conceive the picture to be by Previtali. I am not aware to what master Mr. Stirling assigns it.

JORDAENS.—The Satyr in the fable indignant at the man for blowing hot and cold with the same breath. A good picture, in so far differing from the many repetitions of the subject, that it is not executed with much glazing colour, but solidly painted.

PAUL VERONESE.—The Baptism of Christ. The motives artificial, but the execution in a warm colour, solid and spirited.

ALONSO CANO.—Two angels. A clear drawing in red chalk.

WATTEAU.—A girl. Full-length figure in black and red chalk. Of lively conception and light and masterly treatment.

LUCA SIGNORELLI.—A Pietà. A large predella. Of very passionate character, and differing from the traditional motives. Broadly painted in powerful colouring.

GASPAR POUSSIN.—1. A landscape, with two Capuchin friars conversing in the foreground. Deeper in the picture a dark, still piece of water, and a view through a cavern. The sky of unusual clearness. A beautiful and poetical picture.

WOUVERMANS.—On the right a ruin, with a gateway, before which are two women and children in shadow. A rider is exercising a brown horse in a circle. Next him is another horseman,

On the left are pedestrians and a horse. A rather dark, but a good and careful picture of his second period.

IL PADOVANINO.—The Ecce Homo. The composition devoid of style, but well painted and in a warm and forcible tone.

DRAWING-ROOM.

TENIERS.—A large landscape, in clear lighting. In the foreground a man, a woman, and child. Of great effect.

NICOLAS POUSSIN (?).—The Finding of Moses. A large picture with a beautiful clear landscape, and differing from his known composition. It hangs too high, however, for a closer opinion.

GAUDENZIO FERRARI.—The Virgin holding the Child on her lap, who is giving St. Peter the keys. On the left is St. Paul. Behind the Virgin is a cave. On each side landscape. A fine picture of the Lombard school, reminding me most of this master.

GASPAR POUSSIN.—2. A landscape with a man reposing in the foreground, and conversing with a standing figure. A transparent and careful picture, with a bright horizon.

CLAUDE LORRAINE.—On the left much foliage. In the foreground Christ and the two disciples on the way to Emmaus. On the right a distant view. In the middle distance buildings, with a hill in the background. A small picture of the most refined charm, throughout transparent and very careful.

LAVINIA FONTANA.—Two girls in a boat, with a youth rowing. On wood. Of very graceful motive and careful treatment. This picture has much of the character of this gifted lady painter.

JAN STEEN.—Christ visiting the sisters at Bethlehem. A rich composition. Treated quite within the range of his art, and resembling his Marriage at Cana in the Aremberg collection at Brussels. In each of these pictures is a large curtain. Signed. On wood. Admirably lighted, and of great power of colour; now, however, in a somewhat neglected condition.

RUBENS.—3. A scene from the history of some Roman Emperor. Above the Emperor, in the sky, is an eagle, with a wreath of laurel. On the left are builders. The background a landscape. On wood. Very spirited.

GUIDO RENI.—St. John the Evangelist, looking up. In an oval. Warmer in feeling than usual, and well finished in a warm and clear tone.

Isaac van Ostade.—On the left the stump of a tree. Before it a man holding a grey horse. On the right a view over a flat country. On wood. Unfavourably hung, but apparently a good picture.

Several French portraits in miniature and enamel. Some appear to be by Petitot.

DINING-ROOM.

Sir Henry Raeburn.—Portrait of Helen Stirling, a little girl seated in the open air. Of much truth of head, warm and clear colouring, and soft treatment. The rest is very sketchily treated.

LIBRARY.

Sir John Watson Gordon.—Portrait of Sir Walter Scott. Almost half-length, but without hands. Of truthful conception, clear colouring, and careful painting.

The Library at Keir is too remarkable a room not to be mentioned. It extends through three apartments in width, and two stories in height, and is entirely lined with the most odoriferous cedar. The cornice, ribs of the groining, and other parts of this multiform apartment, as well as the furniture, are decorated with carved mottoes in every European language, not excepting the proprietor's native Scotch, the study of which would occupy an ordinary length of life very profitably.

COLLECTION OF PICTURES AT DUNMORE PARK,

Near Falkirk ; Seat of the Earl of Dunmore.

I was favoured by Lady Matilda Maxwell with a letter to Lady Dunmore, the mother of the young Earl, and was agreeably surprised when she introduced herself to me as an old acquaintance, having seen me in 1835, on the occasion of my visit to her father, the Earl of Pembroke, at Wilton House. I regretted that my time was so limited as only to permit of a hurried view of the interesting collection.

BILLIARD-ROOM.

Alessandro Turchi, called L'Orbetto.—Psyche looking at the sleeping Cupid by the light of a torch. I am inclined to consider this a good picture by this master.   On copper.   Of striking effect.

GASPAR POUSSIN.—1. A hilly landscape, with figures bathing in the foreground.   Sketchy in treatment, but so grand and poetical in composition that I attribute it to this master.

TINTORETTO.—1. Portrait of Admiral Capello, with a long white beard, and a crimson mantle over his armour.   On the left, next him, architecture, the background dark.   Almost to the knees. Very energetically conceived, and of broad but careful execution in his reddish golden tone.

GIUSEPPE PORTA, called SALVIATI.—Joseph and Potiphar's wife.   She is very vulgarly conceived, but both are coloured in a clear and powerful tone.

JACOB RUYSDAEL.—1. On the right in the foreground is a piece of water with the sun upon it.   On the left a wood with a road leading through it, and a seated figure conversing with one standing.   The sky very clear.   On wood.   The trees rather dark, but the whole of great charm and careful painting.

2. A very small landscape.   On the right a rock between trees, on the left a piece of water.   On wood.   A rather dark but very attractive picture.

ARTUS VAN DER NEER.—The moon is seen rather high in the heavens, and over a canal, on which are various fishing-boats.   In the distance, on both shores, are buildings.   Signed.   On wood. A small but charming picture of the best time of the master.

NICOLAS POUSSIN.—A large landscape with Orpheus and Eurydice bitten by the asp.   A composition differing both in landscape. and figures from the well-known picture in the Louvre, and not less fine.   In respect of grandeur and melancholy of feeling, nobility of lines, and general tone, this picture is closely allied to the admirable landscape with Diogenes and the cup in the Louvre. Gleams of sun are seen piercing the beautiful clouds.

THE GALLERY.

INNOCENZO DA IMOLA.—The Virgin and Child, Joseph and the little St. John.   A genuine but moderate example of this often repeated composition by him.

DANIEL MYTENS.—Charles I. and Henrietta Maria, with a grey horse held by a negro, and some favourite dogs.   Full-length

figures, life-size.   Of simple and unpretending truth, and carefully
carried out in a light, clear tone.

DRAWING-ROOM.

HOBBEMA.—A landscape with a water-mill on the right ; on the
left a group of trees ; behind, in the middle distance, a village in
sunshine.   A clear and charming picture, of moderate size.

TITIAN (?).—The Adoration of the Shepherds.   An attractive
picture, painted in a warm tone, with a fine landscape.   Of THE
SCHOOL OF TITIAN.   For the master himself it is not clever
enough.

VAN DER HELST (?).—Portrait of a boy with hat and feathers.
Too highly hung for an opinion, but, as far as I could judge, not
by Van der Helst, but rather by CUYP, 1.

VELASQUEZ.—Seven peasants with festive garlands leading an
ox along.   Of great humour, and most cleverly treated in a warm,
transparent tone.

RUBENS.—Soldiers maltreating peasants.   Highly dramatic.
A composition somewhat like that in the gallery at Munich.
Although hanging too high to permit of a decided opinion, yet it
looks so well that I am not inclined to dispute the name given.

LE NAIN.—Four men playing at dice, and another figure.   Of
his usual care and truth, but of more powerful colour.

CUYP.—2. A boy holding a grey horse.   A small picture of
the middle and best time of the master.

GASPAR POUSSIN.—2. An upright landscape.   It looks well,
but is too darkly hung.

Two boys, of charming conception and rare depth of colour,
appear to me to be by an Italian master, though I am not able to
give the name.

SIR JOSHUA REYNOLDS.—A boy grasping his sword with his
right hand.   Very powerful.

ALBERT DURER (?).—An altarpiece with wings ; the Nativity,
the Adoration of the Kings, and the Flight into Egypt.   A very
good work by the rare Dutch master WALTHER VAN ASSEN.   The
Nativity is now much sunk.

LODOVICO CARRACCI.—The Visitation.   Of elevated heads and
motives, but the insipid tone recalls the late works of Sebastian
del Piombo.

PARMIGIANINO.—Music, an allegorical figure, and the Graces. Life-size. Mannered in composition, of a cold red in the flesh-tones, and black in the shadows.

GASPAR POUSSIN.—3. A landscape of moderate size. On the right stately trees; on the left a wood. In the middle distance a plain, with hills retiring to the horizon. The composition admirable, the sky unusually cheerful, and the colouring unusually warm.

TITIAN.—A male portrait in crimson dress. This appears fine, but hangs in too high and dark a place.

SEBASTIAN DEL PIOMBO (?).—A very careful landscape, with small figures, representing the entry of Christ into Jerusalem. Decidedly by a skilful Netherlandish hand of the time of Lambert Lombard, and well worthy of attention.

ALESSANDRO ALLORI, called BRONZINO.—Portrait of Cardinal Soderini. Animated, careful, and well-coloured.

GIULIO ROMANO.—The Virgin with the Child, who is caressing the little St. John. The latter is held by St. Catherine. At the side is Joseph. Above are numerous angels. The background landscape. A good composition of very solid execution.

FRANCESCO FRANCIA (?).—The Virgin and Child. A good picture by his son GIACOMO FRANCIA.

DOSSO DOSSI (?).—Adoration of the Shepherds. SCHOOL OF TITIAN, but of merit.

GIULIO ROMANO.—The Conversion of St. Paul. A strange composition of hard forms, and of powerful but gaudy colouring.

MARCELLO VENUSTI.—Christ on the Mount of Olives. The often-repeated composition by Michael Angelo. It hangs too high for an opinion.

LEONARDO DA VINCI (?).—The Virgin holding the Child, who is in the act of benediction. A good picture by GIOVANNI PEDRINI.

ANNIBALE CARRACCI.—A Pietà, with the Virgin, St. John, and the Magdalen. A spirited sketch. The motives very passionate.

FRA BARTOLOMMEO (?).—A large picture. SCHOOL OF ANDREA DEL SARTO. A moderate picture.

DINING-ROOM.

SIR JOSHUA REYNOLDS.—Portrait of a gentleman in Highland costume, with landscape background. Full-length, life-size. As animated in conception as it is solid in painting and powerful in tone.

VANDYCK.—1. Portrait of Henrietta Maria in a white silk dress. Full-length figure, life-size. A very good picture, but representing some other lady.

PYNACKER.—A landscape with a stream and two boats, with men and cattle. On the left a hill. An admirable work.

SALVATOR ROSA.—A large landscape, with Hagar and Ishmael. One of his grand compositions, broad, spirited, and solid in execution.

TINTORETTO.—2. The Finding of Moses. A slight but clever sketch.

PAUL VERONESE.—Martyrdom of St. Catherine. The head noble and the execution careful, but in his less esteemed colouring with the cold reddish lights and grey shadows.

VANDYCK.—2. Perseus and Andromeda. The painter only adopted this subject in order to paint a female Academy model with the greater care. Perseus and the dragon are in the background, and quite subordinate. The picture is now very dirty.

<hr>

THE M'LELLAN GALLERY,

Now the Museum, Glasgow.

The patriotic feeling which induced the late Mr. M'Lellan to bequeath his collection of pictures to the city of Glasgow has been worthily recognised by the erection of a building, containing three noble and well-lighted apartments, in which the pictures are seen by the public, and thus form the basis of a Museum which, with the love of public institutions pervading Great Britain, cannot fail to grow more and more in importance. It is not my intention to repeat here what I have already stated regarding many of these pictures in vol. iii. p. 286; but I feel it incumbent on me, as in the case of the pictures in the Liverpool Institution, to mention equally such as are of minor, as well as of greater importance among those not before alluded to. The numbers in the Catalogue, which I here affix, supersede the necessity of my entering into any particular explanation of each picture.

THE NETHERLANDISH SCHOOL.

This school is represented the most numerously, and also, comparatively speaking, by the largest number of valuable pictures.

4. Dirk van Delen.—Interior of a church in the Norman style.

6. Teniers.—1. Peasants being turned into frogs at the entreaty of Latona. Skilful imitation of a higher style of art.

8. D. D. Blieck, a.d. 1656.—This is the inscription on the interior of a church, erroneously given as "Block" in the Catalogue. This is a good picture painted on wood in the taste of Emanuel de Witte.

11. Jan Baptiste Weenix.—A seaport. A good picture.

13. Simon de Vlieger.—1. An agitated sea. Spirited, true, and of sunny transparency.

14. De Vries.—A landscape. Much in the manner of his master, Ruysdael. Erroneously entitled "John Vredeman de Vries" in the Catalogue.

18. Willem van Aelst.—Still life. Very beautiful. Assigned to "Jan David de Heem" in the Catalogue.

20. Philip Wouvermans.—A barren hilly scene, with a market-cart. A good, and warmly coloured picture of his first manner. Erroneously ascribed to his brother Peter, an inferior painter.

21. Teniers.—2. The Surgeon. Warm in tone, and of careful treatment.

29. Bartholomew Breenberg.—A landscape, with travellers asking their way. A very good picture for him. Warm, powerful, and clear.

32. Judocus de Momper.—A landscape, with the Conversion of St Paul. A clever picture, wrongly assigned to Paul Bril.

34. Nicolas Berghem.—A small winter landscape. Of admirable effect, and of softer forms than usual.

37. Frederic Moucheron.—A small landscape of careful execution.

41. David Vinckeboom.—Landscape with a cow, and the Flight into Egypt. Inscribed with his sign, the Finch. Very nice.

42. Cornelis Poelemberg.—The Expulsion from Paradise. Very warm and clear.

49. Hobbema (?)—In my opinion not by him; but a good landscape of THE SCHOOL OF Ruysdael.

56. LUCAS VAN UDEN.—Landscape; with a Repose in Egypt introduced by HEINRICH VAN BALEN. A good picture.

59. FRANS FLORIS (?).—SS. Catherine and Margaret. Not by him, but by some good master.

58. RUBENS (?).—Christ and St. John, as children. Only the school of Rubens.

64. VANDYKE (?).—A Repose in Egypt, with angels dancing. This composition often occurs. The original is in the Petersburg Gallery. A school copy.

69. SIMON DE VLIEGER.—2. A storm at sea. Good.

99. HOBBEMA (?).—A very large picture. But by some other clever landscape-painter of the school.

105. CASPAR NETSCHER. — Portrait of a lady. Signed, and dated 1671, a circumstance I did not notice in my former mention.

107. MELCHIOR HONDEKOETER.—Poultry. Very powerful, but somewhat dark in parts.

108. JAN STEEN.—A merry party. Genuine, but one of his over-brown pictures.

156. VAN DER POEL.—A fire. Particularly rich, clear, and careful.

172. REMBRANDT.—The painter studying from a female model. Of great power and transparency.

THE ITALIAN SCHOOL.

70. BECCAFUMI.—The Marriage of the Virgin. A slight work.

87. SANDRO BOTTICELLI.—The Annunciation. The figures are small in proportion to the architecture, and the colouring unusually grey, but otherwise a good picture.

93 and 94. BASSANO. The Four Seasons. Crude and coarse, and decidedly by one of the inferior painters of the family.

95. BONIFAZIO (?).—The Woman taken in Adultery. Judging from the highly original conception of the characters, and from the feeling and depth of colour, I am inclined to consider this picture a fine work of the middle period of GIORGIONE. It agrees especially with the Holy Family in the Louvre. A man in Venetian costume, and seen in profile, is conducting the woman before Christ. She, with her right arm upon her breast, repents her crime, and beseeches pardon. Christ seated, and addressed by an old man, is stretching his right hand towards her. . On the right

is a warrior, seen behind, speaking to the High Priest, in lively action. Behind the woman are two other men in conversation. On the right of the background is architecture, on the left a fine landscape. The head of the woman, as well as that of the man leading her, is very spirited—the yellow robe has an empty look from restoration.

98. GUARDI.—1. View of the church of S. Giorgio Maggiore in Venice. Of admirable keeping and clear and delicate tone.

103. GIORGIONE.—2. The Virgin and Child enthroned. Four saints at the side. The background an extensive hilly landscape. I have already described this picture in the possession of the late Edward Solly, Esq. Since then it has unfortunately lost much of its harmony by over-cleaning, and looks much harder; this is especially seen in the figure of the S. Sebastian. Nevertheless I adhere to my original persuasion that it is a work of Giorgione's earlier time. The influence of his master Giovanni Bellini is still seen in the Virgin and Child.

105. TITIAN (?).—Danaë and the Golden Shower. Of graceful motive and rare delicacy of modelling, in a bright tone. But the curtain is too heavy and the landscape too grey for Titian—the feeling of the picture also different. It is, however, by some good master of the Venetian school.

104. ANDREA SCHIAVONE.—The daughter of Herodias hastening to receive the head of John the Baptist. Of landscape treatment and very singular conception; the sketchy handling, however, is spirited.

115. PALMA GIOVANE (?).—The Virgin enthroned, surrounded with saints. This is by an earlier and a better hand than Palma Giovane, although I cannot decide by whom.

114. CANALETTO (?).—View of the Piazzetta, taken on the shore. A rather slight work by GUARDI (2).

118. CIMA DA CONEGLIANO (?).—The Virgin and Child, with two female saints. All I can say is that the picture belongs to the school of Giovanni Bellini.

SALVATOR ROSA. — 1. A landscape with a waterfall. Of very powerful effect.

2. An upright landscape, with lofty trees, with soldiers upon a rock near. Also water and more rocks. Of grand composition and broad treatment.

Besides the picture by Murillo already mentioned, here is a St. Joseph with the Child by Tobar. This Spanish master approaches the style of Murillo, and is very careful in execution.

EARLY GERMAN AND NETHERLANDISH SCHOOLS.

119. A female portrait with a pink in her hand, the fingers of which are well placed. A fine but unfortunately over-cleaned picture of the School of Albert Durer—probably by George Penz. The ground is green. The name of Holbein given to it is false.

120. Aldegrever (?).—This is the very arbitrary title given to a Virgin and Child I have already designated as a delicate work by Patenier.

122. Albrecht Altdorfer.—St. Hubert adoring the crucifix upon the head of the stag. The conception is very curious, the mountainous landscape much finished, and the colouring of great force.

130. Hans Burckmair.—St. Adrian, in front of architecture, the sword in his right hand. On the one side is an anvil, on the other a lion. A careful little picture.

127. Early German School.—A landscape, with David and Bathsheba and several other little figures. This appears worthy of notice, but it hangs too high for any judgment.

132. Matthew Grunewald (?).—The miracle of the Crucifix, or the Mass of Pope Gregory. At the height at which the picture hangs it most recalls the master assigned.

131. Joachim Patenier.—2. Christ taking leave of his mother before his crucifixion. Here wrongly called Christ and the widow of Nain. A careful and remarkable picture by that master.

137. School of Patenier.—The Adoration of the Kings. Of careful execution.

140. Michael Wohlgemuth.—The Adoration of the Kings. This picture is most like the master assigned.

123. School of Bartholomew Zeitbloom.—Christ on the Mount of Olives. A good picture.

FRENCH SCHOOL.

14. Philippe de Champagne.—The Annunciation. Of his later time.

74. Gaspar Poussin.—1. A landscape. Poetical, warm, and clear.

81 (2). A landscape, with two young men in the foreground. Finely felt and very warm in colour.

20. Boucher.—Leda and the Swan. Feeble and disagreeable in sentiment, though skilfully modelled in a silvery tone.

2. Another picture, without a number, by this painter, is here— a boy teaching a girl to play the flute. This is very pretty.

ENGLISH SCHOOL.

25. Zoffany.—A family scene. Two children are dancing. The motives are pleasing, the heads true, but the colouring somewhat heavy.

43. Sir Joshua Reynolds.—Portrait of Miss Linley, afterwards Mrs. Sheridan. A bust-picture in profile. Very animated and of clear and warm colouring.

41. Richard Wilson.—A landscape, with a church. A beautiful picture, of earnest tone and a warm sky.

COLLECTION OF PICTURES AT BOTHWELL CASTLE, LANARKSHIRE,

Seat of the late Lord Douglas.

This collection, which is distributed through the different apartments of the house, once formed half of the collection of the Great Lord Clarendon. This half was selected by the Duchess of Queensberry, and has since then been preserved here. The Duchess's choice was not fortunate, the collection at the Grove, seat of the Earl of Clarendon, vol. ii. p. 454, having retained the larger proportion of the fine pictures. Nevertheless, as I proceed to show, some good works, and a few excellent ones, are here. As regards the portraits by Sir Peter Lely, I can only mention the most remarkable.

BREAKFAST ROOM.

Vandyck.—1. Lord Lindsay, in armour ; his helmet next him. In the background a piece of landscape. Full-length, life-size. The beauty of the left hand shows what this picture once was. The head is much defaced by over-painting.

Sir Peter Lely.—Portrait of Nell Gwynn, seated : to the knees. True and careful ; the colouring clear and delicate.

Four more pictures by Sir Peter Lely are also in this room, and three by Lingelen, a feeble follower of Vandyck.

DINING-ROOM.

Vandyck (?).—Portrait of Charles I. An early copy.

Sir Joshua Reynolds.—Margaret Duchess of Douglas. Full-length, walking in great state. A coronet in her left hand. The background landscape. Of true and refined conception, and solidly painted in his clear tone.

Vandyck (?).—The Earl of Strafford. The same picture of which the finest example is in Wentworth House. An early copy. The head good, the hands weak in drawing and colouring.

Vandyck.—2. James I. in black armour with a blue ribbon of an order. The background architecture and a curtain. Full-length, life-size. This picture can only have been painted by Vandyck from some earlier portrait. It is clear in colour, and the hands particularly delicate.

Of the twelve other portraits in this apartment, five are by Sir Peter Lely and two by Sir Godfrey Kneller.

DRAWING-ROOM.

Vandyck (?).—Henrietta Maria, seated, in a yellow satin dress, with a child in white silk, and a brown dog jumping up to her. The background architecture, curtain, and landscape. Though the composition is decidedly by Vandyck, and the effect of the delicate silvery tones very attractive, yet the forms are too empty for him, the accessories too heavy in tone, and insipid in treatment.

Vandyck.—3. Lady Paulett. Standing, in white satin, a rose in her right hand, the left holding her dress. On the right a curtain of very powerful red ; on the left a ground of one colour. A charming picture, carefully executed in a clear silvery tone.

4. Lord Banning. In black dress, with falling white collar. His left hand on his hip, in his right a black hat. The background has architecture on the right, and, on the left, a view of a landscape. Easy in motive and carefully painted in his brownish tones. The heavy colouring of the landscape and the many details show another hand.

VANDYCK (?).—The Duke of Buckingham in a dress of white silk. By quite another hand than Vandyck's, and more resembling Mytens.

VANDYCK (?).—The Earl of Holland. An early copy.

VANDYCK. — 5. Mrs. Howard, in an orange silk dress. The ground dark. Almost to the knees. The flesh of somewhat insipid tone, but the hands delicate, and the execution careful.

Of the three other portraits in this apartment one is by SIR GODFREY KNELLER.

LIBRARY.

HANS HOLBEIN.—1. Lord Cromwell. Almost in profile, in a black dress trimmed with brown fur, a paper in his left hand, and seated behind a table with a green cover. On this is a book with gilt edges, papers, parchment documents, and a pen. The background is wainscot and a dark green hanging. Of the utmost truth of conception, and, judging from the powerful brown flesh-tone, and the whole treatment, painted about 1530. Half-length.

2. Sir Thomas More, in a gold brocaded coat, and crimson mantle with brown fur, kneeling at a faldstool with folded hands. A little book before him. The expression is elevated, and the picture carefully finished in a warm brownish tone. Both these pictures hang much too high.

3 (?). Erasmus of Rotterdam. An early copy from Holbein.

VAN SOMERS.—Sir Walter Raleigh, with the bâton. True, clear, and careful.

Among the six other pictures here is one by SIR GODFREY KNELLER. The other rooms are full of portraits, but containing none of particular value. A picture containing the portraits of two women, called Vandyck, in a bedroom No. 9, is an early copy. The number of portraits in the house amount to 81.

After this inspection I accompanied my friend Mr. Gibson Craig in a walk through the beautiful and well-kept pleasure-grounds. The ruins of old Bothwell Castle, built of a warm red sandstone, lie very picturesquely on the margin of the rocks over-looking the here small stream of the Clyde. A grand circular tower is particularly conspicuous. The fine trees which ornament each side of the stream have a beautiful effect. A fine collection of heaths in the garden especially attracted our attention.

LETTER X.

Collection of pictures, antiquities, and other objects of art at Alnwick Castle — Objects of art in Newcastle-on-Tyne — Pictures belonging to W. W. Bardon, Esq. — Pictures at Coxlodge Hall — Pictures at Jesmond Cottage — Pictures at Heddon House — Pictures at Ravensworth Castle — Durham Cathedral, and MSS. in the Library — Pictures in Durham — Pictures belonging to the Archdeacon of Durham — Objects of art at Duncombe Park — Pictures at Elvaston Castle — Pictures at Locko Park — Picture belonging to Earl of Warwick — Lincoln Cathedral — Collections of art at Brocklesby — Pictures at Scawby House — Collection at Clumber Park — Collection at Welbeck Abbey — Pictures at Serlby — Collection at Wimpole, seat of the Earl of Hardwicke — MSS. at Cambridge.

COLLECTION OF PICTURES, ANTIQUITIES, AND OTHER OBJECTS OF ART AT ALNWICK CASTLE,

SEAT OF THE DUKE OF NORTHUMBERLAND.

On occasion of my visit to England in 1854 I had the privilege of spending a day at Alnwick Castle as his Grace's guest. This grand residence with its walls and towers has an effect, though not on so colossal a scale, which reminds the spectator of Windsor Castle. Since the period of my visit great alterations have been undertaken, which, while they have increased the appearance of a mediæval fortress externally, have greatly extended and embellished the space within. The Camuccini collection, which the Duke purchased at Rome in 1856, is to be placed in this castle. On this account it appears to me more appropriate to describe the pictures as if already here. They consist of 74 works in number, by far the greater portion belonging to the Italian schools of the 16th and 17th centuries. At the same time, specimens of the 14th and 15th centuries are among them, and some examples of the Netherlandish school of the 17th century. Although the pictures had been known to me in Rome, yet the kindness of the Duke in allowing me to study them again on their arrival in Northumberland House was very acceptable.

I proceed first to notice the schools of central Italy.

GIOTTO.—The half of a Diptych from the Barberini collection, the other half of which is in the Sciarra Colonna Palace. This is divided into four compartments, containing the following representations. 1. Above, Christ and the Virgin; in the centre, a bishop, with angels and saints; below, a church in the form of an octagon, with open doors, and many bending figures. 2. St. Catherine convincing the Doctors of their error. 3. Above, the Coronation of the Virgin, with the folds of the drapery still indicated in gold, as in the Byzantine manner; below, angels and the Apostles. 4. St. Francis receiving the Stigmata, and John the Baptist. This is a relic of the most delicate kind, the heads fine, the motives very speaking, and the execution like the tenderest miniature. At the same time it is far more in the style and form of the early Sienese school, allied as it was to the Byzantine manner, than to that of Giotto. In excellent preservation.

Lo SPAGNA.—To this painter I am inclined to ascribe two small and delicate figures of the Magdalen and St. Catherine, which formerly in separate parts formed portions of a predella attributed to Raphael. Nevertheless, however refined and elevated in feeling, they show both in colouring and treatment rather the hand of Lo Spagna.

RAPHAEL.—The small picture of the Virgin with the Child on her lap, who is holding a pink. It is well known that the charming composition is by Raphael, and of all the numerous specimens of the picture I have seen, none appear to me so well entitled to be attributed to his hand as this. A notice in the Catalogue by Camuccini states this picture to have been painted by Raphael for Maddalena degl' Oddi, in Perugia, by whose heirs it was sold to a Frenchman before 1636, and taken to Paris, where Camuccini purchased it.

GIULIO ROMANO.—1. Portrait of Giuliano de' Medici, brother of Leo X., painted in fresco on a tile, from the original by Raphael. This is very energetically treated in a warm tone.

2. A copy of the Holy Family by Raphael in the Museum at Naples. Very faithful, but rather cool in tone.

GAROFALO.—1. Christ healing the man possessed with evil spirits. Near him are two youths; others are on a ship with two women on the right in the middle distance. From the Aldobrandini collection. A good picture by the master; the heads fine and the colouring warm.

2. Judith adorning herself. Obviously the portrait of a beautiful woman; rather above life-size. The background architecture, with a view of a landscape. The fine features are grandly rendered, and broadly and softly painted in a warm tone. The forms, however, are very full. From the Aldobrandini collection.

ANDREA DEL SARTO.—His own portrait, purporting to be painted for Lorenzo de' Medici. From the Braschi collection. Pleasing and clear, but rather small and tame in conception, and glassy in surface, for this master.

PONTORMO.—1. The Virgin and Child. From the Borghese collection. A warm and careful picture, quite in the style and manner of his master, Andrea del Sarto.

2. The Birth of the Virgin. In all essentials a copy of the fine fresco by Andrea del Sarto in the courtyard of the SS. Annunziata at Florence, but on a small scale. Very careful, but strikingly gaudy in colour.

IL ROSSO.—Portrait of Sebastian del Piombo, with a black cap, and a paper in his hand, on which is a motto. A grey ground. Of noble conception and careful execution, but rather hard in the forms and red in colour. Judging from the authentic portraits of Sebastian del Piombo, this picture represents another person.

IL CAVALIERE D'ARPINO.—A Pietà, with the Virgin and four other figures. From the Borghese collection. An unusually good picture by this mannered painter. The body of Christ is especially noble and refined.

VENETIAN SCHOOL.

GIOVANNI BELLINI and TITIAN.—" I dei venuti a gustare i frutti della terra." This picture, representing the gods assembled in a landscape, is thus described by Giovanni Gherardi de' Rossi. This is one of the four celebrated pictures formerly in the Ludovisi palace—the Bacchus and Ariadne in the National Gallery is another—and was purchased by Camuccini in 1797. It is by far the chief picture in the collection. The gods occupying the foreground are painted by Bellini, and are a specimen of the naïve manner in which he rendered the scenes of ancient mythology. Neither in motives nor character do they bear the slightest impress of an antique form of conception; but are merely common mortals, and in some instances very ugly ones. The skill, however, with which they are coloured and arranged, and the truth and masterly execution of detail, have an admirable effect in the midst of the landscape, finished by Titian, which forms the principal feature in the picture. In poetry of composition, management of light, warm and luminous colouring, and broad and spirited treatment, this landscape, which is without comparison the finest that up to that period had ever been painted, constitutes justly an epoch in the history of art. At the same time the preservation is excellent. Signed " Johanes Bellinus, MDXIII."

TITIAN.—2. Venus seeking to retain Adonis ; a subject which often recurs. This specimen, from the Barberini collection, is much smaller than those in the possession of Lord Elcho and in the National Gallery, and rather to be considered as a kind of sketch, in which, however, the flesh parts are carefully modelled in a full and transparent golden tone, and only the hair and the landscape treated more slightly. This picture surpasses Lord Elcho's in preservation, and that in the National Gallery in beauty. The sky is of especial beauty.

3 (?). Portrait of an Admiral in armour. From the Barberini collection. Spiritedly rendered ; but in this respect, as well as in colour and treatment, obviously a work by TINTORETTO, 1.

4. Male portrait of a member of the Barbarigo family in a furred dress, taken quite in front. The background a piece of landscape. From the Aldobrandini gallery. Somewhat empty in forms, but the hand admirable.

5. Portrait of Pope Paul III., in the form in which it often occurs, but only about half the size of life. From the Casa Altieri. Very animated and decided in forms, but some of the outlines, for instance that of the upper part of the head, very hard and heavy for Titian.

ORAZIO TITIANO.—The Virgin adoring the Child, who is sleeping on a cushion, supported by a saint. The little St. John is kissing the Child's feet. The background landscape. From the Barberini collection. I am too little acquainted with the master to decide whether the name given be correct. At the same time the style of art is very moderate, and the forms empty.

BONIFAZIO.—1. The Virgin holding a book, and contemplating the sleeping Child on the ground. Next him the little St. John.

The background is a pretty landscape. The motives are graceful, and the painting warm and soft.

2. The Virgin holding the Child on her lap, who is giving a cross to the little St. John, brought to him by Elizabeth. On the right are Joseph and Zachariah. In the foreground is a ruin ; in the background landscape. Purchased in 1797 from the Aldobrandini collection. An admirable work of the master ; the heads noble, the colouring clear and golden, and the execution careful.

PARIS BORDONE.—Portrait of a woman with her right breast bare. The ground dark. Half-length. From the Aldobrandini collection. Very animated, and also careful, but too red in colour.

TINTORETTO.—2. An Ecce Homo. The ground dark. A beautiful and well-finished picture.

PAUL VERONESE.—1. The Magdalen kneeling, in a landscape, with three angels. Of intenser feeling and more noble forms than usual, and carefully painted in a warm and transparent tone.

2. The Virgin and Child. Of realistic conception, but carefully executed in a clear tone.

CARLO CAGLIARI.—The repentant Magdalen. Signed. From the Casa Lante. A good picture for him.

FERRARESE SCHOOL.

DOSSO DOSSI.—A picture known by the title " Pianto, riso, ira." This subject is represented by two women fighting, a boy laughing, and another figure making mouths and tearing his hair. To the knees. The conception is very animated, and the forms decided. The execution in a warm brownish tone is very solid.

MAZZOLINO.—Christ driving the Money-changers from the Temple. A very rich composition. In the background, on a gallery, the healing of the lame and the blind man. From the Aldobrandini collection. One of the best works of the master known to me. Of the utmost decision and miniature-like delicacy of execution, and of astonishing glow of colour.

THE ECLECTIC AND NATURALISTIC SCHOOLS, WITH THEIR COTEMPORARIES AND FOLLOWERS.

LODOVICO CARRACCI.—1. Herminia taking refuge with the shepherds. Conceived as a landscape. The heads pleasing, the colouring warm, and the execution careful.

2. St. Francis receiving the Stigmata. Presented by Pope Clement XII. to his nephew Rezzonico. Well composed, but very heavy and grey in colour.

ANNIBALE CARRACCI.—1. Susannah and the Elders. From the Barberini gallery. Somewhat hard in the forms, but of powerful colouring and marrowy painting.

2. Portrait of the well-known philologist, Giulio Cesare Scaligero, extending his hands. The background architecture. The forms decided, and animatedly rendered. The colouring warm. Signed with the painter's name, and with that of the sitter also.

3. John the Baptist in a landscape, kneeling and looking up. Three angels in the sky, blue hills in the background. This picture, the landscape of which is very fine, passes for the united work of Lodovico Carracci and Domenichino. It appears to me, however, judging from style and treatment, rather the work of ANNIBALE CARRACCI.

AGOSTINO CARRACCI.—Tancred baptizing the dying Chlorinda. Conceived as a landscape. The heads noble in expression and form; the drawing very correct, but the flesh tones grey, and the drapery without style.

GUIDO RENI.—The Crucifixion, with the Virgin and St. John. A repetition, on a small scale, of the " Cristo de Capucini" in Rome, painted, according to Malvasia, for Cardinal Gessi, and by his will placed on the side altar of the mortuary chapel in the church of the Maria della Vittoria, from which it was purchased by Camuccini in 1801. It is noble in heads and motives, and carefully carried out. The colouring is unusually lively, almost gaudy. In admirable preservation.

GUERCINO.—Esther before Ahasuerus. A composition of four figures. According to Malvasia, painted in 1639 for Cardinal Onofrio, brother of Pope Urban VIII. From the Barberini collection, and engraved by Strange. The characters very pleasing, the composition happy, and carefully executed in his reddish tones. A chef-d'œuvre of the master.

SCHIDONE.—A boy, in animated action, about to place a wreath on a Death's head. Of unusual power and transparency of chiaroscuro.

DOMENICO FETI.—The blind leading the blind and falling into a ditch. Of animated heads, and very careful execution. Erroneously called Schidone.

MICHAEL ANGELO DA CARAVAGGIO.—The body of St. Stephen lamented. A careful picture, warm in the lights, and dark in the shadows.

PIETRO FRANCESCO MOLA.—St. Bruno, in a landscape. Angels in the sky. Sketch for the well-known picture. Good.

BERNARDO STROZZI.—The youthful Christ teaching in the Temple. To the knees. The Christ is quite realistically conceived, in profile. Of great truth, and carefully executed in powerful tones, which are reddish in the flesh. One of his best pictures.

CARLO MARATTI.—Portrait of Cardinal Antonio Barberino. Carefully painted in a warm tone for him.

VELASQUEZ (?).—Portrait of Peter Alcantara. Differing from this master both in feeling and touch, and more like RIBERA. It is well modelled in a pale tone.

FRENCH SCHOOL.

NICOLAS POUSSIN.—A spirited copy from Raphael's fresco of the Deliverance of St. Peter. Only St. Peter and the angel, however, are given.

CLAUDE LORRAINE.—A harbour by sunset. Painted for Pope Urban VIII. From the Barberini collection. A duplicate is in the Louvre. A rich and delicately carried out composition, with a rather reddish sky. Now quite disfigured by neglect.

NETHERLANDISH SCHOOL.

GERHARD HONTHORST.—Christ mocked. From the collection of Cardinal Salviati. A work of great effect.

SNYDERS.—1 and 2. A wild-boar hunt, and a stag hunt. Large and good pictures.

JAN BREUGHEL.—1. Paradise. A pretty little picture. Signed.

2. Temptation of St. Anthony. Erroneously attributed to Peter Breughel the younger.

PHILIP WOUVERMANS.—On the left a peasant's house. In the foreground a horse. On the right a distant view. A good picture of his first manner, in which the influence of Peter de Laar is distinctly seen.

———

After examining the pictures I proceeded to study the collection of antiquities distributed in the well-lighted rooms of two of the towers. Here the Duke himself, who formed the collection in some measure in his travels, and whose interest in this department is equalled by his knowledge, was good enough to be my cicerone.

EGYPTIAN ANTIQUITIES.

This collection, which was arranged by Sir Gardner Wilkinson, consists chiefly of small objects of choice character.

A circular glass case, in the centre of the apartment, contains a rich collection of scarabæi, arranged according to the dynasties, some of which are remarkable in point of material—as, for instance, a scarabæus of finely-grained granite; others for the workmanship. Of these last there is one in a hard limestone, with a figure, the legs and feet of which are of surprising truth of nature, and so sharply executed that even the nails on the feet are given.

In two other cases, between two windows, are a considerable number of small idols in earthenware, amulets in form of lotus sceptres, symbolical eyes, &c.; also many other objects in cornelian, lapis lazuli, and granite, some of them of very delicate workmanship, especially various groups of three divinities. The best of the whole, however, is a female head with wig-like hair, but with a refined and elevated expression in the gentle mouth, and the whole execution displaying a pure feeling for nature seldom to be found in Egyptian sculptures. Two vases also of oriental alabaster, below the cases, with the heads of the jackal and the cynocephalus or dog-headed baboon, are of particular beauty. In the upper part of the case are Grecian vases in painted terracotta, of fine forms, and some antique glass vessels.

Another case contains slippers, the pallet of a priestess of the name of Tora, a little box with a number of gold rings, with hieroglyphics, statuettes in bronze, and more especially a small tablet of a hard stone, in the centre of which is a deity, and hieroglyphics around. Below the case are two alabaster vases, with the head of a sparrow-hawk, and a human head, in the style of those above mentioned.

A fourth case contains vessels chiefly in alabaster, with the four heads already described, a sphinx in limestone, and fragments of statues.

A series of statuettes of various kinds of stone, of wood, &c., are also preserved here in a glass case. One, richly painted, and with folded wings, in the style of a sarcophagus lid, is particularly remarkable. A small obelisk, too, in a yellowish limestone, is interesting. Below the glass case is the upper part of the statue of Osiris, in green basaltes, of sharp and admirable workmanship.

The following sculptures are on pedestals :—

The lower portion of a statue of a kneeling priest, presenting a prayer written on a tablet for a woman of the name of Servata. Found in the vicinity of Memphis, and of very great antiquity.

A small alabaster altar, of oblong form, with a larger oblong, and a smaller quadrangular hollow, around which are perhaps the earliest hieroglyphics yet discovered. This was the sacrificial altar of the large temple at Karnac, founded by Pharaoh Orta-sen I.

A series of larger and smaller stêle, or monumental columns, with the representation of a door in stone. The moulding of very sharp workmanship, and with considerable remains of the original painting. Many of the stêle also show remains of colour. Also two small fac-similes of obelisks. Some Roman cinerary urns are of great beauty.

The other tower contains in the lower room the upper portion of a very interesting stone Saxon cross, found near Wodens-church, at Alnmouth, Northumberland, in 1789. The very flatly treated body of the Christ is almost destroyed. Next him, and somewhat smaller, are the thieves. Below, and on a larger scale, are Longinus with the spear, and a Jew with the sponge. Below the feet of Christ is a space with ribbon-like interlacings. The proportions of the figures are long ; the workmanship very rude. This cross is considered to belong to the 9th or 10th century. According to the late John Kemble, the Saxon scholar, an inscription upon it contains Meredeh, the name of the artist. A fragment of this cross is given in the Archæologia, vol. x. pl. 36, p. 472.

The upper apartment in this tower is devoted to a very remarkable collection of Roman, Celtic, early Teutonic, and early Christian relics. These have been critically arranged by a profound scholar in this department of archæology—namely, Mr. Albert Way.

A case contains objects in stone—hammers, arrow-heads, &c., of the earliest epoch. In another case we see the specimens in metal of a more advanced period—swords, daggers, keys, &c.

Also a crozier in bronze, the very simple form of which shows its antiquity. Particularly remarkable are several bronze celts and casts of stone forms, intended for bronze casting, which have been found in Wiltshire.

A number of Irish antiquities in bronze, celts, swords, armlets, &c., are very interesting. Among the armlets is one in silver, with pretty ornamentation, found in the Shannon at Athlone. Gilt casts of gold rings and other ornaments, the originals of which are in the Dublin Museum, are also here.

Nor may I omit a very ancient Irish bell in iron.

Next in order is a considerable collection of terracotta vessels, found in England and Ireland. Some of these have very pleasing forms.

A collection of Roman altars and stêle, one with the relief of a horseman, and an inscription. These have all been found in Northumberland.

For the benefit of the lovers of mineralogy, of which I am also one, I must finally mention that a collection of this class is preserved in one of the towers, containing some fine specimens.

After spending the greater portion of the day in these studies, I doubly enjoyed a drive of several hours with his Grace through the magnificent park, which abounds in the most varied views of near and distant scenery, and which led us gradually to a tower erected on a height commanding a magnificent panorama, with the boundless surface of the sea on the one side, seen beneath the influence of a calm sunny day. Particularly beautiful in my eyes was the purple glow of the heather, just then in full blossom. Within the extensive range of the park are also included the ruins of an old convent.

On our return her Grace, who had spent the interim in her Sunday-school, allowed us the refreshment of milk from her dairy, whence we retraced our steps through the "Port of Sally" to the castle. On my inquiring why this gateway was so named, the Duke informed me that on an occasion of war between the English and Scotch, in the middle ages, the English had made a midnight sally through this gate, in which the Scotch king Malcolm was mortally wounded: since which the gateway had retained this name. The next day the Duke went to shoot game on the moors, while I returned to Newcastle to follow the game that most interests me.

OBJECTS OF ART IN NEWCASTLE-ON-TYNE.

I visited Newcastle from Coxlodge Hall, the seat of my since-deceased and lamented friend Mr. John Anderson, who, himself a great lover of art, kindly became my cicerone to all that was worth seeing within reach. The town collection of antiquities is very appropriately placed in the picturesque old castle, and consists chiefly of Roman remains found in the county of Northumberland. The most interesting relic is a Mithraic representation, found near the old Roman wall, at a place called Housesteads, the ancient Borgovicus, about three miles from Newcastle. The zodiac, with Mithras in the centre, is still in great measure preserved, and also one of the youths with the Phrygian cap and the torch, which are peculiar to this kind of monument. But of the bull nothing more than a hoof remains. Other objects, altars, stêles, weapons, &c. Also many Irish celts, presented by the Duke of Northumberland.

The view from this building of the city, lying as it does upon the river Tyne, with its boldly conceived and remarkable bridge, is very striking. The stately erections also for the purposes of commerce, justice, and amusement are proof that Newcastle is a thriving city.

PICTURES BELONGING TO W. W. BARDON, ESQ.

SITTING-ROOM.

GUIDO RENI.—Sketch for his Aurora fresco in the Rospigliosi Palace at Rome. This appears spirited, but hangs too high.

TENIERS.—A woman eating olives; a manservant is helping her to some liquid. Signed. Of spirited execution in a yellowish flesh-tone.

STAIRCASE ON SECOND FLOOR.

MURILLO.—The Baptism of Christ. Full-length, life-size figures. The figure of the Christ is too insignificant, though elevated in motive and expression. This figure is treated in a silvery tone; the St. John, which is more successful, in a reddish flesh-tone. The hands of this latter are particularly fine.

VELASQUEZ.—Head of a boy. Animated in conception and delicate in tone.

DRAWING-ROOM.

HERRERA THE ELDER.—Joseph with the infant Christ, who is holding a stalk of lilies. Pleasingly composed, and of warm and transparent colouring ; the influence of Murillo is obvious.

VELASQUEZ.—Portrait of a cardinal in an arm-chair. Full-length, small figure. A charming picture. The attitude easy, the colouring clear and delicate (for instance the crimson dress of great depth), and spirited and careful in touch.

ARTUS VAN DER NEER.—A fire by moonlight. On wood. The 'fire is somewhat too red ; otherwise a good picture.

NICOLAS POUSSIN.—1. Venus on clouds kissing Cupid ; amorini around. The forms are refined, the motives elevated, the colouring of unusual vivacity and clearness, and the finish great.

2. The companion picture. The subject apparently winter. Venus and the Loves are warming themselves at a brazier. An amorino is descending through the air. A loving couple in the background. Of similar merit as the foregoing.

WILLEM VAN DE VELDE.—A calm sea ; on the right, in front, a boat with two fishermen ; on the left another large boat. On wood. Of great charm, refined and clear.

GREUZE.—A girl caressing a lamb. This hangs too high, but the girl appears to me as delicate in drawing as the lamb is feeble.

FRANZ MIERIS.—The Water-Doctor. The glass over this picture prevents any close examination. The figure of the woman fainted appears to be of great delicacy, the rest feebler.

PAUL VERONESE (?).—This purports to be the sketch for the Marriage of Cana in the Louvre. It is, however, a good picture of the school from that work.

STAIRCASE, FIRST FLOOR.

RUYSDAEL.—A dark wood, with a view through it in the centre. Signed. On wood. This is a spirited picture of his earlier time, but it has become brown. In the foreground are two lofty trees, under which is a sportsman seated with his dog. Behind are a lake and hills. On the foremost shore of the lake are a man and woman with a donkey and sheep. A delicate picture, of warm and clear colouring.

DINING-ROOM.

Rembrandt.—Lucretia with the dagger. Although the lady is a genuine Dutchwoman, yet the expression of grief is well rendered, both in the features and in the pale colouring. The impasto is excellent.

Nicolas Poussin.—3. A landscape with two women conversing by the side of a piece of still water in the foreground. In the middle distance a monument with a seated statue and various buildings. Finely composed and of delicate keeping.

Giacomo Bassano.—Christ driving the Money-changers from the Temple. This picture, which came from Spain, is an unusually good work by the master, being throughout carefully rendered in a very warm and clear tone.

Jan Wynants.—A somewhat large landscape, a sportsman in the foreground. A careful picture, but in that reddish-brown tone which is less preferred.

Gainsborough.—Portrait of a lady as a shepherdess. Delicately conceived and harmoniously carried out in a silvery tone.

Lingelbach.—A good picture in the taste of Wouvermans.

Backhuysen.—Vessels in a storm on a rocky coast. This appears to be a good picture, but its sunken condition allows of no opinion.

Jan Steen.—Five figures, two seated at a meal. The one playing the violin has his own features. Full of humour and of careful painting.

Spanish School.—Christ as Ecce Homo, Pilate, and an executioner. The Christ is very nobly conceived. The other two figures of powerful colouring. The touch is marrowy.

PICTURES AT COXLODGE HALL,

Seat of the late John Anderson, Esq.

DINING-ROOM.

Murillo.—John the Baptist and three Pharisees, to whom he is speaking; the lamb at his feet. The background landscape. Full-length, life-size figures. Formerly, like the Murillo in Mr.

Bardon's possession, in the convent of S. Leandro at Seville. The head of the St. John is noble; the Pharisee next to him, in a dark green dress, and seen in profile, has something grand, and forms a happy contrast with the pale old man with spectacles, in a robe of bright purple. The third, also in profile, has a violet cap, a steel-blue coat, and a yellow mantle. The folds of the drapery are broad in style.

HUCHTENBURGH.—A combat on horseback between Orientals. Signed. Particularly clear and careful.

PALAMEDES.—A party of seven persons, gentlemen and ladies, performing music. A very delicate and clear picture.

NETHERLANDISH SCHOOL.—The Emperor Charles V. as a boy of about eight years old. The delicate pale boy is of very animated conception. The inscription " Carolus Quintus " is doubtless of later date, since he did not become emperor until his 20th year. This picture came from Spain.

TENIERS.—1. A brandy-seller offering a glass of spirits to a woman standing in a doorway. Of delicate silvery tone. The landscape background is especially successful.

2 and 3. Five persons in front of a door by moonlight. Of charming effect in his delicate cool tones. One of those pictures called "un après diner." The companion to it is feebler.

CORNELIS SACHTLEVEN.—Ducks and geese, with some cows, on a piece of water. In the middle distance are two fishermen. The fowls are masterly, and the whole picture carefully finished.

CANALETTO.—1. View of the Giudecca. Clear and powerful.

WILSON.—View in South Wales. Of beautiful lines and striking lighting.

TENIERS.—4. In the foreground a stout man at a meal. Behind are three men eating oysters. Very animatedly conceived and harmoniously carried out in a subdued tone.

CANALETTO.—2. View of the Doge's palace, with a portion of the Riva dei Schiavoni, with the Bucentaur and numerous other vessels. A tent is seen on the Piazzetta. The scene is enlivened with numerous figures. In point of extent, clearness of colouring, and refinement of detail, this is one of his most beautiful pictures. Presented by Catherine II. of Russia, with two others, to the father of Admiral Greig.

SIR THOMAS LAWRENCE.—Portrait of Sir Sidney Smith as a

young man. The fine features are animatedly rendered, and the tone of unusual warmth.

BRACHELAER.—The thief caught stealing grapes. One of the best works of this generally feeble painter of the modern Belgian school.

DRAWING-ROOM.

CANALETTO.—3. The Piazza before the church of SS. Giovanni and Paolo, with the equestrian statue of Colleoni by Verocchio, and the view of a canal in perspective. One of the finest works of the master, of great delicacy of aërial perspective, and of much transparency and freedom of handling.

SIR JOSHUA REYNOLDS.—1. The lady of the Rev. George Hudspath; next to her the head of a large dog. Half-length figure. Animated, clear, and delicate.

2. Sir George Young, Secretary of the War Department, in a red furred dress. The very decided character is admirably rendered, and the colouring of great force.

DUJARDIN.—A male portrait, in profile, in a black dress with white collar, and one hand seen. Of great truth of nature.

CANALETTO.—4. View of the Grand Canal. An admirable picture.

WILSON.—2. Landscape with a piece of water. On the left trees; on the right, in the background, an eminence and ruins, in warm lighting. Of rare truth and clearness.

STAIRCASE.

CUYP.—Three little girls and several sheep in a landscape. One of the girls is making a wreath, the second giving flowers to a sheep, the youngest leading a sheep by a string. In the foreground are some large leaves, painted with the utmost mastery. In the middle distance is a tree and some bushes. In the centre the tower of Dort rising above a wood. The figures life-size. Signed. Of extraordinary truth and wonderful power and clearness of warm colouring.

ALBANO (?).—The Judgment of Paris. Venus in the act of receiving the apple; Paris in front of her. On copper. This differs from Albano in the character of the heads. It is also more decided in the forms, more delicate in the reflected lights of the flesh, and in all these respects recalling rather L'ORBETTO.

COLLECTION OF PICTURES BELONGING TO
MATTHEW ANDERSON, ESQ.,

AT HIS SEAT, JESMOND COTTAGE, NEAR NEWCASTLE.

Mr. Matthew Anderson, brother to my late friend, is an ardent lover of art, and has formed a rich collection of pictures, the majority of which belong to the Flemish and Dutch schools, with some specimens also of the Italian, Spanish, and French schools. I can only mention the principal pictures, and in the order in which I saw them.

CUYP.—Three little girls, life-size, playing with a lamb in the open air. Signed. The children are of great truth and power of colouring, the lamb is the weakest portion.

VANDYCK.—St. Jerome seated in a landscape. Full-length life-size figure. Of the earlier time of the master, and of a transparency allied to Rubens.

ADRIAN VAN OSTADE.—Ninepin-players in the open air. Signed, and dated 1665. A large picture, but unfortunately restored in some parts.

JAN STEEN.—Three men offering presents to a girl. Clear and careful.

GUIDO RENI.—1 and 2. The Annunciation. Half-length figures, in two pictures. Very carefully finished in a delicate silvery tone.

RUBENS.—1 and 2. St. Francis standing, next him a lamb. The companion-picture, another saint in profile, with a dog next him, holding a torch in his jaws. Both pictures of a semicircular form above. Of elevated character, refined tone, and broad treatment, but of rather short and broad proportions. These pictures came from Spain.

WILSON.—A landscape of warm tone, with a piece of clear water, with reflections. An angler in the foreground.

BERGHEM.—A rocky landscape with cattle. Of unusual size. A woman upon a mule, and another carrying a lamb. About 2 ft. 8 in. high, 3 ft. 8 in. wide. Well composed, clear in colour, and broad in treatment.

JAN WYNANTS.—A large landscape. On the left a large tree. Of happy composition, but somewhat scenical in treatment.

TENIERS.—A man and woman in the open air. Signed. Very true and harmonious.

ARY DE VOYS.—A young man in elegant dress looking upwards. Warm, clear, and careful.

WOUVERMANS.—A landscape with a horseman on a road. A charming and clear picture in his first manner, and allied to his master Wynants.

JAN HACKERT.—A wood. Signed, and dated 1665. This picture, though painted in an unusually cool tone, allied to Pynacker, shows the whole charm of the master.

PYNACKER.—A landscape. Cattle are being driven through a ford in the foreground. A bull is refractory. Behind is a wood. Of very powerful effect and solid execution.

SASSOFERRATO.—A good and careful specimen of the frequently repeated picture of the Virgin praying.

TENIERS.—A large and rocky landscape; various figures in the foreground. Of decorative but spirited treatment, and much advantage taken of the red-brown ground.

IL SALAINO.—St. Ann holding the Virgin on her lap, who is stooping down to the Child. The latter is playing with a lamb. A careful repetition, of warm and clear tone and delicate *sfumato*, of the well-known picture ascribed to Leonardo da Vinci in the Louvre.

CAREÑO.—The Immaculate Conception. The subject often treated by Murillo. A particularly good picture for this master, who belonged to the decline of the Spanish school. The angels are especially worthy of observation.

MOYA.—The Virgin and Child and St. Joseph. Half-length figures. Coloured with uncommon force and clearness, obviously under the strong influence of Vandyck.

WILLEM DE HEUSCH.—A rocky landscape, with figures by POELEMBERG. Very pretty.

RIBERA.—The Apostles Simon and James the Less. Of unusually grand and earnest conception, of broad drapery conformable to style, and masterly handling.

TINTORETTO.—St. Augustine writing in a landscape. To the knees. Spirited.

GASPAR POUSSIN.—A finely-composed landscape. In the middle distance a hill and figures. In the foreground a shepherd and his flock.

JAN DAVID DE HEEM.—1. A breakfast, with a large bowl very conspicuous. Signed. An excellent picture of his earlier time.

2. A rich and admirable flower-piece.

DAVID RYCKART.—A party of peasants in an interior. A rich composition of considerable extent, warmth of tone, and careful finish.

BERGHEM.—A landscape with ruins in the centre. In the foreground a shepherd leaning against a white cow. A good work.

BACKHUYSEN.—A slightly-agitated sea, with vessels. Signed L. B. The perfect truth of this picture shows the favourable influence of Ruysdael. An admirable work.

BERKHEYDEN.—View of the Hôtel de Ville at Amsterdam, with numerous figures. A particularly clear and careful picture.

LAIRESSE.—The Coronation of Solomon. A large engraved picture in the taste of Poussin, and of warm tone.

RODRIGO DE MORANDA.—Courtiers amusing themselves with shooting. The companion of the picture in possession of General Fox. Well executed in a silvery tone by this Watteau of the Spanish school.

SPANISH SCHOOL.—Christ bound to the Column. Full-length, life-size. Of dignified and elevated conception, and not unworthy of Murillo in execution.

PHILIP DE KONINGK.—A distant view over a flat country. A picture of delicate tone, and rich in detail.

DE DELFTSCHE VAN DER MEER.—Portrait of an old woman. A picture worthy of Rembrandt, by this rare master.

FRANÇOIS MILET.—A very poetical landscape in the taste of Nicolas Poussin, with good figures by SEBASTIAN BOURDON.

EMANUEL DE WITTE.—Interior of a church. An excellent work by this the greatest of all the Dutch architectural painters.

CONSTANTIN NETSCHER.—Portraits of three children. A beautiful picture, approaching his father.

NICOLAS MAAS.—A cook preparing fish; with numerous accessories. Signed. Very true, warm, and careful.

MARCELLO VENUSTI.—The well-known Holy Family by Michael Angelo, with the Child sleeping on the lap of the Mother. A delicate picture.

SALVATOR ROSA.—A large landscape, with a tree on the left

and a hill on the right. In the foreground three soldiers. Of poetic invention, and with much well-executed detail.

JAN BOTH.—An admirable landscape, with numerous figures introduced by his brother ANDREAS BOTH.

BACKHUYSEN.—2. A slightly-agitated sea, with several large vessels. A good and careful work.

JACOB RUYSDAEL.—An extensive view, with a sandhill conspicuous, and figures and animals by BERGHEM. A small picture of the rarest delicacy.

JAN STEEN.—Cincinnatus found eating a dish of turnips by the ambassadors from Rome. Treated quite within the sphere of his art. Very powerful and careful, but rather gaudy.

RUBENS.—Portrait of his first wife, Catherine Brandt, in a black dress and hat. Very animated, and solidly carried out with a transparency unusual even with him.

JAN VAN GOYEN.—A number of figures amusing themselves on a frozen stream. In truth, power of colour, and careful handling, one of the best pictures of the master known to me, and also of considerable size.

JAN BOTH.—A landscape in sunny evening light. In front a piece of water with the subjects reflected, and with capital figures by ANDREAS BOTH. A very charming picture.

MABUSE.—The Virgin and Child. The best specimen known to me of this often repeated composition.

TENIERS.—An old man with two women in an interior ; another man is looking in. In the background is a fourth figure. Carried out in his cool tones, and in very bright light. The flesh tones alone somewhat opaque.

ARTUS VAN DER NEER.—The moon half hidden by clouds, shining upon a canal and the shore. The sky is one of the finest specimens of his art, and in warmth of tone approaches Rembrandt.

CLAUDE LORRAINE.—On the left are large trees. In the background water and hills. In the foreground three figures and a boy. A charming picture of his earlier time, with the trees of a juicy green, unfortunately rather injured by cleaning.

NICOLAS POUSSIN.—A diminished copy of the fresco, by Domenichino, of the Scourging of St. Andrew, which he so much admired. Very careful and spirited. The master is especially recognisable in the colouring and in the form of the eyes in some of the heads.

SALVATOR ROSA.—2. A hilly landscape, with a dark lake in the centre. Some figures in the foreground. Very dark, but very attractive in poetic feeling.

PIETRO FRANCESCO MOLA.—St. Bruno in ecstacy, in a landscape. A small but good specimen of this subject, which he so often repeated.

DIRK VAN DELEN.—A large and admirable architectural piece, with figures by TENIERS.

GAINSBOROUGH.—A very successful landscape.

PATRICK NASMYTH.—A view of Windsor Castle. Signed, and dated 1826. True, powerful, and careful.

PYNACKER.—A large landscape, with a piece of water in the foreground. On the further shore several figures. Blueish hills in the background.

TENIERS.—Landscape, with harvest. True, clear, and admirably treated.

PICTURES BELONGING TO GEORGE BURDON, ESQ.,

HEDDON HOUSE, NEAR NEWCASTLE.

I owe my introduction to this house also to my late kind friend. Though the Italian pictures are few in number, they are too good to be passed over in silence.

ROMANINO.—Christ bearing his Cross. On wood. About 2 ft. high, and 2 ft. wide. Well composed, and of great power of colour.

GIROLAMO DA SANTA CROCE.—The Virgin, with the Child lying on the ground, adored by St. Francis and by a crowned saint. In the sky are three angels. In the landscape the three Kings. A pretty, warm, and careful picture, of moderate size, corresponding in many respects with a picture by this master (No. 24) in the Museum at Berlin.

DOMENICHINO.—A hilly landscape with a waterfall. A small picture, finely composed and well finished, but it has much darkened.

TITIAN (?).—The Virgin holding the Child on her lap, who is in lively action. The background a beautiful landscape executed in a warm tone. The head of the Madonna rather indifferent. In my opinion a picture of his school.

DOMENICO FETI.—To this painter I am inclined to attribute a picture with three beggar-boys, life-size, in the foreground, on the step of a stair. In the background are monks, apparently distributing gifts, and the heads of several women. The boys are true in motives, admirable in drawing, and in some parts of masterly painting in a clear chiaroscuro.

PICTURES IN RAVENSWORTH CASTLE,

SEAT OF LORD RAVENSWORTH.

This castle has been built in the Norman style, in order to correspond with two towers of that date which had survived. The hall is very successful in effect, and the arrangement of the apartments very appropriate. The number of pictures is not large, but includes a few worthy of attention.

DINING-ROOM.

JAN FYT. — A large boar-hunt. Signed. One of the chief works of this master, who, after Snyders, was the greatest animal-painter in the Netherlandish school. The figures are by another hand, recalling Gerard Honthorst.

GALLERY.

NICOLAS POUSSIN.—1. Rebecca and Eleazar at the well. This is a different composition to that, known by the engraving, in the Louvre, and is of upright form. The motives are very happy ; the red, heavy colouring is an evidence of his earlier time. The sky is very beautiful.

2. A landscape, known by the engraving, of an elevated poetical feeling and careful execution.

GASPAR POUSSIN.—A landscape of fine invention and clever execution.

MICHAEL ANGELO DA CARAVAGGIO.—1, 2, 3, and 4. Four pictures of the same size. Two of them are of those drinking and gambling subjects which show his vulgar realistic element to advantage, while Achilles with the daughters of Lycomedes, and Alexander instructed by Aristotle, being subjects beyond his grasp, are almost ridiculous in conception. All are now very dark.

SOLOMON RUYSDAEL.—A landscape of great truth and rare power for him.

DURHAM.

This city, in point of situation and buildings, is one of the most picturesque I know. The stately cathedral and the old castle (the latter, it is true, greatly restored) form a most imposing mass upon the hill, while the lower part of the city, with the river and bridges, one of which dates from the 13th century, unite to form a scene of peculiar charm. The cathedral is the grandest building of the late Norman style, of the 12th century, existing in England. At the west end are two square towers, and at the junction of nave and transept another. The Gothic roof is of later date, about a hundred years after the original building. The perspective effect of the interior is of wondrous beauty. The ground-plan is distinguished by certain peculiarities. Thus the transept, in addition to the breadth of the centre aisle, has a side aisle. The Lady Chapel also is in the form of a second transept. This chapel, in the early Gothic style, is of great beauty, and one window is of very tasteful tracery. In the choir is a screen of perforated stone-work of the Gothic style of the 14th century, which is very beautiful. A wooden canopy also, once over the font, now in a corner, of the late Gothic forms of the time of Charles I. mingled with those of the Renaissance, deserves notice for its happy design and rich details. Very interesting also is the Galilee Chapel, essentially Norman in construction, which stretches along the breadth of the west end. The capitals of the columns are as original as they are elegant in form. The archivolts are richly decorated, some of them with the zigzag ornament. The Gothic windows are of later introduction. By the removal of the whitewash in a large niche the remains of an original wall-painting have come to view. Two saints at the side show very simple treatment. The form of mitre on the head preserved indicates the 12th century. The fine mouldings, which are of genuine Norman character, in tender and harmonious colouring, are very interesting. A monument of simple form, according to a Latin inscription on the top, contains the bones of the Venerable Bede.

The library of the cathedral, where I was received by the Rev. Mr. Greenwell with the greatest civility, contains the remains of the alb of St. Cuthbert, of gold brocade, discovered and brought here on occasion of a removal of the bones of the saint, once in the choir of the cathedral. The figures of the Apostles and Prophets, with their names, worked upon this garment, attracted my attention in no small degree by the reminiscences of the antique and the masterly execution they display. Among other ecclesiastical garments preserved in a glass case upon the stair I was also especially struck by two of great antiquity, with very tasteful decorations, both in form and colour, on a purple material. In the library also, Roman sculptures and altars, discovered in the vicinity, have found place. It is historically known that cohorts of Syrian and North African troops were stationed for a considerable time about here.

The chief purport of my visit to the library, however, was the study of the miniatures it contains. This study convinced me that a school of miniature-painting existed at Durham for several centuries of the middle ages, which devoted itself more to the practice of beautiful decorations than to the representation of scenes with figures. By this means, however, a rare degree of taste and an admirable technical manner were developed. The numbers attached to the following notices refer to a Latin catalogue printed in 1825 :—

A. ii. 17. The Gospels of John, Luke, and Mark, in this order, quarto, with one column in capital or majuscule letters. Decidedly of the 8th century. The opening words, "In principio," are an example of the Irish Anglo-Saxon mode of ornamentation of the most delicate kind, in the taste of the Cuthbert book in the British Museum. The fillings out of the flourishes and spiral scrolls are purple, the framework of a fine grey. At the opening of the other two Gospels are also beautiful initials, though of smaller size.

A. ii. 16. The Gospels in folio, entirely in majuscule letters. These purport to have been written by the Venerable Bede, and at all events belong to the 8th century. Leaf 37b contains a small flourish in yellow upon a black ground, with a yellow framework.   Above is a human head, in which a feeling for beauty is distinguishable ; below is a dragon.

3. ii. 30. Cassiodorus, Commentary on the Psalms.   Folio, in two columns, also purporting to be by Bede, and also in my opinion at least of the 8th century.   Leaf 81b contains David enthroned, with the inscription " David Rex."   This is coarse and rude, but not like the arbitrary and arabesque-like human figures of Irish art. The motives of the purple mantle are simple and without understanding ; on the lap is a kind of lyre, and two dragons on the arms of the throne.   The border, in eighteen compartments, is formed of very delicate flourishes and dragon-work in light and dark purple, vermilion, and green, quite in the Irish taste.   Leaf 169b contains David with a glory, standing on the two-headed serpent, in a bright purple mantle with simple but well-understood folds, and a yellow coat.   In his left hand is a spear.   The foreshortened foot is very rude.   The border, in ten compartments, is simpler here, but with very elegant scroll-work in black and white.

B. ii. 13. The Psalter, with St. Augustin's Commentary.   Folio, written about 1090, in two columns.   Leaf 102a contains the figure of William, the Bishop of that time, in the act of benediction, with his name written by ; above him the figure of Christ blessing ; below him a small figure of a man, probably the painter, with the name Robert Benjamin inscribed.   The outlines are black and vermilion, the proportions long, the drapery of the bishop painted green.   The initials are formed of scroll and dragon work, in a broad style.

B. iii. 32. A Hymnarium, in small folio, of the 11th century. Leaf 56b contains two bishops enthroned ; below, a monk in a forced attitude, representing, it is believed, Africus, the author of a Latin grammar for the use of the Anglo-Saxons.   Here the Anglo-Saxon character of the miniatures is quite developed.   The outlines are in red, with light shadowings in the same colour, in green, and in blue.

A. iv. 10. The Gospel of St. Matthew with a glossary.   Small folio, written about 1150.   On the first leaf is Christ in the mandorla, in the act of benediction, with a book in his left hand.   In the corners are the signs of the Evangelist represented as human figures with the different heads.   The execution is clear, the border is of a pretty pattern.

A. i. 10. Homilies on the Gospel of St. Matthew, folio, in two columns, written about 1150, with beautiful initials of broad scroll-work in light and harmonious colouring, and fillings out in a delicate blue. Leaf 186a contains an S, formed very ingeniously of a dragon. In the initial A is Christ enthroned, in white drapery, with a gold girdle, his right hand raised, and holding an open book in his left. The ground of a beautiful azure. The indications of the folds are simple but good. Leaf 197 contains an O, with Christ again, smaller, and in the mosaic type. Leaf 221a, St. John the Evangelist, in an O, with a long brown beard, book, and pen, of severe and dignified conception. Besides these are some other figures.

A. ii. 1. The Vulgate. Large folio, four volumes, in two columns, in a strong minuscule letter. This was executed by order of Bishop Hugo, who filled the office in 1153, and died in 1194. Leaf 2a of the first volume contains, above, a beautiful B in a square field of fine blue with white dots. At the opening of the book of Maccabees, in the upper and lower part of an E, is a fierce combat. The proportions are short, the flesh-tones brown, the other colours light and gaudy. The old leather cover of the first book, which is drawn over a later cover, is very remarkable. In the centre is a compartment with beautiful scrollwork, and three compartments with animals in two rows. On the back is a beautiful pattern with animals in the centre, and above and below scrollwork.

A. ii. 19. The Epistles of St. Paul, with a Commentary. A moderate-sized folio, in two columns. The Epistles in a large minuscule letter, the Commentary in a smaller ; written about the second half of the 12th century, and once the property of Bishop Hugo. Both the initials, and the quadrangular compartments they occupy, are of very choice taste, masterly execution, and of the most beautiful colours. This is especially the case with a P and an N. Only occasionally do figures occur ; as, for instance, St. Paul, a half-length figure, according to the traditional type, in an initial, and, leaf 250a, the martyrdom of three saints in a P.

A. iii. 2. The Books of Moses, Leviticus, and Numbers, in a moderate-sized folio, written, according to a notice in the catalogue, before the year 1199. In leaf 87a is a very beautiful initial, in cool, harmonious colours. The chief thing to be observed here is the old original binding, agreeing in all essentials with the one above described. The arrangement is, however, finer here, and eight figures of saints of short proportions occur.

A. iii. 7. The Psalter. A moderate folio, in the very tasteful original cover. On the upper side are horsemen, and an old woman playing the harp. On the lower side are very beautiful decorations of the Greek honeysuckle ornament in excellent style.

A. ii. 10. The Psalter, with a Commentary. Folio, in two columns. The text in large minuscule letters, the Commentary with smaller. Written about 1250-60. Of great refinement of art, both in the figures, where pen-drawing predominates, and in the initials. Leaf 7b, in a B are David and Goliath. Leaf 57a, the Coronation of David. Leaf 254b, Christ enthroned, in the mosaic type. The fillings out of the initials are coloured, for instance, purple. Here is also a kind of panelled ground of great delicacy. As it is ascertained that this manuscript was executed in Durham, it gives a favourable idea of the state of art there at that time.

C. i. 9. The Decretals. Folio, with elegant ornamentation, and few, and, in point of art, moderate vignettes, of the 13th century.

C. i. 14. Commentary on the Decretals by Andreas and three others. Written from about 1320 to 1330. A number of initials in oblong compartments are decorated with animals, weapons, &c., in a very elegant style. Every circumstance shows an English origin. The weapons, for instance, are English.

A. ii. 3. The Vulgate. In folio, two columns. Written in a strong minuscule letter about the beginning of the 14th century. At the beginning is a monk writing; below, the Devil. Many of the heads, in black outlines, have something individual—for instance, that of Jesse. The colours of the quadrangular compartments are of extraordinary brilliancy, especially the azures.

A. i. 18. Petri Berchorii Repertorium Morale. Three volumes folio. Written in two columns, and prior to the year 1362, when the author died. This is adorned with very rich and beautiful borders, all showing signs of an English origin.

A. iii. 32. A missal in a quarto-like folio, in two columns, written in a strong minuscule letter, about 1380-90, containing a Crucifixion, with the Virgin and St. John, of careful modelling and good taste in the drapery, but without feeling in the heads. In the angles the signs of the Evangelists.

Durham also possesses a few collections of pictures, to which Mr. Greenwell most kindly escorted me. In a house belonging to Mr. Fenderson, commanding a magnificent view of the cathedral, I found, among other pictures, a large and poetic landscape, with figures, which I consider to be a NICOLAS POUSSIN; a good landscape by SALVATOR ROSA; and two pretty pictures by ARTUS VAN DER NEER, a night and a day piece.

Among the numerous pictures belonging to the Archdeacon of Durham, I was struck by an altarpiece representing the Adoration of the Shepherds—a remarkable picture of the Netherlandish school of the time of Bernardin van Orley. The flesh tones are pale; the rocks in the background of fantastic forms; and the touch is very melting. A very suspicious signature, with the letters P. B., has led to its being assigned to Perino del Vaga.

St. Bartholomew and another saint—full-length figures, life-size —are excellent pictures, which I am most inclined to attribute to MORETTO OF BRESCIA. They are here wrongly given to Sebastian del Piombo.

A Holy Family, rather coarse in character, I consider a good work by BONIFAZIO. The name of Titian, here given, is too good for it.

The Archdeacon possesses besides copies, by VERRIO, from Raphael's Cartoons at Hampton Court.

In the collection of another gentleman, whose name I have lost, I saw a Christ by CARLO DOLCE—one of the master's choice works; a fine moonlight piece by ARTUS VAN DER NEER; and on the ground floor a good picture of the Lombard school, most probably by LUINI, in which St. Catherine is particularly beautiful.

OBJECTS OF ART AT DUNCOMBE PARK, YORKSHIRE,

SEAT OF LORD FEVERSHAM.

This stately house lies in a wooded country, of a pleasing hilly character. Behind it is a fine terrace, commanding an extensive view.   The beautiful park consists of two divisions, the outer called the Oak Park.

THE HALL.

This space is richly decorated with sculpture, and has an imposing effect.   An antique Molossian dog, of Parian marble, is by far the most remarkable object.   It bears much resemblance to that in the Uffizi at Florence, called the Dog of Alcibiades, but is more animated and of more careful workmanship.   The left fore foot alone is new.

An example of the Discobulus standing at ease—a good Roman work of Parian marble—is also worthy of remark.   The proportions are slenderer, and the development of the body less powerful, than in the well-known statue.   Nose, mouth, and chin, a portion of the throat, and the right hand are new.

Among the busts of celebrated men I remarked those of Pitt and Wellington.

DINING-ROOM.

GUIDO RENI.—1. David and Abigail.   The character of the heads is somewhat modern, but refined ; and the execution of masterly and careful completion in a cool tone.   Engraved by Strange.

JAN BOTH.—On the right a rock, with a waterfall.   A large picture of fine composition.   The distance especially is of airy delicacy.

HOBBEMA.—A large landscape, with rain-clouds.   Signed.   Of pleasing invention, but rather dark in tone.

SALOON.

SIMONE DA PESARO.—I do not understand the subject.   It appears a delicate picture by the master, but hangs too high over a door.

AGOSTINO CARRACCI.—On the left are two nymphs.   Opposite, Pan bound by Cupid.   A spirited work, known by an engraving by himself.   Carefully painted, but of insipid and heavy colouring.

DRAWING-ROOM.

CLAUDE LORRAINE.—1. On the left trees.   On the right cattle near a piece of cool blue water.   In the middle distance a rock with a waterfall, a watermill, and trees. In the distance a bridge, a temple, and water. Of pleasing composition, but the cattle, and also the distance, unusually hard.

2. The companion. In the foreground a large herd of cattle being driven along. On the right trees and much underwood. On the left a distance of cool reddish tone. Of the same quality as the foregoing.

CARLO DOLCE.—Martyrdom of St. Andrew. A very excellent picture of the master. Unusually noble and energetic in dramatic conception, and of great power of clear colouring.

GIACOMO BASSANO.—The Annunciation to the Shepherds. A clear, warm, and careful picture.

DOMENICHINO (?).—Adam and Eve, the latter with Abel on her shoulder. In my opinion a clear and delicate picture by L'ORBETTO.

TITIAN (?).—A careful copy of the Madonna with the rabbit, in the Louvre.

GUIDO RENI.—2. A Charity. A pleasing composition of very careful finish, known by the engraving.

3. St. Catherine with the palm, looking upwards in entreaty. Of fine form and very warm tone.

TITIAN (?).—Holy Family in a landscape. The little St. John is leading a lamb. St. Francis is opposite. There was too little light for me to form an opinion of this picture; but it appears to be a good work much resembling Paris Bordone. The landscape especially is beautiful.

NICOLAS POUSSIN.—A storm. Of poetical feeling, but very dark.

STATE BEDROOM.

TITIAN (?).—Venus and Adonis kissing. At all events only a picture of the school. Most probably by IL CAVALIERE LIBERI. But the light was insufficient for me to judge.

CHARLES LEBRUN.—A Visitation. A very delicate picture by him.

SEBASTIAN BOURDON.—The Child sleeping in a landscape, with Elizabeth and St. John. Very pretty, and quite in the taste of Nicolas Poussin.

GUIDO RENI.—4. Bacchus and Ariadne. This appears to be a

genuine example of this often repeated and somewhat artificial composition.

CARLO MARATTI.—The Virgin in Glory, accompanied by angels. A pleasing and careful picture.

FEDERIGO BAROCCIO.—The Nativity. Pleasing, careful, and of very transparent colouring.

GIOVANNI BELLINI (?).—The Presentation in the Temple. A rich and beautiful composition, carefully executed in a warm tone. Too darkly placed for any opinion, but most probably a work of his scholar BISSOLO.

DRESSING-ROOM.

PHILIP WOUVERMANS.—A large landscape with a falcon-chase in the foreground. Also other men and horses. A very originally composed picture in his second manner.

DOMENICHINO (?).—A large landscape, with a naked fisherman in the foreground. Too cold and hard for him, but a good picture by GRIMALDI.

SALVATOR ROSA.—1 and 2. Two small landscapes. These appear to be good and careful works, but are too highly hung between windows for any decision.

PICTURES AT ELVASTON CASTLE, DERBYSHIRE,
SEAT OF THE EARL OF HARRINGTON.

This stately castle has on the one side the appearance of a building of the middle ages, and on another that of an elegant modern erection. The fine hall is built in the Gothic style. The columns and ribs of the ceiling are gilt, and the various weapons hanging on the columns and walls enhance the mediæval effect. The staircase is also very picturesque. The spacious dining-room is decorated with splendid crimson and gold hangings, presented by a King of Spain to an Earl of Harrington, English ambassador to the court of Madrid. Among the numerous pictures distributed in the different apartments, I found a small number which I am tempted to describe. For the greater convenience of the reader, I annex the numbers as I found them on the pictures.

No. 191. RUTHHART.—A bear-hunt. Of very animated action and carefully painted in powerful colour. Wrongly termed Fyt.

No. 214. Teniers.—Two peasants playing cards, a third looking on. A woman is looking out from behind a wooden partition. Behind, three peasants before a fireplace. The heads, which are kept in a brownish tone, are very lively, and the cool effect agreeable. The treatment is careful, and of good impasto.

A male portrait, without number or name, is an excellent picture of the Netherlandish school, and most probably by Quentin Matsys. The man is attired in a furred garment of a patterned stuff, and a black cap ; to a gold chain round his neck is appended a crucifix, and in his right hand is a flower. The ground is green. The hands are of particular delicacy.

No. 190. Nicolas Maas.—A student in his library, surrounded with books, &c. Full-length. Very animated, and approaching Rembrandt in warmth and power of colour. The execution broad, but careful.

No. 181. Cornelis Jansen.—A female portrait, purporting to be Elizabeth Queen of Bohemia. Dated 1624. A delicate picture of clear colouring and tender execution, but representing another woman.

No. 194. Hoare of Bath.—A drawing with coloured chalks. Philip Earl of Chesterfield, author of the celebrated Letters. The fine features, and good expression of the face, are successfully given.

No. 180. Sir Godfrey Kneller.—John Duke of Marlborough. Of animated conception and careful execution in a warm tone.

No. 192. Carlo Maratti.—Cardinal Bentivoglio. Full-length. Two-thirds life-size. The attitude easy.

No. 146. Gerard Lairesse.—The death of Ananias. A good specimen of that period of the master when he still painted in a warm tone. Erroneously termed Lebrun.

No. 234. Sir Peter Lely.—A male portrait in armour. True, warm, and careful.

Other pictures by this master are here, some of them good, but others belonging to slighter works.

No. 376. Sir Joshua Reynolds.—1. Jane Lady Harrington. Full-length figure, seated. Animated, transparent, and of powerful colour. The background is landscape.

No. 377.—2. Lady Fleming. Full-length standing figure, with

landscape background, in a rose-coloured dress, extending her right hand. The beautiful features are livelily rendered. In some part this picture is unfinished.

No. 346.—3. His own portrait, in very youthful years. Of light local tones, and showing yet an undeveloped stage of his art.

4. The father of the present Earl of Harrington, young and in armour, a drawn sword in his right hand. Next him a black man with a helmet. The background a dark landscape. The expression of the fine features is admirably given. The colouring very powerful.

No. 356. ANNIBALE CARRACCI (?).—Pilate washing his hands. A very moderate picture by LUCA GIORDANO.

No. 317. NICOLAS BERGHEM.—A large landscape in the taste of Both. In the foreground a herd about to cross a ford. Finely composed, but of very broad treatment.

Besides these are some other portraits by GAINSBOROUGH. Upon the whole the pictures are in a neglected condition.

Among the remarkable features at Elvaston are the gardens, laid out in the old French style, with only evergreen trees and shrubs. This was done by the late Earl at an enormous expense. The rarest firs and pines from Canada, China, and the Himalayas are found here. In one part of the grounds is a labyrinth formed of these pines, the thick shade of which is relieved by smooth plots of the freshest verdure. A number of peacocks, and here and there pieces of sculpture, add to the picturesqueness of the scene.

I found Elvaston Castle occupied by numerous guests, and was indebted to the kindness of the Earl and Countess for some days of great enjoyment.

PICTURES AT LOCKO PARK, DERBYSHIRE,

SEAT OF WILLIAM DRURY LOWE, ESQ.

I had the good fortune to make the acquaintance of this gentleman at Elvaston Castle, and found him a great lover of art, and especially of the early Italian schools. I therefore gladly accepted his invitation to visit the pictures at Locko Park, and found my journey richly repaid. I proceed to notice some of the best pictures.

ARTOIS and RUBENS.—A very clear and careful landscape,

with two women and a man, lightly and spiritedly painted by Rubens.

BOURGUIGNON.—1. A very poetic landscape; doubtless a view in the Apennines, with a combat on horseback in the foreground.

2. A fierce combat. Slight, but spirited.

GUERCINO.—St. Peter repentant. Of far more feeling than usually characterises this painter, and also of great force and truth, and of careful finish.

VINCENZO CATENA.—To this master I attribute a capital picture of very original conception, of Christ with the Disciples at Emmaus. St. James is here represented as aged. The figures two-thirds life-size.

MARC ANTONIO FRANCESCHINI.—I am inclined to assign to this master a St. Theresa surrounded with angels, with the angel of Death about to hurl his arrow. It is a type of the weak sentimentality of feeling belonging to this time; but carefully and clearly painted.

MICHAEL ANGELO DA CARAVAGGIO.—The Crowning with Thorns. The Christ is of unusually elevated character for him, and shows the influence of Guido. The picture otherwise displays his power of colour and energy of treatment.

GIUSEPPE D'ARPINO.—The Virgin in Glory, surrounded with angels. A small and very delicate picture by this mannerist.

CANALETTO.—View of the Campo S. Giacomo, not far from the Rialto, with numerous figures. Admirably carried out in very clear colouring. From the Beckford collection.

GASPAR POUSSIN.—A landscape with water, and two figures. Across the water buildings and a hill. Of elevated composition, and unusual warmth of horizon.

ANDREA DEL SARTO.—The Virgin holding the Child, with St. John presenting the globe. Further behind is Joseph. The Virgin is very noble, but the right corner of the Child's mouth is out of drawing. A delicate picture by the master.

JAN BOTH (?).—A landscape, with a large hill conspicuous. This picture looks well, but hangs too high for an opinion.

MARIOTTO ALBERTINELLI.—Christ blessing the kneeling St. John. The Virgin seated on the ground, Joseph behind. Of pleasing heads, and great power of colour, but somewhat gaudy.

DOMENICO GHIRLANDAJO.—1. The profile portrait of Maria

Tornabuoni, who also appears as donatrix in the frescoes of this master, in the tribune of S. Maria Novella, at Florence. The background is a landscape. Another and more careful example of this picture, with some deviations, is in the Berlin Museum.

2. The profile portrait of a young man, perhaps the husband of the foregoing. In the background a hilly landscape. Both portraits are of great truth of feeling, and of uncommon force and clearness of tempera colour. Wrongly termed Masaccio.

CORNELIS JANSEN.—To him I attribute a portrait of Charles I. in youthful years, with a white collar, very animated, and of careful finish.

RUBENS.—Portrait of a young woman, in rich costume with a blueish collar. A purple background. Of refined and lively conception, and carefully executed in his earlier Genoese manner.

HOLBEIN.—Henry VIII., with a portion of one hand, in rich costume. Clear and careful. One of the earlier portraits of this monarch by the painter.

LODOVICO CARRACCI.—The Assumption of the Virgin. A very dramatic composition, under the strong influence of Correggio, whose delicate tones he has successfully imitated in the foremost angels, while the little angels above are of heavy and red colouring. The execution is very careful.

BOURGUIGNON.—3. A fight of horsemen; companion to No. 2. Spirited, but cruder and heavier in tone.

PIETRO DELLA FRANCESCA.—The profile portrait of a youth with light hair, violet cap, and green dress. The ground a dark blue. Refined in feeling, and of careful finish, especially in the hair.

BACCIO BANDINELLI.—Portrait of an old man, larger than life, holding a letter in his right hand, the writing on which agrees with the facsimile of his handwriting in Gaye's Carteggio. Admirably drawn, and of great power.

SEBASTIAN DEL PIOMBO.—Andrea Doria in profile, with a long white beard. Of elevated character, but so slightly painted that the drawing is seen through. This picture has at all events a close affinity to the master assigned.

MORETTO.—To this painter I attribute a male portrait, with the name Bartolommeo Capello, father of Bianca Capello, and the date 1546, April, on a letter he holds in his right hand. He is dressed in the white mantle of an order, and a black coat. The conception is very animated, the hands delicate, the flesh-tones insipid, and the ground of a delicate grey.

ADDITION TO THE COLLECTION OF THE EARL OF WARWICK.

Vol. III. p. 212.

The Virgin, ascending from her tomb, and dropping her girdle to St. Thomas in presence of St. Philip, St. Francis, and St. Paul. The composition of this picture, formerly in the Cathedral at Pisa, belongs, I am convinced, entirely to Raphael; but as regards the execution I only recognise his hand in the St. Thomas, St. Francis, and in some cherubs. He probably left the picture unfinished, like the Madonna del Baldachino in the Pitti Palace, to which it bears much resemblance, on his leaving Florence for Rome in 1508. In the other parts I recognise the hand of his friend Ridolfo Ghirlandajo, who on his departure, as is stated by Vasari, completed another of his pictures.

THE CATHEDRAL AT LINCOLN, AND OTHER BUILDINGS.

To Sir Charles Anderson, under whose hospitable roof at Lea, near Gainsborough, I spent three most agreeable days, I was indebted further for the sacrifice of his time in showing me everything of interest within possible reach. One Sunday morning took us by rail to Lincoln Cathedral, which rose in the distance, an imposing mass, on an elevation in the extensive plain. For situation, size, beauty of proportion, peculiarity of ground-plan, and varied and admirably executed details, this is one of the most remarkable cathedrals in England. The building dates from very different periods. The lower part of the centre of the façade is executed in the Norman, or what we term in Germany the Romanesque style. In the higher portions, and on each side, the early English or Gothic style is observable. At the same time, all three of the doors are carried out in rich Norman taste. This is also the case with the reliefs accompanying them, though these are moderate in point of art. On the other hand, the eleven enthroned statues of

English kings in the gallery in the centre are far later in date, and rather coarse in workmanship. The two quadrangular towers at the sides date, as is evident from the form of the arches, from the 14th century, while the lofty and beautiful tower in the centre shows the purer forms of the Gothic school of the 13th century. On the lower part of this tower, and on various surfaces of wall, is introduced a delicate reticulated ornament. At the end of the stately transepts are circular windows, one of them with tracery of roundish forms, and very beautiful coloured glass, in which azure predominates, belonging to the 13th century; the other with broad leaves, like the circular window in the façade of York, displays the later flamboyant style. A peculiar feature is observable in a second transept behind the choir, abutting on the Lady Chapel, which terminates the building. This chapel is in the purest and richest Gothic taste, and of beautiful proportions. From the figures of angels sculptured in the spandrils of the arches, engraved a few years ago, and published in a work by Mr. Cockerell, it is also called the Angels' Choir. The skill with which the chiefly graceful motives of this sculpture are introduced into the little favourable spaces is quite extraordinary; the style of the drapery also is of rare purity. Of the same high merit, and of the same period, are the now unfortunately mutilated sculptures on the rich doorway on the south side. The rich tracery of the window at the end of the Angels' Choir is very remarkable. It is now filled by very unfortunate modern painted glass, which is however to be replaced by better. Above the transept is a well-formed lantern. The windows of the nave and the aisles, with their three compartments without tracery or coloured glass, have a poor effect. The perspective of the nave is much interrupted by a whimsical arrangement of the groining. On the other hand, the distance of one column from another gives a light and beautiful appearance. A gallery of considerable depth runs round the whole interior. Chapels of various sizes, and other side buildings, exhibit many picturesque details. Particularly interesting is the Galilee Chapel. All necessary restorations and repairs are admirably carried on, and a sum of 1500*l*. a year is set aside for that purpose from the funds of the Cathedral.

In the vicinity is a small but beautiful cloister. The tracery is of very pure taste. On the key-stones of the wooden arches are sculptures of good style, and soft drapery.   They are now, however, almost obliterated.

The Chapter-house, close by, is also in the early English style, and has an admirable effect both within and without.   It is supported in the centre of the interior by a column.   The buttresses on the outside stand out far from the walls, to which they are united by flying arches.   Several buildings in the vicinity are allied in style to the Cathedral, so that they form an harmonious whole.   Not far from the Cathedral, and still higher in position, was the old fortress, of which only the walls survive; within them are now the prison and court of justice.   The garden belonging to these commands a beautiful view of the Cathedral.

The situation of the city, also on undulating ground, is very picturesque.   At one time it boasted of above 50 churches and more than 30,000 inhabitants.   An old house still retains stone ornaments over door and windows of a pure Norman character. Repeated whitewashings have blunted the forms.   It is called the Jews' House.

COLLECTION OF ART AT BROCKLESBY, LINCOLNSHIRE,
SEAT OF THE EARL OF YARBOROUGH.

Besides a considerable number of pictures of the Italian, Netherlandish, and French schools, some of which are very remarkable, are preserved the celebrated Wortley collection of antiques, formerly in Apuldercombe House, in the Isle of Wight, and now passed by inheritance into the possession of Lord Yarborough. Although his Lordship was not at home, the presence of Sir Charles Anderson opened to us all the apartments containing pictures.

ENTRANCE HALL.

TINTORETTO.—A male portrait, almost to the knees.   One of his coarser works.

GIORGIONE (?).—Portrait of a man seated, in gay dress.   Too weak in drawing, and not refined enough in feature, for Giorgione, but a good and interesting picture of the Venetian school.

THE HALL.

SALVATOR ROSA.—1. A combat of horsemen. Spirited, but dark.

SOUTH LIBRARY.

REMBRANDT (?).—A male portrait. A good work of his school.

ZUCCHERO.—Portrait of a young man in a silk dress; most arbitrarily denominated Don Carlos. Of great elegance.

DRAWING-ROOM.

A very stately apartment with rich and tasteful furniture, and beautiful old Sèvres vases, leading into a charming conservatory.

VELASQUEZ (?).—A Spanish officer. A good picture of animated composition, but by another hand.

PAUL VERONESE(?).—Susannah and the Elders. A spirited picture by TINTORETTO.

SEBASTIAN DEL PIOMBO (?).—The Descent from the Cross. A small picture by DANIEL DA VOLTERRA, of beautiful composition, deep feeling in the heads, and careful execution.

GASPAR POUSSIN (?).—A landscape by SALVATOR ROSA (2), in the distance of which he has imitated the manner of Gaspar Poussin. This shows a rare union of power and transparency of colour and beauty of lines. Two figures are in his own style.

PAUL VERONESE.—1. Rebecca and Eleazar at the Well. A charming picture in his clear silvery tones. The Rebecca particularly noble.

RAPHAEL (?).—The Virgin and Child; behind them, on a rich throne, St. Anna standing; above, two angels. On each side of the throne, on a parapet, are reliefs of mythological import, in the taste of Mazzolino da Ferrara. A small picture, on wood. Very original in invention, and by some excellent Ferrarese master.

TITIAN (?).—Cupid playing on the lute. This appears good, but in its position between two windows no opinion can be formed.

PALAMEDESS PALAMEDES.—1 and 2. Two interiors, with figures, are good pictures by him.

ZUCHARELLI.—1 and 2. Two very large landscapes, views in the vicinity of Verona and Vicenza. The excellent keeping, great transparency, and careful finish, render these his chefs-d'œuvre.

Carlo Dolce.—The aged St. Mary Egyptiaca in prayer. Noble in character, and powerful and clear in colour.

Gaspar Poussin.—1. Rocks and caves, through which the light falls, and a waterfall. St. Jerome in the foreground. Highly poetical.

Guido Reni.—The infant Christ sleeping on a cross. A delicate little picture, in tender silvery tones, and of careful execution.

Gaspar Poussin.—2. The companion to the foregoing, and of similar composition and merit.

Paul Veronese.—2. The Emperor Augustus, to whom the Sibyl is showing the Virgin and Child. A spirited picture, of noble forms. The head of the emperor is fine, that of the Sibyl very tender. In the background is architecture in the taste of Palladio. Wrongly called Salviati.

Biscaino.—1 and 2. The Noli me tangere, and Christ with the Woman of Samaria. Small, pleasing, and careful pictures, by this not common master.

Domenico Feti.—The parable of the Vineyard. The same composition as in the Dresden Gallery, but this picture is larger and of more powerful colour.

Paul Veronese.—3. The Annunciation. The figures half life-size. The Almighty and angels in the sky. Very golden in tone, but partially slight in treatment.

Correggio (?).—St. Catherine blessed by the infant Christ. An angel in the sky descending with a palm. A beautiful picture, by his scholar Gandini.

Giacomo Bassano.—The Annunciation to the Shepherds. Figures half life-size. Particularly clear.

Salvator Rosa.—A landscape with a large cave. Spirited, but very dark in the foreground.

Innocenzo da Imola.—The Virgin and Child, SS. Ursula and Anthony of Padua. A genuine but weak picture of the master.

Parmigianino.—The infant Christ sleeping in the cradle. Graceful in motive, delicate in rendering, and of warm colour.

Schidone.—The Virgin and Child. Very dramatic. The sketchy treatment is spirited.

Paolo Veronese.—4. Venus seated in a landscape, and drawing a thorn out of her foot. Almost life-size. Of uncommon warmth and clearness. The horizon of the landscape glowing.

NICOLAS POUSSIN.—Rinaldo and Armida, accompanied by amorini. In the distance the two knights listening. Of fine invention, and executed in a full yellowish flesh tone.

DOMENICHINO.—A landscape. In the foreground the Baptism of Christ. Of poetic conception, and warm and clear colouring.

HEINRICK VAN STEENWYCK.—Interior of a church, with figures by FRANZ FRANCK. Rather large. Of rare power and delicacy, and unusually broad treatment.

GASPAR POUSSIN.—3. On the left, in the foreground, an eminence with trees. Two figures on a road, behind them an extended distance. Delicate, clear, and of great charm.

ALBANO.—Six amorini occupied sharpening their arrows on an anvil, and shooting at a mark. A pleasing and clear picture, which has however suffered.

TIEPOLO.—1 and 2. Two pretty pictures.

GUERCINO.—Painting, represented as a woman of pretty features, with a palette. This hangs too high.

LORD WORSLEY'S ROOM.

SALVATOR ROSA.—A landscape, with a hermit in the foreground. A good picture.

JACOB RUYSDAEL.—A waterfall. In the centre of the picture a hill. A very pleasing picture.

LADY YARBOROUGH'S ROOM.

JAN HACKERT.—A beautiful composition in the taste of Pynacker, with figures and cattle by ADRIAN VAN DE VELDE.

TENIERS.—1. Three fishermen on the sea-shore. Very original. Of grey but delicate tone.

2. A landscape with two shepherds, cows, and sheep, by a piece of dark water. Silvery clouds in the sky. A picture of rare force and clearness, and of very spirited touch.

GASPAR POUSSIN.—4. On the right, in the foreground, trees and two figures by a dark piece of water, on the further shore of which are buildings. The sky of bright and tender colour. An admirable work of the master.

LADY YARBOROUGH'S SITTING-ROOM.

LEONARDO DA VINCI (?).—Christ. The hands of striking motive. A good picture of the school.

BEDROOM NO. 1.

Gaspar Poussin.—5. On the left, in the foreground, a tree ; on the right stately buildings on rising ground. In the foreground a waterfall of moderate dimensions, and three figures. In composition, power, transparency of tone, and execution a picture of the first order.

Pieter Pourbus.—A male portrait; his left hand on the hilt of his sword. To the knees. Inscribed 1549, æt. 35. Wrongly given to Franz Pourbus the elder.

Guido Reni.—The Mater Dolorosa. Head and hands in an oval. Delicate in form, and elevated in expression, but of pale colouring.

BEDROOM NO. 3.

Claude Lorraine.—A sea-coast, with sunrise. On the left a stately edifice and trees, further on a tower, and opposite another tower. In the foreground five figures, and three others, and a fourth at a boat. Of the best time of the master. Of great depth and clearness of the warm but subdued tone. From Apuldercombe House.

Barroccio.—The Magdalen with a skull. A good picture.

Battoni.—The Sacrifice of Iphigenia. A small and rich picture. A good work for him.

THE GALLERY.

Nicolas Poussin.—A sleeping nymph and two satyrs. This appears to be an excellent picture, but it hung too high for any decided opinion.

BEDROOM NO. 7.

Gaspar Poussin.—6. On the right trees, with figures under them. In the middle distance a wooded rising ground with buildings. Of great beauty.

Vandyck.—The Virgin, a noble figure, holding the animated Child in her lap, who is adored by the Magdalen. This picture looks very promising, but the dirty condition in which it is, and the height at which it hangs, forbid a more positive opinion.

STAIRCASE.

Sebastian Bourdon.—1, 2, 3, 4, 5, 6, and 7. The Seven

Works of Mercy, in the taste of Nicolas Poussin, and also of about the size of the Seven Sacraments. The compositions are rich, and in part very successful, but the flesh tones often too red and glassy.

ALBANO.—Joseph and Potiphar's wife. Full-length, life-size figures. Obviously the model for the well-known picture by Cignani in the Dresden Gallery. Of very warm and careful execution, but the expression of Joseph not fortunate. Formerly in the Mocenigo collection, Venice.

ANDREA SACCHI.—The dead Abel. An academy-study of good foreshortening and careful finish in a warm tone. In the distance Cain fleeing. This picture often occurs.

BENEDETTO CASTIGLIONE.—A kind of caravan, with figures of men, and various animals, donkeys, leopards, turkeys, turtles, &c. The large size, rich composition, and careful execution of this picture render it his chef-d'œuvre.

CHARLES LEBRUN.—Perseus and Andromeda. An admirable work of the master. Of poetic composition for him, and powerful and warm colouring.

Unfortunately for me, most of the antique sculptures, which are usually placed in a conservatory, were at the period of my visit in the Exhibition at Dublin. Among those remaining, a head of Niobe, brought to England by Sir William Hamilton, attracted my attention by its noble form, fine expression, and good workmanship.

PICTURES AT SCAWBY, LINCOLNSHIRE,

SEAT OF SIR JOHN NELTHORPE, BART.

In this comfortable house, belonging to the brother-in-law of Sir Charles Anderson, are preserved a few excellent pictures.

DRAWING-ROOM.

JAN BOTH.—A hilly landscape with fir-trees. On the left, almost in the foreground, stately rocks with a road at their foot, enlivened by several figures. In the distance are other hills. The clouds are illumined by the sun. Of rare power and freshness, and very attractive in composition.

NICOLAS POUSSIN.—A landscape with a rocky hill rising on the right, and on the left a piece of water, on which is a boat. An apostle is baptising converts, other figures looking on. The grandeur of the composition agrees with the beauty of the landscape. Attributed to Gaspar Poussin.

RUYSBRAECK.—A landscape with a well in the foreground, a statue and a dolphin, and a piece of water, with figures on the shore. A poetical and very careful work by this clever painter, who seldom figures under his own name.

ROTHENHAMMER.—Christ on the Mount of Olives. An admirable little picture.

HENRICK STEENWYCK.—Interior of a prison by torchlight. Delicate and clear.

ANOTHER ROOM.

MABUSE.—The painter has here treated, with no common enthusiasm, the beautiful story of the Count of Toulouse, so characteristic of the spirit of the middle ages. The purport of the story is to this effect—that, deeply touched with the sense of his Saviour's suffering, the Count of Toulouse felt himself unworthy to enjoy the luxuries and honours of his high station; stripping himself, therefore, of his dignities, he proceeded to the Holy Land in the garb of the humblest pilgrim. The young Count is here represented taking off his shirt, which a servant in a brown furred coat receives, who at the same time is holding the black fur coat which his master has laid aside, and which is partly on the ground. His cap lies there too. Next him stands the stately Bishop of Toulouse in his robes, wiping a tear with his left hand, while with his right hand he covers the nakedness of the Count with his dress. Next behind him are two other men, who finely express their sympathy at the scene. On the right, in the middle distance, through a gate, is seen a man bringing the pilgrim's dress, a short hair garment. On the left the Count appears dressed in it, beginning his journey, the pilgrim's staff in his left hand, his eyes cast up in humble aspiration, and the right hand on his breast. In the background, which consists of buildings and a piece of landscape, he appears again, attacked and beaten by two robbers. The effect of colour is unpleasing, the flesh-tones grey and much broken. The naked legs of the Count are well drawn, the violet colour and embroidery on the Bishop's robe of rare delicacy. Cleaning and varnishing would much improve this fine picture.

RIBERA.—The repentant Peter looking up. Of elevated conception for him, and of masterly and solid painting in a warm tone.

MURILLO.—Two beggar-boys; the one eating grapes, the other a melon. This picture is so transparent and pure, that I am inclined to take it for an original repetition of the well-known picture at Munich.

MELCHIOR HONDEKOETER.—1. A white peacock, a pheasant, a Guinea-hen, and a family of fowls.

2. The companion. Water-fowls, geese, ducks, with young ones in the water. These are masterly pictures, in very powerful colouring, and of considerable size.

JAN WEENIX.—A dead hare, dead birds, and a basket of fruit. The background landscape. A warm and clear picture of forcible colour and masterly treatment, of the best time of the master.

LARGILLIÈRE.—Portrait of a man in a powdered peruke, beckoning with the left hand. Of oval form. Very animated and careful.

COLLECTION OF PICTURES AT CLUMBER PARK, NOTTINGHAMSHIRE,

SEAT OF THE DUKE OF NEWCASTLE.

This collection is especially adorned by fine specimens of the Netherlandish school, and also contains a few by Italian and French masters. Here again the kindness of Sir Charles Anderson procured me the undisturbed inspection of the pictures.

STATE DINING-ROOM.

SNYDERS.—1, 2, 3, 4. Four large pictures with poultry, fruit, and fish. On one of them are figures, by LANGJAN, in the act of selling fish. These are excellent specimens of the master.

JAN WEENIX.—A large landscape, in which is a large urn; in the foreground a dog with dead game. This is a picture of the first class by the master in point of composition, power, truth, mastery of execution, and size.

ZUCHARELLI.—1 and 2. Two landscapes of upright form, with cattle, belong to his best works.

BREAKFAST ROOM.

GAINSBOROUGH.—A beggar child. Naïve and lively in feeling, and of masterly execution.

CLAUDE LORRAINE.—A small wooded landscape, with a piece of water. Of cool tone, with the exception of the warm sky.

DOMENICHINO (?).—A Cardinal seated. To the knees. An excellent picture, but too feeble in colour for Domenichino.

POELEMBERG.—A landscape with ruins, and nymphs close by. Of great delicacy.

JACOB RUYSDAEL.—1. A stormy sea, with breakers in the foreground. Several boats, and one with a red sail : on the left a pier ; on the right, in the distance, a ship. Signed. A very spirited work, of masterly execution.

TITIAN (?).—Portrait of a man in a blue dress. This appears to me to be a good picture by PAUL VERONESE.

HOLBEIN.—A male portrait in a black dress and cap ; the background of landscape character. An admirable work of his middle time.

JAN BREUGHEL.—Spring, represented by the reign of Flora. The goddess herself is by ROTHENHAMMER. An excellent picture of moderate size.

JACOB RUYSDAEL.—2. A wooded eminence, with a house upon it, partly in sunshine ; before it a field and garden in full sunshine. The sky is lightly treated in the taste of Hobbema. An excellent and careful picture of his earlier time.

JAN MOSTAERT.—The Virgin standing in a purple mantle, holding the Child, the lower limbs of whom are covered with a cloth : at the sides are three angels, one of them playing the lute, another extending a pink with a joyful expression : the figures of two angels in stone upon two columns, holding festoons of flowers : through an arch is the view of a landscape and a church ; in the church is seen a rose-coloured carpet worked with gold, of rare delicacy ; a small portion of the picture is broken off above, which interferes with an inscription : in niches are the stone statues of two prophets. One of the most beautiful works of the master, who belongs in point of feeling and technical treatment to the Van Eyck school. About 1 ft. 6 in. high, 1 ft. $\frac{1}{2}$ in. wide.

DINING-ROOM.

TENIERS.—1. A rather large landscape. In front of a house is a maidservant sweeping. Painted in a silvery tone, but the treatment of scenic character.

PHILIP WOUVERMANS. — Landscape, with a stag-hunt. Of highly dramatic composition. This picture belongs to the time of transition from his first to his second manner.

VAN OS.—Flower and fruit piece. Sunny in effect in the style of Van Huysum, and very careful.

CLAUDE LORRAINE.—A small picture, with two trees in the centre, and three cows in front. Of delicate painting in a cool tone.

THE CRIMSON DRAWING-ROOM.

FRANCESCO FURINI.—Sigismunda lamenting over the heart of Tancred. Of deep feeling, and warm and clear colouring.

GASPAR POUSSIN. — 1 and 2. Two very poetic landscapes. Companion pictures.

BATHISTA FRANCO.—The Baptism of Christ. Careful, but cold in feeling and colour.

GUIDO RENI.—Artemisia. In his coldest tones.

RUBENS.—1. A girl smelling a flower. Coarse in character, but clear in colour, and very broad in treatment.

REMBRANDT.—Portrait of a man holding a roll of paper in his right hand, and lifting a curtain with his left. Carefully painted in his bright golden tones.

RUBENS.—2. A woman with a bunch of grapes. Companion to the foregoing, and of the same style. Both belong probably to some series representing the five senses.

3. A Jesuit preaching to a country audience. Very animated, but too highly hung to admit of a closer inspection.

GASPAR POUSSIN.—3. A large landscape, with a large hill in the middle distance ; behind which is the Roman Campagna, terminated by a warm horizon. Of marvellous poetry and transparency, and careful execution.

VAN UDEN and TENIERS.—2. A village, with various figures. This hangs too high, but appears to me rather to be the sole work of Teniers.

LARGE DRAWING-ROOM.

Murillo (?).—The Virgin on the Crescent, surrounded by seven angels ; below, a large landscape.   Painted under the strong influence of Rubens, by some less important painter of the Spanish school.   The Virgin is of vulgar character.

Vandyck. — Rinaldo and Armida.   Full-length, life-size figures.   Of pleasing composition, animated heads, and brownish colouring.   The beautiful landscape is warm in colouring.

Benedetto Castiglione.—The finding of Cyrus.   Full-length, life-size figures.   A very good work of the master.

Delorme.—A good architectural piece.

STAIRCASE.

Snyders.—A lioness tearing a boar.   Of animated and spirited treatment.

ANTE-ROOM.

Holbein.—A male portrait, with a cap and a bâton, purporting to be that of Sir Thomas More.   A very beautiful work, but representing another person.   Too high for a closer view.

CHAPLAIN'S ROOM.

Teniers.—3. A cow-stable ; a woman pouring milk into a pail, and speaking to a man standing before the door ; a boy and a calf are striking objects.   A rather large picture, of great truth, especially a brown cow, and powerfully painted in a clear colour.

4. A landscape.   In the foreground a shepherd playing the flute ; a party in front of a house.   Of sunny effect and careful finish.   It hangs too high.

Gainsborough.—A very successful landscape.

Wilson.—A landscape with a piece of water.   Very attractive.

COLLECTION OF PICTURES AT WELBECK ABBEY,
NOTTINGHAMSHIRE,
Seat of the Duke of Portland.

Although this collection consists principally of pictures of the Netherlandish school, yet good works by Italian, German, French, and English masters are also here.   A rich series of portraits in

miniature is also an attraction in this collection. It was com-
menced by Harley Earl of Oxford, carried on by his son the second
Earl, and further increased by Vertue for the widow of the latter.

ANTE-ROOM.

Caspar Netscher.—Portrait of King William III. Full-
length. This picture appeared to me to have much of the character
of this master, but it hangs too high and in too dark a place to
admit of an opinion.

Melchior Hondekoeter.—1 and 2. Two pictures with water-
fowls and a family of hen and chickens belong to his good works.

Frans Hals.—Portrait of an old woman. Very animated, and,
as far as I could judge, by the master ; but the position was too
unfavourable to decide.

Roland Savery.—An animal-piece. Rich and good.

Vandyck (?).—Charles I. on a horse of pale colour. Like the
picture at Blenheim. Too high for an opinion.

School of Giovanni Bellini.—Holy Family, in a landscape,
with the animated portrait of the donor. It has suffered.

Four pictures of interiors, with figures, appeared interesting, but
hung too high for an opinion.

In this apartment, in a series of frames under glass, is the collection of miniatures. It was very interesting to trace portraits
from the time of Henry VIII. to Queen Anne—among which those
by the hands of Isaac and Peter Oliver, Nicholas Hilliard,
Samuel Cooper, Flatman, Hoskins, Petitot, Zincke, and
Lens, are remarkable.

SMALL DRAWING-ROOM.

Vandyck (?).—Sir Hugh Middleton. A good picture by another artist, allied to Mireveldt, and whose name appears to be on
the frame, though the picture hung too high for me to read it.

Henrick van Steenwyck.—1. A room, with St. Jerome and
his lion. Signed, and dated 1624. Carefully executed in a very
clear and bright tone.

Johann van Calcar (scholar of Titian).—Sketch for the fine
male portrait in the Louvre, here called a Titian. Very interesting, but hung too high.

Sir Joshua Reynolds.—1. The late Duke of Portland, as a

boy, in a landscape. The conception is very animated, the colouring warm, but the forms somewhat empty.

Henrick van Steenwyck.—2. The Deliverance of St. Peter. A large, careful, and warm picture of good effect.

Jan Both.—A large landscape, with a piece of very transparent water. This promises well, but hangs too high.

Vandyck.—1. Sir Kenelm Digby in a purple dress, his wife in blue, and two children. To the knees. The background architecture, a curtain, and a landscape. This is a duplicate of the picture in the possession of the Queen, carefully painted in a warm though somewhat heavy tone.

Carlo Dolce. — St. Cecilia. An excellent picture by the master. The hands resembling those of the same saint in the gallery at Dresden.

Vandyck.—2. Portrait of William of Orange, afterwards William III., as a child, in the open air. I leave this fact unquestioned. At all events it represents a pretty boy of good conception. The sunken state of the picture, and the high position, forbid a further opinion.

Snyders.—1. Two lionesses following a roe. Very animated and masterly, and not inferior to the same composition in the gallery at Munich.

Vandyck.—3. Archbishop Laud. Almost to the knees. Very animated, and of careful painting in a warm tone. The hand is particularly excellent. It hangs very unfavourably.

Gaspar Poussin.—A small landscape, which hangs in a dark place between windows.

LARGE DRAWING-ROOM.

Jacob Ruysdael.—A landscape, with grand oaks and a piece of water. Figures in the foreground. A fine composition, but now dark and brown in tone.

Philip Wouvermans.—A hunting party. A huntsman blowing a bugle. A good but now very dark picture.

Sassoferrato.—The Madonna praying. An excellent example of this often-repeated picture, of very warm tone.

Tintoretto.—Portrait of a man with his left hand on a book, and the right pointing to something. Of very animated feeling and carefully painted.

ANNIBALE CARRACCI.—St. John the Baptist, seated in a land-scape, pointing to Christ, who is seen in the distance. Decidedly realistic, but of great energy, and painted in a brown tone. The landscape is poetic.

WILLEM VAN DE VELDE.—1. A calm, with various small ves-sels. A gun is being fired from a large ship. A delicate picture in a warm tone.

2. The companion. Also a calm sea, with several boats. One of them on the left in the foreground, with its white sail reflected in the water. Admirable.

RAPHAEL (?).—An early and careful copy of Francis I.'s Holy Family, in the Louvre.

PAUL BRIL.—Landscape, with a piece of water. A delicate picture of the best time of the master.

PETER NEEFS.—Interior of a church by candlelight. Of great delicacy.

VANDYCK.—4. A child upon a bed. Of great charm and very lively.

SIR JOSHUA REYNOLDS.—Lord Richard Cavendish, in youthful years. Very true and energetic, and of masterly painting.

RUBENS (?).—An early school copy of the often-repeated Garden of Love, a fine example of which is in the gallery at Dresden, and the original, according to a verbal statement on the part of Sir David Wilkie, in the gallery at Madrid.

GASPAR POUSSIN.—1. A landscape, of upright form. In the foreground two figures reposing.

2. The companion to this, hung too high for a closer inspection.

CLAUDE LORRAINE.—A landscape, with a shepherd and shep-herdess in the foreground. This promises well, but is now dark and sunken.

VANDYCK.—5. An Antwerp senator. To the knees. This looks very inviting, but is too highly and darkly hung.

DINING-ROOM.

JAN GRIFFIER.—A very pretty landscape.

SNYDERS.—2, 3, 4, and 5. Four large pictures, but not of his ᵥest works. The great darkness of the shadows is perhaps occa-ᵢoned by their neglected condition.

TITIAN.—Portrait of a man leaning on his left hand. Spirited in conception, and of masterly execution in a golden tone.

VANDYCK.—6. Lord Strafford. A bâton in his right hand; with the left he is pointing to a helmet next him. The background landscape. Of spirited conception, and executed in the same broken flesh-tones as the picture in Wentworth House. A large inscription in golden letters much defaces it.

HONDEKOETER.—1 and 2. Two good pictures of poultry.

GIACOMO BASSANO. — 1 and 2. Two unusually transparent works.

REMBRANDT (?).—His own portrait, in aged years. Too highly hung for an opinion, but not very promising.

CORNELIS JANSEN (?).—This is called the portrait of the Dutch Admiral Tromp; it is, however, decidedly that of Admiral Ruyter by another and also excellent master.

RUBENS.—1. A Triton with sea-nymphs, and boys carrying festoons of fruit. In chiaroscuro. Spirited.

STAIRCASE.

VAN DER MEULEN.—A siege. Of considerable extent. This appears to be a good picture, but hangs too unfavourably.

GOTHIC HALL.

SIR JOSHUA REYNOLDS.—2, 3, 4, and 5. Four pictures : Charity, Hope, and two other allegorical figures. These are meritorious works, though inferior to those of a similar kind in the possession of Lord Normanton.

6. An angel on clouds, in a large arched space. Of great softness and transparency.

7. William Bentinck, third Duke of Portland, in a red dress, seated thoughtfully before a desk. Of very animated conception.

ENTRANCE HALL.

HOLBEIN.—Portrait of a man in black dress, holding a palm in his left hand, and a small book in a bag, on which are five little red crosses, in his right. The ground green. A most admirable picture, in excellent preservation.

PETER BREUGHEL THE YOUNGER, called HELL BREUGHEL. A tournament between an old woman and a man upon a barrel. A rich composition in his broad comic vein. It hangs between the windows.

GERARD HONTHORST.—The Adoration of the Shepherds. A good picture of the master.

SNYDERS.—1, 2, and 3. Two wild-boar hunts and a bull-fight. Good works.

It is greatly to be desired that these pictures, which have been long in a neglected condition, should be assisted by a little discreet cleaning and fresh varnish. This should be done soon, or in many instances the help would come too late.

PICTURES AT SERLBY, NOTTINGHAMSHIRE,

SEAT OF VISCOUNT GALWAY:

Among the small number of pictures in this house are some of great excellence. Sir Charles Anderson was again my guide on this occasion.

THE HALL.

DANIEL MYTENS.—Charles I. and Henrietta Maria, both still very young, dressed in light cool colours, walking hand in hand on a terrace. On the right Sir Geoffrey Hudson, the dwarf, holding two little dogs. Five other dogs also near. On the left a negro holding a grey horse, a brown horse, and a setter, on which a dwarf is riding. Full-length, life-size figures. The flesh tones silvery and clear, the execution very finished. This picture greatly resembles that at Dunmore Park.

VANDYCK (?).—An early copy of the fine picture in the Louvre of Charles I. standing with his horse. But the horse is here omitted.

DRAWING-ROOM.

HOLBEIN (?).—Portrait of the astronomer Nicolas Kratzer. On wood. An early copy of the Louvre picture, with the same inscription and date, 1528.

A very careful copy of Titian's Entombment in the Louvre in chiaroscuro. I consider this a study by the youthful VANDYCK, 1.

HOLBEIN.—Henry VIII., standing. Full-length, life-size figure. Seen as usual in front, in a coat of red and gold brocade, and a mantle of cloth of gold, trimmed with ermine. A black cap and white feather on his head. The ground dark, and upon it a long inscription with the name of the King and 1543. A genuine, careful, and transparent picture.

VANDYCK.—2. William Russell, first Duke of Bedford, with dark hair; in a red dress, standing; with a black hat in his left hand, the right hand with his glove resting on his side. Next him, in a black dress, with his elbow on a parapet, is Francis Russell, fourth Earl of Bedford. Quite on the left an astrolabe. The background architecture, a curtain, and sky. Of very spirited treatment in a truly luminous and golden flesh tone. The left hand of the Earl, in tone and impasto, approaches the portrait of Gevartius in the National Gallery. Otherwise the treatment is very broad, and in some parts—for example, the white collar— almost careless. Painted about 1630.

2. Lady Catherine Manners, Duchess of Buckingham, with her children. Full-length, life-size figures. She is in a black dress, seated, and holding in the rather weakly drawn left hand a medallion, which hangs round her neck, probably the portrait of her murdered husband. On the left, standing next her, is a little boy; on the right a taller boy, holding his mother's right hand in both his, and looking round at his elder sister, who stands on the left in the foreground in a white dress, a flower in her hand. Further back in an oval is a male portrait. In the background on the right a curtain, on the left a stout pillar. Between these is seen the sky. The execution of this picture is very unequal. The elder boy and the girl are animated, and also transparent in colour; the lady, on the other hand, and the little boy, much duller; the curtain and the carpet almost careless in treatment. This picture may have been painted about 1636.

3. Thomas Herbert, eighth Earl of Pembroke; in a red silk dress, with slashed sleeves, lined with white. His left hand on his hip, the right holding a scarf on the right side of the chest. The ground dark. The head is animatedly painted in a very subdued tone, the execution careful, and the treatment of the materials of the dress masterly.

PANNINI.—Interior of St. Peter's. A large picture, and in every respect one of his best.

REGNIER BRACKENBURG.—1 and 2. Two pictures, representing some persons in a room, and belonging to his clear, rich, and delicate pictures.

COLLECTION OF PICTURES AT WIMPOLE, CAMBRIDGESHIRE,
SEAT OF THE EARL OF HARDWICKE.

I had the pleasure of spending a most agreeable day at Wimpole, in the circle of Lord Hardwicke's amiable family. The house is a stately edifice, containing numerous apartments, among which the large drawing-room lighted from above, the library, and dining-room are conspicuous. The pictures are scattered through various rooms, and consist chiefly of Netherlandish masters. Nor are good specimens wanting of the Italian, French, and English schools.

LARGE DRAWING-ROOM.

SIR THOMAS LAWRENCE.—Lord Hardwicke, uncle of the present Earl, in peer's robes. To the knees. Of unusual truth and clearness of colour, and very solidly painted.

Two children in marble, by RAUCH of Berlin. Repetitions of the figures on the monument to Franck at Halle on the Saal. These are as pleasing in feeling as they are excellent in execution.

SMALL DINING-ROOM.

RUBENS.—Two old men, rather above life-size. On wood. Powerful and clear, in subdued and harmonious colouring, and of broad treatment.

VANDYCK.—1. The painter David Ryckart in a fur cap and furred dress and red waistcoat. Bust picture, on wood. Of the frequent repetitions of this portrait the best, which is to the knees, is in the gallery at Dresden. The specimen here is also animated and careful, but less clear in colour.

SEBASTIAN DEL PIOMBO.—Portrait of a man in a black dress, a paper in his right hand. The serious and dignified individuality is worthily conceived.   The tone of the flesh yellow in the lights and very dark in the shadows.

VANDYCK.—2. Portrait of a woman in black dress, with white collar. A bust picture, with one hand. On canvas. Of animated conception and careful painting. The dirty condition in which the picture now is, permits of no opinion as to the colouring.

JAN VAN RAVESTYN.—The learned Dutchman, Heinrich Spelman, with a light beard, and a cap trimmed with lace on his head ; in black dress and white collar. A bust picture. In the background is the date 1628. According to an inscription on the frame, bequeathed by his heir to the Lord Chancellor Hardwicke. Judging from the style of the very truthful conception, and the clear and soft painting, I am inclined to ascribe it to this painter.

VANDYCK.—3. A male portrait in armour, and a white collar, with the elbow of the right hand, in which he holds a staff, leaning on a parapet, and holding a sword with his left. Upon the parapet his helmet and a mailed glove. The background architecture and a curtain. Full-length figure, life-size. Of animated composition, and broadly treated in a brown tone.

ZUCCHERO.—Sir Walter Raleigh, in silver armour ; a staff in his right hand, a sword in his left. The ground dark, half-length. On canvas. The resolute character is well expressed in his delicate features, and the execution in a cold colour is careful.

VANDYCK.—4. Portrait of a lady, standing, in a black dress. A yellow fan in her right hand, the left touching her dress. The background partly a curtain, partly only black colour. The attitude is not so graceful as usual ; the forms, on the other hand, very decided, and the colouring very clear.

RUBENS.—2. Portrait of the Marchese Spinola in rich armour, with the order of the Golden Fleece, and a white collar. A bust picture. Of refined and animated conception, and carefully painted in clear colouring.

GODFRIED SCHALKEN.—1 and 2. Portrait of a man and his wife. Bust pictures, life-size. These are of truthful and lively conception, and painted in clear but not powerful tones.

THE GALLERY.

CORNELIS JANSEN (?).—Portrait of Ben Jonson, in black dress with a small white collar. He is seated in thought, with his arm on the red arm of the chair, and holding a pen in his right hand. Three books are on the table, one of them open. The background consists of architecture in the taste of the Renaissance, a curtain, and a view in the open air. The style of the elevated conception, the fine drawing, especially of the hands, and the cool but delicate flesh tones, indicate an excellent Italian painter, and more parti- cularly a Venetian. The keeping is good, and the touch solid.

Portrait of the astronomer Tycho Brahe, in a black dress, with his left hand pointing to the back of a book, and with his right showing the spectator the order of St. Lazarus about his neck, as if to say that he had received this as a recognition of his labours. The ground dark. Half-length figure, on canvas. This picture is of animated composition, skilful drawing, and clear colouring, but the painter is not known to me.

CARLO CIGNANI.—Prometheus, strange to say, represented as a tender youth, with the eagle devouring his liver. In expression, form, and colour quite in the manner of Guido. Of careful execution.

ANNIBALE CARRACCI.—Portrait of a monk of very clever look. A bust-picture. On canvas pasted on wood. Very animated, and of masterly painting. I have often met with this head.

PIETRO DELLA VECCHIA.—Abner, above life-size, with the colossal head of Goliah; David next him in hat and feathers. Of astonishing energy in his warm brown tone, and of broad but care- ful painting.

PAUL VERONESE.—The repentant Magdalen looking up to an angel, who is pointing to the sky. The background landscape. Warmer in expression and nobler in forms than usual, and broadly treated in his clear yellowish tones.

ALONZO CANO.—Portrait of the well-known poet Lope de Vega in white coat and white collar; in front of him a palm-branch and a sprig of oak. Bust-picture. The ground dark. The noble and thoughtful features are admirably rendered in delicate drawing and in powerful colouring, which is dark in the shadows and of good impasto.

VANDYCK.—5. Portrait of Henderakas du Booys, in a black dress, with the right hand pointing to the companion-picture of Helena Leonora his wife.

6. Wife of the foregoing, also in black dress and white collar,

and her hands folded. Both are refined in composition, and of broad and masterly painting in a subdued brownish tone. Lord Hardwicke has also Cornelis Fischer's engraving from these pictures.

ROOM NEXT THE GALLERY.

Salvator Rosa.—A rich rocky landscape with water. In the foreground on the shore three warriors. Of poetic invention, but heavy in tone.

Luca Giordano.—Leda and the Swan and two amorini. Very decorously conceived, and of clear and careful painting, obviously in imitation of Titian—a feeling which even extends to the landscape.

Gaspar Poussin.—A rather light landscape, of very dark foreground.

Palma Vecchio.—The Virgin holding the Child on her lap. The right hand of the Child in the right hand of a female saint with light hair kneeling before him, and leaning with her left hand on a book. Behind her the archangel Michael, with the scales in his left hand, the spear in his right. Figures half-life-size. The heads of the Virgin and the saint are of noble character and expression, the landscape pleasing. The colouring is warm, but less clear and powerful than usual; the drawing less firm, and the treatment slighter—all indications of the later time of the master.

Cuyp.—View on the Maas. On the shore in the foreground are six cows, two of them standing; on the river are vessels, and beyond the river the town of Dort with its tower. The transparent sky is of a mild warm tone. The cows are well relieved by their powerful colouring. A good picture in the second manner of the master.

J. H. Koekoek.—1. An agitated sea. In the foreground the coast with a boat. Signed and dated 1835. A picture of great truth of nature and clear colouring by this unequal master.

Marcantonio Franceschini.—A Charity. Pleasing, clear, and careful.

Teniers.—2. The Temptation of St. Anthony in the centre. Sculpture and flowers around by Ferdinand van Kessel. Signed. A pretty little picture.

ANOTHER ROOM.

Rubens.—3. A Roman Charity, or Cimon nursed in prison by his daughter Pera, who is looking round. Though clear and powerful in colour and careful in execution, yet composition and expression are little attractive.

J. H. Koekoek. — 2. An agitated sea, with sailing boats. Signed, and dated 1841. True and transparent.

Teniers.—3. In the foreground an old woman, with a bundle of onions in her lap. Next her, on the floor, another bundle, baskets with apples and figs, a dead heron, and a snipe. Behind are two men at a hearth. The last are only sketched in. In his heavy brown tone, but the woman and the fruit, &c., harmonious and clear.

Jacob Jordaens.—The four Evangelists, without attributes, around a table with books. Of clumsy forms and hard colouring.

Francesco Bassano. — The Exodus of the Israelites. The Almighty in the sky. One of his very dark pictures.

J. H. Koekoek.—3. Companion to the last picture. A similar subject and of similar value.

Philip Wouvermans.—A horseman on a grey horse, next him a woman, a child, and a dog. The sky cloudy. On wood. Signed. A very small but delicate picture.

Teniers.—4. A landscape. Card-players in front of a house. Sketchy, and, with the exception of the sky, very brown.

THE NEXT ROOM.

Peter Neefs.—1 and 2. Interiors of churches. The one treated in a warm, the other in a cool tone. Very good pictures.

Walker.—General Lambert, who commanded under Cromwell. In armour. A bust picture. Animated, and of good colour, but somewhat empty in the forms.

Berghem.—The Annunciation to the Shepherds. Warm and forcible, but of broad and scenic treatment.

LARGE DINING-ROOM.

Sir Joshua Reynolds.—1. The Marquis of Rockingham. In the costume of a knight of the Order of the Garter. The background a curtain. Animated, and admirably coloured, especially the hand. The costume is treated with taste. Full-length, life-size figure.

2. Lord Hardwicke, son of the Chancellor, in his peer's robes, pointing with his right hand to himself. The background a curtain and landscape. Very natural in conception and colouring.

CAMBRIDGE.

Vol. III. p. 451.

During the summer of 1854 I paid a visit to Cambridge in order to complete my knowledge of the manuscripts with miniatures existing in the libraries there. The following seemed to me the most important :—

UNIVERSITY LIBRARY.

De Vita Edovardi Confessoris, folio, 33 leaves (E. E. 359), in a small minuscule in three columns. Each page contains a pen-drawing slightly tinted with blue, red, and green. Although the text is written in French verses, I am convinced that the drawings are by the hand of a very clever English artist of the 12th century. Some of the drawings, particularly at the end, have suffered. Very important for proving the high degree of development of drawing in England at so early an epoch.

A missal (D. D. 4, 17) with miniatures, showing a marked influence of the Byzantine school, by a good English artist about the beginning of the 14th century.

Horarium Virginis Mariæ (N. N. 1), octavo, in a large and full minuscule, one column. The miniatures are by the hand of a clever French artist of the school of Jean Fouquet, and executed about 1490. The ornaments of the borders are very fine.

Letters by Johan Robertet, secretary of the Duke of Bourbon, to Monsieur de Monferrant, chevalier, conseiller et chambellan de Monseigneur le Duc de Bourgogne, 42 leaves, in a full minuscule letter, one column, with miniatures by a good French artist manifestly influenced by the school of the Van Eycks ; about 1470.

TRINITY COLLEGE LIBRARY.

An Evangeliarium (B 10, 4), folio, in a minuscule letter of a moderate size, one column. The canons, occupying 13 pages, are very rich in the ornaments. The ornaments of the borders have a great resemblance to the Anglo-Saxon Manuscripts in the library at Rouen. The fine initials show a strong influence of Irish art. The miniatures, of a decided Anglo-Saxon character, are by a skilful hand. A very rich and important monument of the 10th century.

A Psalter (R 17a), fol., containing the text three times, one with an interlineary Anglo-Saxon version, the second with a French version, the third with a commentary. With four and sometimes five columns, written partly in a large, partly in a small minuscule letter. At the head of each Psalm is a pen-drawing, slightly tinted with blue, green, and red ; sometimes also fully painted with body colours. The initials are of fine forms, and of bright and beautiful colours. The miniatures contain a large number of symbolical and emblematical representations. It is only to be lamented that the inscriptions explaining them are wanting from leaf 4 A to the end. By a Latin inscription we learn that a priest at his desk, L. 170 b, is the " predicator Cadwinus," the writer and the painter of this manuscript (" ingenium cujus libri decus indicat hujus"). Very interesting is the plan of a vast convent with a church near the end of the MS., quite in the Romanesque style. The miniatures are full of bold and happy motives. One of the most important monuments of Anglo-Saxon art of the first half of the 12th century I have met with. Presented to the library by Thomas Neville, Dean of Canterbury and Prefect of Trinity College.

The Apocalypse (R 16, 2), fol., in a minuscule of a moderate size, two columns. Although the text is a French version, I am convinced that the painter of the great number of miniatures in body colours was an Englishman. The inventions are peculiar ; the motives happy and dramatic ; the execution neat and careful. The pictures of the last leaf are not finished. A very interesting monument, executed about 1260-70.

A Missal (B 11, 5), small folio, in a full minuscule, one column. The borders of the calendar, written upon six leaves, contain rich ornaments quite of an English character. The miniatures are executed in the style of art which I have described in the first volume of this work, p. 174, and some of them—for instance, the Bearing of the Cross, and the Crucifixion — are the work of a clever English artist. The portrait of the kneeling donor has great individuality. A fine monument, executed about 1420-1430. Presented by Thomas Coppinger.

Libri Apologetici de omni Statu Humanæ Naturæ docentis a Thoma Cancellario Wellensis Ecclesiæ compilatus, and some other treatises (R 14, 5), small folio, containing 15 drawings in Indian ink, executed with the point of the brush, and only in some accessories slightly coloured. The first represents the Fall of the Angels. The following contain allegorical subjects, with explanations in Latin. On the last we see the author, and perhaps also the painter, presenting his work to Thomas of Beckington, priest of Wells and Bath. These drawings are by a very clever artist in the realistic style, fine, lively, and true to nature in the heads, happy in the motives, indicating in the folds of the draperies the influence of the school of the Van Eycks. One of the best specimens of English art, about 1460-1470, I know.

CORPUS CHRISTI COLLEGE LIBRARY.

An Evangeliarium, folio, written throughout in capitals of a pure Roman character, and containing now only two slight and rough miniatures, which, in composition, recall the paintings in the catacombs at Rome. The tradition that this MS. was sent to England by Pope Gregory the Great may therefore be right.

The fragment of an Evangeliarium, written throughout in capitals. The initials, as well as the whole writing, and the only miniature, representing St. John, show an Irish origin. I think rightly assigned to the 7th century.

The first volume of the Vulgate, a very large folio, with several pictures of moderate art, but excellent execution, and very beautiful and large initials, of peculiar invention. In some places are also good drolleries. I do not agree with those who think this MS. only a little later than the time of William the Conqueror. It can hardly have been executed earlier than about 1200-1220. The pictures and initials have quite an English character.

A French translation of the Apocalypse, a small folio, with many slight miniatures of very clever invention. These, and the style of the ornaments, are of a decided English character, so that I have no doubt of the English origin of this MS. belonging to the first half of the 14th century.

These four Manuscripts were bequeathed to the College by Parker, the Archbishop of Canterbury.

INDEX.

2 M 2

N.

2 N 2

LONDON : PRINTED BY W. CLOWES AND SONS, STAMFORD STREET,
AND CHARING CROSS.